THE POEMS OF
William Dunbar

James IV, King of Scots, from the painting by Daniel Mytens in the collection of Lt.-Colonel William Stirling of Keir, Dunblane. This was originally in the collection of Charles I at Whitehall

THE POEMS OF
William Dunbar

Edited by
JAMES KINSLEY
Professor of English Studies in the University of Nottingham

OXFORD
AT THE CLARENDON PRESS
1979

Oxford University Press, Walton Street, Oxford OX2 6DP

OXFORD LONDON GLASGOW
NEW YORK TORONTO MELBOURNE WELLINGTON
KUALA LUMPUR SINGAPORE JAKARTA HONG KONG TOKYO
DELHI BOMBAY CALCUTTA MADRAS KARACHI
NAIROBI DAR ES SALAAM CAPE TOWN

Published in the United States by
Oxford University Press, New York

British Library Cataloguing in Publication Data

Dunbar, William, b. ca. 1465
(Oxford English texts).
I. Title II. Kinsley, James III. Series
821'.2 PR2265 78-40494
ISBN 0-19-811888-0

Printed in Great Britain
at the University Press, Oxford
by Eric Buckley
Printer to the University

PREFACE

In 1942 I was awarded a copy of Mackay Mackenzie's edition of Dunbar as an Anglo-Saxon essay prize at Edinburgh; and there began one of the most intense literary affections of my life. In 1958 I published a selection of Dunbar's poems and was encouraged, by some reviewers, in the belief that I might one day bring out a complete edition which would be less quaintly antique than the Victorian volumes of the Scottish Text Society and less slap-dash than Mackenzie's. I do not wish to give the impression that this enterprise, now finished, has been heroically sustained over twenty years: for a long time it was a recreation, lightening what Burns called 'the toils and fatigues of a laborious life', and providing, in Dunbar's words, 'sum disport' in 'dirk and drublie dayis'. Indeed, it was more in alarm than in delight that I realized, during a sabbatical term three years ago, that my harmless pleasure was—without design—virtually over; that 'game' had, unnoticed, become 'ernest'; that editing in decades had become a habit.

Why a new edition of Dunbar? I have been more of an editor than anything else for going on thirty years, and I have learnt that it is imprudent to justify oneself at the expense of one's predecessors. But the STS edition, when you can get to it, is unsatisfactory: transcriptions are careless, and have anyhow been largely superseded by the STS editions of the Maitland, Bannatyne, and other manuscripts; collation is spasmodic; the commentary, although learned, is garrulous and outmoded; and the glossary was prepared when *OED* had reached only letter C and William Craigie, who was to be the 'onlie begetter' of the Dictionary of early Scots (*DOST*), was still an assistant in Humanity at St. Andrews. Mackay Mackenzie's edition, though it profited from the *OED* lately complete, was admittedly an emergency job to meet urgent student needs. His text rests on STS transcripts and not on the manuscripts; his collation is fitful and eccentric; despite erudition, good sense, and occasional wit, his notes (they do not amount to a commentary) show an infuriating indifference to the reader's needs; and his glossary is disastrous. Yet so powerful is the appeal of Dunbar—who remains, in spite of all that has been said in favour of Villon and Henryson, the greatest European 'makar' between Chaucer and Spenser—that we have struggled on through obscurity and frustration towards delight: my copy of Mackay Mackenzie is the most battered book I have. The only way, however, to the complete student edition which is needed to feed Scottish culture at one of its roots, is through a scholars' edition in which the problems of text, context, exegesis, and lexicography are squarely faced and in large measure solved.

This is my third large-scale editorial venture. In Dryden, I edited a poet who, although he left almost no autographs, read much of his work in proof and sometimes carefully revised it. Burns not only read proof with care, but left to his editors hundreds of autographs and a correspondence rich in comment on his poems. In editing Dunbar, however, I have been for the first time confronted by a poet who survives mainly in manuscript collections[1] built up on subjective and eclectic principles, from sources of disputable authority, nearly half a century after his death. The early sixteenth-century printings aside, the manuscripts and their textual problems have daily reminded me that I have been editing not only a poet but also the earliest anthologists and editors of that poet. When I was tempted by the notion that Bannatyne and Maitland had, for copy-text, Chepman and Myllar or some other early printings of reasonable authority and now lost, I had Sir William Craigie's reminder that the wide variations in orthography in the Maitland Folio MS are due not only to a variety of scribes but also to variety in the character of Maitland's originals; and there is George Bannatyne's apologia:

ȝe reverend redaris thir workis revolving richt:
Gif ȝe get crymis, correct thame to ȝour micht,
And curs na clark that cunnyngly thame wrait

[1] See *infra*, pp. xiii–xv.

Bot blame me, baldly brocht this buik till licht
In tenderest tyme quhen knawlege was nocht bricht
Bot lait begun to lerne and till translait,
My copeis awld, mankit and mutillait. . . .

Bannatyne and Maitland were not only anthologists, but editors. Much of the variation between their texts is plainly due to the use of relatively different copies; but for both of them Dunbar was what Dryden was to call a poet of 'the last Age', and a good deal of the variation between them is due to their efforts to mend rhyme and rhythm, to make the obscure intelligible, and even on occasion to modernize and to make a Catholic poet palatable to Protestants. The text of Dunbar is both a nightmare and a challenge: these 6,000 lines have cost me more anguish, textually, than the 65,000 lines of Dryden's verse and critical prose. The demands made on the editor as exegetist and lexicographer have been as heavy. Within a small corpus of poetry, Dunbar's range of reference in theme, vocabulary, style, and iconology is immense. I felt, twenty years ago, that editing Dryden had been a liberal education. Editing Dunbar has been no less so; and I am grateful for the experience. I am also grateful for the support, encouragement, and advice of a number of institutions and scholars without whom that experience would have been less satisfying, and the outcome less satisfactory.

I acknowledge with great pleasure my debts to the Librarians of the National Library of Scotland, the British Library (British Museum), and Magdalene College, Cambridge, and to the Town Clerk of Aberdeen, for access to the manuscripts and for photographic copies; Professor William Beattie, formerly Librarian of the National Library of Scotland and editor of the Chepman and Myllar prints in facsimile; the late Sir William Craigie, and his successors Mr. A. J. Aitken and Dr. James Stevenson on the staff of the *Dictionary of the Older Scottish Tongue*—assuredly the greatest single contribution to early Scottish studies in this century—for immense help with the Glossary, and so the Commentary; the University of Nottingham and the Delegates of the Oxford University Press for financing the preparation of a computerized concordance to Dunbar, and to Mr. A. J. Aitken for seeing this through; the British Academy, for the award of a European exchange grant in 1975 to take me to the museums of the Low Countries; the curators of collections in Amsterdam, Antwerp, The Hague, and Utrecht, and especially Dr. A. C. Esmeijer of the Kunsthistorisch Institut, Rijksuniversiteit, Utrecht; the Revd. Professor A. R. C. Leaney and Mr. Philip Bagguley, Nottingham, for help with liturgical problems and for the loan of books; Dr. Bengt Ellenberger of the Swedish School of Economics, Helsinki, for material on Dunbar's 'aureate' verse; Professor J. A. W. Bennett, Cambridge; Professor D. A. Bullough, St. Andrews; Professor Kenneth Cameron, Nottingham, both for advice on place-name problems and for making my study-leaves possible; Professor Denton Fox, Toronto, editor of Henryson; Professor John MacQueen, School of Scottish Studies, University of Edinburgh; Professor Hans Meier, Freiuniversiteit, Amsterdam; Mrs. Stella Newton, the Courtauld Institute, University of London; Professor Alastair Smart, Nottingham, for advice on many iconographical questions; Dr. Karl Inge Sandred, Uppsala Universitet; and Dr. D. M. Wilson, Director of the British Museum. My greatest debt is, again, to my wife.

If I had felt that there was any propriety in inscribing an edition of another man's work, this book would have been affectionately dedicated to the memory of Sir William Craigie.

JAMES KINSLEY

University of Nottingham
1977

CONTENTS

IV. VISIONS AND NIGHTMARES

V. MORALITIES

BIOGRAPHICAL AND TEXTUAL NOTE

LITTLE is known of Dunbar's life. Born *c.* 1460, he was probably of the 'nobill strynd' of the earls of Dunbar and March. He may have been the William Dunbar who took a bachelor's degree at St. Andrews in 1477 and a master's degree in 1479. There is no documentary evidence for his activities between 1479 and 1500: that he was a Franciscan novice, and travelled abroad first as a preaching friar and later in the king's service, are speculative deductions from his poems. In 1501 he was in England, probably in connection with the arrangement of the marriage of James IV and Princess Margaret. He had taken priest's orders by 1504. He was granted a royal pension of £10 in 1500, 'to be pait to him of our soverane lordis cofferis be the thesaurair for al the dais of his life or quhil he be promovit be oure soverane lord to a benefice of xl lib. or abone'. By 1507 this had been raised to £20. He received a 'pensioun most preclair' of £80 in 1510 (see **47**, intro. note). It is unlikely that he followed the king to Flodden in 1513. He seems to have survived into the new reign, and probably acquired his long-sought benefice since his pension disappears from the records after 1513. References to him in the accounts of the lord high treasurer and elsewhere are conveniently gathered in the STS edition, i, pp. cliii–clvi. The fullest discussion of the biographical evidence is in J. W. Baxter, *William Dunbar*, 1952.

TEXT. The poems are preserved in:

(1) a number of black-letter prints which survive in apparently unique copies in the National Library of Scotland, and are mainly the work of Walter Chepman and Androw Myllar in or about 1508. Chepman was an Edinburgh merchant trading overseas in wood and textiles; Myllar, a printer who worked during the years 1503–7 at

Rouen. These two burgesses were granted a patent by James IV on 15 September 1507 'to furnis and bring hame ane prent, with al stuff belangand tharto and expert men to use the samyne'; they were to print the laws, Acts of parliament, chronicles, mass-books 'efter our awin Scottis use'. They set up their press in the Southgait (Cowgate) in Edinburgh. The prints are included in George Stevenson's edition of the Makculloch and Gray MSS, STS, 1918; and published in facsimile, with notes by William Beattie, for the Edinburgh Bibliographical Society, 1950. Dunbar's poems in Chepman and Myllar's prints are **10, 23, 35.** A print apparently from another press, and probably printed in Rouen or by foreign workmen in Scotland (see Beattie, op. cit., pp. xiv–xv), includes part of **14, 38, 62.**

(2) the Asloan MS, a miscellany in verse and prose made in the reign of James V. The Malahide family, Dublin; photographs in the National Library of Scotland. Ed. W. A. Craigie, STS, 2 vols., 1923–4. Dunbar, **2, 3, 52B, 54.**

(3) British Museum MS Arundel 285, a collection of devotional verse and prose made before the Reformation; part of the library of Lord William Howard (1563–1640). Ed. J. A. W. Bennett in *Devotional Pieces in Verse and Prose*, STS, 1955. Dunbar, **3, 5, 6.**

(4) British Museum Royal MSS 58, appendix; an early sixteenth-century English collection of madrigals, motets, etc. Dunbar, **24.**

(5) the Aberdeen Minute Book of Seisins, ii (1503–7), iii (1507–13); Town Clerk's Office, Aberdeen. Dunbar, **31, 65, 73.**

(6) the Bannatyne MS, a large poetical miscellany made by George Bannatyne, an Edinburgh merchant educated at St. Andrews, and completed 'in tyme of pest' towards the end of 1568. Ed. W. Tod Ritchie, STS, 4 vols., 1928–34. Dunbar, **1, 4, 6, 9, 10, 11, 13, 15, 16, 17, 19, 22, 23, 34, 37, 38, 42, 49, 50, 52, 53, 54, 55, 56, 57, 59, 61, 62, 63, 64, 65, 67, 68, 70, 71, 72, 73, 74, 77, 78–80, 81, 82, 83.**

(7) the Maitland Folio MS, Magdalene College, Cambridge, 2553; a poetical miscellany compiled *c.* 1570 for Sir Richard Maitland of Lethington (1496–1586), keeper of the great seal (1562) and a lord of session. The only authority for a large number of Dunbar's court poems. Ed. John Pinkerton, *Ancient Scotish Poems*, 2 vols., 1786; W. A. Craigie, STS, 2 vols., 1919 and 1927. Dunbar, **3, 6, 7, 8, 10, 12, 13, 14, 16, 20, 22, 23, 25, 26, 27, 28, 29, 30, 32, 33, 34, 37, 38, 39, 40, 41, 42, 43, 44, 45, 52, 53, 55, 56, 57, 58, 59, 60, 61, 62, 63, 64, 65, 66, 67, 68, 69, 70, 71, 72, 73, 74, 76, 78–80, 81, 82, 83.**

(8) the Reidpeth MS, University Library, Cambridge, Moore LL. v. 10; a transcript (1622) of the Maitland Folio MS made when that manuscript was more nearly complete than it is now; the only authority for Dunbar, **18, 21, 36, 46, 47, 48, 51, 75.**

For poems apart from those which survive in single manuscripts, what is an editor to use as copy-text? Obviously, priority must be given whenever possible to the Chepman and Myllar prints: here, though in fragmentary form, is the work of a court poet set up by printers under royal authority and perhaps overseen by Dunbar himself. Once we have accustomed ourselves to the idiosyncrasies of the compositors (perhaps foreigners), the quality of their texts is clear. Maitland, it appears, had access to a gathering of poems on life at court which would otherwise have been lost. His Folio is the only authority for eight poems addressed to the king, and more than a dozen other court pieces. Since most of these belong to genres, or express attitudes, which we know would have appealed to George Bannatyne, we may reasonably suppose that they came from a collection of relatively intimate and domestic verse owned by or available to Maitland—servant of James V and Mary, and keeper of the great seal—unknown to Bannatyne, and doubtless of good authority. For all this, and for the copies made by Reidpeth, an editor must be grateful. But otherwise, Maitland is textually weak: conspicuously in **23** where, after collation with Chepman and Myllar and Bannatyne, the Folio MS is seen to be often merely in error; inferior rhetorically, metrically, and in diction and imagery; and at times crudely simplified. It can be said in general terms that, despite Bannatyne's tendency to regulate, simplify, and improve his texts—obvious from a collation of his draft and main manuscripts—he is a better witness than Maitland for poems which they both offer, in specific readings and sometimes in content and sequence.

In editing a poet like Burns it is possible to arrange surviving versions in a relationship, and often in chronological order; and on such a sequence the establishment of a text may depend. With Dunbar, however, it is always difficult to characterize the relationship between a print and a manuscript, or between two manuscript versions—and sometimes impossible. For the copyists have usually, and clearly, been working from markedly different originals, and doubtless with differing degrees of fidelity; and an editor, if his policy is to be properly rigorous, must try to decide which text is the better—that is, closer to a hypothetical authoritative original—and stick to it. He takes over as little as possible from other witnesses, and then only *in extremis*. (The alternative is the magpie eclecticism which can sometimes be seen in Mackay Mackenzie.) This is at once a much simpler, and a much more subjective editorial procedure than any I have followed before, and I admit some unease over it. I have, however, after a great deal of experiment, come to the conclusion that where I have a choice of texts, these are usually based on originals which are widely different, related (in ways which are beyond our comprehension) to each other and to a lost autograph half a century older; and that one or other must be followed with cautious fidelity, as *more likely* to be close to Dunbar on the evidence of vocabulary, imagery, structure, style and rhythm, attitude, and general tone. Of course one has relatively well-founded notions about the authority of the early prints, or about the superiority of Bannatyne as against Maitland: but these will not hold systematically for all texts, since the route of one poem from the poet to the printer or the anthologists may have been different from that of another; and (beyond general considerations) the textual evidence for each poem has to be assessed on its merits. In a way unfamiliar to me, and sometimes unnerving, each poem has been a new textual experience, calling for the fresh exercise of critical judgement; not for the application of a grand strategy, but for flexible common sense. And I am painfully aware that there are few faculties less common than that.

The prints and manuscripts have been closely followed, but þ is here printed *th*, abbreviations by suspension and contraction have been expanded, and *u*, *v*, *i*, *j*, and *w* have generally been given their modern values. Merely scribal devices have been ignored. Indentation, capitalization, and punctuation are editorial. Titles in square brackets are editorial.

The frontispiece portrait of James IV was photographed for my 1958 edition by kind permission of Col. Stirling of Keir, Dunblane. It was originally in the collection of Charles I at Whitehall, 'done after an ancient water coloured piece'—probably a miniature—by the king's portrait painter Daniel Mytens (1590–1642).

I

DIVINE POEMS

1. [Et nobis Puer natus est]

Rorate celi desuper.
Hevins distill ȝour balmy schouris
For now is rissin the brycht day ster
Fro the ros Mary, flour of flouris:
The cleir sone quhome no clud devouris,
Surminting Phebus in the est,
Is cumin of his hevinly touris
Et nobis puer natus est.

Archangellis, angellis and dompnationis,
Tronis, potestatis and marteiris seir,
And all ȝe hevinly operationis,
Ster, planeit, firmament and speir,
Fyre, erd, air and watter cleir
To him gife loving, most and lest,
That come in to so meik maneir
Et nobis puer natus est.

Synarris, be glaid and pennance do
And thank ȝour makar hairtfully,
For he that ȝe mycht nocht cum to
To ȝow is cumin full humly—
Ȝour saulis with his blud to by
And lous ȝow of the Feindis arrest;
And only of his awin mercy
Pro nobis puer natus est.

All clergy do to him inclyne
And bow unto that barne benyng
And do ȝour observance devyne
To him that is of kingis king;
Ensence his altar, reid and sing
In haly kirk with mynd degest,
Him honouring attour all thing
Qui nobis puer natus est.

Et nobis Puer natus est. *Text: MS B (f. 27^r–27^v)*
8 *puer*: power *B* 24, 32, 40 *refrain abbrev. in B*

Celestiall fowlis in the are
Sing with ȝour nottis upoun hicht,
In firthis and in forrestis fair
Be myrthfull now at all ȝour mycht;
For passit is ȝour dully nycht,
Aurora hes the cluddis perst,
The son is rissin with glaidsum lycht
Et nobis puer natus est.

Now spring up flouris fra the rute,
Revert ȝow upwart naturaly
In honour of the blissit frute
That rais up fro the rose Mary;
Lay out ȝour levis lustely,
Fro deid tak lyfe now at the lest
In wirschip of that prince wirthy
Qui nobis puer natus est.

Syng, hevin imperiall, most of hicht,
Regions of air mak armony;
All fishe in flud and foull of flicht
Be myrthfull and mak melody:
All *Gloria in excelsis* cry,
Hevin, erd, se, man, bird and best:
He that is crownit abone the sky
Pro nobis puer natus est.

2. Ane Ballat of Our Lady

HALE, sterne superne; hale, in eterne
In Godis sicht to schyne;
Lucerne in derne for to discerne
Be glory and grace devyne;
Hodiern, modern, sempitern,
Angelicall regyne:

33 fowlis] *corr.* flour *in B* 44 rose Mary: rosemary *B* 45–6 *in margin in B* 51 fishe] *corr.* fiche in *B* *colophon* Finis quod Dumbar *B*

Ane Ballat of Our Lady. *Text: MS Asloan (ff. 303ʳ–304ᵛ). Title from table of contents* *colophon* Quod Dumbar *MS*

Our tern inferne for to dispern
  Helpe, rialest rosyne.
    Ave Maria, gracia plena:
  Haile, fresche floure femynyne;
Ȝerne us guberne, virgin matern
  Of reuth baith rute and ryne.

Haile, ȝhyng benyng fresche flurising,
  Haile, Alphais habitakle;
Thy dyng ofspring maid us to syng
  Befor his tabernakle;
All thing maling we doune thring
  Be sicht of his signakle,
Quhilk king us bring unto his ryng
  Fro dethis dirk umbrakle.
    Ave Maria, gracia plena:
  Haile, moder and maide but makle;
Bricht syng, gladyng our languissing
  Be micht of thi mirakle.

Haile, bricht be sicht in hevyn on hicht;
  Haile, day sterne orientale;
Our licht most richt in clud of nycht
  Our dirknes for to scale:
Hale, wicht in ficht, puttar to flicht
  Of fendis in battale;
Haile, plicht but sicht; hale, mekle of mycht;
  Haile, glorius virgin, hale;
    Ave Maria, gracia plena:
  Haile, gentill nychttingale;
Way stricht, cler dicht, to wilsome wicht
  That irke bene in travale.

Hale, qwene serene; hale, most amene;
  Haile, hevinlie hie emprys;
Haile, schene unseyne with carnale eyne;
  Haile, ros of paradys;
Haile, clene bedene ay till conteyne;
  Haile, fair fresche floure delyce;

Haile, grene daseyne; haile fro the splene
  Of Jhesu genitrice;
    Ave Maria, gracia plena:
  Thow baire the prince of prys;
Our teyne to meyne and ga betweyne
  As humile oratrice.

Haile, more decore than of before
  And swetar be sic sevyne,
Our glore forlore for to restore
  Sen thow art qwene of hevyn;
Memore of sore, stern in aurore,
  Lovit with angellis stevyne;
Implore, adore, thow indeflore,
  To mak our oddis evyne.
    Ave Maria, gracia plena:
  With lovingis lowde ellevyn
Quhill store and hore my ȝouth devore
  Thy name I sall ay nevyne.

Empryce of prys, imperatrice,
  Bricht polist precious stane;
Victrice of vyce, hie genitrice
  Of Jhesu lord soverayne;
Our wys pavys fro enemys
  Agane the Feyndis trayne;
Oratrice, mediatrice, salvatrice,
  To God gret suffragane;
    Ave Maria, gracia plena:
  Haile, sterne meridiane;
Spyce, flour delice of paradys
  That baire the gloryus grayne.

Imperiall wall, place palestrall
  Of peirles pulcritud;
Tryumphale hall, hie trone regall
  Of Godis celsitud;
Hospitall riall, the lord of all
  Thy closet did include;

Bricht ball cristall, ros virginall
Fulfillit of angell fude.
Ave Maria, gracia plena:
Thy birth has with his blude
Fra fall mortall originall
Us raunsound on the rude.

3. The Passioun of Crist

AMANG thir freiris, within ane cloister,
I enterit in ane oritorie;
And kneling doun with ane pater noster
Befoir the michtie king of glorie,
Haveing his passioun in memorie,
Syn to his mother I did inclyne,
Hir halsing with ane gaude flore:
And sudandlie I sleipit syne.

Methocht Judas with mony ane Jow
Tuik blissit Jesu our salvatour
And schot him furth with mony ane schow
With schamefull wourdis of dishonour;
And lyk ane theif or ane tratour
Thay leid that hevinlie prince most hie
With manassing attour messour,
O mankynd, for the luif of the.

Falslie condamnit befoir ane juge
Thay spittit in his visage fayr;
And as lyounis with awfull ruge
In yre thay hurlit him heir and thair
And gaif him mony buffat sair
That it wes sorow for to se;
Of all his claythis thay tirvit him bair,
O mankynd, for the luif of the.

The Passioun of Crist. *Text: MS MF (pp. 203–7) collated with MSS Asloan (As; ff. 290v–292r; ll. 1–32, 41–96 only) and Arundel 285 (Ar; ff. 168r–170r; om. ll. 73–80, 121–8). Title from As and Ar*

1 within] in *As* 3 And kneling] And knelit *As*: Knelland *Ar* 6 to] till *As Ar* 7 Hir halsing] I halsit hir *As* 9 Judas] that Judas *As* 10 *et passim* salvatour] salviour *Ar* 11 ane] a *Ar*: *om. As* 12 With] And *As* of] and *Ar* 19 ruge *As Ar*: rage *MF* 20 hurlit] harlit *As Ar* 21 buffat sair] buffatis bair *Ar* 23 Of all] And of *As*

Thay terandis, to revenge thair tein,
For scorne thai cled him in to quhyt
And hid his blythfull glorious ene
To se quham angellis had delyt;
Dispituouslie syn did him smyt
Saying, Gif sone of God thow be,
Quha straik the now, thow tell us tyt—
O mankynd, for the luif of the.

In tene thay tirvit him agane
And till ane pillar thai him band;
Quhill blude birst out at everie vane
Thay scurgit him bayth fut and hand;
At everie straik ran furth ane strand
Quhilk mycht have ransonit warldis thre;
He baid in stour quhill he mycht stand,
O mankynd, for the luif of the.

Nixt all in purpyr thay him cled,
And syn with thornis scharp and kene
His saikles blude agane thay sched,
Persing his heid with pykis grene;
Unneis with lyf he micht sustene
That croun on thrungin with crueltie,
Quhill flude of blude blindit his ene,
O mankynd, for the luif of the.

Ane croce that wes bayth large and lang
To beir thay gaif this blissit lord;
Syn fullelie, as theif to hang,
Thay harlit him furth with raip and corde;
With bluid and sweit was all deflorde
His face, the fude of angellis fre;
His feit with stanis was revin and scorde,
O mankynd, for the luif of the.

25 *Ar has l. 33* 27 blythfull] blissit *Ar* 29 syn did] syne thai did *Ar* 32 *two folios misplaced in Ar* 33–40 *replaced by ll. 81–8 in As* 35 birst out] out bristit *Ar* 36 him bayth] him agane baith *Ar* 38 Quhilk] *om. Ar* 39 stour] stound *Ar* 43 saikles] precious *As* 46 thrungin] thrung *As* 49 large] gret *As Ar* 50 this] that *As* 51 fullelie] furiusly *Ar* as theif] as ane theif *Ar* to: he *MF*: till *Ar* 54 fre] fair *Ar* 55 revin] rent *As*

Agane thay tirvit him bak and syd
  Als brim as ony baris woid;
The clayth that claif to his cleir hyd
  Thay raif away with ruggis rude
  Quhill fersly followit flesche and blude
That it was pietie for to se;
  Na kynd of torment he ganestude,
O mankynd, for the luif of the.

On to the crose of breid and lenth
  To gar his lymmis langar wax
They straitit him with all thair strenth
  Quhill to the rude thay gart him rax,
  Syn tyit him on with greit irne takkis;
And him all nakit on the tre
  Thay raissit on loft be houris sax,
O mankynd, for the luif of the.

Quhen he was bendit so on breid
  Quhill all his vanis brist and brak,
To gar his cruell pane exceid
  Thay leit him fall doun with ane swak
  Quhill cors and corps and all did crak;
Agane thay rasit him on hie,
  Reddie may turmentis for to mak,
O mankynd, for the luif of the.

Betuix tuo theiffis the spreit he gaif
  On to the Fader most of micht;
The erde did trimmill, the stanis claif,
  The sone obscurit of his licht,
  The day wox dirk as ony nicht,
Deid bodies rais in the cite:
  Goddis deir sone all thus was dicht,
O mankynd, for the luif of the.

57 him bak] him baith bak *Ar* 59 cleir] rycht *Ar* hyd *As*: syd *MF Ar* 61 fersly] furth with *Ar* 66 langar] largear *As Ar* 67 straitit . . . strenth] strait . . . strenthis *Ar* 68 rude] end *Ar* 69 on] up *Ar* 70 him all nakit *As Ar*: at him all nathing *MF* the] a *As* 73–80 *om. Ar* 73 so] all *As* 75 To] Till *As* 79 mak] tak *As* 81–8 *repeated in As* 82 the] his *Ar* 83 stanis claif] craggis raif *As* 84 of] fra *Ar*

In weir that he wes ȝit on lyf
  Thay rane ane rude speir in his syde
And did his precious body ryff
  Quhill blude and watter did furth glyde;
  Thus Jesus with his woundis wyde
As martir sufferit for to de
  And tholit to be crucifyid,
O mankynd, for the luif of the.

Methocht Compassioun, vode of feiris,
  Than straik at me with mony ane stound,
And soir Contritioun, bathit in teiris,
  My visage all in watter drownit;
  And Reuth in to my eir ay rounde,
For schame, allace! Behald, man, how
  Beft is with mony ane bludy wound
Thy blissit salvatour Jesu!

Than rudlie come Remembrance
  Ay rugging me withouttin rest,
Quhilk crose and nalis, scharp scurge and lance
  And bludy crowne befoir me kest;
  Than Pane with passioun me opprest,
And evir did Petie on me pow
  Saying, Behald how Jowis hes drest
Thy blissit salvatour, Chryst Jesu!

With greiting glaid be than come Grace
  With wourdis sweit saying to me,
Ordane for him ane resting place
  That is so werie wrocht for the,
  That schort within thir dayis thre
Sall law undir thy lyntell bow;
  And in thy hous sall herbrit be
Thy blissit salvatour, Chryst Jesu.

94 As martir *As*: Ane marter *Ar*: Ane mertirdome *MF* 96 *colophon* Quod Dunbar *As* 97 vode] wod *Ar* 98 ane stound] astound *Ar* 99 soir *Ar*: for *MF* 100 *follows l. 102 in Ar* 103 ane] *om. Ar* bludy *Ar: not in MF* 107 Quhilk] Quhill *Ar* 108 And] Ane *Ar* 112, 120 Chryst] *om. Ar* 117 That schort] The Lord *Ar*

Than swyth Contritioun wes on steir
And did eftir Confessioun ryn;
And Conscience me accusit heir
And kest out mony cankerit syn;
To rys Repentence did begin
And out at the ȝettis did schow;
Pennance did walk the hous within,
Byding our salvitour Chryst Jesu.

Grace become gyd and governour
To keip the hous in sicker stait
Ay reddie till our salvatour,
Quhill that he come, air or lait;
Repentence ay with cheikis wait
No pane nor pennence did eschew
The hous within evir to debait
Onlie for luif of sweit Jesu.

For grit terrour of Chrystis deid
The erde did trymmill quhair I lay,
Quhairthrow I waiknit in that steid
With spreit halflingis in effray;
Than wrayt I all without delay
Richt heir as I have schawin to ȝow,
Quhat me befell on Gud Fryday
Befoir the crose of sweit Jesu.

4. [Surrexit Dominus de sepulchro]

DONE is a battell on the dragon blak;
Our campioun Chryst confoundit hes his force:
The ȝettis of hell ar brokin with a crak,
The signe triumphall rasit is of the croce,
The divillis trymmillis with hiddous voce,
The saulis ar borrowit and to the bliss can go,
Chryst with his blud our ransonis dois indoce:
Surrexit Dominus de sepulchro.

121–8 *om. Ar* 129 Grace *Ar*: Grudge *MF* 132 Quhill] Quhethir *Ar* 139 that] the *Ar* 140 With . . . halflingis] My . . . hail plungit *Ar* *colophon* Finis quod Dunbar *MF*

Surrexit Dominus de sepulchro. *Text: MS B (f. 35r)*

Dungin is the deidly dragon Lucifer,
The crewall serpent with the mortall stang,
The auld kene tegir with his teith on char
Quhilk in a wait hes lyne for us so lang
Thinking to grip us in his clowis strang:
The mercifull lord wald nocht that it wer so;
He maid him for to felȝe of that fang:
Surrexit Dominus de sepulchro.

He for our saik that sufferit to be slane
And lyk a lamb in sacrifice wes dicht
Is lyk a lyone rissin up agane
And as a gyane raxit him on hicht;
Sprungin is Aurora radius and bricht,
On loft is gone the glorius Appollo,
The blisfull day depairtit fro the nycht:
Surrexit Dominus de sepulchro.

The grit victour agane is rissin on hicht
That for our querrell to the deth wes woundit;
The sone that wox all paill now schynis bricht,
And dirknes clerit, our fayth is now refoundit;
The knell of mercy fra the hevin is soundit,
The Cristin ar deliverit of thair wo,
The Jowis and thair errour ar confoundit:
Surrexit Dominus de sepulchro.

The fo is chasit, the battell is done ceis,
The presone brokin, the jevellouris fleit and flemit;
The weir is gon, confermit is the peis,
The fetteris lowsit and the dungeoun temit,
The ransoun maid, the presoneris redemit;
The feild is win, ourcumin is the fo,
Dispulit of the tresur that he ȝemit:
Surrexit Dominus de sepulchro.

11 his] *corr.* the *in B* 13 clowis: clowss *B* 16, 24, 32 *abbrev. in B*
20 as a gyane: as gyane *B* *colophon* Finis quod Dunbar *B*

5. The Maner of Passyng to Confessioun

O SYNFULL man, thir ar the fourty dayis
That every man sulde wilfull pennence dre:
Oure Lorde Jesu as haly writ sayis
Fastit him self, oure exampill to be.
Sen sic ane mychty king and lorde as he
To fast and pray was so obedient,
We synfull folk sulde be more deligent.

I reid the, man, of thi transgressioun
With all thi hert that thou be penitent;
Thow schrive the clene and mak confessioun
And se thairto that thou be deligent
With all thi synnis into thi mynde presente,
That every syn ma be the selfe be schawin—
To thyne confessour it ma be kend and knawin.

Apon thi body gif thou hes ane wounde
That caussis the gret panis for to feill,
Thair is no leiche ma mak the haill and sounde
Quhill it be sene and clengit every deill;
Rycht sua thi schrift, bot it be schawin weill:
Thow art not abill remissioun for to get,
Wittandlie and thou ane syn forȝet.

Off twenty wonddis and ane be left unhelit,
Quhat avalis the leiching of the laif?
Rycht sua thi schrift, and thair be oucht conselit,
Avalis not thi sely saule to saif.
Nor ȝit of God remissioun for to have.
Of syn gif thou wald have deliverance
Thow sulde it tell with all the circumstance.

Se that thi confessour be wys and discreit,
That can the discharge of every doute and weir,
And power hes of thi synnes compleit.
Gif thou can not schaw furth thi synnes perqueir,
And he be blinde and can not at the speir,

The Maner of Passyng to Confessioun. *Text: BM MS Arundel 285* (*Ar; ff.* 161^{r}–162^{v})
8 the: *not in Ar* 11 that: *not in Ar* 13 ma *ed. conj.*: *not in Ar* 14 confessour: confessioun *Ar* 30 That: Than *Ar*

Thow ma rycht weill in thi mynde consydder
That ane blynde man is led furth be ane uther.

And sa I halde that ȝe ar baith begylde—
He can not speir nor thou can not him tell
Quhen nor how thi conscience thou hes fylde;
Thairfor I reid that thou excus thi sell
And rype thi mynde how every thing befell:
The tyme, the place, and how and in quhat wys,
Sa that thi confessioun ma thi synnes pryce.

Avys the weill or thou cum to the preist
Of all thi synnes, and namelie of the maist,
That thai be reddy prentit in thi breist.
Thow sulde not cum to schryfe the in haist
And syne sit doun abasit as ane beist:
With humyll hert and sad contrycioun
Thow suld cum to thine confessioun.

With thine awin mouth thi synnes thou suld tell;
Bot sit and heir the preist hes not ado.
Quha kennes thi synnes better na thi sell?
Thairfor I reid the, tak gude tent thairto.
Thow knawis best quhair bindis the thi scho;
Thairfor be wys afor, or thou thair cum,
That thou schaw furth thi synnes, all and sum.

Quhair seldin compt is tane and hes a hevy charge,
And syne is rekles in his governance
And on his conscience he takis all to large
And on the end hes no rememberance:
That man is abill to fall ane gret mischance.
The synfull man that all the ȝeir oursettis
Fra pasche to pasche rycht mony a thing forȝettis.

I reid the, man, quhill thou art stark and ȝoung
With pith and strenth into thi ȝeris grene,
Quhill thou art abill baith in mynde and toung,
Repent the, man, and kepe thi conscience clene.
Till byde till age is mony perrell sene.
Small merit is of synnes for to irke
Quhen thou art ald, and ma na wrangis wyrke.

48 hert *ed. conj.: not in Ar* *colophon* Quod Dumbar *Ar*

6. The Tabill of Confessioun

To The, O marcifull salviour myn, Jesus,
My king, my lord, and my redemer sueit,
Befor thy bludy figour dolorus
I schrife me cleyne with humile spreit and meik
That ever I did unto this hour compleit
Baith in word, in wark and in entent.
Falling on face full law befor thy feit
I cry the marcy and laser to repent.

To the my meik sueit salviour I me schrife,
And dois me in thy marcy maist exelling,
Off the wrang spending of my wittis five:
In hering, seing, tuiching, gusting, smelling,
Ganestanding, greving, offending and rebelling
Aganis my lord God omnipotent.
With teris of sorrow fra myn ene distelling
I cry the marcy and laser to repent.

I wrachit synnar vile and full of vice
Off the sevin deidly synnis dois me schrif:
Off prid, invy, of ire and covatice,
Off lichory, gluttony, with sleuth ay till ourdrife,
Exercing vicis ever in all my life
For quhilk, allace, I servit to be schent:
Rew on me, Jesu, for thy woundis five;
I cry the marcy and laser to repent.

The Tabill of Confessioun. *Text: BM MS Arundel 285 (Ar; ff.* 1r–4v*) collated with MSS Ba (pp. 9–11; Bannatyne's draft) and Bb (ff. 17v–19v) and MS MF (pp. 199 203). Title in Ar only. See Commentary*
1 myn] *om. Ba Bb* 4 schrife: Schir *Ar* schrife me cleyne] repent my synnys *Ba Bb*: schryve my syn *MF* spreit and meik] hairt contreit *Ba Bb*: hart and spreit *MF* 6 word, in wark] werk word *Ba*: werk in word *Bb MF* and in] and eik *Bb* 7 thy] *corr.* my *in Ar* 9 meik] *om. Ba Bb* 10 And dois] Committing *Bb* thy *Ba Bb MF: not in Ar* exelling: exellent *Ar*: excellenting *Ba Bb* (*corr. to* excelling): excelling *MF* 12 tuiching, gusting] gusting / tuiching *Ba Bb*: twiching taisting *MF* 13 offending] invying *Ba*: moving *Bb* 14 my lord God] the my God *Ba Bb MF* (and lord *added in margin in Bb*) 15 fra myn] frome my *Ba Bb* 18 dois] do *Ba* 19 invy, of ire] of ire / invye *Ba Bb* 20 till] to *Ba Bb MF*

I schrif me, Lord, that I abusit have
  The sevin deidis of marcy corporall:
The hungry, meit, nor thristy, drink I gaif,
  Vesyit the seik, nor redemit the thrall,
  Herbreit the wilsum, nor nakit cled at all,
Nor ȝit the deid to bery tuke I tent.
  Thow that put marcy abone thi werkis all,
I cry the marcy and laser to repent.

In the sevin deidis of marcy spirituall:—
  To the ignorant nocht gaif I my teching,
Synneris correctioun, nor distitud consall,
  Nor unto wofull wrachis conforting
  Nor unto saulis support of my preching,
Nor wes to ask forgevinnes pacient
  Nor to forgif my nychtburis offending:
I cry the marcy and laser to repent.

Lord, I have done full litill reverence
  Unto the sacramentis sevin of gret renoun:
To that hie eucarist moist of exellence,
  Baptasing, pennence, and confirmacioun,
  Matremony, ordour, and extreme uncioun.
Heirof sa fer as I wes necligent,
  With hert contrit and teris falling doun
I cry the marcy and laser to repent.

25 schrif] confess *Bb* 27 The] To *Ba Bb* nor *Ba Bb*: the *Ar* thristy, drink I] drynk to thristy *Bb* 28 Vesyit] Nor visite *Ba Bb* redemit] did redeme *Ba Bb*: nor ȝit redeme *MF* 30 the deid *Ba Bb MF*: I did *Ar* 31 abone] abuiff *Ba Bb* 33 marcy: mary *Ar* 34 To the ignorant] To ignorantis *Ba Bb*: To ignorant *MF* 37 unto] *followed by* wo (*deleted*) *in Ar* unto saulis] unto my nychtbouris *Ba*: to my nychtbouris *Bb*: on to utheris *MF* support] confort *MF* preching: peching *Ar*: praying *Ba Bb MF* 38 pacient] penitent *Ba Bb* 41–2 *deleted and 43–8 om. in MF* 42 Unto] To *Bb* the . . . sevin of gret] thy . . . of excellent *Ba*: thy . . . excellent of *Bb* 43 To . . . exellence] And of thy halye supper for my sin recompence *Ba*: Thy haly supper for my syn recompence *Bb* eucarist: unacrist *Ar* exellence: exelling *Ar* 44–5 Baptasing . . . uncioun]

Ba has: Gif I for my sin bewaill and mak satisfactioun,
And baptisme als quhilk all my syn wesche doun:
Bb has: And of my gilt the holy satisfactioun,
And bapteme als quhilk all my syn wesche doun

46 sa] als *Ba Bb*

Thy ten commandmentis: a God for to honour,
  Nocht tane in vane, na manslaar to be,
Fader and moder to worschip at all houre,
  To be no theif, the haly day to uphie,
  Nychtburis to luf, fals witnes for to fle,
To leif adultre, to covat na manis rent:
  In all thir, Lord, culpabill knaw I me;
I cry the marcy and laser to repent.

In the twelf artickillis of the treuth: a God to trow—
  The Fader that all wrocht and comprehendit,
And in his only Sone, blissit Jesu,
  Off Mary borne, on croce deid, and discendit,
  The thrid day rais, to the Faderis rycht hand ascendit,
Off quik and ded to cum and hald jugement:
  Into thir pointis, O Lord, quhare I have offendit,
I cry the marcy and lasere to repent.

I trow into the blissit Haly Spreit,
  And in the Kirk—to do as it commandis—
And in the day of dome that we sall ris compleit
  And tak oure flesche agane, baith feit and handis,
  All to be saif into the stait of grace that standis:
Plane I revoik in thir quhair I myswent
  Befor the, juge and lord of sey and landis;
I cry the marcy and laser to repent.

I synnit, Lord, nocht being strang as wall
  In hope, faith, and fervent cherite,
Nocht with the fair foure vertuis cardinall
  Aganis vicis sure anarmyng me:
  With fortitud, prudence and temporance, thir thre,

49–56 *heading* Commandis *in Bb* 49 Thy] The *Ba Bb* a] and *Ba*: ane *Bb*: o *MF* to] till *Ba Bb MF* 50 na manslaar] his name no sleyar *Bb* 55 In all thir] In all this warld *Ba*: Aganis thir preceptis *Bb*: In all this *MF* 57–64 *heading* Articulis creid *in Bb* 57 In the twelf] In *Ba MF*: The *Bb* the] *om. Ba Bb* a] and *Ba*: In *Bb*: Ane *MF* to] I *MF* 58 that all] that all thing *Ba*: that all thingis *Bb*: and all thing *MF* wrocht and] *om. MF* 59 only Sone, blissit] halye blissit sone *Ba Bb*: onlie blissit sone *MF* 60 on] of on *Ba* and] to hell *Bb* 61 rais . . . hand] ryissing to the Fader *Ba Bb*: rysing to the Faderis hand *MF* 63 pointis: pontis *Ar* have] *om. Ba Bb MF* 67 in the day of] to thy *Ba Bb MF* that] *om. MF* 69 into the] in *Ba Bb MF* 70 quhair: quair *Ar* 73 nocht] that nocht *Ba Bb* 74 faith, and] in faith in *Ba Bb*: of faith in *MF* 75 fair] *om. Ba Bb* 77 prudence] *om. MF*

With justice ever in word, werk, and in entent:
To the, Crist Jesu, casting up myn ee,
I cry the marcy and laser to repent.

In the sevin commandis of the Kirk, that is to say
Thy teind to pay, and cursing to eschew,
To keipe the festuall and the fasting day,
The mes on Sonday, the parroche kirk persew,
To proper curat to mak confessioun trew,
Anis in the ȝer to tak the sacrament:
Into thir points quhair I have offendit, sair I rew;
I cry the marcy and laser to repent.

Off syn also into the Haly Spreit,
Off schrift postponit, of syn aganis natour,
Off incontricioun, of confessour undiscreit,
Off ressait synfull of my salviour,
Off undone pennence and satisfactioun sure,
Off the sevin giftis the Haly Gaist me sent,
Off pater noster, and sevin peticionis pure:
I cry the marcy and laser to repent.

Nocht thankand the of gratitud and grace
That thou me wrocht and bocht me with thi ded,
Off this schort tyme remembring nocht the space,
The hevinnis blis, the hellis hiddous feid,
Bot mor trespas, my synnis to remeid
Concluding never all throu myn entent,
Quhois blud on rude for me ran reid,
I cry the marcy and laser to repent.

78 word . . . in] work word or *Ba Bb*: werk wourd and *MF* 81–8 *om. Ba Bb MF* (*81–3 begun and deleted in MF*) 85–6 To . . . sacrament] *transposed in Ar* 89 also into] als aganis *Ba Bb* 90 schrift postponit, of] vertew postponing and *Ba Bb*: schrift postponing of *MF* 91 incontricioun, of] contritioun *Ba Bb* confessour] confessioun *MF* 92 of my] of the my *Ba Bb MF* 93 undone pennence] non repentance *Bb* 94 the Haly] of halie *MF* 95 Off . . . pure] Off sex petitionis in pater noster pure *Ba Bb* and] of *MF* 97 thankand . . . and] thanking . . . nor *Ba Bb MF* 98 bocht me] bocht *Ba Bb* ded] blude *Ba Bb* 99 tyme] lyfe *Ba Bb MF* 100 hiddous feid *Bb*: having confide *Ar*: hidduous sede *Ba*: hidduous feid *MF* 102 never] ever *MF* throu myn] throuch in myne *Ba Bb MF* 103 Quhois] Thow quhois *Ba Bb*: Throw quhois *MF* for me ran reid] ran for men rede *Ba*: ran for my deid *Bb*: for men ran reid *MF*

I knaw me vicius, Lord, and rycht culpabill
In aithis, swering, lessingis and blasflemyng,
Off frustrat speiking in court, in kirk, in tabill,
In word, in will, in wantones expremyng,
Prising my self, and evill my nychtburis demyng;
And so in idilnes my dais I have myspent:
To the wes rent on rude for my redeming,
I cry the marcy and laser to repent.

I have synnit in discimilit thochtis joly,
Up to the hevin extollit in myn entencioun
In hie exaltit arrogance and folly,
Imprudence, derisioun, scorne and vilipencioun,
Presumpcioun, inobedience and contempcioun,
In fals vanglore and deidis necligent:
O thow that deit for my redempcioun,
I cry the marcy and laser to repent.

I have synnit also in reif and opprecioun,
In wrangus gudis taking and posceding
Contrar my ressoun, conscience and discrecioun,
In prodigall spending but reuth of pure folkis neding,
In foule descepcioun, in fals invencionis leding,
To conqueir honour, tresour, land or rent,
In fleschely lust abone messour exceding:
I cry the marcy and laser to repent.

Off mynd dissimilit, Lord, I me confes,
Off feid under ane freindlie continance,

106 lessingis] lesing *Ba Bb* 107 frustrat] frustir Ba *MF* in tabill] or table *Ba*: and table *Bb MF* 108 In . . . wantones] In wordis vyle / in vaneteis *Ba Bb MF* 110 And so] So *MF* I have myspent] I haif spent *Ba*: haif spent *Bb*: have I spent *MF* 111 To the] Thow that *Ba Bb MF* on rude *Ba Bb MF*: *om. Ar* redeming: redempcioun *Ar* 113 have . . . discimilit] synnit in dissaving *Ba MF*: synnit in consaving *Bb* 114 extollit in] extolling *Bb* 116 Imprudence] Proudnes *Ba Bb MF* 119 deit for] deit on rude for *Ba Bb MF* 121 have] *om. Ba Bb MF* and] and in *Ba Bb MF* 122–3 *transposed in Ar* 123 my] gud *Bb* 124 In] Of *Bb* folkis] folk *MF* 125 In . . . leding] *corr.* In foule discepcioun but reuth of pure folkis ne *in Ar* (*deleted*) descepcioun, in] deceptionis *Ba Bb MF* leding] breding *Ba Bb MF* 126 tresour] fre or *MF* or] and *Ba Bb MF* 127 abone] abufe *Ba Bb* 129 Off: O *Ar* 130 ane] a *Ba*: *om. Bb*

Off parsiall juging and perverst wilfulnes,
Off flattering wordis for finyng of substance,
Off fals seling for wrang deliverance
At counsall, sessioun, and at perliament:
Off ever ilk gilt and wickit governance
I cry the marcy and laser to repent.

I schrif me of all cursit cumpany
In all tyme witting and unwiting me;
Off cryminall caus and deid of fellony,
Off ded or slauchter culpabill knaw I me,
Off tiranny, or vengabill cruelte,
In ony wise, deid, counsall or consent:
O deir Jesu that for me deit on tre,
I cry the marcy and laser to repent.

Thoucht I have nocht thi precius feit to kis
As had the Magdalyn quhen scho did marcy craife,
I sall as scho weipe teris for my mys
And every morrow seik the at thi graife,
That seis my hert; as thou hir forgaife,
Thairfor forgife me as synner penitent.
Thy precius body in honour I ressave;
I cry the marcy and laser to repent.

Thow mak me, Jesu, unto the to remember.
I ask thy passioun in me so to abound

131 and] of *MF* 132 Off] In *Ba Bb* for finyng of] and fenȝeing for *MF* 133 seling] solisting *Ba Bb MF* 135 ever ilk] everye *Ba Bb MF* 138 In all tyme] All tyme boith *Ba MF*: All tymes both *Bb* 139 caus and deid] causis and deidis *MF* and deid] of deid *Ba Bb* 140–1 *transposed in Ba Bb MF* 140 Off ded . . . knaw I me] In deid . . . gif I be *Ba*: In hurt . . . gif I be *Bb*: In blude . . . gif I be *MF* 141–2 *transposed in Ar* 141 or] and *Ba Bb* 142 In] Be *Ba Bb MF* wise] maner *Bb* 147 I sall as scho weipe] Allace scho weipit *MF* as scho: eschew *Ar* my] hir *MF* 148 seik] did seik *MF* 149–50 That . . . penitent] *Ba, Bb have*:

Thairfore forgiff me as thow hir forgaiff
That seis my hert as hirris penitent

150 forgife] gif *MF* synner] I am *MF* 151 honour] breist or *Ba Bb MF* 153 Thow] To *Ba Bb MF* unto the to] on the for to *Ba MF*: on the to *Bb* 154 in] *om. Ba Bb* me so to] mynd for to *MF* to: thou *Ar*

Quhill nocht in me unmenȝit be a member
  Bot feiling wo with the of every wound;
  At every straik mak throu my hertis stound
That ever did strenȝe thi fair flesche innocent,
  Sa at na part be of my body sound:
I cry the marcy and laser to repent.

Off all thir synnis that I heir expreme,
  And hes forȝet, to the, Lord, I me schrife,
Appelling fra thy justice court extreme
  Unto thi court of marcy exultive;
  Thou mak my schip in blissit port arrive
That saillis heir in stormes violent,
  And saife me, Jesu, for thy woundis five:
I cry the marcy and laser to repent.

7. [Orisoun]

SALVIOUR, suppois my sensualite
  Subject to syn hes maid my saule of sys,
Sum spark of lycht and spiritualite
Walkynnis my witt, and ressoun biddis me rys;
My corrupt conscience askis, clips and cryis
First grace, syne space for to amend my mys,
Substance with honour doing none suppryis,
Freyndis, prosperite, heir peax, syne hevynis blys.

155 nocht] *om. MF* in] on *MF* in me unmenȝit be] of me unmenȝete be *Ba*: unmenȝeit be in me *Bb* unmenȝit: unmannȝit *Ar* 156 feiling *MF*: felling *Ar*: fall in *Ba Bb* 157 At] And *Ba Bb MF* hertis] hart a *Ba Bb*: hart to *MF* 158 strenȝe] steniȝe *Ba*: stenȝie *Bb*: stryk *MF* 159 be . . . sound] of my bodye be sound *Ba Bb* 160 I cry] Bot crying *Ba Bb* 161 I heir] I did heir *Ba Bb*: I have heir *MF* expreme] expremit *MF* 162 hes] als *Ba Bb* 165 my] thy *MF* arrive] to arryif *Bb* 166 saillis] fallis *MF* 168 I cry] That cryis *Ba Bb MF* *colophon* Heir endis the tabill of confessioun compilit be Mr William Dunber *Ar*: Finis quod Dumbar *Ba Bb*: Heir endis ane confessioun generale compylit be maister Williame Dunbar *MF*

Orisoun. *Text: MS MF* (*p. 326; Reidpeth, f. 40*)
colophon Quod Dumbar *MF*

II

POEMS OF LOVE

8. [Sweit Rois of Vertew]

SWEIT rois of vertew and of gentilnes,
Delytsum lyllie of everie lustynes,
Richest in bontie and in bewtie cleir
And everie vertew that is held most deir,
Except onlie that ȝe ar mercyles:

In to ȝour garthe this day I did persew;
Thair saw I flowris that fresche wer of hew—
Baithe quhyte and rid moist lusty wer to seyne,
And halsum herbis upone stalkis grene:
Ȝit leif nor flour fynd could I nane of rew.

I dout that Merche with his caild blastis keyne
Hes slane this gentill herbe that I of mene
Quhois petewous deithe dois to my hart sic pane
That I wald mak to plant his rute agane,
So confortand his levis unto me bene.

9. [Bewty and the Presoneir]

SEN that I am a presoneir
Till hir that farest is and best,
I me commend fra ȝeir till ȝeir
In till hir bandoun for to rest.
I govit on that gudliest,
So lang to luk I tuk laseir,
Quhill I wes tane withouttin test
And led furth as a presoneir.

Sweit Rois of Vertew. *Text: MS MF (p. 320)*
4 held most *Laing: MF lacks two syllables* *colophon* Quod Dumbar *MF*

Bewty and the Presoneir. *Text: MS B (ff. 214^r–215^r: collated with MS Reidpeth (f. 8; ll. 1–16 only, ending* et quae sequuntur Quod Dumbar)
2, 3 Till] To *R* 5 that] the *R* 6 luk] lurk *R* 7 tane] then *R*

Hir sweit having and fresche bewte
Hes wondit me but swerd or lance;
With hir to go commandit me
Ontill the castell of pennance.
I said, Is this ȝour govirnance,
To tak men for thair luking heir?
Bewty sayis, Ȝa, ser, perchance
Ȝe be my ladeis presoneir.

Thai had me bundin to the ȝet
Quhair Strangenes had bene portar ay
And in deliverit me thairat;
And in thir termis can thai say,
Do wait and lat him nocht away:
Quo Strangenes unto the porteir,
Ontill my lady, I dar lay,
Ȝe be to pure a presoneir.

Thai kest me in a deip dungeoun
And fetterit me but lok or cheyne;
The capitane, hecht Comparesone,
To luke on me he thocht greit deyne.
Thocht I wes wo I durst nocht pleyne
For he had fetterit mony a feir;
With petous voce thus cuth I sene,
Wo is a wofull presoneir.

Langour wes weche upoun the wall
That nevir sleipit bot evir wouke;
Scorne wes bourdour in the hall
And oft on me his babill schuke,
Lukand with mony a dengerous luke:
Quhat is he ȝone, that methis us neir?
Ȝe be to townage, be this buke,
To be my ladeis presoneir.

Gud Houp rownit in my eir
And bad me baldlie breve a bill;

9 Hir] *om. R.* 10 Hes wondit] Thai restit *R* 11 hir] thame *R*
15 Bewty . . . ser] Fresche bewtie said Ȝe *R* 30 a feir: affeir *B*

With Lawlines he suld it beir,
With Fair Service send it hir till.
I wouk and wret hir all my will;
Fair Service fur withouttin feir
Sayand till hir with wirdis still,
Haif pety of ȝour presoneir.

Than Lawlines to Petie went
And said till hir in termis schort,
Lat we ȝone presoneir be schent,
Will no man do to us support;
Gar lay ane sege unto ȝone fort.
Than Petie said, I sall appeir;
Thocht sayis, I hecht, com I ourthort,
I houp to lows the presoneir.

Than to battell thai war arreyit all,
And ay the vawart kepit Thocht;
Lust bur the benner to the wall
And Bissines the grit gyn brocht.
Skorne cryis out, sayis, Wald ȝe ocht?
Lust sayis, We wald haif entre heir;
Comparisone sayis, That is for nocht;
Ȝe will nocht wyn the presoneir.

Thai thairin schup for to defend,
And thai thairfurth sailȝeit ane hour;
Than Bissines the grit gyn bend,
Straik doun the top of the foir tour.
Comparisone began to lour
And cryit furth, I ȝow requeir
Soft and fair and do favour
And tak to ȝow the presoneir.

Thai fyrit the ȝettis deliverly
With faggottis wer grit and huge,
And Strangenes quhair that he did ly
Wes brint in to the porter luge.
Lustely thay lakit bot a juge,

55 com: coim *B*

Sik straikis and stychling wes on steir,
The semeliest wes maid assege
To quhome that he wes presoneir.

Thrucht Skornes nos thai put a prik;
This he wes banist and gat a blek.
Comparisone wes erdit quik
And Langour lap and brak his nek.
Thai sailȝeit fast, all the fek;
Lust chasit my ladeis chalmirleir;
Gud Fame wes drownit in a sek:
Thus ransonit thai the presoneir.

Fra Sklandir hard Lust had undone
His ennemeis, he him aganis
Assemblit ane semely sort full sone,
And rais, and rowttit all the planis:
His cusing in the court remanis,
Bot jalous folkis and geangleiris
And fals Invy that no thing lanis
Blew out on Luvis presoneir.

Syne Matremony that nobill king
Was grevit, and gadderit ane grit ost
And all enermit, without lesing,
Chest Sklander to the west se cost.
Than wes he and his linege lost;
And Matremony withowttin weir
The band of freindschip hes indost
Betuix Bewty and the presoneir.

Be that of eild wes Gud Famis air
And cumyne to continuatioun,
And to the court maid his repair
Quhair Matremony than woir the crowne.
He gat ane confirmatioun,
All that his modir aucht but weir,
And baid still—as it wes resoune—
With Bewty and the presoneir.

90 he: *not in B* 94 Bot] ge *del. in B* 104 Betuix] the *del. in B*

10. The Goldyn Targe

RYGHT as the stern of day begouth to schyne
Quhen gone to bed war Vesper and Lucyne
I raise and by a rosere did me rest;
Up sprang the goldyn candill matutyne
With clere depurit bemes cristallyne
Glading the mery foulis in thair nest;
Or Phebus was in purpur cape revest
Up raise the lark, the hevyns menstrale fyne,
In May in till a morow myrthfullest.

Full angellike thir birdis sang thair houris
Within thair courtyns grene in to thair bouris
Apparalit quhite and rede wyth blomes suete;
Anamalit was the felde wyth all colouris,
The perly droppis schake in silvir schouris,
Quhill all in balme did branch and levis flete;
To part fra Phebus did Aurora grete;
Hir cristall teris I saw hyng on the flouris
Quhilk he for lufe all drank up wyth his hete.

For mirth of May wyth skippis and wyth happis
The birdis sang upon the tender croppis
With curiouse note, as Venus chapell clerkis;
The rosis yong, new spreding of thair knopis,
War powdirit brycht with hevinly beriall droppis
Throu bemes rede birnyng as ruby sperkis;
The skyes rang for schoutyng of the larkis;
The purpur hevyn, ourscailit in silvir sloppis,
Ourgilt the treis, branchis, lef and barkis.

The Goldyn Targe. *Text: Chepman & Myllar print* (*undated*) *collated with MSS B* (*ff.* 345^{r}–348^{v}) *and MF* (*pp. 64–81*). *Heading in print* Here begynnis ane litil tretie intitulit the goldyn targe compilit be Maister Wilyam dunbar
1 begouth] began *B* 2 war] wes *B*: was *MF* 3 rosere] river *MF* 5 cristallyne] cristelling *MF* 7 cape revest] capie vest *MF* 8 raise] sprang *B* fyne] syne *MF* 11 in to] within *B* 12 Apparalit quhite] Apparrellit with quhayte *B* 14 perly] perlit *B* schake] schuke *B MF* 16 To part] Depairt *B MF* 21 note] nottis *B* 22 yong, new] reid now *B*: reid new *MF* 24 birnyng] lemyng *B* 27 lef] leivis *B*

Doune throu the ryce a ryvir ran wyth stremys
So lustily agayn thai lykand lemys
That all the lake as lamp did leme of licht,
Quhilk schadowit all about wyth twynkling glemis
That bewis bathit war in secund bemys
Throu the reflex of Phebus visage brycht:
On every syde the hegies raise on hicht,
The bank was grene, the bruke was full of bremys,
The stanneris clere as stern in frosty nycht.

The cristall air, the sapher firmament,
The ruby skyes of the orient
Kest beriall bemes on emerant bewis grene;
The rosy garth depaynt and redolent
With purpur, azure, gold and goulis gent
Arayed was by dame Flora the quene
So nobily that joy was for to sene;
The roch agayn the rivir resplendent
As low enlumynit all the leves schene.

Quhat throu the mery foulys armony
And throu the ryveris soune rycht ran me by
On Florais mantill I slepit as I lay;
Quhare sone in to my dremes fantasy
I saw approch agayn the orient sky
A saill als quhite as blossum upon spray,
Wyth merse of gold brycht as the stern of day,
Quhilk tendit to the land full lustily
Als falcoune swift desyrouse of hir pray:

And hard on burd unto the blomyt medis
Amang the grene rispis and the redis
Arrivit sche; quhar fro anone thare landis
Ane hundreth ladyes lusty in to wedis,

28 the] *om. B* 29 agayn thai] upoun the *B*: apon thay *MF* 32 That] The *B MF* 34 hegies] ege *B*: hege *MF* raise on] rais hei on *MF* 35 bruke . . . bremys] sone . . . bemis *B* 36 stern] sternis *B* 38 the orient] the reid orient *B* 45 enlumynit] illuminit *B MF* 47 soune rycht] sound that *B MF* 48 as] quhair *B MF* 49 in to] unto *B* 51 A] And *B* als quhite] *om. B* 52 merse] mast *B* 54 Als . . . pray] *om. B* 56 Amang] Amangis *B MF* 58 in to] in till *B MF*

Als fresch as flouris that in May up spredis
In kirtillis grene withoutyn kell or bandis;
Thair brycht hairis hang gletering on the strandis
In tressis clere, wyppit wyth goldyn thredis;
With pappis quhite and mydlis small as wandis.

Discrive I wald, bot quho coud wele endyte
How all the feldis wyth thai lilies quhite
Depaynt war brycht, quhilk to the hevyn did glete?
Noucht thou, Omer, als fair as thou coud wryte,
For all thine ornate stilis so perfyte;
Nor yit thou, Tullius, quhois lippis suete
Off rethorike did in to termes flete:
Your aureate tongis both bene all to lyte
For to compile that paradise complete.

Thare saw I Nature and Venus, quene and quene,
The fresch Aurora, and lady Flora schene,
Juno Appollo, and Proserpyna,
Dyane the goddesse chaste of woddis grene,
My lady Cleo that help of makaris bene,
Thetes, Pallas, and prudent Minerva,
Fair feynit Fortune and lemand Lucina:
Thir mychti quenis in crounis mycht be sene
With bemys blith, bricht as Lucifera.

Thare saw I May, of myrthfull monethis quene,
Betuix Aprile and June hir sistir schene
Within the gardyng walking up and doune,
Quham of the foulis gladdith all bedene;
Scho was full tendir in hir yeris grene.
Thare saw I Nature present hir a goune
Rich to behald and nobil of renoune,

59 in May] in the May *B* 61 hairis . . . gletering] hair . . . glitterand *B MF* 64 Discrive: Distrine *C&M print* 65 feldis . . . thai] flouris . . . thair *B*: feildis . . . thair *MF* 66 war] wes *B*: was *MF* 67 thou, Omer] tholomeir *MF* 68 thine . . . stilis so] thi . . . style most *B*: thi . . . stilis maist *MF* 69 Nor] Na *MF* 70 in to] in till *B MF* 73 and . . . quene] and als dame Venus quene *B* 76 chaste] of chest *B* 78 Thetes] Theses *MF* 80 in] with *B MF* 81 blith, bricht as] bricht blyth as *B*: blyth bricht and *MF* 83 sistir] sisteris *B* 84 gardyng: gardynh *C&M* 86 in] in till *B MF*

Off eviry hew undir the hevin that bene
Depaynt, and broud be gude proporcioun.

Full lustily thir ladyes all in fere
Enterit within this park of most plesere
Quhare that I lay ourhelit wyth levis ronk;
The mery foulis blissfullest of chere
Salust Nature me thoucht on thair manere,
And eviry blome on branch and eke on bonk
Opnyt and spred thair balmy levis donk,
Full low enclynyng to thair quene so clere
Quham of thair noble norising thay thonk.

Syne to dame Flora on the samyn wyse
Thay saluse and thay thank a thousand syse;
And to dame Venus lufis mychti quene
Thay sang ballettis in lufe as was the gyse
With amourouse notis lusty to devise
As thay that had lufe in thair hertis grene;
Thair hony throtis opnyt fro the splene
With werblis suete did perse the hevinly skyes
Quhill loud resownyt the firmament serene.

Ane othir court thare saw I consequent—
Cupide the king wyth bow in hand ybent
And dredefull arowis grundyn scharp and square;
Thare saw I Mars the god armypotent,
Aufull and sterne, strong and corpolent;
Thare saw I crabbit Saturn ald and haire,
His luke was lyke for to perturb the aire;
Thare was Mercurius wise and eloquent,
Of rethorike that fand the flouris faire;

Thare was the god of gardingis, Priapus;
Thare was the god of wildernes, Phanus,
And Janus god of entree delytable;

89 hew undir . . . that] hew that undir . . . hes *B MF* 90 broud] braid *B* 93 ourhelit] heilit *B MF* 95 on] in *B* 96 bonk] blonk *MF* 98 enclynyng . . . so] inclyneand . . . full *B*: inclynit . . . so *MF* 103 ballettis: ballectis *C&M* in] of *B MF* 104 notis lusty] notis most lusty *B MF* 105 thay that] that thai *B* 109 consequent] subsequent *B MF* 110 wyth bow . . . ybent] a bow . . . ay bent *B*: ane bow . . . ay bent *MF* 115 perturb] pturb *C&M* 120 entree delytable] entres dilectable *B*: entres delitabill *MF*

Thare was the god of fludis, Neptunus;
Thare was the god of wyndis, Eolus,
With variand luke rycht lyke a lord unstable;
Thare was Bacus the gladder of the table;
Thare was Pluto the elrich incubus
In cloke of grene—his court usit no sable.

And eviry one of thir in grene arayit
On harp or lute full merily thai playit
And sang ballettis with michty notis clere;
Ladyes to dance full sobirly assayit,
Endlang the lusty ryvir so thai mayit
Thair observance rycht hevynly was to here:
Than crap I throu the levis and drew nere
Quhare that I was rycht sudaynly affrayit,
All throu a luke quhilk I have boucht full dere.

And schortly for to speke, be lufis quene
I was aspyit; scho bad hir archearis kene
Go me arrest, and thay no tyme delayit.
Than ladyes fair lete fall thair mantillis grene;
With bowis big in tressit hairis schene
All sudaynly thay had a felde arayit;
And yit rycht gretly was I noucht affrayit.
The party was so plesand for to sene,
A wonder lusty bikkir me assayit.

And first of all with bow in hand ybent
Come dame Beautee, rycht as scho wald me schent;
Syne folowit all hir dameselis yfere
With mony diverse aufull instrument
Unto the pres; Fair Having wyth hir went,
Fyne Portrature, Plesance, and Lusty Chere.
Than come Resoun with schelde of gold so clere;

123 variand . . . lyke a] variant windis lyk till ane *B*: variand luik lyk till ane *MF* 125 Thare: There *C&M* 126 no sable] un sable *B* 128 or] and *B MF* 134 affrayit: affrayt *C&M* 135 quhilk . . . boucht] that . . . coft *B*: quhilk . . . coft *MF* 136 be] of *B* 139 lete] lute *B* grene: gren *C&M* 140 bowis: lowis *C&M* 141 All] Rycht *B MF* 143 so] to *B* 145 ybent] ay bent *B MF* 147 yfere] in feir *B MF* 149 Unto] On to *MF*

In plate and maille, as Mars armypotent,
Defendit me that nobil chevallere.

Syne tender Youth come wyth hir virgyns ying,
Grene Innocence, and schamefull Abaising,
And quaking Drede wyth humble Obedience:
The goldyn targe harmyt thay no thing;
Curage in thame was noucht begonne to spring;
Full sore thay dred to done a violence.
Suete Womanhede I saw cum in presence;
Of artilye a warld sche did in bring
Servit wyth ladyes full of reverence.

Sche led wyth hir Nurture and Lawlynes,
Contenence, Pacience, Gude Fame and Stedfastnes,
Discrecioun, Gentrise and Considerance,
Levefull Company and Honest Besynes,
Benigne Luke, Mylde Chere and Sobirnes.
All thir bure ganyeis to do me grevance,
Bot Resoun bure the targe wyth sik constance
Thair scharp assayes mycht do no dures
To me, for all thair aufull ordynance.

Unto the pres persewit Hie Degree;
Hir folowit ay Estate and Dignitee,
Comparisoun, Honour, and noble Array,
Will, Wantonnes, Renoun and Libertee,
Richesse, Fredome and eke Nobilitee.
Wit ye thay did thair baner hye display;
A cloud of arowis as hayle schour lousit thay,
And schot quhill wastit was thair artilye,
Syne went abak reboytit of thair pray.

152 plate and] plait of *B MF* 153 that: thas *C&M* 155 Abaising] Abusing *MF* 157 harmyt thay] armit thame *B*: harmit me *MF* 158 Curage] Curagis *MF* 159 sore . . . done] sone . . . do *B*: sone . . . done *MF* 162 wyth] *om. B* 164 Contenence] Continwance *B* 165 Gentrise] Gentilnes *B* 166 Levefull] Lefull *B MF* 168 to] till *MF* 170 assayes . . . do no dures] assay . . . do to me no deirance *B MF* 171 To me, for all thair] For all thair preis and *B MF* 172 Unto] Unto to *B*: One to *MF* persewit: psewit *C&M* 174 Comparisoun: Compisoun *C&M* 180 reboytit of thair] rebutit of the *B*: rebutit of [ ] *MF*

Quhen Venus had persavit this rebute
Dissymilance scho bad go mak persute
At all powere to perse the goldyn targe;
And scho, that was of doubilnes the rute,
Askit hir choise of archeris in refute.
Venus the best bad hir go wale at large;
Scho tuke Presence (plicht ankers of the barge)
And Fair Callyng, that wele a flayn coud schute,
And Cherising for to complete hir charge.

Dame Hamelynes scho tuke in company
That hardy was and hende in archery,
Andároucht dame Beautee to the felde agayn;
With all the choise of Venus chevalry
Thay come and bikkerit unabaisitly;
The schour of arowis rappit on as rayn.
Perilouse Presence that mony syre has slayn
The bataill broucht on bordour hard us by;
The salt was all the sarar, suth to sayn.

Thik was the schote of grundyn dartis kene,
Bot Resoun with the scheld of gold so schene
Warly defendit quho so evir assayit;
The aufull stoure he manly did sustene
Quhill Presence kest a pulder in his ene,
And than as drunkyn man he all forvayit.
Quhen he was blynd, the fule wyth hym they playit
And banyst hym amang the bewis grene;
That sory sicht me sudaynly affrayit.

Than was I woundit to the deth wele nere,
And yoldyn as a wofull prisonnere
To lady Beautee in a moment space;

181 had persavit *MF*: had psavit *C&M*: persavit had *B* 182 Dissymilance] Dissemblance *B MF* persute: psute *C&M* 186 go] to *B* 187 ankers: anker *B MF* 188 coud] can *B*: couth *MF* 191 hardy] hard *B*: hardy *altered to* lady *MF* and] *altered to* rycht *MF* 192 dame] in *B*: in *altered to* dame *MF* 195 as] a *B* 197 bordour hard us] bordour hard me *B*: burde hard me *MF* 199 dartis] arrowis *B* 201 assayit *B MF*: assayes *C&M* 202 stoure] schour *B MF* 203 Quhill *B MF*: Quhilk *C&M* 205 blynd] drukin *B* 206 amang] amangis *B MF* 207 sory] sair *B*: sary *MF* 208 to . . . wele] till . . . full *B*: to . . . full *MF*

Me thoucht scho semyt lustiar of chere
Efter that Resoun tynt had his eyne clere
Than of before, and lufliare of face:
Quhy was thou blyndit, Resoun? quhi, allace!
And gert ane hell my paradise appere,
And mercy seme quhare that I fand no grace.

Dissymulance was besy me to sile,
And Fair Calling did oft apon me smyle,
And Cherising me fed wyth wordis fair;
New Acquyntance enbracit me a quhile
And favouryt me, quhill men mycht go a myle,
Syne tuke hir leve; I saw hir nevir mare.
Than saw I Dangere toward me repair—
I coud eschew hir presence be no wyle.
On syde scho lukit wyth ane fremyt fare

And at the last departing coud hir dresse,
And me delyverit unto Hevynesse
For to remayne; and scho in cure me tuke.
Be this the lord of wyndis, wyth wodenes,
God Eolus, his bugill blew I gesse,
That with the blast the levis all to-schuke;
And sudaynly in the space of a luke
All was hyne went; thare was bot wildernes,
Thare was no more bot birdis, bank and bruke.

In twynklyng of ane eye to scip thai went
And swyth up saile unto the top thai stent
And with swift course atour the flude thai frak;
Thai fyrit gunnis wyth powder violent
Till that the reke raise to the firmament;
The rochis all resownyt wyth the rak,
For rede it semyt that the raynbow brak.
Wyth spirit affrayde apon my fete I sprent
Amang the clewis, so carefull was the crak.

212 tynt had] had tynt *B MF* 213 lufliare] lovarly *B*: lustiar *MF* 216 seme] sene *MF* 217 Dissymulance] Dissemblance *MF* 227 unto] on till *MF* 228, 231 tuke . . . to-schuke *B MF*: take . . . to schake *C&M* 234 bot] *om. B* 236 swyth] swift *B MF* 241 rede] reird *B MF* 243 Amang] Amangis *B*

And as I did awake of my sueving
The joyfull birdis merily did syng
For myrth of Phebus tendir bemes schene;
Suete war the vapouris, soft the morowing,
Halesum the vale depaynt wyth flouris ying,
The air attemperit, sobir and amene;
In quhite and rede was all the felde besene
Throu Naturis nobil fresch anamalyng
In mirthfull May, of eviry moneth quene.

O reverend Chaucere, rose of rethoris all,
As in oure tong ane flour imperiall
That raise in Britane, evir quho redis rycht,
Thou beris of makaris the tryumph riall;
Thy fresch anamalit termes celicall
This mater coud illumynit have full brycht:
Was thou noucht of oure Inglisch all the lycht,
Surmounting eviry tong terrestriall
Alls fer as Mayes morow dois mydnycht?

O morall Gower and Ludgate laureate,
Your sugurit lippis and tongis aureate
Bene to oure eris cause of grete delyte;
Your angel mouthis most mellifluate
Oure rude langage has clere illumynate,
And fair ourgilt oure spech that imperfyte
Stude or your goldyn pennis schupe to write;
This ile before was bare and desolate
Off rethorike, or lusty fresch endyte.

Thou lytill quair, be evir obedient,
Humble, subject, and symple of entent
Before the face of eviry connyng wicht:

244 awake of my sueving] awalk of this swowning *B*: awalk of this swevying *MF* 245 birdis] fowlis *B MF* 247 war . . . soft] was . . . and soft *B*: was [*corr.* with] . . . and soft *MF* 249 attemperit *MF*: attempit *C&M*: intemperit *B* 250 felde] erd *B* 254 ane: and *C&M* 255 Britane] Bartane *MF* 257 Thy . . . celicall] The . . . celestiall *B* fresch: frech *C&M* 258 illumynit have] hafe illuminit *B MF* 263 lippis and tongis] toungis and lippis *B* 264 to] till *B MF* 264–5 *and* 266–70 *transposed in MF* 265 angel mouthis] angelik mowth *B* 267 fair ourgilt] hes ourgilt *B* imperfyte: impfyte *C&M* 268 write: wirte *C&M* 273 face: fare *C&M*

I knaw quhat thou of rethorike hes spent;
Off all hir lusty rosis redolent
Is none in to thy gerland sett on hicht;
Eschame thar of, and draw the out of sicht.
Rude is thy wede, disteynit, bare and rent;
Wele aucht thou be aferit of the licht.

11. [Gude Counsale]

Be ȝe ane luvar, think ȝe nocht ȝe suld
Be weill advysit in ȝour governing?
Be ȝe nocht sa, it will on ȝow be tauld;
Bewar thairwith for dreid of misdemyng.
Be nocht a wreche nor skerche in ȝour spending,
Be layth alway to do amis or schame;
Be rewlit rycht and keip ay this doctring:
Be secreit, trew, incressing of ȝour name.

Be ȝe ane lear, that is werst of all;
Be ȝe ane tratlar, that I hald als evill;
Be ȝe ane janglar, and ȝe fra vertew fall;
Be nevir mair on to thir vicis thrall.
Be now and ay the maistir of ȝour will,
Be nevir he that lesing sall proclame;
Be nocht of langage quhair ȝe suld be still:
Be secreit, trew, incressing of ȝour name.

Be nocht abasit for no wicket tung,
Be nocht sa set as I haif said ȝow heir,
Be nocht sa lerge unto thir sawis sung,
Be nocht our prowd, thinkand ȝe haif no peir;
Be ȝe so wyis that uderis at ȝow leir,
Be nevir he to sklander nor defame,
Be of ȝour lufe no prechour as a freir:
Be secreit, trew, incressing of ȝour name.

274 hes spent *B*: may spent *C&M*: may spend *MF* 275 all] *om. B* 277 thar of] thairfoir *B* 278 disteynit] destitute *B* *colophon* Explicit quod Dumbar of the goldin terge *B*: Explicit the goldin targe compylit be maister William Dunbar *MF*

Gude Counsale. *Text: MS B* (*f. 212*[v])
7 ay *ed.: not in B* 22 nor] *corr.* or to *in B* *colophon* Finis &c. Dumbar *B*

12. [To a Lady, quhone he list to Feyne]

My hartis tresure and swete assured fo,
The finale endar of my lyfe for ever,
The creuell brekar of my hart in tuo,
To go to deathe, this I deservit never;
O man slayar, quhill saule and life dissever
Stynt of ȝour slauchtir; allace, ȝour man am I,
A thowsand tymes that dois ȝow mercy cry.

Have mercie, luif; have mercie, ladie bricht:
Quhat have I wrocht aganis ȝour womanheid
That ȝe suld murdir me, a saikles wicht
Trespassing never to ȝow in word nor deid?
That ȝe consent thairto, O God forbid!
Leif creuelte, and saif ȝour man for schame,
Or throucht the warld quyte losit is ȝour name.

My deathe chasis my lyfe so besalie
That wery is my goist to fle so fast;
Sic deidlie dwawmes so mischeifaislie
Ane hundrithe tymes hes my hairt ouirpast,
Me think my spreit rynnis away full gast
Beseikand grace on kneis ȝow befoir
Or that ȝour man be lost for evermoir.

Behald my wod intollerabill pane
For evermoir quhilk salbe my dampnage;
Quhy undir traist ȝour man thus have ȝe slane?
Lo, deithe is in my breist with furious rage,
Quhilk may no balme nor tryacle asswage
Bot ȝour mercie, for laik of quhilk I de:
Allace, quhair is ȝour womanlie petie?

Behald my deidlie passioun dolorous;
Behald my hiddows hew and wo, allace!
Behald my mayne and murning mervalous
Withe sorrowfull teris falling frome my face:
Rewthe, luif, is nocht, helpe ȝe not in this cace,

To a Lady, quhone he list to Feyne. *Text:* *MS MF* (*pp.* 322–3)
10 ȝe suld murdir: ȝe murdir *MF* *colophon* Quod Dumbar quhone he list to feyne *MF*

For how sould ony gentill hart indure
To se this sycht on ony creature!

Quhyte dow, quhair is ȝour sobir humilnes?
  Swete gentill turtour, quhair is ȝour pete went?
Quhair is ȝour rewthe—the frute of nobilnes,
  Off womanheid the tresour and the rent?
  Mercie is never put out of meik intent,
Nor out of gentill hart is fundin petie,
Sen mercyles may no weycht nobill be.

In to my mynd I sall ȝou mercye cry
  Quhone that my toung sall faill me to speik;
And quhill that nature me my sycht deny,
  And quhill my ene for pane incluse and steik,
  And quhill the dethe my hart in sowndir breik,
And quhill my mynd may think and towng may steir:
And syne, fair weill, my hartis ladie deir!

13. [In Secreit Place]

In secreit place this hindir nycht
I hard ane bern say till a bricht:
My hunny, my houp, my hairt, my heill,
I haif bene lang ȝour lufar leill
And can of ȝow gett confort nane;
How lang will ȝe with denger deill?
Ȝe brek my hart, my bony ane.

His bony berd wes kemd and croppit
Bot all with kaill it wes bedroppit
And he wes townysche, peirt and gukkit.
He clappit fast, he kist, he chukkit
As with the glaikkis he wer ourgane—
Ȝit be his feiris he wald haif fukkit:
Ȝe brek my hairt, my bony ane.

In Secreit Place. *Text: MS B (ff. 103^{v}–104^{r}) collated with MS MF (pp. 310–11; copied in MS Reidpeth, f. 34^{v})*

3 houp . . . hairt] hart . . . hoip *MF* 8 kemd] kemmit *MF*
10 townysche, peirt *MF*: to mich fulich *B* 11 he chukkit] and chukkit *MF*

Quod he, My hairt, sweit as the hunny,
Sen that I born wes of my mynny
I wowit nevir ane uder bot ȝow;
My wame is of ȝour lufe so fow
That as ane gaist I glour and grane;
I trymmill sa, ȝe will not trow:
Ȝe brek my hairt, my bony ane.

Tohie, quod scho, and gaif ane gawf:
Be still, my cowffyne and my cawf,
My new spaind howphyn fra the sowk
And all the blythnes of my bowk;
My sweit swanky, saif ȝow allane
Na leid I luvit all this owk:
Fow leis me that graceles gane.

Quod he, My claver, my curledoddy,
My hony soppis, my sweit possoddy,
Be nocht our bustious to ȝour billie—
Be warme hartit and nocht illwillie;
Ȝour hals, quhyt as quhalis bane,
Gars rys on loft my quhillylillie:
Ȝe brek my hairt, my bony ane.

Quod scho, My clip, my unspaynd jyane
With muderis milk ȝit in ȝour michane,
My belly huddroun, my sweit hurle bawsy,
My honygukkis, my slasy gawsy,
Ȝour musing wald pers ane hairt of stane;
Sa tak gud confort, my gritheidit gawsy:
Fow leis me that graceles gane.

Quod he, My kid, my capircalȝeane,
My bony bab with the ruch brilȝeane,
My tendir girdill, my wally gowdy,
My tirly mirly, my towdy mowdy;

17 wowit . . . uder] never wowit weycht *MF* 22 Tohie: To hie *B*: Tehe *MF* 23 cowffyne] tuchan *MF* 26 swanky] swanking *MF* 28, 42 Fow leis me that] Full leifis me ȝowr *MF* 29 claver, my] claver and my *MF* 32 illwillie] evill wille *MF* 33 hals] heylis *MF* 41 Sa tak] Tak *MF* gawsy] slawsy *MF* 45 girdill] gyrle *MF* 46 towdy] crowdie *MF*

Quhen that our mowthis dois meit at ane
My stang dois storkyn with ȝour towdy:
Ȝe brek my hairt, my bony ane.

Quod scho, Tak me by the hand;
Wylcum, my golk of Maryland,
My chirry and my maikles mynȝeoun,
My sucker sweit as ony unȝeoun,
My strummill stirk ȝit new to spane,
I am applyid to ȝour opinȝoun:
Fow leis me that graceles gane.

He gaif till hir ane appill ruby;
Gramercy, quod scho, My sweit cowhuby.
Syne tha twa till ane play began
Quhilk that thay call the dirrydan,
Quhill bayth thair bewis did meit in ane.
Fow wo, quod scho, Quhair will ȝe, man?
Full leis me that graceles gane.

14. The Tretis of the Tua Mariit Wemen and the Wedo

APON the midsummer evin, mirriest of nichtis,
I muvit furth allane neir as midnicht wes past
Besyd ane gudlie grein garth full of gay flouris
Hegeit of ane huge hicht with hawthorne treis
Quhairon ane bird on ane bransche so birst out hir notis
That never ane blythfullar bird was on the beuche hard.

48 storkyn *MF*: torkin *B* 49 Ȝe brek . . . ane: Ȝe brek &c. *B* 50 scho, Tak] scho now tak *MF* 53 sucker] sowklar *MF* 56 Fow . . . gane: Fow &c. *B*: I luif rycht weill ȝour graceles gane *MF* 57 till] to *MF* 58 Gramercy, quod scho] Quod scho gramercye *MF* 59 Syne . . . till] And thai tway to *MF* 60 that thay] men dois *MF* 61 bayth . . . meit] that thair myrthis met baythe *MF* 62 Fow wo] Wo is me MF 63 Full leis me] Best now I luif *MF* *colophon* Quod Dumbar *MF*: Finis &c. *B* (Quod Clerk *in a different hand*)

The Tretis of the Tua Mariit Wemen and the Wedo. *Text:* (*ll. 1–103*) *MS MF* (*pp. 81–4*); (*ll. 104–530*) *Rouen print* ($a3^r$–$b3^r$) *collated with MS MF* (*pp. 84–96*). *Print lacks first two leaves. Heading in MS MF* Heir beginis the Tretis of the Tua Mariit Wemen and the Wedo Compylit be maister William Dunbar. *Heading and ll. 1–2 re-inked in MS*

2 neir: meid *MF*

Quhat throw the sugarat sound of hir sang glaid
And throw the savour sanative of the sueit flouris,
I drew in derne to the dyk to dirkin efter mirthis;
The dew donkit the daill and dynnit the feulis.
I hard under ane holyn hevinlie grein hewit
Ane hie speiche at my hand with hautand wourdis:
With that in haist to the hege so hard I inthrang
That I was heildit with hawthorne and with heynd leveis.
Throw pykis of the plet thorne I presandlie luikit
Gif ony persoun wald approche within that plesand garding.

I saw thre gay ladeis sit in ane grein arbeir
All grathit in to garlandis of fresche gudlie flouris;
So glitterit as the gold wer thair glorius gilt tressis
Quhill all the gressis did gleme of the glaid hewis.
Kemmit war thair cleir hair and curiouslie sched
Attour thair schulderis doun schyre, schyning full bricht,
With curches cassin thair abone of kirsp cleir and thin.
Thair mantillis grein war as the gress that grew in May sessoun,
Fetrit with thair quhyt fingaris about thair fair sydis.
Off ferlifull fyne favour war thair faceis meik,
All full of flurist fairheid as flouris in June—
Quhyt, seimlie and soft as the sweit lillies
Now upspred upon spray, as new spynist rose;
Arrayit ryallie about with mony riche vardour,
That nature full nobillie annamalit with flouris
Off alkin hewis under hevin that ony heynd knew—
Fragrant, all full of fresche odour fynest of smell.
Ane cumlie tabil coverit wes befoir tha cleir ladeis
With ryalle cowpis apon rawis full of ryche wynis;
And of thir fair wlonkes tua weddit war with lordis,
Ane was ane wedow, I wis, wantoun of laitis.
And as thai talk at the tabill of mony taill sindry
They wauchtit at the wicht wyne and waris out wourdis;
And syn thai spak more spedelie and sparit no matiris.

Bewrie, said the wedo, ȝe woddit wemen ȝing,
Quhat mirth ȝe fand in maryage sen ȝe war menis wyffis;

34–8 *MS faded and defective; readings of beginnings of lines uncertain*
40 *followed in MF by* Aude viduam iam cum interrogatione sua

Reveill gif ȝe rewit that rakles conditioun,
Or gif that ever ȝe luffit leyd upone lyf mair
Nor thame that ȝe ȝour fayth hes festinit for ever,
Or gif ȝe think, had ȝe chois, that ȝe wald cheis better.
Think ȝe it nocht ane blist band that bindis so fast
That none undo it a deill may bot the deith ane?

Than spak ane lusty belyf with lustie effeiris:
It that ȝe call the blist band that bindis so fast
Is bair of blis and bailfull, and greit barrat wirkis.
Ȝe speir had I fre chois gif I wald cheis bettir:
Chenȝeis ay ar to eschew and changeis ar sueit;
Sic cursit chance till eschew, had I my chois anis,
Out of the cheinȝeis of ane churle I chaip suld for evir.
God gif matrimony wer made to mell for ane ȝeir!
It war bot merrens to be mair bot gif our myndis pleisit:
It is agane the law of luf, of kynd and of nature,
Togidder hartis to strene that stryveis with uther:
Birdis hes ane better law na bernis be meikill,
That ilk ȝeir, with new joy, joyis ane maik,
And fangis thame ane fresche feyr unfulȝeit and constant
And lattis thair fulȝeit feiris flie quhair thai pleis.
Cryst gif sic ane consuetude war in this kith haldin!
Than weill war us wemen that evir we war fre;
We suld have feiris as fresche to fang quhen us likit,
And gif all larbaris thair leveis quhen thai lak curage.
My self suld be full semlie in silkis arrayit,
Gymp, jolie and gent, richt joyus and gent:
I suld at fairis be found, new faceis to se,
At playis and at preichingis and pilgrimages greit,
To schaw my renone royaly quhair preis was of folk—
To manifest my makdome to multitude of pepill
And blaw my bewtie on breid quhair bernis war mony,
That I micht cheis and be chosin, and change quhen me
lykit.
Than suld I waill ane full weill our all the wyd realme
That suld my womanheid weild the lang winter nicht;

48 *followed in MF by* Responsio prime vxoris ad viduam 62–5 *last word of each line uncertain* 66 feiris: freiris *MF* 71–2 *MS defective*

And quhen I gottin had ane grome, ganest of uther,
Ȝaip and ȝing, in the ȝok ane ȝeir for to draw,
Fra I had preveit his pitht the first plesand moneth
Than suld I cast me to keik in kirk and in markat
And all the cuntre about kyngis court and uther,
Quhair I ane galland micht get aganis the nixt ȝeir
For to perfurneis furth the werk quhen failȝeit the tother—
A forky fure, ay furthwart and forsy in draucht,
Nother febill nor fant, nor fulȝeit in labour,
Bot als fresche of his forme as flouris in May;
For all the fruit suld I fang thocht he the flour burgeoun.

I have ane wallidrag, ane worme, ane auld wobat carle,
A waistit wolroun na worth bot wourdis to clatter,
Ane bumbart, ane dron bee, ane bag full of flewme,
Ane scabbit skarth, ane scorpioun, ane scutarde behind.
To se him scart his awin skyn grit scunner I think.
Quhen kissis me that carybald, than kyndillis all my sorow—
As birs of ane brym bair his berd is als stif,
Bot soft and soupill as the silk is his sary lume—
He may weill to the syn assent, bot sakles is his deidis.
With gor his tua grym ene ar gladderit all about
And gorgeit lyk tua gutaris that war with glar stoppit;
Bot quhen that glowrand gaist grippis me about
Than think I hiddowus Mahowne hes me in armes.
Thair ma na sanyne me save fra that auld sathane,
For thocht I croce me all cleine fra the croun doun
He wil my corse all beclip and clap me to his breist.
Quhen schaiffyne is that ald schaik with a scharp rasour
He schowis one me his schevill mouth and schedis my lippis,
And with his hard hurcheone scyne sa heklis he my chekis
That as a glemand gleyd glowis my chaftis;
I schrenk for the scharp stound bot schout dar I nought
For schore of that auld schrew—schame him betide.
The luf blenkis of that bogill fra his blerde ene

88 *followed in MF by* Aude vt dicet de viro suo 98 gor his: gor is his *MF* 104 *print begins* me *MF: om. print* 105 schaik] schak *MF*: schalk *Mackenzie* 106 schowis one] chowis *MF* schedis: scheddis *MF*: schendis *print* 107 hurcheone] hurtheone *print* 109 the] that *MF* 111 blerde] bleirit *MF*

As Belȝebub had one me blent abasit my spreit.
And quhen the smy one me smyrkis with his smakes molet
He fepillis like a farcy aver that flyrit one a gillot.
Quhen that the sound of his saw sinkis in my eris
Than ay renewis my noy or he be neir cumand;
Quhen I heir nemmyt his name than mak I nyne crocis
To keip me fra the cummerans of that carll mangit
That full of eldnyng is and anger and all evill thewis.
I dar nought luke to my luf for that lene gib;
He is sa full of jelusy and engyne fals,
Ever ymagynyng in mynd materis of evill,
Compasand and castand cacis a thousand
How he sall tak me with a trawe at trist of ane othir.
I dar nought keik to the knaip that the cop fillis
For eldnyng of that ald schrew that evir one evill thynkis,
For he is waistit and worne fra Venus werkis
And may nought beit worth a bene in bed of my mystirs.
He trowis that ȝoung folk I ȝerne ȝeild, for he gane is,
Bot I may ȝuke all this ȝèr or his ȝerd help.
Ay quhen that caribald carll wald clyme one my wambe
Than am I dangerus and daine and dour of my will;
Ȝit leit I nevir that larbar my leggis ga betueene
To fyle my flesche na fummyll me without a fee gret.
And thoght his pene purly me payis in bed
His purse pays richely in recompense efter;
For or he clyme one my corse, that carybald forlane,
I have conditioun of a curche of kersp all ther fynest,
A goun of engranyt claith right gaily furrit,
A ring with a ryall stane or other riche jowell,
Or rest of his rousty raid, thoght he wer rede wod.
For all the buddis of Johne Blunt, quhen he abone clymis,
Me think the baid deir aboucht, sa bawch ar his werkis.

113 smakes molet: smake smolet *print MF* 115 sound] soundis *MF* his: is *print* 119 eldnyng] elduring *MF* 124 How: Ho *print* trawe at trist: trawe attrist *print*: trew atryst *MF* 125 keik] luik *MF* 126 eldnyng] indilling *MF* 127 waistit: wistit *print* 128 worth: worght *print* 129 ȝerne] warne *MF* for] quhair *MF* 131 Ay] And *MF* 134, 137–45 *endings uncertain in MF* 135 in bed] in to bed *MF* 138 have conditioun] have ane conditioun *MF* curche] curchef *MF* 139 claith right: claitgh ritgh *print* (*recurrent type of error, not recorded infra*) 141 wod: wmyod *print* 143 aboucht, sa bawch: a bouht sa bawth *print* (*recurrent type of error, not recorded infra*)

And thus I sell him solace thoght I it sour think;
Fra sic a syre God ʒow saif, my sueit sisteris deir.

Quhen that the semely had said hir sentence to end
Than all thai leuch apon loft with latis full mery
And raucht the cop round about full of riche wynis
And ralʒeit lang or thai wald rest with ryatus speche.

The wedo to the tothir wlonk warpit ther wordis:
Now fair sister fallis ʒow but fenʒing to tell,
Sen man ferst with matrimony ʒow menskit in kirk,
How haif ʒe farne, be ʒour faith—confese us the treuth—
That band to blise, or to ban—quhilk ʒow best thinkis;
Or how ʒe like lif to leid in to lell spousage?
And syne my self ʒe exeme one the samyn wise,
An I sall say furth the south dissymyland no word.

The plesand said, I protest, the treuth gif I schaw,
That of ʒour toungis ʒe be traist. The tothir twa grantit.
With that sprang up hir spreit be a span hechar.
To speik, quod scho, I sall nought spar; ther is no spy neir.
I sall a ragment reveil fra rute of my hert,
A roust that is sa rankild quhill risis my stomok;
Now sall the byle all out brist that beild has so lang.
For it to beir one my breist wes berdin our hevy;
I sall the venome devoid with a vent large
And me assuage of the swalme that suellit wes gret.

My husband wes a hur maister the hugeast in erd;
Tharfor I hait him with my hert, sa help me our Lord.
He is a ʒoung man ryght ʒaip, bot nought in ʒouth flouris,
For he is fadit full far and feblit of strenth.
He wes as flurising fresche within this few ʒeris,
Bot he is falʒeid full far and fulʒeid in labour.

144 it] eit *MF* 146 to] till *MF* 149 *followed in MF by* Hic bibent et inde vidua Interrogat alteram / mulierem et illa respondet vt sequitur 150 to: *om. print* 152 man] men *MF* menskit: menkit *print*: mensit *MF* 156 ʒe] ʒow *MF* samyn: samy *print* 157 dissymyland] dissembland *MF* 159 tothir] uther *MF* 160, 161 *transposed in MF* 162 fra rute] fra the rute *MF* 164 that . . . lang] that beild hes bein lang *correcting* was burdin our hevie *in MF* 166 devoid] avoyd *MF* 167 the] that *MF* 170 ʒouth] ʒouthis *MF* 172 as] ane *MF*

He has bene lychour so lang quhill lost is his natur,
His lume is waxit larbar and lyis in to swonne.
Wes never sugeorne wer set na one that snaill tyrit,
For eftir sevin oulkis rest it will nought rap anys;
He has bene waistit apone wemen or he me wif chesit,
And in adultre in my tyme I haif him tane oft.
And ȝit he is als brankand with bonet one syde,
And blenkand to the brichtest that in the burgh duellis—
Alse curtly of his clething and kemmyng of his hair
As he that is mare valȝeand in Venus chalmer.
He semys to be sumthing worth, that syphyr in bour,
He lukis as he wald luffit be thoght he be litill of valour;
He dois as dotit dog that damys one all bussis
An liftis his leg apone loft thoght he nought list pische.
He has a luke without lust and lif without curage,
He has a forme without force and fessoun but vertu
And fair wordis but effect, all fruster of dedis.
He is for ladyis in luf a right lusty schadow,
Bot in to derne, at the deid, he salbe drup fundin.
He ralis and makis repet with ryatus wordis
Ay rusing him of his radis and rageing in chalmer;
Bot God wait quhat I think quhen he so thra spekis
And how it settis him so syde to sege of sic materis.
Bot gif him self of sum evin myght ane say amang thaim:
Bot he nought ane is bot nane of naturis possessoris.
Scho that has ane auld man nought all is begylit—
He is at Venus werkis na war na he semys:
I wend I josit a geme and I haif geit gottin;
He had the glemyng of gold and wes bot glase fundin.
Thought men be ferse, wele I fynd, fra falȝe ther curage,
Thar is bot eldnyng or anger ther hertis within.
Ȝe speik of berdis one bewch; of blise may thai sing
That one sanct Valentynis day ar vacandis ilk ȝer:
Hed I that plesand prevelege to part quhen me likit,
To change and ay to cheise agane—than chastite adew!

177 rap] ryd *MF* 182 kemmyng of his hair] kemmit his hair is *MF* 183 As] And *MF* in] in to *MF* 184 semys: sunys *print* 186 as] ane *MF* 187 An] He *MF* list pische] list to pische *MF* 193 repet] rippet *MF* 196 sege] segis *MF* 197 say] sa *MF* 200 na . . . na] na . . . nor *MF* 201 I josit a] I had chosin ane *MF* 204 eldnyng or] endling and *MF*

Than suld I haif a fresch feir to fang in mynn armys;
To hald a freke quhill he faynt may foly be calit.
Apone sic materis I mus at mydnyght full oft
And murnys so in my mynd I murdris my selfin.
Than ly I walkand for wa and walteris about
Wariand oft my wekit kyn that me away cast,
To sic a craudoune but curage that knyt my cler bewte,
And ther so mony kene knyghtis this kenrik within.
Than think I on a semelyar (the suth for to tell)
Na is our syre be sic sevin; with that I sych oft.
Than he ful tendirly dois turne to me his tume person,
And with a ʒoldin ʒerd dois ʒolk me in armys,
And sais, My soverane sueit thing, quhy sleip ʒe no betir?
Me think ther haldis ʒow a hete as ʒe sum harme alyt.
Quoth I, My hony, hald abak and handill me nought sair;
A hache is happinit hastely at my hert rut.
With that I seme for to swoune thought I na swerf tak,
And thus beswik I that swane with my sueit wordis.
I cast on him a crabit e quhen cleir day is cummyn
And lettis it is a luf blenk quhen he about glemys;
I turne it in a tendir luke that I in tene warit
And him behaldis hamely with hertly smyling.

I wald a tendir peronall that myght na put thole,
That hatit men with hard geir for hurting of flesch,
Had my gud man to hir gest; for I dar God suer
Scho suld not stert for his straik a stray breid of erd.
And syne I wald that ilk band that ʒe so blist call
Had bund him so to that bryght quhill his bak werkit;
And I wer in a beid broght with berne that me likit
I trow that bird of my blis suld a bourd want.

Onone quhen this amyable had endit hir speche
Ludly lauchand the laif allowit hir mekle.
Thir gay wiffis maid game amang the grene leiffis:

209 I haif a: I haif I a *print* 210 foly] sillie *MF* 215 that] to *MF* 218 sych: syth *print*: sicht *MF* 221 no] nocht *MF* 224 is] hes *MF* 227 e quhen cleir] and quhen the cleir *MF* 232 hatit] hathit *MF* 237 a] *om. MF* 240 Ludly lauchand: Luly rauthand *print*: Loud lauchand *MF*

Thai drank and did away dule undir derne bewis;
Thai swapit of the sueit wyne, thai swanquhit of hewis,
Bot all the pertlyar in plane thai put out ther vocis.

Than said the weido, I wis ther is no way othir:
Now tydis me for to talk, my taill it is nixt;
God my spreit now inspir and my speche quykkin
And send me sentence to say substantious and noble,
Sa that my preching may pers ȝour perverst hertis
And mak yow mekar to men in maneris and conditiounis.

I schaw ȝow sisteris in schrift I wes a schrew evir,
Bot I wes schene in my schrowd and schew me innocent;
And thought I dour wes and dane, dispitois and bald,
I wes dissymblit suttelly in a sanctis liknes;
I semyt sober and sueit and sempill without fraud,
Bot I couth sexty dissaif that suttillar wer haldin.
Unto my lesson ȝe lyth, and leir at me wit,
Gif you nought list be forleit with losingeris untrew:
Be constant in ȝour governance and counterfeit gud manneris
Thought ȝe be kene, inconstant and cruell of mynd;
Thought ȝe as tygris be terne, be tretable in luf
And be as turtoris in your talk thought ȝe haif talis brukill;
Be dragonis baith and dowis ay in double forme
And quhen it nedis ȝow onone note baith ther stranthis;
Be amyable with humble face as angellis apperand
And with a terrebill tail be stangand as edderis;
Be of ȝour luke like innocentis thoght ȝe haif evill myndis;
Be courtly ay in clething and costly arrayit—
That hurtis ȝow nought worth a hen; ȝowr husband pays for all.

Twa husbandis haif I had, thai held me baith deir;
Thought I dispytit thaim agane thai spyit it na thing.

242 bewis] levis *MF* 243 swapit of] swappit at *MF* 244 *followed in MF by* Nunc bibent et inde prime due Interrogant / viduam et de sua responsione et quomodo / erat 249 that] *om. MF* 252 innocent *MF*: ī nīcrit *print* 258 list be] list befoir be *MF* 260 kene,] kene and *MF* 263 ay] ane *MF* 265 angellis] angell *MF* 270 haif I] I have *MF* thai] that *MF* 271 spyit *MF*: spyt *print*

Ane wes ane hair hogeart that hostit out flewme:
I hatit him like a hund thought I it hid preve;
With kissing and with clapping I gert the carill fone.
Weil couth I krych his cruke bak and kemm his kewt noddill
And with a bukky in my cheik bo on him behind,
And with a bek gang about and bler his ald e
And with a kyind contynance kys his crynd chekis,
In to my mynd makand mokis at that mad fader,
Trouand me with trew lufe to treit him so fair.
This cought I do without dule and na dises tak
Bot ay be mery in my mynd and myrthfull of cher.

I had a lufsummar leid my lust for to slokyn,
That couth be secrete and sure and ay saif my honour
And sew bot at certane tymes and in sicir placis:
Ay quhen the ald did me anger with akword wordis
Apon the galland for to goif it gladit me agane.
I had sic wit that for wo weipit I litill,
Bot leit the sueit ay the sour to gud sesone bring.
Quhen that the chuf wald me chid with girnand chaftis
I wald him chuk cheik and chyn and cheris him so mekill
That his cheif chymys he had chevist to my sone,
Suppos the churll wes gane chaist or the child wes gottin.
As wis woman ay I wrought and not as wod fule,
For mar with wylis I wan na wichtnes of handis.

Syne maryt I a merchand myghti of gudis.
He wes a man of myd eld and of mene statur;
Bot we na fallowis wer in frendschip or blud,
In fredome na furth bering, na fairnes of persoune—
Quhilk ay the fule did forȝet for febilnes of knawlege.
Bot I sa oft thoght him on quhill angrit his hert,
And quhilum I put furth my voce and peddir him callit.

272 hogeart] hachart *MF* 275 krych: keyth *print*: claw *MF*. *See Commentary* 278 chekis] cheik *MF* 282 be] *om. MF* 283 lufsummar] lustiar *MF* 285 at] in *MF* sicir] secreit *MF* 286–7 *MS defective on the left* 287 it] *om. MF* 288 I litill] I bot lytill *MF* 289 gud] the *MF* 292 he *MF*: *om. print* chevist] I wist *MF* 295 wichtnes] vertuousnes *MF* 296 merchand] nĩchand *print* 298 or] nor *MF* 299 na . . . na] nor . . . na *MF*

I wald ryght tuichandly talk be I wes tuyse maryit,
For endit wes my innocence with my ald husband.
I wes apperand to be pert within perfit eild—
Sa sais the curat of our kirk that knew me full ȝing;
(He is our famous to be fals, that fair worthy prelot;
I salbe laith to lat him le quhill I may luke furth.)
I gert the buthman obey—ther wes no bute ellis;
He maid me ryght hie reverens fra he my rycht knew,
For thocht I say it my self the severance wes mekle
Betuix his bastard blude and my birth noble.
That page wes nevir of sic price for to presome anys
Unto my persone to be peir, had pete nought grantit.
Bot mercy in to womanheid is a mekle vertu,
For nevir bot in a gentill hert is generit ony ruth.
I held ay grene in to his mynd that I of grace tuk him,
And for he couth ken him self I curtasly him lerit.
He durst not sit anys my summondis, for or the secund charge
He wes ay redy for to ryn, so rad he wes for blame.
Bot ay my will wes the war of womanly natur:
The mair he loutit for my luf the les of him I rakit,
And eik (this is a ferly thing) or I him faith gaif
I had sic favour to that freke and feid syne for evir.
Quhen I the cure had all clene and him ourcummyn haill
I crew abone that craudone as cok that wer victour.
Quhen I him saw subjeit and sett at myn bydding
Than I him lichtlyit as a lowne and lathit his manneris.
Than woxe I sa unmerciable to martir him I thought,
For as a best I broddit him to all boyis laubour—
I wald haif ridden him to Rome with raip in his heid
Wer not ruffill of my renoune and rumour of pepill.
And ȝit hatrent I hid within my hert all;
Bot quhilis it hepit so huge quhill it behud out.
ȝit tuk I nevir the wosp clene out of my wyde throte

303 tuichandly] twichand in *MF* 308 furth: fueht *print* 309 buthman] bicheman *MF* 310 my] me *MF* 311 severance] soveranis *MF* 315 mercy: nīcy *print* mekle] greit *MF* 318 for he couth] that he culd *MF* 325 cummyn: cūmy *print* 326 wer] was *MF* 327 subjeit . . . myn] subiectit . . . my *MF* sett: soit *print* 329 unmerciable] unmercifull *MF* 331 raip] ane raip *MF* 334 behud] be hid *MF*

Quhill I oucht wantit of my will or quhat I wald desir.
Bot quhen I severit had that syre of substance in erd
And gottin his biggingis to my barne and hie burrow landis,
Than with a stew stert out the stoppell of my hals
That he all stunyst throu the stound, as of a stele wappin.
Than wald I eftir lang first sa fane haif bene wrokin
That I to flyte wes als fers as a fell dragoun.
I had for flattering of that fule fenȝeit so lang,
Mi evidentis of heritagis or thai wer all selit,
My breist that wes gret beild bowdyn wes sa huge
That neir my baret out birst or the band makin.
Bot quhen my billis and my bauchlis wes all braid selit
I wald na langar beir on bridill, bot braid up my heid;
Thar myght na molet mak me moy na hald my mouth in;
I gert the renȝeis rak and rif in to sondir;
I maid that wif carll to werk all womenis werkis
And laid all manly materis and mensk in this eird.
Than said I to my cummaris in counsall about:
Se how I cabeld ȝone cout with a kene brydill—
The cappill that the crelis kest in the caf mydding
Sa curtasly the cart drawis and kennis na plungeing
He is nought skeich na ȝit sker na scippis nought one syd.
And thus the scorne and the scaith scapit he nothir.

He wes no glaidsum gest for a gay lady,
Tharfor I gat him a game that ganyt him bettir.
He wes a gret goldit man and of gudis riche;
I leit him be my lumbart to lous me all misteris,
And he wes fane for to fang fra me that fair office
And thoght my favoris to fynd through his feill giftis.
He grathit me in a gay silk and gudly arrayis,
In gownis of engranyt claight and gret goldin chenȝeis,

337 that] the *MF* 340 throu the] of that *MF* 344 evidentis *MF*: emdentis *print* heritagis]herytage *MF* all] braid *MF* 345 beild bowdyn] beild and bowdin *MF* 347 bauchlis *MF*: bauthles *print; see Commentary* braid] *om. MF* 349 na hald] nor hald *MF* 351 carll] *om. MF* werkis] laubouris *MF* 352 laid all] laid doun all *MF* 356 drawis] drew *MF* 357 skeich na: skeith na *print*: skeycht nor *MF* 359 gest] gaist *MF* a] no *MF* 360–1 *om. MF* 362 my] *om. MF* me all] all my *MF* misteris *MF*: nustīs *print* 363 fra me] fre *MF* 365 a] *om. MF*

In ringis ryally set with riche ruby stonis,
Quhill hely raise my renoune amang the rude peple.
Bot I full craftely did keip thai courtly wedis
Quhill eftir dede of that drupe that docht nought in chalmir;
Thought he of all my clathis maid cost and expense
Ane othir sall the worschip haif that weildis me eftir;
And thoght I likit him bot litill ȝit for luf of othris
I wald me prunȝa plesandly in precius wedis
That luffaris myght apone me luke and ȝing lusty gallandis
That I held more in daynte and derer be ful mekill
Ne him that dressit me so dink; full dotit wes his heyd.
Quhen he wes heryit out of hand to hie up my honoris,
And payntit me as pako proudest of fedderis,
I him miskennyt, be Crist, and cukkald him maid.
I him forleit as a lad and lathlyit him mekle—
I thoght my self a papingay and him a plukit herle;
All thus enforsit he his fa and fortifyit in strenth
And maid a stalwart staff to strik him selfe doune.

Bot of ane bowrd in to bed I sall ȝow breif ȝit.
Quhen he ane hal ȝear wes hanyt, and him behuffit rage,
And I wes laith to be loppin with sic a lob avoir,
Alse lang as he wes one loft I lukit one him nevir
Na leit nevir enter in my thoght that he my thing persit,
Bot ay in mynd ane othir man ymagynit that I haid—
Or ellis had I nevir mery bene at that myrthles raid.
Quhen I that grome geldit had of gudis and of natur
Me thoght him gracelese one to goif, sa me God help.
Quhen he had warit all one me his welth and his substance
Me thoght his wit wes all went away with the laif.
And so I did him dispise; I spittit quhen I saw
That super spendit evill spreit spulȝeit of all vertu.
For weill ȝe wait, wiffis, that he that wantis riches

368 Quhill hely] Quhill all helie *MF* 370 docht: dotht *print* 373 for luf] for the luif *MF* 374 prunȝa] prein *MF* 378 honoris] honour *MF* 383 in] my *MF* 389 Na] And *MF* enter] *om. MF* 390 mynd ane] mynd on ane *MF* 391 at] of *MF* 396 saw] saw him *MF* 397 spendit] expendit *MF* 398 weill] *om. MF* that he] for he *MF*

And valʒeandnes in Venus play is ful vile haldin;
Full fruster is his fresch array and fairnes of persoune,
All is bot frutlese his effeir and falʒeis at the up with.
I buskit up my barnis like baronis sonnis
And maid bot fulis of the fry of his first wif.
I banyst fra my boundis his brethir ilkane;
His frendis as my fais I held at feid evir.
Be this ʒe beleif may I luffit nought him self,
For nevir I likit a leid that langit till his blude;
And ʒit thir wismen, thai wait that all wiffis evill
Ar kend with ther conditionis and knawin with the samin.

Deid is now that dyvour and dollin in erd.
With him deit all my dule and my drery thoghtis;
Now done is my dolly nyght; my day is upsprungin;
Adew dolour, adew; my daynte now begynis.
Now am I a wedow, I wise, and weill am at ese;
I weip as I wer woful, bot wel is me for evir.
I busk as I wer bailfull, bot blith is my hert;
My mouth it makis murnyng and my mynd lauchis;
My clokis thai ar caerfull in colour of sabill
Bot courtly and ryght curyus my corse is ther undir.
I drup with a ded luke in my dule habit,
As with manis daill I had done for dayis of my lif.

Quhen that I go to the kirk cled in cair weid
As foxe in a lambis fleise fenʒe I my cheir.
Than lay I furght my bright buke one breid one my kne
With mony lusty letter ellummynit with gold,
And drawis my clok forthwart our my face quhit
That I may spy unaspyit a space me beside.
Full oft I blenk by my buke and blynis of devotioun
To se quhat berne is best brand or bredest in schulderis
Or forgeit is maist forcely to furnyse a bancat
In Venus chalmir valʒeandly withoutin vane ruse.

399 valʒeandnes] falʒeit anis *MF* play is] play he is *MF* 401 effeir] affect *MF* 403 bot] his *MF* 405 held: heid *print*: had *MF* 408 thai] *om. MF* 412 dolly] dullit *MF* 417 it] *om. MF* 419 ryght] *om. MF* my corse is] is my corps *MF* 421 I *MF: om. print* had done] done had *MF* 427 me beside] be my syd *MF* 429 brand or] branit in *MF*

And as the new mone all pale oppressit with change
Kythis quhilis her cleir face through cluddis of sable,
So keik I through my clokis and castis kynd lukis
To knychtis and to cleirkis and cortly personis.
Quhen frendis of my husbandis behaldis me one fer
I haif a wattir spunge for wa within my wyde clokis,
Than wring I it full wylely and wetis my chekis;
With that watteris myn ene and welteris doune teris.
Than say thai all that sittis about, Se ȝe nought, allace,
Ȝone lustlese led—so lelely scho luffit hir husband;
Ȝone is a pete to enprent in a princis hert,
That sic a perle of plesance suld ȝone pane dre!
I sane me as I war ane sanct and semys ane angell;
At langage of lichory I leit as I war crabit;
I sich without sair hert or seiknes in body:
According to my sable weid I mone haif sad maneris
Or thai will se all the suth; for certis we wemen
We set us all fra the syght to syle men of treuth.
We dule for na evill deid, sa it be derne haldin.

Wise wemen has wayis and wonderfull gydingis
With gret engyne to bejaip ther jolyus husbandis,
And quyetly with sic craft convoyis our materis
That undir Crist no creatur kennis of our doingis.
Bot folk a cury may miscuke that knawlege wantis
And has na colouris for to cover ther awne kindly fautis;
As dois thir damysellis for derne dotit lufe
That dogonis haldis in dainte and delis with thaim so lang,
Quhill al the cuntre knaw ther kyndnes and faith.
Faith has a fair name bot falsheid faris beittir;
Fy one hir that can nought feyne her fame for to saif!
Ȝit am I wise in sic werk and wes all my tyme;
Thoght I want wit in warldlynes I wylis haif in luf
As ony happy woman has that is of hie blude:
Hutit be the halok lase a hundir ȝeir of eild!

435 and cortly] and to courtlie *MF* 437 a wattir] my waltir *MF* clokis] coukis *MF* 439 myn] my *MF* 442 *om. MF* 449 fra *MF*: for *print* 451 wemen *MF*: men *print* 452 bejaip] begaik *MF* 453 convoyis: gvoyis *print*: gydis *MF* 455 miscuke *MF*: mistuke *print* 457 As dois] And dois as *MF* 459 and] of *MF* 461 her fame] hir awin fame *MF* 465 the] that *MF*

I have ane secrete servand rycht sobir of his toung
That me supportis of sic nedis quhen I a syne mak.
Thoght he be sympill to the sicht he has a tong sickir;
Full mony semelyar sege wer service dois mak.
Thoght I haif cair undir cloke the cleir day quhill nyght,
Ȝit haif I solace undir serk quhill the sone ryse.
Ȝit am I haldin a haly wif our all the haill schyre:
I am sa peteouse to the pur quhen ther is personis mony;
In passing of pilgrymage I pride me full mekle—
Mair for the prese of peple na ony perdoun wynyng.

Bot ȝit me think the best bourd quhen baronis and knychtis
And othir bachilleris blith, blumyng in ȝouth,
And all my luffaris lele, my lugeing persewis
And fyllis me wyne wantonly with weilfair and joy:
Sum rownis and sum ralȝeis and sum redis ballatis,
Sum raiffis furght rudly with riatus speche;
Sum plenis and sum prayis, sum prasis mi bewte;
Sum kissis me, sum clappis me, sum kyndnes me proferis;
Sum kerffis to me curtasli, sum me the cop giffis;
Sum stalwardly steppis ben with a stout curage
And a stif standand thing staiffis in mi neiff;
And mony blenkis ben our, that but full fer sittis,
That mai for the thik thrang nought thrif as thai wald.
Bot with my fair calling I comfort thaim all:
For he that sittis me nixt I nip on his finger;
I serf him on the tothir syde on the samin fasson;
And he that behind me sittis I hard on him lene,
And him befor with my fut fast on his I stramp;
And to the bernis far but sueit blenkis I cast:
To every man in speciall speke I sum wordis
So wisly and so womanly quhill warmys ther hertis.

470 quhill] to the *MF* 471 haif I] I have *MF* 473 is *MF: om. print* 474 pilgrymage] pilgramagis *MF* 475 of peple na] of the peaple nor *MF* 478 lugeing *MF*: lugeng *print* 479 And] Sum *MF* 480 rownis *MF*: rowis *print* 488 mai for] may nocht for *MF* 489 Bot] And *MF* 491 serf] schir *MF* 492 sittis *MF: om. print* I hard on him] hard on him I *MF* 493 befor with] before me with *MF* his] *om. MF* 495 speke I] I speik *MF*

Thar is no liffand leid so law of degre
That sall me luf unluffit, I am so loik hertit;
And gif his lust so be lent in to my lyre quhit
That he be lost or with me lig, his lif sall not danger.
I am so mercifull in mynd and menys all wichtis,
My sely saull salbe saif quhen Sabot all jugis.
Ladyis, leir thir lessonis and be no lassis fundin:
This is the legeand of my lif, thought Latyne it be nane.

Quhen endit had hir ornat speche this eloquent wedow,
Lowd thai lewch all the laif and loffit hir mekle,
And said thai sald exampill tak of her soverane teching
And wirk eftir hir wordis, that woman wes so prudent.
Than culit thai ther mouthis with confortable drinkis
And carpit full cummerlik with cop going round.

Thus draif thai our that deir nyght with danceis full noble
Quhill that the day did up daw and dew donkit flouris.
The morow myld wes and meik the mavis did sing,
And all remuffit the myst, and the meid smellit.
Silver schouris doune schuke as the schene cristall,
And berdis schoutit in schaw with ther schill notis.
The goldin glitterand gleme so gladit ther hertis
Thai maid a glorius gle amang the grene bewis.
The soft sowch of the swyr and soune of the stremys,
The sueit savour of the sward, singing of foulis,
Myght confort ony creatur of the kyn of Adam
And kindill agane his curage thoght it wer cald sloknyt.
Than rais thir ryall rosis in ther riche wedis
And rakit hame to ther rest throgh the rise blumys;
And I all prevely past to a plesand arber
And with my pene did report ther pastance most mery.

499 so be] be so *MF* in to] to *MF* 500 lig *MF*: lak *print* not] have no *MF* 502 Sabot] *lacuna in MF faintly filled in with* sall not. *See Commentary* 503 no] nocht *MF* 506 thai] than *MF* 509 ther] *om. MF* 516 schoutit *MF*: shoutit *print* in schaw] in the schaw *MF* schill *MF*: still *print* 517 gladit] glaid *MF* 518 the] thai *MF* 520 sward, singing] swarde and singing *MF* 523, 529 thir *MF*: ryer, ther *print* 526 pastance] pastyme *MF* *colophon* Quod Dunbar *print*: Quod maister Williame Dunbar *MF*

ȝe auditoris most honorable that eris hes gevin
Oneto this uncouth aventur quhilk airly me happinnit:
Of thir thre wantoun wiffis that I haif writtin heir,
Quhilk wald ȝe waill to ȝour wif gif ȝe suld wed one?

15. [Lufis Inconstance]

QUHA will behald of luve the chance
With sueit dissavyng countenance
In quhais fair dissimulance
May none assure;
Quhilk is begun with inconstance
And endis nocht but variance—
Scho haldis with continuance
No serviture.

Discretioun and considerance
Ar both out of hir govirnance,
Quhairfoir of it the schort plesance
May nocht indure;
Scho is so new of acquentance
The auld gais fra remembrance;
Thus I gife our the observans
Of luvis cure.

It is ane pount of ignorance
To lufe in sic distemperance,
Sen tyme mispendit may avance
No creature;
In luve to keip allegance,
It war als nys an ordinance
As quha wald bid ane deid man dance
In sepulture.

Lufis Inconstance. *Text: MS B (f. 281r; following heading* Heir endis the prayis of wemen / And followis the contempt of / Blyndit Luve &c.)

11 the schort] *corr.* with lang *in B* *colophon* Finis *B* (quod Dumbar *in darker ink*)

16. [The Merle and the Nychtingall]

IN May as that Aurora did upspring
With cristall ene chasing the cluddis sable
I hard a merle with mirry notis sing
A sang of lufe with voce rycht comfortable
Agane the orient bemis amiable
Upone a blisfull brenche of lawry grene;
This wes hir sentens sueit and delectable:
A lusty lyfe in luves service bene.

Undir this brench ran doun a revir bricht
Of balmy liquour cristallyne of hew
Agane the hevinly aisur skyis licht,
Quhair did upone the tother syd persew
A nychtingall with suggurit notis new
Quhois angell fedderis as the pacok schone;
This wes hir song, and of a sentens trew:
All luve is lost bot upone God allone.

With notis glaid and glorious armony
This joyfull merle so salust scho the day
Quhill rong the widdis of hir melody,
Saying, Awalk, ȝe luvaris, o this May;
Lo, fresche Flora hes flurest every spray
As Natur hes hir taucht, the noble quene;
The feild bene clothit in a new array:
A lusty lyfe in luvis service bene.

Nevir suetar noyis wes hard with levand man
Na maid this mirry gentill nychtingaill;
Hir sound went with the rever as it ran
Outthrow the fresche and flureist lusty vaill.
O merle, quod scho, O fule, stynt of thy taill,

The Merle and the Nychtingall. *Text: MS B (ff. 283r–284v) collated with MS MF (pp. 165–8)*

1 that] *om. MF* 6 blisfull] blythfull *MF* lawry] *corr.* lawrir *in B* 7 This . . . sentens] Thus . . . sang *MF* 9 bricht] *om. MF* 11 hevinly] *interlined in MF* aisur] *followed by* lusty (*deleted*) *in MF* licht] *corr.* brycht *in MF* 14 angell] angellis *MF* as the] as to the *MF* 17–32 With notis . . . allone.] *om. MF*

For in thy song gud sentens is thair none,
For boith is tynt the tyme and the travaill
Of every luve bot upone God allone.

Seis, quod the merle, thy preching, nychtingale;
Sall folk thair ȝewth spend in to holines?
Of ȝung sanctis growis auld feyndis but faill;
Fy, ypocreit, in ȝeiris tendirnes
Agane the law of kynd thow gois expres
That crukit aige makis on with ȝewth serene,
Quhome Natur of conditionis maid dyvers;
A lusty lyfe in luves service bene.

The nychtingaill said, Fule, remembir the
That both in ȝewth and eild and every hour
The luve of God most deir to man suld be,
That him of nocht wrocht lyk his awin figour
And deit him self fro deid him to succour:
O quhithir wes kythit thair trew lufe or none?
He is most trew and steidfast paramour:
All luve is lost bot apone him allone.

The merle said, Quhy put God so grit bewte
In ladeis with sic womanly having,
Bot gife he wald that thay suld luvit be?
To luve eik Natur gaif thame inclynnyng,
And he of Natur that wirker wes and king
Wald no thing frustir put nor lat be sene
In to his creature of his awin making:
A lusty lyfe in luves service bene.

The nychtingall said, Nocht to that behufe
Put God sic bewty in a ladeis face,
That scho suld haif the thank thairfoir or lufe;

34 sall] Sould *MF* 35 faill *MF*: fable *B* 36 ypocreit] ypocraceis growis *MF* 37 law of kynd] kynd of law *MF* 38 makis on . . . serene] suld nocht . . . be sene *MF* 39 Quhome] Quhilk *MF* 41 Fule] Foull *MF* 42 both] *om.* *MF* ȝewth and eild] eild and ȝouth *MF* 48 him] God *MF* 49 so grit] sic *MF* 50 ladeis] face *interlined in MF* 52 To . . . Natur] And eik nature to luif *MF* 54 nor] na *MF* 55 In to his creature] In creaturis *MF* 58 God sic bewty in] nocht sic luif in to *MF* 59 thairfoir] thairof *MF*

Bot he, the wirker, that put in hir sic grace
Off bewty, bontie, riches, tyme or space
And every gudnes that bene to cum or gone—
The thank redoundis to him in every place:
All luve is lost bot upone God allone.

O nychtingall, it wer a story nyce
That luve suld nocht depend on cherite,
And gife that vertew contrair be to vyce
Than lufe mon be a vertew, as thinkis me;
For ay to lufe invy mone contrair be.
God bad eik lufe thy nychtbour fro the splene,
And quho than ladeis suetar nychbouris be?
A lusty lyfe in lufes service bene.

The nychtingaill said, Bird, quhy dois thow raif?
Man may tak in his lady sic delyt,
Him to forȝet that hir sic vertew gaif
And for his hevin ressaif hir cullour quhyt;
Hir goldin tressit hairis redomyt,
Lyk to Appollois bemis thocht thay schone,
Suld nocht him blind fro lufe that is perfyt:
All lufe is lost bot upone God allone.

The merle said, Lufe is caus of honour ay;
Luve makis cowardis manheid to purchas,
Luve makis knychtis hardy at assey,
Luve makis wrechis full of lergenes,
Luve makis sueir folkis full of bissines,
Luve makis sluggirdis fresche and weill besene,
Luve changis vyce in vertewis nobilnes:
A lusty lyfe in luvis service bene.

The nychtingaill said, Trew is the contrary:
Sic frustir luve it blindis men so far
In to thair myndis it makis thame to vary;

60 he] be *MF* 61 bewty, bontie] bounte, bewte *MF* 62 And] Off *MF* bene] is *MF* 65 it] that *MF* 66 on] in *MF* 68 mon] suld *MF* as thinkis] than think *MF* 74 Man . . . lady] Ane man may in his ladie tak *MF* 75 vertew] bewtie *MF* 76 hevin] ewin *MF* 77 tressit] tressis and *MF* 78 to Appollois] till Apollonis *MF* thocht] quhen that *MF* 81 said] sayis *MF* is caus of] causis *MF* 82 makis] causis *MF* 87 vertewis] vertuous *MF* 90 Sic *MF*: Sie *B* it . . . far] bindis manis hart so sair *MF* 91 myndis] mynd *MF*

In fals vane glory thai so drunkin ar,
Thair wit is went, of wo thai ar nocht war,
Quhill that all wirchip away be fro thame gone—
Fame, guddis and strenth: quhairfoir weill say I dar,
All luve is lost bot upone God allone.

Than said the merle, Myn errour I confes—
This frustir luve all is bot vanite;
Blind ignorance me gaif sic hardines
To argone so agane the varite;
Quhairfoir I counsall every man that he
With lufe nocht in the Feindis net be tone
But luve the Luve that did for his lufe de:
All lufe is lost bot upone God allone.

Than sang thay both with vocis lowd and cleir;
The merle sang, Man, lufe God that hes the wrocht;
The nychtingall sang, Man, lufe the Lord most deir
That the and all this warld maid of nocht;
The merle said, Luve him that thy lufe hes socht
Fra hevin to erd, and heir tuk flesche and bone;
The nychtingall sang, And with his deid the bocht:
All luve is lost bot upone him allone.

Thane flaw thir birdis our the bewis schene,
Singing of lufe amang the levis small,
Quhois ythand pleid ȝit maid my thochtis grene
Bothe sleping, walking, in rest and in travall;
Me to reconfort most it dois availl
Agane for lufe, quhen lufe I can find none,
To think how song this merle and nychtingaill:
All lufe is lost bot upone God allone.

92 vane glory] langar *MF* 94 all] thair *MF* 97 Than . . . Myn] The merle sayis my *MF* 98 This] Sic *MF* all is] is all *MF* 99 me gaif] gaif me *MF* 100 agane] aganis *MF* 102 With] For *MF* net] nek *MF* 103 luve] *om. MF* 106 sang] said *MF* God] him *MF* 107 the Lord] thy God *MF* 108 maid] hes maid *MF* 109 Luve] man luif *MF* thy lufe hes] hes the *MF* 111 sang] said *MF* And . . . the] with all his blude us *MF* 112 him] God *MF* 113 our . . . schene] attour thir feyldis grene *MF* 114 the] thir *MF* 115 ȝit . . . thochtis] in to my thocht is *MF* 117 reconfort most it dois] comfort it dois maist *MF* *colophon* Finis quod Dumbar *B*: Finis quod Dunbar &c. *MF*

17. [Trew Luve]

Now cumis aige quhair ȝewth hes bene
And trew luve rysis fro the splene.

Now culit is dame Venus brand;
Trew luvis fyre is ay kindilland,
And I begyn to undirstand
In feynit luve quhat foly bene:
Now cumis aige quhair ȝewth hes bene
And trew luve rysis fro the splene.

Quhill Venus fyre be deid and cauld
Trew luvis fyre nevir birnis bauld;
So as the ta lufe waxis auld
The tothir dois incres moir kene:
Now cumis aige quhair ȝewth hes bene
And trew lufe rysis fro the splene.

No man hes curege for to wryte
Quhat plesans is in lufe perfyte,
That hes in fenȝeit lufe delyt—
Thair kyndnes is so contrair clene:
Now cumis aige quhair ȝewth hes bene
And trew lufe rysis fro the splene.

Full weill is him that may imprent
Or onywayis his hairt consent
To turne to trew luve his intent
And still the quarrell to sustene:
Now cumis aige quhair ȝewth hes bene
And trew lufe rysis fro the splene.

I haif experience by my sell;
In luvis court anis did I dwell,
Bot quhair I of a joy cowth tell
I culd of truble tell fyftene:
Now cumis aige quhair ȝewth hes bene
And trew lufe rysis fro the splene.

Trew Luve. *Text: MS B (ff. 284v–285v)*
17–18, 29–30, 35–6, 41–2, 47–8, 59–60, 77–8, 83–4 *refrain abbrev. in B*

Befoir quhair that I wes in dreid
Now haif I confort for to speid;
Quhair I had maugre to my meid
I trest rewaird and thankis betuene:
Now cumis aige quhair ȝewth hes bene
And trew lufe rysis fro the splene.

Quhair lufe wes wont me to displeis
Now find I in to lufe grit eis;
Quhair I had denger and diseis
My breist all confort dois contene:
Now cumis aige quhair ȝewth hes bene
And trew lufe rysis fro the splene.

Quhair I wes hurt with jelosy
And wald no luver wer bot I,
Now quhair I lufe I wald all wy
Als weill as I, luvit I wene:
Now cumis aige quhair ȝewth hes bene
And trew lufe rysis fro the splene.

Befoir quhair I durst nocht for schame
My lufe discure nor tell hir name,
Now think I wirschep wer and fame
To all the warld that it war sene:
Now cumis aige quhair ȝewth hes bene
And trew lufe rysis fro the splene.

Befoir no wicht I did complene,
So did hir denger me derene;
And now I sett nocht by a bene
Hir bewty nor hir twa fair ene:
Now cumis aige quhair ȝewth hes bene
And trew lufe rysis fro the splene.

I haif a luve farar of face
Quhome in no denger may haif place,
Quhilk will me guerdoun gif and grace
And mercy ay quhen I me mene:
Now cumis aige quhair ȝewth hes bene
And trew lufe rysis fro the splene.

Unquyt I do no thing nor sane,
Nor wairis a luvis thocht in vane;
I salbe luvit als weill agane,
Thair may no jangler me prevene:
Now cumis aige quhair ȝewth hes bene
And trew luve rysis fro the splene.

Ane lufe so fare, so gud, so sueit,
So riche, so rewthfull and discreit,
And for the kynd of man so meit,
Nevir moir salbe nor ȝit hes bene:
Now cumis aige quhair ȝewth hes bene
And trew luve rysis fro the splene.

Is nane sa trew a luve as He
That for trew lufe of us did de;
He suld be luffit agane, think me,
That wald sa fane our luve obtene:
Now cumis aige quhair ȝewth hes bene
And trew luve rysis fro the splene.

Is non but grace of God I wis
That can in ȝewth considdir this;
This fals dissavand warldis blis
So gydis man in flouris grene:
Now cumis aige quhair ȝewth hes bene
And trew luve rysis fro the splene.

69 luvit als weill: als weill luvit *B* 73–5 *sequence in B ll.* 74 73 75 *but numbered* 2 1 3 *colophon* Finis quod Dumbar

III

POEMS OF COURT LIFE

18. [To the King]

My prince in God, gif the guid grace,
Joy, glaidnes, confort and solace,
Play, pleasance, myrth and mirrie cheir
  In hansill of this guid New ȝeir.

God gif to the ane blissed chance
And of all vertew aboundance
And grace ay for to perseveir
  In hansill of this guid New ȝeir.

God give the guid prosperitie,
Fair fortoun and felicitie,
Evir mair in earth quhill thow ar heir,
  In hansell of this guid New ȝeir.

The heavinlie Lord his help the send
Thy realme to reull and to defend,
In peace and justice it to steir,
  In hansell of this guid New ȝeir.

God gif the blis quharevir thow bownes,
And send the many Fraunce crownes,
Hie liberall heart and handis not sweir,
  In hansell of this guid New ȝeir.

19. [To the King]

Sanct salvatour, send silver sorrow!
It grevis me both evin and morrow
  Chasing fra me all cheritie;
It makis me all blythnes to borrow,
  My panefull purs so priclis me.

To the King. *Text: MS Reidpeth (ff. 2ᵛ–3ʳ)*
11 Evir] *corr.* and *in R*   16 New: *om. R*   *colophon* Quod Dumbar *R*

To the King. *Text: MS B (ff. 113ᵛ–114ʳ)*

Quhen I wald blythlie ballattis breif
Langour thairto givis me no leif;
  War nocht gud howp my hart uphie,
My verry corpis for cair wald cleif;
  My panefull purs so prikillis me.

Quhen I sett me to sing or dance
Or go to plesand pastance,
  Than pansing of penuritie
Revis that fra my remembrance;
  My panefull purs so prikillis me.

Quhen men that hes pursis in tone
Pasis to drynk or to disjone,
  Than mon I keip ane gravetie
And say that I will fast quhill none;
  My panefull purs so priclis me.

My purs is maid of sic ane skyn
Thair will na cors byd it within—
  Fra it as fra the Feynd thay fle.
Quha evir tyne, quha evir win,
  My panefull purs so priclis me.

Had I ane man of ony natioun
Culd mak on it ane conjuratioun
  To gar silver ay in it be,
The Devill suld haif no dominatioun
  With pyne to gar it prickill me.

I haif inquyrit in mony a place
For help and confort in this cace;
  And all men sayis, my lord, that ȝe
Can best remeid for this malice
  That with sic panis prickillis me.

15, 25 *abbrev. in B*   *colophon* Quod Dumbar to the king *B*

20. [Aganis the Solistaris in Court]

Be divers wyis and operatiounes
Men makis in court thair solistationes:
Sum be service and diligence,
Sum be continuall residence;
Sum one his substance dois abyd
Quhill fortoune do for him provyd;
Sum singis, sum dances, sum tellis storyis,
Sum lait at evin bringis in the moryis,
Sum flirdis, sum fenȝeis and sum flatteris,
Sum playis the fuill and all owt clatteris;
Sum man musand be the waw
Luikis as he mycht nocht do with aw;
Sum standis in a nuk and rownes,
For covetyce ane uthair neir swownes;
Sum beris as he wald ga wud
For hait desyr of warldis gud;
Sum at the mes leves all devocion
And besy labouris for premocione;
Sum hes thair advocattis in chalmir
And takis thame selff thairoff no glawmir.
My sempillnes amang the laiff
Wait off na way, sa God me saiff,
Bot with ane humble cheir and face
Refferis me to the kyngis grace;
Me think his graciows countenance
In ryches is my sufficiance.

Aganis the Solistaris in Court. *Text: MS MF* (*p. 8; MFa*: *collated with MSS MFb* (*p. 316*) *and Reidpeth* (*f. 10*)

5 Sum . . . substance] On substance sum men *MFb* 6 Quhill *MFb*: Quhilk *MFa* 11 be] with *MFb* 12 nocht] *om. MFb* 13 in a] in to a *MFb* 15 he] thay *MFb* *colophon* Quod Dumbar *MFa*: Quod Dumbar aganis the Solistaris in court *MFb*

21. [The Magryme]

My heid did ʒak ʒester nicht,
This day to mak that I na micht;
So sair the magryme dois me menʒie,
Perseing my brow as ony ganʒie,
That scant I luik may on the licht.

And now, Schir, laitlie eftir mes,
To dyt thocht I begowthe to dres,
The sentence lay full evill till find—
Unsleipit in my heid behind,
Dullit in dulnes and distres.

Full oft at morrow I upryse
Quhen that my curage sleipeing lyis:
For mirth, for menstrallie and play,
For din nor danceing nor deray,
It will not walkin me no wise.

22. The Dregy of Dunbar Maid to King James the Fowrth being in Strivilling

We that ar heir in hevins glory
To ʒow that ar in purgatory
Commendis us on our hairtly wyis—
I mene we folk in parradyis
In Edinburcht, with all mirrines,
To ʒow of Strivilling in distres
Quhair nowdir plesance nor delyt is
For pety this epistell wrytis.

The Magryme. *Text: MS Reidpeth (f. 6^r)*
5 scant] *interlined in R* 11 oft: off *R* *colophon* Quod Dumbar *R*

The Dregy of Dunbar. *Text: MS B (ff. 102^r–103^v) collated with MS MF (pp. 290–2; Reidpeth, f. 55^v). No title in MF*
title Fowrth: fyift *B* 3 our] *om. MF* 4 in] of *MF* 6 of] at *MF* 7 plesance] plesour *MF* 8 this epistell *MF*: thus ane Apostill *B*

O ȝe heremeitis and hankersaidilis
That takis ȝour pennance at ȝour tablis
And eitis nocht meit restorative
Nor drynkis no wyn confortative
Bot aill, and that is thyn and small,
With few coursis into ȝour hall,
But cumpany of lordis and knychtis
Or ony uder gudly wichtis
Solitar walkand ȝour allone
Seing no thing bot stok and stone;
Out of ȝour panefull purgatory
To bring ȝow to the blis and glory
Off Edinburgh, the mirry toun,
We sall begyn ane cairfull soun,
Ane dirige devoit and meik,
The Lord of blis doing beseik
Ȝow to delyver out of ȝour noy
And bring ȝow sone to Edinburgh joy
For to be mirry amang us;
And sa the dergy begynis thus:

Lectio Prima

The Fader, the Sone, and Haly Gaist,
The mirthfull Mary, virgene chaist,
Of angellis all the ordouris nyne,
And all the hevinly court devyne
Sone bring ȝow fra the pyne and wo
Of Strivilling, every court manis fo,
Agane to Edinburghis joy and blis,
Quhair wirschep, welth and weilfar is,
Pley, plesance and eik honesty:
Say ȝe amen for cheritie.

11 nocht] no *MF* 13 Bot . . . and that] Nor . . . bot that *MF* 14 into] in *MF* 20 and *MF*: of *B* 23 dirige *MF*: dergy *B* 25 noy: nowy *B* 28 And sa the dergy] The dirige *MF* 29 and] the *MF* 30 mirthfull] blissit *MF* 31 ordouris] ordour *MF* 37 and eik] eik and *MF*

Responsio, Tu autem Domine

Tak consolatioun   in ȝour pane,
In tribulatioun   tak consolatioun,
Out of vexatioun   cum hame agane,
Tak consolatioun   in ȝour pane.

Iube Domine benedicere

Oute of distres of Strivilling toun
To Edinburcht blis God mak ȝow boun.

Lectio secunda

Patriarchis, profeitis, and appostillis deir,
Confessouris, virgynis, and marteris cleir,
And all the saitt celestiall;
Devotely we upoun thame call
That sone out of ȝour panis fell
Ȝe may in hevin heir with us dwell
To eit swan, cran, pertrik and plever
And every fische that swymis in rever;
To drynk with us the new fresche wyne
That grew upoun the rever of Ryne,
Fresche fragrant clairettis out of France,
Of Angers and of Orliance,
With mony ane cours of grit dyntie:
Say ȝe amen for cheritie.

Responsorium, Tu autem Domine

God and Sanct Jeill   heir ȝow convoy
Baith sone and weill,   God and Sanct Jeill
To sonce and seill,   solace and joy,
God and Sanct Geill   heir ȝow convoy.

Iube Domine benedicere

Out of Strivilling panis fell
In Edinburcht joy sone mot ȝe dwell.

42 benedicere: benedicite *B*   43 Strivilling] Stirling *MF*   45 and] *om. MF*   47 saitt[hevinlie court *MF*   56 Angers] Angeo *MF*   58 Responsorium] Responsio *MF*   62 Iube Domine benedicere: *om. B*   Strivilling] Stirling *MF*

Lectio tertia

We pray to all the sanctis of hevin
That ar aboif the sterris sevin
ȝow to deliver out of ȝour pennance,
That ȝe may sone play, sing and dance
Heir in to Edinburcht, and mak gud cheir
Quhair welth and weilfair is, but weir;
And I that dois ȝour panis discryve
Thinkis for to vissy ȝow belyve—
Nocht in desert with ȝow to dwell,
Bot as the angell Sanct Gabriell
Dois go betwene fra hevinis glory
To thame that ar in purgatory
And in thair tribulatioun
To gif thame consolatioun
And schaw thame quhen thair panis ar past
Thay sall till hevin cum at last;
And how nane servis to haif sweitnes
That nevir taistit bittirnes,
And thairfoir how suld ȝe considdir
Of Edinburcht blis quhen ȝe cum hiddir
Bot gif ȝe taistit had befoir
Of Strivilling toun the panis soir:
And thairfoir tak in patience
ȝour pennance and ȝour abstinence,
And ȝe sall cum or ȝule begyn
Into the blis that we are in:
Quhilk grant the glorius Trinitie!
Say ȝe amen for cheritie.

Responsorium

Cum hame and dwell   no moir in Strivilling
Frome hiddous hell   cum hame and dwell,
Quhair fische to sell   is non bot spirling;
Cum hame and dwell   no moir in Strivilling.

65 of] in *MF* 69 Heir . . . and mak] And . . . mak *MF* 79 panis ar] pane is *MF* 80 till] to *MF* at last] at the last *MF* 83 suld ȝe] ȝe sould *MF* 86, 93, 96, 97, 101 Strivilling] Stirling *MF* 93 Responsorium] Responsio *MF*

Et ne nos inducas in temptationem de Strivilling:
Sed libera nos a malo illius.
Requiem Edinburgi dona eiis, Domine,
Et lux ipsius luceat eiis.
A porta tristicie de Strivilling,
Erue, Domine, animas et corpora eorum.
Credo gustare statim vinum Edinburgi
In villa viventium:
Requiescant Edinburgi. Amen.
Deus qui iustos et corde humiles
Ex omni eorum tribulatione liberare dignatus es,
Libera famulos tuos apud villam de Stirling versantes
A penis et tristitiis eiusdem,
Et ad Edinburgi gaudia eos perducas
Ut requiescat Strivilling. Amen.

23. The Flyting of Dunbar and Kennedie

SCHIR Johine the Ros, ane thing thair is compild
 In generale be Kennedy and Quinting
Quhilk hes thame self aboif the sternis styld;
 Bot had thay maid of mannace ony mynting
 In speciall, sic stryfe sould rys but stynting;
Howbeit with bost thair breistis wer als bendit
As Lucifer that fra the hevin discendit,
 Hell sould nocht hyd thair harnis fra harmis hynting.

102 *Erue MF: Orna B* *et corpora MF: om. B* 103 *statim*] *not in MF* 105 *Edinburgi. Amen*] *statim. In Edinburgo amen MF. MF adds:*

Domine exaudi orationem meam
Et clamor meus ad te veniat. Oremus

107 *omni*] *not in MF* 110 *eos*] *feliciter MF* 111 *Ut requiescat Strivilling*] *not in MF* *colophon* Heir endis Dumbaris dergy to the king bydand to lang in Stirling *B*: Dumbaris dirige . . . ouir lang in Stirling *MF*

The Flyting of Dunbar and Kennedie. *Text: (ll. 1–315) MS B (ff. 147r–151v, collated with MS MF (pp. 53–79); (ll. 316–552) Chepman & Myllar print (undated) collated with MSS B (ff. 151v–154r) and MF (pp. 79–80, 59–63). Title in B* The Flyting . . . Kennedie / Heir efter followis Jocound and mirrie

1 ane thing thair is] thair is ane thing *MF* 3 thame] thair *MF* 6 Howbeit] Albeit *MF* breistis wer als] breist war als hie *MF* 8 harnis] heid *MF*

The erd sould trymbill, the firmament sould schaik,
  And all the air in vennaum suddane stink,
And all the divillis of hell for redour quaik,
  To heir quhat I suld wryt with pen and ynk:
  For and I flyt, sum sege for schame sould sink,
The se sould birn, the mone sould thoill ecclippis,
Rochis sould ryfe, the warld sould hald no grippis,
  Sa loud of cair the commoun bell sould clynk.

Bot wondir laith wer I to be ane baird,
  Flyting to use for gritly I eschame;
For it is nowthir wynnyng nor rewaird
  Bot tinsale baith of honour and of fame,
  Incres of sorrow, sklander and evill name:
ȝit mycht thay be sa bald in thair bakbytting
To gar me ryme and rais the Feynd with flytting
  And throw all cuntreis and kinrikis thame proclame.

Quod Dumbar to Kennedy.

DIRTIN DUMBAR, quhome on blawis thow thy boist,
  Pretendand the to wryte sic skaldit skrowis?
Ramowd rebald, thow fall doun att the roist
  My laureat lettres at the and I lowis:
  Mandrag, mymmerkin, maid maister bot in mows,
Thrys scheild trumpir with ane threid bair goun,
Say Deo mercy, or I cry the doun,
  And leif thy ryming, rebald, and thy rowis.

Dreid, dirtfast dearch, that thow hes dissobeyit
  My cousing Quintene and my commissar;
Fantastik fule, trest weill thow salbe fleyit;
  Ignorant elf, aip, owll irregular,
  Skaldit skaitbird and commoun skamelar,

10 in vennaum suddane] suld of the venning *MF* (the *in later hand*) 11 of] in *MF* for redour] sall for reddour *MF* (sall *deleted in later hand and* d *prefixed to* reddour) 13 sege] segis *MF* for schame sould sink] suld for schame sink *MF* (*altered in later hand to* suld schame think) 14 mone] sone *MF* thoill] tak *MF* 15 sould hald] micht hald *MF* 18 for] richt *MF* 19 For] At *MF* 21 Incres] Entres *MF* 22 mycht] may *MF* 23 with] in *MF* 24 cuntreis and kinrikis] kinrikis and cuntreis *MF* 27 Ramowd] Raw mowit *MF* fall . . . att] sall . . . to *MF* 31 I cry] I sall cry *MF* 36 aip, owll] owle aip and *MF*

Wan fukkit funling that natour maid ane yrle—
Baith Johine the Ros and thow sall squeill and skirle
And evir I heir ocht of ȝour making mair.

Heir I put sylence to the in all pairtis;
Obey and ceis the play that thow pretendis;
Waik walidrag and verlot of the cairtis,
Se sone thow mak my commissar amendis,
And lat him lay sax leichis on thy lendis
Meikly in recompansing of thi scorne,
Or thow sall ban the tyme that thow wes borne:
For Kennedy to the this cedull sendis.

Quod Kennedy to Dumbar.
Juge in the nixt quha gat the war.

IERSCHE brybour baird, vyle beggar with thy brattis,
Cuntbittin crawdoun Kennedy, coward of kynd;
Evill farit and dryit as Denseman on the rattis,
Lyk as the gleddis had on thy gulesnowt dynd;
Mismaid monstour, ilk mone owt of thy mynd,
Renunce, rebald, thy rymyng; thow bot royis;
Thy trechour tung hes tane ane heland strynd—
Ane lawland ers wald mak a bettir noyis.

Revin, raggit ruke, and full of rebaldrie,
Scarth fra scorpione, scaldit in scurrilitie,
I se the haltane in thy harlotrie
And in to uthir science no thing slie,
Of every vertew void, as men may sie;
Quytclame clergie and cleik to the ane club,
Ane baird blasphemar in brybrie ay to be;
For wit and woisdome ane wisp fra the may rub.

Thow speiris, dastard, gif I dar with the fecht:
ȝe dagone, dowbart, thairof haif thow no dowt.

38 Wan fukkit] Wanfulkit *MF* 42 the] thy *MF* 46 recompansing] recompensatioun *MF* 48 For . . . sendis] *in margin in B* 50 coward] theif *MF* 51 farit] faceit *MF* Denseman] Densmen *MF* 52 had . . . dynd] on thy gule snowt had dynd *MF* 57 raggit] riggit *MF* and] all *MF* 58 Scarth . . . scaldit] Skitterand scorpioun scauld *MF* 63 ay] *om. MF* 65 *preceded by ll. 129–92 in MF* 66 dagone] dragone *MF* dowbart] *added at end of line in MF*

Quhair evir we meit, thairto my hand I hecht
To red thy rebald rymyng with a rowt.
Throw all Bretane it salbe blawin owt
How that thow, poysonit pelour, gat thy paikis;
With ane doig leich I schepe to gar the schowt,
And nowther to the tak knyfe, swerd nor aix.

Thow crop and rute of tratouris tressonable,
The fathir and moder of morthour and mischeif,
Dissaitfull tyrand with serpentis tung unstable,
Cukcald cradoun, cowart, and commoun theif:
Thow purpest for to undo our lordis cheif
In Paislay with ane poysone that wes fell,
For quhilk, brybour, ȝit sall thow thoill a breif:
Pelour, on the I sall it preif my sell.

Thocht I wald lie, thy frawart phisnomy
Dois manifest thy malice to all men;
Fy, tratour theif; fy, glengoir loun, fy, fy!
Fy, feyndly front far fowlar than ane fen!
My freyindis thow reprovit with thy pen;
Thow leis, tratour: quhilk I sall on the preif.
Suppois thy heid war armit tymis ten
Thow sall recryat, or thy croun sall cleif.

Or thow durst move thy mynd malitius—
Thow saw the saill abone my heid up draw;
Bot Eolus full woid and Neptunus,
Mirk and moneles, us met with wind and waw
And mony hundreth myll hyne cowd us blaw
By Holland, Seland, Ʒetland, and Northway coist
In sey desert quhill we wer famist aw:
Ʒit come I hame, fals baird, to lay thy boist.

68 thy] this *MF* 70 that] *om.* *MF* 72 to the tak] tak to the *MF* 74 The] Thow *MF* 75 tyrand] serpent *MF* serpentis tung] teirrand mynd *MF* 77 purpest for to] purposit till *MF* our lordis] the lord thy *MF* 79 For] [For] the *MF* 82 to] till *MF* 83 glengoir loun] ganȝelon *MF* 85 My . . . pen] *om.* *MF* 86 leis] leit *MF* 88 recryat] recry it *MF* or thy] or than thy *MF* 90 abone] abuif *MF* 92 us] wes *B* wind and *MF*: woundis *B* 93 mony] monye ane *MF* blaw] draw *MF* 94 Holland, Seland] hiland forland *MF* Northway] Norroway *MF* 95 sey desert quhill *MF*: desert quhair *B*

Thow callis the rethory with thy goldin lippis;
  Na, glowrand, gaipand fule, thow art begyld.
Thow art bot gluntoch with thy giltin hippis,
  That for thy lounry mony a leisch hes fyld.
  Wan visaged widdefow, out of thy wit gane wyld,
Laithly and lowsy, als lathand as ane leik,
  Sen thow with wirschep wald sa fane be styld—
Haill, soverane senȝeour! Thy bawis hingis throw thy breik.

Forworthin fule, of all the warld reffuse,
  Quhat ferly is, thocht thow rejoys to flyte?
Sic eloquence as thay in Erschry use,
  In sic is sett thy thraward appetyte.
  Thow hes full littill feill of fair indyte:
I tak on me ane pair of Lowthiane hippis
  Sall fairar Inglis mak, and mair parfyte,
Than thow can blabbar with thy Carrik lippis.

Bettir thow ganis to leid ane doig to skomer,
  Pynit pykpuris pelour, than with thy maister pingill.
Thow lay full prydles in the peis this somer
  And fane at evin for to bring hame a single,
  Syne rubbit at ane uthir auld wyfis ingle:
Bot now in winter for purteth thow art traikit—
  Thow hes na breik to latt thy bellokis gyngill;
Beg the ane club for, baird, thow sall go naikit.

Lene larbar loungeour, baith lowsy in lisk and lonȝe;
  Fy, skolderit skyn, thow art bot skyre and skrumple;
For he that rostit Lawarance had thy grunȝe,
  And he that hid sanct Johnis ene with ane wimple,
  And he that dang sanct Augustyne with ane
    rumple

97 thy] the *MF* 98 glowrand] gonnand *MF* 99 gluntoch] glunto *MF* 100 lounry . . . fyld] lymmerie hes money leische befylit *MF* 101 Wan visaged] Vane vagabund *MF* 102 lathand] lauchtane *MF* 104 bawis] ballokis *MF* 106 ferly] marvele *MF* 107 thay in Erschry] thow in eriche dois *MF* 108 thraward] fraward *MF* 114–20 *line-endings defective in MF; supplied from Reidpeth* (*R*) 115 peis this] heit of *R* 116 for] *om. MF* 117 Syne rubbit] And rub it *MF* auld] *om. R* 119 breik]breikis *R* bellokis] balgis *R* 120 club] bratt *R* 121 larbar loungeour] lundyr and lairbair *MF* (baith *deleted*) 122 skyn] skyrne *MF* 124 ene] *corr.* heid *in B*

Thy fowll front had, and he that Bartilmo flaid:
The gallowis gaipis eftir thy graceles gruntill
As thow wald for ane haggeis, hungry gled.

Commirwald crawdoun, na man comptis the ane kers;
Sueir swappit swanky, swynekeper ay for swaittis,
Thy commissar Quintyne biddis the cum kis his ers—
He luvis nocht sic ane forlane loun of laittis.
He sayis thow skaffis and beggis mair beir and aitis
Nor ony cripill in Karrik land abowt;
Uther pure beggaris and thow ar at debaittis—
Decrepit karlingis on Kennedy cryis owt.

Mater annuche I haif, I bid nocht fenʒie,
Thocht thow, fowll trumpour, thus upoun me leid;
Corruptit carioun, he sall I cry thy senʒie.
Thinkis thow nocht how thow come in grit neid
Greitand in Galloway lyk to ane gallow breid,
Ramand and rolpand, beggand koy and ox?
I saw the thair in to thy wathemanis weid
Quhilk wes nocht worth ane pair of auld gray sox.

Ersche katherene, with thy polk breik and rilling,
Thow and thy quene, as gredy gleddis ʒe gang
With polkis to mylne and beggis baith meill and schilling.
Thair is bot lys and lang nailis ʒow amang.
Fowll heggirbald, for henis thus will ʒe hang;
Thow hes ane perrellus face to play with lambis;
Ane thowsand kiddis, wer thay in faldis full strang,
Thy lymmerfull luke wald fle thame and thair damis.

In till ane glen thow hes owt of repair
Ane laithly luge that wes the lippir menis;

127 graceles] gratious *MF* 128 *followed by l. 193 in MF* 129 na man . . . kers] that na man curis ane kers *MF* 130 ay for] fra *MF* 132 nocht sic ane] nane sic *MF* 133 mair] *corr.* thair *in B* 134 Nor] Than *MF* 135 thow are at] thow for wage *MF* 137 Mater . . . haif] I have mater aneuche *MF* 139 he sall I] heir I sall *MF* 140 in grit] in thy grit *MF* 141 to] *om. MF* 142 koy] kow *MF* 143 wathemanis: wachemanis *B*: wathman *MF* 145 polk breik] pok brat *MF* 147 mylne] mill *MF* 149 thus . . . ʒe] ʒit . . . thow *MF* 151 faldis] fauld *MF* 152 lymmerfull] lymmair *MF*

With the ane sowtaris wyfe off blis als bair,
And lyk twa stalkaris steilis in cokis and henis—
Thow plukkis the pultre and scho pullis of the penis.
All Karrik cryis, God gif this dowsy be drownd!
And quhen thow heiris ane guse cry in the glenis
Thow thinkis it swetar than sacrand bell of sound.

Thow lazarus, thow laithly lene tramort,
To all the warld thow may example be
To luk upoun thy gryslie peteous port;
For hiddowis, haw and holkit is thyne ee,
Thy cheik bane bair, and blaiknit is thy ble;
Thy choip, thy choll, garris men for to leif chest;
Thy gane it garris us think that we mon de:
I conjure the, thow hungert heland gaist!

The larbar lukis of thy lang lene craig,
Thy pure pynit thrott peilit and owt of ply,
Thy skolderit skin hewd lyk ane saffrone bag
Garris men dispyt thar flesche, thow spreit of Gy:
Fy, feyndly front! fy, tykis face, fy, fy!
Ay loungand lyk ane loikman on ane ledder;
With hingit luik ay wallowand upone wry
Lyk to ane stark theif glowrand in ane tedder.

Nyse nagus, nipcaik, with thy schulderis narrow,
Thow lukis lowsy loun of lownis aw;
Hard hurcheoun, hirpland hippit as ane harrow,
Thy rigbane rattillis and thy ribbis on raw;
Thy hanchis hirklis with hukebanis harth and haw,
Thy laithly lymis ar lene as ony treis.
Obey, theif baird, or I sall brek thy gaw;
Fowll carrybald, cry mercy on thy kneis.

157 plukkis] pykis *MF* 158 this dowsy be] that deuse war *MF* 160 it] thame *MF* sacrand: seccrind *B*: sacryne *MF* of] that *MF* 161 lene] bene *MF* 162 the] this *MF* 164 For] Full *MF* 165 cheik bane] cheikblaid *MF* 166 Thy . . . garris] Thy choulk, thi chollare, makis *MF* 168 hungert heland] heiland hungart *MF* 169 lukis] linkis *MF* 172 dispyt] dispyse *MF* 173 tykis face, fy] verray tyk face *MF* 175 With . . . wry *MF: om. B* 176 to] till *MF* 178 lowsy loun] lyk ane (lousie *del.*) lowne *MF* 179 hirpland hippit] hippit harpand *MF* 180 ribbis on] ribbis all on *MF* 181 harth] hard *MF* 182 ar] als *MF* 183 baird] carle *MF*

Thow pure pynhippit ugly averill
With hurkland banis holkand throw thy hyd,
Reistit and crynit as hangitman on hill
And oft beswakkit with ane ourhie tyd
Quhilk brewis mekle barret to thy bryd:
Hir cair is all to clenge thy cabroch howis
Quhair thow lyis sawsy in saphron bak and syd,
Powderit with prymros, savrand all with clowis.

Forworthin wirling, I warne the it is wittin
How, skyttand skarth, thow hes the hurle behind;
Wan wraiglane wasp, ma wormis hes thow beschittin
Nor thair is gers on grund or leif on lind.
Thocht thow did first sic foly to me fynd
Thow sall agane with ma witnes than I;
Thy gulsoch gane dois on thy bak it bind,
Thy hostand hippis lattis nevir thy hos go dry.

Thow held the burch lang with ane borrowit goun
And ane caprowsy barkit all with sweit,
And quhen the laidis saw the sa lyk a loun
Thay bickerit the with mony bae and bleit:
Now upaland thow leivis on rubbit quheit;
Oft for ane caus thy burdclaith neidis no spredding,
For thow hes nowthir for to drink nor eit
Bot lyk ane berdles baird that had no bedding.

Strait Gibbonis air that nevir ourstred ane hors,
Bla berfute berne, in bair tyme wes thow borne;
Thow bringis the Carrik clay to Edinburgh cors
Upoun thy botingis hobland, hard as horne;
Stra wispis hingis owt quhair that the wattis ar worne:
Cum thow agane to skar us with thy strais,
We sall gar scale our sculis all the to scorne
And stane the up the calsay quhair thow gais.

185 pure pynhippit *MF*: purehippit *B* 186 holkand . . . thy] holland . . . the *MF* 188 And oft . . . ourhie] And all beskitterrit everie tyme and *MF* 191 sawsy] soust *MF* 192 all with clowis] of no clowse *MF* 195 beschittin] schittin *MF* 196 Nor] Than *MF* or] and *MF* 197 foly] fulty *MF* me *MF*: my *B* 199 Thy] The *MF* 200 go] be *MF* 202 caprowsy] cap roustit *MF* 203 laidis] laddis *MF* 205 on] *corr.* apone *in MF* 207 for . . . eit] to drink nor ȝit to (*interlined*) eit *MF* 213 that] *om. MF*

Off Edinburch the boyis as beis owt thrawis
  And cryis owt ay, Heir cumis our awin queir clerk!
Than fleis thow lyk ane howlat chest with crawis,
  Quhill all the bichis at thy botingis dois bark.
  Than carlingis cryis, Keip curches in the merk—
Our gallowis gaipis—lo! quhair ane greceles gais!
  Ane uthir sayis, I se him want ane sark—
  I reid ȝow, cummer, tak in ȝour lynning clais.

Than rynis thow doun the gait with gild of boyis
  And all the toun tykis hingand in thy heilis;
Of laidis and lownis thair rysis sic ane noyis
  Quhill runsyis rynis away with cairt and quheilis,
  And caiger aviris castis bayth coillis and creilis
For rerd of the and rattling of thy butis;
  Fische wyvis cryis, Fy! and castis doun skillis and skeilis,
  Sum claschis the, sum cloddis the on the cutis.

Loun lyk Mahoun, be boun me till obey,
  Theif, or in greif mischeif sall the betyd;
Cry grace, tykis face, or I the chece and fley;
  Oule, rare and ȝowle—I sall defowll thy pryd;
  Peilit gled, baith fed and bred of bichis syd
And lyk ane tyk, purspyk—quhat man settis by the!
  Forflittin, countbittin, beschittin, barkit hyd,
Clym ledder, fyle tedder, foule edder: I defy the!

Mauch muttoun, byt buttoun, peilit gluttoun, air to Hilhous,
  Rank beggar, ostir dregar, foule fleggar in the flet,
Chittirlilling, ruch rilling, lik schilling in the milhous,
  Baird rehator, theif of nator, fals tratour, feyindis gett,
  Filling of tauch, rak sauch—cry crauch, thow art oursett;

217–22 *MF worn; supplied from Reidpeth* (*R*) 217 Off] In *R* 218 ay] hay *MF* 220 Quhill . . . dois] Sa all the brachattis at thy bottnis *R* 222 gaipis] *om. R* ane] ȝon *R* 226 hingand] hingis *MF* 228 cairt] cartis *MF* 231 skillis] squell *MF* 235 tykis] tyk *MF* fley] *corr.* flee *in MF* 240 fyle] fill *MF* 241 Mauch] Myche *MF* byt *MF*: byle *B* 242 Rank] Bannok *MF* foule] flay *MF* fleggar *MF*: fleggaris *B* 244 rehator] rebeatour *MF* tratour, feyindis] tratour and feyndis *MF* 245 Filling] filine *MF* rak sauch] rak a sauche *MF*

Muttoun dryver, girnall ryver, ȝadswyvar—fowll fell the;
Herretyk, lunatyk, purspyk, carlingis pet,
Rottin crok, dirtin dok—cry cok, or I sall quell the.
Quod Dumbar to Kennedy.

DATHANE deivillis sone and dragone dispitous,
Abironis birth and bred with Beliall,
Wod werwoif, worme and scorpion vennemous,
Lucifers laid, fowll feyindis face infernall,
Sodomyt, syphareit fra sanctis celestiall:
Put I nocht sylence to the, schiphird knaif,
And thow of new begynis to ryme and raif,
Thow salbe maid blait, bleir eit, bestiall.

How thy forbearis come, I haif a feill,
At Cokburnis peth, the writ makis me war,
Generit betuix ane scho beir and a deill:
Sa wes he callit Dewlbeir and nocht Dumbar.
This Dewlbeir, generit of a meir of Mar,
Wes Corspatrik erle of Merche, and be illusioun
The first that evir put Scotland to confusioun
Wes that fals tratour, hardely say I dar.

Quhen Bruce and Balioll differit for the croun
Scottis lordis could nocht obey Inglis lawis;
This Corspatrik betrasit Berwik toun
And slew sevin thowsand Scottismen within thay wawis;
The battall syne of Spottismuir he gart caus,
And come with Edwart Langschankis to the feild
Quhair twelve thowsand trew Scottismen wer keild
And Wallace chest, as the carnicle schawis.

Scottis lordis chiftanis he gart hald and chessone
In firmance fast quhill all the feild wes done

247 purspyk, carlingis] purspyk and carlingis *MF* 252 fowll] and *MF* 255 thow of new begynis] now beginnit of new *MF* 256 bleir eit] bleirit *MF* 258 the writ] as the wryting *MF* 260 Sa . . . callit] Was he and callit *MF* 261 of a meir] on ane meir *MF* 262 Wes] *om. MF* 268 sevin thowsand: vij^{m} *B* within thay] in the *MF* 271 twelve: xij *B* 272 chest, as the carnicle] choissit as us the cronicles *MF*

Within Dumbar, that auld spelunk of tressoun;
Sa Inglis tykis in Scottland wes abone.
Than spulȝeit thay the haly stane of Scone,
The croce of Halyrudhous, and uthir jowellis.
He birnis in hell, body, banis and bowellis,
This Corspatrik that Scotland hes undone.

Wallace gart cry ane counsale in to Perth
And callit Corspatrik tratour be his style;
That dampnit dragone drew him in diserth
And sayd, he kend bot Wallace, king in Kyle:
Out of Dumbar that theif he maid exyle
Unto Edward and Inglis grund agane;
Tigiris, serpentis and taidis will remane
In Dumbar wallis, todis, wolffis and beistis vyle.

Na fowlis of effect amangis tha binkis
Biggis nor abydis for no thing that may be;
Thay stanis of tressone as the bruntstane stinkis.
Dewlbeiris moder, cassin in by the se,
The wariet apill of the forbiddin tre
That Adame eit quhen he tynt Parradyce
Scho eit, invennomit lyk a cokkatryce,
Syne merreit with the Divill for dignite.

Ȝit of new tressone I can tell the tailis
That cumis on nycht in visioun in my sleip:
Archbald Dumbar betrasd the hous of Hailis
Becaus the ȝung lord had Dumbar to keip;
Pretendand throw that to thair rowmis to creip,
Rycht crewaly his castell he persewit,
Brocht him furth boundin and the place reskewit,
Sett him in fetteris in ane dungeoun deip.

276 wes] war *MF* 278 and] with *MF* 283 dampnit] depryvit *MF* in] in till *MF* 286 Unto] On to *MF* 287 Tigiris] Teirandis *R* (*MF faded*) serpentis and taidis] tadis and serpentis *MF* 289–96 *MF partly faded; supplied from Reidpeth* (*R*) 289 effect amangis: effectis amangis *B*: effect of gude amang *MF R* 290 nor abydis] na bydis *R* 294 eit] bayt *R* 295 lyk a] as ane *MF* 298 That] It *MF* 299 Archbald: Archbard *B* 301 throw that to thair] thairthrow to uther *MF* 303 the] his *MF* 304 in ane] in till ane *MF*

It war aganis bayth natur and gud ressoun
That Dewlbeiris bairnis wer trew to God or man,
Quhilkis wer baith gottin, borne and bred with tressoun,
Belgebubbis oyis and curst Corspatrikis clan.
Thow wes prestyt and ordanit be Sathan
For to be borne to do thy kin defame
And gar me schaw thy antecessouris schame;
Thy kin that leivis may wary the and ban.

Sen thow on me thus, lymmer, leis and trattillis
And fyndis sentence foundit of invy,
Thy elderis banis ilk nycht rysis and rattillis:
Apon thy cors vengeance, vengeance thay cry,
Thou art the cause thay may not rest nor ly;
Thou sais for thame few psaltris, psalmis or credis,
Bot geris me tell thair trentalis of mysdedis
And thair ald sin wyth new schame certify.

Insensuate sow, cesse, false Eustase air,
And knaw, kene scald, I hald of Alathya,
And cause me not the cause lang to declare
Off thy curst kyn, Deulber and his allya:
Cum to the croce on kneis and mak a crya;
Confesse thy crime, hald Kenydy the king,
And wyth ane hauthorne scurge thy self and dyng;
Thus dree thy penaunce wyth *deliquisti quia*.

Pas to my commissare and be confest,
Cour before him on kneis, and cum in will,
And syne ger Stobo for thy lyf protest;
Renounce thy rymis, bath ban and birn thy bill,
Heve to the hevyn thy handis, ande hald the still;

305 bayth] *om. MF* 306 or] and *MF* 307 Quhilkis . . . borne] That war bayth borne gottin *MF* 309 prestyt] *blank in MF* 314 sentence foundit] sentence thus foundit *MF* 315 Thy] Thyn *MF* 316 *Chepman & Myllar fragment begins* Apon] And on *B* 318 psaltris, psalmis] psalmes psalteris *MF* 319 trentalis of mysdedis] rentellis and misdeidis *B*: tres-onabill deidis *MF* 323 the cause] the cais *MF* 324 allya: Allya *C&M* 325 kneis: keneis *C&M* 326 the king] thy king *B MF* 328 wyth] *om. B* *deliquisti*] de eli quisti *MF; see Commentary* 332 bill: bull *C&M* 333 hald the] *corr.* hald thy *in MF*

Do thou not thus, bogane, thou salbe brynt
Wyth pik, fire, ter, gun puldre or lynt
  On Arthuris Sete or on ane hyar hyll.

I perambalit of Pernaso the montayn,
  Enspirit wyth Mercury fra his goldyn spere,
And dulcely drank of eloquence the fontayne
  Quhen it was purifit wyth frost and flowit clere;
  And thou come, fule, in Marche or Februere
Thare till a pule, and drank the padok rod
That gerris the ryme in to thy termes glod
  And blaberis that noyis mennis eris to here.

Thou lufis nane Irische, elf, I understand,
  Bot it suld be all trew Scottis mennis lede;
It was the gud langage of this land,
  And Scota it causit to multiply and sprede
  Quhill Corspatrik, that we of tresoun rede,
Thy fore fader, maid Irisch and Irisch men thin,
Throu his tresoun broght Inglise rumplis in:
  Sa wald thy self, mycht thou to him succede.

Ignorant fule, in to thy mowis and mokis
  It may be verifyit that thy wit is thin;
Quhare thou writis Densmen dryit apon the rattis,
  Densmen of Denmark ar of the kingis kyn.
  The wit thou suld have had was castin in
Evyn at thyne ers, bakwart, wyth a staf slong.
Herefore, false harlot, hursone, hald thy tong;
  Deulbere, thou devis the Devill thyne eme wyth
    dyn.

Quhare as thou said that I stall hennis and lammys,
  I latt the witt I have land, store and stakkis;

334 thus] this *MF* bogane] brigane *B*: bogill *MF* 335 pik, fire] pik and fyre *MF* or] and *B MF* 339 dulcely] dulely *B* fontayne] wel and fontane *MF* 340 wyth] fra *MF* 343 the] thy *MF* glod] gude 344 blaberis that] blaberis and billis that *MF* eris] heiris *B* 352 him hun *C&M* 353 mokis] crakkis *MF* 355 apon] on *B MF* 358 thyne thy *B* 360 thyne] thy *B MF* 361 that] *om.* *B MF* 362 land landis *B*

Thou wald be fayn to gnaw, lad, wyth thy gammys,
Undir my burd, smoch banis behynd doggis bakkis:
Thou has a tome purs, I have stedis and takkis;
Thou tynt cultur, I have cultur and pleuch,
Substance and gere; thou has a wedy teuch
On Mount Falconn, about thy crag to rax.

And yit Mount Falconn gallowis is our fair
For to be fylde wyth sik a fruteles face;
Cum hame and hyng on oure gallowis of Aire—
To erd the undir it I sall purchas grace;
To ete thy flesch the doggis sall have na space,
The ravyns sall ryve na thing bot thy tong rutis,
For thou sik malice of thy maister mutis
It is wele sett that thou sik barat brace.

Small fynance amang thy frendis thou beggit,
To stanch the storm wyth haly muldis thou loste;
Thou sailit to get a dowcare for to dreg it,
It lyis closit in a clout on Seland cost;
Sik reule gerris the be servit wyth cald rost
And sitt unsoupit oft beȝond the sey
Criant *caritas* at duris *amore Dei*
Barefut, brekeles, and all in duddis updost.

Deulbere has not ado wyth a Dunbar;
The erl of Murray bure that surname ryght
That evyr trew to the king and constant ware,
And of that kyn come Dunbar of Westfelde knyght.
That successione is hardy, wyse and wycht,
And has na thing ado now wyth the Devile;
Bot Deulbere is thy kyn and kennis the wele
And has in hell for thee a chaumir dicht.

363 gnaw, lad] knaw laird *B* 364 smoch] snoch *B*: smust *MF* 365 purs, I] purs and I *MF* 366 cultur, I] cultyre, and I *MF* 367 Substance] For substance *B* thou has] and ȝow *MF* 371 on] undir *B* 373 na] sum *MF* 375 of] on *MF* 377 amang] amangis *B* 378 the storm] thy scorne *B*: the stormes *MF* 379 sailit to] saill it for to *MF* 382 the] ȝon *MF* 383 *caritas* at duris] at durris Carritas *B* *amore*] pro amore *MF* 385 a] *om. MF* 387 trew . . . ware] trew and constant to the king grace war *B* 388 that *B MF*: tha *C&M* 389 wycht: wyth *C&M*: wicht *B MF* 391 kyn] king *MF* 392 dicht: ditht *C&M*

Cursit croapand craw, I sall ger crop thy tong
And thou sall cry *cor mundum* on thy kneis;
Duerch, I sall dyng the quhill thou dryte and dong
And thou sal lik thy lippis and suere thou leis:
I sall degrade the, graceles, of thy greis,
Scaile the for scorne and shere the of the scule,
Ger round the hede transforme the till a fule
And syne wyth tresone trone the to the treis.

Raw mowit ribald, renegate rehatour,
My linage and fore bearis war ay lele;
It cumis of kynde to the to be a traytoure,
To ryde on nycht, to rug, to reve and stele.
Quhare thou puttis poysoun to me, I appelle
The in that part, preve it, pelour, wyth thy persone;
Clame not to clergy, I defy the, gersone,
Thow sall by it dere wyth me, duerche, and thou dele.

In Ingland, oule, suld be thyne habitacione;
Homage to Edward Langschankis maid thy kyn,
In Dunbar thai ressavit hym, the false nacione:
Thay suld be exilde Scotland mare and myn.
A stark gallowis, a wedy and a pyn
The hede poynt of thyne elderis armes ar;
Wryttyn abone in poesie, Hang Dunbar;
Quarter and draw, and mak that surname thin.

I am the kingis blude, his trew speciall clerk
That nevir yit ymaginit hym offense,
Constant in myn allegeance, word and werk,
Onely dependand on his excellence;

395 Duerch: Duerth *C&M*: derch *B*: Duerche *MF* thou dryte] thow bayt(h) dryt *B*: thou sall dryt *MF* 398 shere . . . the scule] scar . . . thy swle *B* 399 the hede] thy heid *B MF* till] as *B* 400 syne] *om. B* wyth] for *MF* trone the to] gar trone the on *B* 401 rehatour] rebeature *MF* 402 linage and] lenagis *MF* war] was *MF* 403 of kynde] oft *B* 404 rug] rin *B* and] to *B MF* 405 Quhare] Quhen *B MF* 406 preve . . . wyth] and preif . . . with *MF*: and preif it on *B* 407 clergy, I] clergy for I *B* 408 wyth me duerche . . . dele] annuch derch of the deill *B* 409 thyne] thy *B* 410 thy] thyn *MF* 411 thai] *om. B* the] thy *B*: that *MF* 414 thyne] thy *B MF* 415 abone in poesie] in poysie abone *B*: abone be prophecy *MF* 416 that] thy *MF* 417 am the] am of the *MF* blude, his] blude and his *MF* 418 hym] his *B* 419 myn allegeance] mynd in tho(ch)t *B* 420 on] upoun *B*

Traistand to have of his magnificence
Guerdoun, reward and benefice bedene,
Quhen that the ravyns sall ryve out bath thine ene
And on the rattis salbe thy residence.

Fra Etrike Forest furthward to Drumfrese
Thou beggit wyth a pardoun in all kirkis,
Collapis, cruddis, mele, grotis, grisis and geis,
And ondir nycht quhile stall thou staggis and stirkis.
Because that Scotland of thy begging irkis
Thou scapis in France to be a knycht of the felde;
Thou has thy clamschellis and thy burdoun kelde,
Unhonest wayis all, wolroun, that thou wirkis.

Thou may not pas Mount Barnard for wilde bestis,
Nor wyn throu Mount Scarpre for the snawe;
Mount Nycholas, Mount Godart thare arestis
Brigantis sik bois and blyndis thame wyth a blawe.
In Parise wyth the maister buriawe
Abyde, and be his prentice nere the bank
And help to hang the pece for half a frank,
And at the last thy self sall thole the lawe.

Haltane harlot, the devill have gude thou hais!
For fault of puissance, pelour, thou mon pak the;
Thou drank thy thrift, sald and wedsett thy clais;
Thare is na lorde that will in service tak the.
A pak of flaskynnis, fynance for to mak the,
Thou sall ressave in Danskyn of my tailye;
With *de profundis* fend the, and that failye,
And I sall send the blak devill for to bak the.

In to the Katryne thou maid a foule cahute,
For thou bedrate hir doune fra starn to stere;

423 Quhen] Quhair *B* ryve] rug *MF* thine] thy *B MF* 428 ondir] on the *MF* quhile stall thou] quhylis thow stall *B*: quhilk stall thow *MF* 429 that] *om. B* 430 a] *om. B* the] *om. MF* 431 thy clamschellis] the clamschell *MF* 434 Scarpre] scharp *MF* 435 thare] the *B* 436 Brigantis sik bois and] Sic beis of briggand *B* blyndis] bludis *MF* 437 Parise] pairtis *R* the] thy *B* 440 sall] man *B* the lawe] that law *MF* 441 have] a *B MF* 442 mon] ma *B*: man *MF* 443 thrift: trift *C&M* sald and] and als *B* 444 that . . . service] in service that will *B* 446 of] on *MF* 447 fend] sett *B* 448 *line om. MF*

Apon hir sydis was sene that thou coud schute—
  Thy dirt clevis till hir towis this twenty yere:
  The firmament na firth was nevir cler
Quhill thou, Deulbere, devillis birth, was on the see;
The saulis had sonkyn throu the syn of the
  War not the peple maid sa grete prayere.

Quhen that the schip was saynit and undir saile
  Foul brow in holl thou preposit for to pas;
Thou schot, and was not sekir of thy tayle,
  Beschate the stere, the compas and the glas;
  The skippar bad ger land the at the Bas:
Thou spewit and kest out mony a lathly lomp
Fastar than all the marynaris coud pomp,
  And now thy wame is wers than evir it was.

Had thai bene prouvait sa of schote of gune
  By men of were but perile thay had past;
As thou was louse and redy of thy bune
  Thay mycht have tane the collum at the last;
  For thou wald cuk a cartfull at a cast.
Thare is na schip that wil the now ressave;
Thou fylde faster than fyftenesum mycht lave,
  And myrit thaym wyth thy muk to the myd mast.

Throu Ingland, thef, and tak the to thy fute
  And boune with the to have a false botwand;
A horse marschall thou call the at the mute
  And with that craft convoy the throu the land.
  Be na thing argh, tak ferily on hand—
Happyn thou to be hangit in Northumbir

451 sene that thou *B MF*: sene thou *C&M* 452 Thy] The *B* clevis till] clethis to *MF* 453 na] nor *B MF* 454 Deulbere, devillis birth] devillis birth dewlbeir *B*: devilbeir devill birth *MF* 455 The] Thay *MF* sonkyn] suckin *B* throu] all throw *MF* 456 sa] sic *B* 458 holl] how *MF* preposit for] purpost for *B*: purposit *MF* 463 than] nor *B MF* 464 now . . . wers than] ȝit . . . war nor *B* 465 prouvait sa] sa provydit *B*: sa purvait *MF* 468 the collum] na tollum *B* 469 at a] at the *B* 470 wil the] the will *B* 471 fylde] fylit *B*: fild *MF* than] nor *B MF* fyftenesum] fyftein *MF* 472 thy] *om. MF* muk *B MF*: mak *C&M* 474 with the to have] to haif with the *B* 475 marschall: marsehall *C&M* 477 ferily on] frelie upon *MF* 478 Happyn] For happyn *MF* to] *om. MF*

Than all thy kyn ar wele quyte of thy cumbir,
And that mon be thy dome, I undirstand.

Hye souverane lorde, lat nevir this synfull sot
Do schame fra hame unto your nacioun,
That nevir nane sik ane be callit a Scot,
A rottyn crok, louse of the dok, thare doune.
Fra honest folk devoide this lathly lowne;
In sum desert quhare thare is na repaire,
For fylyng and infecking of the aire,
Cary this cankerit corrupt carioun.

Thou was consavit in the grete eclips,
A monstir maid be god Mercurius;
Na hald agayn, na hoo is at thy hips,
Infortunate, false and furius,
Evill schryvin, wan thryvin, not clene na curius;
A myten full of flyting, flyrdom like,
A crabbit, scabbit, evill facit messan tyke,
A schit but wit, schyre and injurius.

Greit in the glaykis gude maister Gilliam gukkis,
Our imperfyte in poetry or in prose,
All clocis undir cloud of nycht thou cukkis;
Rymis thou of me, of rethory the rose?
Lunatike, lymare, luschbald, louse thy hose
That I may touch thy tone wyth tribulation
In recompensing of thy conspiration,
Or turse the out of Scotland; tak thy chose.

Ane benefice quha wald gyve sic ane beste,
Bot gif it war to gyngill Judas bellis;

480 And] For *B* mon] may *MF* 482 nacioun: nacion *C&M* 483 That] Lat *B MF* nane] *om. MF* 484 A] Or *MF* the] thy *MF* 486 In] On *B* 488 Cary] Caus Cary *B* (Caus *apparently added*) corrupt] corruptit *B* 490 god] grit *B* 491, 493 na] nor *B MF* 491 at] in *MF* 494 myten full] myting fule *B* flyrdom like] the flurdome maist lyk *B* 495 A] *om. MF* crabbit, scabbit] *transposed in MF* 496 schyre *MF*: schir *C&M*: schrewit *B* 497 gude] and *MF* Gilliam] Gwilliane *B*: Gibboun *MF* 498 Our . . . prose] Nother parfyte in poecie nor prose *MF* or] and *B* 502 tone] toung *B* 504 thy] the *MF*

Tak the a fidill or a floyte, and geste—
  Undought, thou art ordanyt to not ellis!
  Thy cloutit cloke, thy skryp and thy clamschellis,
Cleke on thy cors, and fare on in to France
And cum thou nevir agayn but a mischance;
  The fend fare wyth the forthwarde our the fellis.

Cankrit Caym, tryit trowane, Tutivillus,
  Marmaidyn, mymmerken, monstir of all men,
I sall ger bake the to the lard of Hill house
  To suelly the in stede of a pullit hen.
  Fowmart, fasert, fostirit in filth and fen,
Foule fond, flend fule, apon thy phisnom fy!
Thy dok of dirt drepis and will nevir dry;
  To tume thy tone it has tyrit carlingis ten.

Conspiratour, cursit cocatrice, hell caa,
  Turk, trumpour, traitour, tyran intemperate;
Thou irefull attircop, Pilate apostata,
  Judas, jow, juglour, lollard laureate;
  Saraȝene, symonyte, provit pagane pronunciate,
Machomete, manesuorne, bugrist abhominabile,
Devill, dampnit dog, sodomyte insatiable,
  With Gog and Magog grete glorificate.

Nero thy nevow, Golyas thy grantsire,
  Pharao thy fader, Egipya thy dame,
Deulbere, thir ar the causis that I conspire,
  Termygantis temptise the, and Vaspasius thine eme;
  Belȝebub thy full brothir will clame
To be thyne air, and Cayphas thy sectour;
Pluto thy hede of kyn and protectour,
  To hell to lede the on lycht day and leme.

507 or a floyte, and] or floyit to *B*: and ane flute and *MF* 510 cors] croce *B* fare on in] syn pas on *MF* 511 mischance: mischanche *C&M* 512 forthwarde] fordwart *B MF* 513 trowane] trowand *MF* 518 fond] fownd *B*: feynd *MF* flend] fleird *B* phisnom fy] phisnomy *B* 519 of dirt drepis . . . nevir] ay drepis of dirt . . . noght *B*: of dirt droppis and nevir gois *MF* 520 tume: tune *C&M*: twme *B*: toyn *MF* has tyrit] wald tyre *B* 521 hell] hellis *B*: and bell *MF* 525 provit] prowd *B* 529, 531 *transposed in MF* 530 Egipya] Egippa *B*: Egiptia *MF* 532 Termygantis] Tarmagant *MF* temptise: tempise *C&M MF* the] *om. B* thine] thy *B MF* 533 will] he will *MF* 534 thyne air] thy air *B* 535 thy hede of] the heid of thy *B* 536 To . . . on] To leid the to hell of *B*

Herode thyne othir eme, and grete Egeas,
  Marciane, Machomete, and Maxencius,
Thy trew kynnismen Antenor and Eneas,
  Throp thy nere nece, and austerne Olibrius,
Puttidew, Baal and Eyobulus:
Thir fendis ar the flour of thy four branchis
Sterand the potis of hell, and nevir stanchis;
  Dout not, Deulbere, *tu es dyabolus*.

Deulbere, thy spere of were but feir thou yelde,
  Hangit, mangit, eddirstangit, strynde *stultorum*,
To me, maist hie Kenydie, and flee the felde,
  Prickit, wickit, convickit lamp *Lollardorum*
  Defamyt, blamyt, schamyt *primas paganorum*.
Out, out, I schout, apon that snowt that snevillis;
Tale tellare, rebellare, induellar wyth the devillis,
  Spynk, sink wyth stynk *ad Tertara termagorum*.
Quod Kennedy to Dumbar:
Juge ȝe now heir quha gat the war.

24. [To Princess Margaret]

Now fayre, fayrest off every fayre,
Princes most plesant and preclare,
The lustyest one alyve that byne:
  Welcum of Scotlond to be quene!

Ȝounge tender plant of pulcritud
Descendyd of imperyalle blode,
Freshe fragrant floure of fayrehede shene:
  Welcum of Scotlond to be quene!

537 thyne] thy *B* 539 kynnismen] kyniswoman *MF* 540 Throp] Ethroup *MF* 541 Eyobulus] Eubalus *B*: eik Eȝobulus *MF* 542 fendis] freyndis *B* flour] flouris *MF* 544, 545 Deulbere] Devilbeir *MF* 546 strynde] stryndie *B*: strynd of *MF* 548 Prickit: Pirckit *C&M*: Pickit *B* wickit, convickit] wickit stickit convickit *B* 549 blamyt, schamyt] *transposed in B* (*line om. and added after* 552) *paganorum*] pagaorium *B*: paginorum *MF* 550 that] thy *MF* 552 *ad Tertara*] ad tertera *C&M*: and Tartara *MF* *colophon Quod . . . war B*: Quod Kennedy to Dunbar *MF*

To Princess Margaret. *Text: BM Royal MSS, no. 58* (*ff.* 17v–18r)

Swet lusty lusum lady clere,
Most myghty kyngis dochter dere,
Borne of a princes most serene:
  Welcum of Scotlond to be quene!

Welcum the Rose bothe rede and whyte,
Welcum the floure of oure delyte,
Oure spreit rejoysyng frome the sone beme:
  Welcum of Scotlond to be quene!
  Welcum of Scotlonde to be quene!

25. [To the King]

SCHIR, for ȝour grace bayth nicht and day
Richt hartlie on my kneis I pray
With all devotioun that I can—
  God gif ȝe war Johne Thomsounis man!

For war it so, than weill war me;
But benefice I wald nocht be;
My hard fortoun wer endit than:
  God gif ȝe war Johne Thomsounis man!

Than wald sum reuth within ȝow rest
For saik of hir, fairest and best
In Bartane sen hir tyme began:
  God gif ȝe war Johne Thomsounis man!

For it micht hurt in no degre
That on so fair and gude as sche
Throw hir vertew sic wirschip wan
  Als ȝow to mak Johne Thomsounis man.

I wald gif all that ever I have
To that conditioun, sa God me saif,
That ȝe had vowit to the swan
  Ane ȝeir to be Johne Thomsounis man.

15 spreit: seqete *MS* (*see Commentary*)

To the King. *Text: MS MF* (*pp. 194–5*)
7 hard: hart *MF* *colophon* Finis quod Dunbar *MF*

The mersy of that sweit meik rose
Suld soft ȝow, thirsill, I suppois,
Quhois pykis throw me so reuthles ran:
  God gif ȝe war Johne Thomsounis man!

My advocat bayth fair and sweit,
The hale rejosing of my spreit,
Wald speid in to my erand than,
  And ȝe war anis Johne Thomsounis man.

Ever quhen I think ȝow harde or dour
Or mercyles in my succour,
Than pray I God and sweit Sanct An
  Gif that ȝe war Johne Thomsounis man!

26. [To the King]

SCHIR, I complane of injuris:
  A refing sonne off rakyng Muris
Hes magellit my making throw his malis
And present it in to ȝowr palis;
  Bot sen he ples with me to pleid
I sall him knawin mak hyne to Calis,
  Bot giff ȝowr henes it remeid.

That fulle dismemberit hes my meter
And poysonid it with strang salpeter,
With rycht defamows speiche off lordis
Quhilk with my collouris all discordis,
  Quhois crewall sclander servis ded;
And in my name all leis recordis:
  Ȝour grace beseik I of remeid.

He has indorsit myn indyting
With versis off his awin hand wryting,
Quhairin baithe sclander is and tressoun;

To the King. *Text: MS MF (pp. 10–11; Reidpeth, f. 11)*
8 dismemberit: dismeberit *MF* 13–14 *completed from R: MF defective*
16 awin] *in margin in MF*

Off ane wod fuill far owt off ressoun
He wantis nocht bot a rowndit heid,
For he has tynt baith wit and ressoun:
Ȝowr grace beseik I off remeid.

Punes him for his deid culpabile,
Or gar deliver him a babile
That Cuddy Rug the Drumfres fuill
May him resave agane this ȝuill,
All roundit in to ȝallow and reid,
That ladis may bait him lyk a buill:
For that to me war sum remeid.

27. [Schir Thomas Norny]

Now lythis off ane gentill knycht
Schir Thomas Norny, wys and wycht
And full off chevelry,
Quhais father was ane giand keyne—
His mother was ane farie queyne
Gottin be sossery.

Ane fairar knycht nor he was ane
On ground may nothair ryd nor gane
Na beire buklar nor brand,
Or cum in to this court, but dreid;
He did full mony valȝeant deid
In Rois and Murray land.

Full mony catherein hes he chaist
And cummerid mony helland gaist
Amang thay dully glennis;
Off the Clan Quhettane twenti scoir
He drave as oxin him befoir
(This deid thocht na man kennis).

18 ressoun] *altered to* seasoun *in margin in MF* *colophon* Quod Dumbar *MF*

Schir Thomas Norny. *Text: MS MF (pp. 3–5; Reidpeth, f. 8)*
4 giand *R*: grand *MF* 5–6, 37–40 *defective in MF; completed from R*
10 to: *not in MF R* 16 Clan: glen *MF* twenti: xx[ti] *MF* *colophon*
Quod Dumbar *MF*

At feastis and brydallis up aland
He wan the gre and the garland—
  Dansit non so on deis;
He hes att werslingis bein ane hunder,
Ȝet lay his body never at under:
  (He knawis giff this be leis).

Was never wyld Robein under bewch
Nor ȝet Roger off Clekniskleuch
  So bauld a berne as he;
Gy off Gysburne, na Allan Bell,
Na Simonis sonnes off Quhynfell
  At schot war never so slie.

This anterous knycht quhar ever he went
At justing and at tornament
  Evermor he wan the gre;
Was never off halff so gryt renowne
Sir Bevis the knycht off Southe Hamptowne:
  (I schrew him giff I le).

Thairfoir Quenetyne was bot a lurdane
That callit him ane full plum jurdane,
  This wyse and worthie knycht;
He callit him fowlar than a full,
He said he was ane licherus bull
  That croynd baith day and nycht.

He wald heff maid him Curris kneff;
I pray God better his honour saiff
  Na to be lychtleit sua:
Ȝet this far furth I dar him prais—
He fyld never sadell in his dais,
  And Curry befyld tua.

Quhairfoir ever at Pesche and Ȝull
I cry him lord off evere full
  That in this regeone duellis;
And verralie that war gryt rycht
For, off ane hy renowned knycht,
  He wanttis no thing bot bellis.

28. [Ane Dance in the Quenis Chalmer]

SIR Jhon Sinclair begowthe to dance
For he was new cum owt of France;
For ony thing that he do mycht
The ane futt ȝeid ay onrycht
  And to the tother wald nocht gree.
Quod ane, Tak up the Quenis knycht!
  A mirrear dance mycht na man see.

Than cam in Maistir Robert Schau:
He leuket as he culd lern tham a,
Bot ay his ane futt did waver;
He stackeret lyk ane strummall aver
  That hopschackellt war aboin the kne;
To seik fra Sterling to Stranaver
  A mirrear daunce mycht na man see.

Than cam in the maister almaser,
Ane hommiltye jommeltye juffler
Lyk a stirk stackarand in the ry;
His hippis gaff mony hoddous cry.
  John Bute the fule said, Waes me,
He is bedirtin; fye, fy!
  A mirrear dance mycht na man se.

Than cam in Dunbar the mackar;
On all the flure thair was nane frackar,
And thair he dancet the dirrye dantoun;
He hoppet lyk a pillie wanton
  For luff of Musgraeffe, men tellis me;
He trippet quhill he tint his panton:
  A mirrear dance mycht na man see.

Than cam in Maesteres Musgraeffe;
Scho mycht heff lernit all the laeffe;

Ane Dance in the Quenis Chalmer. *Text: MS MF (pp. 340–1; Reidpeth, f. 45)*
4 The] *corr.* His *in MF*   23 thair] *interlined in MF*

Quhen I schau hir sa trimlye dance,
Hir guid convoy and contenance,
  Than for hir saek I wissitt to be
The grytast erle or duk in France:
  A mirrear dance mycht na man see.

Than cam in Dame Dounteboir—
God waett gif that schou louket sowr;
Schou maid sic morgeownis with hir hippis,
For lachtter nain mycht hald thair lippis;
  Quhen schou was danceand bisselye,
Ane blast of wind son fra hir slippis:
  A mirrear dance mycht na man se.

Quhen thair was cum in fyve or sax
The Quenis Dog begowthe to rax,
And of his band he maid a bred
And to the danceing soin he him med;
  Quhou mastevlyk abowt ȝeid he!
He stinckett lyk a tyk, sum saed:
  A mirrear dance mycht na man see.

29. [Of James Dog, Kepair of the Quenis Wardrep]

THE wardraipper of Venus boure,
To giff a doublett he is als doure
As it war off ane futt syd frog:
  Madame, ȝe heff a dangerous dog!

Quhen that I schawe to him ȝour markis
He turnis to me again and barkis
As he war wirriand ane hog:
  Madame, ȝe heff a dangerous dog!

42 mirrear: mirrar *MF* *colophon* Quod Dunbar of a dance in the quen[is] chalmer *MF*

Of James Dog. *Text: MS MF* (*p. 339; Reidpeth, f. 44*^{r})
colophon Quod Dunbar of James Dog Kepair of the Quenis wardrep *MF*

Quhen that I schawe to him ȝour wrytin
He girnis that I am red for bytin;
I wald he had ane havye clog:
  Madame, ȝe heff ane dangerous dog!

Quhen that I speik till him freindlyk
He barkis lyk ane midding tyk
War chassand cattell throu a bog:
  Madam, ȝe heff a dangerous dog!

He is ane mastive, mekle of mycht,
To keip ȝour wardroippe over nycht
Fra the grytt Sowdane Gog ma Gog:
  Madam, ȝe heff a dangerous dog!

He is ower mekle to be ȝour messan;
Madam, I red ȝou get a less ane;
His gang garris all ȝour chalmeris schog:
  Madam, ȝe heff a dangerous dog!

30. [Of the said James, quhen he had plesett him]

O GRACIOUS Princes, guid and fair,
Do weill to James ȝour wardraipair
Quhais faythfull bruder maist freind I am:
  He is na dog; he is a lam.

Thocht I in ballet did with him bourde
In malice spack I nevir ane woord
Bot all, my dame, to do ȝour gam:
  He is na dog; he is a lam.

Ȝour hienes can nocht gett ane meter
To keip ȝour wardrope, nor discreter
To rewle ȝour robbis and dres the sam:
  He is na dog; he is a lam.

Of the said James. *Text: MS MF (pp. 339–40; Reidpeth, f. 44v)*
colophon Quod Dunbar of the said James quhen he had plesett him *MF*

The wyff that he had in his innis,
That with the taingis wald braek his schinnis,
I wald schou drownet war in a dam:
He is na dog; he is a lam.

The wyff that wald him kuckald mak,
I wald schou war bayth syd and back
Weill batteret with ane barrou tram:
He is na dog; he is ane lam.

He hes sa weill doin me obey
In till all thing, thairfoir I pray
That nevir dolour mak him dram:
He is na dog; he is a lam.

31. [Gladethe thoue, Queyne of Scottis Regioun]

GLADETHE thoue, queyne of Scottis regioun;
ȝing tendir plaunt of plesand pulcritude,
Fresche flour of ȝouthe new germyng to burgeoun,
Our perle of price, our princes fair and gud,
Our charbunkle chosin of hye imperiale blud,
Our roys riale most reverent under croune,
Joy be and grace on to thi selcitud:
Gladethe thoue, queyne of Scottis regioun.

O hye triumphing peradis of joy,
Lod steir and lamp of eivry lustines;
Of port surmounting Pollexen of Troy,
Dochtir to Pallas in angellik brichtnes;
Mastres of nurtur and of nobilnes,
Of fresch depictour princes and patroun,
O hevin in erthe of ferlifull suetnes:
Gladethe thoue, queyne of Scottis regione.

Gladethe thoue, Queyne of Scottis Regioun. *Text: Aberdeen Minute Book of Seisins (ii; 1503–7). See Commentary*
colophon quod Dunbar *MS*

Of thi fair fegour Natur micht rejois
That so the kervit withe all hir curiys slicht;
Scho has the maid this verray wairldis chois,
Schawing one the hir craftis and hir micht
To se quhow fair sche couthe depant a wicht,
Quhow gud, how noble of all condicioun,
Quhow womanly in eivry mannis sicht:
Gladethe thoue, queyne of Scottis regioun.

Roys red and quhit, resplendent of colour,
New of thi knop at morrow fresche atyrit
One stalk ȝet grene, O ȝing and tendir flour
That with thi luff has all this regioun firit;
Gret Gode us graunt that we have long desirit—
A plaunt to spring of thi successioun,
Syne witht all grace his spreit to be inspirit:
Gladethe thoue, queyne of Scottis regioun.

O precius Mergreit, plesand cleir and quhit,
Moir blitht and bricht na is the beriall schene,
Moir deir na is the diamaunt of delit,
Moir semly na is the sapheir one to seyne,
Moir gudely eik na is the emerant greyne,
Moir riche na is the ruby of renowne,
Fair gem of joy, Mergreit of the I meyne:
Gladethe thoue, queyne of Scottis regioun.

32. [To the Quene]

MADAM, ȝour men said thai wald ryd
And latt this Fasterennis evin ower slyd;
Bott than thair wyffis cam furth in flockis
And baid tham betteis soin abyd
Att haem, and lib tham of the pockis.

To the Quene. *Text MS MF (p. 342; Reidpeth, f. 46)*
1 ȝour] *corr.* said *in MF* said: sad *MF* 4 soin: som *MF* 8 felde: fedle *MF*

Nou propois thai, sen ȝe dwell still,
Off Venus feest to fang ane fill,
Bott in the felde preiff thai na cockis;
For till heff riddin hed bein les ill
Nor latt thair wyffis breid the pockis.

Sum of ȝour men sic curage hed,
Dame Venus fyre sa hard tham sted,
Thai brak up durris and raeff up lockis
To get ane pamphelet on a pled
That thai mycht lib tham of the pockis.

Sum that war ryatous as rammis
Ar nou maid tame lyk ony lammis,
And settin down lyk sarye crockis;
And hes forsaekin all sic gammis
That men callis libbin of the pockis.

Sum thocht tham selffis stark lyk gyandis
Ar nou maid waek lyk willing wandis
With schinnis scharp and small lyk rockis;
And gottin thair bak in bayth thair handis
For ower offt libbin of the pockis.

I saw coclinkis me besyd
The ȝoung men to thair howses gyd,
Had bettir lugget in the stockis;
Sum fra the bordell wald nocht byd
Quhill that thai gatt the Spanȝie pockis.

Thairfoir, all ȝoung men, I ȝou pray,
Keip ȝou fra harlottis nycht and day—
Thai sall repent quhai with tham ȝockis;
And be war with that perrellous play
That men callis libbin of the pockis.

28 Had] *corr.* and *in MF* *colophon* Quod Dunbar *MF*

33. [Ane Blak Moir]

LANG heff I maed of ladyes quhytt;
Nou of ane blak I will indytt
That landet furth of the last schippis;
Quhou fain wald I descryve perfytt
My ladye with the mekle lippis:

Quhou schou is tute mowitt lyk ane aep
And lyk a gangarall onto graep,
And quhou hir schort catt nois up skippis,
And quhou schou schynes lyk ony saep,
My ladye with the mekle lippis.

Quhen schou is claid in reche apparrall
Schou blinkis als brycht as ane tar barrell;
Quhen schou was born the son tholit clippis,
The nycht be fain faucht in hir querrell—
My ladye with the mekle lippis.

Quhai for hir saek with speir and scheld
Preiffis maest mychttelye in the feld
Sall kis and withe hir go in grippis,
And fra thyne furth hir luff sall weld—
My ladye with the mekle lippis.

And quhai in felde receaves schaem
And tynis thair his knychtlie naem
Sall cum behind and kis hir hippis
And nevir to uther confort claem:
My ladye with the mekle lippis.

Ane Blak Moir. *Text: MS MF* (*pp. 341–2; Reidpeth, f. 45*^{v})
9 schou: *om. MF* 21 felde: fedle *MF* *colophon* Quod Dunbar of ane blak moir *MF*

34. [Epetaphe for Donald Oure]

IN vice most vicius he excellis
That with the vice of tressone mellis;
Thocht he remissioun
Haif for prodissioun,
Schame and susspissioun
Ay with him dwellis.

And he evir odious as ane owle,
The falt sa filthy is and fowle;
Horrible to natour
Is ane tratour
As feind in fratour
Undir a cowle.

Quha is a tratour or ane theif
Upoun him selff turnis the mischeif;
His frawdfull wylis
Him self begylis,
As in the ilis
Is now a preiff.

The fell strong tratour Donald Owyr
Mair falsett had nor udir fowyr
Rownd ylis and seyis;
In his suppleis
On gallow treis
3itt dois he glowir.

Falsett no feit hes nor deffence
Be power, practik nor puscence;
Thocht it fra licht
Be smord with slicht,
God schawis the richt
With soir vengence.

Epetaphe for Donald Oure. *Text: MS B (draft, pp. 53–4) collated with MS MF (pp. 11–12; Reidpeth, f. 11)*
6 Ay] *om. MF* 8 filthy] terribill *MF* 11 As] Ane *MF* 14 turnis] rynnes *MF* 19–24, 25–30 *sequence in MF*: 25–30, 19–24 *in B* 20 had nor] hes thane *MF* 21 Rownd *MF*: Rowme *B* ylis] *corr.* jylis *in B* 24 3itt dois he] Now he dois *MF* 26 power] puir *MF* puscence] piscence *MF* 27 licht] *corr.* slicht *in B*

Off the falis fox dissimulatour
Kynd hes every theiff and tratour;
Eftir respyt
To wirk dispyt
Moir appetyt
He hes of natour.

War the fox tane a thowsand fawd
And grace him gevin als oft for frawd,
War he on plane
All war in vane,
Frome hennis agane
Micht non him hawd.

The murtherer ay murthour mais,
And evir quhill he be slane he slais;
Wyvis thus makis mokkis,
Spynnand on rokkis—
Ay rynnis the fox
Quhill he fute hais.

35. The Ballade of ane right noble victorius and myghty lord Barnard Stewart lord of Aubigny, erle of Beaumont roger and Bonaffre, consaloure and chamerlane ordinare to the maist hee, maist excellent, and maist Crystyn prince Loys king of France, knyght of his ordoure, Capitane of the kepyng of his body, Conquereur of Naplis and umquhile constable general of the same: Compilit be Maistir Willyam Dumbar at the said lordis cumyng to Edinburghe in Scotland send in ane ryght excellent embassat fra the said maist Crystin king to our maist souverane lord and victorius prince James the ferde kyng of Scottis.

32 every] all reffar *MF* 36 He hes] Thai heff *MF* 38 als . . . frawd] *corr. to* ay quhen he cald *in MF; Reidpeth* 42 Micht none] Nane mycht *MF* 43 murtherer ay murthour] *corr.* murderaser and martyr *in MF: line om. Reidpeth* *colophon* Finis. Quod Dunbar for Donald Oure Epetaphe *B*: Quod Dumbar *MF*

The Ballade of . . . Barnard Stewart lord of Aubigny. *Text: Chepman & Myllar print* (*c.* *9 May 1508*)

RENOWNIT, ryall, right reverend and serene
  Lord, hie tryumphing in wirschip and valoure,
Fro kyngis downe most Cristin knight and kene,
  Most wyse, most valyand, moste laureat hie victour:
  On to the sterris upheyt is thyne honour;
In Scotland welcum be thyne excellence
  To king, queyne, lord, clerk, knight and servatour,
Withe glorie and honour, lawde and reverence.

Welcum, in stour most strong, incomparable knight,
  The fame of armys and floure of vassalage;
Welcum in were moste worthi, wyse and wight;
  Welcum, the soun of Mars of moste curage;
  Welcum, moste lusti branche of our linnage,
In every realme oure scheild and our defence;
  Welcum, our tendir blude of hie parage,
With glorie and honour, lawde and reverence.

Welcum, in were the secund Julius,
  The prince of knightheyd and flour of chevalry;
Welcum, most valyeant and victorius;
  Welcum, invincible victour moste wourthy;
  Welcum, our Scottis chiftane most dughti:
Wyth sowne of clarioun, organe, song and sence
  To the atonis, lord, Welcum all we cry
With glorie and honour, lawde and reverence.

Welcum, oure indeficient adjutorie
  That evir our naceoun helpit in thare neyd,
That never saw Scot yit indigent nor sory
  Bot thou did hym suport with thi gud deid;
  Welcum therfor abufe all livand leyd
Withe us to live and to maik recidence,
  Quhilk never sall sunye for thi saik to bleid;
To quham be honour, lawde and reverence.

Is none of Scotland borne fathfull and kynde
  Bot he of naturall inclinacioune
Dois favour the withe all his hert and mynde,
  Withe fervent, tendir trew intencioun,
  And wald of inwart hie effectioun

But dreyd of danger de in thi defence
  Or dethe or schame war done to thi persoun;
To quham be honour, lawde and reverence.

Welcum, thow knight moste fortunable in feild,
  Welcum, in armis moste aunterus and able
Undir the soune that beris helme or scheild;
  Welcum, thow campioun in feght unourcumable;
  Welcum, most dughti, digne and honorable,
And moist of lawde and hie magnificence
  Nixt undir kingis to stand incomparable;
To quham be honour, lawde and reverence.

Throw Scotland, Ingland, France and Lumbardy
  Fleys on weyng thi fame and thi renoune,
And our all cuntreis undirnethe the sky
  And our all strandis fro the sterris doune;
  In every province, land and regioune
Proclamit is thi name of excellence
  In every cete, village and in toune,
Withe glorie and honour, lawd and reverence.

O feyrse Achill in furius hie curage,
  O strong invincible Hector undir scheild,
O vailyeant Arthur in knyghtli vassalage,
  Agamenon in governance of feild,
  Bold Henniball in batall to do beild,
Julius in jupert, in wisdom and expence:
  Most fortunable chiftane bothe in yhouth and eild,
To the be honour, lawde and reverence.

At parlament thow suld be hye renownit
  That did so mony victoryse opteyn;
Thi cristall helme withe lawry suld be crownyt,
  And in thy hand a branche of olyve greyn;
  The sueird of conquis and of knyghtheid keyn
Be borne suld highe before the in presence,
  To represent sic man as thou has beyn
With glorie and honour, lawde and reverence.

47 incomparable: incompable *C&M*   69 knyghtheid: knyghteid *C&M*

Hie furius Mars the god armipotent
  Rong in the hevin at thyne nativite;
Saturnus doune withe fyry eyn did blent
  Throw bludy visar men manasing to gar de;
  On the fresche Venus keist hir amourouse e;
On the Marcurius furtheyet his eloquence;
  Fortuna maior did turn hir face on the
Wyth glorie and honour, lawde and reverence.

Prynce of fredom and flour of gentilnes,
  Sweyrd of knightheid and choise of chevalry,
This tyme I lefe for grete prolixitnes
  To tell quhat feildis thow wan in Pikkardy,
  In France, in Bertan, in Naplis and Lumbardy,
As I think eftir withe all my diligence,
  Or thow departe, at lenthe for to discry
With glorie and honour, lawd and reverence.

B in thi name betaknis batalrus,
  A able in feild, R right renoune most hie;
N nobilnes and A for aunterus,
  R ryall blude; for dughtines is D;
  V valyeantnes, S for strenewite:
Quhoise knyghtli name so schynyng in clemence
  For wourthines in gold suld writtin be
With glorie and honour, lawd and reverence.

36. [Elegy on Bernard Stewart Lord of Aubigny]

ILLUSTER Lodovick, of France most Cristin king,
  Thow may complain with sighis lamentable
The death of Bernard Stewart, nobill and ding,
  In deid of armes most anterous and abill,
  Most mychti, wyse, worthie and confortable
Thy men of weir to governe and to gy:
  For him, allace, now may thow weir the sabill
Sen he is gon, the flour of chevelrie.

Elegy on Bernard Stewart. *Text: MS Reidpeth* (*ff.* 6^v–7^r)
3 Stewart: stewar *R*

Complaine sould everie noble valiant knycht
  The death of him that douchtie was in deid,
That many ane fo in feild hes put to flight
  In weris wicht, be wisdome and manheid.
  To the Turkas sey all land did his name dreid
Quhois force all France in fame did magnifie;
  Of so hie price sall nane his place posseid
For he is gon, the flour of chevilrie.

  O duilfull death, O dragon dolorous!
  Quhy hes thow done so dulfullie devoir
The prince of knychtheid, nobill and chevilrous,
  The witt of weiris, of armes and honour,
  The crop of curage, the strenth of armes in stour,
The fame of France, the fame of Lumbardy,
  The chois of chiftanes, most awfull in airmour,
The charbuckell, cheif of every chevelrie!

Pray now for him all that him loveit heir,
  And for his saull mak intercessioun
Unto the Lord that hes him bocht so deir
  To gif him mercie and remissioun
  And namelie we of Scottis natioun,
Intill his lyff quhom most he did affy,
  Forȝett we nevir into our orisoun
To pray for him, the flour of chevelrie.

37. [The Wowing of the King quhen he wes in Dumfermeling]

THIS hindir nycht in Dumfermeling
To me wes tawld ane windir thing:
That lait ane tod wes with ane lame
And with hir playit and maid gud game,
Syne till his breist did hir imbrace
And wald haif riddin hir lyk ane rame:
And that me thocht ane ferly cace.

10 in deid: indeid *R* 13 Turkas: turk *R* 21 stour: stoir *R*
23 chois: schois *R* *colophon* Quod Dumbar *R*

The Wowing of the King quhen he wes in Dumfermeling. *Text: MS B* (*f. 116*^{r}–*116*^{v}) *collated with MS MF* (*pp. 335–7; Reidpeth, f. 58, ll. 1–14 only*). *Title from B*: Followis the wowing . . . Dumfermeling

2 windir] wondrous *MF* 4 gud] grit *MF*

He braisit hir bony body sweit
And halsit hir with fordir feit;
Syne schuk his taill with quhinge and ȝelp
And todlit with hir lyk ane quhelp;
Syne lowrit on growfe and askit grace;
And ay the lame cryd, Lady, help!
And that me thocht ane ferly cace.

The tod wes nowder lene nor skowry—
He wes ane lusty reid haird lowry,
Ane lang taild beist and grit with all;
The silly lame wes all to small
To sic ane tribbill to hald ane bace;
Scho fled him nocht—fair mot hir fall—
And that me thocht ane ferly cace.

The tod wes reid, the lame wes quhyte;
Scho wes ane morsall of delyte—
He lovit na ȝowis auld, tuch, and sklender;
Becaus this lame wes ȝung and tender
He ran upoun hir with a race,
And scho schup nevir for till defend hir:
And this me thocht ane ferly cace.

He grippit hir abowt the west
And handlit hir as he had hest;
This innocent that nevir trespast
Tuke hert that scho wes handlit fast,
And lute him kis hir lusty face;
His girnand gamis hir nocht agast:
And that me thocht ane ferly cace.

He held hir till him be the hals
And spak full fair, thocht he wes fals;
Syne said and swoir to hir be God
That he suld nocht tuich hir prenecod;
The silly thing trowd him, allace—
The lame gaif creddence to the tod:
And that me thocht ane ferly cace.

9 with] with his *MF* 16 He] Bot *MF* 20 hir] him *MF* 27 schup] preissit *MF* 28–63 *refrain abbrev. in B* 28 this] that *MF* 36 hir . . . him *MF*: him . . . hir *B* 37 full] rycht *MF* he] hes *MF*

I will no lesingis put in vers
Lyk as thir jangleris dois rehers,
Bot be quhat maner thay war mard
Quhen licht wes owt and durris wes bard;
(I wait nocht gif he gaif hir grace,
Bot all the hollis wes stoppit hard,
And that me thocht ane ferly cace.)

Quhen men dois fleit in joy maist far
Sone cumis wo, or thay be war:
Quhen carpand wer thir two most crows
The wolf he ombesett the hous
Upoun the tod to mak ane chace;
The lamb than cheipit lyk a mows:
And that me thocht ane ferly cace.

Throw hiddowis ȝowling of the wowf
This wylie tod plat doun on growf,
And in the silly lambis skin
He crap als far as he micht win
And hid him thair ane weill lang space;
The ȝowis besyd thay maid na din:
And that me thocht ane ferly cace.

Quhen of the tod wes hard no peip
The wowf went all had bene on sleip;
And quhill the bell had strikkin ten
The wowf hes drest him to his den,
Protestand for the secound place;
And this report I with my pen,
How at Dumfermling fell the cace.

43 lesingis] lesing *MF* 56 that] this *MF* 58 on] a *MF* 66 bell *MF*: tod *B* 70 fell] *corr.* thair *in B* *colophon* Quod Dumbar *B MF*

38. The Tesment of Maister Andro Kennedy

I MAISTER Andro Kennedy
Curro quando sum vocatus
Gottin with sum incuby
Or with sum freir *infatuatus*;
In faith I can nought tell redly
Unde aut ubi fui natus,
Bot in treuth I trow trewly
Quod sum dyabolus incarnatus.

Cum nichill sit certius morte,
We mon all de quhen we haif done;
Nescimus quando vel qua sorte
Na Blind Allane wait of the mone;
Ego pacior in pectore
This night I myght not sleip a wink;
Licet eger in corpore
Ȝit wald my mouth be wet with drink.

Nunc condo testamentum meum,
I leiff my saull for evirmare
Per omnipotentem Deum
In to my lordis wyne cellar,
Semper ibi ad remanendum
Quhill domisday without dissever
Bonum vinum ad bibendum
With sueit Cuthbert that luffit me nevir.

Ipse est dulcis ad amandum;
He wald oft ban me in his breith
Det michi modo ad potandum
And I forgif him laith and wraith;
Quia in cellario cum cervisia
I had lever lye baith air and lait
Nudus solus in camesia
Na in my lordis bed of stait.

The Tesment of Maister Andro Kennedy. *Text: Rouen print* (*b*5^r–*b*6^v) *collated with MSS B* (*ff*. 154^r–155^v) *and MF* (*pp*. 135–8). *Title from B colophon*
1 Andro] Walter *MF* 7 in] be my *MF* 9 *certius*: cercius *print* 10 quhen we haif *B*: man that is *print MF* done] dome *MF* 12 Na] Nor *B* 27 *modo*] potum *MF* 29 *cervisia*] servitia *MF* (*cf. l.* 112) 32 Na] Nor *B*

A barell bung ay at my bosum
  Of warldis gud I bad na mair.
Corpus meum ebriosum
  I leif on to the toune of Air;
In a draf mydding for evir and ay
  Ut ibi sepeliri queam
Quhar drink and draff may ilka day
  Be cassyne *super faciem meam:*

I leif my hert that nevir wes sicir
  Sed semper variabile
That nevir mare wald flow nor flicir
  Consorti meo Iacobe:
Thought I wald bynd it with a wicir
  Verum deum renui;
Bot and I hecht to teme a bicker
  Hoc pactum semper tenui.

Syne leif I the best aucht I bocht
  Quod est Latinum propter caupe
To hede of kyn, bot I wait nought
  Quis est ille, than I schrew my scawpe:
I callit my lord my heid, but hiddill,
  Sed nulli alii hoc dixerunt;
We weir als sib as seve and riddill
  In una silva que creverunt.

Omnia mea solacia
  Thai wer bot lesingis all and ane,
Cum omni fraude et fallacia
  I leif the maister of Sanct Antane—

34 Of . . . mair] *corr.* In steid of ane braid bowstair *in B* gud] welth *MF*
35 *Corpus*] Et corpus *B* 36 on] in *B* 39 ilka] every *MF*
40 *additional lines in MF*:

Thair wald I be bereit me think
Or beir my bodie *ad tabernam*
Quhair I may feill the savour of drink
Syn sing for me *requiem eternam*

43 nor] and *B* 44 *Iacobe*] *corr.* Iacobi *in B* 49 bocht] coft *MF*
51 To hede of kyn] To the heid of my kin *B* 53 callit] tald *B* my heid] *om. MF* 54 *dixerunt*] sciverunt *B*

Willelmo Gray sine gratia,
Myne awne deir cusing as I wene
Qui nunquam fabricat mendacia
Bot quhen the holyne growis grene.

My fenȝening and my fals wynyng
Relinquo falsis fratribus,
For that is Goddis awne bidding—
Dispersit dedit pauperibus.
For menis saulis thai say thai sing
Mencientes pro muneribus:
Now God gif thaim ane evill ending
Pro suis pravis operibus.

To Jok Fule my foly fre
Lego post corpus sepultum;
In faith I am mair fule than he,
Licet ostendit bonum vultum:
Of corne and catall, gold and fe,
Ipse habet valde multum,
And ȝit he bleris my lordis e
Fingendo eum fore stultum.

To Master Johne Clerk syne
Do et lego intime
Goddis malisone and myne—
Ipse est causa mortis mee.
War I a dog and he a swyne
Multi mirantur super me,
Bot I suld ger that lurdane quhryne
Scribendo dentes sine de.

Residuum omnium bonorum
For to dispone my lord sall haif
Cum tutela puerorum,
Ade, Kytte and all the laif.

61 *Willelmo*] William *B*: Willielmus *MF* 63 *mendacia*] mendatia *print* 68 *Dispersit dedit*] Dispersit et dedit *MF* 69 thai sing] and sing *B* 76 *ostendit*] ostendo *B* 77 gold] *corr.* geir *in B* 84 *Ipse*] Nam ipse *B* 92 Ade] baith Ade *B*

In faith I will na langar raif:
Pro sepultura ordino
On the new gys, sa God me saif,
Non sicut more solito:

In die mee sepulture
I will nane haif bot our awne gyng,
Et duos rusticos de rure
Berand a barell one a styng;
Drynkand and playand cop out evin
Sicut egomet solebam;
Singand and gretand with hie stevin
Potum meum cum fletu miscebam.

I will na preistis for me sing
Dies illa dies ire,
Na ȝit na bellis for me ring
Sicut semper solet fieri;
Bot a bag pipe to play a spryng
Et unum ail wosp *ante me*;
In stayd of baneris for to bring
Quatuor lagenas cervisie,
Within the graif to set sic thing
In modum crucis juxta me
To fle the fendis, than hardely sing
De terra plasmasti me.

39. [To the King]

THIS waverand warldis wretchidnes,
The failȝeand and frutles bissines,
The mispent tyme, the service vane,
For to considder is ane pane.

95 On] *corr.* But *in B* 98 nane haif] have nane *MF* 104 *miscebam*: missebam *print* 107 Na . . . na] Nor . . . no *MF* 111 baneris] torchis *B*: baneir *MF* 112 *cervisie*] servicie *MF* 115 fendis] devill *MF* *colophon* Explicit *print*: Heir endis the tesment of Maister Andro Kennedy / Maid be Dumbar quhen he wes lyk to dy *B*: finis quod Kennedie *MF*

To the King. *Text: MS MF (pp. 178–81; Reidpeth, f. 27)*

The slydand joy, the glaidnes schort,
The feynȝeid luif, the fals confort,
The sweit abayd, the slichtfull trane,
For to considder is ane pane.

The sugurit mouthis with myndis thairfra,
The figurit speiche with faceis tua,
The plesand toungis with hartis unplane,
For to considder is ane pane.

The labour lost and liell service,
The lang availl on humill wyse,
And the lytill rewarde agane,
For to considder is ane pane.

Nocht I say all be this cuntre,
France, Ingland, Ireland, Almanie,
Bot als be Italie and Spane,
Quhilk to considder is ane pane.

The change of warld fro weill to wo,
The honourable use is all ago
In hall and bour, in burgh and plane,
For to considder is ane pane.

Beleif dois liep, traist dois nocht tarie;
Office dois flit and courtis dois vary;
Purpos dois change as wynd or rane;
Quhilk to considder is ane pane.

Gud rewle is banist our the bordour
And rangat ringis but ony ordour
With reird of rebaldis and of swane;
Quhilk to considder is ane pane.

The pepill so wickit ar of feiris,
The frutles erde all witnes beiris,
The ayr infectit and prophane;
Quhilk to considder is ane pane.

13 The labour: The liell labour *MF*

The temporale stait to gryp and gather,
The sone disheris wald the father
And as ane dyvour wald him demane;
  Quhilk to considder is ane pane.

Kirkmen so halie ar and gude
That on thair conscience, rowme and rude,
May turne aucht oxin and ane wane;
  Quhilk to considder is ane pane.

I knaw nocht how the Kirk is gydit,
Bot beneficis ar nocht leill devydit:
Sum men hes sevin and I nocht ane;
  Quhilk to considder is ane pane.

And sum unworthy to browk ane stall
Wald clym to be ane cardinall—
Ane bischoprik may nocht him gane;
  Quhilk to considder is ane pane.

Unwourthy I amang the laif
Ane kirk dois craif and nane can have;
Sum with ane thraif playis passage plane;
  Quhilk to considder is ane pane.

It cumis be king, it cumis be quene,
Bot ay sic space is us betwene
That nane can schut it with ane flane;
  Quhilk to considder is ane pane.

It micht have cuming in schortar quhyll
Fra Calȝecot and the new fund Yle,
The partis of Transmeridiane;
  Quhilk to considder is ane pane.

It micht be this, had it bein kynd,
Cuming out of the desertis of Ynde
Our all the grit se oceane;
  Quhilk to considder is ane pane.

It micht have cuming out of all ayrtis
Fra Paris and the Orient partis,
And fra the ylis of Aphrycane;
  Quhilk to consydder is ane pane.

It is so lang in cuming me till,
I dreid that it be quyt gane will—
Or bakwart it is turnit agane;
  Quhilk to considder is ane pane.

Upon the heid of it is hecht
Bayth unicornis and crownis of wecht;
Quhen it dois cum, all men dois frane;
  Quhilk to considder is ane pane.

I wait it is for me provydit,
Bot sa done tyrsum it is to byd it,
It breikis my hairt and birstis my brane;
  Quhilk to considder is ane pane.

Greit abbais grayth I nill to gather
Bot ane kirk scant coverit with hadder,
For I of lytill wald be fane;
  Quhilk to considder is ane pane.

And for my curis in sindrie place
With help, Sir, of ȝour nobill grace,
My sillie saule sall never be slane
  Na for sic syn to suffer pane.

Experience dois me so inspyr,
Off this fals failȝeand warld I tyre
That evermore flytis lyk ane phane;
  Quhilk to considder is ane pane.

The formest hoip ȝit that I have
In all this warld, sa God me save,
Is in ȝour grace, bayth crop and grayne,
  Quhilk is ane lessing of my pane.

76, 80, 84 *abbrev. in MF* 81 it: *om. MF* *colophon* Finis quod Dumbar &c. *MF*

40. [To the King]

OFF benefice, Sir, at everie feist
  Quha monyast hes makis maist requeist;
  Get thai not all, thai think ȝe wrang thame:
Ay is the ouir word of the geist,
  Giff thame the pelffe to pairt amang thame.

Sum swelleis swan, sum swelleis duke,
And I stand fastand in a nuke
  Quhill the effect of all thai fang thame;
Bot Lord! how petewouslie I luke
  Quhone all the pelfe thai pairt amang thame.

Off sic hie feistis of sanctis in glorie
Baithe of commoun and propir storie
  Quhair lairdis war patronis, oft I sang thame
Charitas pro Dei amore;
  And ȝit I gat na thing amang thame.

This blynd warld ever so payis his dett,
Riche befoir pure spraidis ay thair nett,
  To fische all watiris dois belang thame;
Quha na thing hes can na thing gett,
  Bot ay as syphir sett amang thame.

Swa thai the kirk have in thair cure—
Thai fors bot litill how it fure,
  Nor of the buikis or bellis quha rang thame;
Thai pans nocht of the prochin pure
  Hed thai the pelfe to pairt amang thame.

So warryit is this warldis rent
That nane thairof can be content
  Off deathe quhill that the dragoun stang thame;
Quha maist hes than sall maist repent,
  With largest compt to pairt amang thame.

To the King. *Text: MS MF (a; pp. 321–2) collated with MFb (pp. 8–9; Reidpeth, f. 10)*

8–10, 13–15, 18–20 thame . . . thame] thane . . . thane *MFb* 13 lairdis war] lord was *MFb* 17 spraidis . . . nett *MFb*: spendis . . . mett *MFa* 21 have in thair] had in to *MFb* 23 or] nor *MFb* 26 warryit *MFb*: variant *MFa* warldis] warld *MFb* 27 That . . . be] That men off it ar never *MFb* 29 than sall maist] maist dois thane *MFb* 30 With largest] And hes maist *MFb* *colophon* Quod Dumbar *MFa MFb*

41. [To the King, quhone mony Benefices vakit]

SCHIR, at this feist of benefice
Think that small partis makis grit service,
And equale distributioun
Makis thame content that hes ressoun—
And quha hes nane ar plesit na wyis.

Schir, quhiddir is it mereit mair
To gif him drink that thristis sair,
Or fill a fow man quhill he birst
And lat his fallow de a thrist
Quhilk wyne to drynk als worthie war?

It is no glaid collatioun
Quhair ane makis myrrie, ane uther lukis doun;
Ane thristis, ane uther playis cop out:
Lat anis the cop ga round about
And wyn the covanis banesoun.

42. [To the King]

SCHIR, ȝit remember as befoir
How that my ȝouthe is done forloir
In ȝour service with pane and greiff;
Gud conscience cryis reward thairfoir:
Exces of thocht dois me mischeif.

Ȝour clarkis ar servit all aboute
And I do lyke ane rid halk schout
To cum to lure that hes na leif,
Quhair my plumis begynnis to mowt:
Exces of thocht dois me mischeiff.

To the King, quhone mony Benefices vakit. *Text: MS MF (a; p. 316) collated with MS MFb (pp. 7–8; Reidpeth, f.* 9^{v}*)*
5 plesit na] plesit on na *MFb* 8 quhill] quhilk *MFb* *colophon* Quod Dumbar quhone . . . vakit *MFa*: Quod Dumbar *MFb*

To the King. *Text: MS MF (pp. 295–6, 309: see infra, ll. 76–85; Reidpeth, f. 34, ll. 76–85 only) collated with MS B (ff.* 94^{v}*–*95^{v}*)*
1 ȝit *B*: ȝe *MF* as] as of *B* 2 is] I *B* 7 rid] reid *B* 9 mowt] brek out *B*

Forȝet is ay the falcounis kynd,
Bot ever the myttell is hard in mynd;
Quhone the gled dois the peirtrikis preiff
The gentill goishalk gois undynd:
Exces of thocht dois me mischeiff.

The pyat withe the pairtie cote
Feynȝeis to sing the nychtingale note,
Bot scho can not the corchet cleiff
For hasknes of hir carleche throte:
Exces of thocht dois me mischeiff.

Ay fairast feddiris hes farrest foulis;
Suppois thai have na sang bot ȝowlis
In sylver caiges thai sit at cheif;
Kynd native nestis dois clek bot owlis:
Exces of thocht dois me mischeiff.

O gentill egill, how may this be?
Quhilk of all foulis dois heast fle,
Ȝour leggis quhy do ȝe not releif
And chirreis thame eftir thair degre?
Exces of thocht dois me mischeiff.

Quhone servit is all uther man,
Gentill and sempill, of everie clan—
Kyne of Rauf Colȝard and Johnne the reif—
No thing I gett nor conqueis can:
Exces of thocht dois me mischeif.

Thocht I in courte be maid refuse
And have few vertewis for to ruse,
Ȝit am I cum of Adame and Eve
And fane wald leif as utheris dois:
Exces of thocht dois me mischeif.

11 Forȝet] Forsett *B* 12 myttell] mittane *B* 13 Quhone] Of quhome *B* the peirtrikis] prectikis *B* 14 undynd] unkynd *B* 16 the pairtie] hir pretty *B* 17 nychtingale] nychtingalis *B* 18 not] nevir *B* 23 at cheif *B*: but greif *MF* 24 nestis] nest *B* 25 *et passim: refrain abbrev. in B* 27 Quhilk] That *B* 28 do] will *B* 29 thame] *om. B* 33 Kyne . . . Colȝard *B*: Raf Coilȝearis kynd *MF* 34 nor conqueis] na conquest *B* 38 cum] cumin *B*

Or I sould leif in sic mischance,
Giff it to God war na grevance
To be ane pykthank I wald preif,
For thai in warld wantis na plesance:
Exces of thocht dois me mischeif.

In sum pairt of my selffe I pleinȝe
Quhone utheris dois flattir and feynȝe;
Allace, I can bot ballattis breif,
Sic barnheid leidis my brydill reynȝe:
Exces of thocht dois me mischeiff.

I grant my service is bot lycht;
Thairfoir of mercye and not of rycht
I ask ȝou, Sir, no man to greiff,
Sum medecyne gif that ȝe mycht:
Exces of thocht dois me mischeiff.

Nane can remeid my maledie
Sa weill as ȝe, Sir, veralie:
With ane benefice ȝe may preiff,
And gif I mend not haistalie
Exces of thocht lat me mischeif.

I wes in ȝouthe on nureice kne
Cald dandillie, bischop, dandillie;
And quhone that age now dois me greif
A sempill vicar I can not be:
Exces of thocht dois me mischeif.

Jok that wes wont to keip the stirkis
Can now draw him ane cleik of kirkis
With ane fals cairt in to his sleif
Worthe all my ballattis under the byrkis:
Exces of thocht dois me mischeif.

Twa curis or thre hes uplandis Michell
With dispensationis in ane knitchell
Thocht he fra nolt had new tane leif;

46 of] on *B* 47 utheris] udir folkis *B* 49 leidis] biddis *B* 56 Nane can] May nane *B* 58 With ane] For with a *B* 62 Cald] *om. B* 72 in] bund in *B*

He playis with totum and I with nychell:
Exces of thocht dois me mischeiff.

How sould I leif, and I not landit,
Nor ȝit withe benefice am blandit?
I say not, Sir, ȝow to repreiff,
Bot doutles I go rycht neir hand it:
Exces of thocht dois me mischeiff.

As saule in to purgatorie
Leifand in pane with hoip of glorie,
So is my selffe ȝe may beleiff
In hoip, Sir, of ȝour adjutorie:
Exces of thocht dois me mischeiff.

43. [To the King]

SCHIR, lat it never in toune be tald
That I suld be ane Ȝowllis ȝald.

Suppois I war ane ald ȝaid aver
Schott furth our clewch to squische the clever
And hed the strenthis off all Strenever,
I wald at Ȝoull be housit and stald:
  Schir, lat it never in toune be tald
  That I suld be ane Ȝowllis ȝald.

I am ane auld hors, as ȝe knaw,
That ever in duill dois drug and draw;
Gryt court hors puttis me fra the staw
To fang the fog be firthe and fald:
  Schir, lat it never in toune be tald
  That I suld be ane Ȝowllis ȝald.

76–85 on p. 309 in MF (leaf misplaced) 76 and I] that is *B* 77 am] am I *B* 81 in to] is heir in *B* 82 with] and *B* 83 So . . . may] Seand my self I haif *B* *colophon* Quod Dumbar *MF*: Finis quod Dumbar *B*

To the King. *Text: MS MF (p. 18; ll. 1–32; Reidpeth, f. 14) and MS Reidpeth (f. 1r–1v; ll. 33–76). See Commentary*
1 toune: toume *MF* 3 ȝaid] *corr.* ȝald *in MF* 5 Strenever: Strenneverne *MF* 7–8 *refrain abbrev. in MF R*

I heff run lang furth in the feild
On pastouris that ar plane and peld;
I mycht be now tein in for eild,
My bekis ar spruning he and bald:
  Schir, lat it never in toune be tald
  That I suld be ane ʒowllis ʒald.

My maine is turned in to quhyt,
And thair off ʒe heff all the wyt:
Quhen uthair hors hed brane to byt
I gat bot gris, grype giff I wald:
  Schir, lat it never in towne be tald
  That I suld be ane ʒowllis ʒald.

I was never dautit in to stabell;
My lyff hes bein so miserabell,
My hyd to offer I am abell
For evill schoud strae that I reiv wald:
  Schir, lat it never in towne be tald
  That I suld be ane ʒowllis ʒald.

And ʒett suppois my thrift be thyne,
Gif that I die ʒour aucht within
Lat nevir the soutteris have my skin
With uglie gumes to be gnawin:
  Schir, lat it nevir in toun be tald
  That I suld be ane ʒuillis ʒald.

The court hes done my curage cuill
And maid me ane forriddin muill;
ʒett to weir trapperis at the ʒuill
I wald be spurrit at everie spald:
  Schir, lat it nevir in toun be tald
  That I suld be ane ʒuillis ʒald.

Now lufferis cummis with larges lowd;
Quhy sould not palfrayis thane be prowd,
Quhen gillettis wilbe schomd and schroud
That riddin ar baith with lord and lawd?
  Schir, lat it nevir in toun be tald
  That I suld be ane ʒuillis ʒald.

30 For . . . wald *Reidpeth: MF faded* 32 *MF ends (quire lost)* 37–8 *et passim: refrain abbrev. in R*

Quhen I was ȝoung and into ply
And wald cast gammaldis to the sky,
I had beine bocht in realmes by
Had I consentit to be sauld:
  Schir, lat it nevir in toun be tald
  That I suld be ane Ȝuillis ȝald.

With gentill hors quhen I wald knyp
Thane is thair laid on me ane quhip;
To colleveris than man I skip
That scabbit ar, hes cruik and cald.
  Schir, lat it nevir in toun be tald
  That I suld be ane Ȝuillis ȝald.

Thocht in the stall I be not clappit
As cursouris that in silk beine trappit,
With ane new hous I wald be happit
Aganis this Crysthinmes for the cald.
  Schir, lat it nevir in toun be tald
  That I suld be ane Ȝuillis ȝald.

Respontio Regis

Efter our wrettingis, thesaurer,
Tak in this gray hors, auld Dumbar,
Quhilk in my aucht with service trew
In lyart changeit is his hew:
Gar hows him new aganis this Ȝuill
And busk him lyk ane bischopis muill,
For with my hand I have indost
To pay quhatevir his trappouris cost.

44. [To the King]

SCHIR, ȝe have mony servitouris
And officiaris of dyvers curis:
Kirkmen, courtmen and craftismen fyne,
Doctouris in jure and medicyne,

68 q: Dumbar *R*

To the King. *Text: MS MF (pp. 196–8)*

Divinouris, rethoris and philosophouris,
Astrologis, artistis and oratouris,
Men of armes and vailʒeand knychtis
And mony uther gudlie wichtis;
Musicianis, menstralis and mirrie singaris,
Chevalouris, cawandaris and flingaris,
Cunʒouris, carvouris and carpentaris,
Beildaris of barkis and ballingaris,
Masounis lyand upon the land
And schipwrichtis hewand upone the strand,
Glasing wrichtis, goldsmythis and lapidaris,
Pryntouris, payntouris and potingaris—

And all of thair craft cunning
And all at anis lawboring,
Quhilk pleisand ar and honorable
And to ʒour hienes profitable
And richt convenient for to be
With ʒour hie regale majestie,
Deserving of ʒour grace most ding
Bayth thank, rewarde and cherissing.

And thocht that I amang the laif
Unworthy be ane place to have
Or in thair nummer to be tald,
Als lang in mynd my work sall hald,
Als haill in everie circumstance,
In forme, in mater and substance,
But wering or consumptioun,
Roust, canker or corruptioun,
As ony of thair werkis all—
Suppois that my rewarde be small.

Bot ʒe sa gracious ar and meik
That on ʒour hienes followis eik
Ane uthir sort, more miserabill
Thocht thai be nocht sa profitable:
Fenʒeouris, fleichouris and flatteraris,
Cryaris, craikaris and clatteraris,

10 flingaris] *preceded by blank in MF* 36 eik] *corr.* reik *in MF*

Soukaris, groukaris, gledaris, gunnaris,
Monsouris of France (gud clarat cunnaris),
Inopportoun askaris of Yrland kynd,
And meit revaris, lyk out of mynd,
Scaffaris and scamleris in the nuke,
And hall huntaris of draik and duik,
Thrimlaris and thristaris as thai war woid,
Kokenis, and kennis na man of gude;
Schulderaris and schovaris that hes no schame,
And to no cunning that can clame,
And can non uthir craft nor curis
Bot to mak thrang, Schir, in ȝour duris,
And rusche in quhair thay counsale heir
And will at na man nurtir leyr;
In quintiscence eik, ingynouris joly
That far can multiplie in folie—
Fantastik fulis bayth fals and gredy,
Off toung untrew and hand evill diedie;
(Few dar of all this last additioun
Cum in Tolbuyth without remissioun).

And thocht this nobill cunning sort
Quhom of befoir I did report
Rewardit be, it war bot ressoun
Thairat suld no man mak enchessoun;
Bot quhen the uther fulis nyce
That feistit at Cokelbeis gryce
Ar all rewardit, and nocht I,
Than on this fals warld I cry, Fy:
My hart neir bristis than for teyne,
Quhilk may nocht suffer nor sustene
So grit abusioun for to se
Daylie in court befoir myn e.

And ȝit more panence wald I have
Had I rewarde amang the laif.
It wald me sumthing satisfie
And les of my malancolie,
And gar me mony falt ourse
That now is brayd befoir myn e.

85 Or: And *MF* *colophon* Quod Dunbar *MF*

My mind so fer is set to flyt
That of nocht ellis I can endyt,
For owther man my hart to breik
Or with my pen I man me wreik;
And sen the tane most nedis be—
In to malancolie to de
Or lat the vennim ische all out—
Be war anone, for it will spout
Gif that the tryackill cum nocht tyt
To swage the swalme of my dispyt.

45. [To the King]

COMPLANE I wald, wist I quhome till,
Or unto quhome darett my bill;
Quhidder to God, that all thing steiris,
All thing seis and all thing heiris,
And all thing wrocht in dayis seveyne;
Or till his Moder, Quein off Heveyne;
Or unto wardlie prince heir downe
That dois for justice weir a crownne:—
Off wrangis and off gryt injuris
That nobillis in thar dayis induris,
And men off vertew and cuning,
Off wit, and wysdome in gydding,
That nocht cane in this cowrt conquys
For lawte, luiff, nor lang servys.

Bot fowll, jow-jowrdane-hedit jevellis,
Cowkin kenseis and culroun kevellis;
Stuffettis, strekouris and stafische strummellis,
Wyld haschbaldis, haggarbaldis and hummellis,
Druncartis, dysouris, dyvowris, drevellis,
Misgydit memberis off the Devellis;
Mismad mandragis off mastis strynd,
Crawdones, couhirttis, and theiffis off kynd;

To the King. *Text: MS MF (pp. 16–18; Reidpeth, f. 13^{v})*
4 All] *corr.* And *in MF* 16 Cowkin] *corr.* Couth quhennis *in MF* culroun *Pinkerton*: cukoun *MF* 19 dyvowris: dyowris *MF* 21 strynd] *altered to* skynd *in MF*

Blait-mouit bladȝeanes with bledder cheikis,
Clubfacet clucanes with clutit breikis;
Chuff midding churllis, cuming off cart fillaris,
Gryt glaschewe-hedit gorge-millaris,
Evill horrible monsteris fals and fowll:—
Sum causles clekis till him ane cowll,
Ane gryt convent fra syne to tys,
And he him selff exampill of vys;
Enterand for geir and no devocioun—
The Devill is glaid off his promocioun.
Sum ramyis ane rokkat fra the roy
And dois ane dastart sa destroy;
And sum that gaittis ane personage
Thinkis it a present for a page,
And on no wayis content is he
My lord quhill that he callit be.

Bot quhow is he content or nocht
(Deme ȝe abowt in to ȝowr thocht)
The lerit sone off erll or lord
Upone this ruffie to remord,
That with all castingis hes him cled
His erandis for to ryne and red?
And he is maister native borne
And all his eldaris him beforne,
And mekle mair cuning be sic thre
Hes to posseid ane dignite,
Saying his odius ignorance
Panting ane prelottis countenance,
Sa far above him set at tabell
That wont was for to muk the stabell—
Ane pykthank in a prelottis clais
With his wavill feit and wirrok tais,
With hoppir hippis and henches narrow
And bausy handis to beir a barrow;
With lut schulderis and luttard bak
Quhilk natur maid to beir a pak;
With gredy mynd and glaschane gane,

34 sa *ed. conj.: see Commentary*
56 beir: be *MF*

Mell-hedit lyk ane mortar stane,
Fenȝeing the feris off ane lord—
And he ane strumbell, I stand ford;
And ever moir as he dois rys,
Nobles off bluid he dois dispys,
And helpis for to hald thame downe
That thay rys never to his renowne.

Thairfoir, O prince maist honorable,
Be in this meter merciabill,
And to thy auld servandis haff e
That lang hes lipinit into the.
Gif I be ane off tha my sell,
Throw all regiones hes bein hard tell,
Off quhilk my wrytting witnes beris;
And ȝete thy danger ay me deris:
Bot efter danger cumis grace,
As hes bein herd in mony plece.

46. [To the Lordis of Chalker]

My lordis of chalker, pleis ȝow to heir
My coumpt, I sall it mak ȝow cleir
But ony circumstance or sonȝie;
For left is nether corce nor cunȝie
Off all that I tuik in the ȝeir.

For rekkyning of my rentis and roumes
Ȝe neid not for to tyre ȝour thowmes,
Na for to gar ȝour countaris clink,
Na paper for to spend nor ink
In the ressaveing of my soumes.

I tuik fra my lord thesaurair
Ane soume of money for to wair:
I cannot tell ȝow how it is spendit,
Bot weill I waitt that it is endit;
And that me think ane coumpt our sair.

64 Nobles: And nobles *MF* 70 That lang *R: MF faded* 71 I be . . . tha *R: MF faded* *colophon* Quod Dumbar &c *MF*

To the Lordis of Chalker. *Text: MS Reidpeth (f. 6r–6v)*
8 clink: clank *R* *colophon* Quod Dumbar *R*

I trowit the tyme quhen that I tuik it
That lang in burgh I sould have bruikit;
  Now the remanes ar eith to turs:
  I have na preiff heir bot my purs,
Quhilk wald not lie and it war luikit.

47. [To the Lord Thesaurair]

I THOCHT lang quhill sum lord come hame
Fra quhom faine kyndnes I wald clame;
His name of confort I will declair:
  Welcome, my awin lord thesaurair!

Befoir all rink of this regioun
Under our roy of most renoun,
Of all my mycht, thocht it war mair,
  Welcom, my awin lord thesaurair!

Ȝour nobill payment I did assay,
And ȝe hecht sone without delay
Againe in Edinburgh till repair:
  Welcom, my awin lord thesaurair!

Ȝe keipit tryst so winder weill,
I hald ȝow trew as ony steill;
Neidis nane ȝour payment till dispair:
  Welcom, my awin lord thesaurair!

Ȝett in a pairt I was agast,
Or ȝe the narrest way had past
Fra toun of Stirling to the air;
  Welcom, my awin lord thesaurair!

Thane had my dyt beine all in duill,
Had I my wage wantit quhill Ȝuill,
Quhair now I sing with heart onsair:
  Welcum, my awin lord thesaurair!

To the Lord Thesaurair. *Text: MS Reidpeth* (*ff*. 5^v–6^r)
5 rink] *altered to* raik *in R*

Welcum my benefice and my rent,
And all the lyflett to me lent;
Welcum my pensioun most preclair:
  Welcum, my awin lord thesaurair!

Welcum, als heartlie as I can,
My awin dear maister, to ȝour man,
And to ȝour servand singulair:
  Welcum, my awin lord thesaurair!

48. [To Aberdein]

BLYTH Aberdeane, thow beriall of all tounis,
  The lamp of bewtie, bountie and blythnes,
Unto the heaven ascendit thy renoun is
  Off vertew, wisdome and of worthines;
  He nottit is thy name of nobilnes
Into the cuming of oure lustie quein,
  The wall of welth, guid cheir and mirrines:
Be blyth and blisfull, burgh of Aberdein.

And first hir mett the burges of the toun
  Richelie arrayit as become thame to be,
Of quhom they cheset four men of renoun
  In gounes of velvot, ȝoung, abill and lustie,
  To beir the paill of velves cramase
Abone hir heid, as the custome hes bein;
  Gryt was the soundis of the artelȝie:
Be blyth and blisfull, burgh of Aberdein.

Ane fair processioun mett hir at the port
  In a cap of gold and silk full pleasantlie,
Syne at hir entrie with many fair disport
  Ressaveit hir on streittis lustilie;
  Quhair first the salutatioun honorabilly
Of the sweitt Virgin guidlie mycht be seine,
  The sound of menstrallis blawing to the sky:
Be blyth and blisfull, burgh of Aberdein.

26 lyflett] *filling blank in R* *colophon* Quod Dumbar *R*

To Aberdein. *Text: MS Reidpeth* (*f.* 7^r^–7^v^)

3 ascendit *conj. Laing: blank in R* 15 soundis: sound *R. See Commentary*

And syne thow gart the orient kingis thrie
  Offer to Chryst with benyng reverence
Gold, sence and mir with all humilitie
  Schawand him king with most magnificence;
  Syne quhow the angill with sword of violence
Furth of the joy of paradice putt clein
  Adame and Ev for innobedience:
Be blyth and blisfull, burcht of Aberdein.

And syne the Bruce that evir was bold in stour
  Thow gart as roy cum rydand under croun,
Richt awfull, strang, and large of portratour,
  As nobill, dreidfull, michtie campioun;
  The royall Stewartis syne, of great renoun,
Thow gart upspring with branches new and greine,
  Sa gloriouslie, quhill glaidid all the toun:
Be blyth and blisfull, burcht of Aberdein.

Syne come thair four and tuentie madinis ȝing
  All claid in greine of mervelous bewtie
With hair detressit as threidis of gold did hing,
  With quhyt hattis browderit all rycht bravelie,
  Playand on timberallis and singand rycht sweitlie;
That seimlie sort in ordour weill besein
  Did meit the quein, hir saluand reverentlie:
Be blyth and blisfull, burcht of Aberdein.

The streittis war all hung with tapestrie;
  Great was the pres of peopill dwelt about,
And pleasant padgeanes playit prattelie;
  The legeis all did to thair lady loutt,
  Quha was convoyed with ane royall routt
Off gryt barrounes and lustie ladyis schene;
  Welcum, our quein, the commones gaif ane
    schout:
Be blyth and blisfull, burcht of Aberdein.

35 and] *corr.* full *in R* 37 royall Stewartis *ed. conj.*: nobill Stewartis *conj. Laing: blank in R. See Commentary* 43 gold: cold *R* 44 browderit all: all browderit *R* 47 saluand: husband *R* 54 schene: *blank in R*

At hir cuming great was the mirth and joy
For at thair croce aboundantlie rane wyne;
Untill hir ludgeing the toun did hir convoy;
Hir for to treit thai sett thair haill ingyne.
Ane riche present thai did till hir propyne,
Ane costlie coup that large thing wald contene,
Coverit and full of cunȝeitt gold rycht fyne:
Be blyth and blisfull, burcht of Aberdein.

O potent princes, pleasant and preclair,
Great caus thow hes to thank this nobill toun
That for to do the honnour did not spair
Thair geir, riches, substance and persoun,
The to ressave on maist fair fasoun;
The for to pleis thai socht all way and mein:
Thairfoir sa lang as quein thow beiris croun,
Be thankfull to this burcht of Aberdein.

49. [To the Quene]

O LUSTY flour of ȝowth, benyng and bricht,
Fresch blome of bewty, blythfull, brycht and schene,
Fair lufsum lady, gentill and discret,
Ȝung brekand blosum ȝit on the stalkis grene,
Delytsum lilly, lusty for to be sene:
Be glaid in hairt and expell havines;
Bair of blis, that evir so blyth hes bene,
Devoyd langour and leif in lustines.

Brycht sterne at morrow that dois the nycht hyn chace,
Of luvis lychtsum day the lyfe and gyd,
Lat no dirk clud absent fro us thy face,
Nor lat no sable frome us thy bewty hyd
That hes no confort quhair that we go or ryd
Bot to behald the beme of thi brychtnes;
Baneis all baill and into blis abyd;
Devoyd langour and leif in lustines.

63 Coverit] *corr.* Cunȝeitt *in R* *colophon* Quod Dumbar *R*
To the Quene. *Text: MS B (f. 238v)*
10 day the *conj. Laing: B defective*

Art thow plesand, lusty, ȝoing and fair,
  Full of all vertew and gud conditioun,
Rycht nobill of blud, rycht wyis and debonair,
  Honorable, gentill, and faythfull of renoun,
  Liberall, lufsum and lusty of persoun;
Quhy suld thow than lat sadnes the oppres?
  In hairt be blyth and lay all dolour doun,
Devoyd langour and leif in lustines.

I me commend with all humilitie
  Unto thi bewty blisfull and bening,
To quhome I am and sall ay servand be
  With steidfast hairt and faythfull trew mening
  Unto the deid without depairting;
For quhais saik I sall my pen addres,
  Sangis to mak for thy reconforting,
That thow may leif in joy and lustines.

O fair sweit blossum, now in bewty flouris,
  Unfaidit bayth of cullour and vertew;
Thy nobill lord that deid hes done devoir,
  Faid nocht with weping thy vissage fair of hew;
  O lufsum lusty lady, wyse and trew,
Cast out all cair and comfort do incres;
  Exyll all sichand, on thy servand rew;
Devoyd langour and lef in lustines.

21 persoun] *corr.* renoun *in B* 24 *abbrev. in B* 37 wyse and trew] *corr.* fair of hew *in B* 38 out all] *repeated in B*

IV

VISIONS AND NIGHTMARES

50. [The Thrissill and the Rois]

QUHEN Merche wes with variand windis past
And Appryll had with hir silver schouris
Tane leif at Nature with ane orient blast;
And lusty May, that muddir is of flouris,
Had maid the birdis to begyn thair houris
Amang the tendir odouris reid and quhyt,
Quhois armony to heir it wes delyt:

In bed at morrow sleiping as I lay
Me thocht Aurora with hir cristall ene
In at the window lukit by the day
And halsit me, with visage paill and grene;
On quhois hand a lark sang fro the splene:
Awalk, luvaris, out of ȝour slomering;
Se how the lusty morrow dois up spring.

Me thocht fresche May befoir my bed upstude
In weid depaynt of mony divers hew,
Sobir, benyng, and full of mansuetude,
In brycht atteir of flouris forgit new,
Hevinly of color, quhyt, reid, broun and blew,
Balmit in dew and gilt with Phebus bemys
Quhill all the hous illumynit of hir lemys.

Slugird, scho said, Awalk annone for schame,
And in my honour sum thing thow go wryt;
The lork hes done the mirry day proclame
To rais up luvaris with confort and delyt;
Ȝit nocht incress thy curage to indyt,
Quhois hairt sum tyme hes glaid and blisfull bene,
Sangis to mak undir the levis grene.

Quhairto, quod I, Sall I uprys at morrow,
For in this May few birdis herd I sing?
Thai haif moir caus to weip and plane thair sorrow,

The Thrissill and the Rois. *Text: MS B (ff. 342^v–345^r)*

Thy air it is nocht holsum nor benyng;
Lord Eolus dois in thy sessone ring;
So busteous ar the blastis of his horne,
Amang thy bewis to walk I haif forborne.

With that this lady sobirly did smyll
And said, Uprys and do thy observance;
Thow did promyt in Mayis lusty quhyle
For to discryve the Ros of most plesance.
Go se the birdis how thay sing and dance,
Illumynit our with orient skyis brycht
Annamyllit richely with new asur lycht.

Quhen this wes said, depairtit scho, this quene,
And enterit in a lusty gairding gent;
And than me thocht full hestely besene
In serk and mantill eftir hir I went
In to this garth, most dulce and redolent
Off herb and flour and tendir plantis sueit
And grene levis doing of dew doun fleit.

The purpour sone with tendir bemys reid
In orient bricht as angell did appeir
Throw goldin skyis putting up his heid,
Quhois gilt tressis schone so wondir cleir
That all the world tuke confort fer and neir
To luke upone his fresche and blisfull face,
Doing all sable fro the hevynnis chace.

And as the blisfull soune of cherarchy
The fowlis song throw confort of the licht,
The birdis did with oppin vocis cry,
O luvaris fo, away thow dully nycht,
And welcum day that confortis every wicht;
Haill May, haill Flora, haill Aurora schene,
Haill princes Natur, haill Venus luvis quene.

Dame Nature gaif ane inhibitioun thair
To fers Neptunus and Eolus the bawld
Nocht to perturb the wattir nor the air,

46 eftir hir *conj. Allan Ramsay*: full haistely *B* 57 soune: sonne *B*

And that no schouris scharp nor blastis cawld
Effray suld flouris nor fowlis on the fold;
Scho bad eik Juno, goddes of the sky,
That scho the hevin suld keip amene and dry.

Scho ordand eik that every bird and beist
Befoir hir hienes suld annone compeir,
And every flour of vertew, most and leist,
And every herb be feild, fer and neir,
As thay had wont in May fro ȝeir to ȝeir
To hir thair makar to mak obediens,
Full law inclynnand with all dew reverens.

With that annone scho send the swyfte ro
To bring in beistis of all conditioun;
The restles suallow commandit scho also
To feche all fowll of small and greit renown;
And to gar flouris compeir of all fassoun
Full craftely conjurit scho the ȝarrow,
Quhilk did furth swirk als swift as ony arrow.

All present wer in twynkling of ane e—
Baith beist and bird and flour—befoir the quene:
And first the Lyone, gretast of degre,
Was callit thair, and he most fair to sene
With a full hardy contenance and kene
Befoir dame Natur come, and did inclyne
With visage bawld and curage leonyne.

This awfull beist full terrible wes of cheir,
Persing of luke and stout of countenance,
Rycht strong of corpis, of fassoun fair but feir,
Lusty of schaip, lycht of deliverance,
Reid of his cullour as is the ruby glance:
On feild of gold he stude full mychtely
With flour delycis sirculit lustely.

This lady liftit up his cluvis cleir
And leit him listly lene upone hir kne,
And crownit him with dyademe full deir

67 scharp *conj. Schipper: see Commentary* 78 swyfte: swyft *B* 92 full] *corr.* wes *in B*

Off radyous stonis most ryall for to se,
Saying, The king of beistis mak I the,
And the chief protector in woddis and schawis:
Onto thi leigis go furth, and keip the lawis.

Exerce justice with mercy and conscience,
And lat no small beist suffir skaith na skornis
Of greit beistis that bene of moir piscence;
Do law elyk to aipis and unicornis,
And lat no bowgle with his busteous hornis
The meik pluch ox oppress for all his pryd,
Bot in the ȝok go peciable him besyd.

Quhen this was said, with noyis and soun of joy
All kynd of beistis in to thair degre
At onis cryit lawd, Vive le roy,
And till his feit fell with humilite;
And all thay maid him homege and fewte,
And he did thame ressaif with princely laitis,
Quhois noble yre is *parcere prostratis*.

Syne crownit scho the Egle king of fowlis,
And as steill dertis scherpit scho his pennis,
And bawd him be als just to awppis and owlis
As unto pacokkis, papingais or crennis,
And mak a law for wycht fowlis and for wrennis;
And lat no fowll of ravyne do efferay
Nor devoir birdis bot his awin pray.

Than callit scho all flouris that grew on feild,
Discirnyng all thair fassionis and effeiris;
Upone the awfull Thrissill scho beheld
And saw him kepit with a busche of speiris;
Concedring him so able for the weiris,
A radius croun of rubeis scho him gaif
And said, In feild go furth and fend the laif.

And sen thow art a king, thow be discreit;
Herb without vertew thow hald nocht of sic pryce
As herb of vertew and of odor sueit;

119 *parcere: proceir B: see Commentary*

And lat no nettill vyle and full of vyce
Hir fallow to the gudly flour delyce,
Nor latt no wyld weid full of churlichenes
Compair hir till the lilleis nobilnes:

Nor hald non udir flour in sic denty
As the fresche Ros of cullour reid and quhyt;
For gife thow dois, hurt is thyne honesty,
Conciddering that no flour is so perfyt,
So full of vertew, plesans and delyt,
So full of blisfull angeilik bewty,
Imperiall birth, honour and dignite.

Than to the Ros scho turnyt hir visage
And said, O lusty dochtir most benyng,
Aboif the lilly illustare of lynnage,
Fro the stok ryell rysing fresche and ȝing,
But ony spot or macull doing spring;
Cum, blowme of joy, with jemis to be cround,
For our the laif thy bewty is renownd.

A coistly croun with clarefeid stonis brycht
This cumly quene did on hir heid inclois,
Quhill all the land illumynit of the licht:
Quhairfoir me thocht all flouris did rejos,
Crying attonis, Haill be thow richest Ros,
Haill hairbis empryce, haill freschest quene of flouris;
To the be glory and honour at all houris.

Than all the birdis song with voce on hicht,
Quhois mirthfull soun wes mervelus to heir:
The mavys song, Haill Rois most riche and richt
That dois up flureis undir Phebus speir;
Haill plant of ȝowth, haill princes dochtir deir;
Haill blosome breking out of the blud royall,
Quhois pretius vertew is imperiall.

The merle scho sang, Haill Rois of most delyt,
Haill of all flouris quene and soverane;
The lark scho song, Haill Rois both reid and quhyt,
Most plesand flour of michty cullouris twane;

The nychtingaill song, Haill Naturis suffragene
In bewty, nurtour and every nobilnes,
In riche array, renown and gentilnes.

The commoun voce uprais of birdis small
Apone this wys: O blissit be the hour
That thow wes chosin to be our principall;
Welcome to be our princes of honour,
Our perle, our plesans and our paramour,
Our peax, our play, our plane felicite:
Chryst the conserf frome all adversite.

Than all the birdis song with sic a schout
That I annone awoilk quhair that I lay,
And with a braid I turnyt me about
To se this court, bot all wer went away.
Than up I lenyt, halflingis in affrey,
And thus I wret, as ȝe haif hard to forrow,
Off lusty May upone the nynte morrow.

51. [Ane Dreme]

THIS hinder nycht halff sleiping as I lay
Me thocht my chalmer in ane new aray
Was all depent with many divers hew
Of all the nobill storyis, ald and new,
Sen oure first father formed was of clay.

Me thocht the lift all bricht with lampis lycht,
And thairin enterrit many lustie wicht—
Sum ȝoung, sum old, in sindry wyse arayit;
Sum sang, sum danceit, on instrumentis sum playit,
Sum maid disportis with hartis glaid and lycht.

Thane thocht I thus, This is ane felloun phary,
Or ellis my witt rycht woundrouslie dois varie;
This seimes to me ane guidlie companie,
And gif it be ane feindlie fantasie
Defend me, Jhesu and his moder Marie!

189 nynte: nynt *B* *colophon* Explicit, quod Dumbar *B*

Ane Dreme. *Text: MS Reidpeth* (*R; ff.* 3^v–5^r)

13 This: Thus *R* 14 feindlie: freindlie *R* (*see Commentary*)

Thair pleasant sang nor ȝett thair pleasant toun
Nor ȝett thair joy did to my heart redoun;
  Me thocht the drerie damiesall Distres
  And eik hir sorie sister Hivines
Sad as the leid in baid lay me abone.

And Langour satt up at my beddis heid
With instrument full lamentable and deid;
  Scho playit sangis so duilfull to heir,
  Me thocht ane houre seimeit ay ane ȝeir;
Hir hew was wan and wallowed as the leid.

Thane com the ladyis danceing in ane trece,
And Nobilnes befoir thame come ane space
  Saying, withe cheir bening and womanly,
  I se ane heir in bed oppressit ly;
My sisteris, go and help to gett him grace.

With that anon did start out of a dance
Twa sisteris callit Confort and Pleasance,
  And with twa harpis did begin to sing;
  Bot I thairof mycht tak na rejoseing,
My heavines opprest me with sic mischance.

Thay saw that I not glader wox of cheir,
And thairof had thai winder all but weir;
  And said ane lady that Persaveing hecht,
  Of Hevines he fiellis sic a wecht
Ȝour melody he pleisis nocht till heir—

Scho and Distres hir sister dois him greve.
Quod Nobilnes, Quhow sall he thame eschew?
  Thane spak Discretioun, ane lady richt bening:
  Wirk eftir me and I sall gar him sing
And lang or nicht gar Langar tak hir leve.

And then said Witt, Gif thai work not be the,
But onie dout thai sall not work be me.
  Discretioun said, I knaw his malady,
  The strok he feillis of melancholie—
And Nobilnes, his lecheing lyis in the.

23 so] *corr.* full *in R* 28 Saying: Seing *R* 29 se: sa *R* 36 glader wox] *altered to* glaider wax *in R* 39 fiellis] *corr.* fellis *in R* 48 malady: melody *R* 50 his] *not in R*

Or evir this wicht at heart be haill and feir
Both thow and I most in the court appeir,
  For he hes lang maid service thair in vane;
  With sum rewaird we mane him quyt againe
Now in the honour of this guid new ȝeir.

Weill worth the, sister, said Considerance,
And I sall help for to mantene the dance:
  Thane spak ane wicht callit Blind Effectioun—
  I sall befoir ȝow be with myne electioun;
Of all the court I have the governance.

Thane spak ane constant wycht callit Ressoun
And said, I grant ȝow hes beine lord a sessioun
  In distributioun, bot now the tyme is gone—
  Now I may all distribute myne alone;
Thy wrangous deidis did evir mane enschesoun.

For tyme war now that this mane had sum thing
That lange hes bene ane servand to the king,
  And all his tyme nevir flatter couthe nor faine
  Bot humblie into ballat wyse complaine
And patientlie indure his tormenting.

I counsall him be mirrie and jocound;
Be Nobilnes his help mon first be found.
  Weill spokin, Ressoun my brother, quoth Dis-
    cretioun;
  To sett on dies with lordis at the cessioun
Into this realme ȝow war worth mony ane pound.

Thane spak anone Inoportunitie:
Ȝe sall not all gar him speid without me,
  For I stand ay befoir the kingis face;
  I sall him deiff or ellis my self mak hace
Bot gif that I befoir him servit be.

56 said] *corr.* & *in R* 65 Thy] *corr.* The *in R* evir] *corr.* nevir *in R* 73 quoth: with *R* 74 dies] *corr.* dress *in R* 76 Inoportunitie: Inoportunititie *R*

Ane besy askar soonner sall he speid
Na sall twa besy servandis out of dreid,
  And he that askis nocht tynes bot his word,
  Bot for to tyne lang service is no bourd,
Ȝett thocht I nevir to do sic folie deid.

Thane com anon ane callit Sir Johne Kirkpakar,
Off many cures ane michtie undertaker;
  Quod he, I am possest in kirkis sevin,
  And ȝitt I think thai grow sall till ellevin
Or he be servit in ane, ȝone ballet maker.

And then, Sir Bet-the-Kirk: Sa mot I thryff,
I haif of busie servandis foure or fyve,
  And all derect unto sindrie steidis
  Ay still awaitting upoun kirkmenes deidis
Fra quham sum tithingis will I heir belyff.

Quod Ressoun than, The ballance gois unevin
That thow, allece, to serff hes kirkis sevin,
  And sevin als worth kirk not haifand ane;
  With gredines I sie this world ourgane,
And sufficience dwellis nocht bot in heavin.

I have not wyt thairof, quod Temperance;
For thocht I hald him evinlie the ballance
  And but ane cuir full micht till him wey,
  Ȝett will he tak ane uther and gar it suey;
Quha best can rewll wald maist have governance.

Patience to me—my freind—said, Mak guid cheir
And on the prince depend with humelie feir;
  For I full weill dois knaw his nobill intent:
  He wald not for ane bischopperikis rent
That ȝow war unrewairdit half ane ȝeir.

Than as ane fary thai to duir did frak,
And schot ane gone that did so ruidlie rak
  Quhill all the aird did raird the ranebow under;
  On Leith sandis me thocht scho brak in sounder,
And I anon did walkin with the crak.

95 sum] *interlined in R* 106 me] *corr.* said *in R* 107 humelie] *altered to* hevinelie *in R* 108 full] *corr.* knaw *in R* 109 He: Ȝe *R* 112 that] *corr.* may *in R* rak] *altered to* crak *in R* 115 anon] amon *corr.* amen *in R* *colophon* Quod Dumbar *R*

52. [Fasternis Evin in Hell]

[A]

OFF Februar the fyiftene nycht
Full lang befoir the dayis lycht
I lay in till a trance;
The Dance — And than I saw baith hevin and hell:
Me thocht amangis the feyndis fell
Mahoun gart cry ane dance
Off schrewis that wer nevir schrevin
Aganis the feist of Fasternis evin
To mak thair observance;
He bad gallandis ga graith a gyis
And kast up gamountis in the skyis
That last came out of France.

Lat se, quod he, Now quha begynnis:
With that the fowll sevin deidly synnis
Begowth to leip at anis.
Pryd — And first of all in dance wes Pryd
With hair wyld bak and bonet on syd
Lyk to mak waistie wanis,
And round abowt him as a quheill
Hang all in rumpillis to the heill
His kethat for the nanis;
Mony prowd trumpour with him trippit—
Throw skaldand fyre ay as thay skippit
Thay gyrnd with hiddous granis.

Heilie harlottis on hawtane wyis
Come in with mony sindrie gyis,
Bot ȝit luche nevir Mahoun

Fasternis Evin in Hell. A. The Dance. *Text: MS B (ff. 110r–111r) collated with M MF (pp. 12–16; carelessly copied in MS Reidpeth, f. 11v; see also infra, B. 121 ff textual note). MF text in 6-line stanzas. Marginal headings in B only*

1 Februar] Feber-ȝeir *MF* 4 than] thair *MF* 5 amangis] amang *M* 6 Mahoun] The Devyll *MF* 7 nevir schrevin] nevir weill schrevin *Reidpe* (*MF faded*) 8 Aganis] Agane *MF* 11 gamountis in] gambaldis to *M* 12 That . . . of] As verlottis dois in *MF* 16 wes] cam *MF* 17 hai bair *B MF* wyld] collit *MF* 18 waistie: vaistie *B*: waste *MF* 20 the] till his *MF* 21 kethat] keithe cot *MF* 26 sindrie] haltand *M*

Quhill preistis come in with bair schevin
nekkis—
Than all the feyndis lewche and maid
gekkis,
Blak Belly and Bawsy Broun.

Yre
Than Yre come in with sturt and stryfe;
His hand wes ay upoun his knyfe—
He brandeist lyk a beir:
Bostaris, braggaris and barganeris
Eftir him passit in to pairis
All bodin in feir of weir;
In jakkis and stryppis and bonettis of steill,
Thair leggis wer chenȝeit to the heill,
Frawart wes thair affeir;
Sum upoun uder with brandis beft,
Sum jaggit uthiris to the heft
With knyvis that scherp cowd scheir.

Invy
Nixt followit in the dance Invy
Fild full of feid and fellony,
Hid malyce and dispyte;
For pryvie hatrent that tratour trymlit:
Him followit mony freik dissymlit
With fenȝeit wirdis quhyte,
And flattereris in to menis facis,
And bakbyttaris of sindry racis
To ley that had delyte,
And rownaris of fals lesingis—
Allace, that courtis of noble kingis
Of thame can nevir be quyte.

Avaryce
Nixt him in dans come Cuvatyce,
Rute of all evill and grund of vyce,
That nevir cowd be content;

28 Quhill] Quhilk *MF* schevin] swache *MF* 29 feyndis] Devillis *MF* 35 passit] *followed by* all *deleted in B* 37 stryppis *MF*: scryppis *B* 40 uder] uthairis *MF* 41 uthiris] uthair *MF* 43 followit in the dance: in the dance followit *B MF* 44 Fild] All *Reidpeth* (*MF faded*) 46 that] the *MF* 48 wirdis] vordis and *MF* 50 of sindry racis] in secreit places *MF* 52 And rownaris] And still rowneris *MF* 53 courtis] court *MF* 55 Nixt him in dans] Nyxt eftir him *MF*

Catyvis, wrechis and ockeraris,
Hud pykis, hurdaris and gadderaris,
  All with that warlo went;
Out of thair throttis thay schot on udder
Hett moltin gold, me thocht a fudder,
  As fyreflawcht maist fervent;
Ay as thay tomit thame of schot
Feyndis fild thame new up to the thrott
  With gold of allkin prent.

Sweirnes

Syne Sweirnes at the secound bidding
Come lyk a sow out of a midding—
  Full slepy wes his grunȝie;
Mony sweir bumbard belly huddroun,
Mony slute daw and slepy duddroun,
  Him servit ay with sounȝie:
He drew thame furth in till a chenȝie,
And Belliall with a brydill renȝie
  Evir lascht thame on the lunȝie.
In dance thay war so slaw of feit
Thay gaif thame in the fyre a heit
  And maid thame quicker of counȝie.

Lichery

Than Lichery that lathly cors
Berand lyk a bagit hors—
  And Lythenes did him leid:
Thair wes with him ane ugly sort
And mony stynkand fowll tramort
  That had in syn bene deid.
Quhen thay wer entrit in the dance
Thay wer full strenge of countenance
  Lyk turkas birnand reid;
All led thay uthir by the tersis,
Suppois thay fycket with thair ersis
  It mycht be na remeid.

62 Hett . . . thocht] Off meltyne gold mair thane *MF* 65 new up] u
new *MF* 70 bumbard] lumberd *MF* 78 And . . . counȝie] Tham
quikkar for to cunȝe *MF* 79 Than] Syne *MF* 80 Berand . . . a bagit
Come berand . . . ane bawkit *MF* 81 And] Sic *MF* Lythenes *MF*
Ydilnes *B* 82 wes with] followit *MF* 83 And mony stynkand] Fu
mony a stinking *MF* 84 in syn] in syne *corr.* on syd *in MF* 87 Ly
turkas] With tortchis *MF* 88 All led thay] Ilk ane lad *MF* 89 fycket
fyllit *MF*

Gluttony

Than the fowll monstir Glutteny
Off wame unsasiable and gredy
To dance he did him dres:
Him followit mony fowll drunckart
With can and collep, cop and quart,
In surffet and exces;
Full mony a waistles wallydrag
With wamis unweildable did furth wag
In creische that did incres:
Drynk! ay thay cryit, with mony a gaip—
The feyndis gaif thame hait leid to laip—
Thair lovery wes na les.

Na menstrallis playit to thame but dowt
For glemen thair wer haldin owt
Be day and eik by nycht—
Except a menstrall that slew a man;
Swa till his heretage he wan
And entirt be breif of richt.

THAN cryd Mahoun for a heleand padȝane:
Syne ran a feynd to feche Makfadȝane
Far northwart in a nuke.
Be he the correnoch had done schout
Erschemen so gadderit him abowt
In hell grit rowme thay tuke.
Thae tarmegantis with tag and tatter
Full lowd in Ersche begowth to clatter
And rowp lyk revin and ruke.
The Devill sa devit wes with thair ȝell
That in the depest pot of hell
He smorit thame with smuke.

92 Off wame] Withe waine *MF* 93 he] thair *MF* 94 drunckart] *corr.* drunckard *in B* 99 creische] *corr.* creis *in B* 101 feyndis] Devellis *MF* 103 menstrallis] menstrell *MF* 106 that] *om. MF* 107 his] *om. MF* 108 And entirt] Entering *MF* 109 Than cryd Mahoun] Mahoune cryit *MF* 110 Syne . . . to feche] That . . . and fetchit *MF* 116 in Ersche begowth] begowthe in Irsche *MF* 120 with smuke] with a smuik *MF* *colophon* Quod Dumbar *MF*

[B] The Turnament

NIXT that a turnament wes tryid
That lang befoir in hell wes cryid
  In presens of Mahoun;
Betuix a telȝour and ane sowtar,
A pricklous and ane hobbell clowttar,
  The barres wes maid boun.
The tailȝeour baith with speir and scheild
Convoyit wes unto the feild
  With mony lymmar loun
Off seme byttaris and beist knapparis,
Off stomok steillaris and clayth takkaris—
  A graceles garisoun.

His baner born wes him befoir
Quhairin wes clowttis ane hundreth scoir,
  Ilk ane of divers hew
And all stowin out of sindry webbis;
For quhill the Greik sie flowis and ebbis
  Telȝouris will nevir be trew.
The tailȝour on the barrowis blent;
Allais, he tynt all hardyment,
  For feir he chaingit hew;
Mahoun come furth and maid him knycht—
Na ferly thocht his hart wes licht
  That to sic honor grew.

B. The Turnament. *Text: MS B (ff. 111^r–112^v) collated with MSS MF (pp. 161–5) and Asloan (As; ff. 210^r–211^v). MF opens with* The Dance, *supra, ll. 1–12 and 109–20, with these main variants:* [The Dance] 6 Mahoun cryit eftir ane daunce 12 Of the new use of France 109 He bad first play the heyland padȝan 116 So loud 118 Mahown *and proceeds with ll. 121 ff. Text in MF and As in 6–line stanzas. Marginal heading in B only*

121 Nixt . . . tryid] Syn till ane turnament fast thai hyit *MF* 125 hobbell] howell *MF*: coble *As* 126 The] Thar *As* 129 mony] mony a *As* 130–1 Off . . . Off] With . . . With *MF* knapparis . . . clayth takkaris] gnapparis . . . cat knapparis *As* 131 clayth] beif *deleted in B* clayth takkaris] wit clipparis *MF* 134 ane hundreth] mony *MF* 135 divers] sindrie *MF* 137 Greik sie] greit se *MF*: se flud *As* flowis] fillis *MF As* 139 tailȝour] buthman *As* 141 feir] dreid *MF* 142 come furth and] to confort him *MF*: him comfort *As* 143 lycht] wicht *MF*

The tailȝeour hecht hely befoir Mahoun
That he suld ding the sowtar doun
  Thocht he wer strang as mast;
Bot quhen he on the barrowis blenkit
The telȝouris curage a littill schrenkit,
  His hairt did all ourcast.
Quhen to the sowtar he did cum
Off all sic wirdis he wes full dum,
  So soir he wes agast.
In harte he tuke ȝit sic ane scunner
Ane rak of fartis lyk ony thunner
  Went fra him, blast for blast.

The sowtar to the feild him drest;
He wes convoyid out of the west
  As ane defender stout.
Suppois he had na lusty varlot,
He had full mony lowsy harlott
  Round rynnand him aboute.
His baner wes of barkit hyd
Quhairin Sanct Girnega did glyd
  Befoir that rebald rowt;
Full sowttarlyk he wes of laitis,
For ay betuix the harnes plaitis
  The uly birstit out.

Quhen on the telȝour he did luke
His hairt a littill dwamyng tuke,
  He mycht nocht rycht upsitt;
In to his stommok wes sic ane steir,
Off all his dennar quhilk he coft deir
  His breist held deill a bitt.

145 The tailȝeour] He maid ane *MF*: He *As* hely] *om. MF* 147 strang] wicht *As* mast] maist *MF* 149 curage *As MF*: hairt *B* 151 Quhen . . . did] And quhen he saw the souter *MF As* 152 full] *om. MF As* 154 In . . . ȝit] In till his hart wes *MF*: For he in hart tuke *As* scunner *MF*: scummer *B* 156 Went fra him] He leit of *MF* 159 ane] the *MF*: a *As* 162 Round] Fast *As* 163 of] ane *MF*: a *As* 165 that rebald] the foulsum *MF* 167 betuix] betwene *As* the] his *MF* 168 birstit out] furth couth spout *MF* 169 Quhen on the telȝour] Upon the tailȝour quhen *MF As* 170 dwamyng] wamling *MF*: dwalmyng *As* 171 He . . . rycht] Scantlie he micht *MF*: Uneis he mycht *As* 172 to] till *As* 173 quhilk he coft] that cost him *MF As* 174 deill] never *MF As*

To comfort him or he raid forder
The Devill off knychtheid gaif him order,
  For sair syne he did spitt;
And he about the Devillis nek
Did spew agane ane quart of blek—
  Thus knychtly he him quitt.

Than fourty tymis the Feynd cryd, Fy!
The sowtar rycht effeiritly
  Unto the feild he socht.
Quhen thay wer servit of thair speiris,
Folk had ane feill be thair effeiris
  Thair hairtis wer baith on flocht.
Thay spurrit thair hors on adir syd,
Syne thay attour the grund cowd glyd,
  Than thame togidder brocht:
The tailȝeour that wes nocht weill sittin,
He left his sadall all beschittin
  And to the grund he socht.

His harnas brak and maid ane brattill,
The sowtaris hors start with the rattill
  And round about cowd reill;
The beist, that frayit wes rycht evill,
Ran with the sowtar to the Devill
  And he rewardit him weill.
Sum thing frome him the feynd eschewit—
He went agane to bene bespewit,
  So stern he wes in steill.

176 The Devill] Mahoun *MF* 177 sair syne] *corr.* sawour *in B*: savour syn *MF*: stynk than *As* 178 the Devillis] Mahounis *MF* 180 Thus] So *As* 181 Than] And *MF* 182 rycht] furth *As* effeiritly] abaisitly *MF* 184 of] with *As* 185 Folk . . . feill] Thay micht weill ken *MF* 187 thair hors on] upon *MF As* 188 Syne thay] The hors *MF As* grund] grene *As* cowd] did *MF As* 189 Than] And *MF As* 190 that wes nocht] wes nocht *MF*: was no thing *As* 191 his] the *MF As* 192 grund] erde *MF* 193 harnas . . . and maid] birnis . . . with sic *MF*: birnis . . . and maid *As* 194 the] ane *MF* 195 cowd] did *MF As* 196 The beist . . . frayit wes] The hors . . . wes effrayit *MF*: This beist was affrayit *As* rycht] full *As* 197 Ran] Than *MF* 198 And he rewardit] And thair he warit *MF*: And thar revardit *As* 199 the feynd] Mahoun *MF* 200 went . . . to bene bespewit] trowit . . . to have bein spewit *MF*: trowit . . . to be bespewit *As* 201 stern] strenyt *As*

He thocht he wald agane debait him;
He turnd his ers and all bedret him
  Evin quyte frome nek till heill.

He lowsit it of with sic a reird
Baith hors and man he straik till eird,
  He fartit with sic ane feir:
Now haif I quitt the, quod Mahoun.
Thir new maid knychtis lay bayth in swoun
  And did all armes mensweir.
The Devill gart thame to dungeoun dryve
And thame of knychtheid cold depryve,
  Dischairgeing thame of weir;
And maid thame harlottis bayth for evir—
Quhilk still to keip thay had fer levir
  Nor ony armes beir.

I had mair of thair werkis writtin
Had nocht the sowtar bene beschittin
  With Belliallis ers unblist;
Bot that sa gud ane bourd me thocht,
Sic solace to my hairt it rocht,
  For lawchtir neir I brist;
Quhairthrow I walknit of my trance.
To put this in rememberance
  Mycht no man me resist,
For this said justing it befell
Befoir Mahoun, the air of hell:
  Now trow this, gif ȝe list.

Heir endis the sowtar and tailȝouris war maid be the nobill poyet Maister William Dumbar

204 Evin quyte] Quyt *MF*: Quyte our *As* frome . . . till] fra . . . to *MF As* 205 of] *om. As* 206 he straik till] he blew till *MF*: flawe to the *As* 207 fartit] fart *MF As* 209 Thir . . . knychtis lay bayth] That . . . knycht wes laid *MF*: The . . . knycht lay in to *As* 210 mensweir] foirsweir *MF As* 211 The Devill] Mahoun *MF* 212 cold] did *MF*: to *As* 213 of] all *MF As* 214 bayth] ay *MF*: agane *As* 215 Quhilk] Sic *MF* 216 Nor . . . beir] Than . . . to beir *MF*: Na . . . beir *As* 217 mair] *corr.* writtin *in B* 220 that] thair *MF* 221 it rocht] thair socht *MF As* 223 Quhairthrow] And quhen *MF* 224 To] *corr.* And *in B* 226 For . . . justing] To tell the case how *MF*: To dyt how all this thing *As* 227 air] devill *MF* 228 Now trow this] Schiris trow it *MF As* *colophon* the sowtar] *corr.* justing and the war *in B* *colophon* Finis quod Dunbar *MF*: Quod Dunbar *As*

Followis the Amendis maid be him to the telʒouris and sowtaris for the turnament maid on thame

[C] BETUIX twell houris and ellevin
I dremed ane angell came fra hevin
With plesand stevin sayand on hie,
Telʒouris and sowtaris, blist be ʒe.

In hevin hie ordand is ʒour place
Aboif all sanctis, in grit solace,
Nixt God grittest in dignitie;
Tailʒouris and sowtaris, blist be ʒe.

The caus to ʒow is nocht unkend;
That God mismakkis, ʒe do amend
Be craft and grit agilitie;
Tailʒouris and sowtaris, blist be ʒe.

Sowtaris, with schone weill maid and meit
Ʒe mend the faltis of illmaid feit,
Quhairfoir to hevin ʒour saulis will fle;
Telʒouris and sowtaris, blist be ʒe.

Is nocht in all this fair a flyrok
That hes upoun his feit a wyrok,
Knowll tais, nor mowlis in no degrie,
Bot ʒe can hyd thame; blist be ʒe.

And ʒe tailʒouris with weilmaid clais
Can mend the werst maid man that gais
And mak him semely for to se;
Telʒouris and sowtaris, blist be ʒe.

Thocht God mak ane misfassonit man
Ʒe can him all schaip new agane
And fassoun him bettir be sic thre;
Telʒouris and sowtaris, blist be ʒe.

C. Amendis. *Text: MS B (ff.* 112^{v}*–*113^{r}*) collated with MS MF (p. 317). Heading in B only*

5–8 *om. MF* 12, 16, 24, 28, 32, 36 *abbrev. in B* 13 schone weill maid] weill maid schune *MF* 14 illmaid] evill maid *MF* 17 this fair] the land *MF* 18 his feit] hir fute *MF* 19 nor . . . no] or . . . na *MF* 20 Bot] *corr.* telʒ *in B* 25 man] swayne *MF* 27 And . . . bettir] With bettir fassoun *MF*

Thocht a man haif a brokin bak,
Haif he a gude tailȝour, quhattrak,
That can it cuver with craftis slie;
Telȝouris and sowtaris, blist be ȝe.

Off God grit kyndnes may ȝe clame
That helpis his peple fra cruke and lame,
Supportand faltis with ȝour supple;
Tailȝouris and sowtaris, blist be ȝe.

In erd ȝe kyth sic mirakillis heir,
In hevin ȝe salbe sanctis full cleir
Thocht ȝe be knavis in this cuntre:
Telȝouris and sowtaris, blist be ȝie.

53. [The Antechrist]

Lucina schynnyng in silence of the nicht,
The hevin being all full of sternis bricht,
To bed I went; bot thair I tuke no rest;
With havy thocht I wes so soir opprest
That sair I langit eftir dayis licht.

Off Fortoun I complenit hevely
That scho to me stude so contrariously;
And at the last, quhen I had turnyt oft,
For weirines on me ane slummer soft
Come with ane dremyng and a fantesy.

Me thocht Deme Fortoun with ane fremmit cheir
Stude me beforne, and said on this maneir:
Thow suffer me to wirk gif thow do weill,
And preis the nocht to stryfe aganis my quheill
Quhilk every warldly thing dois turne and steir.

30 gude tailȝour *MF*: gude crafty telȝour *B* 31 craftis] crafte *MF* *colophon* Quod Dumbar *B*: Quod Dumbar quhone he drank to the Dekynnis for amendis to the bodeis of thair craftis *MF*

The Antechrist. *Text: MS B (ff. 133ʳ–134ʳ) collated with MS MF (pp. 334–5; Reidpeth, f. 42ᵛ)*

2 being all] all being *MF* 4 I . . . soir] so sair I wes *MF* 5 dayis] the dayis *MF*

Full mony ane man I turne unto the hicht
And makis als mony full law to doun licht;
Up on my staigis or that thow ascend
Trest weill thy truble neir is at ane end,
Seing thir taikinis; quhairfoir thow mark thame rycht.

Thy trublit gaist sall neir moir be degest,
Nor thow in to no benifice beis possest,
Quhill that ane abbot him cleith in ernis pennis
And fle up in the air amangis the crennis
And as ane falcone fair fro eist to west.

He sall ascend as ane horreble grephoun;
Him meit sall in the air ane scho dragoun;
Thir terrible monsteris sall togidder thrist
And in the cludis gett the Antechrist
Quhill all the air infeck of thair pusoun.

Undir Saturnus fyrie regioun
Symone Magus sall meit him, and Mahoun,
And Merlyne at the mone sall him be bydand,
And Jonet the weido on ane bussome rydand
Off wichis with ane windir garesoun.

And syne thay sall discend with reik and fyre
And preiche in erth the Antechrystis impyre;
Be than it salbe neir this warldis end.
With that this lady sone fra me did wend;
Sleipand and walkand wes frustrat my desyre.

Quhen I awoik, my dreme it wes so nyce,
Fra every wicht I hid it as a vyce
Quhill I hard tell be mony suthfast wy
Fle wald ane abbot up in to the sky
And all his fethreme maid wes at devyce.

16 man] *om. MF* turne unto the] set upone *MF* 17 als] *om. MF* to doun] doun to *MF* 18 ascend] do ascend *MF* 19 neir is] is neir *MF* 21 neir moir] never *MF* 22 beis] *om. MF* 24 amangis] amang *MF* 34 bussome rydand] busum hame rydand *MF* 35 windir] wondrus *MF* 38 Be] And *MF* 39 sone . . . did] did schortlie fra me *MF* 40 Sleipand . . . desyre *MF: om. B*

Within my hairt confort I tuke full sone;
Adew, quod I, My drery dayis ar done;
Full weill I wist to me wald nevir cum thrift
Quhill that twa monis wer sene up in the lift,
Or quhill ane abbot flew aboif the mone.

54. Ane Ballat of the Fenȝeit Freir of Tungland How he fell in the Myre fleand to Turkiland

As ȝung Awrora with cristall haile
  In orient schew hir visage paile
A swenyng swyth did me assaile
  Off sonis of Sathanis seid;
Me thocht a Turk of Tartary
Come throw the boundis of Barbary
And lay forloppin in Lumbardy
  Full lang in waithman weid.
Fra baptasing for to eschew
Thair a religious man he slew
And cled him in his abeit new
  For he cowth wryte and reid.
Quhen kend was his dissimulance
And all his cursit govirnance
For feir he fled and come in France
  With littill of Lumbard leid.
To be a leiche he fenyt him thair,
Quhilk mony a man micht rew evirmair,
For he left nowthir seik nor sair
  Unslane, or he hyne ȝeid;
Vane organis he full clenely carvit;
Quhen of his straik so mony starvit,
Dreid he had gottin that he desarvit
  He fled away gud speid.

49 sene up] first sene *MF* 50 aboif] abone *MF* *colophon* Quod Dumbar *B MF*

Ane Ballat of the Fenȝeit Freir of Tungland. *Text: MS B (ff. 117^{r}–118^{v}) collated with MS Asloan (As; ff. 211^{v}–212^{v}; ll. 1–69 only). Title in As* Of the fenȝeit fals frer of tungland. *Text in 8-line stanzas in B*

1 with] with hir *As* 4 Off] With *As* 6 throw the boundis] out of the land *As* 9 to] till *As*

In Scotland than the narrest way
He come his cunnyng till assay;
To sum man thair it was no play,
  The preving of his sciens;
In pottingry he wrocht grit pyne;
He murdreist mony in medecyne;
The jow was of a grit engyne
  And generit was of gyans.
In leichecraft he was homecyd;
He wald haif for a nicht to byd
A haiknay and the hurtmanis hyd,
  So meikle he was of myance.
His yrnis was rude as ony rawchtir,
Quhair he leit blude it was no lawchtir;
Full mony instrument for slawchtir
  Was in his gardevyance.

He cowth gif cure for laxatyve
To gar a wicht hors want his lyve;
Quha evir assay wald, man or wyve,
  Thair hippis ȝeid hiddy giddy.
His practikis nevir war put to preif
Bot suddane deid or grit mischeif;
He had purgatioun to mak a theif
  To dee withowt a widdy.
Unto no mess pressit this prelat
For sound of sacring bell nor skellat;
As blaksmyth bruikit was his pallatt
  For battering at the study.
Thocht he come hame a new maid channoun
He had dispensit with matynnis channoun,
On him come nowther stole nor fannoun
  For smowking of the smydy.

Me thocht seir fassonis he assailȝeit
To mak the quintessance, and failȝeit;
And quhen he saw that nocht availȝeit
  A fedrem on he tuke

30 mony in] in to *As* (mony *in margin in B;* in *corr.* to) 46 suddane] sudand *As* 49 this] the *As*

And schupe in Turky for to fle;
And quhen that he did mont on he
All fowill ferleit quhat he sowld be
 That evir did on him luke.
Sum held he had bene Dedalus,
Sum the menatair marvelus,
Sum Martis blak smyth Vulcanus
 And sum Saturnus kuke;
And evir the cuschettis at him tuggit,
The rukis him rent, the ravynis him druggit,
The hudit crawis his hair furth ruggit:
 The hevin he micht not bruke.

The myttane and Sanct Martynis fowle
Wend he had bene the hornit howle;
Thay set aupone him with a ȝowle
 And gaif him dynt for dynt.
The golk, the gormaw and the gled
Beft him with buffettis quhill he bled;
The sparhalk to the spring him sped
 Als fers as fyre of flynt.
The tarsall gaif him tug for tug,
A stanchell hang in ilka lug,
The pyot furth his pennis did rug,
 The stork straik ay but stynt;
The bissart, bissy but rebuik,
Scho was so cleverus of hir cluik
His bawis he micht not langar bruik,
 Scho held thame at ane hint.

Thik was the clud of kayis and crawis,
Of marleȝonis, mittanis, and of mawis,
That bikkrit at his berd with blawis
 In battell him abowt;
Thay nybbillit him with noyis and cry,
The rerd of thame rais to the sky,
And evir he cryit on Fortoun, Fy:
 His lyfe was in to dowt.

63 fowill] fowlis *As* 67 blak *As: not in B*

The ja him skrippit with a skryke
And skornit him as it was lyk;
The egill strong at him did stryke
  And rawcht him mony a rowt:
For feir uncunnandly he cawkit
Quhill all his pennis war drownd and drawkit;
He maid a hundreth nolt all hawkit
  Beneth him with a spowt.

He schewre his feddreme that was schene
And slippit owt of it full clene
And in a myre up to the ene
  Amang the glar did glyd;
The fowlis all at the fedrem dang
As at a monster thame amang
Quhill all the pennis of it owsprang
  In till the air full wyde.
And he lay at the plunge evirmair
Sa lang as any ravin did rair;
The crawis him socht with cryis of cair
  In every schaw besyde;
Had he reveild bene to the ruikis
Thay had him revin all with thair cluikis.
Thre dayis in dub amang the dukis
  He did with dirt him hyde.
The air was dirkit with the fowlis
That come with ȝawmeris and with ȝowlis,
With skryking, skrymming, and with scowlis
  To tak him in the tyde.
I walknit with the noyis and schowte,
So hiddowis beir was me abowte;
Sensyne I curs that cankerit rowte
  Quhair evir I go or ryde.

104 with] *corr.* quha *in B* *colophon* finis quod Dumbar *B*

55. [How Dunbar wes desyrd to be ane Freir]

THIS nycht befoir the dawing cleir
Me thocht Sanct Francis did to me appeir
With ane religious abbeit in his hand,
And said, In this go cleith the my servand;
Reffus the warld, for thow mon be a freir.

With him and with his abbeit bayth I skarrit
Lyk to ane man that with a gaist wes marrit;
Me thocht on bed he layid it me abone,
Bot on the flure delyverly and sone
I lap thairfra, and nevir wald cum nar it.

Quoth he, Quhy skarris thow with this holy weid?
Cleith the thairin, for weir it thow most neid;
Thow that hes lang done Venus lawis teiche
Sall now be freir and in this abbeit preiche:
Delay it nocht, it mon be done but dreid.

My brethir oft hes maid the supplicationis
Be epistillis, sermonis and relationis,
To tak the abyte, bot thow did postpone;
But ony proces cum on thairfoir annone,
All sircumstance put by and excusationis.

Quod I, Sanct Francis, loving be the till,
And thankit mot thow be of thy gude will
To me, that of thy clayis ar so kynd;
Bot thame to weir it nevir come in my mynd:
Sweit confessour, thow tak it nocht in ill.

In haly legendis haif I hard allevin
Ma sanctis of bischoppis nor freiris, be sic sevin;
Off full few freiris that hes bene sanctis I reid;
Quhairfoir ga bring to me ane bischopis weid
Gife evir thow wald my sawle gaid unto hevin.

How Dunbar wes desyrd to be ane Freir. *Text: MS B (f. 115ʳ–115ᵛ) collated with MS MF (pp. 333–4; Reidpeth, f. 42). Heading in B only* Followis how Dumbar wes desyrd to be ane freir

11 with] at *MF* 13 lang done . . . lawis] done lang . . . law *MF*
16–20 My . . . excusationis] *follows l. 30 in B and MF* 18 the] this *MF*
19 ony] forder *MF* 21–5 *om. MF*

Gif evir my fortoun wes to be a freir
The dait thairof is past full mony a ȝeir;
For into every lusty toun and place
Off all Yngland, frome Berwick to Kalice,
I haif in to thy habeit maid gud cheir.

In freiris weid full fairly haif I fleichit;
In it haif I in pulpet gon and preichit
In Derntoun kirk and eik in Canterberry;
In it I past at Dover our the ferry
Throw Piccardy, and thair the peple teichit.

Als lang as I did beir the freiris style
In me, God wait, wes mony wrink and wyle;
In me wes falset with every wicht to flatter
Quhilk mycht be flemit with na haly watter—
I wes ay reddy all men to begyle.

This freir that did Sanct Francis thair appeir,
Ane fieind he wes in liknes of ane freir;
He vaneist away with stynk and fyrie smowk;
With him me thocht all the hous end he towk,
And I awoik as wy that wes in weir.

56. [Renunce thy God and cum to me]

THIS nycht in my sleip I wes agast:
Me thocht the Devill wes tempand fast
The peple with aithis of crewaltie,
Sayand, as throw the mercat he past,
Renunce thy God and cum to me.

32 past] gone *MF* a] *om. MF* 38 eik] *om. MF* 41 Als] So *MF* 45 I . . . reddy] Reddie wes I *MF* to begyle] for to bakbyte *MF* 49 hous end *MF*: houshend *B* *colophon* Quod Dumbar *B MF*

Renunce thy God and cum to me. *Text: MS B (ff.* 132^{v}*–*133^{r}*) collated with MS MF (pp. 55–7; Reidpeth, f.* 18^{v}*). See Commentary*

1–5 This nycht . . . me.] *MF opens*:

Dremand me thocht that I did heir
The comowne peiple bane and sweir
Blasfemiand Godis majestie;
The Devill ay rowndand in thair eir,
Renunce ȝour God and cum to me.

5 Renunce thy] Renunce ȝour *MF passim*

Me thocht as he went throw the way
Ane preist sweirit be God verey
Quhilk at the alter ressavit he;
Thow art my clerk, the Devill can say,
Renunce thy God and cum to me.

Than swoir ane courtȝour mekle of pryd
Be Chrystis windis bludy and wyd,
And be his harmes wes rent on tre;
Than spak the Devill hard him besyd,
Renunce thy God and cum to me.

Ane merchand his geir as he did sell
Renuncit his pairt of hevin and hell;
The Devill said, Welcum mot thow be,
Thow salbe merchand for my sell;
Renunce thy God and cum to me.

Ane goldsmith said, The gold is sa fyne
That all the workmanschip I tyne—
The Feind ressaif me gif I le:
Think on, quod the Devill, that thow art myne;
Renunce thy God and cum to me.

Ane tailȝour said, In all this toun
Be thair ane better weilmaid goun
I gif me to the Feynd all fre;
Gramercy telȝour, said Mahoun,
Renunce thy God and cum to me.

6–15 Me thocht . . . me.] *not in MF; but cf. ll. 81–5 infra, textual note*
16–20 Ane merchand . . . me.] *MF has*:

> The marchand sweiris mony aithe
> That never man saw better clayth
> Na fynnar silk cum owr the se:
> To sweir, quod Sathan, be nocht layth;
> To sell my geir I will have the.

20–80 *refrain abbrev. in B* 21–5 Ane goldsmith . . . me.] *not in MF* 26 Ane tailȝour said] The tailȝour sayis *MF* 27 weilmaid] schappin *MF* 28 all] als *MF* 29 said] quod *MF*

Ane sowttar said, In gud effek,
Nor I be hangit be the nek
Gife bettir butis of ledder ma be:
Fy, quod the Feynd, thow sairis of blek;
Ga clenge the clene and cum to me.

Ane baxstar sayd, I forsaik God
And all his werkis evin and od
Gif fairar stuff neidis to be:
The Dyvill luche and on him cowld nod,
Renunce thy God and cum to me.

Ane fleschour swoir be the sacrament
And be Chrystis blud maist innocent,
Nevir fatter flesch saw man with e:
The Devill said, hald on thy intent;
Renunce thy God and cum to me.

The maltman sais, I God forsaik,
And that the Devill of hell me taik
Gif ony bettir malt may be,
And of this kill I haif inlaik:—
Renunce thy God and cum to me.

Ane browstar swoir the malt wes ill—
Baith reid and reikit on the kill
That it will be na aill for me,
Ane boll will nocht sex gallonis fill:—
Renunce thy God and cum to me.

31 Ane sowttar said] The sowter sayis *MF* 32 Nor I be hangit] The Devill mot hang him *MF* 34 Fy, quod the Feynd] The Feind sayis fy *MF* 35 Ga clenge the clene and] Ga wysche the weill syn *MF* 36 Ane baxstar sayd] The bakstar sayis *MF* 38 Gif . . . be] That better breid did na man se (did *interlined*) *MF* 39 luche] said *MF* cowld *MF*: qw^{t} *B* 40 Renunce . . . me] With thy licht lewis cum unto me *MF* 41–4 Ane fleschour . . . intent] *MF has*:

The fleschour sweiris, Be Godis woundis
Come never sic beif into thir bowndis
Na fattar mottoune can nocht be;
Fals, quod the Feind, and till him rowndis

46–50 The maltman . . . me.] *MF has*:

Be Goddis blud, quod the taverneir,
Thair is sic wyine in my selleir
Hes never come in this cuntrie;
Ȝit, quod the Devill, thow sellis our deir;
With thy fals met cum downe to me.

The smyth swoir, Be rude and raip,
In till a gallowis mot I gaip
Gif I ten dayis wan pennyis thre,
For with that craft I can nocht thraip:—
Renunce thy God and cum to me.

Ane menstrall said, The Feind me ryfe
Gif I do ocht bot drynk and swyfe;
The Devill said, Hardly mot it be—
Exers that craft in all thy lyfe,
Renunce thy God and cum to me.

Ane dysour said with wirdis of stryfe
The Devill mot stik him with a knyfe
Bot he kest up fair syisis thre:
The Devill said, Endit is thy lyfe;
Renunce thy God and cum to me.

Ane theif said, God, that evir I chaip,
Nor ane stark widdy gar me gaip
Bot I in hell for geir wald be:
The Devill said, Welcum in a raip;
Renunce thy God and cum to me.

The fische wyffis flett and swoir with granis
And to the Feind, saule, flesch and banis
Thay gaif thame with ane schowt on hie:
The Devill said, Welcum all att anis;
Renunce thy God and cum to me.

Me thocht the devillis als blak as pik
Solistand wer as beis thik;

51–60 Ane browstar . . . me.] *not in MF* 61 Ane . . . ryfe] The menstrall sayis, That ever I thryve *MF* 63 said . . . be] sayis, Than I counsall the *MF* 64 that] *corr.* thy *in MF* 65 Renunce . . . me] Syn cum and play ane spring to me *MF* 66–70 Ane dysour . . . me.] *not in MF* 71–5 *follows later in MF: see infra* 76 with granis] thair menis *MF* 77 saule] gaif *MF* 78 Thay . . . hie] Sa did the hukstaris hailellie *MF* 81–5 Me thocht . . . me.] *MF has*:

The rest of craftis grit ethis swair
Thair wark and craft had na compair,
Ilk ane into thar qualitie;
The Devill sayis, Thane withouttin mair
Renunce ȝour God and cum to me.

Ay tempand folk with wayis sle,
Rownand to Robene and to Dik,
Renunce thy God and cum to me.

The theif sayis, That ever I scaip . . . [*as ll. 71–5, supra*]

The cowrt man did grit aithis sweir
He wald serve Sathan for sevin ȝeir
For fair claythis and gold plaintie;
The Devill said, Thair is sum for geir
Wald renunce God and dwell with me.

To bane and sweir na staittis stud a,
Man or woman, grit or sma,
Ryche and pur, nor the clargie;
The Devill said than, Of commoun la
All mensworne folk man cum to me.

colophon Quod Dumbar *B MF*

V

MORALITIES

57. [Quhat is this Lyfe?]

QUHAT is this lyfe bot ane straucht way to deid,
 Quhilk hes a tyme to pas and nane to duell;
A slyding quheill us lent to seik remeid,
 A fre chois gevin to paradice or hell,
 A pray to deid, quhome vane is to repell;
A schoirt torment for infineit glaidnes—
Als schort ane joy for lestand hevynes.

58. [This Warld unstabille]

I SEIK about this warld unstabille
To find ane sentence convenabille,
 Bot I can nocht in all my wit
 Sa trew ane sentence fynd off it
As say, it is dessaveabille.

For ȝesterday I did declair
Quhow that the seasoun soft and fair
 Com in als fresche as pako fedder;
 This day it stangis lyk ane edder,
Concluding all in my contrair.

Ȝisterday fair up sprang the flouris,
This day thai ar all slane with schouris;
 And fowllis in forrest that sang cleir
 Now walkis with a drery cheir,
Full caild ar baith thair beddis and bouris.

Quhat is this Lyfe? *Text: MS MF (p. 310) collated with MS B (f. 75v)*
 1 bot] *om. B* straucht] draucht *B* to deid] to the deid *B* 2 a] *om. B*
3 seik] win *B* *colophon* Quod Dumbar *MF*: Finis *B*

This Warld unstabille. *Text: MS MFa (pp. 5–6; inaccurately copied in MS Reidpeth, f. 8v) collated with MS MFb (p. 315)*
 7 seasoun] *marginal corr. of* sessione *in MFa*: sasoun *MFb: om. R* 11 up] *om. MFb*

So nixt to summer winter bein;
Nixt eftir confort, cairis kein,
  Nixt dirk mednycht the mirthefull morrow,
  Nixt efter joy aye cumis sorrow;
Sa is this warld, and ay hes bein.

59. [All erdly Joy returnis in Pane]

OFF LENTREN in the first mornyng
Airly as did the day up spring
Thus sang ane bird with voce upplane:
All erdly joy returnis in pane.

O man, haif mynd that thow mon pas;
Remembir that thow art bot as
And sall in as return agane;
All erdly joy returnis in pane.

Haif mynd that eild ay followis ȝowth,
Deth followis lyfe with gaipand mowth
Devoring fruct and flowring grane;
All erdly joy returnis in pane.

Welth, warldly gloir and riche array
Ar all bot thornis laid in thy way
Ourcoverd with flouris in ane trane;
All erdly joy returnis in pane.

Come nevir ȝit May so fresche and grene
Bot Januar come als wod and kene;
Wes nevir sic drowth bot anis come rane:
All erdly joy returnis in pane.

16 So . . . bein *MFb R: MFa defective* *colophon* Quod Dumbar *MFa MFb*

All erdly Joy returnis in Pane. *Text: MS B (f. 48ᵛ) collated with MS MF (pp. 319–20)*

3 upplane] out plane *MF* 7 return] revert *MF* 8, 12, 16, 20, 28, 32, 40 erdly] warldlie *MF* 8, 16, 20, 28, 32, 36 *abbrev. in B* 11 flowring] flowrit *MF* 13 warldly: wardly *B* 14 laid] *om. MF* 15 Ourcoverd . . . in: Ourcoverd . . . laid in *B*: Coverit . . . laid for *MF* 17 ȝit *om. MF*

Evirmair unto this warldis joy
As nerrest air succeidis noy;
Thairfoir quhen joy ma nocht remane
His verry air succeidis, pane.

Heir helth returnis in seiknes
And mirth returnis in havines,
Toun in desert, forrest in plane;
All erdly joy returnis in pane.

Fredome returnis in wrechitnes,
And trewth returnis in dowbilnes
With fenȝeit wirdis to mak men fane;
All erdly joy returnis in pane.

Vertew returnis in to vyce
And honour in to avaryce;
With cuvatyce is consciens slane:
All erdly joy returnis in pane.

Sen erdly joy abydis nevir,
Wirk for the joy that lestis evir;
For uder joy is all bot vane:
All erdly joy returnis in pane.

60. [Vanitas Vanitatum et omnia Vanitas]

O WRECHE, be war: this warld will wend the fro
  Quhilk hes begylit mony greit estait;
Turne to thy freynd, belief nocht in thy fo,
  Sen thow mon go, be grathing to thy gait;
  Remeid in tyme and rew nocht all to lait;
Provyd thy place, for thow away man pas
  Out of this vaill of trubbill and dissait:
Vanitas vanitatum et omnia vanitas.

21 unto . . . warldis] to . . . warldlie *MF*   31 fenȝeit] feynȝeand *MF* to mak] and makis *MF*   38 that] the *MF*   *colophon* Quod Dumbar *B MF*

Vanitas Vanitatum et omnia Vanitas. *Text: MS MF (pp. 195–6)* *colophon* Finis quod Dunbar *MF*

Walk furth, pilgrame, quhill thow hes dayis licht;
  Dres fra desert, draw to thy duelling place;
Speid home, for quhy anone cummis the nicht
  Quhilk dois the follow with ane ythand chaise;
  Bend up thy saill and win thy port of grace;
For and the deith ourtak the in trespas
  Than may thow say thir wourdis with, Allace:
Vanitas vanitatum et omnia vanitas.

Heir nocht abydis, heir standis nothing stabill;
  This fals warld ay flittis to and fro;
Now day up bricht, now nycht als blak as sabill,
  Now eb, now flude, now freynd, now cruell fo,
  Now glaid, now said, now weill, now in to wo,
Now cled in gold, dissolvit now in as;
  So dois this warld transitorie go:
Vanitas vanitatum et omnia vanitas.

61. [Memento Homo quod cinis es]

Memento homo quod cinis es—
Think, man, thow art bot erd and as;
Lang heir to dwell na thing thow pres,
For as thow come sa sall thow pas.
Lyk as ane schaddow in ane glas
Hyne glydis all thy tyme that heir is;
Think, thocht thy bodye ware of bras,
Quod tu in cinerem reverteris.

Worthye Hector and Hercules,
Forcye Achill and strong Sampsone,
Alexander of grit nobilnes,
Meik David and fair Absolone
Hes playit thair pairtis, and all are gone
At will of God that all thing steiris:
Think, man, exceptioun thair is none
Sed tu in cinerem reverteris.

Memento Homo quod cinis es. *Text: MS B (ff. 47ʳ–47ᵛ) collated with MS MF (pp. 193–4)*

5 as] till *MF* 6 glydis all thy] gais the *MF* 12 Meik] King *MF* 13 playit . . . pairtis] past . . . tyme *MF* 14 God] him *MF*

Thocht now thow be maist glaid of cheir,
Fairest and plesandest of port,
Ȝit may thow be within ane ȝeir
Ane ugsum ugelye tramort;
And sen thow knawis thy tyme is schort
And in all houre thy lyfe in weir is,
Think, man, amang all uthir sport,
Quod tu in cinerem reverteris.

Thy lustye bewte and thy ȝouth
Sall feid as dois the somer flouris;
Syne sall the swallow with his mouth
The dragone death that all devouris:
No castell sall the keip, nor touris,
Bot he sall seik the with thy feiris;
Thairfore remembir at all houris
Quod tu in cinerem reverteris.

Thocht all this warld thow did posseid,
Nocht eftir death thow sall posses,
Nor with the tak bot thy guid deid
Quhen thow dois fro this warld the dres:
So speid the, man, and the confes
With humill hart and sobir teiris,
And sadlye in thy hart inpres
Quod tu in cinerem reverteris.

Thocht thow be taklit nevir so sure
Thow sall in deathis port arryve,
Quhair nocht for tempest may indure
Bot ferslye all to spumis dryve.
Thy ransonner with woundis fyve
Mak thy plycht anker and thy steiris
To hald thy saule with him on lyve
Cum tu in cinerem reverteris.

20 ugelye: uglye *B*: horrible *MF* 22 lyfe] dait *MF* 27 the] he *MF* 28 that all devouris *MF: added in B in later hand* 30 seik] feche *MF* 34 death] deid *MF* 36 this warld the] the cuntre *MF* 37 So] Go *MF* 38 With . . . teiris] Tak this to spur the quhen thow sweiris *MF* 44 ferslye] freschlie *MF* spumis dryve: spumis dryff *MF*: speiris [ ] *B* 45 ransonner with woundis] ransoun with his woundis *MF* 46 anker] ankeris *MF* 48 *Cum*] *Quod MF* *colophon* Finis quod Dumbar *B*: Finis &c. *MF*

62. [Timor Mortis conturbat me]

I THAT in heill wes and gladnes
Am trublit now with gret seiknes
And feblit with infermite:
Timor mortis conturbat me.

Our plesance heir is all vane glory,
This fals warld is bot transitory,
The flesch is brukle, the Fend is sle:
Timor mortis conturbat me.

The stait of man dois change and vary,
Now sound, now seik, now blith, now sary,
Now dansand mery, now like to dee:
Timor mortis conturbat me.

No stait in erd heir standis sickir;
As with the wynd wavis the wickir
Wavis this warldis vanite:
Timor mortis conturbat me.

One to the ded gois all estatis,
Princis, prelotis and potestatis,
Baith riche and pur of al degre:
Timor mortis conturbat me.

He takis the knychtis in to feild
Anarmyt undir helme and scheild,
Victour he is at all melle:
Timor mortis conturbat me.

That strang unmercifull tyrand
Takis one the moderis breist sowkand
The bab full of benignite:
Timor mortis conturbat me.

Timor Mortis conturbat me. *Text: Rouen print* ($b3^r$–$b4^v$) *collated with MSS B* (*ff.* 109^r–110^r) *and MF* (*pp.* 189–92)

1 heill] heilth *MF* 6 bot transitory] bot ane transitorie *MF* 8 *et seq.*] *refrain abbrev.* Timor et cetera *in print and from l. 16 in B:* Timor domini . . . me *MF 52, 56* 9 *et passim* and: et *print* 15 Wavis this] So wannis this *B*: Swa waveris the *MF* vanite: vainte *print* 17 One to the ded] Unto the deth *B* 21 to feild] to the feild *B*: the feild *MF* 22 undir] bayth with *MF* 25 That] The *MF* unmercifull] unvynsable *B* 26 Takis *B MF*: Tak *print*

He takis the campion in the stour,
The capitane closit in the tour,
The lady in bour full of bewte:
Timor mortis conturbat me.

He sparis no lord for his piscence,
Na clerk for his intelligence;
His awfull strak may no man fle:
Timor mortis conturbat me.

Art magicianis and astrologgis,
Rethoris, logicianis and theologgis—
Thame helpis no conclusionis sle:
Timor mortis conturbat me.

In medicyne the most practicianis,
Lechis, surrigianis and phisicianis,
Thame self fra ded may not supple:
Timor mortis conturbat me.

I se that makaris amang the laif
Playis heir ther pageant, syne gois to graif;
Sparit is nought ther faculte:
Timor mortis conturbat me.

He has done petuously devour
The noble Chaucer of makaris flour,
The monk of Bery, and Gower, all thre:
Timor mortis conturbat me.

The gud Syr Hew of Eglintoun
And eik Heryot and Wyntoun
He has tane out of this cuntre:
Timor mortis conturbat me.

That scorpion fell has done infek
Maister Johne Clerk and James Afflek
Fra balat making and trigide:
Timor mortis conturbat me.

33 lord] lordis *MF* 34 Na] Nor *B MF* clerk for his] clerkis for thair *MF* 43 ded] deth *B* 45 that] the *B MF* amang] amangis *B* 46 pageant] padȝanis *B MF* 54 And eik: Et eik *print*: Ettrik *B*: Etrik *MF* 57 That] The *MF* fell] *om. MF* 58 Afflek] Auchinlek *MF*

Holland and Barbour he has berevit;
Allace that he nought with us levit
Schir Mungo Lokert of the Le:
Timor mortis conturbat me.

Clerk of Tranent eik he has tane
That maid the anteris of Gawane;
Schir Gilbert Hay endit has he:
Timor mortis conturbat me.

He has Blind Hary and Sandy Traill
Slane with his schour of mortall haill
Quhilk Patrik Johnestoun myght nought fle:
Timor mortis conturbat me.

He has reft Merseir his endite
That did in luf so lifly write,
So schort, so quyk, of sentence hie:
Timor mortis conturbat me.

He has tane Roull of Aberdene
And gentill Roull of Corstorphin—
Two bettir fallowis did no man se:
Timor mortis conturbat me.

In Dunfermelyne he has done roune
With Maister Robert Henrisoun;
Schir Johne the Ros enbrast has he:
Timor mortis conturbat me.

And he has now tane last of aw
Gud gentill Stobo and Quintyne Schaw
Of quham all wichtis has pete:
Timor mortis conturbat me.

Gud Maister Walter Kennedy
In poynt of dede lyis veraly—
Gret reuth it wer that so suld be:
Timor mortis conturbat me.

61 and] *om. MF* 62 nought with us] with us nocht *MF* 65 Clerk] The clerk *MF* 66 of Gawane] of Ser Gawane *B* 67 Hay] Gray *B* 70 his] the *MF* schour] schot *B* 71 fle *MSS: print defective* 74 lifly] lustie *MF* 75 of] so *MF* 81 In] *corr.* And *in B* done roune] ta[n]e broun *B* (*in different ink*) 82 With Maister] With gud Maister *B* 85–8 And . . . *me*] *om. MF* 89 Gud] And *B* 91 so suld be] he suld de *MF*

Sen he has all my brether tane
He will naught lat me lif alane;
On forse I man his nyxt pray be:
Timor mortis conturbat me.

Sen for the ded remeid is none
Best is that we for dede dispone
Eftir our deid that lif may we:
Timor mortis conturbat me.

63. [Into this Warld may none assure]

QUHOME to sall I complene my wo
And kyth my kairis on or mo?
I knaw nocht amang riche nor pure
Quha is my freynd, quha is my fo,
For in this warld may none assure.

Lord how sall I my dayis dispone?
For lang service rewarde is none,
And schort my lyfe may heir indure
And lossit is my tyme bygone;
Into this warld ma none assure.

Oft falsett rydis with ane rowt
Quhen trewth gois on his fute abowt
And lak of spending dois him spur;
Thus quhat to do I am in dowt:
Into this warld may none assure.

Nane heir bot riche men hes renoun
And bot pure men ar pluckit doun
And nane bot just men tholis injure;
Sa wit is blindit and ressoun:
Into this warld may none assure.

98 dede] deth *B* 99 deid] deth *B* *colophon* Quod Dunbar quhen he wes sek &c. *print*: Quod Dumbar *B*: Finis quod Dunbar &c. *MF*

Into this Warld may none assure. *Text: MS B (ff. 84ʳ–85ʳ) collated with MS MF (pp. 331–3; Reidpeth, f. 40ᵛ)*

15 *et passim*] *refrain abbrev. in B* 17 bot] *om. MF* 20 Into] For in *MF*

Vertew the court hes done dispyis;
Ane rebald to renoun dois ryis
And cairlis of nobillis hes the cure
And bumbardis brukis the benifyis:
Into this warld may none assure.

All gentrice and nobilitie
Ar passit out of he degre;
On fredome is laid foirfaltour;
In princis is thair no pety:
For in this warld may none assure.

Is non so armit in to plait
That can fra truble him debait;
May no man lang in welth indure
For wo that evir lyis at the wait:
Into this warld may none assure.

Flattry weiris ane furrit goun
And falsett with the lordis dois roun
And trewth standis barrit at the dure
And exul is honour of the toun:
Into this warld may none assure.

Fra everilk mowth fair wirdis proceidis;
In every hairt disceptioun breidis;
Fra everylk e gois lukis demure
Bot fra the handis gois few gud deidis:
Into this warld may none assure.

Toungis now ar maid of quhyte quhaill bone
And hairtis ar maid of hard flynt stone
And ene ar maid of blew asure
And handis of adamant laith to dispone:
Into this warld may none assure.

Ʒit hairt with hand and body all
Mon anser deth quhen he dois call
To compt befoir the juge future;

24 the] *om. MF* 25, 30, 35, 40, 45, 50, 60 Into] So in *MF* 34 evir lyis] lyis ever *MF* 37 lordis *MF*: lord *B* 39 And exul] Exylit *MF* honour *MF: om. B* 43 everylk] everie *MF* lukis *MF*: luke *B* 48 ar maid of blew *MF*: of amiable blyth *B* 51 with hand] and handis *MF*

Sen all ar deid or than de sall,
Quha suld in to this warld assure?

No thing bot deth this schortly cravis,
Quhair fortoun evir as fo dissavis
With freyndly smylingis of ane hure
Quhais fals behechtis as wind hyne wavis:
Into this warld may none assure.

O quha sall weild the wrang possessioun
Or the gold gatherit with oppressioun
Quhen the angell blawis his bugill sture,
Quhilk unrestorit helpis no confessioun?
Into this warld may none assure.

Quhat help is thair in lordschippis sevin
Quhen na hous is bot hell and hevin,
Palice of licht or pitt obscure
Quhair ȝoulis ar hard with horreble stevin?
Into this warld may none assure.

Ubi ardentes anime,
Semper dicentes sunt, Ve, ve!
Sall cry Allace, that wemen thame bure,
O quante sunt iste tenebre!
Into this warld may none assure.

Than quho sall wirk for warldis wrak
Quhen flude and fyre sall our it frak,
And frely fruster feild and fure
With tempest kene and hiddous crak?
Into this warld may none assure.

Lord, sen in tyme sa sone to cum
De terra surrectourus sum,
Reward me with non erdly cure—
Tu regni da imperium:
In to this warld may non assure.

54 than] *om. MF* 58 of] lyk *MF* 62 the gold gatherit] gadderit gold *MF* 72 *sunt MF: om. B* 79 hiddous] thundir *MF* 81 in] the *MF* 83 non] na *MF* 84 *Tu . . . imperium*] Bot me ressave *in regnum tuum MF* 85 In to] Sen in *MF* *colophon* Finis quod Dumbar *B*: Quod Dumbar *MF*

64. [For to be Blyth me think it best]

FULL oft I mus and hes in thocht
How this fals warld is ay on flocht,
Quhair no thing ferme is nor degest;
And quhen I haif my mynd all socht
For to be blyth me think it best.

This warld evir dois flicht and vary;
Fortoun sa fast hir quheill dois cary
Na tyme bot turne can it tak rest,
For quhois fals change suld none be sary;
For to be blyth me thynk it best.

Wald man considdir in mynd rycht weill
Or Fortoun on him turn hir quheill
That erdly honour may nocht lest,
His fall less panefull he suld feill;
For to be blyth me think it best.

Quha with this warld dois warsill and stryfe
And dois his dayis in dolour dryfe,
Thocht he in lordschip be possest
He levis bot ane wrechit lyfe;
For to be blyth me think it best.

Off warldis gud and grit riches
Quhat fruct hes man but mirines?
Thocht he this warld had eist and west
All wer povertie but glaidnes;
For to be blyth me thynk it best.

Quho suld for tynsall drowp or de,
For thyng that is bot vanitie,

For to be Blyth me think it best. *Text: MS B (f. 98^v) collated with MS MF (p. 337 Reidpeth, f. 43); ll. 1–9 repeated and struck out in B (f. 115^v)*

6 evir dois flicht] dois ever chynge *MF* 7 hir] the *MF* 8 bot turne] in turning *MF* it *MF: om. B* 11 man *MF*: men *B* considdir in mynd rycht] in mynd considdir *MF* 12 on him turn hir] turnit on him the *MF* 14 he suld] sould he *MF* 15, 20, 35 *abbrev. in B* 16 Quha] *corr* Quhen *in B* 16–20 Quha . . . best.] *om. MF* 21 warldis gud] wardlie guddis *MF* 24 wer] is bot *MF* 27 For] Off *MF*

Sen to the lyfe that evir dois lest
Heir is bot twynklyng of ane e;
For to be blyth me think it best.

Had I for warldis unkyndnes
In hairt tane ony havines
Or fro my plesans bene opprest,
I had bene deid lang syne, dowtles;
For to be blyth me think it best.

How evir this warld do change and vary,
Lat us in hairt nevir moir be sary
Bot evir be reddy and addrest
To pas out of this frawdfull fary;
For to be blyth me think it best.

65. [Without Glaidnes avalis no Tresure]

Be mery, man, and tak nocht fer in mynd
The wavering of this wrechit vale of sorow;
To God be hummle and to thi frend be kyind,
And with thi nichtbour glaidlie len and borow—
His chance this nycht, it may be thine to morow.
Be mery, man, for any aventure;
For be wismen it has bene said afforow,
Without glaidnes avalis no tresure.

Mak gude cheir of it that God the sendis,
For warldis wrak but weilfar nocht avalis;
No thing is thine sauf onlie that thow spendis—
The remanent of all thow brukis with balis;
Seik to solace quhen saidnes the assalis,

28 dois] sall *MF* 31 warldis] warldlie *MF* 33 fro] for *MF* 36 do] dois *MF* 37 in hairt nevir moir] no moir in hart *MF* 38 evir] ay *MF* *colophon* &c. Quod Dunbar *B*: Quod Dumbar *MF*

Without Glaidnes avalis no Tresure. *Text: Aberdeen Minute Book of Seisins (iii, 1510–11) collated with MSS B (f.* 98^{r}*–*98^{v}*) and MF (pp. 221–2)* 2 vale] warld *B* 4 nichtbour] nychtbouris *B* 5 this nycht: this *Aberdeen*: to nycht *B*: the nicht *MF* 6 Be mery, man] Be blyth in hairt *B*: Be glaid in hart *MF* 7 be] oft with *B MF* it] *om. MF* 9 Mak gud] Mak the gud *B MF* that *B MF: om. Aberdeen* 10 warldis wrak . . . nocht] welth . . . no thing the *MF* 11 thing] gude *B MF* that] bot *B* 12 The . . . all] Remenant all *B*: The remanent thow *MF* with] bot with *B MF* 13 Seik to] Seik thow to *MF*

Thy lyfe in dolour ma nocht lang indure;
Quharfor of confurt set up all thi salis:
Without glaidnes avalis no tresure.

Follow pete, flie trubill and debait,
With famous folkis hald thi company;
Be cheritable and hummle of estait,
For warldis honour lestis bot ane cry;
For truble in erd tak no malancoly:
Be rich in patiens, gife thoue in gudis be pur;
Quha levis mery, he levis michtely:
Without glaidnes avalis no tresur.

Thow seis the wrechis set with sorow and care
To gaddir gudis all thar liffis spaice,
And quhen thar baggis ar full thar self ar bar,
And of thar riches bot the keping hes
Quhill uthiris cum to spend it that hes grace
Quhilk of the wynning no labour hed na cur;
Thairfoir be glaid, and spend with mirrie face:
Without glaidnes avalis no tresure.

Thocht all the wrak that evir hed levand wicht
War onlie thine, no mor thi pert dois fall
Bot met and clacht, and of the laif ane sicht—
Ȝit to the juge thow sall mak compt of all;
Ane raknyng richt cummis of ane ragment small;
Be just and joyus, and do to none injur,
And treuth sall mak the strang as ony wall:
Without glaidnes avalis no tresure.

14 Thy . . . lang] In dolour lang thy lyfe ma nocht *B*: For lang in dolour thi dayis may nocht *MF* 15 Quharfor] Thairfor *MF* 17–40 *sequence in MF 33–40, 25–32, 17–24* 17 Follow] Follow on *B MF* pete] peis *MF* 18 thi] the in *MF* 19 hummle] meik *MF* of] in thyne *B MF* 20 For] All *MF* warldis] warldly *B MF* honour] plesour *MF* 23 mery] mirrelie *MF* michtely *B MF*: michely *Aberdeen* 25 the] thir *B MF* 26 all] in all *B* 27 And quhen] *om. MF* self] selfis *B* ar] ar alwayis *MF* 28 thar] the *MF* the *B MF*: *om. Aberdeen* 29 uthiris cum *B*: tothir *Aberdeen*: ane cum eftir *MF* 30 the] thy *B* no . . . na] tuik bot lytill *MF* 31 Thairfoir . . . mirrie face *MF: om. Aberdeen*: Tak thow example and spend with mirrines *B* 33 wrak] werk *B* 34 no mor . . . fall] of it no more have sall *MF* 35 and clacht] drynk clais *B*: and clayth *MF* 36 mak] gif *B* 37 richt] ryche *MF* ragment *B MF*: regiment *Aberdeen* 39 And] Than *MF* as ony *B MF*: has *Aberdeen* *colophon* Quod Dumbar *B MF*

66. [He hes anewch that is Content]

QUHO thinkis that he hes sufficence,
Off gudis hes no indigence;
Thocht he have nowder land nor rent,
Grit mycht nor hie magnificence,
He hes anewch that is content.

Quho had all riches unto Ynd
And wer not satefeit in mynd,
With povertie I hald him schent:
Off covatyce sic is the kynd;
He hes anewch that is content.

Thairfoir I pray ȝow, bredir deir,
Not to delyt in daynteis seir;
Thank God of it is to the sent,
And of it glaidlie mak gud cheir:
Anewch he hes that is content.

Defy the warld, feynȝeit and fals,
Withe gall in hart and hunyt hals;
Quha maist it servis maist sall it repent;
Off quhais subchettis sour is the sals:
He hes aneuch that is content.

Giff thow hes mycht, be gentill and fre;
And gif thow standis in povertie,
Off thine awin will to it consent
And riches sall returne to the:
He hes aneuch that is content.

And ȝe and I, my bredir all,
That in this lyfe hes lordschip small,
Lat langour not in us imprent;
Gif we not clym we tak no fall:
He hes aneuch that is content.

He hes anewch that is Content. *Text: MS MF (p. 307) collated with MS Reidpeth (R; f. 5r–5v). See Commentary*

2 Off] And of *R* 4 hie] ȝitt *R* 6 had all riches] all the riches had *R* 7 in mynd] in his mynd *R* 11 Thairfoir . . . ȝow] Quhairfoir thocht thow my *R* 12 to delyt in] servit be with *R* 15 Anewch he hes] He hes enowch *R* 16 the] this *R* 17 hunyt] hony in *R* 18 maist sall *R*: sall sonast *MF* it] *om. R* 19 subchettis] surcharge *R* 23 thine] thy *R* 24 riches sall returne] it sall riches turne *R* 27 That in] Within *R* lordschip] lordschippis *R* 28 not in us imprent] nane in us be lent *R*

For quho in warld moist covatus is
In warld is purast man, I wis,
And moist nedy of his intent;
For of all gudis no thing he hes
That of no thing can be content.

67. [Thyne awin Gude spend]

MAN, sen thy lyfe is ay in weir
And deid is evir drawand neir,
The tyme unsicker and the place,
Thyne awin gude spend quhill thow hes space.

Gif it be thyne, thy self it usis;
Gif it be nocht, the it refusis—
Ane uthir of it the proffeit hes;
Thyne awin gud spend quhill thow hes spais.

Thow may to day haif gude to spend
And hestely to morne fra it wend
And leif ane uthir thy baggis to brais;
Thyne awin gude spend quhill thow hes space.

Quhill thow hes space se thow dispone
That for thy geir, quhen thow art gone,
No wicht ane uder slay nor chace;
Thyne awin gude spend quhill thow hes space.

Sum all his dayis dryvis our in vane,
Ay gadderand geir with sorrow and pane,
And nevir is glaid at ȝule nor Pais;
Thyne awin gude spend quhill thow hes space.

31 in . . . covatus] that leist contentit *R* 33 moist nedy of] neidfullest in *R* 34 thing he hes] no this is his *R* *colophon* Quod Dumbar *MF R*

Thyne awin Gude spend. *Text: MS B (f. 136r–136v) collated with MS MF (pp. 225–6)*

2 evir] sicker *MF* 4 *et passim* Thyne . . . spend] Man spend thy gud *MF* 5–16 *sequence in MF 9–12, 5–8, 13–16* 5–6 usis . . . refusis] use . . . refuse *MF* 6 the] thow *MF* 8 quhill: *altered to* quhen *in B* 10 hestely to morne] to morne haistelie *MF* 12–28, 36 *refrain abbrev. in B* 14 geir] gude *MF* 15 No wicht] Nocht with *MF* 19 nevir is . . . nor] utheris ar . . . and *MF*

Syne cumis ane uder glaid of his sorrow
That for him prayit nowdir evin nor morrow
And fangis it all with mirrynais;
Thyne awin gude spend quhill thow hes space.

Sum grit gud gadderis and ay it spairis,
And eftir him thair cumis ȝung airis
That his auld thrift settis on ane es;
Thyne awin gude spend quhill thow hes space.

It is all thyne that thow heir spendis,
And nocht all that on the dependis,
Bot his to spend it that hes grace;
Thyne awin gud spend quhill thow hes spais.

Trest nocht ane uthir will do the to
It that thy self wald nevir do,
For gife thow dois, strenge is thy cace;
Thyne awin gud spend quhill thow hes space.

Luke how the bairne dois to the muder,
And tak example be nane udder
That it nocht eftir be thy cace;
Thyne awin gud spend quhill thow hes space.

68. [Cuvetyce]

FREDOME, honour and nobilnes,
Meid, manheid, mirth and gentilnes,
Ar now in cowrt reput as vyce;
And all for caus of cuvetice.

22 nowdir] nor *MF* 23 mirrynais] mirrey face *MF* 25 ay] all *MF* 26 thair] *om. MF* 28 Thyne . . . space] Man &c. *B* 29 heir spendis] dispendis *MF* 30 on the] thow *MF* 31 it] he *MF* 33–6, 37–40 *transposed in MF* 35 thy] the *MF* 38 example] ȝour sampill *MF* *colophon* Quod Dumbar *B*: Finis *MF*

Cuvetyce. *Text: MS B (ff. 64v–65r) collated with MS MF (pp. 6–7; Reidpeth, f. 9)*
3 reput as] all reput *MF*

All weilfair, welth and wantones
Ar chengit in to wretchitnes,
And play is sett at littill price;
And all for caus of covetyce.

Halking, hunting and swift hors rynning
Ar chengit all in wrangus wynnyng;
Thair is no play bot cartis and dyce:
And all for caus of covetyce.

Honorable houshaldis ar all laid doun;
Ane laird hes with him bot a loun
That leidis him eftir his devyce;
And all for caus of covetyce.

In burghis, to landwart and to sie,
Quhair was plesour and grit plentie,
Vennesoun, wyld fowill, wyne and spyce,
Ar now decayid thruch covetyce.

Husbandis that grangis had full grete,
Cattell and corne to sell and ete,
Hes now no beist bot cattis and myce;
And all thruch caus of covettyce.

Honest ʒemen in every toun
War wont to weir baith reid and broun,
Ar now arrayit in raggis with lyce;
And all for caus of cuvetyce.

And lairdis in silk harlis to the heill
For quhilk thair tennents sald somer meill
And leivis on rutis undir the ryce;
And all for caus of cuvetyce.

10 Ar] Is *MF* 11 and] *corr.* all *in MF* 12, 16, 28, 32, 36, 40 *abbrev. in B* 13 all] *om. MF* 17 burghis] townnes *MF* 18 was plesour] thair was play *MF* 20 Ar . . . thruch] Is now bot cair and *MF* 23 beist] guidis *MF* 24 thruch] for *MF* 25 Honest ʒemen] *not in MF (defective)* 26 War . . . baith] That wont war to weir *MF* 27 in . . . with] withe . . . and *MF* 29 And lairdis] Lordis *MF* heill *MF*: eill *B* 30 thair . . . meill] the tennenttis haiff sauld thair seill *MF*

Quha that dois deidis of petie
And leivis in pece and cheretie
Is haldin a fule, and that full nyce;
And all for caus of cuvetyce.

And quha can reive uthir menis rowmis
And upoun peur men gadderis sowmis
Is now ane active man, and wyice;
And all for caus of cuvetyce.

Man, pleis thy makar and be mirry,
And sett not by this warld a chirry;
Wirk for the place of paradyce,
For thairin ringis na cuvettyce.

69. [In Winter]

IN to thir dirk and drublie dayis
Quhone sabill all the hevin arrayis,
  With mystie vapouris, cluddis and skyis,
  Nature all curage me denyis
Off sangis, ballattis and of playis.

Quhone that the nycht dois lenthin houris
With wind, with haill and havy schouris,
  My dule spreit dois lurk for schoir;
  My hairt for langour dois forloir
For laik of Symmer with his flouris.

I walk, I turne, sleip may I nocht;
I vexit am with havie thocht;
  This warld all ovir I cast about,
  And ay the mair I am in dout
The mair that I remeid have socht.

35 haldin] now *MF* 37 And quha can reive] Quha reiff can *MF* 38 gadderis] gadder *MF* 42 not by] nocht off *MF* 44 thairin] thair *MF* *colophon* Finis *B*: Quod Dumbar *MF*

In Winter. *Text: MS MF (MFa; pp. 318–19) collated with MSS MFb (p. 3; ll. 23–50) and Reidpeth (f. 1r; ll. 1–22); see Commentary*
7 with] and *R* 9 *om. R* 11 may] can *R* 14 ay] evir *R*

I am assayit on everie syde;
Despair sayis, Ay in tyme provyde
And get sum thing quhairon to leif,
Or with grit trouble and mischeif
Thow sall in to this court abyd.

Than Patience sayis, Be not agast;
Hald Hoip and Treuthe within the fast
And lat Fortoun wirk furthe hir rage,
Quhome that no rasoun may assuage
Quhill that hir glas be run and past.

And Prudence in my eir sayis ay,
Quhy wald thow hald that will away?
Or craif that thow may have mo space,
Thow tending to ane uther place
A journay going everie day?

And than sayis Age, My freind, cum neir
And be not strange, I the requeir;
Cum brodir, by the hand me tak;
Remember thow hes compt to mak
Off all thi tyme thow spendit heir.

Syne Deid castis upe his ȝettis wyd
Saying, Thir oppin sall the abyd;
Albeid that thow wer never sa stout,
Undir this lyntall sall thow lowt—
Thair is nane uther way besyde.

For feir of this all day I drowp:
No gold in kist nor wyne in cowp,
No ladeis bewtie nor luiffis blys
May lat me to remember this,
How glaid that ever I dyne or sowp.

22 *R ends: MFb begins* 24 Quhome: Quhone *MFa*: Quhen *MFb* 26 my] myne *MFb* 28 mo: no *MSS* 29 to] till *MFb* 33 by] and be *MFb* 34 hes compt] hes ane compt *MFb* 36 Syne] Thane *MFb* 37 abyd] byd *MFb* 40 nane] no *MFb*

Ȝit quhone the nycht begynnis to schort
It dois my spreit sum pairt confort
Off thocht oppressit with the schowris;
Cum lustie Symmer with thi flowris,
That I may leif in sum disport.

70. [Ane wirkis Sorrow to him sell]

He that hes gold and grit riches
And may be into mirrynes,
And dois glaidnes fra him expell
And levis in to wrechitnes:
He wirkis sorrow to him sell.

He that may be but sturt or stryfe
And leif ane lusty plesand lyfe,
And syne with mariege dois him mell
And bindis him with ane wicket wyfe:
He wirkis sorrow to him sell.

He that hes for his awin genȝie
Ane plesand prop, but mank or menȝie,
And schuttis syne at ane uncow schell
And is forfairn with the fleis of Spenȝie:
He wirkis sorrow to him sell.

And he that with gud lyfe and trewth,
But varians or uder slewth,
Dois evir mair with ane maister dwell
That nevir of him will haif no rewth:
He wirkis sorrow to him sell.

47 pairt] thing *MFb* (*margin*) *colophon* Quod Dumbar *MFa MFb*

Ane wirkis Sorrow to him sell. *Text: MS B* (*ff.* 115^{v}–116^{r}) *collated with MS MF* (*pp.* 212–13)

4 in to wrechitnes] daylie in distres *MF* 9 bindis him with] weddis syn *MF* 12 mank] mak *MF* 13 syne] *om. MF* 14 And is] *om. MF* 15 He wirkis . . . sell] *abbrev. in B*: I gif him to the Devill of hell *MF* 17 uder] ordour *MF* 19 nevir . . . no] never mair will of him *MF* 20 He wirkis . . . sell]. *abbrev. in B*

Now all this tyme lat us be mirry
And sett nocht by this warld a chirry;
Now quhill thair is gude wyne to sell,
He that dois on dry breid wirry
I gif him to the Devill of hell.

71. [Thir Ladyis fair that in the Court ar kend]

THIR ladyis fair
That makis repair
And in the court ar kend,
Thre dayis thair
Thay will do mair
Ane mater for till end
Than thair gud men
Will do in ten
For ony craft thay can;
So weill thay ken
Quhat tyme and quhen
Thair menes thay sowld mak than.

With littill noy
Thay can convoy
Ane mater fynaly
Richt myld and moy,
And keip it coy
On evyns quyetly;
Thay do no mis—
Bot gif thay kis
And keipis collatioun,
Quhat rek of this?
Thair mater is
Brocht to conclusioun.

22 by] on *MF* 23 Now] And *MF* 25 *colophon* Quod Dumbar *B*: Finis *MF*

Thir Ladyis fair that in the Court ar kend. *Text: MS B (f. 261ʳ–261ᵛ) collated with MS MF (pp. 324–5; Reidpeth, ff. 38ᵛ–39ʳ)*

6 till] to *MF* 10 So] For *MF* 16 Richt] 3it *MF* 17 And] Thai *MF* 23 Thair] The *MF*

Wit ȝe weill
Thay haif grit feill
Ane mater to solist,
Trest as the steill,
Syne nevir a deill
Quhen thay cum hame ar mist.
Thir lairdis ar,
Methink, richt far
Sic ladeis behaldin to
That sa weill dar
Go to the bar
Quhen thair is ocht ado.

Thairfoir I reid
Gif ȝe haif pleid
Or mater in to pley,
To mak remeid
Send in ȝour steid
Ȝour ladeis grathit up gay.
Thay can defend
Evin to the end
Ane mater furth expres;
Suppois thay spend
It is unkend—
Thair geir is nocht the les.

In quyet place
Thocht thay haif space
Within les nor twa howris,
Thay can, percaice,
Purches sum grace
At the compositouris.
Thair compositioun
With full remissioun
Thair fynaly is endit;
With expeditioun
And full conditioun
Thair seilis ar to pendit.

25 Wit ȝe] Ȝe may wit *MF* 30 ar] is *MF* 50 Thocht] And *MF* 53 sum] sic *MF* 56 With full remissioun] without suspitioun *MF* 59 conditioun] remissioun *MF* 60 Thair . . . pendit] And selis thairto appendit *MF*

Alhaill almoist
Thay mak the coist
With sobir recompens;
Richt littill loist,
Thay get indoist
Alhaill thair evidens.
Sic ladyis wyis
Thay ar to pryis,
To say the veretie,
Swa can devyis
And none suppryis
Thame nor thair honestie.

72. [In Prays of Wemen]

Now of wemen this I say for me,
Off erthly thingis nane may bettir be.
Thay suld haif wirschep and grit honoring
Off men aboif all uthir erthly thing.
Rycht grit dishonour upoun him self he takkis
In word or deid quha evir wemen lakkis,
Sen that of wemen cumin all ar we;
Wemen ar wemen and sa will end and de.
Wo wirth the fruct wald put the tre to nocht,
And wo wirth him rycht so that sayis ocht
Off womanheid that may be ony lak,
Or sic grit schame upone him for to tak.
Thay us consaif with pane, and be thame fed
Within thair breistis thair we be boun to bed;
Grit pane and wo and murnyng mervellus
Into thair birth thay suffir sair for us;
Than meit and drynk to feid us get we nane
Bot that we sowk out of thair breistis bane.

68 Thay ar] Ar all *MF* 70 Swa] Sic *MF* 71 none *MF*: not 72 nor] throw *MF* *colophon* Finis quod Dumbar *B*: Quod Dumbar *MF*

In Prays of Wemen. *Text: MS B* (*f.* 278[v]) *collated with MS MF* (*pp.* 294–5)
1 Now of wemen] Off wemen now *MF* 4 erthly] warldlie *M*
17 we] *corr.* thai *in MF* 18 that] it *MF*

Thay ar the confort that we all haif heir—
Thair may no man be till us half so deir;
Thay ar our verry nest of nurissing.
In lak of thame quha can say ony thing,
That fowll his nest he fylis, and for thy
Exylit he suld be of all gud cumpany;
Thair suld na wyis man gif audience
To sic ane without intelligence.
Chryst to his fader he had nocht ane man;
Se quhat wirschep wemen suld haif than.
That Sone is Lord, that Sone is King of Kingis;
In hevin and erth his majestie ay ringis.
Sen scho hes borne him in hir halines
And he is well and grund of all gudnes,
All wemen of us suld haif honoring,
Service and luve, aboif all uthir thing.

73. [Tway Cummeris]

RYCHT airlie on Ask Weddinsday
Drynkand the wyne satt cumeris tway;
The tane cowth to the tother complene:
Graneand and suppand cowd scho say,
This lang Lentern makis me lene.

On cowch besyd the fyre scho satt—
God wait gif scho wes grit and fatt;
ȝit to be feble scho did hir fene
And ay scho said, Cummer, latt preif of that:
This lang Lentern makis me lene.

20 till] to *MF* 23 fowll] fule *MF* 24 he] *om. MF* 26 ane] a fule *MF* 27 he had nocht] had not *MF* 33 of us suld] sould of us *MF* *colophon* Quod Dumbar *B*: Quod Dumbar in prays of women *MF*

Tway Cummeris. *Text: MS B (f. 137ʳ) collated with the Aberdeen Minute Book of Seisins (AMB; ii, 1503–7), MSS MF (pp. 57–8) and Reidpeth (f. 19ᵛ). See Commentary*

1 Rycht] *om. MF* Ask] als *MF* 2 Drynkand] At *MF* 3 cowth to the tother] to the tother cold *MF* 4 Graneand] Sichand *MF* cowd] couth *AMB*: can *MF* 5 makis] it makis *AMB passim*: hes maid *MF* 6 On . . . fyre] One couch befor the fyir *AMB:* Besyd the fyr quhair that *MF* 7 wes] wair *AMB* 9 And ay scho said] Ay scho said *AMB*: Sayand ay *MF* Cummer *AMB MF: del. in B* 10 This . . . me] That lentrune sall nocht mak us *MF*

My fair sweit cummer, quod the tuder,
ȝe tak that nigirtnes of ȝour muder;
All wyne to test scho wald disdane
Bot mavasy, scho bad nane uder:
This lang Lentern makis me lene.

Cummer, be glaid both evin and morrow
Thocht ȝe suld bayth beg and borrow,
Fra our lang fasting ȝe ȝow refrene
And latt ȝour husband dre the sorrow:
This lang Lentern makis me lene.

ȝour counsale, cummer, is gud, quod scho;
All is to tene him that I do,
In bed he is nocht wirth a bene.
Fill fow the glas and drynk me to;
This lang Lentern makis me lene.

Off wyne out of ane choppyne stowp
Thay drank twa quartis sowp and sowp,
Off drowth sic exces did thame strene;
Be than to mend thay had gud howp:
This lang Lentroun makis me lene.

11 My . . . quod] Fair gentill cumer said *MF* 13 All] Ill *MF* wald] did *MF* 14 scho bad nane] and nan drink *AMB* 15, 20, 25 *abbrev. in B* This . . . me] That lentrune suld nocht mak hir *MF* 16 glaid] blythe *MF* 17, 19 *transposed in MF* 17 Thocht . . . borrow] The gud quhar [one] ȝe beg or borrow *AMB*: And I shall find ȝow God to borrow *MF* 18 ȝe] *om. AMB MF* refrene] referne *MF* 20 This . . . me] That lentrune sall nocht mak ȝow *MF* 21 ȝour . . . quod] Fair gentill cumer than said *MF* 24 fow] anis *AMB: om. MF* glas] *corr.* cop *in AMB:* cop comer *MF* me to] to me *AMB* 25 This . . . me] That lentrune sall nocht mak us *MF* 26 Off wyne] Thir twa *MF* 27 twa] thre *MF* quartis sowp] quartis bot soup *AMB* 28 Off . . . strene] Sic drouthe and thrist was thame betwene *MF* strene *AMB*: constrene *B* 29 Be] Bot *MF* 30 This . . . lene] That lang lentrin suld nocht mak tham leen *AMB:* That lentrune swld nocht mak thame lene *MF* *colophon* Quod Dumbar *MSS*

74. [Tydingis hard at the Sessioun]

ANE murlandis man of uplandis mak
At hame thus to his nychtbour spak:
Quhat tydingis, gossep—peax or weir?
The tother rownit in his eir,
I tell ȝow this undir confessioun:
Bot laitly lichtit of my meir
I come of Edinburch fra the sessioun.

Quhat tythingis hard ȝe thair, I pray ȝow?
The tother answerit, I sall say ȝow;
Keip this all secreit, gentill brother—
Is na man thair that trestis ane uther;
Ane commoun doar of transgressioun
Of innocent folkis prevenis a futher:
Sic tydingis hard I at the sessioun.

Sum with his fallow rownis him to pleis
That wald for invy byt of his neis;
His fa sum by the oxstar leidis;
Sum patteris with his mowth on beidis
That hes his mynd all on oppressioun;
Sum beckis full law and schawis bair heidis
Wald luke full heich war not the sessioun.

Sum bydand the law layis land in wed,
Sum super expendit gois to his bed,
Sum speidis for he in court hes menis;
Of parcialitie sum complenis,
How feid and favour flemis discretioun;
Sum speikis full fair and fasly fenis:
Sic tythingis hard I at the sessioun.

Tydingis hard at the Sessioun. *Text: MS B (f. 59r–59v) collated with MS MF (pp. 314–15; Reidpeth, f. 37)*

4 tother] uther *MF* his eir *MF*: heir *B* 10 all] in *MF* 11 that trestis] trowis *MF* 16 invy] anger *MF* 20 law] laich *MF* 22 the] *om. MF* 23 super expendit] superspendit *MF* 25 Of parcialitie sum *MF*: Sum of parcialitie *B*

Sum castis summondis and sum exceptis;
Sum standis besyd and skaild law keppis;
Sum is continuit, sum wynnis, sum tynis;
Sum makis him mirry at the wynis;
Sum is put owt of his possessioun;
Sum herreit and on creddens dynis:
Sic tydingis hard I at the sessioun.

Sum sweiris and forsaikis God;
Sum in ane lambskin is ane tod;
Sum in his toung his kyndnes tursis;
Sum cuttis throttis, and sum pykis pursis;
Sum gois to gallous with processioun;
Sum sanis the sait, and sum thame cursis:
Sic tydingis hard I at the sessioun.

Religious men of divers placis
Cumis thair to wow and se fair facis;
Baith Carmeleitis and Cordilleris
Cumis thair to genner and get ma freiris,
And ar unmyndfull of thair professioun—
The ȝungar at the eldar leiris:
Sic tydingis hard I at the sessioun.

Thair cumis ȝung monkis of he complexioun,
Of devoit mynd, luve and affectioun,
And in the courte thair hait flesche dantis
Full faderlyk with pechis and pantis;
Thay ar so humill of intercessioun,
All mercyfull wemen thair eirandis grantis:
Sic tydingis hard I at the sessioun.

32 him] thame *MF* 33 Sum is] And sum *MF* 35, 49 *abbrev. in B* 36 and] and sum *MF* 38 in] on *MF* 39 cuttis . . . pykis] kervis . . . cuttis *MF* 40 Sum gois to gallous] To gallows sum gais *MF* 46 ma] *om. MF* 47 And ar unmyndfull] As is the use *MF* 50 he] het *MF* 52 hait] proud *MF* 55 eirandis] errand *MF* *colophon* Finis quod Dumbar *B*: Quod Dumbar *MF*

75. [To the Merchantis of Edinburgh]

QUHY will ȝe merchantis of renoun
Lat Edinburgh ȝour nobill toun
For laik of reformatioun
The commone proffeitt tyine, and fame?
  Think ȝe not schame,
That onie uther regioun
Sall with dishonour hurt ȝour name?

May nane pas throw ȝour principall gaittis
For stink of haddockis and of scaittis,
For cryis of carlingis and debaittis,
For fensum flyttingis of defame;
  Think ȝe not schame,
Befoir strangeris of all estaittis
That sic dishonour hurt ȝour name?

Ȝour stinkand scull that standis dirk
Haldis the lycht fra ȝour parroche kirk;
Ȝour foirstair makis ȝour housis mirk
Lyk na cuntray bot heir at hame;
  Think ȝe not schame,
Sa litill polesie to wirk
In hurt and sklander of ȝour name?

At ȝour hie croce quhar gold and silk
Sould be, thair is bot crudis and milk;
And at ȝour trone bot cokill and wilk,
Pansches, pudingis of Jok and Jame;
  Think ȝe not schame,
Sen as the world sayis that ilk
In hurt and sclander of ȝour name?

Ȝour commone menstrallis hes no tone
Bot Now the Day dawis, and Into Joun;

To the Merchantis of Edinburgh. *Text: MS Reidpeth (ff. 1ᵛ–2ᵛ)*
7 hurt] *corr.* quyt *in R*   15 scull] *corr.* stull *in R: see Commentary*
25 Jame: James *R*

Cunningar men man serve Sanct Cloun
And nevir to uther craftis clame;
  Think ȝe not schame,
To hald sic mowaris on the moyne
In hurt and sclander of ȝour name?

Tailȝouris, soutteris and craftis vyll
The fairest of ȝour streittis dois fyll,
And merchandis at the stinkand styll
Ar hamperit in ane hony came;
  Think ȝe not schame,
That ȝe have nether witt nor wyll
To win ȝourselff ane bettir name?

Ȝour burgh of beggeris is ane nest,
To schout thai swentȝouris will not rest;
All honest folk they do molest,
Sa piteuslie thai cry and rame;
  Think ȝe not schame,
That for the poore hes nothing drest,
In hurt and sclander of ȝour name?

Ȝour proffeit daylie dois incres,
Ȝour godlie workis les and les;
Through streittis nane may mak progres
For cry of cruikit, blind and lame;
  Think ȝe not schame,
That ȝe sic substance dois posses
And will not win ane bettir name?

Sen for the court and the sessioun
The great repair of this regioun
Is in ȝour burgh, thairfoir be boun
To mend all faultis that ar to blame,
  And eschew schame;
Gif thai pas to ane uther toun
Ȝe will decay, and ȝour great name.

31 serve] *corr.* schow *in R* 37 streittis: streit *R* 46 rame] *corr.* lament *in R*

Thairfoir strangeris and leigis treit,
Tak not over mekill for thair meit,
And gar ȝour merchandis be discreit;
That na extortiounes be, proclame
  All fraud and schame;
Keip ordour and poore nighbouris beit,
That ȝe may gett ane bettir name.

Singular proffeit so dois ȝow blind,
The common proffeit gois behind;
I pray that Lord remeid to fynd
That deit into Jerusalem,
  And gar ȝow schame;
That sumtyme ressoun may ȝow bind
For to [win bak to] ȝow guid name.

76. [Dunbar at Oxinfurde]

To speik off science, craft or sapience,
  Off vertew, morall cuning or doctryne,
Off jure, off wisdome or intelligence,
  Of every studie, lair or disciplyne:
  All is bot tynt, or reddy for to tyne.
Nocht using it as it suld usit be—
  The craft excersing, considering nocht the fyne:
Ane peralous seiknes is vane prosperite.

The curius probacion logicall,
  The eloquence off ornat rethorye,
The naturall science filosophicall,
  The dirk apirance off astronamy,
  The theologgis sermon, the fablis off poetrye—
Withowt guid lyff, all in the selff dois de
  As Mayis flouris dois in September drye:
Ane peralows lyff is vane prosperite.

67 proclame: proclameid *R* 73 fynd] *corr.* send *in R* 77 win bak to *conj.: blank in R* *colophon* Quod Dumbar *R*

Dunbar at Oxinfurde. *Text: MS MF (a; pp. 9–10; Reidpeth, f. 10v) collated with MFb (pp. 317–18)*
7 craft] craist *MFb* 10 rethorye] *corr.* oratrie *in MFb* 11 science] off *del. in MFa* 13 fablis *MFb*: fable *MFa* 14 selff: salff *MFa* 15 Mayis] Maii *MFb*

Quhairfoir ȝe clerkis grytast off constance,
Fullest off science and off knaleging,
To us be mirrouris in ȝowr governance
And in owr dirknes be lampis in schining,
Or thane in frustar is ȝowr lang lerning.
Gyff to ȝowr sawis ȝour deidis contrar be
Ȝowr maist accusar is ȝour awin cuning:
Ane peralows seiknes is vane prosperite.

77. [He Rewlis weill that weill him self can Gyd]

To dwell in court, my freind, gife that thow list,
For gift of fortoun invy thow no degre;
Behold and heir and lat thy tung tak rest—
In mekle speiche is pairt of vanitie;
And for no malyce preis the nevir to lie;
Als trubill nevir thy self, sone, be no tyd
Uthiris to reiwll, that will not rewlit be:
He rewlis weill that weill him self can gyd.

Bewar quhome to thy counsale thow discure,
For trewth dwellis nocht ay for that trewth appeiris;
Put not thyne honour into aventeure—
Ane freind may be thy fo as fortoun steiris:
In cumpany cheis honorable ſeiris
And fra vyld folkis draw the far on syd;
The psalme sayis, *Cum sancto sanctus eiris*:
He rewlis weill that weill him self can gyd.

Haif pacience thocht thow no lordschip posseid,
For hie vertew may stand in law estait;
Be thow content, of mair thow hes no neid;
And be thow nocht, desyre sall mak debait
Evirmoir, till deth say to the than, Chakmait:

17 clerkis grytast] clarkis and grittest *MFb* 20 owr *MFb*: ȝowr *MFa* in *MFb*: off *MFa* 21 frustar is ȝowr] *corr. to* vain is all ȝour *in MFa* *colophon* Quod Dumbar *MFa*: Quod Dumbar at Oxinfurd *MFb*

He Rewlis weill that weill him self can Gyd. *Text: MS B (ff. 68ʳ–69ʳ)*
4 speiche: speice *B* 14 vyld] *altered to* vyle *in B*

Thocht all war thyne this warld within so wyd,
Quha can resist the serpent of dispyt?
He rewlis weill that weill him self can gyd.

Fle frome the fallowschip of sic as ar defamit
And fra all fals tungis fulfild with flattry,
Als fra all schrewis, or ellis thow art eschamit;
Sic art thow callit, as is thy cumpany:
Fle perrellus taillis foundit of invy;
With wilfull men, son, argown thow no tyd,
Quhome no ressone may seis nor pacify:
He rewlis weill that weill him self can gyd.

And be thow not ane roundar in the nuke,
For gif thow be, men will hald the suspect;
Be nocht in countenance ane skornar, nor by luke,
Bot dowt siclyk sall stryk the in the neck:
Be war also to counsall or coreck
Him that extold hes far him self in pryd;
Quhair parrell is but proffeit or effect
He rewlis weill that weill him self can gyd.

And sen thow seyis mony thingis variand,
With all thy hart treit bissines and cure;
Hald God thy freind, evir stabill be him stand;
He will the confort in all misaventeur;
And be no wayis dispytfull to the peure
Nor to no man do wrang at ony tyd:
Quho so dois this, sicker I ȝow asseure,
He rewlis weill that sa weill him can gyd.

46 do: to *B* *colophon* Finis quod Dumbar *B*

78–80. [Of Discretioun]

78. [Discretioun in Asking]

Off every asking followis nocht
Rewaird, bot gif sum caus war wrocht;
And quhair caus is, men weill ma sie,
And quhair nane is, it wilbe thocht:
In asking sowld discretioun be.

Ane fule, thocht he haif caus or nane,
Cryis ay, Gif me, in to a drene;
And he that dronis ay as ane bee
Sowld haif ane heirar dull as stane:
In asking sowld discretioun be.

Sum askis mair than he deservis;
Sum askis far les than he servis;
Sum schames to ask (as braidis of me)
And all withowt reward he stervis:
In asking sowld discretioun be.

To ask but service hurtis gud fame;
To ask for service is not to blame;
To serve and leif in beggartie
To man and maistir is baith schame:
In asking sowld discretioun be.

He that dois all his best servyis
May spill it all with crakkis and cryis—
Be fowll inoportunitie;
Few wordis may serve the wyis:
In asking sowld discretioun be.

Discretioun in Asking. *Text: MS B* (*f. 61^r–61^v*) *collated with MS MF* (*pp. 259–60;* *Reidpeth, f. 21^r*) *and Bannatyne's draft* (*d; pp. 45–6*)

1 Off] Eftir *MF* 2 war] be *MF* 3 And . . . weill] And be thair caus as men *MF* weill] *om. d* 4 And . . . is] And be thair naine *MF* 6 thocht] quhidder *MF* 7 Gif me] gif me gif me *MF* drene] rane *MF* 8 ay] on *MF* 9 as stane] as ane stane *d*: as a stane *MF* 11 askis] gifis *MF* deservis] desyris *d* 12 far] *om. d* far les than] na thing bot it *MF* 13 as] and *d MF* 14 withowt reward he] without gwerdoun *d*: within his guardoun *MF* stervis] servis *MF* 15, 30, 35 *abbrev. in B* 16–20 *not in MF* 21 dois . . . best] makis . . . maist *MF* his] thair *d* 22 May . . . all] He may it tyne *MF* 23 Be fowll inoportunitie] In fuliche oportunitie *MF* 24 serve] suffice to *d MF*

Nocht neidfull is, men sowld be dum;
Na thing is gottin but wordis sum;
Nocht sped but diligence we se;
For nathing it allane will cum:
In asking sowld discretioun be.

Asking wald haif convenient place,
Convenient tyme, lasar and space
But haist or preis of grit menȝie,
But hairt abasit, but toung rekles:
In asking sowld discretioun be.

Sum micht haif ȝe with littill cure,
That hes oft Nay with grit labour;
All for that tyme not byd can he,
He tynis baith eirand and honour:
In asking sowld discretioun be.

Suppois the servand be lang unquit,
The lord sumtyme rewaird will it;
Gife he dois not, quhat remedy?
To fecht with fortoun is no wit:
In asking sowld discretioun be.

79. [Discretioun in Geving]

To speik of gift or almous deidis.
Sum gevis for mereit and for meidis,
Sum warldly honour to uphie
Gevis to thame that nothing neidis:
In geving sowld discretioun be.

26 Nocht . . . is, men sowld] Not . . . in asking that men *MF* 27 Na] For no *MF* gottin] wone *d* 28 Nocht sped] Now speche *MF* 31–5 *follow l. 45 in MF* 33 or] but *d MF* 34 abasit, but . . . rekles] rekles or . . . abasit *MF* 36–8 Sum . . . he] *MF has:*

Sum hes so muche he takis no cure
That of the wynning tuke na labure
Bot for his tyme no moir hes he

38 that] his *d* 41 unquit] unservit *MF* 42 The . . . will] Sum tym the maister will reward *MF* rewaird will] rewardis *d* 44 fecht] flytt *MF* *colophon* Finis of asking. Followis discretioun of geving *B*: Endis discretioun in asking. Foll. Giving *d*

Discretioun in Geving. *Text: MS B (ff. 61ᵛ–62ᵛ) collated with MS MF (pp. 260–1; Reidpeth, f. 21ᵛ) and Bannatyne's draft (d; p. 46)*

1 gift] giftis *MF* 2 and for] and sum for *MF*

Sum gevis for pryd and glory vane,
Sum gevis with grugeing and with pane,
Sum gevis in practik for supple,
Sum gevis for twyis als gud agane:
In geving sowld discretioun be.

Sum gevis for thank and sum for threit,
Sum gevis money and sum gevis meit,
Sum gevis wordis fair and sle;
Giftis fra sum ma na man treit:
In geving sowld discretioun be.

Sum is for gift sa lang requyrd
Quhill that the crevar be so tyrd
That, or the gift deliverit be,
The thank is frustrat and expyrd:
In geving sowld discretioun be.

Sum gevis to littill full wretchitly
That his giftis ar not set by
And for a huidpyk haldin is he,
That all the warld cryis on him, Fy:
In geving sowld discretioun be.

Sum in his geving is so large
That all ourlaidin is his berge:
Than vyce and prodigalite
Thairof his honour dois dischairge:
In geving sowld discretioun be.

Sum to the riche gevis geir
That micht his giftis weill forbeir,

6–10 *follow l. 15 in MF* 6 and glory] gloir and *MF* 7 grugeing] grwnsching *MF d* 10, 15, 20, 25, 40, 55, 60 *abbrev. in MF* 8 in] on *d*: for *MF* for] and *MF* 9 gud] mekle *d* 11 and . . . threit *MF*: sum chereit *B*: and sum for cherite *d* 12 and] *om. MF* 14 Giftis] And giftis *MF* ma na] can no *MF* 15, 20, 30, 35, 45, 50, 55 *abbrev. in B* 16 is for gift] for his giftis *MF* 17 that] *om. d MF* crevar] persewarc *MF* 21 to littill full] so lytill and *MF* full] and full *d* 22 That his] That all his *MF* 23 And for a] And for sic *d*: Sa grit ane *MF* he: hie *B* 27 ourlaidin] our ladynnit *MF* 28 Than vyce] Throw want *MF* 29 dois] *om. d* 31–5 *not in MF* 31 gevis geir] gevis his geir *d*

And thocht the peur for falt sowld de
His cry nocht enteris in his eir:
In geving sowld discretioun be.

Sum givis to strangeris with faces new
That ȝisterday fra Flanderis flew,
And to awld servandis list not se
War thay nevir of sa grit vertew:
In geving sowld discretioun be.

Sum gevis to thame can ask and plenȝie,
Sum gevis to thame can flattir and fenȝie,
Sum gevis to men of honestie
And haldis all janglaris at disdenȝie:
In geving sowld discretioun be.

Sum gettis giftis and riche arrayis
To sweir all that his maister sayis,
Thocht all the contrair weill knawis he;
Ar mony sic now in thir dayis:
In geving sowld discretioun be.

Sum gevis gudmen for thair kewis,
Sum gevis to trumpouris and to schrewis,
Sum gevis to knaiffis awtoritie;
Bot in thair office gude fundin few is:
In geving sowld discretioun be.

Sum givis parrochynnis full wyd,
Kirkis of Sanct Barnard and Sanct Bryd,
To teiche, to rewill and to ouirsie,
That hes na witt thame selffe to gyde:
In geving sowld discretioun be.

33 *d breaks off* (*leaves missing*) 34 His: Is *B* 36 with] and *MF* faces *MF*: face *B* 38 to . . . se] will not pay auld servandis fee *MF* 39 War thay] Thocht thai be *MF* 41–2 *transposed in MF* 41 ask and] craftlie *MF* 46 gettis] giffis *MF* 48 all . . . he: all . . . hie *B*: he ken weill the contrarie *MF* 49 Ar . . . thir] So is thair mony now a *MF* 51 gevis] giffis to *MF* kewis: gud kewis *B*: thewis *MF* 53 knaiffis *MF*: knaw his *B* 54 fundin] fund *MF* 57 Kirkis] Curches *MF* 58 To . . . and to] The peple to teche and *MF* 59 hes na . . . selffe *MF*: he na wit hes thame *B* *colophon in B* Finis of discretioun of geving. Followis discretioun in taking

80. [Discretioun in Taking]

EFTIR geving I speik of taking,
Bot littill of ony gud forsaiking.
Sum takkis our littill awtoritie
And sum our mekle, and that is glaiking:
In taking sowld discretioun be.

The clerkis takis beneficis with brawlis,
Sum of Sanct Petir and sum of Sanct Pawlis;
Tak he the rentis, no cair hes he
Suppois the Divill tak all thair sawlis:
In taking sowld discretioun be.

Barronis takis fra the tennentis peure
All fruct that growis on the feure
In mailis and gersomes rasit ouirhie,
And garris thame beg fra dure to dure:
In taking sowld discretioun be.

Sum takis uthir mennis takkis
And on the peure oppressioun makkis,
And nevir remembris that he mon die
Quhill that the gallowis gar him rax:
In taking sowld discretioun be.

Sum takis be sie and sum be land
And nevir fra taking can hald thair hand

Discretioun in Taking. *Text: MS B (ff. 62ᵛ–63ʳ) collated with MS MF (pp. 261–2; Reidpeth, f. 22ᵛ)*
1 I] we will *MF* 2 ony gud] na gude giftis *MF* 6 The] Thir *MF* 8 Tak . . . hes] Sett he the rent na cure giffis *MF* 11 Barronis . . . fra the] Thir baronis . . . frome thair *MF* 12 fruct] fructis *MF* 13 In] *om. MF* rasit] ar rasit *MF* 15 *additional lines in MF*:

Thir merchandis takis unlesum win
Quhilk makis thair pakkis oftymes full thin;
Be thair successioun ȝe may see
That ill won geir riches not the kin:
In taking &c.

16 mennis: mens *B* 17 on] to *MF* 19 Quhill: Quhilk *B* 20, 25, 30 *abbrev. in B* 21 Sum . . . sum] Pairt . . . part *MF* sum: *om. B* 22 nevir . . . can hald thair] parte . . . can not hald his *MF*

Quhill he be tit up to ane tre;
And syne thay gar him undirstand
In taking sowld discretioun be.

Sum wald tak all his nychbouris geir;
Had he of man als littill feir
As he hes dreid that God him see,
To tak than sowld he nevir forbeir:
In taking sowld discretioun be.

Sum wald tak all this warldis breid
And ȝit not satisfeit of thair neid
Throw hairt unsatiable and gredie;
Sum wald tak littill, and can not speid:
In taking sowld discretioun be.

Grit men for taking and oppressioun
Ar sett full famous at the sessioun,
And peur takaris ar hangit hie,
Schamit for evir and thair successioun:
In taking sowld discretioun be.

81. [May na Man now undemit be]

MUSING allone this hinder nicht
Of mirry day quhen gone was licht
Within ane garth undir a tre,
I hard ane voce that said on hicht,
May na man now undemit be.

23 to] on *MF* 24 syne] than *MF* 26–30, 31–5 *transposed in MF* 28 hes . . . God] dois God quha dois *MF* 29 than . . . nevir] it all he wald not *MF* 31 warldis] warld on *MF* 32 ȝit . . . neid] not ȝit can be satisfeid *MF* 35 *additional lines in MF*:

Stude I na mair aw of man nor God
Than suld I tak bayth evin and od;
Ane end of all thing that I see—
Sic justice is not worthe ane clod:
In taking &c.

37 Ar: At *B* at] on *MF* 38 And peur] Quhair small *MF* 39 Schamit] Thai ar schamit *MF* *colophon* Finis quod Dumbar *B*: Finis *MF*

May na Man now undemit be. *Text: MS B (ff. 63v–64r) collated with MS MF (two versions: MFa, pp. 168–70; MFb, pp. 313–14)*
2 licht] the nicht *MFa* 4 that said] say *MFb*

For thocht I be ane crownit king
ȝit sall I not eschew deming;
Sum callis me guid, sum sayis thai lie,
Sum cravis of God to end my ring,
So sall I not undemit be.

Be I ane lord and not lord lyk,
Than every pelour and purspyk
Sayis, Land war bettir warit on me;
Thocht he dow not to leid a tyk,
ȝit can he not lat deming be.

Be I ane lady fresche and fair
With gentillmen makand repair
Than will thay say, baith scho and he,
That I am jaipit lait and air;
Thus sall I not undemit be.

Be I ane courtman or ane knycht
Honestly cled, that cumis me richt,
Ane prydfull man than call thay me;
Bot God send thame a widdy wicht
That can not lat sic demyng be.

Be I bot littill of stature
Thay call me catyve createure,
And be I grit of quantetie
Thay call me monstrowis of nature;
Thus can I not undemit be.

And be I ornat in my speiche
Than Towsy sayis I am sa streiche,
I speik not lyk thair hous menȝie.

6 be] wer *MFb* 7 sall] sould *MFb* 8 thai *MFa MFb:* I *B* 9 cravis of] prayis *MFa*: prayis to *MFb* ring] regnne *MFb* 10 So sall] Thus can *MFb* 13 warit] set *MFa* 17 gentillmen] plesand men *MFb* 18 say] sweir *MFb* he: hie *B* 20 Thus] So *MFb* 21 I *MFa MFb: om. B* 22 that . . . richt] as cummis richt *MFa*: eftir my mycht *MFb* 26–30 Be I bot . . . undemit be] *om. MFa* (Be I lytill of stature *del.*) 26 Be I bot] And be I *MFb* 27 Thay call me] Than call thai me a *MFb* 28 grit of] off grit *MFb* 30 Thus] So *MFb* 30, 35 *abbrev. in B* 32 sa streiche: sa screiche *B*: so striche *MFa*: our streche *MFb* 33 speik] mute *MFb* thair hous] to thair *MFb*

Suppois hir mowth misteris a leiche
ȝit can I not undemit be.

Bot wist thir folkis that uthir demis
How that thair sawis to uthir semis,
Thair vicious wordis and vanite,
Thair tratling tungis that all furth temis,
Sum wald lat thair demyng be.

War nocht the mater wald grow mair
To wirk vengeance on ane demair,
But dout I wald caus mony de,
And mony catif end in cair
Or sum tyme lat thair deming be.

Gude James the ferd, our nobill king,
Quhen that he was of ȝeiris ȝing
In sentens said full subtillie,
Do weill, and sett not by demyng,
For no man sall undemit be.

And so I sall with Goddis grace
Keip his command in to that cace,
Beseiking ay the Trinitie
In hevin that I may haif ane place;
For thair sall no man demit be.

34 mowth] mulls *MFb* misteris a] mister ane *MFa*: mistiris ane *MFb* 36, 37 uthir] utheris *MFa MFb* 37 to] till *MFb* 40 Sum wald] Sum tyme wald *MFa*: Wald sum tyme *MFb* 41–5 War . . . deming be *MFa: not in B* 41 mair] the mair *MFb* 43 I wald caus] thair wald rycht *MFb* 46 Gude] *om. MFa MFb* our nobill] of Scotland *MFb* 47 Quhen . . . was] Quhone he wes bot *MFb* 48 In . . . full] This subsequent said *MFb* 51 I sall] sall I *MFb* 53 Beseiking] Beseikand *MFa MFb* ay] ever *MFb* *colophon* Finis quod Dumbar *B* Finis *MFa*: Quod Stewarte *MFb*

82. [How sould I Governe me]

How sould I rewill me or in quhat wys
I wald sum wyse man wald devys,
Sen I can leif in no degre
Bot sum my maneris will dispys:
Lord God, how sould I governe me?

Giff I be lustye, galland and blythe,
Than will thai say on me full swythe
ȝone man, out of his mynd is he
Or sum hes done him confort kythe:
Lord God, how sould I governe me?

Giff I be sorrowfull and sad
Than will thai say that I am mad;
I do bot drowpe as I wald de,
So will thai deyme, bayth man and lad:
Lord God, how sall I governe me?

[Be I liberall, gentill and kynd,
Thocht I it tak of nobill strynd,
ȝit will thai say, baythe he and he,
ȝon man is lyke out of his mynd:
Lord God, how sall I governe me?]

Giff I be lustie in myne array
Than lufe I paramoris, say thai,
Or in my mynd is proud and he,
Or ellis I haif it sum wrang way:
Lord God, how sall I governe me?

How sould I Governe me. *Text: MS MF (pp. 323–4; Reidpeth, f. 38) collated with MS B (ff. 65^{v}–66^{v}). Sequence in MF 1–25, 36–40, 26–30, 31–5, 41–50; in B 1–15, 21–50 (om. 16–20)*

1 in] *om. B* 3 Sen I can] I can not *B* 4 my maneris will] will my maneris *B* 5 sould] sall *B passim* 6 lustye, galland] galland lusty *B* and *B*: ane *MF* 8 ȝone . . . mynd] That owt of mynd ȝone man *B* 14 So . . . deyme] Thus . . . say *B* lad *B*: laid *MF* 16–20 *not in B* 21 myne] *om. B* 23 mynd] hairt *B* 24 Or . . . way *B: om. MF*

And gif I be not wele besene
Than twa and twa sayis thame betwene,
Evill gydit is ȝon man, par de—
Be his clething it may be sene:
Lord God, how sould I governe me?

Gif I be sene in court our lang
Than will thai quhispir thame amang,
My freindis ar not worthe ane fle
That I sa lang but gwerdon gang:
Lord God, how sould I governe me?

In court rewaird gif purches I,
Than have thai malice and invy;
And secreitlie on me thai lie
And dois me sklandir privaly:
Lord God, how sould I governe me?

How sould my gyding be devysit?
Gif I spend litle I am dispysit;
Be I courtas, nobill and fre,
A prodigall man than am I prysit:
Lord God, how sould I governe me?

Sen all is jugit, bayth gud and ill,
And no mannis toung I may had still,
To do the best my mynd salbe;
Lat everie man say quhat he will,
The gratious God mot governe me.

26 And gif . . . wele besene] Gif . . . weill als besene *B* 28 Evill gydit s . . . par de] That evill he gydis . . . trewlie *B* 29 Be his clething] Lo be his laithis *B* 32 quhispir] murmour *B* 34 gwerdon] reward *B* 36 In . . I: And gif sum tyme rewarde gif I *MF*: In court rewaird than purches I *B* 8 on me thai] thay on me *B* 39 sklandir] hinder *B* 41 How ould . . . be] I wald . . . war *B* 43 Be I courtas, nobill] Gif I be nobill entill *B* 44 than am I] I am so *B* 46 Sen all is jugit] Now juge thay ne *B* 47 no . . . may] I may no mans tung *B* *colophon* Quod Dumbar *MF*: Finis quod Dumbar *B*

83. [Foure Maner of Men ar evill to Pleis]

FOURE maner of men ar evill to pleis.
Ane is that riches hes and eis,
Gold, silver, corne, cattell and ky,
And wald haif pairt fra uthiris by.

Ane uthir is of land and rent
So grit a lord and so potent
That he may not it rewill nor gy
And ȝit wald haif fra uthiris by.

The thrid dois eik so dourly drink
And aill and wyne within him sink
Quhill in his wame no rowme be dry,
And ȝit wald haif fra uthiris by.

The last that hes of nobill blude
Ane lusty lady fair and gude,
Boith vertewis, wyis and womanly,
Bot ȝit wald haif ane uthir by.

In erd no wicht I can persaif
Of gude so grit aboundance haif,
Nor in this warld so welthfull wy,
Bot ȝit he wald haif uthir by.

Bot ȝit of all this gold and gud
Or uthir conȝie to conclude:
Quha evir it haif, it is not I;
It gois fra me to uthiris by.

Foure Maner of Men ar evill to Pleis. *Text: MS B (a; f. 66^v^, ll. 1–24) collated with MSS Bb (Bannatyne's draft, p. 47; ll. 9–24) and Reidpeth (f. 3)*

1 maner: mener *Ba* men] folkis *R* pleis *R*: ken *Ba* 3 corne, cattell] cattell cornis *R* 4 And] *corr.* Ȝett *in R* 6 so] ane *R* 7 he may not it] may nother *R* 8 And ȝit] Ȝet he *R* 9–12, 13–16 *transposed in R* 9 The thrid] Ane uther *R* eik] *om. Bb* 11 wame] vane *R* 12 *abbrev. in Ba* And ȝit] Bot he *R* fra uthiris] ane uthir *Bb* 13 The last] Ane is *R* 14 lusty] nobill *R* 16 Bot] And *R Bb* 20 Bot ȝit he . . . uthir] Bot he . . . frome utheris *R* 23 Quha] Quhar *corr.* Ȝett *in R* 24 fra] frome *R* 24 *additional lines in R*:

And nemlie at this Chrystis mes
Quharevir Schir Gold maid his regres,
Of him I will no larges cry:
He ȝeid fra me till utheris by.

colophon Finis *Ba Bb*: Quod Dumbar *R*

REFERENCES AND ABBREVIATIONS

For references to manuscripts and early prints of Dunbar's poems see pp. xi–xiii. References to modern printings are mainly to the editions by David Laing (2 vols., 1834; supplement, 1865); John Small, Æ. J. G. Mackay, and W. Gregor (STS, 3 vols., 1884–9); J. Schipper (Vienna, 1892–4); and W. Mackay Mackenzie (1932). Early Scotch texts are quoted mainly from the editions of the Scottish Text Society (STS), English ones from the editions of the Early English Text Society (EETS). The Bible is quoted, with appropriate numbering, in the Vulgate text.

Aquinas, *Summa*	S. Thomas Aquinas, *Summa Theologiae*, Blackfriars edn., 60 vols., 1964–76.
Baxter	J. W. Baxter, *William Dunbar: a Biographical Study*, 1952.
Cal. Doc. Scot.	*Calendar of Documents relating to Scotland*, ed. J. Bain, iv (1888).
Chaucer	*The Works of Geoffrey Chaucer*, ed. F. N. Robinson, 1957 (*CT*, Chaucer's *Canterbury Tales*).
Devotional Pieces	*Devotional Pieces in Verse and Prose from MS Arundel 285 and MS Harleian 6919*, ed. J. A. W. Bennett, STS, 1955.
DOST	*A Dictionary of the Older Scottish Tongue*, ed. W. A. Craigie and A. J. Aitken *et al.*, 1931– .
Flowering	*The Flowering of the Middle Ages*, ed. Joan Evans, 1966.
Gaselee	*The Oxford Book of Medieval Latin Verse*, ed. Stephen Gaselee, 1937.
Henryson	quoted from the edition of the poems prepared by Denton Fox for Oxford English Texts.
Irlande	Johannes de Irlandia, *The Meroure of Wyssdome composed for the use of James IV. King of Scots A.D. 1490*, 2 vols., STS, 1926, 1965.
James I, *The Kingis Quair*	ed. John Norton-Smith, 1971.

Lapidaries	*English Mediæval Lapidaries*, ed. Joan Evans and Mary S. Serjeantson, EETS, 1933.
LHTA	*Accounts of the Lord High Treasurer of Scotland*, ed. T. Dickson and J. Balfour Paul, 6 vols. (1473–1538), 1877–1905.
Mackenzie	Dunbar's *Poems*, ed. W. Mackay Mackenzie, 1932.
Mackie	R. L. Mackie, *King James IV of Scotland*, 1958.
McRoberts	*Essays on the Scottish Reformation 1513–1625*, ed. David McRoberts, 1962.
Migne	*Patrologiae cursus completus; series latina*, ed. J.-P. Migne, 1844–55.
MLR	*The Modern Language Review.*
OED	*The Oxford English Dictionary.*
Pitscottie	Robert Lindesay of Pitscottie, *The Historie and Cronicles of Scotland*, ed. Æ. J. G. Mackay, 3 vols., STS, 1899–1911.
Raby, *CLP*	F. J. E. Raby, *A History of Christian-Latin Poetry from the beginnings to the close of the Middle Ages*, 1953, 1966.
Raby, *SLP*	F. J. E. Raby, *A History of Secular Latin Poetry in the Middle Ages*, 2 vols., 1957.
RES	*The Review of English Studies.*
Sarum Missal	*The Sarum Missal*, ed. J. Wickham Legg (1916), 1969.
SATF	Société des anciens Textes Français.
Scott	Tom Scott, *Dunbar: a critical Exposition of the Poems*, 1966.
SHR	*The Scottish Historical Review.*
Smith	Janet M. Smith, *The French Background of Middle Scots Literature*, 1934.
SND	*The Scottish National Dictionary*, ed. William Grant and David Murison, 10 vols., 1929–76.
Tilley	M. P. Tilley, *A Dictionary of the Proverbs in England in the Sixteenth and Seventeenth Centuries*, 1950.
Whinney	Margaret Whinney, *Early Flemish Painting*, 1968.

Whiting — B. J. Whiting, *Proverbs, Sentences, and Proverbial Phrases from English Writings mainly before 1500*, 1968.

Woolf — Rosemary Woolf, *English Religious Lyric in the Middle Ages*, 1968.

COMMENTARY

I

DIVINE POEMS

1. *Et nobis Puer natus est.* A triumph in Dunbar's celebratory style. The hymn is built out of the first two parts of the *Te Deum* and the *Benedicite* (ll. 9–16 *n.*), from which 'the turning of narrative into hortatory invocation' in a Nativity poem and the 'enumeration of planets, elements, birds, and animals' are apparently derived (Woolf, p. 306). Miss Woolf draws attention to a group of English carols which celebrate the Incarnation through the *Te Deum*; e.g.

Cherubyn and seraphyn alsoo,
Tronis, potestates, and many moo
Fulle sweetly sunge to that Lorde tho,
Te Deum Laudamus

(R. L. Greene, *The Early English Carols*, 1935, nos. 295, 297, 300, 301). On the ballade stanza see **3**, intro. note. The refrain *Et nobis puer natus est* is part of the introit for Christmas Day (*Sarum Missal*, p. 29) —'. . . et filius datus est nobis cuius imperium super humerum eius et uocabitur nomen eius magni consilii angelus'— derived from Isa.ix. 6.

1. Isa. xlv. 8, 'Rorate, coeli, desuper, et nubes pluant justum: aperiatur terra, et germinet salvatorem'; a recurring versicle in the Advent services and offices.

3–7. *the brycht day ster.* Cf. Rev. xxii. 16, 'Ego Jesus . . . sum radix, et genus David, stella splendida et matutina'. *The cleir sone* [*sol*]: Migne, ccxix, 'index de nominibus Christi'; cf. Mal. iv. 2; S. Ambrose in Raby, *CLP*, p. 35, sts. 1–2, 8; *English Hymnal*, no. 52. Christ is the new dawn, the true 'Aurora radius and bricht . . . the glorius Appollo' (**4.** 21–2 *n.*), the true sun surmounting the planetary sun Phoebus (cf. Chaucer, *CT*, II. 11–12; James I, *The Kingis Quair*, st. 72). With l. 4, cf. **2.** 8 *n.*

9–16. *Archangellis . . . potestatis*: five of the nine hierarchies of heaven, elaborated in the Middle Ages from such texts as Col. i. 16, where *throni*, *dominationes*, and *potestates* are angelic or demonic powers 'peopling the universe and controlling the planets' (C. F. D. Moule in *Peake's Commentary*, 1962, p. 991); Aquinas, *Summa*, 1a. 108. 5. See also **50.** 57 *n.* Moving in this stanza from the hierarchies through the 'marteiris seir' to the 'hevinly operationis', Dunbar is summoning all the powers in the universe, from 'hevin imperiall' (l. 49) to earth, to celebrate the Nativity of Creator and Redeemer in love. He fuses the Pauline terms with first the *Te Deum*— '. . . tibi omnes angeli, tibi coeli, et universae potestates . . . proclamant . . . Pleni sunt coeli et terra majestatis gloriae tuae . . . Te martyrum candidatus laudat exercitus . . .'—and then with the *Benedicite* (cf. Ps. cxlviii, *Laudate dominum de coelis*): 'Benedicite, angeli domini, domino: benedicite, coeli, domino . . . omnes virtutes domini . . . sol et luna . . . stellae coeli . . . omnis imber et ros . . . omnes spiritus dei . . . Benedicite, ignis et aestus, domino . . . Benedicat terra dominum.'

11. *operationis*. Cf. Gower, *Confessio Amantis*, vii. 1281–3, 'Upon sondri creacion / Stant sondri operacion / Som worcheth this, som worcheth that'.

25–32. *All clergy*, etc. Cf. *Benedicite*: 'sacerdotes domini . . . benedicite, servi domini, domino'.

33–40. *Celestiall fowlis*, etc. Cf. *Benedicite*: 'benedicite, omnes volucres coeli, domino'. Dunbar gives a Christian application to the convention of dawn bird-song (cf. **10.** 1–27, **16.** 1–16, **50.** 1–14).

41–8. *Now spring up flouris*, etc. Cf. *Benedicite*: 'benedicite, universa germinantia in terra, domino'.

43–4. *the blissit frute . . . Mary*. Cf. the Angelic Salutation, 'Ave Maria, gratia plena; dominus tecum: benedicta tu in mulieribus, et benedictus fructus ventris tui Jesus'. See **2.** 8 *n*.

47–8. *that prince wirthy . . . natus est*. Cf. Isa. ix. 6, 'Parvulus enim natus est nobis... princeps pacis'; Rev. i. 5, 'princeps regum terrae, qui dilexit nos et lavit nos a peccatis nostris in sanguine suo'.

49. *hevin imperiall, most of hicht*: *coelum empyreum*, the highest heaven and the dwelling of God and his angels; Dante's

ciel ch'è pura luce;
Luce intellettual piena d'amore,
Amor di vero ben pien di letizia,
Letizia che trascende ogni dolzore.
Qui vederai l'una e l'altra milizia
Di Paradiso . . .

(*La Divina Commedia*, 'Paradiso', xxx. 39–44.). Cf. **2.** 25; Aquinas, *Summa*, 1a. 61, 4, 2, 'id dicatur coelum empyreum. Unde Isidorus dicit quod supremum coelum est coelum angelorum' (on Deut. x. 14); ibid. 1a. 102, 2, 1, 'coelum empyreum est supremum corporalium locorum, et est extra omnem mutabilitatem'.

53. *Gloria in excelsis . . . Hevin*, *erd*, etc. The *hymnus angelicus* sung after the *kyries* in the Mass: 'Gloria in excelsis deo. Et in terra pax hominibus bone uoluntatis. Laudamus te . . .' (Luke ii. 14).

55. *He that is crownit abone the sky.* Cf. Rev. xix. 11–12, 'Et vidi coelum apertum . . . in capite ejus diademata multa, habens nomen scriptum, quod nemo novit nisi ipse'.

2. *Ane Ballat of Our Lady.* A celebration of the Blessed Virgin Mary, 'thesaurus Dei' (S. Bernard of Clairvaux); a poetic analogue to paintings of the Coronation of the Virgin, in a catalogue of types (cf. Alanus de Insulis, *Anticlaudianus* (Raby, *CLP*, p. 299), 'Haec est stella maris, vitae via, porta salutis . . .'). On poems in honour of the Virgin, 'probably . . . the largest and also the most ornate and rhetorical section of the religious lyric in the fifteenth century', see Woolf, ch. viii. The substance of Dunbar's poem is thoroughly traditional; I have illustrated it mainly from verse and prose devotions of his own time.

Aureate diction and internal rhymes are conventional in hymns to the Virgin, notably in the work of the French *rhétoriqueurs* (see Smith, pp. 75–6); but this poem is one of Dunbar's most accomplished pieces of virtuosity, each stanza built on the repeated module a_4b_3 round an *Ave Maria, gracia plena* anaphora with triple internal rhyme and and supplementary alliteration.

The Angelic Salutation *Ave Maria* (see **1**. 43–4 *n.*) is drawn from Luke i. 28 and 42; the supplication 'Sancta Maria, mater Dei, ora pro nobis peccatoribus, nunc et in hora mortis nostrae' was added in the sixteenth century.

1. *sterne superne.* Cf. *infra*, ll. 26, 53, 70; Gaselee, no. 43, ll. 7–12; Lydgate, *Stella Celi Extirpauit* (ii), 'Thou glorious sterre this world to enlumyne . . . Thou splendaunt sterre, of sterris moost souereyne'; Lydgate's *Ballade at the Reverence of Our Lady*, st. 4, and *Ave Maria*, st. 2. In art, a single star is the symbol of the Virgin, worn on her mantle at shoulder or breast.

2. *In Godis sicht to schyne.* Cf. *Devotional Pieces*, pp. 284–5, 'O ȝe twa gemmes of the hevin, Mary and Ihonne; O ȝe twa lanternis schyning hevinly befor God'.

3. *Lucerne in derne.* Cf. *Devotional Pieces*, p. 295, ll. 42–3, 'Haill, brichtest sterne, / Haill, licht lucerne'; Irlande, i. 99, 'hire haly saule was a bricht licht of paradice full of wertu and grace . . . *Dixit deus: Fiat lux, et facta est lux.* And, of the licht cloude þat God maid, fyrst he maid the hevinly, and . . . of þe licht and cleire body virginale of þis lady he maid the haly body of Jhesu, and, as in þe licht may be na myrknes, sua in þe bodely nature of the virgin was na fylth nor syn'; *infra*, ll. 27–8.

4. *glory and grace*: the state of beatitude. Cf. Aquinas, *Summa*, 1a. 62, 'de perfectione angelorum in esse gratiae vel gloriae'.

5. *Hodiern . . . sempitern.* Cf. Heb. xiii. 8, 'Jesus Christus heri, et hodie: ipse et in saecula'.

6. *Angellicall regyne*: a patristic title. The coronation of the Virgin by Christ, prefigured in Solomon's enthronement of his mother at his right hand (1 Kgs. ii. 19), is a common theme in medieval art. Cf. George Ferguson, *Signs and Symbols in Christian Art*, 1961, pls. 27, 28, and X; Marion Lawrence, 'Maria Regina', *Art Bulletin*, vii (1924–5), 150–61; *Flowering*, pp. 288–9; Irlande, i. 148, 'This lady full of grace was cled with the werraye sone of God; all the kyrk and hale waurld is vndir hire powere and subieccioune, and sche is crovnit quene of angellis, of men and all manere of creaturis'.

7. *Our tern inferne for to dispern.* See *infra*, ll. 29–30, 51–2 *nn.*

8. *rosyne.* Floral imagery applied to the Virgin derives from the Song of Songs. On the tradition see Woolf, pp. 287–90 and references; cf. *infra*, ll. 40–3, 79.

11, 22. *virgin matern . . . moder and maide but makle*: Dante's 'vergine madre, figlia del tuo figlio' (*Paradiso*, xxxiii. 1). Cf. *Ave maris stella* (Gaselee, no. 29), ll. 2–3, 'Dei mater alma / atque semper virgo'; the ME lyric *I syng of a mayden that is makeles*, 'Moder and mayden was never non but che— / Wel may swych a lady Godes moder be'; Irlande, i. 97; Woolf, pp. 130–3.

14, 16. *Alphais habitakle . . . his tabernakle*: Rev. i. 8, 'Ego sum α et ω, principium et finis, dicit dominus Deus: qui est, et qui erat, et qui venturus est, omnipotens'. The virgin as 'templum Dei' (cf. Raby, *CLP*, p. 366) is prefigured in the Old Testament tabernacle: 'Per sanctificationem autem tabernaculi, de qua dicitur, *Sanctificavit tabernaculum suum Altissimus* [Ps. xlvi. 4], videtur significari sanctificatio matris Dei, quae tabernaculum Dei dicitur, secundum illud Psalmi, *In sole posuit tabernaculum suum* [Ps. xix. 5]' (Aquinas, *Summa*, 3a. 27, 2). Cf. Gaselee, no. 18, ll. 13–16 (*English Hymnal*, no. 214, v. 3); Lydgate, *Ballade at the Reverence of Our Lady*, st. 20; *The Fyfftene Ioyes*, st. 19, 'Of þe Holy Gooste, O þowe chossine tabarnacle'. See *infra*, ll. 77–8 *n.*

25. *hevyn on hicht.* See **1.** 49 *n.*

27–8. *Our licht . . . scale.* See *supra*, l. 3 *n.*; cf. *Devotional Pieces*, p. 8, l. 14, 'Haill, beyme to skaill of ded the dirk vmbrakill'.

29–30. *wicht in ficht . . . battale.* The Virgin's dominion over Satan and her defence of sinners in their battle against him, derived from exegesis of God's judgement on Eve and the Serpent (Gen. iii. 15), is illustrated in numerous miracle-stories and in the visual arts. She is often represented crowned, treading on a devil or dragon: e.g.

Geertgen tot Sin Jans's *Virgin in Glory* (Whinney, pl. 58*a*); early sixteenth-century wood carvings in the Aartsbisschoppelijk Museum, Utrecht. The Madonna del Soccorso is represented with a club, chasing away a devil; the Santa Maria della Vittoria appears in the sky above a battle, or victorious and enthroned. Cf. Woolf, pp. 284–5; Lydgate, *Ave Jesse Virgula*, l. 7, 'glorious mayde, with whom no fiend maye stryve', and *Fyfftene Ioyes*, st. 5, 'O qwene of heven, of helle eke Emparesse'; Villon, *Ballade pour prier Nostre Dame*, 'Emperiere des infernaulx paluz'; *Devotional Pieces*, pp. 327 and 334; Irlande, i. 98.

31. *plicht*: main anchor, the symbol of Christian hope 'quam sicut anchoram habemus animae tutam ac firmam, et incedentem usque ad interiora velaminis' (Heb. vi. 19). Cf. Lydgate, *To Mary the Queen of Heaven*, st. 7, 'Of hope our Anker, at the hauene of lyff taryue'. For other maritime metaphors applied to the Virgin see *Devotional Pieces*, pp. 281 (ll. 83–4, 90) and 332 (l. 297).

34. *Haile, gentill nychttingale*. Cf. Lydgate, *Ballade at the Reverence of Our Lady*, st. 12, 'O curteys columbe, replet of all mekenesse, / O nyghtyngale, with thi notys newe'.

40. *ros of paradys*: i.e. without thorns, which it grew after the Fall. Cf. Alanus de Insulis, *Anticlaudianus* (Raby, *CLP*, p. 299), the Virgin 'nescia spineti florens rosa, nescia culpae / gratia'; Irlande, i. 152, 'This haly lady was maid in þe orient, as paradice. . . . Sche was the werray hevinly paradice, þat all herbis and treis of wertu florist in till'; *supra*, l. 8 *n*.

42. *floure delyce*: a variety of lily; symbol of royalty in France, and of purity; given in Christian art to the Virgin as queen of heaven. It is often carried by the angel in pictures of the Annunciation and Adoration, or placed prominently in a vase. See Whinney, pls. 2*a*, 6, 15, 28, 32*a*, 34, 47, 85*b*. In Jacobello del Fiore's *Virgin and Child Enthroned* (late fifteenth century; Aartsbisschoppelijk Museum, Utrecht) the throne is entwined with lilies and backed by a bank of them; in the *Death of the Virgin* in the *Middelrijns Altaar* (*c*. 1410, same museum) an apostle holds a long-stalked lily over her bed.

43. *grene daseyne*: 'the emperice and flour of floures alle' (Chaucer, Prologue to *The Legend of Good Women*, F 185); in the fifteenth century, introduced in paintings of the Adoration as typifying the innocence of the Child.

47–8. *ga betweyne . . . oratrice*. On Mary as intercessor see Woolf, pp. 119–20, and A. Caiger-Smith, *English Medieval Mural Paintings*, 1963, pp. 34–5. Cf. next note.

51–2. *Our glore forlore . . . restore*: as 'blest *Marie*, second *Eve*' (Milton, *Paradise Lost*, v. 387). Cf. Christ as 'novissimus Adam' (1 Cor. xv. 45). Raby (*CLP*, p. 367) cites the *Mariale*:

Evae crimen nobis limen
paradisi clauserat,
haec, dum credit et obedit,
coeli claustra reserat.

'And sene be the mediacioune of this glorius lady and virgin was maid pes, alliance and confederacioune betuix God and man, angellis and man, and amang þe hevinly wertuis, Therfor, in gret honoure of þis lady and virgin, the angell of God mycht, salusand and honorand hir say, *Aue maria* . . . And þis concord is betakynnit in þat, þat þis name "eva" is changit in the wourd of salutacioune "Aue" . . . And the pane, that man was oblist to, sone eftir was turnit in glore eternall' (Irlande, i. 143).

53. *stern in aurore*. Cf. Lydgate, *To Mary the Queen of Heaven*, st. 4, 'Glad Aurora, kalendis of cleer day, / Of Phebus vprist, massager most enteer'.

54. *angellis stevyne*. Cf. the pious Franciscan parody of the *Te Deum* in honour of Mary (Raby, *CLP*, p. 375):

tibi omnes angeli, tibi caeli et universae potestates,
tibi cherubin et seraphin humili nobiscum voce proclamant,
virgo, virgo, virgo virginum sine exemplo.

56. *mak our oddis evyne*: have our sins forgiven at the Judgement; in representations of which the Virgin intercedes and sometimes tips the scales in the weighing of souls. Cf. A. Caiger-Smith, *English Medieval Mural Paintings*, 1963, pp. 58 ff.; Van der Weyden's *Last Judgment* (Whinney, pl. 31); *Flowering*, pp. 255 (224, 233, 234, 236).

62. *Bricht polist precious stane*. Cf. Marbod's *Stella maris* (Gaselee, no. 48), l. 3, 'gemma decens . . . perfecta decore'; *Devotional Pieces*, p. 298, 'Thou polist gem without offence / Thou bair the lambe of innocence'; Lydgate, *To Mary the Queen of Heaven*, st. 2, *Ave Jesse Virgula*, sts. 8 and 9, and *Ballade at the Reverence of Our Lady*, sts. 5, 13, 14, 19.

65. *pavys fro enemys*. Cf. Lydgate, *Testament*, st. 2, 'Iesus . . . Ageyn all enemyes sheld, paveys, and defence'.

71. *Spyce*. Cf. Ecclus. xxiv. 17 ff.; S. of S. iv. 12–16, 'Hortus conclusus soror mea sponsa . . . veni, Auster, perfla hortum meum, et fluant aromata illius'.

72. *the gloryus grayne*: Christ, figured in his own metaphor, 'dico vobis, nisi granum frumenti, cadens in terram, mortuum fuerit . . . multum fructum affert' (John xii. 24–5). Cf. *Ave Gloriosa* (*Devotional Pieces*,

p. 294), 'Haill, grane maist glorius / That is or euer hes bene: / Off the, Mary, I mene'.

73 *wall*: well. The sealed well or fountain is a common symbol of the virginity of Mary (S. of S. iv. 12); but Dunbar is using the metaphor as Irlande does in 'This lady . . . was þe well and merour of all chastite, purite and virginite' (i. 103). Cf. *Devotional Pieces*, p. 279, 'well of life and forgevinnes, well of heill and of grace, well of piete and indulgence, well of consolacioun and blithnes'. *place palestrall*: palace, misusing *palestrall* for *palatial*. STS editors cite a hymn, 'Sacratum palatium Dei convocaris'. Dunbar may have misread or faultily recalled Troilus' 'feste and pleyes palestral' (athletic games) (Chaucer, *Troilus and Criseyde*, v. 304).

74, 76. With the rhymes cf. *Devotional Pieces*, p. 297, 'Specull of pulcritude . . . Schawand thy celsitude / With glore and gratitud'.

75. *hie trone regall*. Cf. *supra*, l. 6 *n*. The Virgin is the throne of the true Solomon (cf. 1 Kgs. x. 18). So in the *Victorine Sequences* (Raby, *CLP*, p. 367), lxxiii. 36:

> tu thronus es Salomonis,
> cui nullus par in thronis
> arte vel materia;
> ebur candens castitatis,
> aurum fulvum charitatis
> praesignant mysteria.

77–8. *the lord . . . Thy closet did include*. The Virgin is typified in the 'porta clausa' of Ezek. xliv. 1–3 (see Raby, *CLP*, pp. 373–4). Cf. *supra*, ll. 14, 16 *n*.; Geoffrey de Vinsauf, *Poetria Nova*, ll. 1208–10, 1515–17:

> Filius univit se nostrae, clausus in aula
> Virginis; inclusit uterus quem claudere mundus
> Non potuit . . .
> qui clam discendit in aulam
> Virginis et foribus clausis egressus ab aula
> Virginea, porta clausa;

The Myrrour of Our Ladye (1450), 'Went the sonne of God oute of the pryvy closet of the maydens wombe' (*OED*); Lydgate, *Ballade at the Reverence of Our Lady*, st. 5; *Devotional Pieces*, p. 295; Irlande, i. 99, 'þe king of hevin, of angellis and of glore maid him ane nobile palace, þat is the waurld . . . bot his gret chaumere of rest, quiet and plesaunce, quhare he likit best and was maist secret, was þis haly lady and virgin'.

79. *cristall*: in medieval art, the symbol of the Immaculate Conception. Cf. *Devotional Pieces*, p. 294, 'Haill cumly cristell cleir / Abone the ordouris nyne'.

80. *Fulfillit of angell fude*: part of the medieval legend. Cf. Aquinas, *Summa*, ed. cit., li (1969), 85.

3. *The Passioun of Crist.* This hortatory narrative of the Passion is framed in a Good Friday vision, followed by a simple form of meditation. It is rudimentary religious pageant (note l. 142); 'þer ben mony þousaund of pepul þat couþ not ymagen in her hert how Crist was don on þe rood, but as þai lerne hit be syȝt of ymages and payntours' (fifteenth-century preacher quoted in V. A. Kolve, *The Play called Corpus Christi*, 1966; see ch. 8). The typical fifteenth-century poem on the Passion is based on the narrative of events from the betrayal to the crucifixion and burial; Dunbar's stops with Christ's death. The common source of such poems is the Latin meditations—mainly Franciscan, e.g. Ubertino of Casale's *Arbor Vitae Crucifixae* (early fourteenth century), the devotional writing of S. Bonaventura (d. 1274), James of Milan's *Stimulus Amoris*, and above all the *Meditationes Vitae Christi* formerly attributed to Bonaventura but probably by John de Caulibus of San Gemignano. Cf. Raby, *CLP*, pp. 419–21. (An English metrical version was made by Robert Manning of Brunne (*c.* 1315–30), and a partial prose version by the Carthusian Nicholas Love (*ante* 1410; *The Mirrour of the Blessed Lyf of Jesu Christ*, ed. L. F. Powell, 1908; see Elizabeth Zeeman in *RES*, N.S. vi (1955), 113–27). References *infra* are to Isa Ragusa's translation of a fourteenth-century manuscript in the Bibliothèque Nationale (Ital. 115), *Meditations on the Life of Christ*, 1961. On Franciscan meditations see John Moorman, *A History of the Franciscan Order . . . to the Year 1517*, 1968, pp. 260 ff.)

For an account of fifteenth-century poems in this kind, and an admirable short critique of Dunbar's poem, see Woolf, pp. 183–238 (esp. 233–4). The stanza is the standard ballade (ababbcbc) derived from the troubadour stanza (abababab); cf. Lydgate's *Cristes Passioun*, from which Dunbar probably derived his refrain (Lydgate's l. 49, 'Al this was doon, O man, for love of the'). See also **1, 9, 61**.

Dunbar follows the Gospel narratives, directly or otherwise, in the following passages and details: ll. 11–12, Matt. xxvi. 47, Mark xiv. 43 and 48; 13, 'lyk ane theif', Matt. xxvi. 55, Mark xiv. 48, Luke xxii. 52; 17–22, Matt. xxvi. 67, Mark xiv. 65; 27–8, Mark xiv. 65, Luke xxii. 64; 29–32, Matt. xxvi. 67–8, Mark xiv. 65, Luke xxii. 63–4; 36, Matt. xxvii. 26, Mark xv. 15; 41–8, Matt. xxvii. 29–30, Mark xv. 17–19, Luke xxiii. 11, John xix. 2–3; 81–6, Matt. xxvii. 50–2, Luke xxiii. 44–5; 89–92, John xix. 34; 118–20, see note. Details not derived from biblical sources are therefore ll. 25–6, 33–5, 49–80 (the Crucifixion); see notes.

7. *gaude flore*: the hymn *Gaude flore virginali.*

9–12. *Methocht Judas . . . dishonour.* Medieval artists associate Judas closely with the violence of the Jews and Roman soldiers, in grouping and in gesture; e.g. BM Add. MS 17868 (thirteenth-century Psalter), f. 24; Add. MS 39627 (Gospel book, 1356), f. 204ᵛ; fourteenth-century Italian panels of the Passion in the National Gallery.

13–14. *lyk ane theif*, etc. Cf. *Devotional Pieces*, p. 255, 'Bund as ane theif so wes ȝou harlit and led'; p. 262, 'Leid as ane tyk and theif lyke'.

19. *as lyounis.* Cf. *Meditations*, p. 325, the chief priests and elders 'rejoice like lions that have taken their prey'.

20. *thay hurlit him heir and thair.* Cf. Manning's *Meditations*, ll. 425 ff.:

> Þe cursed houndes runne hym aboute,
> And drowe hym furþe, now yn, now oute;
> Sum bynte hym, sym blyndyþ hym . . .

26. *For scorne . . . in to quhyt.* So in Bosch's *Christ mocked* (Nat. Gallery; Whinney, pl. 73) and in the *Middelrijns Altaar* (*c.* 1410) in the Aartsbisschoppelijk Museum, Utrecht. Cf. *Meditations*, p. 328, 'Herod, thinking him a fool, in derision he had him dressed in white, and sent him back to Pilate . . . He was regarded by everyone not only as a criminal but as a fool'; *Devotional Pieces*, p. 235, 'the quhit coit and purpour claith gaif him for scorne'.

27–8. *And hid . . . delyt.* Cf. Bromyard, *Summa praedicantium* (cited in Woolf, p. 223), 'Quod caput illud, cuius pulchritudo nullo termino metitur, spinis coronaretur. Et quod facies, quam Angeli desiderant prospicere, a Iudeis conspueretur.' There is a wealth of illustration of the blindfolding of Christ: e.g. the fourteenth-century fresco at Horsham Church; BM Add. MS 42130, f. 92ʳ; BM Add. MS 47682, f. 29ᵛ (W. Hassall, *The Holkham Bible*, 1954, pl. f. 29ᵛ, p. 127); BM MS Roy. 2.B.VII, f. 248ᵛ. One of the most dramatic representations in painting is Grünewald's *Verspottung Christi* (1504; Munich).

29. *syn did him smyt.* Cf. *The Wakefield Pageants*, ed. A. C. Cawley, 1958, no. 6, 'Coliphizacio', ll. 388 ff.; V. A. Kolve, *The Play called Corpus Christi*, 1966, p. 185.

33–4. *In tene . . . him band.* Christ appears with hands bound, or bound hand and foot, in many manuscripts and paintings. He is often bound with violence (e.g. in the fourteenth-century altar-piece now in Stockholm's Staters Historiska Museum, where the binding is done by a hooded man getting extra purchase by putting his foot on the Lord's knee). Binding is not invariable in illustrations of the flagellation, but it is common. Cf. Lydgate, *The Fifteen Ooes of Christ*, l. 60; *Cristes Passioun*, l. 29, 'Bounde to a peleer by violent sturdynesse'; Willi Kurth, *The Complete Woodcuts of Albrecht Dürer*, 1963 edn., pl. 122; *Meditations*, pp. 326, 329, the elders threw Jesus into 'a kind of prison . . . There they bound him to a stone column, of which afterwards a part was broken away: it is preserved to this day, as I know from a brother of ours, who saw it'; 'Jesus is stripped and bound to a column and scourged . . . The *Historia* [of Peter Comestor] says that the column to which he was bound shows the traces of his bleeding.'

42–8. *syn with thornis*, etc. Cf. Lydgate, *A Seying of the Nightingale*, sts. 19–20:

> . . . A crowne of thorne þat throbbed thorugh his breyne,
> And al þe blood of his body spent;
> His hevenly eyeghen, allas, deeþe haþe eblent . . .
> Þis war þe saame which þat Isaye
> Saugh frome Edome came with his clooþe depeynt
> Steyned in Bosra, eeke did him aspye
> Baaþed in blood, til he gan wexen feynt.

The Crown of Thorns is often depicted with intense violence in late medieval art. The crown is forced on with a pole wielded by two men in the *Middelrijns Altaar* (*c.* 1410; Aartsbisschoppelijk Museum, Utrecht); in a fifteenth-century panel in the Rijksmuseum, Amsterdam, a narrative of Christ's life in eighteen scenes, two men force the crown on with a pole, one lifting both feet off the ground to increase his weight. Cf. Bosch's *Christ crowned with Thorns*, Musée Royale, Antwerp; Altdorfer's *S. Sebastian* altar-piece (1509–18). Two torturers with crossed poles appear on the Doberan reredos (1360–6), and three men with crossed poles in the Cologne altar-piece by the Master of S. Veronica (*c.* 1440); see Gertrud Schiller, *Iconography of Christian Art*, ii (1972), pls. 251–6.

49. *Ane croce . . . lang*: *Meditations*, p. 331 (citing Peter Comestor's *Historia*); Manning's *Meditations*, ll. 563–4, 'A cros was fet furþ, boþe long and grete, / þe lengþe þerof was fyftene fete'.

52. *Thay harlit him furth with raip and corde*: elaborating the Vulgate uses of *ducere* in the Passion narratives (Matt. xxvii. 2 and 31, Mark xv. 20, Luke xxiii. 26 and 32). Cf. *Ludus Coventriae*, EETS, p. 294, 'leyn þe crosse in hese necke to berynt and drawyn hym forth with ropys'; *York Plays*, ed. L. T. Smith, 1885, p. 336; M. D. Anderson, *Drama and Imagery in English Medieval Churches*, 1963, p. 215; Dürer's woodcuts (edn. cit., pl. 216).

54. *His face, the fude of angellis*. STS editors cite the hymn *Ecce panis angelorum*. Cf. *Salve caput cruentatum* (*English Hymnal*, no. 102, ll. 5–8); **2.** 80 *n*.

58. *brim as ony baris*: proverbial; Whiting, B390.

59–62. *The clayth*, etc. An apocryphal incident, common in medieval literature. Woolf, pp. 226–7; the fifteenth-century poem *Ihesu that alle this worlde hast wroghte*,

> Thi bodyly wounde were woxe al drye,
> The purpure þer-to was cleved ful fast.
> They rente it of with a grete haste,
> And þat was, good Lord, more peyne to þe
> Than al þe scourgynge þat was now past,
> And þus þi blode þou sched for me;

Manning's *Meditations*, ll. 615–18:

> Hys cloþys cleuyn on hys swete body;
> Þey rente hem of as þey were wode;
> Hys body aȝen ran alle on blode.

65–9. *On to the crose*, etc. For the tradition that Christ was stretched and tied to the cross before being nailed cf. the Passion pageant in the Chester plays (*Ten Miracle Plays*, ed. R. G. Thomas, 1966, pp. 118–19, ll. 121 ff.); *The Northern Passion*, EETS, ll. 2776 ff.; the representations described in Anderson, op. cit., p. 148; *Devotional Pieces*, pp. 262–3:

> Behald, how with þair rapis teuch
> The Iowis fell my lymmes oute dreuch,
> For that na lymme was meit aneuch
> Vnto þe bore . . . .

74. *all his vanis brist and brak*. Cf. *Devotional Pieces*, p. 256, ll. 46–7:

> Naikit and paill, ded on þe croce þou hang,
> Thy wanis burssin, þi senonis schorn þan.

76–80. *Thay leit him fall doun*, etc. Cf. Nicholas Love, *Mirrour*, ed. L. F. Powell, 1908, p. 239: they 'so nailed hym faste on the crosse; and after with all hir myȝt lifte uppe the crosse with hym hangynge also hye as they myȝt and than lete hym falle doun into the morteys. In the whiche falle as thou myȝt vndirstonde all the synowes to be broken to his souereyne peyne.'

84. *The sone obscurit of his licht*. In illustrated manuscripts the sun and moon are often shown (as disks, or personified), veiled, turned away, in clouds, or held in the draped hands of angels at the Crucifixion.

85. *dirk as ony nicht*: proverbial; Whiting, N103.

86. *Deid bodies rais*: Matt. xxvii. 52. Adam is commonly represented rising from a sarcophagus below the Cross. There is a vivid representation of the dead rising in numbers from five broken sarcophagi in the Bibl. Ambrosiana, Milan (L. 58, fifteenth-century miscellany, f. 54v); cf. Laborde, *Étude sur la Bible Moralisée*, iv (1921), pl. 647.

92. *blude and watter*: symbols of the major sacraments, Baptism and the Eucharist; 'mortuo Christo lancea percutitur latus, ut profluant sacramenta quibus formetur Ecclesia' (cited in E. Mâle, *The Gothic Image*, 1961 edn., p. 187 and refs.).

97–8. *Methocht Compassioun . . . stound.* Cf. *Devotional Pieces*, 'The Passioun of Christ' (also in the Bannatyne and Makculloch MSS), p. 255:

> Compatience persis, reuth and marcy stoundis
> In myddis my hert, and thirlis throw þe vanis.

97–112. *Methocht Compassioun*, etc. Cf. **6.** 157–9.

105–8. *Than rudlie . . . kest*: a memorial of the *arma Christi*, instruments of the Passion; there is perhaps a hint here of the *imago pietatis* (see Woolf, pp. 184–5, 208–9). Cf. Lydgate's *Testament*, st. 109, 'Behold the spere . . . the reed spyre gall and eysel fett', etc. See C. Carter, 'The *Arma Christi* in Scotland', *Proc. Soc. Antiquaries of Scotland*, xc (1956–7), 116–29, pls. x-xv. Of the thirty or so representations of the *arma Christi* which survive (mainly in stone) from the late Middle Ages in Scotland, the closest to Dunbar's selection of instruments is a tomb recess in the Aisle of the Holy Blood in S. Giles', Edinburgh, showing the heart within the crown of thorns, column and whip, nails, spear, and sop (ibid., p. 126). This aisle was formed about 1513.

118–19. *undir thy lyntell . . . in thy hous*: referring to the risen Saviour in the Eucharist. *hous*: the body; 2 Cor. v. 1, 'terrestris domus nostra'; cf. 2 Pet. i. 13, Mark xiv. 58. *lyntell*: echoing Matt. viii. 8, 'Domine, non sum dignus ut intres sub tectum meum' (Luke vii. 6; cf. **69.** 36–40), modified to become a communion prayer in the Middle Ages (see J. A. Jungmann, *Public Worship*, transl. Clifford Howell, 1957, p. 143).

4. *Surrexit Dominus de sepulchro.* This great hymn is 'made up largely of a triumphal series of definitions and consequences of the redemptive victory and rising of Christ' (Woolf, p. 307); public, celebratory, it was perhaps written for choral singing. It is built of traditional images and ideas; but it uniquely illustrates Dunbar's skill in interweaving rhyme and alliteration on a metrical base of fluid strength, and his ability (as Dryden said admiringly of Virgil) to maintain majesty in the midst of plainness. It is made out of the spoken language; but it is 'speech of unanswerable and thundering greatness' (C. S. Lewis, *English Literature in the Sixteenth Century*, 1954, p. 96).

The basis of ll. 1–16 and 33–40 is the *Descensus Christi ad Inferos* (? second century) which, together with *Acta Pilati* (fourth century), makes up the *Evangelium Nicodemi*. The legend of Christ's triumphal descent into hell between his crucifixion and his resurrection is based scripturally—if erroneously—on 1 Pet. iii. 19, 'in quo et his qui in carcere erant spiritibus veniens praedicavit', and iv. 6; cf. Matt. xxvii. 52–3; Acts ii. 24, 'quem Deus suscitavit, solutis doloribus inferni', and ii. 31, 'quia neque derelictus est in inferno'. The *Evangelium Nicodemi* was known throughout Europe in Latin and vernacular versions; see W. H. Hulme, *The Middle English Harrowing of Hell and Gospel of Nicodemus*, EETS. The *Harrowing* is represented in the mystery-play cycles (York, no. 37; Towneley, no. 25; Coventry, no. 33; Chester, no. 18). For the dramatizing of the legend in the Church's ceremonies see Karl Young, *The Drama of the Medieval Church*, 1962, i. 149–77.

Dunbar follows iconographic tradition in merging the themes of (1) resurrection from the tomb and (2) the harrowing of hell. So, e.g., a twelfth-century Psalter-hymnal in the Bibliothèque de la Ville, Amiens (19, f. 9v), shows Christ rising from the sarcophagus with his bannered cross-staff and treading on a horned Satan (Ps. xci. 13, 'conculcabis leonem et draconem')—transfixing him with the cross-staff in his right hand, and with the left hand grasping a group of naked figures emerging from hell-mouth. The fourteenth-century Gisle Gradual (Gymnasium Carolinum, Osnabrück) shows Christ with bannered cross-staff standing on the Devil and the gates of hell (cf. *infra*, l. 20 *n*.). See further W. H. Hulme, op. cit., pp. lxiv–lxv; Emile Mâle, *The Gothic Image*, 1961 edn., pp. 224–7; cf. S. Fulbert's *Chorus novae Jerusalem* (*English Hymnal*, no. 139).

The refrain *Surrexit Dominus de sepulchro* is a versicle from the Mass for Easter Day (*Sarum Missal*, pp. 135, 137); it opens an anonymous Easter hymn in the Bannatyne MS (f. 34v). The stanza, a decasyllabic octave with refrain, is based on a French form (cf. *One Hundred Ballades, Rondeaux and Virelais*, ed. Nigel Wilkins, 1969, nos. 51, 52, 62); it was a common Middle English stanza, and popular with Dunbar (cf. **6**, **11**, **16**, **31**, **35**, **36**, **48**, **49**, **60**, **65**, **76**, **77**).

1. *Done is a battell on the dragon blak*. Cf. Lydgate, *The Dolerous Pyte of Crystes Passioun*, l. 42, 'Fauht with Sathan a myhty strong batayl', and *Cristes Passioun*, l. 57, 'I ffought for the a fful greet batayll / Ageyn Sathan the tortuous serpent'. The scriptural source of the 'dragon blak' and the 'deidly dragon Lucifer' (l. 9) is Rev. xx. 2–3, 'et apprehendit draconem, serpentem antiquum, qui est Diabolus et Satanas'; Rev. xii. 9.

3. *the ȝettis of hell ar brokin*. The *Descensus* relates the coming of Christ to the gates: 'subito facta est vox ut tonitruum et spiritualis clamor: *Tollite portas, principes, vestras, et elevamini, portae aeternales, et introibit rex gloriae*. [Ps. xxiv. 7.] Haec audiens inferus dixit ad Satan

principem: Recede a me et exi de meis sedibus foras; si potens es praeliator, pugna adversum regum gloriae . . .' (text in Young, op. cit. i. 149). See **69**. 36–40 *n*.

5. *The divillis trymmillis*. Cf. *Ros Mary* (Mackenzie, no. 87), ll. 41–8.

9–10. *the deidly dragon Lucifer*. See *supra*, l. 1 *n*. *The crewall serpent . . . stang*: Gen. iii; Rev. xii. 9, 'draco ille magnus, serpens antiquus, qui vocatur Diabolus et Satanas, qui seducit universum orbem', and xx. 2–3; 1 Cor. xv. 55, 'Ubi est mors victoria tua? ubi est mors stimulus tuus?'

11–12. *The auld kene tegir*, etc. Cf. Hrabanus Maurus (Migne, cxi. 219), 'Tigris autem mystice significat astutiam Diaboli. Inde in Job scriptum est: *tigris periit*, *eo quod non haberet praedam*, *et catuli leonis dissipati sunt*' (Job iv. 11).

17–18. *He for our saik*, etc. One type of the Crucifixion is Moses offering a lamb before the tabernacle (Lev. iii); another, the Passover (Exod. xii. 3). Cf. Isa. liii. 5, 7; Acts viii. 32; 1 Pet. i. 19 and ii. 24; Rev. v. 6.

19. *lyk a lyone rissin up agane*. The lion of Judah is a type of the Resurrection (Gen. xlix. 9, Num. xxiv. 9); so in the fifteenth-century Serbian Psalter in the Staatsbibliothek, Munich (f. 98r; Ps. lxxi), Christ-Logos appears asleep on a mattress with a sleeping lion beside him. Cf. Raby, *CLP*, p. 356; in the bestiaries the lion cub is brought to life by its father's breath on the third day—a type of the Resurrection. Cf. S. Fulbert's *Chorus novae Jerusalem*, st. 2 (Raby, p. 263); Adam of S. Victor's *Easter Sequence*, st. 13 (ibid., p. 353): 'sic de Iuda leo fortis / fractis portis dirae mortis / die surgens tertia'. The dramatic contrast between the slain lamb and the risen lion may have been suggested by Rev. v. 5–6: 'Ne fleveris: ecce vicit leo de tribu Iuda, radix David . . . Et vidi, et ecce . . . agnum stantem tamquam occisum.'

20. *as a gyane raxit him on hicht*: the antitype of Samson, breaking the gates of hell as Samson bore off the gates of Gaza (Judg. xvi. 3). In illustrations of the Resurrection Samson often appears carrying away the gates. Cf. Adam of S. Victor's *Easter Sequence*, st. 12 (Raby, *CLP*, p. 353): 'Samson Gazae seras pandit / et asportans portas scandit / montis supercilium.'

21–2. *Aurora . . . Appollo*. Christ is the sun of righteousness risen with healing in his wings (Mal. iv. 2), here identified with the god of the sun. See **1**. 3–7 *n*. Cf. Huizinga on the monstrance (*The Waning of the Middle Ages*, 1955 rpt., p. 202); Grünewald's *Isenheim Altarpiece* (Resurrection) and Alastair Smart's comments in *The Renaissance and*

Mannerism outside Italy, 1972, p. 158; *Devotional Pieces*, p. 274:

> On loft is ryssyn þe gret illumynar,
> The lampe þat lychtnes euery regioun.
> Thy glorius birth, þe blisfull orient sone,
> With ioy is partit fra þe subtell nycht . . .

27–8. *The sone*, etc. Cf. **3.** 84–5.

29. *The knell of mercy*: an allusion to the ringing of bells on Easter Day. Cf. Langland, *Piers Plowman*, B. xviii. 424–5: Truth, Righteousness and Peace—

> Tyl þe daye dawed þis damaiseles daunced,
> That men rongen to þe resurexion . . .

31. *The Jowis . . . errour*. Cf. Luke xxiii. 34, 'Jesus autem dicebat· Pater, dimitte illis: non enim sciunt quid faciunt'.

34–6. *The presone brokin . . . the dungeoun temit*. Cf. the *Canticum Triumphale* sung in Easter processions (Young, op. cit. i. 151): 'Cum rex gloriae Christus infernum debellaturus intraret, et chorus angelicus ante faciem ejus portas principum tolli praeciperet, sanctorum populus, qui tenebatur in morte captivus, voce lacrimabili clamaverat: Advenisti desiderabilis, quem expectabamus in tenebris, ut educeres hac nocte vinculatos de claustris. Te nostra vocabant suspiria; te larga requirebant tormenta; tu factus es spes desperatis, magna consolatio in tormentis'; Abelard, in Raby, *CLP*, p. 322.

5. *The Maner of Passyng to Confessioun*. An exhortation to penitence, written for 'fourty dayis' of Lenten discipline. The stanza is the French *chant-royal*, associated with poems in honour of God or the Virgin, and with the poetical contests at Rouen when a 'king' was elected; used by Chaucer in *Troilus and Criseyde* and by James I in *The Kingis Quair*. Cf. **12, 50, 57.**

3–7. *Oure Lorde Jesu . . . deligent*. Matt. iv. 1–2; cf. the *Rathen Manual* (*c.* 1490) for Ash Wednesday (ed. Duncan MacGregor, 1905, p. 19), 'Concede nobis quesumus Domine presidia milicie Christiane sanctis inchoare ieiuniis: et contra spirituales nequicias expugnaturi, continencie muniamur auxiliis, per Christum'.

8–14. *I reid the . . . knawin*. 'The first [condicioun] that a man examyn his conscience and record all the synnis that he has committit of the quhilkis he has nocht had perfyte contricioun na maid confessioun. . . . The secund that the persoun haue displesans and detestacoun of all thir synnis that he has distinct memor of. The thrid that the persone haue generale displesance and detestacoun of all synnis forȝet be him or hire Or that thai committit be Ignorance' (*Asloan MS*, STS, i. 12; a treatise 'Of Penance' attributed to John Irlande).

20–1. *Thow art not abill . . . forȝet.* Cf. Aquinas, *Summa*, 3a. 87, 1, 'Exigitur autem ad remissionem peccati mortalis perfectior poenitentia, ut scilicet homo actualiter peccatum mortale commissum detestetur, quantum in ipso est, scilicet diligentiam adhibeat ad rememorandum singula peccata mortalia, ut singula detestetur'.

35. *ane blynde man . . . uther.* Cf. Matt. xv. 14; Whiting, B350.

47. *abasit as ane beist*: passive, dejected. Whiting, B125.

48. *sad contrycioun*: the first act of penitence. 'contritio . . . est in corde, et sic pertinet ad interiorem poenitentiam; confessio autem est in ore, et satisfactio in opere . . .' (Aquinas, *Summa*, 3a. 89, 1, 3, and 90, 2, 1).

54. *Thow knawis . . . scho*: proverbial; cf. Chaucer, *CT*, III. 491–4, IV. 1553; Tilley, M129.

61. *abill . . . mischance.* For the idiom cf. Henryson, *Testament of Cresseid*, l. 84, 'I haue pietie thow suld fall sic mischance'.

64–70. *I reid the . . . wyrke.* Cf. Irlande, 'Of Penance', 'I se that part of peple and namelye ȝoung folk in thair strenth ȝouthhed and wantoness deferris thair pennance to thair eild, craband the hie maieste of God and puttand thaim in perill of perpetuall dampnacoun' (*Asloan MS*, STS, i. 3; cf. i. 61–4. The 'perils' are set out on pp. 5–6).

6. *The Tabill of Confessioun.* This poem, in a common genre and written no doubt as an aid for penitents rather than for Dunbar's private use, survives and is attributed to Dunbar in four manuscript versions: one in BM MS Arundel 285 (*c.* 1540), a Roman Catholic devotional book belonging to the Howard family (*Devotional Pieces*, STS); a draft and a second version in the Bannatyne MS; and one in the Maitland Folio MS. The Arundel MS is the earliest of these; despite some errors, and metrical irregularities, its readings are generally superior (e.g. at ll. 4, 6 and 78, 12, 13, 19, 25, 27, 37, 38, 55, 73, 74, 91, 108, 158, 159); and it provides an orthodox Catholic text whereas the other MSS alter and omit to accommodate Protestant susceptibilities (see ll. 4, 43–8, 81–8, 90, 93, 140).

Professor Bennett notes (*Devotional Pieces*) that the poem follows the general sequence of the form of confession found in early printed primers—e.g. the Sarum Primer (1538; Maskell, *Monumenta Ritualia Ecclesiae Anglicanae*, 1882, iii. 296); the York Primer (1536; Wordsworth, *Horae Eboracenses*, Surtees Society, 1920, p. 150), and *Hortulus Animae* (1540 edn., p. 120). I quote below from the Table of Confession transcribed in the Asloan MS (*c.* 1515) 'efter Master Ihon Irland', who returned to Scotland from his Paris professorship *c.* 1483 and became confessor to James IV (see Irlande, introduction). On the stanza see **4.**

1–6. *To The . . . entent.* 'I synfull persone humilie confessis and schryvis me to God almychti my fader makere ransomere and saluatore . . . Of all the synnis that I haue done spoken and thocht sen I was borne . . .' (*Asloan MS*, STS, i. 66).

9–16. *To the . . . repent.* 'First I haue synnit Aganis my maker in my V wittis of nature that God of his grace has gevyne me to vse wele in his seruice to his honour and my profet. In myn eyne seand . . . abusand myn eres and heryng . . . with my mouth spekand and man-swerand the haly name of God . . . makand lesingis and detractionis . . . Allswa I confess me that I haue synnit in the abusioun of my handis doand evill werkis' (*Asloan MS*, i. 66–8).

17–24. *I wrachit synnar . . . repent.* 'Allswa I confess me of the Vij dedly and capitale synnis committit be me aganis my creator and Redemptour be myn Ingratitude aganis my proffet and the gud of my saull; and first in the gret and foull syn of pryde . . .' (*Asloan MS*, i. 69). See the sequence in **52**, *infra*.

23. *thy woundis five.* The Resurrection appearances add the wounds in Christ's hands and feet (Luke xxiv. 39) to the opening of his side. These are a popular theme in medieval devotional verse (Woolf, pp. 224 ff.).

25–40. *I schrif me . . . repent.* 'Allswa I haue nocht completit nor fulfillit the Vij deidis and werkis of cherite and mercy The quhilkis ar double, corporall and spirituale' (*Asloan MS*, i. 75). The seven 'deidis of marcy corporall' are (i) feeding the hungry; (ii) giving drink to the thirsty; (iii) clothing the naked; (iv) harbouring the stranger; (v) visiting the sick; (vi) ministering to the prisoner; (vii) burying the dead. Matt. xxv. 35–6. The seven 'deidis of marcy spirituall' are traditionally (i) converting the sinner; (ii) instructing the ignorant; (iii) counselling the doubtful; (iv) comforting the sorrowful; (v) bearing wrongs patiently (l. 38; misunderstood by Bannatyne); (vi) forgiving injuries; (vii) praying for the living and the dead.

41–8. *Lord, I have done*, etc. 'Allswa I haue offendit nocht honorand the glorius passioun of Ihesu nor the vij sacramentis of haly kirk havand verteu of his glorius passioun' (*Asloan MS*, i. 77). This stanza is begun, deleted, and abandoned in Maitland's MS (1570/1586). *The Confession of the Faith and Doctrine, Belevit and professit be the Protestantis of Scotland* (1560) declared (art. xxi) 'that we now . . . have twa chiefe Sacramentes onelie instituted be the Lord *Jesus*, and commanded to be used of all they that will be reputed members of his body, to wit, Baptisme and the Supper or Table of the Lord *Jesus*, called the Communion of his Body and his Blude'.

49–56. *Thy ten commandmentis*: Exod. xx. 1–17, Deut. v. 6–21. Cf. *Asloan MS*, i. 74.

57–72. *In the twelf artickillis of the treuth . . . repent.* 'The xij artikillis of the treuth. Allswa I haue synnit aganis God almychti nocht trowand in him . . . first nocht trowand in the artikle of his hie and Infinit powere De omnipotencia . . . nocht trowand thre personis in a diuinite . . .' (*Asloan MS*, i. 75–7; where Irlande runs on into a diffuse paraphrase of the Apostles' Creed).

73–80. *I synnit . . . repent.* For the theological virtues of faith, hope, and charity see 1 Cor. xiii. 13, Gal. v. 5–6, Col. i. 4–6, 1 Thess. i. 3; Aquinas, *Summa*, 1a, 2ae, 62. For the cardinal virtues, *justitia*, *prudentia*, *temperentia*, and *fortitudo*, see Aquinas, *Summa*, 1a, 2ae, 61.

73. *strang as wall*: proverbial; Whiting, W13–W18.

81–8. *In the sevin commandis . . . repent.* 'Allswa I grant that I haue offendit God my creatour and my modere the haly kirk nocht obeyand to the commandementis of it falland in cursing . . .' (*Asloan MS*, p. 78).

86. *Anis in the ȝer . . . sacrament*: the minimum prescribed by the Fourth Lateran Council (1215), and normal practice in the later Middle Ages.

89. *syn . . . into the Haly Spreit*: Mark iii. 28–30.

94. *the sevin giftis the Haly Gaist me sent*: Isa. xi. 2–3, 'Et requiescet super eum spiritus Domini: spiritus sapientiae, et intellectus, spiritus consilii, et fortitudinis, spiritus scientiae, et pietatis, et replebit eum spiritus timoris Domini'. 'Allswa I haue synnit gretly nocht havand nor vsand in my defalt The vij hie and mychti giftis of the haly gast . . .' (*Asloan MS*, i. 77).

95. *paternoster, and sevin peticionis*: Matt. vi. 9–13.

105. *I knaw me vicius*, etc. Dunbar moves from offences against and abuses of schematized laws, virtues, etc. to a more expansive and specific catalogue of sins of speaking (ll. 105–12), thought, and intention (ll. 113–20), and ill deeds inspired by greed, lust, anger, and envy (ll. 121–44).

108. *wantones*: arrogance. Cf. Henryson, *Testament of Cresseid*, l. 549, 'Sa efflated I was in wantones'.

134. *sessioun*. See **74**, intro. note.

140–2. *Off ded . . . consent.* 'I haue committit slauchter other be mynd or in deid be my counsall support or assistence or in word' (*Asloan MS*, p. 74). Despite dominical admonitions against sin committed in the heart (cf. Matt. v. 27–8), Bannatyne and Maitland try to lighten the burden with 'gif I be'.

146. *Magdalyn*: Luke viii. 2, Mark xv. 40 and xvi. 1 ff. (cf. l. 148);

traditionally identified with Mary the sister of Martha, and with the woman who washed Christ's feet with tears and anointed them (Luke vii. 37–50).

157–9. *At every straik . . . sound.* Cf. **3.** 97–112.

164. *thi court of marcy exultive.* Cf. Ps. xxxiii (for All Saints' Day), 1, 18–19, 22: 'Exultate justi in Domino . . . Ecce oculi Domini super metuentes eum . . . ut eruat a morte animas eorum . . . Fiat misericordia tua, Domine, super nos: quemadmodum speravimus in te.'

165–7. *mak my schip . . . woundis five.* Cf. Lydgate, *Testament*, st. 21:

At welles five licour I shal drawe
To wasshe the ruste of my synnes blyve

. . . . . .

I mene the welles of Crystes woundes five
Wherby we cleyme, of mercyful piete,
Thorow helpe of Iesu at gracious port taryve,
There to haue mercy, knelyng on our kne.

7. *Orisoun.* 1–4. *Salviour . . . biddis me rys.* Cf. Douglas, *King Hart*, ll. 761–8, 'Ressoun come: Schir king I reid ȝe ryse', etc.

6–8. *First grace . . . blys.* Echoing the absolution at prime and compline, 'Misereatur vestri omnipotens Deus, et, dimissis peccatis vestris, perducat vos ad vitam aeternam'; cf. *Scottish Book of Common Prayer*, 'May the almighty and merciful Lord grant unto you pardon and remission of all your sins, time for true repentance, amendment of life, and the grace and comfort of the Holy Spirit'.

II

POEMS OF LOVE

8. *Sweit Rois of Vertew.* This fine lyric was probably written for music. The stanza takes the rhyme-scheme of one kind of rondeau ($aabba_5$). It is a variant of the common $aabab_4$ stanza (**81**; cf. Wyatt's 'My lute awake'). See also **51, 53, 55.**

2, 8–9. *Delytsum lyllie*, etc. Cf. **49.** 4–5.

10. *rew*: (*ruta graveolens*) an evergreen shrub, the bitter leaves of which were used for medicinal purposes from the fourteenth century. Dunbar's is the first recorded use of this word (*OED rue* sb.[2]; OF *rue*) with a punning allusion to 'rue', sorrow, pity (*OED rue* sb.[1]; OE *hrēow*). Mrs. Bawcutt has drawn attention to *The Lay of Sorrow*, ll. 51–2: 'In my garding . . . All peiciens now fynd I nocht but rewe' (*Speculum*, xxix (1954), 708–26).

9. *Bewty and the Presoneir.* The trope of a lover held in thrall by love, or to his mistress's beauty and virtue, is derived from *Le Roman de la Rose*, ll. 1951 ff.; cf. the Chaucerian *Romaunt of the Rose*, ll. 1927 ff., and esp. ll. 1967–72:

> And if ye lyst of me to make
> Youre prisoner, I wol it take
> Of herte and will, fully at gree.
> Hoolly and pleyn Y yelde me
> Withoute feynyng or feyntise,
> To be governed by youre emprise . . .

Priscilla Bawcutt, in her commentary on the comparable allegory of *King Hart* (Gavin Douglas, *Minor Poems*, STS, p. lxxxv), cites also Baudouin de Condé, *Prisons d'Amours*, and Philippe de Remi, *Salu d'Amours*. For a parallel see Hall's account of the pageant 'Fortresse Dangerus' at the English court, 1512 (Sydney Anglo, *Spectacle, Pageantry and Early Tudor Policy*, 1969, p. 118). Dunbar extends the metaphor of the prisoner into a concise allegory of courtship and marriage, perhaps after the design of a similar court pageant. The ultimate source of the allegory is the psychological drama of *Le Roman de la Rose*, describing a lover's vision of his attempt to possess his lady's love (symbolized by the Rose): he is aided by Franchise, Pity, and Belacueil (Fair Welcome), symbols of her generosity and readiness to accept him;

and opposed by Danger, Chastity, Fear, and Slander, symbols of her defensive reticence and her dread of dishonour. Dunbar modifies the formula. The lover is imprisoned by the lady's beauty, and secured by her reticence and indifference; he counter-attacks (ll. 41 ff.) with the conventional auxiliaries, and gains her love (ll. 57–88); and the consequent assaults of Slander and Envy (ll. 89 ff.) are repelled by Matrimony—an extension of the traditional campaign of *amour courtois*, which ends in possession.

On the standard ballade stanza, see **3**, intro. note.

The fragment in the Reidpeth MS, preceded by eleven poems by Dunbar, is ascribed to him (doubtless on the authority of the Maitland Folio MS); the only complete extant version, in the Bannatyne MS, is anonymous. This has encouraged some critics to question Dunbar's authorship. But the poem is not improbably an exercise by the author of **10**; the words and phrases in it which do not occur elsewhere in the Dunbar canon do not, in my view, constitute a substantial case against ascription to Dunbar (ll. 4, 'bandoun'; 5, 'govit'; 7, 'test'; 18, 'Strangenes'; 23, 'dar lay'; 28, 'thocht . . . deyne' (the only citation in *DOST*); 38, 'methis'; 39, 'be this buke'; 44, 'Fair Service'; 55, 'ourthort'; 60, 'gyn'; 78, 'stychling'; 81, 'prik'; 83, 'erdit'; 85, 'the fek'; 86, 'chalmirleir'; 95, 'lanis'; 106, 'continuation'); and there is a significant number of correspondences (see *infra*) with others of Dunbar's poems.

5–6. *I govit . . . tuk laseir*. In the psychology of love, desire begins with seeing. Cf. **10**. 134–5, 202 ff.; Chaucer, *Troilus and Criseyde*, i. 271 ff., ii. 533–6, 624 ff., and *CT*, I. 1074 ff., 'He cast his eye upon Emelya, / And therwithal he bleynte and cride, "A!" / As though he stongen were unto the herte . . .'.

8. *led furth as a presoneir*. Cf. **10**. 208–10.

9. *Hir sweit having and fresche bewte*. Cf. **10**. 145–9, **16**. 49–50.

13. *Is this ȝour govirnance*. Cf. **15**. 9–10.

18. *Strangenes*: the outpost of the lady's defences; a variant of Danger (porter in the *Roman de la Rose*; cf. **10**. 223–8, **17**. 55 ff.; Chaucer, *Troilus and Criseyde*, ii. 1376; Gower, *Confessio Amantis*, iii. 1537–1612; C. S. Lewis, *The Allegory of Love*, 1938, pp. 364–6); and the antithesis of Belacueil (Fair Welcome) who has 'no straungenesse . . . in him sen' (the Chaucerian *Romaunt of the Rose*, ll. 3609–11). Cf. Douglas, *King Hart*, ll. 303–4, 'Dame Chaistetie hir chalmarere bot dout, / And Strangenes hir portare can weill scorne'.

22. *unto*: in the office of.

27. *Comparesone*: distinction, a courtly quality (cf. **10**. 174); the lady's assessment of how far the lover falls short of the ideal.

30. *feir*: adversary. For this sense cf. Douglas, *Eneados*, X. xii. 115, 'to the erth ourthrawyn he hes his feir'.

33–4. *Langour*: dispirited indifference, the antithesis of the lover's 'Bissines' (l. 60). Cf. the personification in **51.** 21–5; Douglas, *King Hart*, ll. 261–2, 'Langour he lay vpon the wallis but sleip, / But meit or drink the watche horne he blew'.

39. *townage*: uncourtly; cf. **13.** 10. *be this buke*: an oath sworn on the Gospels.

41. *Gud Houp rownit.* Cf. Lydgate, *The Temple of Glass*, l. 892; James I, *The Kingis Quair*, st. 113; (?) Robert Semple, '. . . Than cumis Gud Hoip with lachand cheir / and biddis me lat all sorrowis swage / Quhen I think on my lady deir' (*Ballatis of Luve 1400–1570*, ed. John MacQueen, 1970, pp. 116–18).

49. *Petie*: the traditional feminine virtue, which urges surrender to the lover in order to prevent him dying of unrequited or unconsummated love. Cf. **12.** 28, **14.** 315–16, 497–502, *nn.*, **74.** 55. In *King Hart* (ll. 337 ff.) the king and his company 'vpone dame Pietie cry', and Danger advises her mistress, Dame Plesance: 'keip Pietie fast . . . no licence to hir len. / May scho wyn out, scho will play ȝow a cast'.

55. *Thocht*: the lover's application in courtship; to be distinguished from Reason (**10.** 151–3, 199–216), a defence against falling into love's thrall.

60. *Bissines*: cf. **16.** 85.

65. *Thai . . . schup for to defend.* Cf. **37.** 27.

74. The relative pronoun is frequently omitted.

77. *Lustely . . . juge*: they dispensed cheerfully, vigorously, with any arbiter.

78. *stychling*: rustling: Cf. Douglas, *Palice of Honour*, l. 308, 'the stychlyng of a mows out of presence'.

86. *Lust chasit my ladeis chalmirleir*: an apparently original way of representing possession. Cf. *King Hart*, quoted *supra*, l. 18 *n.*

87. *Gude Fame wes drownit.* See **14.** 284 *n.*

96–101. *Blew out . . . Than wes he and his linege lost.* Cf. Douglas, *King Hart*, ll. 217–21, 'This courtlie king and all his cumlie ost . . . out thay blew, with brag and mekle bost . . . / That lady and hir lynnage suld be lost'. For illustrations of the custom of denouncing publicly by blowing a horn see quotations from the *Acts of Parliament* in *DOST*, s.v. *blaw*, 3b.

99. *all enermit.* Cf. **62.** 21–2.

10. *The Goldyn Targe.* Dunbar's theme is the failure of 'Resoun with schelde of gold' to defend him from 'Venus chevalry': 'Than was I woundit to the deth wele nere, / And yoldyn as a wofull prisonnere / To lady Beautee' (ll. 208–10). The poem, written in the ample nine-line stanza (aabaabbab$_5$) used by Chaucer in the *compleynt* in *Anelida and Arcite*, similarly by Henryson in *The Testament of Cresseid*, and by Gavin Douglas in *The Palice of Honour* (*c.* 1501), is a more elaborate allegory of love than **9.** Dunbar uses the main conventions of the *locus amoenus* (ll. 1–45), the dream vision (ll. 46 ff.), and the double company of actors (ll. 55 ff., 109 ff.) familiar from *Le Roman de la Rose*, Chaucer's Prologue to *The Legend of Good Women*, *The Flower and the Leaf*, and elsewhere. (On the *locus amoenus* or paradisal park in classical and medieval allegory see Raby, *SLP*, ii. 17–18; E. Curtius, *European Literature and the Latin Middle Ages*, 1963 edn., pp. 195 ff.; J.A.W. Bennett, *The Parlement of Foules*, 1957, ch. ii; Paul Piehler, *The Visionary Landscape*, 1971, esp. pp. 77–82; Dagmar Thoss, *Studien zum Locus Amoenus im Mittelalter*, 1972. Cf. **50.** 44 ff.) *The Goldyn Targe* was chosen by Sir David Lindsay to exemplify Dunbar's 'language at large' (*Testament of the Papyngo*, ll. 17–18); and Denton Fox, in the best modern study of the poem, considers it a conscious poetic *tour de force*. Dunbar uses the rich tradition of the love allegory parasitically: 'his immediate concern is with the technical and rhetorical manipulation of the form, not with the "meaning" of the genre . . . for which it had been devised' (*Eng. Lit. Hist.* xxvi (1959), 311–34).

Some of Dunbar's sources, and analogues in the courtly tradition, are indicated in F. Mebus, 'Beiträge zu . . . *The Goldin Terge*', in *Englische Studien*, xxxix (1908), 40–69. R. D. S. Jack draws attention to parallels (some plausible) between Dunbar's psychomachia and Lydgate's in *Reson and Sensuallyte*, in *Studies in Scottish Literature*, viii (1971), 222–6.

The primary text of *The Goldyn Targe* is the Chepman and Myllar print which, in addition to its early date and probable authority, is remarkably free from substantive error despite the difficulty of the language. The two manuscript versions are inferior, with many readings which look like simplifications or 'improvements' (Bannatyne MS, ll. 1, 8, 14, 29, 47, 48, 52, 73, 80, 81, 89, 103, 105, 109, 110, 128, 145, 147, 202, 236, 241, 257; Maitland Folio MS, ll. 3, 14, 29, 47, 48, 80, 89, 103, 109, 110, 128, 145, 147, 202, 236, 241); misreadings and other errors (Bannatyne, ll. 11, 16, 21, 22, 28, 34, 51, 54, 65, 76, 123, 126, 157, 159, 164, 205, 207, 213; Maitland, ll. 7, 8, 16, 34, 67, 78, 81, 96, 155, 157, 159, 216); and metrical clumsiness (Bannatyne, ll. 12, 36, 38, 170, 182, 258; Maitland, ll. 170, 182, 258). The two MSS agree in many places against the print, and probably derive from a common source other than the print (ll. 16, 22, 29, 32, 47, 48, 56, 61, 65, 68, 80, 89, 103, 104, 110 (cf. 145), 120, 128, 135, 141, 147, 152, 159, 170, 171, 182, 192, 197, 202, 208, 217, 236, 241, 245, 247, 258).

1–9. *Ryght as the stern*, etc. Cf. Lydgate, *Troy Book*, i. 1198–1201:

> The nyȝt ypassed, at springyng of þe day,
> Whan þat þe larke with a blissed lay
> Gan to salue the lusty rowes rede
> Of Phebus char, þat so freschely sprede
> Vpon þe bordure of þe orient . . .

2. *Vesper and Lucyne*: the star shining in the west before sunrise, and the moon. Cf. *infra*, l. 79, and **53.** 1 *n.* STS edd. cite Cicero, *De Natura Deorum*, ii. 27, 'Luna a *lucendo* nominata sit, eadem est enim *Lucina*'.

4–6. *the goldyn candill matutyne*: the sun. Cf. OE *heofon-candel*, *daeg candel*, etc; Chaucer, *Complaint of Mars*, l. 7, 'Lo! yond the sunne, the candel of jelosye'; Lydgate, *Two Nightingale Poems*, EETS, p. 8, 'This oure of morow cleped matutyne'. *With clere depurit bemes cristallyne.* Cf. Douglas, *The Palice of Honour*, Prologue, ll. 46–7, 'Richt hailsome was the sessoun of the ȝeir. / Phebus furth ȝet depured bemis cleir'. On the association of beauty and light see J. Huizinga, *The Waning of the Middle Ages*, 1955 edn., pp. 270–1. *Glading the mery foulis in thair nest.* Cf. the song to May in Douglas, *Palice*, Prologue, l. 78, 'Thy mirth refreschis byrdis in thair nestis'.

7. *in purpur cape revest*: echoing Virgil's description of Elysium, *Aen.* vi. 638–71, 'aether et lumine vestit purpureo'. Cf. Lindsay, *The Monarche*, ll. 146–7, Phoebus' 'donke impurpurit vestiment nocturnall / With his imbroudit mantyll matutyne'. 'Purpre that we calle red representeth the fire' (Caxton, 1489; *OED*).

10. *houris*: services at set times; here, matins. Cf. **50.** 5; Jean de Condé, *La Messe des Oisiaus* (thirteenth century); the Chaucerian *Romaunt of the Rose*, ll. 670–6, 'These briddes . . . songe her song as faire and wel / As angels don espirituel'.

14–15. *The perly droppis schake in silvir schouris*, etc. Cf. Chaucer, *CT*, I. 1496, 'The silver dropes hangynge on the leves'; Lydgate, *Reson and Sensuallyte*, ll. 140–1, 'And the siluer dropes rounde / Lych perles fret vpon the grene'. But for the association of flowery *trees* (ll. 11–12), bird song, and 'silvir schouris' of dew, cf. Douglas, *The Palice of Honour*, Prologue, ll. 21–7:

> The birdis sat on twystis and on greis
> Melodiously makand thair kyndlie gleis
>
> . . . . .

> Amang the branchis of the blomed treis,
> And on the Laurers siluer droppis lyis.

16. *To part fra Phebus did Aurora grete.* Cf. Lydgate, *Assembly of the Gods*, st. 37; *The Floure of Curtesy*, ll. 36–42; and *Troy Book*, iii. 2745–6, 'Whan Aurora with sylver dropes schene / Her teares shadde upon the freshe grene'.

17–18. *Hir cristall teris.* Cf. **16.** 1–2, **50.** 9–10, **54.** 1–2. Lines 17–18 are a variation on Chaucer, *The Legend of Good Women*, ll. 773–5:

> Tyl on a day, whan Phebus gan to cleere,
> Aurora with the stremes of hire hete
> Hadde dreyed up the dew of herbes wete . . .

20. *the tender croppis.* Cf. Chaucer, *CT*, I. 7.

23–4. *powdirit brycht with hevinly beriall droppis*, etc. See **31.** 34 *n.*; cf. **48.** 1. *powdirit*: spangled, a heraldic term. Cf. Lydgate, *Assembly of the Gods*, l. 266, 'A mantell . . . purfylyd with poudryd hermyne'; Douglas, *Eneados*, VIII. vii. 150; Spenser, *The Faerie Queene*, III. ii. 25. For 'hevinly beriall' and 'throu bemes rede birnyng' cf. *Lapidaries*, p. 28: 'Berille is a stone þat is a colour like to water . . . when þe sonne shyneth, and cometh of þe lande of Inde. The riall berill casteth fire ayein þe sonne. . . . When þe sonne shyneth þervppon, hit taketh fervent heete. . . . Seynt Iohn seith þat in þe appocalipse he sawe þe berill þe eyght stone on þe foundement of þe lastyng Cite' (Rev. xxi. 20).

25. *The skyes rang for schoutyng of the larkis.* Cf. Chaucer, *The Parlement of Foules*, ll. 309–15; Douglas, *The Palice of Honour*, Prologue, ll. 22–4, 'The birdis . . . schill noitis fordinned all the skyis'.

26. *ourscailit in silvir sloppis. Ourscailit* has been glossed as 'covered in scales' and as 'skailed', scattered. *Sloppis* is conjecturally glossed in *OED* as 'slaps', openings, hence breaks in the clouds, patches of sky (s.v. *slap* sb.[2] 1*c*). But these would not be silver. Denton Fox (art. cit.) reads *slops*, 'loose outer garments', and glosses 'trailing clouds'. There seems to be no evidence for the early use of *slop* = splash. But the sense is apparently a mackerel-sky, dappled over with small clouds (cirro-cumulus).

27. *lef.* I am reluctant to follow Bannatyne and emend to the more obvious plural *leivis* (as the printer must have been tempted to do) against Maitland and the print. I read *lef*, which is metrically easier than *leivis*, as collective—leafage, foliage.

28–33. *Doune throu the ryce*, etc. 'Down through the bushes a river ran in streams, so delightfully meeting these pleasant rays of light that all the water shone like a lamp; which so reflected all around with twinkling gleams that the boughs were bathed in other rays . . .' Cf. Lindsay, *The Monarche*, ll. 171, 4138, 5336, 'the reflex of Phebus bemes brycht'. On the application of 'lake' to *flowing* water see *DOST*, s.v. *lake* n.[2] 3.

35. *bremys*: bream; probably the common carp bream (*abramis brama*). 'A fish not familiar in Scotland, but giving the alliteration' (Mackenzie); but cf. *LHTA*, i. 305, payment to 'the fyschare that brocht bremys to the Kyng' (1496).

36. *stanneris*: pebbles, gravel. Cf. Douglas, *Palice*, l. 1150, 'beriall stremis rinnand ouir stanerie greis'. With the imagery of green bank and shining pebbles cf. the Chaucerian *Romaunt of the Rose*, ll. 125–9:

> Tho saugh I well
> The botme paved everydell
> With gravel, ful of stones shene.
> The medewe softe, swote and grene,
> Beet right on the watir syde.

But the images of reflection in the stanza almost certainly derive from the *Romaunt*, ll. 1553–629. With the simile in l. 36 cf. Chaucer, *CT*, I. 267–8; Lydgate, *Reson and Sensuallyte*, ll. 1004–5, 'they yaf as gret a lyght / As sterris in the frosty nyght'; Lindsay, *Deploratioun*, l. 146.

37–45. Behind the heraldic colours and artificial illumination of this setting is Dunbar's 'joy in clear water and the clear lights of Northern sun under a washed sky. . . . The transparent quality [he] gives all his lights may seem faintly unnatural to an English reader . . . but Dunbar was a man of East Scotland, where light does give that sense of being seen through crystal' (Agnes Mure Mackenzie, *Scottish Literature to 1714*, 1933, pp. 92, 93).

37. *the sapher firmament*. See **31**. 36 *n*.

39. *emerant bewis grene*. Cf. **31**. 37 *n*.

42, 48. *dame Flora the quene . . . Florais mantill*. Cf. Lydgate, *The Complaint of the Black Knight*, l. 1, and *Fall of Princes*, i. 538–9: 'And fresshe Flora, which is of floures queene, / Hir lyuere made off a perpetuel greene'.

51. *A saill als quhite as blossum upon spray*. The simile is proverbial cf. Chaucer, *CT*, I. 3323–4; Whiting, B383. The imagery here was perhaps suggested by Douglas, *Palice of Honour*, ll. 1358–61:

> And secundlie I saw ane lustie Barge
> . . . . . .
> This gudelie Carwell, taiklit traist on raw,
> With blanschite saill, milk quhite as ony snaw.

But cf. Skelton's dream of 'a shyppe goodly of sayle . . . with takelyng ryche and of hye apparayle', dropping anchor and displaying an allegorical company to the poet (*Bowge of Court*, ll. 29 ff.; unique copy of 1st edn., 1499, in Nat. Lib. Scotland).

52. *merse of gold*: the round-top or top-castle surrounding the lower masthead, adorned with 'mers clathes' or coloured hangings. The armorial artist Alexander Chalmers was paid ten French crowns in April 1506 for painting the merse of a royal ship (*LHTA*, iii. 189).

55. *hard on burd*: close at hand—alongside the shore.

60–2. *In kirtillis . . . thredis*. Cf. the Chaucerian *Romaunt of the Rose*, ll. 776–9:

> Ful fetys damyseles two,
> Ryght yonge, and full of semelyhede,
> In kirtles, and noon other wede,
> And faire tressed every tresse . . .

kirtillis grene: May dress; see **14.** 24 *n.*; cf. **48.** 42. For a fine early illustration see *Les Très Riches Heures du Duc de Berry*, ed. J. Longnon and R. Cazelles, 1969, 6, 'May'.

61–3. *Thair brycht hairis*, etc. Conventional romance description; see **14.** 19–22 *n.*

64–72. *Discrive I wald, bot quho coud*, etc. *Occupatio* or *occultatio*; what is told by pretending to omit it (*Ad Herennium*, iv. 37). Cf. Chaucer, *The Book of the Duchess*, ll. 895 ff.; *CT*, I. 2919–66. Dunbar's descriptive catalogue follows in l. 73 with the stock formula 'Thare saw I'; cf. Chaucer, *The House of Fame*, ll. 1214 ff.; *CT*, I. 1995 ff.

65. *thai lilies quhite*: the company of ladies, flower-like in green kirtles with white and gold above. The allusion is misunderstood and lost in the MSS.

67–8. *Omer . . . thine ornate stilis*. A common though ill-founded tribute; Dunbar's only reference to Homer. Cf. Lydgate, *Amor Vincit Omnia*, st. 5, 'The Greke Omerus with his sugre mowth / Tullius put out for al theyr eloquence'; Douglas, *Palice of Honour*, ll. 895–7:

> Thair saw I weill in Poetrie ygroundit
> The greit Homeir, quhilk in Greik langage said
> Maist eloquentlie, in quhome all wit yboundit.

69–70. *Tullius*. Cicero's *De Inventione* (the 'Rhetorica nova'), and the *Ad Herrenium* ('Rhetorica vetus') attributed to him were among the most popular medieval textbooks on rhetoric. See H. Rashdall, *The Universities of Europe in the Middle Ages*, ed. Powicke and Emden,

1936, i. 248 and iii. 155. Cf. Hawes, *The Pastime of Pleasure*, ll. 1156–69, on aureate diction,

> the well of fruytfulnesse
> Which Vyrgyll claryfyed and also Tullyus
> With latyn pure, swete and delycyous.

73. *Nature and Venus, quene and quene*: juxtaposed by Chaucer in *The Parlement of Foules*, ll. 260 ff., (see J. A. W. Bennett's study of the poem, 1957, pp. 111 ff.). Cf. Douglas, *Palice of Honour*, Prologue, ll. 91–3:

> O Nature, Quene, and O ȝe lustie May,
> Quod I tho: how lang sall I thus foruay, [err
> Quhilk ȝow and Venus in this garth deseruis? [serve

75. *Juno Appollo.* Despite the print—'Juno Apollo / and Proserpyna' —editors punctuate 'Juno, Appollo', and deplore the intrusion of the god into a catalogue of goddesses. But Dunbar knew that Apollo was the sun-god (cf. **4.** 21–2 *n.*). I suspect that 'Appollo' is to be taken as an appellative for Juno, 'goddes of the sky' (**50.** 69), possibly (though erroneously) on the model of 'Phoebus Apollo' (cf. Virgil, *Aen.* iii. 251).

76. *Dyane . . . grene*: an echo of Chaucer, *CT*, I. 2297, 'O chaste goddesse of the wodes grene'.

77. *My lady Cleo . . . bene*: the muse of history (cf. Douglas, *Palice of Honour*, ll. 854–5, 'Lady Cleo, quhilk craftelie dois set / Historyis auld'), but invoked by James I with the other muses, 'with your bryght lanternis wele conuoye / My pen' (*The Kingis Quair*, st. 19). Dunbar probably recollects Chaucer, *Troilus and Criseyde*, ii. 8–11:

> O lady myn, that called art Cleo,
> Thow be my speed fro this forth, and my Muse,
> To ryme wel this book til I have do;
> Me nedeth here noon other art to use.

78. *Thetes*: the sea deity Thetis, mother of Achilles. *Pallas, and prudent Minerva*: one and the same, however; Greek and Latin names for 'the Quene of Sapience' (Douglas, *Palice of Honour*, ll. 241–2).

79. *Lucina.* See *supra*, l. 2 *n.*

81. *Lucifera*: the planet Venus; the morning star.

82–6. *May, of myrthfull monethis quene . . . in hir yeris grene.* Cf. Chaucer, *Troilus and Criseyde*, ii. 50; James I, *The Kingis Quair*, st. 65, 'fresche May . . . flour of monethis all . . . oure quene'. Mebus (art. cit.) quotes Lydgate, 'May among moneths sitte lyk a queene, / Hir sustir April wattryng hir gardynes'. D. W. Robertson (*Preface to Chaucer*, 1969 rpt., p. 257) notes that 'kalendars sometimes show May as a young girl holding flowers (fig. 105)'.

83. *sistir*: old plural form 'corrected' by Bannatyne.

87–90. *Thare saw I Nature . . . proporcioun*. Cf. **50**. 15–21. The association of a rich gown with Nature is derived ultimately from Alanus de Insulis, *De Planctu Naturae* (see Raby, *SLP*, ii. 18). Cf. Lydgate, *Reson and Sensuallyte*, ll. 347 ff.; the Chaucerian *Romaunt of the Rose*, ll. 888 ff. Line 90 echoes Lydgate, *Complaint of the Black Knight*, ll. 162–3, 'the best ther of brede . . . wel ymade by good proporsioun'.

95. *Salust Nature*. Cf. Chaucer, *The Parlement of Foules*, ll. 673–6, 'But fyrst were chosen foules for to synge . . . To don to Nature honour and plesaunce'.

102–5. *And to dame Venus . . . hertis grene*. Cf. James I, *The Kingis Quair*, sts. 33–5; Venus' 'virginum choream' in the pastourelle *Ubi primum vidi amicam* (Raby, *SLP*, ii. 239).

109. *consequent*: in the print only. Cf. Lindsay, *Deploratioun . . . of Quene Magdalene*, l. 121, 'The Senatouris, in ordour consequent'.

111. *dredefull arowis grundyn scharp and square*. Cf. Douglas, *King Hart*, ll. 108–10, 'The grundin dairtis, scharp and bricht to se', etc.

112. *Mars the god armypotent*. Mars 'dysposeth the soul to unstedfaste sytte and lyghtnes, to wrathe, and to boldnes, and to other coleryke passions. Under him is conteined warre, bataile, prisonne and enmyte. And he tokeneth wrathe . . .' (Bartolomaeus Anglicus; Maurice Hussey, *Chaucer's World*, 1967, p. 114 and pl. 78). Cf. Virgil, *Aen*. ix. 717; Chaucer, *CT*, I. 1982, translating Boccaccio's 'armipotente'; **35**. 73. Dunbar seems to have been the first to assemble a company of Roman deities in a courtly love meadow (W. A. Neilson, *The Origins and Sources of the Court of Love*, 1899, p. 164).

114–15. *crabbit Saturn . . . air*. Traditionally 'an evyll willed planete, colde and drye' (Bartolomaeus Anglicus); cf. Chaucer, *CT*, I. 2467, and Henryson, *The Testament of Cresseid*, ll. 151 ff., Saturn 'as ane busteous churle on his maneir / Come crabitlie with auster luik and cheir . . . his lyart lokkis lay . . . ouirfret with froistis hoir', with Denton Fox's notes in his edition of the *Testament*, 1968. *lyke for to perturb the aire*. Cf. **23**. 9–12.

118–20. *Priapus*: presided over the fertility of fields and flocks, and his phallic image protected gardens and vineyards (cf. Chaucer, *The Parlement of Foules*, ll. 253–9). *Phanus*: Faunus, deity of fields and fertility (cf. Chaucer, *CT*, I. 2925–8). *Janus*: deity of gates and doors, his emblem a key (cf. Chaucer, *Troilus and Criseyde*, ii. 77, 'Janus, god of entree').

125–6. *Pluto the elrich incubus . . . no sable*. Pluto, here in fairy green, is king of faery also in the romance of *Sir Orfeo* and in Chaucer, *CT*, IV. 2038–41 and 2226 ff. Dunbar probably adds the emphatic 'usit no sable' to show that he knew Pluto as the classical king of the 'derke peyne' (cf. Chaucer, *The House of Fame*, ll. 1511–12). Pluto is apparently called an incubus here because of his rape of Proserpina. Cf. **38**. 3–8, and *n.*

131. *mayit.* Cf. Malory, *Works*, ed. E. Vinaver, 1947, iii. 1120, 'So hit befelle in the moneth of May, quene Gwenyver called unto her ten knyghtes . . . and she gaff them warnynge that early uppon the morn she wolde ryde on maynge into woodis and fyldis . . . "And I warne you . . . that ye all be clothed all in gryne, othir in sylke othir in clothe".'

135. *a luik quhilk I have boucht full dere.* See **9**. 5–6 *n.*

136–7. *be lufis quene / I was aspyit.* Cf. Chaucer, *The Book of the Duchess*, ll. 816–19, 835–41.

141. *felde*: i.e. of battle.

145–98. The attacking force is made up of a number of platoons, each broadly representing a group of related feminine qualities, and most of them personified in *Le Roman de la Rose* and the literature derived from it: (i) Beauty with her supporters Fair Demeanour, Fine Appearance, Delight, and Pleasing Countenance (ll. 145–50); (ii) Youth with her characteristic qualities of innocence, modesty, fear, and obedience (ll. 154–9); (iii) Womanliness with other virtues of character—Breeding, Humility, Restraint, etc. (ll. 160–7); (iv) High Degree and qualities of rank (ll. 172–6; for Comparisoun, see **9**. 27 *n.*); (v) Dissimulation, with Physical Presence and Fair Greeting (see **9**. 18 *n.*; cf. James I, *The Kingis Quair*, st. 97), Affection and Familiarity, Beauty and Acquaintance (ll. 182–222; qualities of sexual appeal). Cf. Peter Dronke, *Medieval Latin and the . . . Love Lyric*, 1968, ii. 367–9.

151, 183, 200. *schelde of gold . . . the goldyn targe*: perhaps suggested by Lydgate's *Pilgrimage of the Life of Man* (EETS, i. 224), where the main part of the Christian's armour against sin is a targe of prudence and 'rihtful jugement'.

176. *Richesse*: 'An high lady of gret noblesse / And gret of prys in every place' (Chaucerian *Romaunt of the Rose*, ll. 1033 ff.).

177. *thay did thair baner hye display.* Cf. Chaucer, *CT*, I. 966.

179. *quhill wastit . . . artilye.* Cf. Blind Hary, *Wallace*, iv. 579, 'Be that his arrous waistyt war and gayne'.

187–9. *Presence*: physical closeness. *Fair Callyng*: Guillaume de Lorris's Bialacoil in *Le Roman de la Rose* but, as Denton Fox points out (art. cit., p. 328), more wanton in Dunbar (cf. **14.** 489 ff.). The metaphor of 'plicht ankers' is distracting.

190. *Hamelynes*: intimacy. Cf. *The Freiris of Berwik* (Mackenzie, p. 186), ll. 157–8; Lindsay, *Ane Satyre of the Thrie Estaits*, ed. Kinsley, 1954, p. 184—'Let never preists be hamelie with ʒour wyfis. / My wyfe with preists . . . maid me nine tymes cuckald on ane nicht'—and the dramatic representation of Hamelines on pp. 49–50, 57–8.

193. *the choise of Venus chevalry*. Cf. **35.** 82.

202–10. *The aufull stoure*, etc. The poet's reason is no defence against the sight and closeness of his lady (see **9.** 5–6 *n.*; *supra*, l. 135); and it is banished to the greenwood (l. 206; cf. *Harry, harry, hobbillschowe*, Bannatyne MS, f. 120r, ll. 109–10, 'I haif bene baneist vndir þe lynd / This lang tyme'). So the Chaucerian *Romaunt of the Rose*, ll. 3332 ff.:

With that word Resoun wente hir gate,
Whanne she saugh for no sermonynge
She myght me fro my foly brynge.
Thanne dismaied, I lefte all sool,
Forwery, forwandred as a fool . . .

215. *gert ane hell my paradise appere*. Cf. the *Romaunt of the Rose*, ll. 3621–2, 4136–7, 4743–4, love 'Also a swete helle it is / And a soroufull paradys'; Chaucer, *CT*, I. 1223–6, 1236–7.

223–8. *Than saw I Dangere*, etc. Deprived of Resoun, the lover for a time enjoys his lady's affection; but he is rejected by a sudden reticence and thrown into despair. On *Dangere* see **9.** 18 *n.*

230. *God Eolus, his bugill blew*. Cf. **50.** 33–5; Chaucer, *The House of Fame*, ll. 1636–54, Eolus

Took out hys blake trumpe of bras,
That fouler than the devel was,
And gan this trumpe for to blowe
As al the world shulde overthrowe . . .

Douglas, *Eneados*, vii, Prologue, l. 67, 'So bustuusly Boreas his bugill blew'; Skelton, *The Crowne of Lawrel*, st. 34.

235. *In twynklyng of ane eye*: proverbial; Whiting, T547. Cf. **50.** 85, **64.** 29.

238–43. *Thai fyrit*, etc. Cf. **51.** 111–15.

249. *The air attemperit, sobir and amene*. Cf. the Chaucerian *Romaunt of the Rose*, ll. 130–1; Chaucer, *The Book of the Duchess*, ll. 339–43, and *The Parlement of Foules*, ll. 204–10.

251, 257. *Naturis nobil fresch anamalyng . . . fresch anamalit termis celicall*. Denton Fox comments (art. cit., p. 333) on ll. 253–70: 'What we have here . . . is theory and example; the theory being the stanzas stating that poetry should be like enamel and the example being the rest of the poem. Subject, style and aesthetic theory all coalesce . . . 'anamalit' is simultaneously a characteristic of the garden [cf. l. 13], of the hard and brilliant style . . . and of the sort of poetry that Dunbar strives to make.'

253–70. *O reverend Chaucere*, etc. Fifteenth-century poets had established this critical view of Chaucer and Gower as an inevitable formula. Cf. Lydgate, *Troy Book*, ii. 4697 ff., and iii. 4237; Hoccleve, *Regement of Princes*, ll. 1962–3 and 2084–6; James I, *The Kingis Quair*, st. 197:

> Vnto the inpnis of my maisteris dere,
> Gowere and Chaucere, that on the steppis satt
> Of rethorike quhill thai were lyvand here,
> Superlatiue as poetis laureate
> In moralitee and eloquence ornate
> I recommend my buik . . .

See further Caroline Spurgeon, *Five Hundred Years of Chaucer Criticism and Allusion*, 1925, i.

259. *oure Inglisch*: until Flodden (1513) the usual name for the vernacular of lowland Scotland as well as of England, distinguished from Gaelic or 'Ersche' (cf. **23.** 107–12). Gavin Douglas, however, makes a distinction between English and Scots in the Prologue to *Eneados*, i (1513), 105 ff.:

> And ȝit forsuyth I set my bissy pane
> As that I couth to mak it braid and plane,
> Kepand na Sudron bot our awyn langage,
> And spekis as I lernyt quhen I was page.
> . . . . . .
> [Bot] me behufyt quhilum or than be dum
> Sum bastard Latyn, French or Inglys oyss
> Quhar scant was Scottis . . .

262. *O morall Gower*: traditional address, first used by Chaucer in *Troilus and Criseyde*, v. 1856. Cf. Hawes, *The Pastime of Pleasure* (Spurgeon, op. cit., i. 67):

> As morall Gower, whose sentencious dewe
> Adowne reflareth, with fayre golden beames,
> And after Chaucers all abrode doth shewe,
> Our vyces to clense . . .

Douglas, *Palice of Honour*, l. 920. See J. H. Fisher, *John Gower*, 1965, pp. 3–8. *Ludgate laureate*: i.e. worthy of a laurel crown for poetry. Cf. **35.** 4–5. On Lydgate's early reputation as 'the most dulcet sprynge / of famous rethoryke' (Stephen Hawes), see W. F. Schirmer, *John Lydgate*, 1961, pp. 255–7.

266. *Oure rude langage has clere illumynate.* Cf. Chaucer on Petrarch, *CT*, IV. 31–3.

271. *Thou lytill quair.* The *envoi de quare*, a modest address to book or poem, was a common way of ending. Cf. Chaucer, *Troilus and Criseyde*, v. 1786; James I, *The Kingis Quair*, st. 194; and J. Norton-Smith, *Lydgate: Poems*, 1966, pp. 175–6.

274. *I knaw . . . spent*: 'I know that you have striven to show all the eloquence you have (but) . . . .'

278–9. *Rude is thy wede*, etc. Cf. Geoffrey de Vinsauf, *Poetria Nova*, ll. 63–5 (on *poesis*):

caveat sibi, ne caput hirtis
crinibus, aut corpus pannosa veste, vel ulla
ultima displiceant . . .

11. *Gude Counsale.* The Bannatyne MS adds 'ffinis' to l. 24: 'ffinis &c. dumbar' is subscribed in lighter ink and possibly in a different hand; but the slight difference in the ascription may be due merely to cramping at the foot of a full page. On the stanza see **4**, intro. note. For the extension of the code of *amour courtois* from sexual mores to a general moral rule see, e.g., Andreas Capellanus, *De Amore* (transl. J. J. Parry, 1941).

7. *ay*: my addition. The line needs a syllable here, and a verb + 'ay' is common in Dunbar. Note also the movement between 'never' and 'always' in the poem (ll. 6, 12–14, 22).

8. *Be secreit.* See **14.** 284 *n.*

15. *Be nocht of langage*: 'don't speak'.

18. *Be nocht . . . heir*: 'don't be so regarded, assessed, as I have said—a liar, trattler, etc.'.

19. *sa lerge . . . sung*: in this context of fame and esteem (ll. 17–20), probably 'so lavish to those who flatter you with songs'.

12. *To a Lady, quhone he list to Feyne.* Though in the more extravagant modes of courtly poetry it is hard to tell 'ernest' from 'game', this is manifestly a parody of the poetry of *amour courtois* (cf. Scott, pp. 59–60). The first three stanzas read gravely enough; but the tone becomes hysterical, and rhetorical extravagance preposterous, with the melodrama of ll. 22–8, 29–32, and rises to a climax in the final stanza. The standard by which to measure Dunbar's seriousness is the beautifully controlled courtly complaint to a 'sweit rois of gentilnes' (**8**). On the stanza see **5**.

1–2. *My hartis tresure . . . ever.* Cf. **14.** 500 *n.*; Chaucer, *CT*, I. 2775–6, 2780:

> Allas, myn hertes queene! allas, my wyf!
> Myn hertes lady, endere of my lyf!
> . . . . . .
> Fare wel, my swete foo, myn Emelye!

On the use of the oxymoron in love poetry see Robinson's note on Chaucer, *Troilus and Criseyde*, i. 411.

5–6. *man*: lover, vassal in love's service. Cf. James I, *The Kingis Quair*, st. 63, 'Quhen sall your merci rew vpon your man / Quhois seruice is yit vncouth vnto yow'; Lindsay, *The Historie of Squyer Meldrum*, ed. Kinsley, 1959, ll. 955–8:

> Madame, gude-morne;
> Help me, ȝour man that is forlorne.
> Without ȝe mak me sum remeid,
> Withouttin dout I am bot deid.

7. *mercy.* See **9.** 49 *n.*, **14.** 315–16, 497–502, *nn.*; cf. **13.** 1–7.

15–16. *so besalie / That wery is my goist to fle.* Cf. James I, *The Kingis Quair*, st. 173, 'O besy goste ay flikering to and fro . . .'; Chaucer, *Troilus and Criseyde*, iv. 302–3, 'O wery goost . . . Why nyltow fleen . . .'.

24. *undir traist*: legal phrase, maintaining the theme of vassalage. Cf. Skene, *Regiam Majestatem. The Auld Lawes . . . of Scotland*, 1609, ii. 131: '*Slauchter vnder trust.* Murther . . . of our Soveraine Lords leiges, quhere the persone slaine is vnder the trust, credit, assurance, and power of the slayer, is treason and lese majestie'.

28. *womanlie petie.* See **9.** 49 *n.*

31. *mayne and murning.* Cf. Henryson, *Fabillis*, l. 1555, 'Brekand his hart with sair murning and mane'.

34–5, 40–2. *For how*, etc. Cf. Chaucer, *CT*, I. 1761, 'pitee renneth soone in gentil herte'; *Troilus and Criseyde*, i. 898–900:

> sith thy lady vertuous is al,
> So foloweth it that there is som pitee
> Amonges alle thise other in general.

For later references see Whiting, H273, P243.

37. *Swete gentill turtour.* See **14.** 262 *n.*

13. *In Secreit Place.* This poem is a concise dramatic illustration of the satirical attitude to the conventions of *amour courtois* more elaborately expressed in **14.** It follows the tradition of the *chanson daventure*, in' which the wooing of a country girl by a clerkly lover is described in dialogue; and it opens in courtly style with the poet *en cachette* (cf. **14.** 11 ff.), listening to a 'bern' and a 'bricht' and a plaint against 'danger'. But the two are no more courtly lovers than are the 'tua mariit wemen and the wedo': he is a backstairs fornicator, familiar with the terms and postures of *amour courtois* but foul in person and manners; she is a giggling kitchen girl. The stanza (aabbcbc$_4$ with refrain) is a French form; cf. **26, 28, 37, 74.** In **13** the dialogue has two refrains.

The stanza form, the tonal correspondence between this poem and **14,** the parody, and the sheer skill of the exercise, encourage me to accept the ascription to Dunbar in the Maitland Folio MS (the attribution to Clerk in the Bannatyne MS is added in a different hand). I have, however, followed Bannatyne's text, except in a few places. Bannatyne's reading in l. 10 is clumsy and unrhythmical, and looks like an attempt to read a difficult manuscript; the omission of 's-' in l. 48 destroys the alliteration and the sense. Maitland's reading at l. 17 is attractive; but his readings in ll. 28, 29, 42, 50, 60, 63 look like attempts at smoothing, and those in ll. 33, 46, 61 are quite probably errors. At l. 61 he misses the metaphor

2. *bern.* See **14.** 74 *n. bricht*: poetical; cf. **14.** 181, 236.

6. *denger*: disdain. See **9.** 18 *n.*, **10.** 223–8 *n.*; cf. **17.** 39, 56, 62.

7. *ȝe brek my hart.* See **14.** 500 *n.*

10. *townysche*: uncourtly; cf. **9.** 39. Bannatyne's 'to mich' may be a misreading of 'touniche'.

12. *glaikkis*: amorous folly. The main sense is 'foolishness'; see *DOST*, s.v. *glaik*, *glaiker*, *glaiks*, *glaikit*. *DOST* glosses *glaikkis* here as 'sensual desire'; but 'ȝit be his feiris' in l. 13 implies some opposition between 'clappit . . . kist . . . chukkit' and 'wald haif fukkit'. There were signs, in the way he went on, that he intended more than this amorous play.

15. *sweit as the hunny*: common proverb; see Whiting, H430.

18–19. *My wame . . . grane*: a ludicrous contrast between 'fow' and 'gaist'.

23. *cowffyne*: obscure. *Tuchan* (Maitland Folio MS) is a stuffed calf-skin used to encourage the cow to give milk; but this makes 'and my cawf' tautological and destroys the alliteration. *Cowffyne* is perhaps related to 'coffe, coife', a rascal.

29. *claver . . . curledoddy*: clover . . . ribwort plantain or wild scabious. The endearments in this stanza are in ludicrous juxtaposition: (honey) clover—plantain; bread dipped in honey—sheep's head broth. Cf. *infra*. ll. 33–4 *n.*

32. *warme hartit*. Cf. **14.** 498 and *n*.

33–4. *ȝour hals . . . quhillylillie*. The neck is a stock erotic zone in romance. *Quhalis bane*: i.e. ivory from the walrus etc.; a poetic simile. Cf. *Pearl*, l. 212, 'Her ble more blaȝt þen whalleȝ bon'; *Squier of Lowe Degre*, l. 527, 'Lady, as whyte as whales bone'. The romantic tribute is however negated by the physical crudity of l. 34.

38. *belly huddroun*: heifer-belly, big-bellied glutton. Cf. **52.** 70. *hurle bawsy*: obscure. Cf. the spirit Hurlbasie conjured up in *The Freiris of Berwik* (Mackenzie), l. 495; **52.** 30; **23.** 194 ('hurle' = skitters). Obviously an offensive endearment, like *belly huddroun*.

39. *honygukkis*: sweet idiot. Still current in Lothian. *slasy gawsy*: obscure. *Gawsy* is common in eighteenth- and nineteenth-century Scots, 'handsome, portly, jolly' (*SND*), but is not recorded in *DOST*.

44. *brilȝeane*: obscure; in the context probably obscene (cf. ll. 46–8).

45. *girdill*: (?) *fig*. belt, that which binds. Maitland's *gyrle* may be (as in modern Scots) a variant of *girdill*, not = 'girl'. *gowdy*: (?) 'goldie', gold piece.

46, 48. *tirly mirly . . . towdy mowdy*: prob. for *pudendum muliebre*; cf. Burns, *Poems and Songs*, ed. Kinsley, 1968, note on **109.** 64, 'Jeany Mitchel's tirlie-whirlie'.

51. *golk of Maryland*: 'cuckoo of fairy-land'; a daft appropriation from the burlesque tale of Mayiola or Mayok, the 'golk of Maryland' and daughter of 'the king of fary', who was wooed for seven years by the king of Babylon (Bannatyne MS, ff. 142ᵛ–143ʳ).

52. *mynȝeoun*: darling, lover. Cf. Lindsay, *The Historie of Squyer Meldrum*, 1959, ll. 232–4:

> Ladies of him wes amorous.
> He was ane Munȝeoun for ane Dame,
> Meik in Chalmer lyk ane lame.

53. *sweit as ony unȝeoun*: a ludicrous simile.

57. *appill ruby*: a variety of apple. Cf. *Exch. Rolls*, v. 186 (1445), 'pro centum pomis ruby pro rege' (*DOST*).

58. *cowhuby*: prob. a pejorative term; booby, fool. Cf. Lindsay, *The Tragedie of the Cardinall*, ll. 379–82:

> Nor to fantastyke fenȝeit flatteraris
> . . . . .
> Of cowhubeis, nor ȝit of clatterraris,
> That in the kirk can nouther sing, nor saye . . .

60. *dirrydan*: i.e. copulation. Cf. **28.** 24. For similar sexual applications of dance-names in later Scots cf. Allan Ramsay's *Lucky*

Spence's Last Advice, l. 69, 'the auld Game *Taunty Raunty*'; *The Reels o' Bogie* (*The Merry Muses of Caledonia*, 1959 edn., pp. 127–8); *The Bob o' Dumblane* and *The Reel o' Stumpie* in Burns, *Poems and Songs*, ed. Kinsley, 1968, nos. 513 and 573.

61. *bewis*: branches; limbs.

14. *The Tretis of the The Tua Mariit Wemen and the Wedo.* Dunbar's experimental interest in developing a comic contrast between a conventional form and a freshly chosen theme, and his sense of a contradiction between the artifices of *amour courtois* and the realities of the sexual relationship (cf. **13**), are most fully illustrated in the *Tretis*. Formally, the poem is a *dêbat* on love and marriage. Three ladies are discovered in a decorated garden bower, celebrating the festival of Midsummer Eve. The poet, following the convenient habit of many courtly predecessors, creeps up and *en cachette* behind a hedge listens to their conversation. The Wedo assumes the role of president of the court, and sets her companions a *demande d'amour* (ll. 41–8). The others take up the question in turn, and answer it pragmatically by recounting their experiences in marriage. When the Wedo has made her contribution, the discussion is resolved in wine and laughter, and the trio 'rakit hame to ther rest'. The poet turns to the reader with a satiric *demande d'amour* of his own (ll. 529–30). The ladies, splendidly dressed and furnished with fine vessels and wine, have the beauty of romance heroines. Cf. ll. 34, 36, 150, 243, 252, 443, 523. The Wedo has an ideal 'galland' who 'couth be secrete and sure and ay saif my honour' (ll. 283–4, 466). She cultivates 'baronis and knychtis' and 'bachilleris' (ll. 476–7). She professes 'pitee' and shows 'mercy' to a desperate lover (ll. 315–16, 497–500). But these are only jocular echoes of the sentiment of *amour courtois*. Her 'honour' is an accessible commodity, her exercise of 'pitee' indiscriminate. She is less a courtly lover than an amateur harlot (ll. 476–83). Her application of the rules and terminology of *amour courtois* is deliberately comic. In social station, and in many of her attitudes and habits, she is sister to Chaucer's Wife of Bath. She married a widower merchant, a mere 'buthman' (ll. 296, 309). She has the Wife's appetite and uninhibited self-confession, her love of proverbial wisdom and her irrepressible spirits, her fancy for fine clothes which 'hely raise my renoune amang the rude peple' (ll. 365–8), her pride in social position, and her fondness for pilgrimages 'mair for the prese of peple na ony perdoun wynyng' (ll. 472–5). Her two companions, though 'weddit . . . with lordis' (l. 36), are revealed as coarse, lecherous, and cruel. Ideal beauty is exposed as the whited sepulchre of lust and greed; what seems to be of the bower is seen to belong to the street; and three drinking, jesting gossips cynically pretend, as part of their festive joke, allegiance to courtly love.

In the *Tretis*, the old alliterative line is used on two different levels. It is a vehicle both for coarse description and self-expression, and for ornamental scene-painting. It is probable that Dunbar had models for the abusive alliterative verse of the *Tretis* and the *Flyting* (**23**). Mr. Thorlac Turville-Petre has drawn my attention to the association of the alliterative line with invective—e.g. Darius on Alexander in *The Wars of Alexander*:

> Ane amlaȝe, ane asaleny, ane ape of all othire,
> A wirling, a wayryngle, a wawil-eȝid shrewe,
> Þe caitifeste creatour þat cried was euire

(cf. *infra*, ll. 89–99). It is much more certain that by the time of James IV the alliterative line was associated chiefly with sophisticated types of poetry (cf. W. A. Craigie, 'The Scottish Alliterative Poems', *Proc. Brit. Acad.* xxvi (1943). In the prologue to the *Tretis* Dunbar shows his familiarity with the diction and devices of the 'Alliterative Revival'. For forty lines the smooth, rapid run of the verse and the 'enamellit termis' give the listener what he expects in this measure, and seem to set the tone of the poem. Metre, diction, and the external character of the three women harmonize. Then the alliterative line is turned to a new and unexpected use in the speech of the first Wife. The centre of the *Tretis* is the contrast between appearance and reality, between the ideal world of courtly poetry and the 'spotted actuality' of the three women's minds and habits; and to this end a metrical form with courtly associations is suddenly turned into the medium of erotic reminiscence.

A number of literary traditions coalesce in the *Tretis*. (1) The courtly code and style discussed *supra*. (2) Anti-feminist writing in Latin and the vernaculars, from S. Jerome on. See Robinson's summary in his edition of Chaucer, 1957, p. 698; F. L. Utley, *The Crooked Rib*, 1944; John Peter, *Complaint and Satire in Early English Literature*, 1956, pp. 30 ff., 86 ff. Dunbar probably owes a direct debt to Lydgate's *Pain and Sorrow of Evil Marriage*; see ll. 70–2 *n.*; and cf. st. 7:

> wyfes gladly be
> Dyvers of hert, full of duplicite,
> Right mastirfull, hasty and eke proude,
> Crabbed of langage when þei lust cry lowde.

(3) Gossip or ale-wife dialogue; cf. *Evangiles des Quenouilles*, ed. Jannet, 1855; *Talk of Ten Wives on their Husbands' Ware* (*c.* 1475), in F. J. Furnivall, *Jyl of Breyntford's Testament*, Ballad Society, VIIa

(1871), pp. 6, 29–33; *Gossips' Meeting* in R. L. Greene, *A selection of English Carols*, 1962, no. 86; Skelton, *The Tunning of Eleanor Rummynge*. The convention survived in folk-song; cf. *Our John's brak Yestreen*, in *The Merry Muses of Caledonia* (*c.* 1800; ed. G. Legman, 1965, p. 76 and notes). (4) The convention of the eaves-dropping poet, derived from the *chanson d'aventure* and the French court poets. This provides the framework of the *Tretis*. (5) The *chanson de mal mariée*, to which the matter of Dunbar's dialogue owes a good deal, though he is working on a much bigger scale. There is usually but a single complainant; but one *chanson* has three wives (Smith, pp. 39–40). Cf. H. E. Sandison, *The Chanson d'Aventure in Middle English*, 1913, pp. 13, 54–6.

I have followed the 'Rouen' print for the main part of my text (ll. 104–530); this is early and generally good, most of its errors being minor mistakes by the printer. Lines 1–103, now missing from the print, are based on the Maitland Folio MS. This differs from the print much less substantially than we might expect for such a long and difficult text—and mainly in obvious misreadings, careless transcription, and attempts to 'improve' either sense or metre.

Title. *Tretis*: narrative, tale; cf. Chaucer, *Troilus and Criseyde*, iv. 666–70, 'The whiche tale . . . this tretis'. Title from the Maitland Folio MS, but possibly Dunbar's.

1. *the midsummer evin*: S. John's Eve, 23 June; traditionally a time of bonfire and celebration, later condemned as one of several 'superstitious days' (*DOST*; 1577). See M. M. Banks, *British Calendar Customs: Scotland*, iii (1941), 15 ff.; cf. A. R. Wright, *British Calendar Customs: England*, iii (1940), 6 ff.

4. *hawthorne treis*. With this whole passage cf. the formal garden in James I, *The Kingis Quair*, sts. 31 and 33:

> . . . in the corneris set
> Ane herber grene with wandis long and small
> Railit about; and so with treis set
> Was all the place, and hawthorn hegis knet,
> That lyf was non walking there forby
> That myght within scarse ony wight aspye.
> . . . . .
> And on the smalle grene twistis sat
> The lytill suete nyghtingale . . .

10. *donkit . . . dynnit*: 'made damp . . . made a din'. Cf. *The Complaynt of Scotland* (EETS, pp. 38–9), 'the fresche den . . . hed maid dikis and dailis verray donc . . . the dyn that the foulis did' (Mackenzie).

19–22. *So glitterit*, etc. Conventional romance description. Cf. **10.** 61–2, **16.** 77, **48.** 43; *The Geste Hystoriale of . . . Troy*, l. 9135, 'The faire heris of that fre flammet of gold'; Chaucer, *The Hous of Fame*, ll. 1386–7, 'Hir heer, that oundy was and crips, / As burned gold hyt shoon to see', and *The Parlement of Foules*, ll. 267–8, 'Hyre gilte heres with a golden thred / Ibounden were, untressed as she lay'; Lydgate, *Troy Book*, ii. 4741–4 (on Cresseid):

Hir sonnysche her, liche Phebus in his spere,
Bounde in a tresse, briȝter þanne golde were,
Doun at hir bak, lowe doun be-hynde,
Whiche with a þrede of golde sche wolde bynde;

and with ll. 21–2 cf. Hawes, *Pastime of Pleasure*, ll. 2035–7:

Her heer was downe so clerely shynynge
Lyke to the golde late puryfyde with fyre,
Her heer was bryght as the drawen wyre.

20. *all the gressis did gleme*. Cf. Henryson, *Fabillis*, ll. 868–9:

The ground wes grene, and as the gold it glemis,
With gresis growand gudelie, grit and gay.

23. *curches . . . of kirsp*: a prominent and usually valuable part of a woman's dress, often bejewelled, and covering the head or breast. Cf. *infra*, ll. 137–8; **23.** 221; *Sir Gawain and the Green Knight*, ll. 954–6:

Kerchofes of þat on, wyth mony cler perleȝ,
Hir brest and hir bryȝt þrote bare displayed,
Schon schyrer þen snawe þat schedeȝ on hilleȝ.

24. *mantillis grein*: May dress; cf. **10.** 59–60, 139, and **48.** 42. The colour was common; but it is perhaps intended here to signify freshness and sexual vigour. Cf. **10.** 86, 105, 127, 155; Douglas, *Eneados*, i, Prologue, l. 321, 'Greyn gentill ingynys and breistis curageus'; Clerk, Bannatyne MS, f. 255^{r}, l. 26, 'Thocht luve be grene in gud curage'; *infra*, l. 67 *n*.

25. *Fetrit with thair quhyt fingaris*. Cf. Geoffrey de Vinsauf, *Poetria Nova*, ll. 593–5:

Confluat in tenues digitos substantia mollis
Et macra, forma teres et lactea, linea longa
Et directa; decor manuum se jactet in illis.

27. *All full . . . flouris*. Cf. Holland, *Buke of the Howlat* (*c.* 1450; Bannatyne MS, f. 302), l. 6, 'The feildis flourischit and fret full of fairheid'.

31. *annamalit with flouris*. Cf. **10.** 250–1.

35. *ryalle cowpis*: sumptuous wine cups of gold or silver, probably with covers of the kind to be seen in the British Museum medieval collections; cf. **48.** 61–3.

36. *wlonkes*: lovely ladies. The OE epithet (splendid, fine) survived as a conventional adjective in alliterative verse; cf. *The Wars of Alexander*, l. 508, 'a worthi wedow and a wlonk'; *The Awntyrs of Arthur*, l. 347, 'wlonkest in wede'. The only substantive use recorded in *OED* prior to Dunbar is in the *Morte Arthur* (*c.* 1400), l. 3338, 'Thane I went to that wlonke, and wynly hire gretis'. But see T. Turville-Petre, *The Alliterative Revival*, 1977, p. 81. Cf. *infra*, l. 150; not otherwise used by Dunbar.

37. *wantoun*: perhaps here merely 'sportive, given to broad jesting' (cf. **10.** 175, and *infra*, l. 49 *n.*); but there is probably a suggestion too of 'given to amorous dalliance' (cf. *infra*, l. 479, and **28.** 25.

39. *wauchtit at the wicht wyne*: 'quaffed the potent wine in large draughts'. *Waucht* is a strong verb for a lady's drinking. Cf. Douglas, *Eneados*, VII. ii. 89–90, 'in flacon and in skull / Thai skynk the wyne, and wauchtis cowpis full'; and later uses by Allan Ramsay (*On seeing the Archers*, ll. 99–100, 'How hearty went these Healths about! / How blythly were they waughted out!') and Burns (*Auld Lang Syne*, l. 23, 'a right gude-willie-waught'). The exposure has now begun, with the poet, like Pepys, wondering 'to see how the ladies did tipple' (*Diary*, 23 April 1661).

41–8. *Bewrie*, etc. A *demande d'amour*; cf. *infra*, ll. 527–30.

44. *leyd*: person, man. Common in alliterative phrases; cf. Henryson, *Fabillis*, l. 2283, 'Fy on the leid that is not leill and lufit', and *The Testament of Cresseid*, l. 449, 'my face, / To luik on it, na leid now lyking hes'.

49. *ane lusty . . . lustie*: 'a fair one . . . merry'. Cf. Henryson, *The Bludy Serk*, ll. 8–11, 'A lusty lady ȝing . . . Off lusty laitis and he honour'.

51. *blis and bailfull . . . barrat*. With the alliterative pattern cf. Rolland, *The Court of Venus*, iv. 378, 'Now may I bruik with greit barret and baill'; Subdert in Bannatyne MS, f. 145^{v}, l. 19, 'Without barrett or baill'; Maitland Folio MS, p. 224, 'In baill be blyth for þat is best / In barret gif þow be bowne to byd/Lat comfort . . .; Stewart, *Chron.*, l. 2490, 'The baill, the barrat, and the daylie beir . . . of ȝoung and ald' (*DOST*).

53. *changeis ar sueit*. Cf. Erasmus, *Adagia*, I. vii. 44, 'Jucunda vicissitudo rerum', and citations.

58–63. *agane the law of luf, of kynd and of nature*, etc. These terms were commonly interchangeable; see the appendix on 'Natura, Nature and Kind' in J. A. W. Bennett, *The Parlement of Foules*, 1957. Bennett shows succinctly that 'almost all the diverse medieval conceptions of Nature find a place in our last medieval poet' Dunbar. With the Wife's sentiment here cf. **16.** 52–6. Dunbar's immediate model for complaint against the repeal of the 'golden laws of nature' was probably Lydgate's *Floure of Curtesye*, sts. 7–10:

> . . . Than thought I thus, 'Alas, what may this be,
> That euery foule hath his lyberte
> Frely to chose after his desyre
> Eueryche his make thus, fro yere to yere!
>
> The sely wrenne, the tytemose also,
> The lytel redbrest, haue free election
> To flyen yfere and togyther go
> Where as hem lyst, aboute enuyron,
> As they of kynde haue inclynacion,
> And as Nature, emperesse and gyde,
> Of euery thyng lyste to prouyde.
>
> But man alone, alas, the harde stounde,
> Ful cruelly, by kyndes ordynaunce,
> Constrayned is, and by statute bounde,
> And debarred from al suche plesaunce.
> What meneth this? What is this purueyaunce
> Of God aboue, agayne al right of kynde,
> Withoute cause so narowe man to bynde?'

The ultimate source is Ovid, *Metamorphoses*, x. 320 ff.; cf. Donne, *Elegies*, xvii. 38–49, and *The Progresse of the Soule*, ll. 191–210.

60. *bernis*. See *infra*, l. 74 *n*.

65. *weill war us*. For this usage cf. James I, *The Kingis Quair*, st. 53.

67. *curage*: (here) sexual desire, energy. Cf. *supra*, l. 24 *n*.; *infra*, ll. 188, 203, 215, 485; **32.** 11–15; and Henryson, *The Testament of Cresseid*, ll. 29–35, on remedying 'in the auld the curage doif and deid'.

69. *jolie and gent*, *richt joyus and gent*. Mackenzie emends to '. . . joyus, and gentryce', which is syntactically difficult. The repetition of 'gent' in the MS is defensible: it throws emphasis on 'richt joyus'.

70–2. *I suld at fairis*, etc. Cf. Chaucer, *CT*, III. 555–9; Lydgate, *The Pain and Sorrow of Evil Marriage*, sts. 15–16, on 'wyves . . . vnstable':

> They hem reioise to see and to be sayne,
> And to seke sondry pilgremages;
> At grete gaderynges to walken vpon the playne,
> And at staracles to sitte on hie stages . . .

Of ther nature they gretly hem delite,
With holy face fayned for the nones,
In seyntuaries ther frendes to visite,
More than for relikkes or any seyntis bones
. . . . .
To kys no shrynes, but lusty yong images;

and Lindsay, *Ane Dialogue*, ll. 2653 ff.:

. . . I haue sene pass one meruellous multytude,
ȝong men and wemen, flyngand on thare feit,
Under the forme of feynit sanctytude,
For tyll adore one Image in Loreit.
Mony came with thare marrowis for to meit,
Committand thare fowl fornicatioun . . .

On plays and pilgrimages in Scotland see Denis McKay, in McRoberts, pp. 107–9.

74. *bernis*: fellows; lovers. OE *beorn*, a warrior; used in this sense as late as Blind Hary's *Wallace*, e.g. iv. 310, vi. 652; Dunbar's **27.** 27 (satirically); and in Douglas, *Eneados*, VIII. viii. 146, etc. Usually poetic and alliterative in Scots. Dunbar uses *berne* also for 'lover'; cf. **13.** 2; *infra*, ll. 237, 429, 494.

81. *in kirk and in markat*: i.e. in every public place. So used later in Scots law and in common parlance (see *SND*, s.v. *kirk* n.[1] II. 1).

85. *A forky fure* (Maitland). This reading is difficult. Mackenzie in his glossary takes *forky* to be a variant of 'forcy(e)', 'forsy', and follows *DOST* in conjecturing that *fure* = 'man'. But although there is a similar repetition for emphasis *supra*, l. 69, the repetition of 'forsy' here seems less natural. I prefer 'forthy' (forward, enterprising, bold; cf. Rolland, *The Sevin Sages*, l. 8749, 'Alexander peirt, furthie, and masculine'). *Fure*, conjecture apart, has two established senses: 'to bear, go, fare'; 'a furrow'. Two emendations seem possible: (1) 'Ay forthy to fure'; (2) 'Ay forthy in fure'. The second part of the line has an equine image (cf. ll. 79, 114, 387), and sexual metaphors from ploughing are widespread in folk-poetry. (2) is the more attractive alternative, both in meaning and in matching the syntactical pattern of the rest of the line; but ploughing was normally done by teams of oxen, being less 'forthy' than horses. Cf. **50.** 110–12. Horses were, however, used in the plough in some parts of Scotland; Dr. D. M. Wilson, Director of the British Museum, has drawn my attention to illustrations of horse-ploughing in English manuscripts; and we have Lydgate's assurance that 'The plouh, the cart myht no thyng doo / Withouten hors dayly ye may see, / Tilthe wer lost, ne wer hors parde' (*Debate of the Horse*, st. 16).

87. *als fresche . . . May*. Cf. **10**. 58–9; Whiting, F306.

88. *burgeoun*: make to bud, grow; possibly a sexual metaphor.

89. *wobat*: the hairy oubit, caterpillar. Cf. Alexander Scott's *ȝe blindit luvaris luke* (Bannatyne MS, ff. 289–90):

> Swa ladeis will nocht sounȝe [bother
> With waistit wowbattis rottin,
> But prowdly thay will prounȝe [deck themselves
> Quhair geir is to be gottin.

The aged and repulsive husband of a young wife is a stock figure in medieval comic and satiric literature. Cf. Ovid, *Amores*, iii. 7; Boccaccio, *Decameron*, ii. 10; the detailed description of Agapes' husband in Boccaccio, *Ameto* (extracts in Bryan and Dempster, *Sources and Analogues of Chaucer's Canterbury Tales*, 1941, pp. 339–40); and Chaucer, *CT*, IV. 1818–57.

94. *carybald*: origin and sense obscure; the connotation is obviously repulsive. Cf. **23**. 184; *The Flyting between Montgomerie and Polwart* (*c*. 1585), l. 523, 'ȝon caribald, ȝone catiue execrabill'.

96. *soft . . . as the silk*: a fresh application of a poetical cliché; Whiting, S313.

101. *Mahowne*: a shortened form of 'Mahomet'; apparently taken to be a false god, a devil worshipped by heathens, hence Satan.

105. *schaik* (MF *schak*). Mackenzie emends to *schalk*, but I retain the MS reading. Mr. A. J. Aitken comments in a letter: 'as orthographic "reverse" spelling variants of *schalk* these are, though unusual, perhaps not impossible'.

108. *as a glemand gleyd*. Cf. Whiting, G152.

111. *bogill*: hobgoblin, nightly spectre; origin uncertain (cf. Welsh *bwg*, ghost; *bwgwl*, terror). Dunbar's is the first recorded use. Gavin Douglas (1513) twice takes 'bogles' with 'brownies' (*Eneados*, i, Prologue, l. 273; vi, Prologue, ll. 17–18); but Dunbar's image is perhaps clarified from Stewart's *Croniklis* (1535), l. 46888, 'Ane laithlie lene tramort . . . like ane bogill all of ratland banis'.

112. *Belȝebub*: a derogatory form (god of flies) of *Baal-zebul* (god of the lofty dwelling), a Syrian deity (2 Kgs i. 2); Satan (cf. Mark iii. 22–5, 'scribae . . . dicebant: Quoniam Beelzebub habet: et quia in principe daemoniorum ejicit daemonia. Et . . . dicebat illis: Quomodo potest Satanas Satanam ejicere?'). Cf. **23**. 533.

113–16. *And quhen . . . gillot*: 'and when the scoundrel simpers at me with his rogue's muzzle, he puts out his lower lip like a farcied (diseased) cart-horse that leers at a mare'. *Smy*: cf. Douglas, *Eneados*, xiii, Prologue, l. 131, 'Ʒa, smy, quod he, Wald thou eschape me swa?'; *smake*: cf. *Misc. Wodrow Soc.* (1844; *OED*), p. 438, 'calling them lownes, smaicks, seditious knaves'; *fepillis*: cf. *Peblis to the Play* (Maitland Folio MS, p. 161), 'He fippillit lyk ane faderles fole . . . "be still, my sweit thing" '. The emendation of *smake smolet* to *smakes molet* was proposed by E. J. Dobson and Patricia Ingham in *Medium Ævum*, xxxvi (1967), 38, taking *mol(l)et* as a diminutive of 'mull', a lip (cf. 'gull', 'gullet'; Maitland's reading at **81.** 34). Erroneous division is not uncommon; and sense apart, the alliterative stress on the final syllable is infrequent in Dunbar. With *mull/mol(l)et* cf. Scots *mulet/molet*, a mule; *infra*, l. 349; *mollet* and other words relating to bridles, etc., in *DOST*, pt. xxiv, 343.

128. *beit . . . of my mystyrs*: 'relieve . . . my sexual wants'; cf. Maitland Quarto MS, f. 27:

> Of Venus play past is the heit
> For I may not the misteris beit
> Of Meg nor Mald;
> For ane ȝoung lass I am not meit,
> I am sa auld.

nought . . . worth a bene: Whiting, B92; **73.** 23.

132. *dangerus*. See **9.** 18 *n.*, **10.** 223–8; cf. *infra*, l. 253.

135–6. *pene . . . purse*. Cf. Kennedy's use of 'pen' and 'purs' in his poem against 'mouth thankles' (the vulva) in *Maitland Folio MS*, STS, i. 365, ll. 31–2.

138. *a curche of kersp*: *supra*, l. 23 *n.*

139. *engranyt claith*: cloth dyed in cochineal, usually scarlet or crimson (cf. *infra*, l. 366; *OED*, s.v. *engrain*).

141. *rousty raid*. *OED* glosses *rousty* as 'lacking in alertness . . . through old age' (s.v. *rusty* a.[1] 5); but the metaphor may be otherwise: 'foray with a rusted weapon'. With this use of *raid* cf. *infra*, ll. 194, 391.

142. *Johne Blunt*: stupid John. Cf. **38.** 73; Lindsay, *Ane Satyre of the Thrie Estaits*, l. 1689, 'Iohne-Fule, ȝe raif'; *Kitteis Confessioun*, l. 76, 'droukin schir Johne Latynelesse'; Bannatyne MS, f. 94^r, l. 52, 'Thus said Iohine Vponland'.

146. *the semely*: ironic; cf. *infra*, ll. 150, 158 ('the plesand'). As a quasi-substantive the word has serious poetic associations: cf. the *York Mystery Plays* (ed. L. Toulmin Smith, 1885), xlvii. 6, 'And to þat semely schall ȝe saye / Off heuene I haue hir chosen quene'; *Le Morte Arthur*, ll. 636–9 (on the Maid of Astolat), 'The feyrest lady that is on

lyff . . . a semely for to see'. The tone of the following lines (147–50) is one of violence and uproar.

153. *be ȝour faith*: honestly, in truth.

155. *lif . . . spousage*. Cf. Wyntoun, *Orygynale Cronykil* (*c.* 1420), vii. 269, 'wyth hyr hys lyff / In lel spowsale he thowcht to lede'.

160–7. *With that sprang up*, etc. The voice of the second Wife rises at once into rabid 'flyting'. Cf. Dunbar's melodramatic prologue in **23.** 9 ff.

162. *ragment*: long discourse. Cf. Lindsay, *Answer to the Kingis Flyting*, l. 1, 'Redoutit Roy, your ragment I haif red'.

164. *beild*: suppurated. Cf. *infra*, l. 345; Gilbert of the Haye, *Buke of the Law of Armys*, 1456 (STS, i. 59), Caesar's 'hert rais in his breste and belit sa, that unes mycht he lest for ire'.

168. *hur maister*: frequenter of whores, 'keeper', rather than brothel-owner. Cf. *Edinburgh Burgh Records*, 1560 (iii. 65), 'Carying of the saidis bordelaris, houremaisteris, and harlottis throw the toun in ane carte' (*DOST*); Pitscottie, ii. 141, 'the bischope of Murray quhilk ever was ane hure maister all his dayis and committit huredome and adullterie . . . saying he wald nocht put away his hure'.

176. *Wes never sugeorne*, etc. 'Rest—abstinence—was never worse (more futilely) imposed than on that tired snail . . .'.

186–7. *as dotit dog*, etc. Cf. Chaucer, *CT*, X. 858 ff., 'thise olde dotardes holours [lechers], yet wol they kisse though they may nat do. . . . Certes they been lyk to houndes; for an hound, whan he comth by the roser or by othere [bushes], though he may nat pisse, yet wole he heve up his leg and make a contenauce to pisse'.

197–8. *Bot gif . . . possessoris*: 'unless he himself, some evening, might (assay) have a go at one among them; but he is not one, but *none* of those who possess sexual power'. The negative pattern in l. 198 is strongly emphatic. With this use of 'natur' cf. *supra*, l. 174, and *infra*, l. 392.

201. *geit*: jet bead. Cf. Edinburgh Testaments (Reg. House), iii. 363b, 1575, 'Counterfute perlis for masking . . . cailȝeit geit' (*DOST*).

202. *glemyng of gold . . . bot glase*. Whiting, G282.

203. *curage*. See *supra*, ll. 24, 67 *nn*.

206. *sanct Valentynis day*. The association with courtship may derive from the pagan festival (February) of Lupercalia; cf. Chaucer, *The Parlement of Foules*, ll. 680 ff.

10. *freke*: man (usually a fighting man); poetical, common in lliterative verse.

32. *geir*. See **71**. 48 *n*.

38. *that bird . . . want*: 'that girl (the 'peronall', 'bryght') would not e able to jest about *my* bliss'.

39. *amyable*: ironic; cf. *supra*, ll. 146, 158.

43. *swanquhit*: a poetical quasi-substantive contrasting with *swapit f*, 'tossed off'.

49–50. *Sa that my preching*, etc. The Wedo, like the second Wife, pens with an invocation: she promises, not invective, but a mock ermon—'soverane teching' to help the others to 'wirk eftir hir wordis' ll. 507–8). Images of, and hypocritical pretensions to piety recur in ier speech; e.g. ll. 249–50 and 251–5, 306–8, 414–50, 470–5, 97–504.

51. *schrew*. Cf. Chaucer, *CT*, IV. 2428, 'of hir tonge, a labbyng hrewe is she'.

52. *schene in my schrowd*: 'fair in my gown'; a stock alliterative hrase. Cf. *Golagros and Gawane* (*c*. 1470), l. 553, 'Schaip the evin to he schalk in thi schroud schene'.

61. *as tygris be terne*. Cf. Chaucer's advice in the *envoi* to the Clerk's ale (*CT*, IV. 1198–9), 'And sklendre wyvis . . . Beth egre as is a ygre yond in Ynde'; the Scots poem abusing women (*c*. 1500; Nat. ib. Scot. Advocates MS 1. 1. 6), ll. 15–16, 'Als terne as tygir, of ung vntollerable— / O thow violent virago vennemouss'.

62. *And be . . . brukill*: 'and be like turtle-doves in your talk, although our sexual parts are frail—yield readily'. The turtle-dove typifies onjugal affection and fidelity (cf. Lydgate, *Ballade at the Reverence of Our Lady*, st. 12; Holland, *The Buke of the Howlat*, Bannatyne MS, . 303^{r}, ll. 127–8, 'þe turture trewest / Ferme faithfull and fest'), and implicity (cf. the Chaucerian *Romaunt of the Rose*, l. 1219; Lydgate, *Reson and Sensuallyte*, ll. 5368, 5987; Tilley, D572–4). With Dunbar's use of *talis* cf. Langland, *Piers Plowman*, A. iii. 120, 'She is ykil of hire tail . . . As Commoun as þe Cartewey to knave and to lle'; *Cocke Lorelles Bote* (*c*. 1515), l. 14, 'Many whyte nonnes with vhyte vayles / That was full wanton of theyr tayles'. Generally taken s one sense of 'tail' (OE *tæȝl*, a horse's tail), i.e. the other end from the ead; but cf. Fr. *taille*, cut, division.

69. *nought worth a hen*: Tilley, H426. Cf. Chaucer, *CT*, III. 1112; he Chaucerian *Romaunt of the Rose*, l. 6856.

273. *hatit . . . like a hund*: a curious but not uncommon alliterative comparison; cf. Whiting, H585.

274. *kissing and . . . clapping*: a stock alliterative phrase. Cf. **13.** 11; *The Buik of Alexander*, ii. 1971–2, 'I am our ald to clap or kis / Maydin that ȝoung and ioly is'; Lindsay, *Ane Satyre of the Thrie Estaits*, l. 489, 'To kis hir and clap hir, sir, be not affeard'.

275. *krych*: scratch. The print reading *keyth* is not otherwise known, and is probably a paleographic error for *krych*, a variant spelling of 'critch', 'cratch' (origin obscure), to scratch (the Maitland Folio MS reads *claw*), which the context requires. The emendation was proposed by E. J. Dobson and Patricia Ingham in *Medium Ævum*, xxxvi (1967), 38.

277. *bler his ald e*: hoodwink, beguile him. Cf. **38.** 79; Chaucer, *CT*, I. 3865, 'With bleryng of a proud milleres ye'; Henryson, *Fabillis*, ll. 2040–1, 'ȝe sal se / Giff I can craft to bleir ȝone carlis ee'; Whiting, E217.

283. *I had a lufsummar leid*, etc. Cf. Chaucer, *CT*, III. 303–5.

284. *That couth . . . saif my honour*. The traditional concern for reputation. Insistence on a lover's being 'secrete and sure' is a recurrent theme in the literature of *amour courtois*: 'qui non celat, non amat'. Cf. **9.** 87–96; Chaucer, *Troilus and Criseyde*, iii. 943–4, 'So werketh now in so discret a wise / That I honour may have and he plesaunce'. This quasi-courtly language is in obvious contrast to 'my lust for to slokyn' in l. 283.

301. *Bot I . . . hert*: 'but I often thought of him till his heart grew angry'.

305. *within perfit eild*: 'before I was fully of age'.

307. *prelot*: implying that the 'curat' (properly the priest with cure of souls in the parish) has been advanced to some ecclesiastical dignity, perhaps as prior or abbot. *famous*: reputable; cf. **65.** 18.

311–12. *the severance . . . my birth noble*. Probably the Wedo is to be understood as exaggerating; she shares the Wife of Bath's pre-occupation with social status. Cf. the bastard daughter of the parson ('ycomen of noble kyn') in Chaucer's Reeve's Tale (*CT*, I. 3942–68), 'Ther dorste no wight clepen hire but "dame" '.

315–16. *mercy . . . gentill hert . . . ruth*. See **9.** 49 *n.*; *infra*, ll. 497–502 *n.*; **12.** 40–2; **74.** 55, where the use is again cynical. The sentiment in l. 316 is recurrent in Chaucer; see *CT*, I. 1761, and Robinson's note, and ibid. V. 483.

319. *durst not sit anys my summondis*: 'dares not once disregard my summons, command'. Cf. *Rauf Coilȝear*, l. 99, 'Durst scho neuer sit summoundis that scho hard him say' (so Icel. *sitjæ*). *Charge*: injunction; cf. Douglas, *Eneados*, IV. vi. 6, 'Astonyst he wes to syt sa hie a charge'.

326. *as cok that wer victour*. Cf. **32.** 8.

332. *Wer not*: 'were it not for . . .'.

337–42. *Bot quhen*, etc. Cf. Chaucer, *CT*, III. 204–14, 409–17.

338. *hie burrow landis*: high buildings on his holdings of burgh land; tenements.

344. *Mi evidentis . . . selit*: 'till the documents securing the inheritance were sealed'.

345. *beild*: swollen with rage. Cf. *supra*, l. 164 *n.*

347. *bauchlis*. The print has *bauthles*, which *DOST* is unable to gloss; but the print often confuses *c* and *t*. The vb. 'bauchill', to denounce openly, has a quasi-legal force (see quots. in *DOST*), which suggests that Dunbar's substantive *bauchlis* = documents discrediting the husband.

353–8. *Than said I*, etc. Cf. the humiliation of the husband in Chaucer, *CT*, III. 534–42.

362. *lumbart*: (Lombard) financier; often pejorative. Cf. *Colkelbie Sow* (Bannatyne MS, f. 358r), 'A lunatik, a sismatyk / An heretyk, a purspyk / A lumbard, a lolard / Ane vsurar, a bard . . .'.

366. *engranyt claight*. See *supra*, l. 139 *n.*

382. *plukit herle*: plucked heron; hunted with falcon (Chaucer, *CT*, V. 1196–7) and roasted and eaten with ginger.

384. *maid a stalwart staff . . . doune*. Cf. Chaucer, *Troilus and Criseyde*, . 740–2; Whiting, S652; and *The Buik of Alexander*, iii. 6487, 'I gadder the wande quhairof I fale', translating 'Or ai cuelli la verge dont je serai batus' (*Les Vœux du Paon*, l. 4734).

386. *hanyt*: unused; or (more strongly) held back. The main sense is to fence, enclose. Cf. Rolland, *Seven Sages*, l. 8945, 'I have not hanit to hant . . . The companie of ȝone fair ladie'.

389. *thing*: sexual parts. Cf. *infra*, l. 486; Chaucer, *CT*, III. 121; Jonson, *The Alchemist*, v. i, 'The Boy . . . with the great thing'.

391. *raid*. Cf. *supra*, ll. 141, 194.

397. *super spendit*: '(who has) laid out beyond his means'. Cf. **74.** 23.

401. *up with*: 'upward course' (Mackenzie, following *OED*); but the reference is plainly sexual: climax.

408–9. *thai wait . . . samin*: 'they believe that all evil wives are known by their dispositions and are recognized for what they are by these'.

413–21. *Adew dolour*, etc. Cf. Chaucer, *CT*, III. 587–92:

> Whan that my fourthe housbonde was on beere
> I weep algate, and made sory cheere,
> As wyves mooten, for it is usage,
> And with my coverchief covered my visage,
> But for that I was purveyed of a make,
> I wepte but smale, and that I undertake;

Henryson, *Fabillis*, ll. 509–15, 'Ceis sister off ȝour sorrow . . . Syne chant this sang, Wes never wedow sa gay!'

421. *manis daill*: sexual intercourse. Cf. Irlande, i. 78, 'in paradice þai had nocht carnale daile to giddir'.

422–39. *Quhen that I go to the kirk*, etc. See *supra*, ll. 70–2 *n*.

423. *As foxe in a lambis fleise*: proverbial (Matt. vii. 15); Whiting, W474. Cf. **74**. 37.

424–5. *my bright buke . . . ellummynit with gold*: a manuscript primer or devotional book (l. 428). The Wedo's ability to read, and her possession of such a book, are evidence of her status and wealth. On manuscript illumination in Scotland in the early sixteenth century see McRoberts, p. 215. James IV paid for 'certane bukis of illumynin gold' in 1507 (*LHTA*, iii. 278) and for 'illumnyng' his 'evangelist buke' in 1508 (ibid., iv. 41). *one my kne*: she sits on a stone bench at the side (cf. l. 440); the bulk of the congregation stand (McRoberts, p. 105).

430–1. *a bancat / In Venus chalmir*: sexual metaphors. Cf. *Blowbol's Testament* (*c*. 1508), 'He gaf me many a good certacioun . . . That he had laboured in Venus secret celle'.

432–5. *And as the new mone*, etc. Cf. Chaucer, *Troilus and Criseyde* i. 174–7:

> Nas nevere yet seyn thyng to ben preysed derre,
> Nor under cloude blak so bright a sterre
>
> As was Criseyde, as folke seyde everichone
> That hir behelden in hir blake wede.

436–43. *Quhen frendis*, etc. Cf. the Wife of Bath in *CT*, III. 587 ff.

449. *of treuth*: away from the truth.

464. *happy*: fortunate. Cf. Gilbert of the Haye, *Buke of the Law of Armys* (STS, i. 81), 'he that is nocht in the grace of God sall nocht be hardy in bataill na happy'.

465. *Hutit . . . eild*: 'derided may the guileless lass [i.e. one without 'wylis . . . in luf'] be till she is a hundred years old'.

469. *semelyar sege*. Cf. *Rauf Coilȝear*, ll. 716–17, 'Thar was seruit in that saill seigis semelie, / Mony Senȝeorabill Syre on ilk syde seir'.

474. *passing of pilgrymage*. See *supra*, ll. 70–2 *n*.

477. *othir bachilleris blith*. Cf. Holland, *Buke of the Howlat*, l. 689, 'squyeris and bachelaris blyth'.

478. *lugeing*: here a town house, residence; cf. **48.** 59.

489. *fair calling*: address, welcome. Cf. Bialacoil in the *Roman de la Rose* (Chaucerian version, ll. 2979 ff.), the Lover's 'warrant' for entry into the 'roseir'; **10.** 188 and 218.

497–502. *Thar is . . . jugis*. The salon for 'baronis and knychtis' is exposed as a brothel; and the Wedo whose social superiority to her husband was a source of discord satisfies her lust where she chooses. Cf. Sensualitie in Lindsay, *Ane Satyre of the Thrie Estaits* (ed. Kinsley, 1954, p. 49), 'And ȝit I am of nature sa towart / I lat no luiffer pas with ane sair hart'. Such passages are obscene adaptations of the portrait of Fraunchise in the *Roman de la Rose* (Chaucerian version, ll. 1211–31):

> . . . And if a man were in distresse,
> And for hir love in hevynesse,
> Hir herte wolde have full gret pite,
> She was so amiable and fre.
> For were a man for hir bistad,
> She wolde ben right sore adrad
> That she dide over-gret outrage,
> But she hym holpe his harm to aswage.
> Hir thought it elles a vylanye.

499. *lust . . . lent*. Cf. Douglas, *Eneados*, xii, Prologue, l. 200, 'Myne hart is lent apon sa gudly wight'.

500. *his lif sall not danger*: the conventional threat of the supplicating lover in *amour courtois*. Cf. **13.** 1–7; and Chaucer's parody of the stock situation in the Miller's Tale (*CT*, I. 3276–84):

> And prively he caughte hire by the queynte,
> And seyde, Ywis, but if ich have my wille,
> For deerne love of thee, lemman, I spille. . . .

502. *Sabot*: God. The Maitland Folio reading 'sall not' is a hopeless effort at emendation. I altered to 'sa God' in my 1958 edition. But E. J. Dobson and Patricia Ingham are clearly right (*Medium Ævum*, xxxvi (1967), 38–9) to retain the print reading *Sabot* as a form of 'Sabaoth' ('Dominus sabaoth', Lord of hosts; Isa. i. 9, Rom. ix. 29, Js. v. 4). The Greek and Latin forms, being indeclinable, were not

recognized as genitives, and gave rise to ME 'Lord God Sabaoth', 'oure lorde Sabaoth'. The form *Sabot* seems a confusion of 'sabaoth' and 'sab(b)ot', sabbath. See *OED*, s.vv. *sabaoth* and *sabbath*.

503. *be no lassis fundin*. Cf. *supra*, l. 465.

504. *This is the legeand . . . nane*: an ironic reference to the saint's life (*legenda*); these were collected and commonly read as part of public worship.

515. *Silver schouris . . . cristall*. Cf. **10**. 14.

527–30. *ȝe auditoris*, etc. A *demande d'amour*.

15. *Lufis Inconstance*. The stanza, made up of a repeated $a_4a_4a_4b_2$ and working throughout the poem on two rhymes, is formally close to the French *virelai* (cf. Nigel Wilkins, *One Hundred Ballades, Rondeaux and Virelais*, 1969, nos. 24, 25, 34).

13. *new*: changeable, given to novelty. Cf. **10**. 220–2.

16. *The Merle and the Nychtingall*. For an account of the medieval literary debate in Latin see H. Walther, *Das Streitgedicht in der lateinischen Literatur des Mittelalters*, 1920; Raby, *SLP*, ii. 282 ff. Disputations between or among birds are common enough in medieval French and English literature; see the introductions to *The Owl and the Nightingale*, the most notable bird *débat* in English, ed. J. W. H. Atkins (1922) and E. G. Stanley (1960). Dunbar probably knew Lydgate's *The Churl and the Bird*; and he may have known Sir Thomas Clanvowe's *Cuckoo and Nightingale* (*c*. 1403), a *débat* on love between two birds in a May landscape. But this is a 'Book of Cupid God of Love' and has no religious reference (Chaucer, *Works*, ed. W. W. Skeat, vii, 1897). For other didactic birds in medieval Scots see the Bannatyne MS, ff. 44r–45r ('Furth throw ane forrest as I fure') and ff. 53r–55r ('Walking allone amang thir levis grene', on 'Man mend thy lyfe and restoir wrangus geir'). Cf. **59**. For the stanza see **4**.

The Maitland Folio MS omits ll. 17–32; and the two manuscripts may have had different sources. Maitland is inferior: there are lines metrically or otherwise defective (7, 9, 42, 49, 52, 74, 92); there are hints of scribal simplification (38, 59, 62, 78); and there are nonsensical readings at ll. 36, 58, 77, 78.

1–2. *Aurora . . . With cristall ene*: the rosy-fingered Dawn who opens the gates of the east and chases Nox and Somnus before her (l. 2) and scatters the dew; she has snowy eyelids. Cf. **1**. 36–40, **10**. 5, 14–18, **50**. 9–10, **54**. 1–2.

3. *merle*: blackbird. For the association of this bird with May cf. Henryson, *The Testament of Cresseid*, ll. 425–30; Bannatyne MS, f. 218r:

> Quhen Flora had ourfret þe firth
> In May of every moneth quene,
> Quhen merle and mavis singis with mirth
> Sueit melling in þe schawis schene,
> Quhen all luvaris reiosit bene . . .

4. *comfortable*: pleasant, delightful. Cf. Lindsay, *Deploratioun*, st. 18, silk and gold, in cullouris comfortabill'.

5. *blisfull . . . lawry*: not apparently significant here. The laurel is the emblem of martial or poetic distinction and immortality; cf. *The Flower and the Leaf*, ll. 267–73, 302–17, and esp. 505–18 (Chaucer, *Works*, ed. W. W. Skeat, vii, 1897). The bird in Lydgate, *The Churl and the Bird*, sings from a 'fressh laurer'.

13. *A nychtingall.* Popular with poets, this bird was presumably no more familiar north of the English midlands in Dunbar's day than it is now. The description in l. 14 suggests that Dunbar had not seen the nightingale (though it *does* sing by day as well as by night). Dunbar celebrates Christian love through the bird traditionally associated most closely with erotic love. Cf. James I, *The Kingis Quair*, sts. 54 ff.; E. K. Chambers in *Early English Lyrics*, 1907, p. 270: 'The nightingale, indeed, plays a conspicuous part in all this [Provençal] poetry. His song is the symbol of amorous passion, and he himself is appealed to as the confidant and adviser of lovers, the go-between who bears messages from heart to heart.'

17–19. *With notis glaid*, etc. Cf. Lydgate, *The Churl and the Bird*, st. 11:

> It was a verray heuenly melodie
> Euen and morwe to here the briddis song.
> And the soote sewgred armonye
> Of vncouth warblis and tewnes drawe along,
> That al the gardeyn of the noise rong.

25. *Of ȝung sanctis . . . faill.* Cf. *Middle English Sermons* (EETS, . 159), 'Itt is a comond proverbe bothe of clerkes and of laye men, younge seynt, old dewell". And so thei arn disceyveyd . . .'.

8. *makis on*: makes one, agrees.

4–5. *That him . . . succour*: Gen. i. 26–7, 'Et ait: Faciamus hominem d imaginem et similitudinem nostram . . .'; Preface for Easter (*Sarum Missal*, p. 213), 'Ipse enim verus est agnus qui abstulit peccata mundi. Qui mortem nostram moriendo destruxit et vitam resurgendo reparavit.'

47. *He is . . . paramour*: a not uncommon figure. Cf. the *Legends of the Saints* (STS, l. 1118), 'My dere lord Ihesu Criste . . . þat is my luf and paramor'.

70. *God bad . . . splene*: Deut. vi. 5, 'Diliges dominum Deum tuum ex toto corde tuo'; Matt. xxii. 37. Cf. **17**, refrain.

77. *goldin tressit hairis*. Cf. **14.** 19–22 *n.*

78. *Appollois*: of the god of light. Cf. **4.** 21–2 *n.*

85. *Luve . . . bissines*. Cf. **9.** 60.

17. *Trew Luve*. The contrast and conflict between fleshly and spiritual love are inevitably common themes in medieval literature. See Chaucer, *Troilus and Criseyde*, v. 1835–55 and Robinson's note; cf. Gower, *Confessio Amantis*, viii. 3138–72; **16.** Six-line stanzas are uncommon; this one combines two triplets (the second made up of a linking line and a couplet refrain). Cf. **43.**

3. *Now culit is dame Venus brand*. For the figure of Venus' torch or fire cf. the Chaucerian *Romaunt of the Rose*, ll. 3705 ff.; Chaucer, *Troilus and Criseyde*, i. 436, 445, 490, and *CT*, IV. 1723–8:

> And Venus laugheth upon every wight
> . . . . .
> And with hire fyrbrond in hire hand aboute
> Daunceth biforn the bryde and al the route.

On the 'cooling' of this fire cf. Henryson, *The Testament of Cresseid*, ll. 29–33:

> Thocht lufe be hait, ȝit in ane man of age
> It kendillis nocht sa sone as in ȝoutheid,
> Of quhome the blude is flowing in ane rage;
> And in the auld the curage doif and deid
> Of quhilk the fyre outward is best remeid . . .

6. *trew luve rysis fro the splene*. See **16.** 70 *n.*

8. *Trew . . . bauld*. Cf. *Rauf Coilȝear*, l. 222, 'ane bricht fire was byrnand full bald'; *Legends of the Saints*, x. 469, 'the fyre that bald can byrne'.

22. *the quarrell to sustene*. Cf. the French jousting term, 'soutenir la gageure'.

39, 56, 62. *denger*: disdain. See **9.** 18 *n.*; cf. **10.** 223–8, **13.** 6.

57. *I sett nocht by a bene*: proverbial; Whiting, B82–B92.

64. *mercy*: the divine mercy replacing the 'feynit' mercy of a mistress (cf. **14.** 315–16, 497–502, *nn.*).

67–8. *Unquyt . . . vane*: 'I neither do nor say anything unrewarded, nor do I expend a thought of love in vain'.

88. *in flouris grene*: in the flourishing time of life. Cf. Douglas, *King Hart*, l. 705, 'Strenth said, Now I am grene and in my flouris'; Rolland, *Seven Sages*, l. 4125, '. . . in my flouris of ȝouthheid blumand grene'.

III

POEMS OF COURT LIFE

18. *To the King.* This is probably an early poem—fresh, light-hearted, optimistic—in anticipation of James's generosity to his court on Handsel Monday (*han(d)sel*, a good-luck gift, especially one given at the beginning of the year). New Year poems were popular in France; Janet Smith cites Deschamps, *Balade qui parle des estraines du jour de l'an*, and a number of *étrennes* from Christine de Pisan to noble patrons (p. 65). Cf. Lydgate, *Ballade* 'on a new-year's gift of an eagle, presented to King Henry VI':

> . . . Moste noble Prynce, which in especyal
> Excelle alle oþer, as maked is memorye,
> Þis day beo gif to youre estate ryal,
> As I sayde erst, honnour, conquest, victorye—
> Lyche as þis egle haþe presented to your glorye . . .

The stanza (aabb_4 with refrain) is the French *kyrielle*, and one of Dunbar's commonest; cf. **24, 25, 29, 30, 39, 47, 52C, 59, 62, 67, 68, 83.**

1. *My prince in God.* Mackenzie wrongly inserts a comma after *prince*; but see *DOST*, prep. *in*, 6c.

18. *Fraunce crownes*: the French gold *écu*, worth about two-thirds of a pound Scots; cf. *Acts of the Parliaments of Scotland*, 33b (1451), 'the crown of France hauand a crowned flowre-deluce on ilk side of the scheild'.

19. *To the King.* Perhaps the earliest of Dunbar's petitions to James IV. The witty begging poem addressed to a noble patron is common in medieval literature; there are examples in the work of Machaut, Deschamps, and Froissart, and Dunbar probably knew Chaucer's *Complaint to his Purse* (*envoi* addressed to Henry IV) and Lydgate's *Letter to Gloucester*, 'Riht myhty prynce':

> Tokne of mornyng, weryd clothys blake,
> Cause my purs was falle in gret rerage,
> Lynyng outward, his guttys wer out shake,
> Oonly for lak of plate and of coignage . . .

Cf. E. R. Curtius, *European Literature in the Latin Middle Ages*, 1953, Excursus vii; K. J. Holzknecht, *Literary Patronage in the*

Middle Ages (1923; rpt. 1966), esp. pp. 94 ff. (on commissioned ʼriting in England and Scotland, with Lydgate 'about as near the rofessional poet as is found in the Middle Ages'), 170 ff. ('rewards'), nd 191 ff. (the 'epistle mendicant', with notable examples from ʼhaucer, Hoccleve, and Lydgate). But Dunbar is far from typical. 1) His services to James seem to have been (*a*) sacerdotal (perhaps as onfessor and mentor, occasionally writing hymns or devotional oetry for court use); (*b*) diplomatic or secretarial. He was in England 1 1501, probably in connection with negotiations for the royal etrothal (Baxter, p. 85), and seems to have been a member of a iission to Denmark (**23**). It is perhaps to service of this kind that)unbar refers in **42**. 1–3, **43**. 9–10, **44**. 67 ff. Only occasionally does e claim recompence as a poet (cf. **42**. 46–50, **44**. 25 ff.); and nowhere oes he reflect the bardic tradition of the Celts, where reward was xpected not merely for the well-wrought lay but also for the cele-ration of the deeds and virtues of a noble house (see J. E. Caerwyn Villiams, *Proc. Brit. Academy*, lvii (1971), 87 ff.). (2) There is no ecord of general literary service to the king, in, e.g., translation: one r two poems celebrate court occasions in the high style, and a number ncluding **23**) were probably written for James's entertainment, but)unbar seems for the most part to have written out of his own moods ıd concerns. (3) There is almost nothing of the poetical excercise in ıese petitions—little encomium and no flattery (cf. **51**. 66–70):)unbar claims what he thinks is due to long service and merit, and es his own neglect as a manifestation—intensely felt—of an unjust ıd corrupt court.

The stanza ($aabab_4$ with refrain) is identified by Schipper as an ometrical tail-rhyme stanza shortened by one verse (*History of English ersification*, 1910, pp. 308–9), one of Dunbar's commonest forms: . **32**, **33**, **40**, **42**, **56**, **63**, **64**, **66**, **70**, **73**, **78**, **79**, **80**, **81**, **82**.

Sanct salvatour: i.e. Christ, to whom the collegiate church at St. ndrews, where Dunbar may have been educated, was dedicated in ıe 1450s. *send silver sorrow*: an imprecation against silver.

2. *cors*: coin with a cross on one side.

). *Aganis the Solistaris in Court*. The metre is the OF *vers octosyllabe* ought into English poetry through Anglo-Norman.

solistationes: petitions, devices for attracting royal attention.

Sum singis . . . storyis. On entertainers at court see *LHTA*, i. lix ff.

moryis: 'Moorish' dance performed in the guise of blackamoors or otesques (Flem *mooriske dans*, F *danse moresque*); sometimes—in

England at any rate—incorporating a hobby-horse, Robin Hood, et (Joseph Strutt, *The Sports and Pastimes of the People of England*, 183 pp. 223–4, 254). Royal payments are recorded in 1501–2 and 1503– for instance, 'to the men that brocht in the morice dance, and to tha menstralis', and 'to Colin Campbell and his marowis that brocht in th moris dauns' (*LHTA*, ii. 135, 414).

12. *with aw*: withal, along with the rest.

21. *The Magryme.* The stanza is a variant of the common form aaba (see **19**); cf. **41, 46, 58, 69.**

6–10. *And now . . . distress.* Cf. Douglas, *Eneados*, i, Prologue, l 19–22: 'Quhy suld I than with dull forhed and vayn, / With rud engyne and barrand emptyve brayn . . . Presume to write'. *Schir* James IV. *in my heid behind*: in the third cell of the brain (memory The middle cell was reason's, and the front fantasy's (cf. Chaucer, *CT* I. 1376).

14. *din nor danceing nor deray.* Cf. *Chrystis Kirk on the Grene*, ll. 1– 'Was nevir in Scotland hard nor sene / Sic dansing nor deray'; Dougla *Eneados*, XIII. viii. 75–7, 'Than ioy and myrth, with dansyng an deray, / Full mery noys and sovndis of gam and play / Abuf the brygh starnys hie vpwent'.

22. *The Dregy of Dunbar . . . Strivilling.* During Lent James I often retired to the Franciscan Observant house he had built Stirling (Mackie, pp. 117, 154, 231). *Dirige* ('dregy') is the openin word of the antiphon at matins in the Office of the Dead (Ps. v. 'Dirige, Deus meus, in conspectu tuo viam meam'); Dunbar's poem an epistolary parody—and its ending an adaptation—of parts of th office, contrasting the purgatorial austerities of the Franciscans wit the celestial delights of the court at Edinburgh. The poet and h fellows are represented as an apostle and a heavenly choir. The parod begins at l. 29. The office had vespers, matins (with three nocturn each with three psalms and three lessons), and lauds. Dunbar's *lection* are three prayers to the 'saitt celestiall', each with a choral respons

Parody of divine offices and of prayers and creeds was a commo diversion in the later Middle Ages. In Latin there are, for instanc the *officium lusorum* (an elaborate parody of the Mass) and oth profane lyrics in the *Carmina Burana* (Raby, *SLP*, ii. 277–8); i French, the Mass was perverted to the celebration of Venus in Jean d Condé's *Messe des Oiseaux*. Smith (p. 68) draws attention to fifteent century parodies, *La Paternostre des Verollez*, *La Paternostre d Angloys*, *Letanie des bons Compaignons*, *De Profundis des Amoreu*

Cf. W. A. Neilson, *The Origins and Sources of the Court of Love*, 1899, pp. 220–7.

The poem is in paragraphed couplets. The responses are in French *triolet* form, eight lines set as four, with the first line repeated as a fourth and ll. 1–2 repeated as 7–8.

18. *stok and stone*: alliterative tag; cf. Chaucer, *Troilus and Criseyde*, iii. 589 (properly idols of wood and stone).

19–28. *Out of ȝour panefull purgatory*, etc. Cf. *infra*, ll. 106–11 *n.*

31. *the ordouris nyne*. See **1**. 9–16 *n.*

32–5. *And all . . . joy and blis*. Cf. the antiphon in the burial service, 'In paradysum deducant te angeli in suum conuentum suscipiant te martyres et perducant te in ciuitatem sanctam Ierusalem' (*Sarum Missal*, p. 447).

38, 58. *Say . . . cheritie*: versicle followed by response, probably echoing Ps. xl. 11 (third nocturn at matins in the Office of the Dead), 'Tu autem Domine ne longe facias miserationes tuas a me: misericordia tua et veritas tua semper susceperunt me'.

43, 63. *Iube Domine benedicere*: from the Ordinary of the Mass, before the Gospel (*Sarum Missal*, p. 218).

45. *Patriarchis*: Abraham, Isaac, Jacob, and Jacob's twelve sons (Gen. xii ff.; cf. Acts vii. 8 and Heb. vii. 4).

51. *cran*: now a rare migrant from E. Europe, but common in marshland in Britain until the seventeenth century. Cf. *LHTA*, i. 182, ii. 132; **53**. 24; Pitscottie, i. 337, Atholl's banquet for James V.

52. *every fische that swymis in rever*. 'It is impossible to describe the immense quantity of fish. The old proverb says already *piscinata Scotia*. Great quantities of salmon, herring, and . . . stock fish, are exported. The quantity is so great that it suffices for Italy, France, Flanders, and England' (John Major, *De Gestis Scot.*, 1518; G. Gregory Smith, *The Days of James IV*, 1890, pp. 61–2).

55. *clairettis*. See **44**. 42 *n.*

56. *Angers and . . . Orliance*: Angers and Orléans, on the Loire.

59. *Sanct Jeill*: S. Giles (Aegidius), patron saint of beggars; to him the High Kirk in Edinburgh is dedicated. Cf. Lindsay, *Ane Satyre of the Thrie Estaits*, ed. Kinsley, 1954, p. 176: '*Pauper*: I pray to God and sweit Sanct Geill . . .'.

66. *the sterris sevin*: the Pleiades. Cf. Lydgate, *Troy Book*, ii. 3323, 'Pliades, þe sevene sterris briȝt'; Douglas, *Eneados*, viii, Prologue, ll.

150–1, 'The Pleuch, and the polys, the planettis began, / The sun, the Sevyn Starnys, and the Charl Wayn . . .'.

74. *Sanct Gabriell*: archangel; the messenger of divine comfort.

97–8. *Et ne nos inducas . . . illius*: petitions from the *Pater noster*.

99–100. *Requiem . . . eiis*. Cf. the opening antiphon in the Mass for the Dead, 'Requiem eternam dona eis Domine, et lux perpetua luceat eis' (*Sarum Missal*, p. 431).

101–2. *A porta . . . corpora eorum*. Cf. the versicle and response at vespers (Office of the Dead), 'Requiem eternam. V. A porta inferi. ℟. Erue Domine animas eorum'.

103–4. *Credo . . . viventium*. Parodying Ps. xxvii. 13, 'Credo videre bona Domini in terra viventium'; antiphon in the second nocturn at matins in the Office of the Dead, and versicle and response in the burial service (*Sarum Missal*, pp. 446, 450).

106–11. *Deus qui . . . Strivilling*: 'God, who deigns to free the just and humble in heart from all their tribulation, free your servants who live in the town of Stirling from its pains and sorrows, and bring them to the joys of Edinburgh that Stirling may be at rest'. Cf. the alternative prayer at vespers in the Office of the Dead (*in die depositionis defuncti*): 'Deus, cui proprium est misereri semper . . . jubeas eam a sanctis angelis suscipi, et ad patriam paradisi perduci; ut . . . non poenas inferni sustineat, sed gaudia aeterna possideat.'

23. *The Flyting of Dunbar and Kennedie*. This is the earliest surviving example of a 'flyting'—a blend of primitive literary criticism and lampoon apparently popular in fifteenth- and sixteenth-century Scotland. It is not the only evidence of lively dispute among Scotch literati: Dunbar rails against Mure, who 'indorsit myn indyting / With versis off his awin hand wryting' (**26**), and Gavin Douglas in his *Eneados* (STS, iv. 192) remarks 'detractouris intil every place' who 'or evir thai reid the wark, byddis byrn the buke'. Few other 'flytings' have survived: James V 'flyted' Sir David Lindsay (Lindsay, *Works*, STS, i. 101), and Montgomerie and Polwart's *Flyting* is cited by James VI in *Ane Schort Treatise*, 1584 (STS, i. 81), to illustrate '*Rouncefallis* or *Tumbling* verse' for 'flyting or Inuectiues'—which may point to an established fashion. The antecedents of the form are obscure. Suggested models closest to Dunbar in time and place include the Provençal *sirvente* and *tenso* (*dèbat*; see **16**) and *partimen* (*jeu-parti*); see Smith, pp. 51–7, for a cautious argument in favour of Continental influence; cf. E. K. Chambers on the 'minstrel repertory' in *The Medieval Stage*, 1903, i. 79–81. Dunbar may well have known he invectives of the Italian humanist Poggio Bracciolini (1380–1459) gainst Filelfo and Lorenzo Valla, named among the poets in Gavin)ouglas, *Palice of Honour* (*c.* 1501), ll. 1232–3: 'And Poggius stude vith mony girne and grone / On Laurence Valla spittand and cryand y!' Skelton was probably also writing in a Continental tradition in his xchanges with Garnesche (*c.* 1515), although Maurice Pollet reads hese (*John Skelton*, 1971, p. 76) as imitations of Scotch 'flyting'; and here is a Latin tradition in invective from S. Jerome to Dunbar's ontemporary Erasmus.

Whether or not Dunbar was directly influenced by Continental nodels, it seems very unlikely that the 'flyting' style and vocabulary ised here, rhetorically mature and assured, and linguistically rich and aried, are his invention. Kennedy and his 'cousing Quintene' (l. 34) ad 'ane thing . . . compild', which apparently was not only a 'bost' ll. 3, 6) but 'bakbytting' (l. 22); and it is Kennedy, not Dunbar, who as the first brutally accomplished innings in the *Flyting*. It may be lausibly argued that Kennedy (and probably Quintene) wrote not out f Continental but out of Gaelic tradition. Dunbar associates the ubious craft of 'flyting' with bards (ll. 17–21, 49, 120); and although is pejorative use of *ba(i)rd* is reflected in early acts against vagabond ninstrels ('bardis, or sic lik utheris rynnaris aboute', 'sornaris, bardis, naisterfull beggaris or fenȝeit fulys'; 1449, 1457, *Acts of the Parlia-nents of Scotland*, 1814–75, ii. 36 and 51), there is some evidence that oards' were specifically associated with invective. Cf. *infra*, ll. 105–8; Iolland, *The Buke of the Howlat* (*c.* 1450), l. 811, 'The bard . . . itterlye coud ban'; *Aberdeen Ecclesiastical Records*, 1562, 'All com-noun skoldis, flyttaris, and bardis to be baneist'; the translation of ON *kāld*, a poet, into English *scold*. In Holland's *Buke of the Howlat* (ll. 91–804) the Rook comes as 'a bard out of Irland with "banachadee" God's blessing]', speaking a gallimaufry of Scots and Gaelic, citing he Irish kings and threatening to *ryme* (Asloan MS; Bannatyne MS, ryve') if he is denied food and drink. Cf. Spenser, *View of the Present tate of Ireland*, 1596, 'None dare displease [the Bardes] for feare to unne into reproch throughe their offence, and to be made infamous in he mouthes of all men'; J. E. Caerwyn Williams, in *Proc. Brit. Academy*, lvii (1971), 116–17. The Celtic associations were still live 1 1574, when an Act was passed that 'na Irische and hieland bairdis nd beggaris be brocht . . . in the lawland' (*Acts*, iii. 89). The practice f satire by Gaelic bards, in both Ireland and Scotland, is old. Alter-ations between poets go well back in tradition, and the *aoir*, a poetical ıvective, survived from the medieval Irish period down to modern mes. The *Flyting* of Dunbar and Kennedy 'is as typical of the *aoir* as ny Gaelic example could be' (James Ross, 'A Classification of Gaelic

Folk-Song', *Scottish Studies*, i (1957), 119–21 and 149; cf. John MacInnes, 'The Oral Tradition in Scottish Gaelic Poetry', ibid. xii (1968), 33–40). The *Flyting* indeed 'reflects a common human resort under passion to improvised abuse' (Mackenzie, p. xxxii); Mackenzie illustrates the 'psychology' of the genre from a novel of 1931, and a jocular but freely abusive 'flyting' habit between a Scot and an Englishman in Burma in the Second World War is recorded in J. H. Williams, *Elephant Bill*, 1950, ch. 13. But the poetic mode of satire exemplified in the *Flyting* probably came into the Scottish court from Gaelic tradition before the time of Dunbar.

The *Flyting* may have been developed in a series of attacks and counter-attacks circulated in manuscript at court; it may, at least in its final form, have been recited before the king as a stylized duel in verse. As it has survived, it consists of Dunbar's initial challenge (ll. 1–24), Kennedy's counter-challenge (ll. 25–48), and a sustained piece of invective from each poet (ll. 49–248, 249–552). The stanza ($ababbccb_5$) is not used elsewhere in Dunbar's extant poems. Alliterative four-stress patterns are interwoven with the syllabic metre, and the last stanzas of each poet's main contribution (ll. 233–48, 545–52) have additional internal rhyme. There is in Dunbar's sections an astonishing variety of language: melodramatic rhetoric, a 'langage rude' of calculated harshness and fine precision in the caricature of Kennedy, and a wildly vituperative climax which is just as much a *tour de force* in diction as any passage in the 'aureate' poems. For a discussion of Schipper's unnecessary but at one time influential rearrangement of the text of the *Flyting*—an exercise in 'arbitrary ingenuity'—see Baxter, Appendix VI.

I have followed the Chepman and Myllar print from l. 316, where the fragment begins, as the version contemporary with (and possibly overseen by) Dunbar. For the first part of the poem I have followed Bannatyne, which is not only more legible than the Maitland Folio, but is properly ordered. Maitland's scribe took his text from a copy which had two leaves interchanged (ll. 65–128, 129–192), and so got these sets of stanzas in the wrong order; and when Reidpeth copied the MS he added further confusion (see W. A. Craigie, *The Maitland Folio Manuscript*, STS, ii. 69–70). Sequence apart, the differences between these two main MSS are numerous; and the many variants in Bannatyne against the Chepman and Myllar print suggest that the first part of the Bannatyne version (ll. 1–315) too was not copied, however carelessly, from the lost opening of the print. Bannatyne is not at all points superior to Maitland—sometimes weaker in diction or metre and sometimes obviously erroneous. Generally, however, the Maitland Folio MS is inferior to Bannatyne: weaker rhetorically or in metre

explicable; and Dunbar says only that the voyage was stormy, not that he was off course. I read the stanza as an account of a rough, dark voyage from northern Holland up the west coast of Jutland and round into the Kattegat past Zealand; and thereafter to the south of Norway on the return journey—the destination being Denmark, with which Scotland at this time had active diplomatic relations. Dr. Karl Sandred of Uppsala supports my identification of *Ȝetland* with Jutland.

99. *gluntoch with thy giltin hippis*: (a) bare-kneed (Highlander) with your yellowed hips (Gael *glùn*, knee; Mackenzie).

104. *Thy bawis . . . breik.* The kilted Highlander has no *breik*; cf. *infra*, l. 119.

105. *of all the warld reffuse.* Cf. Chaucer, *Troilus and Criseyde*, i. 570, 'That am refus of every creature'.

106–12. *Quhat ferly is*, etc. A clear enough statement that 'flyting' is a Celtic craft. See **10.** 259 *n*.

109. *fair indyte*: the high 'aureate' style. Cf. **10.** 262–70.

112. *Carrik*: the southern district of Ayrshire, largely Gaelic-speaking until the Reformation. See W. L. Lorimer, 'The Persistence of Gaelic in Galloway and Carrick', *Scottish Gaelic Studies*, vi (1949), 114–36; John MacQueen, 'The Gaelic Speakers of Galloway and Carrick', *Scottish Studies*, xvii (1973), 17–33.

113. *leid ane doig to skomer.* Cf. *Master of Game* (*c.* 1400), xx, 'teche þe childe to leede þe houndes to scombre twyse on þe daye' (*OED*).

123–6. *For he . . . flaid.* A tradition passed down from S. Ambrose has it that S. Laurence, commanded by the Roman prefect to hand over the Church's treasure, distributed it among the poor with 'These are the treasure of the Church', and was martyred by roasting on a gridiron. There is a fresco of his life and martyrdom in the Church of S. Lorenzo in Rome. There are frescos in England at Abbots Langley and Frindsbury. *sanct Johnis ene*: almost certainly a reference to John the Baptist. The notion that he was blindfolded before being beheaded may be an echo of the blindfolding of Christ. In the Luttrell Psalter (*c.* 1340; BM Add. MS 42130, f. 53^{v}) S. John is represented at his prison window, before his executioner, with a head-dress; and alongside is a grotesque wearing a wimple. Bellenden, in his translation of Boece's *History* (*c.* 1531), repeats the traditional story that the English, not approving the preaching of Augustine of Canterbury, 'sewit fische talis on his abilȝeament. Vtheris allegis þai dang him with skaitt rumpillis . . . God tuke on þame sic vengeance þat þay and all þair posterite had lang talis mony ȝeris eftir'. *Scotichronicon*, ix. 32. S. Bartholomew is said to have been flayed alive at Albanopolis in Armenia, and then crucified. He is portrayed carrying a knife, and sometimes with a human skin over one arm. Cf. the Luttrell Psalter, ff. 107v and 108r; Berenson, *Italian Pictures*, 1932, p. 242; O. Sirén, *Giotto*, 1917, ii, pl. 194. With l. 124 cf. *Legends of the Saints*, STS, ii. 251, 'Dowchtir . . . lene me þi curch to heile me, / Till þat myn hewid of strikin be'.

128. *ane haggeis*: the first Scotch reference to this variety of pudding, apparently popular in England in the fifteenth century. It derives much of its emblematic virtue from Burns's *Address*. For an eighteenth-century recipe see Burns, *Poems and Songs*, ed. Kinsley, 1968, iii. 1221–2. Dunbar seems to disparage the haggis as peasant fare. On the *hungry gled* see **42**. 13 *n*.

129. *na man comptis the ane kers*: proverbial; Whiting, C546.

130. *swappit*: whopping, great big (?).

131. *kis his ers*: an act of homage, in mimicry of the witchrite of kissing the Devil's arse (*osculum infame*). Cf. **33**. 23; the comedy of the contractual kiss in Lindsay, *Ane Satyre of the Thrie Estaits*, ed. Kinsley, 1954, p. 115; *Gammer Gurton's Needle*, 1575, II. i. 68 ff.

133. *skaffis*: scrounge. Perhaps from the Du and G *schaffen*, to procure food; brought in by soldiers from Continental campaigns.

139. *senȝie*: war-cry. See *DOST*, s.v. *ensenȝe*. Cf. Barbour, *Brus*, xv. 497, 'Than his ensenȝe he can hye cry'; Douglas, *King Hart*, l. 222, 'Thay cryit on hicht thair seinȝe wounder lowde'. Dunbar's use of the formula is ironic: he will display Kennedy in his 'true colours' in what follows.

143. *wathemanis weid*: outlaw's dress (*waith*, hunting). Cf. **54**. 8; *The Murning Maiden*, ll. 64–9 (Maitland Folio MS, p. 303):

In waithman weyd Sen I ȝow find
In this wod walkand ȝour alone
Ȝour mylk quhyt handis we sall bind
Quhill that the blude burst fra the bone
Chargeand ȝow to prwsoun
To the kingis deip dwngoun . . .

145. *Ersche katherene*: Highland reiver. Cf. **10**. 259, **52**. 113–14 *nn*. *rilling*. Cf. Blind Hary, *Wallace*, i. 215–19, 'Thow Scot . . . Ane Ersche mantill it war thi kynd to wer . . . Rouch rewlyngis apon thi harlot fete'.

149–52. *Fowll heggirbald . . . damis. heggirbald* is obscure; the image in ll. 150–2 is of a predatory fox or wolf.

154. *Ane laithly luge . . . menis*: identified by editors as the house of Glentig (Tig Water is a tributary of the River Stinchar in Carrick);

according to Paterson (*Life and Poems of Dunbar*, 1860, p. 24), acquired by Kennedy from John Wallace in 1504. But the transaction is not documented (see Baxter, pp. 75–6), and there is no evidence of Glentig having been a leper-house. Dunbar is probably romancing; Kennedy's reply (*infra*, ll. 361–7) has the ring of truth about it.

158. *dowsy*. Cf. More (1529), 'Beeing so dowsie drunke, that he could neither stande nor reele' (*OED*).

161. *lazarus*: here not (as commonly) a leper (Luke xvi. 20; cf. Henryson, *Testament of Cresseid*, ll. 343, 531), but a resurrected corpse (John xi. 17, 43–4); n.b. *tramort*, and cf. ll. 167, 175–6.

164–5. *For hiddowis, haw . . . ble*. Cf. Henryson, *Testament of Cresseid*, ll. 337–41.

171. *lyk ane saffrone bag*: orange-red, yellow. Saffron was used for colouring, flavouring, and medicinally. Cf. Whiting, S11; *infra*, l. 191.

172. *spreit of Gy*: the spirit of Guido de Corvo, which haunted his widow and was ultimately exorcized by four Dominican friars (*Scotichronicon*, xiii. 6–9; Mackenzie).

184. *carrybald*. See **14.** 94 *n*.

187. *Reistit . . . hill*. Cf. *supra*, l. 51.

188. *beswakkit . . . tyd*. Cf. Douglas, *Eneados*, I. iii. 22–3, 'Heich as a hill the iaw of watir brak / And in ane hepe cam on thame with a swak'.

192. *clowis*: 'the dried flower-bud of *Caryophyllus aromaticus*, much used as a pungent aromatic spice' (*OED*).

193. *wirling*. Origin unknown; but cf. *The Wars of Alexander* (1400/1450), l. 1733, 'A selly noumbre of wrichis and wirlingis' (*OED*).

194. *the hurle behind*: diarrhoea. Cf. Stewart in the Bannatyne MS, f. 140v, 'They haif the hurle ay behind / The stynk that thay mak in the wind / Will Flanderis infeck'.

196. *gers on grund or leif on lind*. Burlesque application of common alliterative phrases.

199. *Thy gulsoch gane . . . bind*. I take this metaphor of a jaundiced face bound to Kennedy's back as a grotesque way of saying that his jaundice has run into a flux. Cf. *Gilbert of the Haye's Prose Manuscript* (1456; STS, ii. 139), 'Wateris of pulis and dubbis . . . engenderis evill collis [bilious humours] that byndis mannis body and mistemperis it . . .'.

205. *rubbit quheit*: wheat rubbed in the hands to extract the grain. Cf. *supra*, ll. 116–17.

209. *Strait Gibbonis air.* In 1503 a payment was made to 'Strait [stingy] Gibbon' by royal command; *LHTA*, ii. 395. He was possibly a court jester.

211. *Edinburgh cors.* See **75.** 22 *n.*

212. *hard as horne.* Cf. Lydgate, *The Assembly of the Gods*, l. 618; Whiting, H481.

217. *as beis owt thrawis*: a stock simile. Cf. Chaucer, *CT*, III. 1693, 'Right so as bees out swarmen from an hyve'; Whiting, B117.

218. *our awin queir clerk.* Cf. *infra*, l. 417 *n.*

219. *lyk ane howlat chest with crawis.* Cf. **54.** 69 ff.

221. *Keip curches in the merk*: 'hide your finery'; see **14.** 23 *n.*

225. *gild.* Cf. Douglas, *Eneados*, I. xi. 107–8 (transl. Virgil's l. 747), 'The gyld and ryot Tyrryanys dowblit for ioy, / Syne the rerd followit of the ȝonkeris of Troy'.

233. *Mahoun.* See **14.** 101 *n.*

236. *rare*: i.e. in lamentation; cf. Barbour, *Brus*, v. 97; Douglas, *Eneados*, V. xi. 26, 'al togiddir gan to weip and rair'. *defowll*: the literal sense is of trampling underfoot; cf. *Brus*, ii. 359; Kennedy, *The Passioun of Crist*, l. 444 (*Devotional Pieces*, p. 22).

241. *Hilhous*: an obscure allusion to Sir John Sandilands of Hillhouse near Edinburgh.

243. *Chittirlilling. DOST* glosses 'obscure term of abuse'; but probably a playful variant (for rhyming) of *chitterling*, pig's guts (cf. l. 241, *mauch muttoun*).

244. *rehator.* See also l. 401. Origin and meaning obscure; but cf. Douglas, *Eneados*, XIII. vi. 117 (transl. 'improbus', wicked, vile).

245. *rak sauch*: 'stretch-the-withy', 'gallows-bird'. Cf. *Satirical Poems of the Reformation* (1570), xii. 56, 'For this foule deid ȝour seid man rak ane sauch' (*OED*, s.v. *saugh*).

248. *cry cok*: admit defeat. Cf. Douglas, *Eneados*, xi, Prologue, ll. 119–20, 'Becum thow cowart, crawdoun recryand, / And by consent cry cok, thy ded is dycht'.

249. *Dathane deivillis sone*: son of the devil Dathan, who with Abiron (l. 250) rebelled against Moses and was swallowed up in the earth (Num. xvi).

250. *Beliall.* See **52.** 74 *n.*

256. *blait . . . bestiall.* For the sense of beaten into ox-like submissiveness cf. Stewart, *Buik of the Croniklis*, 1535, l. 12880, 'calland ws sa bestiall bodeis blait . . . But mycht and strenth'.

257. *thy forbearis*: the earls of Dunbar and March, descended from Gospatrick, Earl of Northumberland, who retired into Scotland in 1068 after the Conquest and in 1072 was given the manor of Dunbar and lands in the Merse by Malcolm Canmore. Patrick, eighth Earl of Dunbar and first Earl of March (d. 1308), adhered to the interest of Edward I of England (ll. 261–4, 270). His part in opening Berwick to Edward's attack (ll. 267–8) is told in Blind Hary's *Wallace* (the 'carnicle' of l. 272), i. 78 ff.: 'Eduard entrit and gert sla hastely / Off man and wiff vii thousand and fyfty, / And barnys als.' For the Battle of Spottismuir (Dunbar, 1296; ll. 269–72) see *Wallace*, viii. 180 ff.

258. *Cokburnis peth*: in Berwickshire, where a tower belonged originally to the earls of March.

261. *a meir of Mar*. *DOST* cites Major's *Historia*, 1740, vi. 14, 'Many Scots are wont privately to compare the Stewarts to the horses of Mar, which are good when they are young but bad when they are old'.

262–3. *be illusion*, etc. Cf. *Wallace*, vii. 5–6, the 'Inglismen . . . With suttelte and wykkit illusione / The worthi Scottis to put to confusione.'

270. *Edwart Langschankis*: Edward I, so nicknamed in the chroniclers. Cf. *infra*, l. 410.

277–8. *Than spulȝeit thay . . . jowellis*. Cf. *Wallace*, i. 115 ff.

281–4. *Wallace gart cry . . . king in Kyle*. *Wallace*, viii. 1–22: 'Corspatrik'

Lychtly . . . lowch, in scorn as it had beyn,
And said he had sic message seyldyn seyne:
'That Wallace now as gouernour sall ryng,
Her is gret faute off a gud prince or kyng.
That king off Kyll I can nocht wndirstand.
Off him I held neuir a fur off land . . .

289. *fowlis of effect*. Cf. Holland, *The Buke of the Howlat*, l. 165, 'Thir ar fowlis of effect, but fellony or feid'.

299–304. *Archbald Dumbar . . . deip*. In 1446 'Attour Archebald Dunbar seigit the castell of Haillis [near Haddington] in Lowtheane and at the first assault he wan the samin and slew them all that he fand thairin. He schortlie thairefter was beseigit be James Douglas in quhois will he put himself and the castell but ony farder debaitt' (Pitscottie, i. 56). George, eleventh Earl of Dunbar and March, had his earldom and estates forfeited in 1435; Hepburn of Hailes was one of those sent to take possession of March's castle at Dunbar, and remained there as constable. Archibald Dunbar, possibly a son of the eleventh Earl, seems to have been taking his revenge.

308. *Belgebubbis oyis.* See **14.** 112 *n.*; cf. *infra*, l. 533.

309. *Thow wes prestyt and ordanit be Sathan.* A slur on Dunbar's true ordination (cf. *infra*, ll. 505–8), which took place before 15 August 1500, when he was awarded a pension of £10 'for al the dais of his life or quhil he be promovit be oure soverane lord to a benefice of xl lib.' (Baxter, p. 61), and possibly much earlier.

319. *trentalis*: 'great numbers'; a trental is properly a set of thirty requiem masses for the repose of a soul.

321–2. *cesse, false Eustase air . . . Alathya.* An allusion to the *Ecloga Theoduli*, a Carolingian Latin pastoral familiar as a textbook in the Middle Ages (Raby, *SLP*, i. 228–9). It describes a poetical contest between an Athenian shepherd Pseustis, who draws on pagan mythology, and Alithia, a shepherdess of the line of David, who counters with biblical analogues. Cf. Chaucer, *The House of Fame*, l. 1228. *hald of*: am a vassal, tenant, of. For this sense cf. the *Asloan MS* (STS, i. 194), 'Thai held of him in Yngland, richt as the Ynglis king held and suld hald of the king of Fraunce'.

328. *deliquisti quia.* 'because you have sinned'. The Maitland Folio MS reading 'de eli quisti quia' is perhaps a clumsy echo of Ps. xxii. 1, 'Deus, Deus meus, respice in me: quare me dereliquisti'. This is not a penitential psalm, and has no relevance here.

330. *cum in will*: not sacramental, but military; 'submit to his will'. Cf. Blind Hary, *Wallace*, x. 289–90, 'And kep thaim in, quhill thai for hungyr sor / Cum in his will or ellis de tharfor'.

331. *Stobo.* See **62.** 86 *n.*

333. *Heve . . . handis*: a posture of prayer and thanksgiving. Cf. Gilbert of the Haye, *Buke of Knychthede*, STS, p. 10; *Wallace*, xii. 544, 'Heyffyt wp thar handis and thankit God off grace'.

336. *Arthuris Sete*: a hill (822 ft.) immediately south of Holyrood in Edinburgh.

337–40. *I perambalit*, etc. See **35.** 78 *n.*

346–8. *Bot it suld . . . sprede*: Kennedy's reply to ll. 105 ff.

351. *Inglise rumplis.* See *supra*, ll. 123–6 *n.* (quotation from Bellenden).

355–6. *Quhare thou writis*, etc. See *supra*, l. 51 *n.* The king's father, James III, had married Princess Margaret of Denmark in 1468. A mission was sanctioned in 1489 to renew the alliance between the two countries (*Acts of the Parliaments*, ii. 214), and Sir James Ogilvie concluded a treaty of peace and alliance in Denmark on 21 June 1492.

360. *thou devis . . . dyn*. Cf. **52.** 118 (Dunbar's small revenge?).

368. *Mount Falconn*: the gallows-hill of Paris. Dunbar, according to Kennedy, was soon to travel to France and Italy. Cf. *infra*, ll. 433–40.

378. *muldis*: graves, burial mounds, where Dunbar lost his 'small ynance' in the sea off Zealand (*supra*, ll. 90–6 *n*.).

381. *reule*: conduct. For this sense cf. *York Mystery Plays*, ed. L. Toulmin Smith, 1885, xxvi. 31–2, 'þer is a ranke swayne / Whos rule s noȝt right'.

386–8. *The erl of Murray . . . Westfelde knyght*. Patrick, ninth Earl of Dunbar and March, became Earl of Moray when his wife, Lady Agnes Randolph, assumed the title of Countess of Moray on the death of her brother in 1346. Kennedy is, however, selective; he does not nention Archibald Earl of Moray, who was killed fighting against ames II in May 1455 and attainted of treason. The earldom was then ested in the crown, and conferred by James IV on his natural son ames Stewart in 1501. James de Dunbar, cousin and heir of Thomas, hird Earl of Moray (d. *c*. 1430), was father of Sir Alexander Dunbar of Westfield.

394. *cry cor mundum on thy kneis*: Ps. li. 1, 10, 'Miserere mei, Deus . . . Cor mundum crea in me'; said at lauds on the first Sunday in Lent.

397. *degrade . . . greis*: deprive . . . academic degrees. If Dunbar was he man of that name listed in the records of St. Andrews as a 'deterninant' (bachelor) in 1477, he probably matriculated in 1475 and he raduated Master of Arts in 1479.

98. *Scaile . . . and shere the of the scule*: 'dismiss . . . and cut you off rom the university'.

99. *round the hede*: 'crop-head'. Cf. **26.** 18–19 *n*.

00. *trone . . . to the treis*: (?) pillory. *trone*: weighing-beam often ssociated with a pillory (cf. **75.** 24 *n*.). For this use of the verb cf. William Stewart, *To the King* (Maitland Folio MS, p. 299), ll. 49–50, Than trasoun man be thrwnit to ane tre / And mwrthour markit for is grit mischeiff'.

01. *rehatour*. See *supra*, l. 244 *n*.

04. *ryde on nycht*: 'ride out under cover of dark'. Cf. *infra*, l. 428.

05. *Quhare . . . poysoun to me*: *supra*, ll. 77–8.

07. *Clame not to clergy*: 'do not claim your ecclesiastical status'.

09. *oule*. See **34.** 7 *n*.; cf. *supra*, l. 36.

10. *Edward Langschankis*. See *supra*, l. 270 *n*.

417. *I am the kingis blude*. See *supra*, intro note. *his trew speciall clerk* Walter may have acted as deputy for Lord Kennedy of Dunure hereditary bailie of Carrick (Baxter, p. 63). He is described in ar action of 1491 as 'pretendit bailye depute of Carrik' (*Acts of the Lord of Council*, i, 1478–1495, 212a).

424. *on the rattis . . . residence*. See *supra*, l. 51 *n*.

425–30. *Fra Etrike Forest . . . felde*. See **55**, intro. note and ll. 31–40 Whether these escapades as an itinerant preacher are truth or fiction Kennedy seems to have known of Dunbar's poem.

431. *clamschellis . . . burdoun*: the scallop shells and staff of the pilgrin 'knycht of the felde' (a derisive title; cf. *chevalier de cuisine*). *kelde* is o uncertain sense. *DOST* conjectures 'caused or allowed to cool' (*kele*, tc cool); Mackenzie glosses 'coloured', prob. from *kele*, red ochre fo marking sheep.

433–5. *Mount Barnard*, etc. Alpine places on the pilgrim ways tc Rome.

435–6. 'On Mount Niklaus . . . brigands stop such fellows as you anc blind them . . .'.

437–8. *buriawe*: hangman; cf. *supra*, ll. 367 ff.

441. *the devill . . . hais*: 'may the Devil take the property you have'

446. *Danskyn*: Danzig, ludicrously far from Dunbar's intended route There was a Scotch trading colony there.

447. *de profoundis*: the opening of one of the penitential psalms (cxxx) used in the Office of the Dead.

449. *In to the Katryne*. M. P. MacDiarmid has suggested that thi was on the voyage of 1490 (*supra*, intro. note). The same ship carriec ambassadors to France in the summer of 1491 (*LHTA*, i. 179), fron North Berwick, and Dunbar may have been one of the company. Bu if he was indeed put ashore sick 'at the Bas' (l. 461), he had not beer long aboard. However, the allusion in l. 466 supports MacDiarmid' conjecture, for the *Katryne* was captured by the French in 1490.

468. *collum* ship (? = *collvin*). Cf. Stewart, *Buik of the Croniklis*, l 5034, 'Ane navin larg, With craik [ship], colvine, with mony bark anc barge'.

474. *a false botwand*. Obscure; but apparently a stave or other evidenc of function or identity; cf. *infra*, ll. 475–6.

475. *horse marschall*: man in charge of horses (cf. *LHTA*, i. 305, i 330).

481. *Hye souverane lorde*: James IV.

484. *thare doune*: in England.

489. *Thou was consavit in the grete eclips*. Taken by editors as evidence that Dunbar was born in 1460. But Denton Fox shows (*PQ*, xxxix (1960), 414–15) that the total eclipse of the sun of 18 July 1460 would not have been noticeable north-west of Italy, and that there was no 'grete eclips' visible in Scotland between 1441 and 1468, though Dunbar was certainly born within that time. This encourages scepticism about all the 'biographical' data in the *Flyting*.

494. *myten*. Cf. Bannatyne MS, f. 140r, 'Thow Sathanas seid . . . Mandrag, mymmerkyn and mismaid mytting'.

497. *gukkis*. *DOST* glosses as 'a jocular title' (cf. **13.** 39); but this is probably the verb, 'talks, behaves foolishly'.

505–6. *Ane benefice . . . beste*. Apparently the first (unfulfilled) promise of a benefice came with Dunbar's pension in 1500 (Baxter, pp. 61, 210 *et passim*). *to gyngill Judas bellis*: for treachery. The image is perhaps that of an ass (*beste*) with bells.

513. *Caym*: Cain (Gen. iv); in the Middle Ages, a demon. *Tutivillus*: a demon who gathered up the words mumbled or syncoped by careless clerks, and those of people who talked in church; familiar from miracle plays, misericords, and other church decoration. See M. D. Anderson, *Drama and Imagery in British Churches*, 1963, pp. 173–7 and pls. 16*b* and 24*d*; G. L. Remnant, *A Catalogue of Misericords in Great Britain*, 1969, pp. 19 (Ely, no. 2), 114 (Gayton, Northants, no. 3), 132 (New College, Oxford, no. 27), and 141 (Enville, Staffs., no. 2); and Neville Denny in *Medium Ævum*, xliii (1974), 255, 259.

515. *the lard of Hill house*. See *supra*, l. 241 *n*.

517. *Fowmart*: polecat; term of abuse. Cf. Bannatyne MS, f. 139v, 'Cum furth fowmart and face thy flytting'. *fasert*: hermaphrodite fowl; coward. Cf. Rolland, *The Court of Venus*, Prologue, l. 203, '[als] uncontrair his complexioun / As ane fasert to fecht with ane falcoun'.

522. *Turk*: Muslim, pagan. Cf. **54.** 5; *infra*, ll. 525–6.

523. *attircop*: spider. Cf. 'like to the venemous attercope, who . . . drinkes up the corrupt and poysonable humors' (*DOST*; 1586).

524. *lollard laureate*: 'champion heretic'. Cf. Gilbert of the Haye, *Buke of the Law of Armys* (1456), iv (STS, i. 12), 'a man that traistis to lollardis and fals prechouris and takis to his fude the sedis of errouris and herisy'.

525. *symonyte*: one who traffics in benefices, emoluments, etc. (Acts viii. 9–24).

528. *Gog and Magog*. See **29.** 19 *n*.

529. *Golyas*: the Philistine champion Goliath (1 Sam. xvii).

530. *Egipya*: in the *Testamentum Josephi*, the name of Potiphar's wife (cf. Gen. xxxix. 7 ff.).

532. *Termygantis*: Tervagant, one of three Sacracen gods (cf. *La Chanson de Roland*, ll. 611, 2467–8, 2696–7, 'Pleignent lur deus Tervagan e Mahum / E Apollin dunt il mie nen unt'); hence, a devil. Cf. **52.** 115. *Vaspasius*: the Roman emperor Vespasian.

533. *Belȝebub*. See **14.** 112 *n*.

534. *Cayphas*: the high priest who condemned Jesus (Matt. xxvi. 57 ff., John xi. 49–53 and xviii. 14 ff.).

535–6. *Pluto . . . leme*. See **10.** 125–6 *n*. *on . . . leme*: by daylight and torchlight.

537. *Egeas*: the proconsul who martyred S. Andrew (Bruce Dickins, *TLS*, 21 Feb. 1924).

538. *Marciane*: probably Marcion of Sinope (d. *c*. 160), initiator of the heresy that the Gospel was one of love, excluding the Law. *Maxencius*: the cowardly and luxurious son of Maximianus, drowned after his rebellion against Constantine in A.D. 317; executioner of S. Catherine of Alexandria.

539. *Antenor*: betrayer of Troy by the wooden horse; *Eneas*, represented in the Middle Ages (e.g. in Chaucer's *Legend of Good Women*, iii) as the betrayer of Dido.

540. *Throp*: Criseyde, who was unfaithful to Troilus. Cf. Lydgate, *Fall of Princes*, Prologue, ll. 281–7; Chaucer 'In youthe . . . made a translacioun / Off a book which callid is Trophe / In Lumbard tunge . . . Gaff it the name of Troilus & Cresseide' (Bruce Dickins, *TLS*, 10 July 1924). *Olibrius*: the Roman prefect who martyred S. Margaret at Antioch (Mackenzie).

541. *Puttidew*: the Wandering Jew, who pushed Jesus (F *boute-dieu*) on the *via dolorosa* and was doomed to wander the earth until the Last Day (Bruce Dickins, *TLS*, 14 Dec. 1935). *Eyobulus*: Aurelius Eubulus, officer to the emperor Elagabalus, torn to pieces by the soldiers and people (Dion Cassius, *Hist*., lxxx. 21).

548. *lamp Lollardorum*. Kennedy returns to the charge of lollardry (see *supra*, l. 524).

552. *ad Tertara termagorum*: to the hell of the devils (*supra*, l. 532 n.).

24. *To Princess Margaret*. One of two fragementary part-songs written to celebrate the marriage of Margaret Tudor to James IV in 1503 (see **50**, *nn.*) and surviving in English manuscripts—'brought back doubtless by returning wedding guests' (H. M. Shire, *Song, Dance and Poetry of the Court of King James VI*, 1969, pp. 2–3), and the earliest datable court-song in Scots. One of the musical parts is marked in above the words in the manuscript (BM Royal MSS 58, no. 21; early sixteenth century). On the stanza see **18.**

Although anonymous in the MS, this poem is traditionally attributed to Dunbar. There is nothing in it to make the attribution improbable; and although the diction and imagery are conventional enough, ascription is in my view justified by the parallels noted below. (**31** and **49**, cited below, are of uncertain authorship but are equally likely to be Dunbar's.)

2. *Princes most plesant and preclare.* Cf. **48.** 65.

5–6. *Ȝounge tender plant . . . blode.* Cf. **2.** 73–4, **50.** 166–8, **31.** 2–5.

7. *Fresche . . . shene.* Cf. **2.** 10, **50.** 142, 160, **14.** 18, 27.

9. *Swet lusty lusum lady clere.* Cf. **10.** 98, **48.** 6, 54, **49.** 37, **83.** 14.

13. *the Rose bothe rede and whyte.* Cf. **8**, **25.** 21, **50**; see **50.** 141–3 *n.*

14. *the floure of oure delyte.* See **2.** 42 *n.*

15. *Oure . . . beme*: in the MS, hypermetrical, obscure, and a weak rhyme; but the musical notation in the MS corresponds to the text. It is probable that the music was not part of the original composition, and simply follows a corrupt transcript of the poem. I emend to 'spreit', with a glance forward to **25.** 26; but the line is still not quite intelligible. For 'frome' read 'as'?

25. *To the King.* An address to James IV, asking him to accept the queen's petition on Dunbar's behalf. On the stanza see **18.** *Johne Thomsounis man*: a fellow who yields to the wishes of his wife (Joan; origin unknown). Cf. Scott, *Old Mortality*, ch. xxxviii: 'D'ye think I am to be John Tamson's man, and maistered by women a' the days o' my life?'

19. *vowit to the swan.* The chivalric practice of making vows, to a bird of symbolic or heraldic significance, to carry out a great deed dates from the early fourteenth century. Edward I and his son swore to God and two swans on 22 May 1306 that they would punish Robert Bruce. See *The Buik of Alexander*, ed. R. L. Graeme Ritchie, STS, i. xxxviii–xl.

21–4. *The mersy*, etc. See **50**, intro. note.

31. *sweit Sanct An*: mother of the Virgin Mary, and the subject of a popular cult in the late Middle Ages. If Dunbar wrote with the Mass

for the feast of S. Anne (26 July) live in his mind, he may have been recalling the introit and offertory (Ps. xlv. 1 and 9): '. . . dico ego opera mea regi'; 'Filiae regum in honore tuo. Astitit regina a dextris tuis in vestitu deaurato.'

26. *To the King*. 'Raking Mur' was apparently a 'raiker about', a vagabond, but is not otherwise known. Cf. Dalrymple's translation of Leslie's *Historie of Scotland* (1596), STS, i. 121, 'Reivers, raikers, herrieris of the ground'. On the stanza see **13.**

6. *hyne to Calis*: from here to, as far as, Calais. Probably proverbial; cf. Whiting, C6.

9. *salpeter*: potassium nitrate, used medicinally. The earliest quotation in *OED* is from *LHTA*, ii. 139 (1501), 'ij pund salt petir to the leich'.

18–19. *rowndit heid*: cropped head. Cf. **23.** 399.

24. *Cuddy Rug the Drumfres fuill*. 'Cuddy Rig', 'Cudde fule', 'English Cuddy' performed before the king in Dumfries in September 1504 (*LHTA*, ii. 457).

26. *ȝallow and reid*: the royal livery.

27. *Schir Thomas Norny*. A piece of domestic ridicule in the form of a parody of the romances, using the romance tail-rhyme stanza (cf. J. Schipper, *History of English Versification*, 1910, pp. 296 ff.) and conventional tags and diction, as Chaucer had done in the Tale of Sir Thopas; and following Chaucer's example in the satiric twist of the short line, and in the absurd allusions to 'faerie'. Parallels are recorded below.

'Sir' Thomas Norny was a member of the royal household. In my 1958 edition I followed Baxter in taking Norny to be a *miles gloriosus* about the court: although he is 'lord off evere full', the one thing he lacks is the jester's bells (ll. 49–54). But l. 54 is ironic; Norny was a court fool (J. H. Eddy, 'Sir Thopas and Sir Thomas Norny', *RES*, N.S. xxii (1971), 401–9). He is given the title of 'Schir' in *LHTA* almost exclusively in entries for 1505–7, and this was probably a short-lived joke initiated by Dunbar's poem. He does receive costly and elegant court dress from the king (e.g. *LHTA*, iii. 307). But he is issued with the jester's red and yellow colours in 1504 (*LHTA*, ii. 320, 321, 329), twice along with the fool Curry (*infra*, l. 43 *n.*); and an entry for 1511–12 (*LHTA*, iv. 184) records 'item, to Thomas Norny, fule, in elimose [alms] at his passage to Sanct James, iiij Franch crownis'.

1–6. *Now lythis*, etc. Cf. Chaucer's opening, *CT*, VII. 712–17:

Listeth, lordes, in good entent,
And I wol telle verrayment
Of myrthe and of solas;
Al of a knyght was fair and gent
In bataille and in tourneyment,
His name was sire Thopas.

6. *Gottin be sossery*. Cf. **38**. 1–4. Sir Thopas sought an elf-queen as leman (*CT*, VII. 787–800).

7–9. *Ane fairar knycht . . . brand*. Cf. Chaucer, loc. cit., ll. 804–6:

For in that contree was ther noon
That to him durste ride or goon,
Neither wyf ne childe . . .

12. *Rois and Murray land*: conveniently remote. Norny was in the north with the king late in 1505.

16. *Quhettane*: Chattan; a clan which 'hevely trublit' the north, and was one of the combatants in the battle of the clans at Perth in 1396. See the close of Scott's *Fair Maid of Perth*, and his note xiv. *scoir*: group of twenty; sheep and cattle were counted orally to twenty and recorded by a notch on a stick (cf. l. 17).

22. *werslingis*: no more appropriate to a Scotch 'knight' than to Sir Thopas.

25–30. *Was never wyld Robein*, etc. The conventional comparison with acknowledged heroes of romance (cf. Chaucer, *CT*, VII. 897–902; Bryan and Dempster, *Sources and Analogues of Chaucer's Canterbury Tales*, 1958, pp. 556–9). But 'wyld Robein under bewch' and the others from Sherwood Forest are heroes of popular balladry, not of chivalric romance. Roger of Clekniskleuch, unidentified, was presumably associated with Robin Hood. Guy of Gisburne was an ally of the sheriff of Nottingham, slain by Robin Hood; there survive on this episode a ballad, and a fragmentary dramatic piece dating from *c.* 1475 (Child, *Popular Ballads*, no. 118). 'Allan Bell' is probably Adam Bell, the hero of 'Mery it was in grene forest' (Child, no. 116). 'Simonis sonnes of Quhynfell' are unidentified; but a dance with this name is mentioned in *Colkelbie's Sow* (*c.* 1500; Bannatyne MS, f. 359^v^). Municipal pageants, in Scotland as elsewhere, were under the command of a lord of misrule, who sometimes gave place to Robin Hood or Little John imported from the south; but in 1555 the puritanical Estates 'ordanit that in all tymis cumming na maner of persoun be chosin Robert Hude nor Lytill Johne, Abbot to unressoun, Quenis of May nor utherwyse, nouther in Burgh nor to landwart in ony tyme to cum' (Anna J. Mill, *Medieval Plays in Scotland*, 1927, pp. 21–33).

27. *berne*. Cf. **14.** 74 *n.*

31–5. *This anterous knycht . . . gre.* Cf. Chaucer, loc. cit., l. 909, 'he was a knyght auntrous'; *Ipomadon* (A), ed. Kölbing, 1889, ll. 16–18: 'Thereffore in þe world where euer he went / In justys or in turnamente / Euer more the pryce he wan.' *Sir Bevis*: hero of a fourteenth-century romance (Chaucer, loc. cit., l. 899).

37. *Quenetyne*. See **23**, intro.; apparently the author of an earlier skit on Norny.

43. *Curris kneff*: a mere assistant to the court fool Curry who, with his wife Daft Anne of Linlithgow, seems to have turned folly to comfortable profit in the king's service (*LHTA*, iii, index).

28. *Ane Dance in the Quenis Chalmer.* This poem illustrates the personalities and manners of Margaret's retinue, and was perhaps written for her entertainment. Sir John Sinclair (ll. 1–7) of Dryden appears frequently in the Treasurer's accounts from 1490 on, playing bowls and cards with the king (cf. *LHTA*, ii. 112, 459). He was (with Dunbar) on a mission to England when the betrothal of James IV and Margaret was being negotiated in 1501 (*LHTA*, ii. 121); and he was still in the queen's service in 1513 (Baxter, p. 161). Robert Shaw (ll. 8–14) was a court physician whose name appears in the records 1502–8 (*LHTA*, ii. 436, 477); he may have been the Master Robert Shaw who became a priest and said his first mass in James's presence in May 1508 (*LHTA*, iv. 41). The *maister almaser* (ll. 15–21) may have been the Englishman Dr. Babington who was concerned in the queen's marriage arrangements in 1503, remained in Scotland as her almoner, was nominated Dean of Aberdeen in December 1505, and had died by May 1507 (Baxter, pp. 161–2). John Bute the fool (ll. 19–20) appears in the records from 3 November 1506 (*LHTA*, iii. 301, 308 ff.). Mrs. Musgrave (ll. 26, 29–35) has not been identified; she may have been the wife of a Sir John Musgrave who came up from England with the queen in 1503 (STS edn., i. ccl–ccli), but there was a Lady Musgrave at court in September 1501 (*LHTA*, ii. 120). Dame Dounteboir (ll. 36–42) was falsely identified as the wife of the queen's wardrober James Dog (cf. Baxter, p. 162); see *infra*, l. 36 *n.* On James Dog (l. 44) see **29**, **30.**

The probable identification of the 'maister almaser' as Dr. Babington, and the emergence of Bute the fool in late 1506, suggest a date of mid 1506 for the poem. On the stanza see **13.**

4, 10, 16–17. The irregular metre matches the awkward movements of the dancers; contrast the smooth description of Dunbar's own 'dirrye dantoun' and of the favoured Mrs. Musgrave (ll. 23–35).

13. *Stranaver*: far north in Sutherland; typifying remoteness. Cf. **43.** 5.

24. *dirrye dantoun*: a lively dance. For a metaphorical application of the term see **13.** 60 *n.*

36. *Dame Dounteboir*: a disparaging name for a lady of the court. Cf. Lindsay, *Ane Supplicatioun . . . in Contemptioun of Syde Taillis* (women's long-train dresses; *c.* 1540), colophon, 'Quod Lyndesay, in contempt of the syde taillis / That duddrounis and duntibouris throw the dubbis traillis'; John Knox's references to 'old dountybowris . . . that long had served in the Court' and to 'Madame Raylie, maistres to the Quenis dontiboures (for maides that court could not then beare)' (*History of the Reformation in Scotland*, 1558–66; *DOST*, s.v. *duntibour*).

44. *The Quenis Dog*. See **29,** intro. note. The pun on his name is applied proverbially in l. 48 (cf. Whiting, H592).

45. *of his band he maid a bred*: 'from his dog-chain he made a spring'.

29. *Of James Dog, Kepair of the Quenis Wardrep*. This and **30** concern Dunbar's attempt (ultimately successful) to get a doublet out of the keeper of the queen's wardrobe. James Dog had been groom of the king's wardrobe (*LHTA*, i. 240, 387, ii. 20, 29). He passed into the queen's service in a position of great responsibility, with the charge of furnishings, tapestries, and the like as well as liveries, and with control of payments in kind to court servants. He evidently remained in this post at least until 1527 (*LHTA*, v. 314). 'The Queen seems to have ordered Dunbar a doublet. . . but Mr. Doig, having scrupled, was *hitched into a rime*, and thus stands as a skeleton in the Surgeons Hall of Fame' (John Pinkerton, *Ancient Scotish Poems*, 1786, ii. 408). On the stanza see **18** *n.*

3. *ane futt syd frog*: a cloak long enough to reach the feet. Cf. Douglas, *Eneados*, VII. x. 29–31, 'he that was cheif duke'

> In rob ryall vesti, that hait Quyryne,
> And rich purpour, eftir the gys Gabyne,
> Gyrd in a garmont semly and fut syde;

translating Virgil's 'ipse Quirinali trabea cinctuque Gabino / insignis . . . consul' with Ascensius's gloss 'circumcingente altera extremitate'.

5. *markis*: device, seal. Margaret's letter-seal shows her crowned, seated, 'before her a hound or brachet leaping up' (BM. Catalogue of Seals, no. 14899).

17. *ane mastive*. Cf. **28.** 47.

19. *Sowdane*: Muslim potentate; hence, a pagan ruler. *Gog ma Gog*: the twelve-foot chief of the giants of Albion destroyed by Brute when

he came to Britain with the Trojan remnant. See Geoffrey of Monmouth, *History of the Kings of Britain*, transl. Lewis Thorpe, 1969, pp. 53–4. Cf. **23.** 528; *The Manere of the Crying of ane Play*, ll. 37–40 (with Dunbar's rhymes; Mackenzie, no. 86); Spenser, *The Faerie Queene*, III. ix. 50; Norman Cohn, *The Pursuit of the Millennium*, 1970 edn., pp. 32 and 334.

30. *Of the said James, quhen he had plesett him.* 'If so, whether was it most dangerous to displease, or to please Dunbar?' (Pinkerton, op. cit., ii. 409). There *was* a James Lam as well as a James Doig at court (*LHTA*, ii. 308).

23. *dram.* Cf. Douglas, *Eneados*, iv, Prologue, l. 158, 'to be dram / Or forto drowp lyke a fordullyt ass'.

31. *Gladethe thoue, Queyne of Scottis Regioun.* This poem survives only in the Aberdeen Minute Book of Seisins in the Town Clerk's office, vol. ii (1503–7); on the same page is **73. 31** forms a left-hand column on the page, with **73** on the right; the ascription 'q dunbar' appears below the centre of the last stanza of **73**, and directly to the right of the final line of **31.** It is almost certainly not in the same hand as **73**: it *may* have been added by the scribe of **31**, but since it is in a larger and grander style than the two poetical texts, I take it as probably an attribution of both poems to Dunbar by a later hand. The authorship of **73** is not in dispute; and there is strong internal evidence for Dunbar's authorship of **31.** In the style and diction there is nothing uncharacteristic of Dunbar; the marriage of rhyme and alliteration is typical of Dunbar; and verbal figurative parallels with poems indisputably by him are noted below (**24** is probably, but not certainly, Dunbar's).

The entries preceding and following these two poems in the Minute Book are dated 25 October 1505 and 28 March 1506; and although the sequence in the manuscript is not systematically chronological, the expectation expressed in ll. 29–31 confirms a date before February 1506/7, when the queen's first child was born. On the stanza see **4.**

2–5. *Ȝing tendir plaunt . . . pulcritude . . . imperiale blud.* Cf. **2.** 73–4, **14.** 87–8, **24.** 5–7, **50.** 166–8.

3. *Fresche flour of ȝouthe.* Cf. **2.** 10 and 42, **50.** 142 and 160. *germyng.* Cf. Caxton, *Golden Legend* (1483), 'whan the brannches been cut of the knotte that remayneth . . . It germeth and bryngeth forth newe buddes' (*OED*).

4. *Our perle of price.* Cf. **14.** 443, **50.** 180. Dunbar puns on the name of Queen Margaret, echoing Matt. xiii. 46, 'Inventa autem una

pretiosa margarita, abiit, et vendidit omnia quae habuit, et emit eam'. *our princes fair and gud.* Cf. **30.** 1.

5. *charbunkle.* See **36.** 24 *n.*

6. *Our roys riale*: so symbolized in **50**; cf. **14.** 523.

7. *selcitud.* Cf. **2.** 76.

10. *Lod steir and lamp*: paragon and luminary. Cf. Lindsay, *Testament of the Papyngo*, ll. 491–2, 'he wes myrrour of humylitie, / Lode sterne and lampe of liberalytie', and *Ane Dialog*, 4931, 'lod sterre and lumynare'; the undated sixteenth-century romance *Clariodus*, ii. 365, 'Lodstar of luve, and lampe of lustieheid' (*DOST*). *lamp of eivry lustines.* Cf. **8.** 2, **48.** 2.

11. *surmounting*: a strong term; cf. **10.** 260–1. *Pollexen*: Polyxena, the beautiful daughter of Priam, beloved of Achilles.

12. *Dochtir to Pallas in angellik brichtnes.* Cf. **10.** 78 *n.* Pallas was bright-eyed (γλαυκῶπις).

13. *Mastres of nurtur . . . nobilnes.* Cf. **50.** 173–4.

17–21. *Of thi fair fegour*, etc. Cf. **10.** 251, **14.** 31.

19. *this verray wairldis chois.* Cf. **10.** 193, **35.** 82; Fowler (*c.* 1590), 'The fairest face of feminine, yea, of the world the chose' (*DOST*).

25. *Roys red and quhit.* Cf. **8.** 8, **24.** 13; see **50.** 141–3 *n.*

27. *One stalk . . . flour.* Cf. **8.** 9, **49.** 4.

33. *Mergreit*: a play on 'Margaret'/'margarite', a pearl (cf. *supra*, l. 4); opening a stanza of lapidary metaphor. *cleir and quhit*: 'Their colour is very white, but as if a little light were shining through it, and so they gleam although they are white' (Albertus Magnus, *Mineralia*, ii. 2; transl. D. Wyckoff, 1967, p. 105).

34. *blitht and bricht . . . beriall schene.* Cf. **10.** 23, 39; **48.** 1. The beryl is correctly described by Pliny (*Hist. Nat.* xxxvii. 20. 76–9) but —because Pliny gives one of its colours as aquamarine—confused by medieval writers with rock crystal (waterclear quartz); see Albertus Magnus, *Book of Minerals*, transl. Wycoff, p. 76. *blitht.* Cf. *Lapidaries*, p. 125, 'This berell norosheth loue betwixt man and woman. The water that thes stones ar washen in ar good for sore eyen, and being drunke it doth away heuenes of hart and sighings'. *bricht . . . schene.* For Dunbar, beryl typifies translucent brightness. Cf. **10.** 23–4 *n.* With the sequence in ll. 34–6 cf. *Rauf Coilȝear*, l. 465, 'Stanes of beriall cleir / Dyamountis and sapheir'.

35. *the diamaunt of delit.* 'God ȝaue many fayre vertues and grace to þe diamond'; 'it droweth to him vertues many one . . . It accordeth man and woman of loue together' (*Lapidaries*, pp. 83, 121).

36. *sapheir*: 'a ston ryȝt comly one a ryng vpone a kyngis fynger; and God haue ȝeve to him myche grace'. 'It is good for kings, queenes and great lords'; 'þe saphir is of þe color of hevene . . . þe secund fundament in the heuenly Ierusalem . . . and for he is so noble and excellent, þerfor he is clepid gemma gemmarum, as it wer chef of precios stones' (*Lapidaries*, pp. 100, 120, 101). Cf. **10.** 37.

37. *gudely . . . the emerant grene.* Cf. *Lapidaries*, pp. 85, 121: 'Esmeraude is a ston þat ouerpasseth al þe grennesse of grenhede . . . comeþ owte of the lond of Tyre by a water of paradis. Nero haþe a myrrour of þis ston wherein he loked, and he wyst by þe vertu of þis stone al þat he wole seke or deseyre'; 'God gaue it such vertue; And to a man þat kepeth it, his body and members should be euer cleane and without euell.' Cf. **10.** 39.

38. *riche . . . the ruby of renowne*: the climax of Dunbar's catalogue. 'It overcometh all ye mervealous stones of beuty . . . of so gentle coulor lyk a burning cole. He is lord and king of stones and of all gemms. It hath ye vertue of xii stones. It is of so great value and price yt he yt beareth it ageinst ye people yey have all manner of joy of his comming. . . . It is sayd yt this stone is in ye fleme of paradice' (*Lapidaries*, pp. 123–4). Cf. **10.** 24, **36.** 24 *n.*, **50.** 132.

39. *gem of joy.* Cf. **50.** 153.

32. *To the Quene.* The title was added by Pinkerton. His conjecture is reasonable, in view of the mode of address (cf. **29**) and in the absence of alternatives. On the stanza see **19.**

'This piece is a singular one to be addrest to a queen. Some words in it I shall not, and others I confess, I cannot explain' (Pinkerton, *Ancient Scotish Poems*, 1786, ii. 410). 'The pockis' (syphilis) became widespread in Scotland in the closing years of the fifteenth century—possibly introduced by Perkin Warbeck's 'great army of valiant captaines of all nations . . . thieves, robbers, and vagabonds' in 1496–7 (Hall; R. S. Morton, 'Some Aspects of the early History of Syphilis in Scotland', *British Journal of Venereal Diseases*, xxxviii (1962), 175–80). The 'Grandgore Act' of 1497 required all those infected with 'this contagius seiknes' to assemble on Leith sands for transportation to the island of Inchkeith in the Firth of Forth, 'thare to remane quhill God prouyde for thair health' (*Burgh Records of Edinburgh*, i (1869), 71). Curiously, the subject provoked a good deal of poetry in Latin and the vernaculars.

1–2. *ryd . . . slyd*: ride out 'on the splore', and let the court festivities of Fastern's Eve (cf. **52.** 1 ff.) slip by; cf. Chaucer, *CT*, IV. 82, 'Wel ny alle othere cures leet he slyde'; *Troilus and Criseyde*, v. 351–2, 'laten slide / The tyme'. Around 'Fasteringis Evin' in 1505, for instance, the Treasurer paid out for 'tournaying', 'gisaris', 'dansaris', and taubronaris' (*LHTA*, ii. 476–7).

4. *betteis soin abyd*: shortly, at once, submit to remedies, repairs. *DOST* records *beit* n. only for the repair of a ship; but cf. the vb. *be(i)t*, *bette*, to relieve, make good, repair.

5. *lib*: cure by a potion or charm. Cf. Henryson, *Sum Practysis of Medecyne*, ll. 18–21:

> Is nowdir fevir nor fell that our the feild fure,
> Seiknes nor sairnes, in tyme gif I seid,
> Bot I can lib thame and leiche thame fra lame and lesure,
> With salwis thame sound mak . . .

The alternative gloss in *DOST*, 'appar., to treat for venereal disease by cutting the chancres' (following the STS editors), takes *lib* as 'geld', 'cut', it seems on the sole evidence of Dunbar's line. But it would soon have been obvious that surgery was ineffectual; and at this time mercury, sarsaparilla, and guaiacum were being imported from the Continent as treatment (Morton, art. cit.).

7. *Venus feest*. With the metaphor cf. **14.** 430–1 and *n.*

8. *na cockis*. Cf. **14.** 326.

11. *curage*: sexual energy. See **14.** 67 *n.*

15. *lib tham of the pockis*: here and in the rest of the poem (ll. 19–20, 34–5), apparently a metaphor for illicit intercourse. It has been argued (see esp. Scott, p. 164, and the correspondence in *TLS*, 20 January 1966 *et seq.*) that Dunbar plays on *pockis*=(1) syphilis, (2) money-bags, (3) scrotums. This would I think be uncharacteristic. Scott's notion of intercourse as a cure for venereal disease—'a theory, magical and superstitious, but a primitive apprehension of the principle of inoculation'—is merely speculative: in speaking of fornication as 'libbin of the pockis' there may be no more than an ironic popular jest. (The metaphorical use of 'the hair of the dog that bit me' goes back to the sixteenth century; cf. Whiting, H21, and Tilley, H237; Pope, *The Rape of the Lock*, v. 19–20, 'Oh! if to dance all Night . . . charm'd the Small-pox'.)

16. *ryatous as rammis*. Cf. **37.** 6.

17. *tame . . . lammis*. Cf. **30**, refrain. Proverbial; Whiting, L36.

18. *crockis*: old ewes. Cf. **23.** 248.

20, 35. *That men callis*: i.e. figuratively, and vulgarly. Cf. **13.** 60.

24. *gottin . . . handis*: so emaciated that they can span their backs with two hands.

30. *the Spanȝie pockis*: known also as the French or Italian pox, and 'the seiknes of Napillis'.

33. *Ane Blak Moir*. There are references to negresses at court in 1504 and 1511–13 (*LHTA*, ii. 465, 469; iv. 401), presumably enjoying in the royal service a benevolent form of the black slavery which became common and fashionable in southern Europe during the fifteenth century (see l. 3); cf. *infra*, l. 8 *n.*, and Dürer's drawing of the negress Katharina (1521; Uffizi). But the occasion of Dunbar's poem was almost certainly a tournament held in 1507 and repeated more elaborately in 1508. The instigator was a French visitor, the Sieur de la Bastie. He left for France in January 1506–7 with the illuminated proclamation of a 'justing of the wild knycht for the blak lady' to be held in August. The *Emprise du Chevalier Sauvage à la Dame Noire* offered a challenge to all comers for five weeks in a field near the castle at Edinburgh which was allegorically decorated (see Baxter, p. 165). The tournament was repeated on 31 May 1508. A full account is given by Pitscottie (i. 242–4). The 'heill lordis and barronis' of Scotland were commanded, and attended with 'money gentilmen out of Ingland France and Denmark'. 'Amang the rest thair come ane knycht and ane lady callit the quhyt rois . . . the king gart set the haill justing and callit the samyn the turnament of the black knicht and the black lady and . . . iustit him selff dissaguysed onknawin and he was callit the blak knicht. . . . He wan the lady frome thame all for he was verie puissant and strenthie on horsback and faucht and iustit with all kynd of weaponis. . . . Evirie barroun was comm[e]ndit be the iudge and the harrauldis as thay vsit thame selff vith thair weponis as was givin to thame eftirward be the king for thair reward and adwancment of thair honour the quhilk weaponis war of fyne gold or of siluir or than doubill ovir gilt . . . This turnament and iusting beand indureit the space of xl dayis . . . the king causit to mak ane gret triumphe and bancat in Halyrudhous quhilk lestit the space of thrie dayis . . . And . . . at the hennest [hindmost] bancat pheirs [farce, entertainment] and play vpone the thrid day thair come ane clwdd out of the rwffe of the hall as appeirit to men and opnit and cleikkit vp the blak lady in presence of thame all that scho was no moir seine bot this was done be the art of Igramancie . . .' Dunbar's response (and probably his contribution) to these elaborate ceremonies, starting from the original contrast between the 'quhyt rois' and the 'blak moir', is characteristically novel and ribald. On later poems on the courtship of the black and the white see John Cleveland, *Poems*, ed. B. Morris and E. Withington, 1967, p. 101. For the stanza see **19.**

8. *catt*: cat-like, snub. Cf. the portrait of one of Cosimo de Medici's negro *femmine bestiali* (*c.* 1450; Margaret Aston, *The Fifteenth Century: The Prospect of Europe*, 1968, p. 60).

11. *claid in reche apparrall.* The lady sat in a 'chair triumphale' adorned with red taffeta; she wore a gown of gold-flowered damask, with bordering in green and yellow taffeta, and black sleeves and gloves. Her attendants were dressed in white coats and green and yellow taffeta gowns. (*LHTA*, iv. 64, 129.)

14. *be fain*: with willingness, gladly.

23. *kis hir hippis.* Cf. **23.** 131 *n.*

34. *Epetaphe for Donald Oure.* The Macdonalds, Lords of the Isles, were descended from the Norwegian Somerled, thane of Argyll, and were virtually independent of the Scottish kings until the reign of James IV. John, eleventh Earl of Ross and Lord of the Isles, was forfeited for treasonable communication with England in 1475, restored in 1476, and again forfeited in 1493. His natural son Angus Og married Mary, daughter of the first Earl of Argyll; but Angus's son Donald 'Owre' (Gael *odhar*, dun, brown) or Dubh (black) was held by the government to be 'bastard and unlawfull'. Donald must have been known to Dunbar; after the forfeiture of the Lordship of the Isles he was held at court in James IV's service (*LHTA*, i. 273, 342, 380, 381). He escaped in 1501, and in 1503 led a serious insurrection of Macdonalds, Camerons, Macleans, and Macleods in Badenoch. He was defeated and imprisoned again in 1505, and was in Stirling Castle in 1507 (*LHTA*, iii. lxxxii and 415). Dunbar's poem dates from this time. Its tone, says Mackenzie, 'is unnecessarily malignant towards one who had known no personal freedom save for the few years he was "out" against the Government. He was partly the victim, partly the instrument of higher powers.' The emphatically rhythmical stanza, with its alliterative phrases below the four-stress lines, is related to *rime couée*. It is admirably suited to the precipitate violence of Dunbar's feeling.

I have preferred the draft text in the Bannatyne MS, but I have followed Maitland's sequence in ll. 19–30. In the Maitland Folio MS the reading at l. 8 spoils the alliterative pattern; l. 14 is apparently a misreading; l. 32 is metrically inferior; and ll. 36, 38 look like editorial 'improvements'.

7. *odious as ane owle*: the type of the unnatural rebel and usurper. The owl tried to deprive the eagle of its sovereignty (Nicholas Pergamus, *Dialogus Creaturarum*, 82); in one of the *Fabulae* of Odo of Sherington the falcon tries, like James IV here, to raise the owlet in his nest, but 'de ovo te eduxi, de natura non potui'. For these and other references

see M. P. MacDiarmid, 'Richard Holland's Buke of the Howlat', *Medium Ævum*, xxxviii (1969), 277–90. Cf. **23.** 36.

22. *suppleis*: punishment, torture. (*OED*'s first quotation is from Blount, 1656).

25. *feit*: standing-ground, base.

31–2. *Off . . . tratour*: 'every thief and traitor has the nature of the false fox, the dissimulator'.

45–8. *Wyvis thus . . . hais.* Cf. Tilley, F627; Henryson, *Fabillis*, ll. 826–7, 'Now find I weill this prouerb trew', quod he, / "Ay rinnis the foxe, als lang as he fute hais" '.

35. *The Ballade of . . . Barnard Stewart lord of Aubigny.* The Stuarts were one of several Scotch families who in the fifteenth century gave distinguished service to the kings of France. Sir John Stuart of Darnley (d. 1429), lord of Castlemilk, entered the French service *c.* 1422 and became seigneur of Aubigny in 1425. Bernard (or Bérault) Stuart (*c.* 1447–1508) was his grandson, third Seigneur d'Aubigny, and captain of Charles VIII's Scots Guard. He led the French force in support of Henry VII at Bosworth in 1485. He served Charles as ambassador to Scotland and Rome, and as governor of Calabria (1494) and Naples (1501), where he was imprisoned (1503–4) after his defeat by the Spaniards at Seminara. In 1508 he was sent to Scotland by Louis XII to confirm the French alliance, and died there on 11 June (see **36**). In Scotland 'he was weill ressawit witht the king and consall . . . and the kingis grace treittit him werie weill and gentellie, and sett him ewer at the tabill witht him self and maid him iudge in all his iusting and tornamentis, callit him father of weir because he was practissit in the samin' (Pitscottie, i. 241–2). See Lady Elizabeth Cust, *The Stuarts of Aubigny*, 1891. For an account of Aubigny's military career, and his acclaim as 'ung bon chevalier et sage, bon et honorable', 'ung tres gentil et vertueux capitaine', 'un grand chevalier sans reproche', see Douglas Gray, 'A Scottish "Flower of Chivalry" and his Book'—a French treatise of the art of war—*Words 4* (Wellington, N. Zealand), Jan. 1974, pp. 22–34. He is portrayed on a medal by Spinelli (G. F. Hill, *Corpus of Italian Medals of the Renaissance before Cellini*, 1930, pl. 155). Dunbar's *Ballade* was probably written and published as part of the official reception of Aubigny in May 1508. On the stanza see **4.** Beaumont-le-Roger (heading) is near Bernay, south of le Havre; *Bonaffre* is apparently Bouafles.

1–2. *Renownit . . . valoure.* It is of course possible to punctuate with a comma after 'serene'; but the run-on (rare in early Scots) makes a more powerful rhetorical opening, and the resultant pause after 'Lord' makes better metrical sense of l. 2.

7. *servatour*: perhaps merely 'servant'; but probably in the rare sense of 'squire, page'. Cf. Fabyan, *Chron.* (*c.* 1513), 1533, vii. 124, 'v. C. men of armys, wyth a servyture to eueryche spere'.

8. *Withe glorie*, etc. An echo of Theodulph's Palm Sunday processional hymn, *Gloria laus et honor tibi sit, rex Christe, redemptor* (Gaselee, no. 27).

17. *the secund Julius*: the first of Dunbar's comparisons of Aubigny with some of the Nine Worthies (Joshua, David, Judas Maccabaeus; Hector, Alexander, Julius Caesar; Arthur, Charlemagne, Godfrey of Bouillon). See *infra*, ll. 58, 59, 62; sections on *Les Vœux du Paon*, where the vogue of the Nine Worthies began, in *The Buik of Alexander*, ed. R. L. Græme Ritchie, STS, vol. 1; and Gollancz's edition of *The Parlement of the Thre Ages*, 1915.

22. *clarioun*: the 'folded' trumpet which came in during the fifteenth century (*New Oxford History of Music*, iii (1960), 477).

58. *invincible . . . undir scheild.* Cf. **62.** 21–2.

67–8. *cristall*: bright as crystal. Aubigny deserves to be crowned with the laurel of victory (cf. Chaucer, *CT*, I. 1027, 'With laurer crowned as a conquerour'; Lydgate, *Assembly of Gods*, l. 791) and the olive of peace (cf. Gilbert of the Haye, *The Buke of the Law of Armys*, STS, p. 39, 'gert put up on a spere a branch of ane olyve tree in takenyng of pes').

73. *Mars . . . armipotent.* See **10.** 112 *n.*

75–6. *Saturnus . . . manasing to gar de.* See **10.** 114–15 *n.*; cf. Saturn's words in Chaucer, *CT*, I. 2453 ff., 'Myn is the stranglyng and hangyng by the throte . . . My lookyng is the fader of pestilence'.

77. *fresche Venus.* Cf. Chaucer, *CT*, I. 2386, 'faire, yonge, fresshe Venus free'; *The Complaint of Mars*, l. 26.

78. *Marcurius*: Mercury, god of eloquence, 'of fayre spekynge and of wisdom' (Bartholomaeus Anglicus). See Henryson, *Testament of Cresseid*, ed. Denton Fox, 1968, ll. 239–52 and notes; cf. **23.** 337–40.

79. *Fortuna maior*: a figure of the stars in geomancy, marked out ::⋅⋅, which resembles figures made by some of the last stars of Aquarius and the first of Pisces. Cf. Dante, *La Divina Commedia*, 'Purgatorio', xix. 4–6; Chaucer, *Troilus and Criseyde*, iii. 1415–26, and Robinson's note.

82. *Sweyrd . . . chevalry.* Cf. **10.** 193.

36. *Elegy on Bernard Stewart Lord of Aubigny.* On Bernard Stuart third Seigneur of Aubigny, see **35.** Aubigny fell ill while travelling from Edinburgh to Stirling, and died on 11 June 1508 (*Exchequer Rolls* xiii. 123). In his will of 8 June he directed that his body should be buried in the church of Blackfriars, Edinburgh (*DNB*). On the stanza see **4.**

1. *Illuster Lodovick*: Louis XII (1462–1515), 'Father of the people'.

6. *to governe and to gy*: stock alliterative phrase in the romances. Cf. Lydgate, *On the Departing of Thomas Chaucer*, l. 5; Douglas, *King Hart*, l. 20.

7–8. *For him . . . chevelrie.* Christopher Brookhouse (*Studies in Scottish Literature*, vii (1969), 123) compares Deschamps, *Ballade sur la Mort de Bertrand du Guesclin*, 'Chascun pour vous doit noir vestir et querre; / Plourez, plourez flour de chevalerie'.

10. *douchtie . . . in deid*: stock. Cf. *DOST*, *douchty* adj. 2.

13. *the Turkas sey.* I emend *turk* to the disyllabic form used by Gavin Douglas in 'apon hir schulder the giltyn bow Turcas' (*Eneados*, XI. xiii. 11). Aubigny was feared as far as the Black Sea, the fringe of Asia.

17–18. *O dragon . . . devoir.* See **4.** 1, 9–10, *nn.*; cf. **40.** 28, **61.** 28. 1 Pet. v. 8, 'adversarius vester diabolus . . . quaerens quem devoret'.

20. *witt of weiris.* Cf. *Golagros and Gawane* (*c.* 1475; Chepman and Myllar, 1508), l. 1050, 'Gawane, the wit of our were'.

21. *crop*: highest part of a tree; highest manifestation. Cf. Chaucer, *Troilus and Criseyde*, v. 25, 'she that was the sothfast crop and more [top and root] / Of al his lust or joies'.

24. *charbuckell*: ruby. Cf. Albertus Magnus, *Book of Minerals* (transl. Dorothy Wyckoff, 1967), ii. 1 (p. 61), 'they say that the carbuncle is the noblest, having the powers of all other stones; because it receives a power similar to that of the Sun, which is more noble than all other heavenly powers' (cf. pp. 77–8); *Lapidaries*, p. 21, 'Rubye . . . is of suche lordeschippe þt when he þat bereth hym cometh amonge men, all thei shul bere hym honeur and grace and all shul bere hym ioye of his presence'; p. 110, 'þe man þat bereþ þis ston schal be never overcom in ple ne in batayl'; pp. 123–4, 'he is lord and king of stones and of all gemms . . . It is sayd yt this stone is in ye fleme of paradice'. Cf. **31.** 5, 38 *n.*

37. *The Wowing . . . in Dumfermeling.* This energetic and coarsely witty beast-fable celebrates an amorous exploit, presumably involving one or more people well known at court, in Dunfermline in Fife. The tradition that the *tod* (fox) was James IV himself, who had a palace at Dunfermline, rests entirely on the king's libertine reputation and Bannatyne's title. Baxter points out (p. 51) that 'this is not the only place where Bannatyne has implicated King James without the confirmation of internal evidence', and that James's hair was brown, not red (ll. 16, 22). But there are reddish-browns; and the evidence for James's colouring is only Mytens's copy of 'an ancient water coloured piece' (probably a miniature) from the sixteenth century. The identities of fox, lamb, and wolf remain uncertain. The tradition of the beast-fable had lately been much enriched, at Dunfermline, by Dunbar's older contemporary Henryson (see John MacQueen, *Robert Henryson*, 1967, ch. 4 and appendices). On the stanza see **13. 13** and **37** have affinities not only of form but of occasion and tone; both are ironic rather than directly moralistic like Henryson's *Fabillis*. Dunbar here makes subtler satiric use of the refrain.

6. *riddin hir lyk ane rame*. Cf. **32.** 16.

12. *lowrit*: cowered. These lines show close observation of canine behaviour.

16. *lowry*: Lawrence; a name first given to the fox (Reynard in England and on the Continent) in Henryson's *Fabillis*.

19. *To sic . . . ane bace*: probably a sexual quibble on 'treble / triple instrument', 'bass / support'. It is otherwise difficult to see why the natural attribution of *tribbill* to the *lame* and *bace* to the *tod* has been inverted.

39. *prenecod*: pin-cushion; still current as a metaphor for the female genitals. Cf. 'pin-case', 'pintle-box'.

50–1. *Quhen men dois fleit*, etc. Proverbial; Whiting, J58. With this transitional *sententia* cf. Burns, *Tam o' Shanter*, ll. 59 ff., 'But pleasures are like poppies spread . . .'.

55. *The lamb than cheipit lyk a mows*: an ambiguous cry, to meet the expectations of both male lovers. Cf. Iphigenia in Dryden's *Fables* (*Poems*, ed. Kinsley, 1958, iv. 1749):

> Thus while he spoke he seiz'd the willing Prey,
> As *Paris* bore the *Spartan* Spouse away:
> Faintly she scream'd, and ev'n her Eyes confess'd
> She rather would be thought, than was Distress'd.

59. *in the silly lambis skin*: i.e. covered in retreat by the lamb, who has to receive the wolf as a second suitor (ll. 67–8). For the figure of a fox rather than a wolf in sheep's clothing, cf. **14.** 423, **74.** 37.

38. *The Tesment of Maister Andro Kennedy*. Andro Kennedy was apparently a drunken court physician (cf. ll. 57–8); *LHTA*, ii. 61,

158. The attribution to Dunbar rests on Bannatyne's colophon. Correspondences with other poems, ascribed on better evidence to Dunbar, are few: with ll. 3–4 cf. **23.** 244 and **27.** 6; with the rhymes in ll. 41–5 cf. **62.** 13–14; with l. 77 cf. **83.** 3. There is, on the other hand, no evidence, in diction or tone, for rejecting the traditional attribution. The stanza is of the cross-rhymed four-line type, doubled, and with variable rhyme-scheme (abababab, ababacac, ababcdcd, ababbcbc), common in medieval French and English poetry.

Dunbar manages an echo of the great twelfth-century *Confessio*, 'Meum est propositum in taberna mori, / ubi vina proxima morientis ori'; but his intention is comic, and he tries the popular burlesque exercise of writing in two languages. His alternate lines in Scots and Latin are not precisely macaronic, except on occasion (cf. ll. 4, 110): a more orthodox example is the *Polemo-Middinia* attributed to Drummond of Hawthornden, in which vernacular words are given Latin terminations and worked into a Latin context.

The poem belongs to the genre of the satiric testament, popular in late medieval France. The history of the genre runs from the Latin prose *Testamentum Porcelli* and verse *Testamentum Asini*: it includes Walther von der Vogelweide's *Vermächtnis*, fourteenth-century Spanish wills in verse, Deschamps's *Autres Lettres envoyees par Eustache, lui estant malade, et la maniere de son Testament par esbatement*, Jean Regnier's *Livre de la Prison*; *Le grand Testament de Taste-vin, roy des pions*; and pre-eminently Villon's two works. On the tradition see W. H. Rice, *The European Ancestry of Villon's Satirical Testaments*, 1941, esp. pp. 141 ff. Reference is often made from Dunbar to Villon; but Villon's *Le Lais* (40 stanzas) and *Le Testament* (186 stanzas with interspersed ballades) are on a different scale from that of **38**, intensely personal, and 'satirical' at a much deeper level. The testament was a fairly popular form (serious or satiric) in Scots; cf. Henryson's *Testament of Cresseid*, the testament in Lindsay's *Historie of Squyer Meldrum*, and his *Testament and Complaynt of our Soverane Lordis Papyngo*.

3. *Gottin with sum incuby*. 'Multique . . . de quorum fide dubitandum non est, audisse confirmant, sylvanos et faunos, quos vulgo incubos vocant, improbos saepe exstitisse mulieribus et earum appetitisse et peregisse concubitum' (S. Augustine, *De Civitate Dei*, xv. 23). Cf. *The Ynglis Cronikle* (*Asloan MS*, STS, i. 204), 'The erll Galfryd of Angeoss was Incobus and gottin betuix a devill and his modere in mannis likness'. With the amiable alternative of 'sum freir *infatuatus*' in l. 4 cf. the Wife of Bath's 'lymytour' saying his office: 'Ther is noon oother incubus but he, / And he ne wol doon hem but dishonour' (Chaucer, *CT*, III. 873–81).

8. *dyabolus incarnatus*: 'a fiend in human form'. Denton Fox notes the

clash between 'the idiotic and redundant pomposity' of l. 7 and 'the preposterously different pomposity' of l. 8 (in D. S. Brewer, *Chaucer and Chaucerians*, 1970, p. 184).

12. *Na Blind Allane . . . mone*: apparently proverbial. Cf. Lindsay, *The Tragedie of the Cardinall* (1546), ll. 395–6, 'I understude no science Spirituall, / No more than did blynd Alane of the Mone'.

24. *sueit Cuthbert*: not identified.

28. *laith and wraith*. Cf. Wyntoun, *Orygynale Cronykil* (*c.* 1420), iii. 231–2; ix. 3001; viii. 2287–8, 'Willame the Walayis / Persawyd how he wes in gret leth / Had wyth the Cwmynys in thare wreth'.

31. *camesia*: chemise, shirt.

40. *Thair wald I*, etc. (Added in Maitland Folio MS.) These lines may derive from a draft of the sentiments ultimately enshrined in ll. 98–116.

49. *the best aucht*: the most valuable possession, 'claimed by the superior on the death of a tenant' (*DOST*); here a *caupe* (l. 50; Gael *colpa*, a mature grazing beast).

55. *als sib . . . riddill*: proverbial. Cf. *The Thre Prestis of Peblis* (*c.* 1500), l. 476, 'I am to you als sib as seif is to ane riddil'.

60. *Sanct Antane*: the preceptory of S. Antony, founded in 1435 by Robert Logan of Restalrig; situated at the south-west corner of St. Antony's Wynd, Leith, and destroyed at the Reformation.

68. *Dispersit dedit pauperibus*: Ps. cxii. 9.

73. *Jok Fule*. Cf. **14.** 142.

79. *bleris . . . e*: deceives; proverbial. See **14.** 277 *n*.

81. *Master Johne Clerk*: not at all necessarily the poet lamented in **62.** 58; as the alleged cause of Kennedy's death (l. 84), he was presumably an incompetent physician. He seems to have misread or falsely transcribed *dentes* in some medical context (l. 88).

92. *Ade*: Adam. *Kytte*: familiar form of Katherine.

101. *cop out evin*: quite emptying the bowl.

104. *Potum . . . miscebam*: Ps. cii. 9.

105–16. *I will na preistis*, etc. Mackenzie cites the *Testament de Taste-vin, roy des pions* (topers): 'Aupres de taverne la belle / Qu'on plante sur sa servelle [head] / Un sep de la meilleure vigne'; but with the spirit of the stanza cf. the Archpoet's *Aestuans intrinsecus* (*c.* 1163), ll. 41–8 (Gaselee, no. 66):

> Meum est propositum in taberna mori,
> ubi vina proxima morientis ori:
> tunc cantabunt laetius angelorum chori
> 'Sit Deus propitius huic potatori'.
>
> Poculis accenditur animi lucerna,
> cor imbutum nectare volat ad superna:
> mihi sapit dulcius vinum in taberna
> quam quod aqua miscuit praesulis pincerna.

Dies illa dies ire: the sequence for the burial of the dead attributed to the Franciscan Thomas of Celano (*c.* 1250).

110. *ail wosp*: bunch of straw used as a sign for an alehouse.

111–12. *In stayd of baneris . . . cervisie.* Cf. the 'Testament' which ends Lindsay's *Historie of Squyer Meldrum* (*c.* 1552), where it is decreed that the squire's banner shall be carried at his funeral to music, followed by his arms and horse 'in ordour triumphall' (ed. Kinsley, 1959, p. 68).

116. *De terra plasmasti me.* Cf. Ps. cxix. 73.

39. *To the King.* Here as in **62** (but far less effectively) Dunbar moves from a melancholy view of the human scene to his own personal concern. This poem was written after 1498 (see l. 62 *n.*), and indeed after 1503 if the reference in l. 57 is specifically to James IV and Margaret (but surely not after the award of a pension in 1510). On the stanza see **18.**

1–8. *This waverand warldis wretchidnes*, etc. Cf. (?) Jacopone da Todi, *De Contemptu Mundi* (Raby, *CLP*, pp. 435–6):

> Cur mundus militat sub vana gloria
> cuius prosperitas est transitoria?
> tam cito labitur eius potentia,
> quam vasa figuli, quae sunt fragilia . . .
>
> quam breve festum est haec mundi gloria!
> ut umbra hominis sic eius gaudia,
> quae semper subtrahunt aeterna praemia,
> et ducunt hominem ad dura devia . . .

7. *sweit abayd*: plausible, adroit delay.

10. *figurit*: rhetorical, 'fine'. Cf. Blind Hary, *Wallace*, vi. 57, 'Fortoun him schawit hyr fygowrt doubill face'; Whiting, F8, F12 ('Trust not him that has two faces and two tongues'), F13 ('Two

faces in one hood'). Dunbar is, however, echoing Chaucer, *Troilus and Criseyde*, v. 897–9:

> And but if Calkas lede us with ambages,
> That is to seyn, with double wordes slye,
> Swiche as men clepen a word with two visages . . .

21. *The change . . . to wo.* Cf. Chaucer, *Troilus and Criseyde*, i. 1–5, 'The double sorwe of Troilus to tellen . . . how his aventures fellen / Fro wo to wele, and after out of joie'.

23. *In . . . plane.* Cf. **59.** 27–8.

26. *Office.* For this sense cf. Maitland Folio MS, p. 20, 'in court . . . with the hieast placeit / In honour, office or in dignitie'.

42–3. *rowme and rude*: space and extent. The image is probably proverbial. Cf. the seventeenth-century proverbs, 'to have a wide conscience, as one may swing a cat in't' (Tilley, C603a; 1666), and 'a Traveller to Rome must have . . . a conscience as broad as the Kings highway' (Tilley, W888; 1617).

49. *ane stall*: i.e. of a canon or other minor dignitary.

55. *Sum . . . passage plane*: while Dunbar receives nothing at the hand-out of preferments, some others, making off with a whole load of twenty-four ['sheaves'], demand unobstructed passage.

62. *Calȝecot*: Calicut on the Malabar coast; the first place in India visited by Pedro de Covilhão in 1486 and by Vasco da Gama in 1498. Newfoundland, *the new fund Yle*, was discovered by John Cabot in 1497, and by *c.* 1500 was in use as a fishery base by the French and Portuguese. (It has, however, been argued that Bristol fishermen sailed to N. America earlier—in the 1480s; see *The Times*, 15 April 1976, p. 14, and D. B. Quinn's letter of 30 April. Professor Quinn suggests to me that Dunbar's is the first British reference to the New World in literature.)

63. *Transmeridiane*: the region beyond the meridian in the Atlantic which separates the New from the Old World (*OED*; Dunbar is the only citation).

65. *be this . . . kynd*: 'by this time . . . in accord with the natural order'.

66, 69. *Cuming*: (have) come.

67. *the grit se oceane*: the *mare oceanum* (Caesar, *De Bello Gallico*, iii. 7; OF *mer oceane*), opposed to the Mediterranean inland sea. The phrase 'grit se oceane' occurs in Sir Gilbert of the Haye's translation of the *Buik of Alexander* (Taymouth MS, *c.* 1460) and in the Asloan MS (STS, i. 154) (*DOST*).

70. *Paris*: Persia; probably a scribal error.

71. *Aphrycane*: Africa. *Ylis* are shown on fifteenth-century maps off the north-west coast of Africa; see, e.g., illustrations from Schedel (1493) and Martellus (*c.* 1490) in Margaret Aston, *The Fifteenth Century*, 1968, nos. 2 and 34.

78. *unicornis and crownis of wecht*: gold coins first issued by James III, bearing the figure of a unicorn on the obverse (cf. *Exchequer Rolls*, ix. 549 (1487), 'in denariis aureis vocatis unicornys'); and gold crowns of standard weight.

86. *hadder*: heather; for centuries a common thatch. Cf. *Misc. Spalding Club*, v. 23, 'xxxii thraw of thak hathir to Sanct Clementis kirk' (1467); 'As to the roofing or theiking or heddering of the new kirk' (1599; *DOST*).

89–92. *And for my curis . . . pane*: 'My innocent soul will never perish or suffer torment for the sin of having livings in various places with the help, Sir, of your noble grace'; ironic.

95. *phane*: weather-vane. Cf. Whiting, V5; Lydgate, *Reson and Sensuallyte*, ll. 6180–1, 'They turne nat as doth a phane / With vnwar wynde'.

99. *bayth crop and grayne*: completely.

100. *lessing of my pane*. Cf. *The Buik of Alexander*, ii, Prologue, l. 20, 'myne intent / To get lessing of my torment'.

40. *To the King*. In this poem the movement is the converse of that in **39**: here 'the personal complaint of Dunbar is widened into satire of the court in general, and that satire is universalized . . . the turning of real values upside down. Yet the note of self-pity is still there, and muffles the force of the poem' (Scott, p. 102). On the stanza see **19**.

2. *Quha monyast hes*: 'Those who have most already'.

4–5. *Ay is the ouir word*, etc. The phrasing survives in later lyric, e.g. Burns's fragment 'The Night was still' (*Poems and Songs*, ed. Kinsley, 1968, no. 133):

Sae merrily they danc'd the ring,
  Frae e'enin till the cocks did craw,
And aye the owerword o' the spring
  Was, Irvine's bairns are bonnie a'.

6–7. *Sum swelleis swan . . . nuke*. Figurative: the swan symbolizes high living in a rich benefice, the duck a good living; Dunbar 'fasts' (Mackenzie).

12. *commoun and propir*. The *commune sanctorum* is the office for saints who have no individual office (*proprium sanctorum*) of their own.

20. *syphir*: the cipher in algorism. With the metaphor cf. *Mum and the Sothsegger* (*c.* 1405), 'Þan satte summe as siphre doth in awgrym, / Þat noteth a place and no þing availith'; *Secular Lyrics of the XIVth and XVth Centuries*, ed. R. H. Robbins, 1952, no. 138, 'And ye in your Armes so truly hym knyt, / And I lyke a syphyr syt you by'.

23. *Nor . . . quha rang thame*: nor who administered the sacraments.

26–8. *So warryit . . . dragoun stang thame.* See **4.** 9–10 *n.*; cf. **36.** 17–19, **61.** 28.

41. *To the King, quhone mony Benefices vakit.* On the stanza see **21.**
2. *small partis makis grit service*: 'small portions serve many'.

42. *To the King.* On the stanza see **19.** I have followed the Maitland Folio text here; Bannatyne's is manifestly careless and inferior.

6. *clarkis*: scribes, secretaries; if clerics, then in court roles inferior to Dunbar's.

7. *rid halk*: the little red merlin (*falco columbarius*). Had Dunbar red hair?

12. *myttell*: some less noble bird of prey; listed in an Act of 1457 with 'foulys of reif as ernys [eagles], bussards, gleddis' (*DOST*).

13. *gled*: the kite (*milvus milvus*); notoriously greedy and cowardly, preying on the ground on rodents, partridges, chickens and offal. Cf. **23.** 52, 128, 237; Lydgate, *Fall of Princes*, iv. 2952, 'With roial egles a kite may nat flee'.

14. *gentill goishalk*: (*astur palumbarius*) the first of Chaucer's 'egles of a lowere kynde' in *The Parlement of Foules*, ll. 330–6. Cf. Holland, *The Buke of the Howlat* (Bannatyne MS, f. 305r), ll. 327–8, 'Goshalkis were gouernouris of þe grit ost, / Chosin chiftanis chevelrus in chairgis of weiris'.

16. *pairtie cote.* Cf. *LHTA*, i. 225 (1494), 'v½ quarteris of crammesyn satyne to be half a party dowblat'.

18. *the corchet cleiff*: 'split the crotchet into quavers'. Cf. Chaucer, *CT*, I. 3377, Absolon 'syngeth brokkynge as a nyghtyngale'.

21. *fairast feddiris hes farrest foulis*: proverbial. Cf. *The James Carmichaell Collection of Proverbs in Scots* (sixteenth century), ed. M. L. Anderson, 1957, no. 503; and later Fergusson, *Hame Content*, l. 68, and Burns, *Here's to thy Health*, l. 25.

24. *owlis.* See **34.** 7 *n.*

33. *Rauf Colȝard and Johnne the reif*: heroes of two popular Scotch tales of the fifteenth century: the first unwittingly entertains Charlemagne, is knighted, and becomes marshal of France; the second likewise entertains Edward I and his family are rewarded.

38. *Ȝit am I cum of Adame and Eve*: proverbial; Whiting, A37.

62. *dandillie, bischop, dandillie*: possibly a nursery song.

69. *ballattis under the byrkis*: love-songs and light poems.

74. *He playis . . . nychell*: 'he gets all in this game of chance, I get nothing'. A *totum* was a four-sided disk made for a spinning toy, with a letter inscribed on each side: T (*totum*), A (*aufer*), D (*depone*), N (*nihil*, '*nichell*'), the player's fortune being set by the letter uppermost when the toy fell. Cf. Joseph Strutt, *The Sports and Pastimes of the People of England*, 1833, pp. 385–6.

43. *To the King.* With the metaphor of the old horse, which Dunbar develops with great artistry, sympathy, and thoroughness, cf. Chaucer's Reeve (*CT*, I. 3867–9):

> But ik am oold, me list not pley for age;
> Gras tyme is doon, my fodder is now forage;
> This white top writeth myne olde yeris . . .

The stanza form is uncommon; cf. **17.** Editors have disarranged the true sequence of these stanzas, opening the poem with ll. 45–68. But the text in the Maitland Folio MS begins clearly in the middle of a page (18) with the opening refrain 'Schir, lat it never . . . Ȝowllis ȝald', and the first five stanzas ('Suppois I war', etc.)—obviously Dunbar's beginning, with his key proposition to the king. The remainder of the poem was on a quire of the Maitland Folio MS now lost; it was extant in Reidpeth's time, but misplaced to follow p. 2. Reidpeth began his own MS with Dunbar's **69**, which he transcribed as far as l. 22 (the foot of Maitland's page, now also lost); and then, misled by the misplaced quire, he proceeded without a break to **43.** 33–76. When he later reached Maitland's p. 18, he transcribed **43.** 1–32, where Maitland's text reaches the foot of the page, and the point at which his earlier transcript had begun.

2. *Ȝowllis ȝald.* The wit of the poem derives from this special use of *ȝald*, an old horse, to denote anyone who was not wearing a new garment at Christmas. The phrase survives in modern Scots in the north-east, as 'eelshard'; cf. modern 'paseyad', someone with nothing new to wear for Easter; and A. S. C. Ross in the *Saga-Book* of the Viking Society, xii (1937), 1–18. Payments were made to Dunbar on 27 January 1505–6 'for caus he wantit his goun at Ȝule—v lib.', and on 4

January 1506–7 'in recompensatioun for his goun—v lib.' (*LHTA*, iii. 181, 361). On the court at Christmas, its dress and entertainment, see *LHTA*, i. ccxxxvii ff.

5. *Strenever*. Cf. **28.** 13 *n*.

10. *drug and draw*: a common alliterative phrase. Cf. Wyntoun, *Orygynale Cronykil*, i. 1619, 'Hors he gert bath drwg and drawe'; Henryson, *Fabillis*, ll. 2749–50, 'His hors, his meir, he man len to the laird, / To drug and draw in cairt and cariage'.

12. *fang the fog*: get at the grass left out in the fields in the winter. *be firthe and fald*: 'by wood and field'; a common alliterative phrase. Cf. Henryson, *Robene and Makyne*, ll. 95–6; Douglas, *Eneados*, vii, Prologue, l. 162, 'Quhen frostis doith ourfret baith firth and fald'.

36. *uglie gumes*: i.e. those of the cobblers. Cf. **52.** 130.

45. *larges lowd*: ceremonial giving of presents at a festive season. See *DOST*, s.v. *larges*, 3; cf. *LHTA*, iv. 325 (1511–12), 'To Ylay herold, in the name of the officiaris of armez, for thair crying larges one New ȝeir day, deliverit eftir the ald . . . use, x Franch crounis'.

46–8. *palfrayis* . . . *gillettis*: saddle-horses (like Dunbar) . . . mares (with a *double-entendre* in l. 48).

53–4. *I had beine bocht* . . . *sauld*: while on the king's service abroad?

60. *cruik and cald*: lameness and the cold (as sickness). Cf. **52**C. 34 and *The Cursing of Sir Johine Rowlis* (Bannatyne MS, f. 104v), ll. 49–50, 55–6:

> Kald kanker feister or feveris
> Brukis byllis blobbis and bleistiris
> . . . .
> Seattica and Arrattica
> The cruke the cramp the Colica.

69. *Respontio Regis*. There seems no reason to dispute (as some commentators have done) the ascription of these lines to James IV in the MS. If Dunbar himself had hopefully provided a *responsio regis*, he would I think have done so—more wittily but with more difficulty—in the stanza of his petition.

44. *To the King*. A vivid and in part satiric picture of the activity of town and court around James IV (cf. *LHTA*, i. clxxxviii ff.): and, against it, Dunbar's complaint of neglected merit rising into rage. We can probably date the poem after September 1507, when the king licensed the first Scotch printers, if we read *pryntouris* (l. 16) in the modern sense. (The context does of course allow the word its older sense of 'coiner'; but the coiners have I think gone with the carvers at

l. 11.) Chepman and Myllar undertook to 'furnis and bring hame ane prent, with al stuff belangand tharto' from France, 'and expert men to use the samyne', to print the laws and acts, chronicles, mass-books, legends of Scotch saints and other books. The earliest dated book printed in Scotland is a Chepman and Myllar, 4 April 1508.

4. *Doctouris in jure and medicyne.* The Universities of St. Andrews and Glasgow had faculties of canon law, and there was some provision for medicine; but some of James's 'doctouris' came from England and the Continent. One 'Dutch doctor' certainly came via Sweden in 1505 (*LHTA*, iii. 103, 168, 176–9, 190); and 'the lang Doctor of Denmark' received a pension in 1511 (*LHTA*, iv. 267–8).

6. *artistis*: perhaps alchemists; cf. **62**. 37–40 *n*.

7. *Men of armes and vailȝeand knychtis.* In the *Calendar of State Papers* (*Spain*), i (1862), there is a letter (no. 210) from the Spanish ambassador Pedro de Ayala (1498) containing much invaluable comment on life in Scotland, the king, and his court. He describes James's 'men of armes' as 'very good soldiers'. 'The King can assemble, within thirty days, 120,000 horse. . . . There is much emulation among them as to who shall be best equipped, and they are very ostentatious . . .' James was fond of tourneys; cf. **33**. intro. note, and Lindsay on James's court in *The Complaynt of the Papyngo*, ll. 486–7, 493–6, 500–4:

> Allace! quhare bene that rycht redoutit Roye,
> That potent prince, gentyll king James the Feird
>
> . . . . .
>
> Duryng his tyme so Iustice did preuaill,
> The Savage Iles trymblit for terrour;
> Eskdale, Euisdale, Liddisdale, and Annerdale
> Durste nocht rebell, doutyng his dyntis dour
>
> . . . . .
>
> And of his court, throuch Europe sprang the fame,
> Of lustie Lordis and lufesum Ladyis ȝing,
> Tryumphand tornayis, iustyng, and knychtly game,
> With all pastyme, accordyng for ane kyng:
> He wes the glore of princelie governyng.

9. *Musicianis . . . singaris.* James IV loved musical entertainment, and song both sacred and secular. He set up a chapel-royal in 1501 (see Charles Rogers, *History of the Chapel Royal of Scotland*, 1882; Frank Ll. Harrison, *Music in Medieval Britain*, 1958, pp. 14–15, 26, 37, 193–4). 'After mass,' says Pedro de Ayala (*CSP*, *Spain*, i, no. 210, 25 July 1498), the king 'has a cantata sung, during which he sometimes despatches very urgent business'. James played the lute and monochord, which went with him about the country (*LHTA*, i. 329; 1497); an organ also was carried on royal progresses (e.g., *LHTA*, i.

269, 336; ii. 117, 125, 128–9, 407). James encouraged country singers liberally; 'wemen . . . about simmer treis singand' was one of many pleasant customs put down at the Reformation. On New Year's Day 1507 payment was 'giffin to divers menstrales, schawmeris, trumpetis, taubronaris, fithelaris, lutaris, harparis, clarscharis [Gael harpers], pipars, extending to lxix persons' (*LHTA*, iii. 360)—large if perhaps not easily harmonized household music; and in the same year, the Treasurer's accounts mention minstrels from France, Ireland, England, and Italy, Italian pipers, dancers and guisers, singers, and a 'Franch quhissillar' (*LHTA*, iii and iv, indexes).

10. *Chevalouris*: defined for me by Mrs. Helena M. Shire, from a reference in the Red Book of Ossory, as 'blackleg minstrels who played outside union regulations'; *cawandaris* remain obscure.

11. *Cunȝouris*: coiners from the king's 'cunȝehouse' (mint).

12. *Beildaris . . . ballingaris.* On 13 August 1506 James IV wrote to Louis XII: 'For a long time past we have been busy with the building of a fleet for the protection of our shores. . . . Since there is a greater abundance of building material in your realm, we have sent our men thither to fetch beams and oakwood from a friendly nation, and to bring shipwrights to us. . . . Order this fleet, me and my people, whither you will; you will find no one readier to obey, either for vow or honour' (*Epistolae . . . Regum Scotorum*, 1722, i. 39; transl. G. Gregory Smith, *The Days of James IV*, 1890, pp. 103–4). James's finest achievement in shipbuilding was the *Great Michael*, completed in 1511 (*LHTA*, iv. lv and 313). This enterprise 'wasted a' the wuids of Scotland to big her, and danged a' the men in Scotland to launch her'. She was, says Pitscottie, 'the greattest scheip and maist of strength that ewer saillit in Ingland or France. . . . all the wryghtis of Scottland, ȝe and money wther strangeris, was at hir devyse. . . . Scho was xij scoir of futtis of length and xxxv futte withtin the wallis; scho was ten fute thik in the waill, cuttit jeastis of aik witht hir wallis and burdis on ewerie syde sa stark and thik that na canon could gang throw hir'. She carried a ship's company of 300, with 120 gunners and 'ane thowsand men of weir' (Pitscottie, i. 251–2). There is a model reconstruction of the *Great Michael* in the Royal Scottish Museum (see Mackie, facing p. 212).

13. *Masounis lyand upon the land.* See *LHTA*, i. cclxiii ff., ii. 269–81. James built or repaired castles at Dunbar, Inverness, Tarbert, and Loch Kilkerran (*LHTA*, i. 323 *et passim*, 376, 215, clxv), and added halls at Methven, Lochmaben, and Dingwall (*LHTA*, i. 276, ii. 278). At the Palace of Holyrood, chapel, gallery, and great hall were built by 1503 (*LHTA*, ii. 87, 269, 273); the northern tower (all that now

survives of James's building) was finished in 1505 (*LHTA*, iii. 84, 85, 86). Stirling Castle was strengthened, and refined by a 'Kingis hous' with gardens (*LHTA*, i. 276 ff.); Linlithgow was given a chapel, hall, and galleries (*LHTA*, i. 195, 204); and in 1501, alongside Falkland Castle, a palace to serve as a hunting lodge with a game preserve, began building (*LHTA*, ii. 87–9, 424, 425, 461, iii. 82, 295, 298).

16. *Pryntouris*. See *supra*, intro. note. *payntouris*. There were portrait-painters at court (see plates in Mackie); but there were probably many more artists engaged in the decoration of churches and royal houses. *potingaris*: apothecaries, employed as alchemists. See *infra*, ll. 55–6 *n.*

25–34. *And thocht that I . . . my rewarde be small.* Mock-modesty—for the *topos* see E. R. Curtius, *European Literature and the Latin Middle Ages*, 1963 edn., pp. 83–5—rising to a climacteric declaration of merit, and ending in a brief but devastating sarcasm. (l. 34). The claim in ll. 28–33 is familiar in Renaissance verse.

41. *groukaris*, *gledaris*: obscure (unless *gledaris* are related to the *gled*, kite, figuring ravenous greed; see **42.** 13 *n.*). *gunnaris*: probably included with the 'uthir sort' instead of the 'men of armes' (l. 7) because of their origin and (for Dunbar) deplorable expense. James's artillery French as well as Scotch, was celebrated not only for its quality but also for its cost: that of the *Great Michael* was particularly 'great and costlie to the king' (Pitscottie, i. 251). The gunnery experts are intruders like the foreigners in ll. 42–3. There are references in *LHTA*, 1507–13, to such as 'George the Almane gunnar', 'Hannis', 'Wolf' and Frenchmen who received payments of drinksilver and taffeta and hose.

42. *Monsouris . . . cunnaris*: connoisseurs of claret, the staple wine in Scotland until the introduction, in the eighteenth century, of 'that other liquor called port' (David Hume). Cf. **22.** 55–6; *LHTA*, i ccix ff. There were Frenchmen of every rank at court, from noblemen to gardeners, priests to minstrels, doctors to shipwrights and black-smiths (*LHTA*, ii, index).

43. *Inopportoun askaris of Yrland kynd.* The attributive is probably intended to distinguish the 'Irland-men' from their Gaelic-speaking Scotch relatives, the 'Irischemen' (see *DOST*, s.vv. *Irischeman*, *Irland-man*), who of course did not stand in any higher esteem with Dunbar Men of Ireland recorded in *LHTA*, in receipt of pay and other rewards include friars and priests, minstrels, a falconer, a lathenar, and a lorimer

44. *lyk out of mynd*: as if out of their wits, apparently mad.

46. *hall huntaris of draik and duik*: scroungers round the hall tables.

48. *kennis na man of gude*: acknowledge, respect no man of importance

55–6. *ingynouris joly*: alchemists. James zealously collected books 'learned in the philosophy of the true alchemy' (*Epist. Regum Scot.* i. 119), and alchemical materials (see *LHTA*, iii and iv, indexes, 'quinta essencia'). *quintiscence*: alchemy. The 'fifth element' or quintessence is the substance of the celestial spheres and luminaries, not subject to the four primary qualities, and influencing the earth in mysterious ways. The charlatan Damian (see **54**) 'causet the king to believe that he, be multiplyinge [increasing the precious metals by transmutation of the baser metals] and utheris his inventions, would make fine gold of uther metall, quhilk science he callit the quintassence; quhairupon the king maid greit cost, bot all in vaine' (Bishop Leslie, *Historie of Scotland . . . 1436–1561*). For an account of alchemy in Scotland see John Read, *Prelude to Chemistry*, 1939; cf. E. J. Holmyard, *Alchemy*, 1957; intro. to Norton's *Ordinal of Alchemy*, ed. John Reidy, EETS, 1975.

60. *Tolbuyth.* See **75**, intro. note.

66. *Cokelbeis gryce*: a farcical popular tale of a feast; Bannatyne MS, ff. 357ʳ–365ʳ; mentioned in Douglas, *Palice of Honour* (*c.* 1501), l. 1712; and summarized in T. F. Henderson, *Scottish Vernacular Literature*, 1910, pp. 85–90.

79. *My mind so fer is set to flyt.* Cf. **23.** 9–24.

45. *To the King.* A cannily oblique request to the king for 'grace' towards the poet, in the form of a 'complaint' against social—mainly ecclesiastical—'climbers' at court. Dunbar opens sarcastically on behalf of nobles and other men of merit who receive no justice from the king (ll. 1–14). He moves into a violent catalogue of rascals, in the alliterative 'flyting' style (ll. 15–27)—a rhetorical *tour de force*, whatever its relationship to the social realities. This is followed (ll. 28–38) by three illustrations of clerical corruption; and by the exemplary portrait of a 'ruffie' in 'a prelottis clais' lording it over the true aristocracy (ll. 39–66)—a portrait which is, I suspect, specific. Dunbar quietly insinuates his own claim for 'grace' in the final paragraph; he is himself 'of nobill strynd' (cf. **82.** 17). The witty shape and tone of the poem, and the calculated fever of the 'flyting' catalogue, do not deserve Gregory Smith's criticism, 'eminently lacking in seriousness' (*The Transition Period*, p. 55; quoted by Mackenzie). He regards ll. 15 ff. as 'a quagmire of verbal eccentricities', 'in all probability . . . a study in fifteenth-century nonsense'; but this is basing literary judgement on the inadequacy of philological evidence. In fact, only half a dozen of these 'abusive terms' defy explanation.

15. *jow-jowrdane-hedit jevellis*: 'infidel po-headed ruffians'.

16. *kenseis*: apparently 'rascals'. Cf. *Colkelbie Sow*, l. 351, 'Curris, kenseis and knavis' (Bannatyne MS, f. 359v); a 'flyting' in the Bannatyne MS, f. 139v, 'Fals clatterand kensy, kukald knaif'. *Cowkin* is obscure; it may mean 'shitten' (cf. Glossary, *cuk*). *Culroun* (MS *cukoun*) is almost certainly correct—'rascally'; cf. Douglas, *Eneados*, viii, Prologue, l. 43, 'Calland the colȝar a knafe and culron ful qweir'.

17. *stafische*: unmanageable, unruly (cf. Douglas, *Eneados*, XII. vi. 134, Thymetes' 'staffage, skeich and hedstrang hors'). *strummellis*: obscure, but elsewhere in Dunbar a pejorative word for a horse or stirk (cf. **13.** 54, **28.** 11; *infra*, l. 62); perhaps 'low-bred, worthless beasts'.

18. *hummellis*: merely recorded in *DOST*; but following *strummellis* this may be a contemptuous figurative use of 'Hummill / hommill', hornless.

25. *Chuff midding churllis*. Mackenzie hyphenates *chuff-midding* and glosses 'chaff-dungheap'. But the Scots forms of 'chaff' are 'caf(f)e', 'caiff, 'ca(l)f', 'cauf'; cf. **14.** 355. I follow *DOST* in taking *chuff* to be an attributive use of the noun, = a base, surly fellow; cf. **14.** 290; Henryson, *Fabillis*, ll. 2037–8, 'ȝone verray churlische chuff . . . will not giff us ane hering off his creill'. I take *midding* with *churllis*, which accords with *cart fillaris* (? dung carters).

34. *And dois . . . destroy*: metrically defective in the MS; I have supplied 'sa'. I take the sense of ll. 33–4 to be sarcastic: 'One gets a bishop's rochet out of the king by clamour and so—by disguise—puts an end to a stupid sot'. In 1487 James III had been granted the privilege, by Innocent VIII, 'of virtually nominating to bishoprics and monasteries with an income of more than two hundred florins' (McRoberts, pp. 43–4).

62. *strumbell*. See *supra*, l. 17 *n*.

46. *To the Lordis of Chalker*. The 'Lordis Auditouris' or 'Lordis of Chekker' were appointed by commission to hold the annual audit; and as the Court of Exchequer to hear matters concerning the royal revenues. Dunbar's grants and allowances came not from the Chekker but from the Lord High Treasurer (see **47**; cf. *infra*, ll. 11–12). He is using the occasion of the midsummer audit humorously to draw attention to his parlous financial state. On the stanza see **21**.

4. *corce*: coin with a cross on one side. Cf. **19.** 21–2.

47. *To the Lord Thesaurair*. Dunbar's pension was increased dramatically by James IV to £80 a year on 26 August 1510 in 'a lettre maid to maister William Dunbar of the gift of ane yerely pensioun . . . to be pait to him at Mertymes and Witsonday of the kingis cofferis be the thesaurare that now is and beis for the tyme or quhill he be promovit to benefice of 100 lib. or abone etc. with command to the said thesaurare to pay the sammyn and to the auditouris of chakker to allow etc. at Edinburgh the xxvi day of August the yere forsaid. Per signaturam' (*Register of the Privy Seal of Scotland*, i (1488–1529), 1908, p. 323; 'Per signaturam' indicates a letter with James's signature directing the Keeper of the Privy Seal). The first payment would be made at Martinmas (11 November; the Treasurer's accounts for this year do not survive); cf. ll. 21–4. Andrew Stewart, Bishop of Caithness (1502–17) and abbot *in commendam* of Kelso, was Lord High Treasurer from 1 October 1510 till October 1512. For an account of his office see Thomas Dickson in *LHTA*, i. xiii–xxxvi. On the stanza see **18.**

1. *thocht lang*: 'wearied, yearned'. Cf. *To the Gouvernour in France* (anonymous in the Bannatyne MS, f. 78r; sometimes attributed to Dunbar), ll. 35–6: 'Thy tardatioun causis us to think lang, / For of þi cuming we haif rycht grit dispair'.

5. *rink*: men of valour, knights. The correction *raik* in Reidpeth's MS has been related to *rike*, rich; but the poetical *rink* may stand. Cf. *Golagros and Gawane* (*c.* 1475; Chepman and Myllar, *c.* 1508), ll. 9–11: 'Dukis and digne lordis douchty and deir / Sembillit to his summoune, / Renkis of grete renoune . . .'.

18–19. *the narrest way . . . to the air*: the shortest way to the circuit court of justice (passing Edinburgh by).

25–7. *Welcum . . . most preclair*. Commentators have fretted over the implication that Dunbar had received benefice and stipend ('rent') as well as his pension. But I take the stanza only as a shout of delight over (*a*) the 'pensioun most preclair' in lieu of the (probably more modest) benefice with 'rent' and 'lyflett' that he had been seeking; and (*b*) the prospect, given some substance in the king's letter, of an ultimate benefice of '100 lib. or abone'.

48. *To Aberdein*. Queen Margaret's ceremonial entry into Aberdeen took place in May 1511. Dunbar seems to have been in attendance (cf. **65**, intro. note). Civic preparations for this event are recorded in the burgh records (ed. J. Stuart, Spalding Club, xii, 1844). On 30 April 'it was statut and ordanit . . . for the clenging of the toune agane the quenys cumming, that the belman pas throw all the hail toune, and command and chairg all maner of personis, that has ony myddingis upon the forgait befor thair yettis and daioris, to devoid, red, and cleng the samyn . . .'. On 4 May 'the prouest, bailȝeis, counsaill, and communite . . . warnit be the handbell and the officiaris oppinly throw the haill townne, gatherit, and circualy inquerit, be Normond of Lesly and

Gilbert Prestoun, officiaris, all in one voice, concordand, grantit, and frely consentit to ressave oure soverane lady the queyne, als honorablie as ony burgh of Scotland, except Edinburgh allanerlie, and to mak als larg expensis thereapone as the prouest and counsail diuiss, for the honour of the towne and plesour of his gud grace' (p. 81). The pageants described in Dunbar's poem (ll. 21–40, 51) were probably presented by the town guilds, and are not described in the burgh records. See Anna J. Mill, *Medieval Plays in Scotland*, 1927, pp. 99–100. 'The enhancing of royal entries with pageantry was a tradition common to England, France, the Low Countries, and Italy; and everywhere in the fifteenth and early sixteenth century we encounter the same archways across city streets, assemblages of pageant castles, genealogical trees, tabernacles, mountains, fountains, and gardens, and the same groups of allegorical personages . . . augmented with a generous admixture of biblical and historical exempla' (Sydney Anglo, *Spectacle, Pageantry, and Early Tudor Policy*, 1969, p. 6 *et passim*). See also E. K. Chambers, *The Mediaeval Stage*, 1903, ii. 166 ff.; *Renaissance Triumphs*, ed. Margaret McGowan, 4 vols., 1976. On the stanza see **4.**

1. *beriall*: beryl. See **31.** 34 *n.* Cf. Lindsay, *Ane Satyre of the Thrie Estaits*, ed. Kinsley, 1954, p. 44: 'Fair ladie Sensualitie, / The buriall of all bewtie / And portratour preclair.'

15. *Gryt . . . artelȝie*: metrically defective; I emend to '. . . soundis . . .' as the most conservative solution (cf. **14.** 115, 'sound/soundis'). *Was* is a possible plural, though I am tempted to emend to *war*.

21. *the salutatioun*: the first of the guild pageants (Luke i. 28). 25–8: Matt. ii. 9–12; Gen. iii. 23–4.

35. *of portratour*: in form, appearance. Cf. Lindsay, quoted *supra*, l. 1 *n.*; Pitscottie, ii. 17, Lennox was 'ane strang man of personage weill schapin in portratour, that is to say weill braint [upright] in legis and armes weill schoulderit . . .'.

37. *royall Stewartis*. Laing (1834 edn.) is almost certainly right to supply the 'Stewartis' here; but the repetition of 'nobill' in two lines is unlikely. I emend to *royall*: (1) with 'royall . . . great renoun' cf. **47.** 6; (2) Bruce is logically followed by the *royal* Stewarts ('syne'), whose line began with Robert II (1316–90), seventh Steward and son of Bruce's daughter Marjorie.

42. *claid in greine*. See **14.** 24 *n.*

43. *hair detressit . . . hing*. See **14.** 19–22 *n.*

45. *timberallis*: dim. of *timbre*, a tambourine. Cf. the Chaucerian *Romaunt of the Rose*, ll. 769–75; Gower, *Confessio Amantis*, vi

1843–5, 'Wher as sche [the queen] passeth be the strete / Ther was ful many a tymber bete / And many a maide carolende'.

49. *To the Quene.* This poem has no title or ascription in the Bannatyne MS. The language and tone are courtly; but through the conventions thrust an affection and devoted concern. Though Queen Margaret was not the only lady of the court to be widowed prematurely at this period, Laing reasonably suggested that l. 35 refers to the death of James IV at Flodden in 1513, and attributed the poem to Dunbar. For subject and author, Margaret and Dunbar are strong candidates. In 1513 the queen was still only twenty-four, a 'lusty flour of ʒouth' as she had been when she came north to her marriage, but a blossom now flowering 'in bewty . . . unfaidit bayth of cullour and vertew' (ll. 1–2, 33–4); and Dunbar was her man, 'servand', and poet (ll. 25–32). There is strong internal evidence for his authorship. (1) He uses this stanza in a number of poems indisputably his (see **4**), and the interweaving of rhyme and alliterative patterns is characteristic. (2) There are few words in the poem that do not occur elsewhere in his work, and these are not in any way atypical—'lychtsum', 'baneis all baill', 'debonair', 'mening' (ll. 10, 15, 19, 28). (3) There are numerous correspondences between this poem and others indisputably his, in image and diction. These are noted below (with references to **24** and **31**, which are technically *dubia*, in parenthesis). On the same kind of evidence as for **31**, I accept Laing's attribution.

1–2. *O lusty flour . . . schene.* Cf. **2.** 13, **14.** 477, **48.** 6, **50.** 149–51.

4–5. *ʒung brekand blosum . . . sene.* Cf. **8.** 2 and 8–9, [**31.** 27], **50.** 166–7.

6. *Be glaid . . . and expell havines.* Cf. **70.** 3.

7. *Bair of blis.* Cf. **14.** 51, **23.** 155.

9–12. *Brycht sterne . . . hyd.* Cf. **14.** 432–3, **16.** 1–2, **50.** 50–6.

13. *quhair that we go or ryd.* Cf. **27.** 8, **54.** 128.

19–21. *nobill of blud . . . gentill . . . Liberall.* Cf. **82.** 16–17.

29. *Unto the deid.* Cf. **62.** 17.

31. *Sangis to mak.* Cf. **50.** 27–8.

35. *deid hes done devoir.* Cf. **61.** 28, **62.** 49.

37. *lufsum lusty lady.* Cf. [**24.** 9], **83.** 13–14.

IV

VISIONS AND NIGHTMARES

50. *The Thrissill and the Rois.* Included by Allan Ramsay in *The Ever Green* (1724) with the title 'The Thistle and the Rose . . . A Poem in Honour of Margaret, Daughter to *Henry* the VII. of *England*, Queen to James the IV. King of *Scots*'. Henry VII first offered Margaret to James in June 1495, during the Perkin Warbeck affair; reopened negotiations in September 1499 and procured a bull of dispensation because James and Margaret were fourth-degree cousins; and concluded three treaties with the Scotch ambassadors on 24 January 1502, on the Border, peace and confederation, and the marriage. Immediately the treaty was signed, a marriage by proxy took place; but James was not to claim his bride before 3 September 1503, when she would be thirteen years and ten months old. Margaret set out for Scotland in July 1503, and was married at Holyrood on 8 August. On the negotiations, progress, and ceremonies, see *LHTA*, ii. liii ff.; Mackie, pp. 90–112; J. D. Mackie, *The Earlier Tudors 1485–1558*, 1966, pp. 157 ff.; Baxter, pp. 113–18; modernized excerpts in Agnes Mure Mackenzie, *Scottish Pageant*, i (1952), 109 ff.

Dunbar's poem manifestly refers to the royal marriage (see esp. ll. 92–8, 113–19, 148–68); and he dates it explicitly 9 May (ll. 188–9). It was possibly written in May 1502, two months after the return of the embassy from London; but more probably in May 1503, when preparations were being made for the wedding, and Henry had just ratified the treaty (4 May; *Cal. Doc. Scot.* iv, no. 1703). In the setting of his dream and the description of Nature's parliament Dunbar owes much to the example of Chaucer's *Parlement of Foules*, and he borrows Chaucer's stanza (see **5**, intro. note). The poem is 'a triumph of fruitful obedience to conventions. By one convention the political match becomes an instance of *l'amour courtois*, and this, by another convention, becomes of course a May morning dream. By a third convention, that of heraldry, we bid farewell to men and women and talk instead about a lion, an eagle, a thistle, and a rose; and the goddess Natura, out of Alanus, Chaucer, and others, as the patroness of flowers, beasts, and lovers alike, interlocks the whole' (C. S. Lewis, *English Literature in the Sixteenth Century*, 1954, p. 91). The climax of the poem is Nature's injunction to the rulers of the beasts, birds and plants —King James in three heraldic representations—and the celebration of the rose. The thistle and the rose were already associated as emblems of the marriage: the new windows of Holyrood Palace carried the arms of Scotland and England with a thistle and a rose interlaced through a crown (Leland, *De Rebus Britannicis Collectanea*, 1774, iv. 295), and James's marriage contract was bordered in intertwined roses, thistles, and marguerites (*Cal. Doc. Scot.* iv. 340). Despite a few defects in metre and sense, Bannatyne's is a good text, perhaps copied from a print issued for the wedding celebrations. (**10**, which does survive in a Chepman and Myllar print, follows **50** in the Bannatyne MS.)

2. *Appryll*: trisyllabic, after 'averill' (*DOST*, s.v. *aperell*).

4. *May, that muddir is of flouris*. Cf. Douglas, *The Palice of Honour* (*c.* 1501), ll. 65–6, 'Maternall moneth lady and maistres / Tyl euery thing adoun respirature'; Chaucer, *Troilus and Criseyde*, ii. 50–2:

> In May, that moder is of monthes glade,
> That fresshe floures, blew and white and rede,
> Ben quike agayn, that wynter dede made . . .

5. *houris*. See **10.** 10 *n.*

6. *odouris*: fig. flowers (*denominatio*).

9. *Aurora with hir cristall ene*. See **16.** 1–2 *n.*, **54.** 1–2.

15–21. *May . . . In weid depaynt*, etc. See **10.** 87–90 and *n.*

19. *broun*: dark-coloured, dusky. Cf. *Tayis Bank* (Bannatyne MS, f. 229r), ll. 17–18, 'About all blomet wes my bour / With blossummes broun and blew'.

22–3, 36–7. *Slugird . . . Uprys and do thy observance*. Cf. Chaucer, *CT*, I. 1042–5:

> . . . May wole have no slogardie a-nyght.
> The sesoun priketh every gentil herte,
> And maketh hym out of his slep to sterte,
> And seith, Arys, and do thyn observaunce.

33–5. *Lord Eolus*. See **10.** 230 *n.*

44. *a lusty gairding gent*: the pleasance, or *locus amoenus*. See **10**, intro. note.

49. *levis . . . fleit*: leaves wet with the dew flowing down.

51. *bricht as angell*. Cf. Barbour, *Brus*, viii. 233–4, 'glitterand as thai war lik / Till angellis he of hevinis rik'; xii. 425–6, 'The Inglis men . . . richt as angelis schane brichtly'.

56. *all sable fro the hevynnis chace*. Cf. **16.** 1–2 *n.*

57. *cherarchy*: hierarchy. Cf. **1.** 9–16 *n.*; cf. *Asloan MS*, 'Ane Extract of the Bibill', STS, i. 299–300, 'the ix ordouris Angell

archangell throni dominacionis principatus potestates virtutes cherubin & seraphin Thrys thre the thrinfald celestiale cherarchijs'. For the 'blisfull soune' cf. Lindsay's *Dreme* (1528), ll. 519–25:

In Ordouris nyne thir spretis glorious
  Ar deuydit, the quhilkis excellently
Makis louyng, with sound melodious,
  Syngand Sanctus rycht wounder feruentlye.
  Thir ordouris nyne thay are full plesandlye
Deuydit into Ierarcheis three,
  And three Ordouris in everilk Ierarchie.

63. *Haill princes Natur, haill Venus.* Cf. **10.** 73 ff.; Douglas, *Eneados*, xii, Prologue, ll. 246–9:

The larkis, lowd releschand in the skyis,
Lovys thar lege with tonys curyus,
Baith to Dame Natur and the fresch Venus,
Rendryng hie lawdis in thar obseruance.

Dunbar's Dame Nature is able to give 'ane inhibitoun', to bid and ordain (ll. 64–70, 71–2), as the supreme power here, 'vicaire of the almyghty Lord' (Chaucer, *The Parlement of Foules*, l. 379; following Alanus de Insulis). Cf. Alanus' ode to Nature:

O dei proles, genetrixque rerum,
vinculum mundi, stabilisque nexus.
gemma terrenis, speculum caducis,
    lucifer orbis.

pax, amor, virtus, regimen, potestas,
ordo, lex, finis, via, lux, origo,
vita, laus, splendor, species, figura,
    regula mundi

(Raby, *CLP*, p. 301; see the appendix on 'Natura, Nature, and Kind' in J. A. W. Bennett, *The Parlement of Foules*, 1957, pp. 194–212).

64–6. *Dame Nature . . . air.* Cf. Douglas, *The Palice of Honour*, ll. 46–54 ('a garding of plesance'):

Richt hailsome was the sessoun of the ȝeir.
. . . . . .
God Eolus of wind list nocht appeir,
Nor auld Saturne, with his mortall speir
And bad aspect contrair till euerie plant.
Neptunus nold within that Palice hant . . .

67. This line is metrically defective in the MS. Editors have interpolated 'snell' (which has the demerit of not occurring elsewhere in Dunbar) and *scharp* (which is tolerable).

83. *ȝarrow*: milfoil, said to be used by witches to give them speed on night rides.

34. *swift as ony arrow*: proverbial; Whiting, A186.

35. *twynkling of ane e*: proverbial; Whiting, T547.

)1–8. *curage leonyne*. Cf. Chaucer, *CT*, VII. 2646, Alexander 'was . . . ful of leonyn corage'. In the heraldic symbolism of ll. 92–8 Dunbar follows the example of the French *rhétoriqueurs*, notably Chastellain (Smith, p. 63). The lion represents majesty, mercy, and watchfulness (George Ferguson, *Signs and Symbols in Christian Art*, 1961 edn., pp. 21–2); and the royal arms of Scotland. See the illustrations in Mackie, facing pp. 36, 148; cf. Holland, *The Buke of the Howlat* (1450; Bannatyne MS, ff. 302^{r}–310^{v}), ll. 365–73:

> Thairwith linkit in a lyng be leirit men approvit [line
> He bure a lyoun as lord of gowlis full gay
> Maid maikles of mycht on mold quhair he movit
> Rycht rampand as roy ryell of array
> Of pure gold wes the grund quhair the grym hovit
> With dowble tressour about flowrit in fay
> And flourdelycis on loft that mony leid lovit
> Of gold signet and set to schaw in assay
> Our souerane of Scotlandis armis to knaw.

119. *Quhois noble yre is parcere prostratis*. The MS has '*proceir* . . .'; but Dunbar is quoting, rather clumsily, part of a motto associated with the armorial bearings of the kings of Scots, 'parcere prostratis scit nobilis ira leonis' (cf. Henryson, *Fabillis*, ll. 929–30, where the lion assures his subjects 'I lat ȝow wit, my micht is merciabill / And steiris nane that ar to me prostrait'). The motto is derived from Pliny, *Nat. Hist.* viii. 19, 'Leoni tantum ex feris clementia in supplices; prostratis parcit'. Dunbar's sense is clear, if elliptical; and I do not take Douglas Young's advice (*SHR*, xxxviii (1959), 14) to emend *is* to *scit*.

120. *the Egle king of fowlis*: the emblem of royal liberality. The eagle was said to share its prey among the other birds, 'as a king taketh heed to a community' (Bartholomaeus Anglicus; Robert Steele, *Mediæval Lore*, 1905, p. 118).

129. *the awfull Thrissill*: the emblem of armed power.

132. *rubeis*: or carbuncles. See **36.** 24 *n*.

141–3. *Nor hald non udir flour . . . honesty*: timely advice to James, who was about this time dallying with both Janet, daughter of Lord Kennedy, and one 'L. A.' or 'M. L. A.' (*LHTA*, ii. 366, 370, 380). *reid and quhyt*: a stock phrase, but specially appropriate to the daughter of Elizabeth of York and the Lancastrian Henry VII. On the red and white rose of union, devised in 1486 and prominent throughout the Tudor age, see Sydney Anglo, *Spectacle, Pageantry, and Early Tudor Policy*, 1969, pp. 24, 36–7, 347. *honesty*: reputation. Nature's appeal to the 'Thrissill' is appropriate: it was sometimes an emblem of fidelity, and is carried as such (Professor Alastair Smart assures me) in Dürer's self-portrait of 1493 (Louvre; Marcel Brion, *Dürer*, 1964 edn., p. 10).

144–7. *no flour is so perfyt*, etc. So Bartholomaeus Anglicus, *De Proprietatibus Rerum*, transl. Trevisa (xvii. 136), 'Among alle floures of the worlde the floure of the rose is cheyf and beeryth the pryce. And therfore ofte the cheyf partye of man: the heed is crownyd wyth floure of roses as Plinius sayth. And by caus of vertues and swete smelle and sauour, for by fayrnesse they fede the syghte . . .' (Anglo, op. cit. p. 24).

51. *Ane Dreme.* Dunbar here uses the devices of the dream allegory to urge his claim to a benefice; the poem is not an artistic success, for the narrow personal concern suits ill with the broad, general, and august associations of allegory—'more of a curiosity than an achievement' (Scott, p. 154). On the stanza see **8.**

1–2. *halff sleiping . . . Me thocht.* See **52.** 3 *n. aray*: decoration, furnishing. Cf. Lindsay, *The Historie of Squyer Meldrum*, ll. 883–4, 'his Chalmer weill arrayit / With dornik work on buird displayit'.

5. *formed was of clay.* Translating Gen. ii. 7, 'Formavit igitur dominus Deus hominem de limo terrae . . .' (*limus*, mud).

12. *varie*: wander in derangement. Cf. Douglas, *Palice of Honour* Prologue, l. 101, 'My dasyt heid quham lake of brane gart veray'.

14. *feindlie*: diabolical. In the context Dunbar must have written *feindlie*; Reidpeth's 'freindlie', if not a mere slip, seems to be an alteration in erroneous accord with 'guidlie companie' (l. 13).

18. *Distres*: affliction, sorrow; personified in the *Roman de la Rose*. Cf. the Chaucerian *Romaunt*, ll. 4997–9.

20. *Sad as the leid*: heavy as lead. Cf. Douglas, *Eneados*, XII. vi 148, 'assaill with strakis sad'; Whiting, L123.

21. *Langour.* See **9.** 33–4 *n.*

25. *wan and wallowed as the leid*: proverbial; cf. Chaucer, *CT*, VIII 727–8, 'my colour . . . wan and of a leden hewe'; *Thewis of Gud Women* (*c.* 1475), 'And vallowit on the morn as lede' (Whiting, L134); ibid. L115–18, 122, 126).

43. *Discretioun.* Cf. **10.** 165.

51. *haill and feir*: whole and well. Common phrase; cf. Barbour, *Brus* iii. 92, ix. 231.

54–5. *sum rewaird . . . ȝeir.* See **18** *n.*

56. *Considerance*: consideration. Cf. **10.** 165, **15.** 9–10.

58. *Blind Effectioun*: ignorant, undiscerning inclination, partiality.

61–4. *Ressoun . . . may all distribute*. Cf. **41**. 1–5.

65. *Thy . . . enschesoun*: 'people always challenged your unjust deeds'.

68. *all his tyme nevir flatter couthe*: on the evidence of the extant poems, notably true.

86. *Kirkpakar*: one who gathers kirks as into a pack.

94. *deidis*: deaths.

102. *him*: for him (Dunbar).

103–4. *And but ane cuir*, etc. When Temperance might 'weigh out' to Dunbar one (? the only vacant) benefice, Dunbar intemperately asks for another one.

109–10. *He wald not . . . half ane ȝeir*. By Dunbar's time royal nomination of bishops had replaced election by chapter in Scotland (the final confirmation being made, of course, by the Pope); and the crown enjoyed the temporalities of a see during a vacancy (see M. Mahoney in McRoberts, pp. 43–4). Patience here assures the poet (ironically) that the king would not, for his own profit, delay the nomination of a beneficed priest to a vacant bishopric, if this meant holding up Dunbar's preferment.

111–15. *Than as ane fary*, etc. A similar device ends the dream in **10**. 235–43.

52. *Fasternis Evin in Hell*. These twenty tail-rhyme stanzas (cf. **27**) have always been printed as two separate poems closely related in form and theme—entitled 'The Dance of the Sevin Deidly Synnis' and 'The Turnament of the Tailliour and the Sowtar'—with the quatrains of 'Amendis . . . to the telȝouris and sowtaris' (**52** [C] as a supplement. In the Bannatyne MS the stanzas form a continuous sequence, with marginal titles, 'The dance' and 'The turnament'; and the 'Amendis' follow. In the Maitland Folio MS the first part (ll. 1–120) is on pp. 12–16, followed by two other poems by Dunbar; on pp. 161–5 Maitland repeats the first and last parts of 'The dance' (ll. 1–12, 109–20) and passes on to 'The turnament'. The compilers of both MSS thus recognized the essential unity of this material, and I have restored it under a single editorial title with continuous line-numbering. It constitutes an infernal vision in four parts: a prologue (ll. 1–12) in which the Devil calls for a dance of the unshriven to inaugurate Fastern's Even, the last day of carnival before Lent; the dance of the seven deadly sins (ll. 13–108); 'a heleand padȝane' called for by the Devil (ll. 109–20); and a burlesque 'turnament . . . in presens of Mahoun'.

The precise dating in the first stanza suggests that the 'vision' took place in 1507, when Fastern's Even fell on 16 February (see Baxter, pp. 154–6).

[A] 3. *a trance*: an intermediate state between sleep and waking (cf. Lydgate, *Ballade on an Ale Seller*, l. 5; *The Assembly of Gods*, ll. 14–16, Morpheus 'toke me by the sleue / And as I so lay half in a traunse / Twene slepyng and wakyng he bad me aryse'); sometimes, as here, with 'great apprehension or dread of coming evil' (*OED*). Cf. **51.** 1–5.

6. *Mahoun*: Satan; see **14.** 101 *n*.

8. *Fasternis evin*: the eve of the Lenten fast; Shrove Tuesday. Cf. Barbour, *Brus*, x. 437–41:

The folk that tym wes halely
Into the hall at thair dansyng,
Synging, and othir wayis playing:
As apon Fastryn evyn is
The custom to mak joy and blis.

11. *gamountis in the skyis*. The *gamount* (F *gambade*) was a spring or caper, here part of the masquerade (*gyis*). Cf. Lindsay, *Complaynt . . . to the Kingis Grace*, ll. 181–2, 'Castand galmoundis with bendis and beckis / For wantones, sum brak thair neckis'.

14. *the fowll sevin deidly synnis*. Aquinas, *Summa*, 1a. 2ae. 84. The motif of the Sins is common in medieval painting, carving, and tapestry; in didactic literature; and in dramatic entertainments: see M. W. Bloomfield, *The Seven Deadly Sins*, 1952. They may have had a place in the pageants and guisings which were popular at James IV's court (see Baxter, pp. 152–3). But to present this pageant in hell before an audience of devils, and to throw it, not into the formal allegorical procession of the painters and poets, but into the wild swirl of a dance, seem to be original notions of Dunbar's. He revitalizes a commonplace theme by a novel blend of allegorical vision with both comedy and horror. Each Sin has here a human entourage: the pageant represents both sin and its consequences. The obvious relationship between sin and disease was utilized by moralists and poets, and Dunbar probably knew the comparisons in Gower's *Miroir de l'omme*, i. So Pryd leads his victims in a frenzy through scalding fire; the followers of Yre wound one another in madness; Invy, with whom jaundice was associated, 'for pryvie hatrent . . . trymlit'; the followers of Cuvatyce and Gluttony—sins both related to dropsy—are filled up with molten gold and hot lead; the lethargy associated with Sweirnes becomes torture in the dance; and the followers of Lichery are lepers painfully linked to one another in obscene lust. The carnival of the Sins, and the dancing pace they set, are the agony of the sinners.

16. *Pryd*: 'initium omnis peccati est superbia' (Ecclus. x. 15); Aquinas, *Summa*, 1a. 2ae. 84, 2.

17–21. *With hair wyld bak*, etc. A portrait of a gallant. Pride is represented in many Prudentius MSS in a flowing mantle and a head-dress (*Psychomachia*, ll. 178 ff.). The *bonet on syd* is presumably not the small cap with turned-up brim common in Holbein's work, but the large bonnet with plumes (cf. the somewhat later illustrations in James Laver, *Costume of the Western World: Early Tudor*, 1951, pls. 23, 24). The *kethat* is an obscure garment; the context suggests a voluminous mantle. With the association of extravagance in dress and *waistie wanis* cf. Chaucer, *CT*, X. 416 (Superbia); the anonymous *Off ladeis bewties to declair* (Maitland Folio MS, p. 51), 'Thair beltis thair brochis and thair ringis / Makis bigginis bair at hame'.

30. *Blak Belly and Bawsy Broun*: apparently two fiends. Two of the devil-torturers in Roull's *Cursing* (*c.* 1500) are Brownie (ll. 107–8) and Bellie Basie (l. 260); Maitland Folio MS, pp. 143, 148.

31–42. *Yre*. 'Of Ire . . . cometh werre, and every manere of wrong that man dooth to his neighebor . . . eek manslaughtre' (Chaucer, *CT*, X. 561). In Deguileville's *Pèlerinage de la vie humaine*, translated by Lydgate (ll. 15544 ff.) and probably known to Dunbar, Wrath appears as an armed man; and in other descriptions of the Sins he is placed under the influence of Mars. Brueghel's drawing of *Ira* (1557; Uffizi, Florence) has war as its main theme, with Ira fully armed in the fore-ground and supported by two men 'bodin in feir of weir' carrying a monstrous knife (H. A. Klein, *Graphic Worlds of Peter Brueghel the Elder*, 1963, pl. 43).

33. *lyk a beir*. Dunbar glances at the traditional association of the Sins and animals (cf. *infra*, ll. 68, 80; Bloomfield, op. cit., Appendix I). A fifteenth-century English drawing of 'saules that war dampned' shows some 'tothed as bares and thai signifie manslaers and misferers in wil or in dede and ireful' (ibid., p. 221). Cf. Capgrave, *Life of S. Katharine* (*c.* 1450), EETS, p. 379, 'Venemous in anger was he as a bere'. In Brueghel's *Ira*, the sin is attended by a bear which is gnawing at a victim's leg. See also D. W. Robertson, *Preface to Chaucer*, 1969, pp. 153 ff.

41–2. *Sum jaggit . . . scheir*. Cf. Wyntoun, *Orygynale Cronykil*, iv. 1075, 'Wyth a knyff wp to the hefft / He steykyd hym'.

43. *Invy*: here associated with *pryvie hatrent* and 'bakbytting'. Envy is not a passive or interior sin. In a fifteenth-century manuscript of Deguileville's *Pèlerinage*, f. 68r (Bibl. Royale, Brussels, 10176–8), a pilgrim is shown turning away from three vices: Envy on hands and knees holding two spears towards the pilgrim, Treason and Slander

riding on Envy's back. Slander points a spear, strung with three human ears.

48. *quhyte*: insincere. Cf. Chaucer, *Troilus and Criseyde*, iii. 901 and 1567; James I, *The Kingis Quair*, st. 136, 'thoughtis blak hid vnder wordis quhite'; Henryson, *Fabillis*, ll. 600–1, 'This fenȝeit foxe may weill be figurate / To flatteraris with plesand wordis quhyte'; Douglas, *Eneados*, I. xi. 34, Cupid's 'dissemblit slekit wordis quhite'.

56. *Rute of all evill*: 1 Tim. vi. 10, 'Radix enim omnium malorum est cupiditas'. For innumerable proverbial applications see Whiting, C491.

58. *ockeraris*. The usurer's hut is central in Brueghel's *Avaritia* (BM; 1556; Klein, op. cit., pl. 40).

61–6. *Out of thair throttis . . . fervent*. Cf. the miser vomiting gold in Lochner's altar-piece of the Last Judgement (*c.* 1430) in Cologne (*Flowering*, p. 228) and the thirteenth-century wall-painting at Chaldon, Surrey (ibid., p. 236). The punishment in ll. 64–6 is familiar in literature from classical times to the Renaissance (e.g. in Ford's *'Tis Pity she's a Whore*, 1633, III. vi. 8 ff., on hell where burning oil is poured down the drunkard's throat and 'the usurer / Is forc'd to sup whole draughts of molten gold'. I know of no clear iconographical illustration; but the (now destroyed) fourteenth-century fresco in the Church of the Holy Cross, Felstead, probably represented Avarice being tortured in the same way.

68. *lyk a sow*. The pig is commonly associated with Lust. In Brueghel's *Accidia* (1557; Albertina, Venice) the attendant animal is a sleeping ass; but there is a massive pig in the left foreground (Klein, op. cit., pl. 46).

70. *belly huddroun*. Cf. **13**. 38.

74. *Belliall*: 'iniquity'; personified in 2 Cor. vi. 15, 'Quae autem conventio Christi ad Belial?'; and taken from this and the 'filii Belial' in Judg. xix. 22, 1 Sam. ii. 12, etc., to be the name of a devil. Cf. **23**. 249–50.

76. *slaw of feit*. Some writers on the Sins located Sloth in the feet. Christ's wounds were sometimes interpreted as defences from the vices, and his feet were said to be nailed against Sloth (Bloomfield, op. cit., pp. 167–8, 189; Woolf, p. 225).

79–80. *Lichery . . . lyk a bagit hors*. The pig and the goat are the common emblems of Lust. But the horse symbolizes sensuous passion, *libido*, in Plato (*Phaedrus*, 253); and the motif survived in medieval and Renaissance art. I have seen a MS of Alexander Laicus, *In Apocalipsin*, showing Luxuria as a horse; and in numerous MSS of

Prudentius' *Psychomachia* Luxuria is shown riding or driving horses. See Edgar Wind's discussion of the reliefs on the fountain in Titian's 'Sacred and Profane Love' in *Pagan Mysteries in the Renaissance*, 1958, ch. ix; D. W. Robertson, *Preface to Chaucer*, 1962, pp. 30, 253–4, and figs. 7, 8, 63. Cf. Valeriano's chapter on 'meretricia procacitas' in *Hieroglyphica*, 1575, iv. 24, citing (*inter alia*) Virgil, *Georgics*, iii. 266 ff., 'Scilicet ante omnes furor est insignis equarum, / Et mentem Venus ipsa dedit . . .', Ps. xxxii. 9, and Jer. v. 8, 'Equi amatores, et emissarii facti sunt; unusquisque ad uxorem proximi sui hinniebat'. Cf. Dunbar's own simile in **14.** 114. Literary authority aside, the stallion is familiar as a fertility symbol in folk ritual and magic; and his nature justifies Dunbar's comparison.

86–7. *full strenge of countenance . . . reid*: i.e., showing early signs of leprosy, which was associated with lechery (see Denton Fox's introduction to Henryson, *The Testament of Cresseid*, 1968, pp. 25 ff., and references; S. N. Brady, *The Disease of the Soul: Leprosy in Medieval Literature*, 1974). *turkas birnand reid.* Cf. Douglas, *Eneados*, VIII. vii. 185, 'And with the grippand turcas oft also / The glowand lump thay turnyt to and fro'.

110. *Makfadȝane*: a type-name (cf. 'Paddy', 'John Bull'), perhaps suggested by Blind Hary's account of the campaign against Makfadȝan in *Wallace* (ed. M. P. McDiarmid, STS, note on vii. 626).

112. *correnoch*: properly a lament (Gael *corranach*); in Scots of this period, a loud outcry (see *DOST*, s.v. *corenoch*).

113–14. *Erschemen . . . in hell*, etc. See **10.** 259 *n.* Dunbar in several places expresses the lowlander's contempt for the Gaelic-speaking highlander; cf. **23.** 145–68; Bannatyne MS, f. 162[v], 'How the first Helandman of God was maid / of Ane horss turd in Argylle as is said'.

115. *tarmegantis.* See **23.** 532 *n.*

118. *The Devill . . . ȝell.* Cf. **23.** 360.

119. *depest pot of hell.* Cf. the *Excommunicacio generalis*, 'And as the lycht of this candeill passis fra the sycht of yow, sa be thair saulis condempnit fra all spirituall lycht and leime of hevinne to remanne in the deipe pott of hell . . .' (*Rathen Manual* (*c.* 1490), ed. Duncan MacGregor, 1905, p. 28); T. Spencer, 'Chaucer's Hell', *Speculum*, ii. 179 ff. For a *fabliau* in which heaven is cleared of the garrulous Welsh see Peter Rickard *et al.*, *Medieval Comic Tales*, 1972, pp. 55–6.

[B] 121. *Nixt that a turnament wes tryid.* The horror of the dance has been dissolved in the comedy of ll. 109–20, and a smooth transition made to the farce which here follows. The mock-tournament poem, popular in Renaissance Scotland, is derived from (*a*) parody of chivalric romance (cf. **27** and *nn.*), and (*b*) the medieval tradition of 'brawl' poetry, in which peasant merry-making at a wedding or some other public occasion reaches its climax in licentious and violent farce. The first Scotch exemplars of this genre are the fifteenth-century *Christis Kirk on the Green* and *Peblis to the Play*—though earlier examples may be lost. See G. F. Jones, '*Christis Kirk* . . . and the German Peasant-Brawl', *Pub. Mod. Lang. Assn.* lxviii (1953), 1101–25. The history of the brawl in Scots from *Christis Kirk* and beyond is well recorded by A. H. Maclaine in *Studies in Scot. Lit.* ii (1964–5; 4 parts); see also my Warton Lecture on 'Robert Burns and the Peasantry, 1785', *Proc. Brit. Acad.* lx (1974). Dunbar here derides both the timorous 'crafts', who are not up to heroics, and the grave and extravagant farce of the tournament itself (see **33** and *nn.*; cf. J. Huizinga, *The Waning of the Middle Ages*, 1955 edn., pp. 82–4, and Sydney Anglo, 'Anglo-Burgundian Feats of Arms . . . 1467', *Guildhall Miscellany*, ii (1965), 271–83). Two mock-tournaments written at the Scottish court in the reigns of James V and Mary are Sir David Lindsay's *Justing betuix James Watsoun and Jhone Barbour*, *Servitouris* (1538) and Alexander Scott's *Justing and Debait . . . betuix William Adamsone and Johine Sym* (*c.* 1560).

124–5. *Betuix . . . clowttar*: pejorative synonyms follow the craft-names. Dunbar chooses his unheroic protagonists on good authority; cf. the translation of parts of Vegetius, *De re militari*, in 1494 (? by Adam Loutfut, Kintyr Pursuivant), 'Barbouris, soutaris, writaris and talȝeouris, and their awin craft be weill consideryt, thai are na worth for battell, for he may never weil strike with ax or swerd that suld haf a licht hand to hald rasour, nedil, or pen . . .' (*Studies in Scot. Lit.* viii (1971), 178).

129–31. *mony lymmar loun*, etc. Like the Sins in the dance just ended, both Tailor and Soutar are accompanied by a supporting rabble. In the Tailor's entourage are subsidiary workers in his trade: seam cutters, cutters of basting-thread (used to stitch quilting loosely), those who work protective steel into horses' pectoral covers, and those who tack cloth.

137. *the Greik sie*: the tideless Mediterranean.

138. *Telȝouris will nevir be trew*. Cf. Whiting, T13. The dishonesty of the crafts is a commonplace; cf. Maitland Folio MS, p. 338, 'Tak a wobster that is leill / And a myllar that will not steill'.

147. *mast*: 'the greatest' is a possible reading (cf. *DOST*, s.v. *mast(e* n.[4]). But comparison with the size and strength of a ship's mast was proverbial; see Whiting, M396–400.

161. *harlott*: knave, rascal (as *supra*, l. 25). Cf. Bellenden's translation

of Boece's *History*, 1821 edn., i. cviii, 'Gif ony churle or velane the dispise, Bid hence him harlot'.

164–8. *Sanct Girnega*: a devil placed with Gog and Magog, 'Julius apostata / prince pluto and quene cokatrice' in Roull's *Cursing* (Maitland Folio MS, p. 143); and introduced in *The Flytting betuix the Sowtar and the Tailȝour* (Bannatyne MS, ff. 139^{v}–141^{r}) as 'that grym gaist', the sowtars' 'girnand god grit Garnega', who aids them in battle by spewing 'ane pynt at a pant / Off fowll uly ba'.

194. *start*. Editors read 'scart' (the Asloan MS has *scarrit*); but in all other uses of *scare* in Dunbar the MSS have *sk-* forms.

201. *So stern he wes in steill*: i.e., the Sowtar; a ludicrous application of a romance tag. *He* in ll. 200–7 is the Devil.

215. *still*: style.

220. *that sa gud ane bourd me thocht*. This coarse comedy, to which Dunbar seems to have been addicted, is typically medieval; cf. Chaucer, *CT*, the Prologue to and close of the Summoner's Tale. Excretory jokes were common; Dunbar's *dénouement* of 'Belliallis ers unblist' perhaps owes something to the belief that homage is paid, in the witch rites, by kissing the Devil's posterior. Cf. Lindsay, *Ane Satyre of the Thrie Estaits*, ed. Kinsley, 1954, p. 115.

[C] *The Amendis*. A tail-piece to the preceding poem. The place and the occasion are suggested by Maitland's colophon (see l. 40, textual note). Cf. the amends offered to James Dog (**30**); but note the pawky satiric aside in l. 39. As Geoffrey de Vinsauf advises (*Poetria Nova*, ll. 431–3),

> Contra ridiculos si vis insurgere plene,
> Surge sub hac specie: lauda, sed ridiculose;
> Argue, sed lepide gere te, sed in omnibus apte.

On the stanza see **18**.

53. *The Antechrist*. This dream-poem, opening conventionally but running on into sombre burlesque, derides the projected flights of the alchemist John Damian, abbot of Tungland, from the heights of Stirling Castle in 1507. Damian was an Italian, first recorded in *LHTA* in 1501–2 as a 'medicinar' and 'Franch leich' (ii. 395, 144, 139); but he 'had sa craftie and curious ingin to begyl, that he persuadet the king of his gret cunning in al thing natural, cheiflie in that politik arte, quhilk quha knawis tha cal him an alcumist; bot his intentioun only was to milk purses' (John Leslie, *Historie of Scotland*, transl. Dalrymple, STS, ii. 125). He received money and equipment from James IV for alchemy, and was made abbot of Tungland in 1504. In 1507 he 'tuik in hand to flie with wingis', probably to regain the declining royal favour. On this catastrophic experiment see **54.** Damian nevertheless kept his place in the royal household, receiving gifts and alchemical equipment and making money from the king at cards in 1507–8; getting five years' study leave in September 1508; and returning in 1513 to help with the mining of gold at Crawford in Lanarkshire (*LHTA*, iv. 79, 83, 89, 90, 101, 103, 111, 112, 122, 408). On the stanza see **8.** I have preferred Bannatyne's text to that in the Maitland Folio MS, which is metrically clumsy at ll. 5, 16, 17, 18, 34, 39.

1. *Lucina*: the moon; properly the goddess who presided over labour in child-birth, identified with Diana (= Luna, the moon); cf. **10.** 2 *n.* Diana was also identified with Hecate, the Greek moon-goddess and goddess of enchantment (cf. *infra*, ll.31–5).

10. *fantesy*: 'Deme Fortoun', the illusory substance of the 'dremyng'. Cf. **10.** 49, **51.** 14–15. Dunbar's dream is an *oraculum* as defined by Macrobius, in which it is revealed 'what will or will not transpire, and what action to take or to avoid' (*Commentary on the Dream of Scipio*, transl. W. H. Stahl, 1966, pp. 87–8, 90).

14–15. *my quheill . . . steir.* Cf. Boethius, *De Consolatione Philosophiae*, ii, pr. 2 (transl. Chaucer): Fortune says 'stidfastnesse is uncouth to my maneris. Swich is my strengthe, and this pley I pleye continuely. I torne the whirlynge wheel with the turnynge sercle; I am glad to chaungen the loweste to the heyeste, and the heyeste to the loweste.' See H. R. Patch, *The Goddess Fortuna in Mediaeval Literature*, 1927, pp. 147–77; F. P. Pickering, *Literature and Art in the Middle Ages*, 1970, pp. 206–22. The Middle English references are cited in Whiting, F506. For an extended account in Scots see James I, *The Kingis Quair*, ll. 57 ff., 1109 ff., and *nn.* Cf. **10.** 79, **64.** 7–8, **69.** 23–5.

18. *staigis*: steps. Cf. *The Mirror for Magistrates* (1559), 'Warwick', i, 'happy knyghtes / Whom Fortune stalde vpon her stayles stage'. Contrast **61.** 14.

21. *Thy trublit gaist. Cf.* James I, *The Kingis Quair*, st. 173, 'O besy goste ay flikering to and fro, / That neuer art in quiet nor in rest . . .'; following Chaucer, *Troilus and Criseyde*, iv. 302, 'O wery goost, that errest to and fro . . .'.

24. *crennis.* See **22.** 51 *n.*

26. *grephoun*: part lion, part eagle; symbolizing evil forces, especially the persecutors of Christianity; an incarnation of Satan (Louis Réau, *Iconographie de l'Art Chrétien*, i (1955), 88).

29. *the Antechrist*: Christ's chief enemy, to come at the end of history (1 John ii. 18, 22, iv. 3); often identified with the composite beast from the sea in Rev. xiii. 1–2, 'super capita eius nomina blasphemiae.

Et bestia quam vidi, similis erat pardo, et pedes eius sicut pedes ursi, et os eius sicut os leonis' (cf. Dunbar's winged dragon and griffon). Antichrist would be an appropriate offspring: he was commonly portrayed as 'a demon or dragon flying in the air surrounded by lesser demons, or trying to fly aloft in order to prove himself God and being hurled to his death by God' (Norman Cohn, *The Pursuit of the Millennium*, 1970 edn., pp. 33–6 and pl. 1).

31. *Saturnus fyrie regioun*: farthest away from the earth. Cf. **35.** 75–6; but see **10.** 114–15 *n.*

32. *Symone Magus sall meit him.* J. A. W. Bennett notes (*Medium Ævum*, xxvi (1957), 196) that Simon Magus (Acts viii. 9) came to represent the 'false Christ' (cf. *infra*, ll. 36–8), and that according to a story in the *Acts of Peter and Paul*, popularized by the *Golden Legend*, he tried to demonstrate his magical powers to Nero by flying up to heaven with the support of demons. At S. Peter's prayers he was dashed to the ground and fatally injured. Cf. Bishop Leslie on Damian (*Historie*, STS, ii. 125): 'al war lyk to cleiue of lauchter, that quha lyk another Icarus wald now flie to hevin, rycht now lyk another Simon Magus mycht nott sett his fute to the Erde'.

33. *Merlyne at the mone.* It was commonly believed that devils and sorcerers lived beneath the moon, which was subject to supernatural influences. On the Welsh prophet Myrddin, who became the Arthurian wizard Merlin, see *Arthurian Literature in the Middle Ages*, ed. R. S. Loomis, 1959, chs. 3, 19, 23, 37.

54. *Ane Ballat of the Fenȝeit Freir of Tungland.* Like **53** this is a burlesque vision ridiculing John Damian, the French or Italian 'medicinar' and alchemist, whom James IV made abbot of Tungland in March 1504, and his taking 'in hand to flie with wingis' in 1507. For his career at court see **53.** On *rime couée*, here using triplets instead of couplets, see **27.**

'The day cumis', says Bishop Leslie; 'to baith his schouders he couples his wings, that of dyvers foulis he had provydet, fra the hicht of the castel of Sterling as he wald tak jornay, he makis him to flie up in the air; bot or he was weil begun, his veyage was at an end, for this deceiver fel doun with sik a dade, that the bystanders wist not quhither tha sulde mair meine his dolour, or mervel of his dafrie. Al rinis to visit him, tha ask the Abbot with his wings how he did. He ansuers that his thich bane is brokne, and he hopet never to gang agane; al war lyk to cleiue of lauchter, that quha lyk another Icarus wald now flie to hevin, rycht now lyk another Simon Magus mycht nott sett his fute to the Erde. This notable Abbot, seing himselfe in sik derisioun, to purge his crime, and mak al cleine, the wyte he lays on the wings, that tha war not uttirlie egle fethiris bot sum cok and capoune fethiris, sais he, war amang thame, nocht convenient to that use' (*Historie*, STS, ii. 125).

1–2. *As ȝung Awrora . . . paile.* See **16.** 1–2 *n.* Dunbar starts conventionally, with a dawn dream.

4. *sonis of Sathanis seid.* The suggestion that Damian is a *diabolus* perhaps owes something to the habit of presenting devils in feathered costume (the standard dress of unfallen angels) in comic scenes in the mystery plays (cf. Allardyce Nicoll, *Masks, Mimes and Miracles*, 1931, p. 189). The banns for the Chester plays refer to 'The devill in his feathers, all ragged and rente'. Cf. the feathered and winged devil, with three-taloned feet and hands, on a misericord at Gayton St. Mary's, Northants. G. L. Remnant, *A Catalogue of Misericords in Great Britain*, 1969, p. 114 and pl. 16*b*; M. D. Anderson, *Drama and Imagery in English Medieval Churches*, 1963, pp. 167–70.

5. *a Turk of Tartary*: a Moslem, a devil; Mahomet being regarded as a false god. Cf. **14.** 101, **52.** 6.

6. *Barbary*: barbarian (Saracen) territory.

7–8. *forloppin . . . in waithman weid*: renegade, fugitive . . . in outlaw's dress. Cf. **23.** 143 *n.*

11. *cled him in his abeit.* On 'fenȝeit' friars see **55**, intro. note.

16. *Lumbard leid*: the medical learning of Bologna; with Paris, the archetype of the medieval university and, from the middle of the thirteenth century, a notable centre of medicine (Rashdall, *The Universities of Europe in the Middle Ages*, ed. Powicke and Emden, 1936, i, ch. iv, esp. pp. 233–47).

21. *Vane organis*: jugular or 'organic' veins. *he full clenely carvit*: perhaps a reminiscence of Chaucer's 'in myn herte is korven every veyne' (*The Parlement of Foules*, l. 425); an ironic compliment typical of anti-medical satire.

31. *jow*: (Jew) infidel; cf. **23.** 524, **45.** 15.

32. *generit was of gyans.* Cf. the anonymous fantasy of the 'grit gyre carling' (ogress) in the Bannatyne MS (f. 136), ll. 22–5, 'The carling now . . . Is mareit with Mahomyte . . . scho is quene of Jowis'. The association of giants and devilish practices rests on the medieval exegesis of Gen. vi. 1–4 ('Gigantes autem erant super terram in diebus illis . . .') and Isa. xiv. 9 ('Infernus subter conturbatus est in occursum adventus tui, suscitavit tibi gigantes'). Cf. *Beowulf*, ll. 106–13.

34–6. *He wald haif . . . myance*: 'he was so resourceful that he would have, for one night's attendance, a horse and the wounded man's skin as payment'.

37. *yrnis*: surgical instruments (*DOST*, s.v. *irne*, 2. e); still current in Midlothian.

44. *hiddy giddy*: in a turbulent whirl, topsy-turvy. Cf. Lindsay, *Ane Satyre of the Thrie Estaits*, ed. Kinsley, 1954, p. 182, 'Quha drinks of that aill . . . It will gar all his harnis rage . . . It gart my heid rin hiddie giddie'.

50. *sacring bell*: used at the elevation of the Host. The *skellat*, a small hand-bell, is not obviously distinct. (It has been suggested to me that the 'sacring' bell was that in the steeple; but this use of the term seems to be post-Reformation).

51. *bruikit*: blackened with the smoke of the alchemist's furnace. The origin of the word is obscure. Cf. Douglas, *The Palice of Honour*, l. 652, 'with blek my face thay bruik'; Chaucer, *CT*, VIII. 663–72, 'Why artow so discoloured of thy face? . . . I am so used in the fyr to blowe / That it hath chaunged my colour'.

53–4. *channoun . . . channoun*: dignitary (properly, one of the secular clergy of a cathedral or collegiate church) . . . rule, prescription.

55. *stole nor fannoun*: two strips of silk, one worn round the neck and the other over the left arm, as liturgical vestments.

58. *quintessance*. See **44.** 55–6 *n.*

65–8. *Sum held . . . kuke*: a crazily logical series of alternatives. Daedalus made artificial wings for himself and his son Icarus, by which they escaped from the Labyrinth which Daedalus had constructed for the enclosure of the man-bull Minotaur on Crete; cf. Henryson, *Fabillis*, l. 887, 'The Minotaur, ane Monster mervelous'. Damian's 'bruikit' head above his 'fedrem' suggests to the birds that he is some sort of celestial blacksmith or cook. On Saturn see **10.** 114–15 *n.*

73. *Sanct Martynis fowle*: possibly the martin, supposedly so named because it comes in spring and departs at Martinmas; or, more appropriately in the context, the migrant hen-harrier (*circus cyaneus*), known in France as 'oiseau de Saint-Martin' and a bird of prey.

76. *dynt for dynt*. Cf. Wyntoun, *Orygynale Cronykil*, vii. 2055.

80. *as fyre of flynt*: a tag; cf. Barbour, *Brus*, xiii. 36; *The Buik of Alexander*, ii. 4867; Blind Hary, *Wallace*, iv. 285.

98. *skornit him as it was lyk*: 'derided him, as might be supposed'. The jay is characterized by its jarring, disconnected note and its (apparently mocking) imitation of other animal and bird calls. Its stock epithet in

Scots is 'jangling' (see *DOST*, s.v. *ja*). Cf. Chaucer, *The Parlement of Foules*, l. 346, 'the skornynge jay'.

123. *With skryking . . . scowlis.* Cf. Holland, *The Buke of the Howlat* (Bannatyne MS, f. 302r), ll. 66–7, 'Sum bird will bay at my beke and sum will me byte / Sum skirpe me with scorne, sum skyrme at myn e'.

125–8. *I walknit . . . ryde.* A satiric variant of Chaucer's ending of *The Parlement of Foules*:

> And with the shoutyng, whan the song was do
> That foules maden at here flyght awey,
> I wok, and othere bokes tok me to . . .

Cf. **10.** 238–43, **50.** 183–9, **51.** 111–15.

55. *How Dunbar wes desyrd to be ane Freir.* This lightly satiric dream-vision has often been taken as evidence that Dunbar was at one time a Franciscan friar, or (less improbably) that he had been a Franciscan novice; that he wandered naughtily abroad in friar's habit (ll. 31–45), and now pretends to be startled by the appearance in his dream of the dress he had abused. For the arguments see Mackenzie, pp. xx–xxi; Baxter, pp. 26–40. There is, however, no other 'evidence' that Dunbar had ever been even a novice; and when the whole corpus of his poetry is considered as in some sense an expression of his nature and attitudes, the behaviour he describes in this vision is manifestly out of 'character'. He is capable of envy, anger, uncharitableness, and coarseness, but not of this sustained sacrilegious masquerade. (For those who are tempted to read medieval poetry of a 'personal' kind, like Dunbar's, as biography, there is an admirable caveat in Professor George Kane's Chambers Memorial Lecture for 1965 on 'The Autobiographical Fallacy in Chaucer and Langland Studies'). On the internal evidence, this poem is a comic *jeu d'esprit* on the belief that 'daemones in hoc aere caliginoso sunt ad nostrum exercitum' and 'portant secum ignem gehennae quocumque vadant' (Aquinas, *Summa*, 1a. 64, 4); a modest but neat contribution to the volume of satire against friars in the late Middle Ages (see Arnold Williams, 'Chaucer and the Friars', *Speculum*, xxviii (1953), 499–513; John Peter, *Satire and Complaint in Early English Literature*, 1956, pp. 80 ff.; John Moorman, *A History of the Franciscan Order*, 1968, ch. 38). The call to amendment of life and doctrine in ll. 12–15 is reminiscent of, for instance, Chaucer's fiction in the Prologue to *The Legend of Good Women*, F. 319 ff. The claim in ll. 33–40 is manifestly a fictional exaggeration; the admissions in ll. 36–45 are, in miniature, the same kind of destructive self-exposure as Chaucer uses in the Pardoner's Prologue (*CT*, VI. 329–462), and exemplify a not uncommon device used against the friars—satirizing them from an assumed posture within the Order (see A. G. Rigg, 'William Dunbar: The "Fenyeit Freir"', *RES*, N.S. xiv (1963), 269–73). The poem is a 'feigning' about *falset*: the action is a dream-vision with an extravagant, lying confessional fantasy (ll. 33–45) within it; the apparition of S. Francis is a fiend (friars are sometimes represented with devils on their shoulders; see *Flowering*, pp. 50, 62); the key symbol is the friar's habit, the sheep's clothing disguising the wolf (note the cynical reference to the 'bischopis weid' at ll. 29–30); and indeed the theme of the whole poem is the falseness of the friars against whom the text was often directed, 'attendite a falsis prophetis, qui veniunt ad vos in vestimentis ovium, intrinsecus autem sunt lupi rapaces: a fructibus eorum cognoscetis eos' (Matt. vii. 15–16). On the stanza see **8**.

16–18. *My brethir . . . postpone*. Taken by some as autobiographical. But although the *epistillis* may have been private letters, the *sermonis* and *relationis* suggest public and general attempts at recruitment.

23. *that of thy clayis ar so kynd*. S. Francis impulsively sold his father's goods to finance the restoration of San Damiano, and was required by the bishop to restore what he owed to his father. Francis laid at the bishop's feet not only what he owed in money, but also the clothes he had from his father, 'wishing to say only "Our Father, which art in heaven", not "my father, Peter Bernardone"' (Moorman, op. cit., p. 7).

25. *confessour*: the title which the saint bears in the Calendar, indicating that his virtue was signalized by miracles.

34. *Kalice*: Calais, English till 1558.

38. *Derntoun*: Darlington, Co. Durham (see Bruce Dickins in *MLR*, xxviii (1933), 507), where the Bishop of Durham founded a collegiate church in the twelfth century.

42. *In me . . . wes mony wrink*. Cf. Henryson, *Fabillis*, l. 2167, 'the foxe and all his wrinkis'.

47. *Ane fieind*: one of 'these contaminated and abandoned spirits [who] wander over the whole earth and contrive a solace for their own perdition by the destruction of men. Therefore they fill every place with snares, deceits, frauds, and errors . . . and terrify men's souls with dreams, harass their minds with frenzies . . .' (Lactantius, *Inst. Div.* ii. 15; *Ante-Nicene Christian Library*, XXI (1871), i. 128).

56. *Renunce thy God and cum to me*. The versions of this poem in the Maitland Folio and Bannatyne MSS are markedly different. I have adopted Bannatyne's text. It is, however, likely that neither version represents a finished poem; there are inconsistencies and clumsinesses in both, and in both some stanzas may have been interpolated (the catalogue device invites this).

Mackenzie follows earlier editors in seeing both texts as 'retouched and added to by later admirers', with a consequent loss of symmetry and coherence. The shorter version in Maitland is, for Mackenzie, a 'self-contained little poem on a definite subject, the oaths of the "commone people" ', with a series of exempla from the crafts; to this have been added, to the detriment of the original design, the closing stanzas on the thief, courtier, clergy, and all *staittis*. In his view the Bannatyne text takes the revision further—dropping the stanzas at the end, on the courtier *et al.*, because of their 'impropriety', and interpolating new stanzas on the same theme at the beginning (ll. 6–15); amplifying the list of *exempla* (ll. 21–5, 46–60, 66–70) clumsily, with the refrain 'simply tagged on'; and introducing a 'new motive of "devillis . . . as beis thik" ' (ll. 81–5).

'All this', says Mackenzie, 'is hypothetical'. It has the additional demerit of being unnecessary. (1) Apart from Maitland's ending—about which Mackenzie is probably right to be suspicious—the Maitland Folio version, if earlier than Bannatyne's and closer to Dunbar's original, should be clearly superior to Bannatyne's. I do not think that it is so, in general terms: and there are arguably inferior readings in Maitland at ll. 19–20, 28, 32, 35, 39. (2) The sequence in Bannatyne is logical and well ordered (cf. Baxter, pp. 111–12). Dunbar's dream is of the Devil in the market-place (ll. 1–5), listening to oaths and enticing the blasphemers into his service by taking their blasphemies and asseverations seriously (cf. Chaucer's Friar's Tale; *CT*, III. 1301 ff.). He begins with the priest and courtier, who blaspheme against God in mindless habit, and the merchant; and proceeds down through the crafts who swear falsely in pursuit of profit (ll. 21–60) to the outer fringes of the market-place—to minstrel, dicer, thief, fish-wife (ll. 61–80). (3) Mackenzie rightly points to the irregularity in the use of the refrain at ll. 50, 55, 60—and these stanzas may of course be interpolated; but they are not uncharacteristic of Dunbar, and the refrain may be effectively read as the Devil's recurrent, intrusive whisper. (4) Lines 81–5 do not introduce a 'new motive'; the solitary figure of the Devil is, at the climax of the dream, multiplied into a diabolical horde which throngs the market-place. On the stanza see **19.**

3. *aithis of crewaltie*: violent oaths. Baxter notes the frequent legislation against 'grevous and abominabill aithis, sweiring, execratiounis, and blasphematioun of the name of God; sweirand in vane be his precius blude, body, passioun, and woundis; Deuill stick, cummer,

gor, roist, or ryfe thame; and sic uthers ugsume aithis and execratiounis aganis the command of God' (1551; Baxter, p. 111).

17. *Renuncit . . . hell*: repudiated the Judgement.

32. *Nor I*: may I.

37. *evin and od*: a commonplace; Whiting, O18.

44. *hald on thy intent*: 'keep up your tactics'.

46. *The maltman.* He prepared barley and other grain for the brewer by steeping, germinating, and drying in a kiln.

51–4. *Ane browstar swoir . . . fill.* The maltster's customer, the ale-seller, is equally dishonest in swearing that the malt is quite worthless: a *boll* (a grain measure of variable capacity) of it will not produce six gallons of ale, let alone a 'sexterne' of a dozen (*DOST*, s.v. *boll* n.[1] (a)).

56. *rude and raip*: instruments of Christ's passion; cf. **3.** 33 ff.

71–3. *Ane theif said . . . be*: 'O God, may I always escape; nor may a strong gallows-rope make me gape—unless I am to enjoy wealth in hell'. For the construction 'God . . . nor' without a verb cf. Henryson, *Fabillis*, l. 2121, 'Nou God nor that I hang'.

82. *as beis thik*: proverbial; Whiting, B167.

V

MORALITIES

57. *Quhat is this Lyfe?* On the rhyme-royal stanza see **5.** With l. 1 cf. Chaucer, *CT*, I. 2777, 'What is this world? what asketh men to have? . . .'; Seneca, *De Consolatione ad Polybium*, xi. 3, 'tota vita nihil aliud quam ad mortem iter est'.

3. *a slyding quheill . . . remeid*: 'a moving wheel given to us to seek our salvation'.

58. *This Warld unstabille.* A nice example of commonplace made memorable, and moving, by craftsmanship. With the sentiment cf. **62.** 5–16. For the stanza see **21.**

8. *als fresche as pako fedder.* Cf. **16.** 14.

10. *Concluding . . . contrair*: 'coming to an end quite against what I had said'.

16. *So nixt . . . bein*: a melancholy inversion of the familiar medieval commonplace, 'after wynter foloweth grene May' (Chaucer, *Troilus and Criseyde*, iii. 1062; Whiting, W372).

19. *efter joy aye cumis sorrow*: proverbial; Whiting, J58.

59. *All erdly Joy returnis in Pane.* On the stanza see **18.** The sentiment in the refrain is proverbial: cf. Chaucer, *CT*, VII. 3205; Gower, *Confessio Amantis*, v. 191–4; Henryson, *The Prais of Aige*, l. 26, 'of erdly ioy ay sorow is the end'; Douglas, *Eneados*, iv, Prologue, ll. 220–1, 'wil I repeyt this vers agane, / Temporal ioy endis wyth wo and pane'; Whiting, J58–61. On didactic birds see **16,** intro. note.

4. *returnis in*: 'turns into'. Cf. Douglas, *Eneados*, IV. viii. 99–100, 'furthȝet wynys gude / Onon returnyt into laithly blude'.

5–7. *O man . . . agane.* Cf. Horace, *Sat.* II. vi. 97, 'vive memor quam sis aevi brevis'; **61,** intro. note.

10–11. *Deth . . . grane.* Cf. **4.** 9–12 *n.*; Lydgate, quoted in **62.** 70 *n.*

19. *Wes nevir . . . rane*: proverbial; Whiting, D417.

27. *plane*: treeless waste.

60. *Vanitas Vanitatum et omnia Vanitas.* A rhetorical mosaic of moral commonplaces, but powerfully felt. The refrain is from Eccles. i. 2. On the stanza see **4.**

7. *this vaill of trubbill*: Ps. lxxxiv. 5–6, 'Beatus vir, cuius est auxilium abs te . . . in valle lacrymarum in loco, quem posuit'. Cf. *Prymer* (*c.* 1400), 'To the we syȝen gronynge and wepynge in this valeye of teeres' (*OED*).

9–15. *Walk furth, pilgrame*, etc. The scriptural basis of the common medieval sententia of the pilgrimage of life is Heb. xi. 13, 'Juxta fidem defuncti sunt omnes . . . confitentes quia peregrini et hospites sunt super terram'; 1 Pet. ii. 11. Cf. Chaucer, *CT*, I. 2847–8, 'This world Nys but a thurghfare ful of wo, / And we been pilgrymes, passynge to and fro'; Chaucer, *Truth*, ll. 17–20:

> Her is non hoom, her nis but wildernesse:
> Forth, pilgrim, forth! Forth, beste, out of thy stal!
> Know thy contree, look up, thank God of al;
> Hold the heye wey . . .

Guillaume de Deguileville's *Pèlerinage de la Vie humaine* (1330–1) was translated by Lydgate in 1426–8.

17–24. *Heir nocht abydis . . . vanitas.* Cf. esp. **61, 62.** 5–16; and the large number of phrases on the pattern 'now day . . . now nycht' cited in Whiting, N179. *als blak as sabill.* See Whiting, S1.

61. *Memento Homo quod cinis es.* Lines 1, 8, and the refrain are from the Mass for Ash Wednesday: '*Deinde distribuantur cineres sacerdote dicente.* Memento [homo] quia cinis es et in cinerem reuerteris' (*Sarum Missal*, p. 51 and n.; Gen. iii. 19). Cf. 'Erthe oute of erthe is wondirly wroghte' in *Early English Lyrics*, ed. E. K. Chambers and F. Sidgwick, 1907, no. xciv, with 'memento homo . . .' as epigraph. I have preferred Bannatyne's as the stronger and less conventional text. On the stanza see **3.**

5–6. *Lyk as ane schaddow . . . is.* Cf. Job viii. 9, 'sicut umbra dies nostri sunt super terram'; Ps. cxliv. 4; and numerous quotations from religious literature in Whiting, S182, S185.

7–8. *Think . . . reverteris.* Cf. **60.** 22–3; Job vi. 12, 'nec fortitudo lapidum fortitudo mea, nec caro mea aenea est'; Whiting, B511.

9–16. *Worthye Hector*, etc. The *ubi sunt* motif common in medieval elegiac verse. Cf. **62**; Villon, *Le Testament*, st. xl and the following ballades of *dames* and *seigneurs Du temps jadis*: 'Et meure Paris ou Elayne, / Quicunques meurt, meurt a douleur . . .'; Dictes moy ou, n'en quel pays, / Est Flora la belle Romaine . . . Mais ou sont les neiges d'antan', etc.

13. *Hes playit thair pairtis*. Cf. **62.** 45–6.

14. *God that all thing steiris*. Cf. **53.** 14–15.

15. *exceptioun thair is none*. Cf. Villon, *Le Testament*, st. xxxix: 'Je congois que povres et riches, / Sages et folz, prestres et laiz . . . Mort saisit sans excepcion'.

20. *ugsum ugelye tramort*. Cf. **23.** 161, **52.** 83. The metre requires a trisyllabic spelling of 'uglye' (not uncommon in the fifteenth century).

26. *feid . . . flouris*. Cf. Whiting, F317.

28. *the dragone death*. Cf. **4.** 1, 9–10, *nn.*, **36.** 17–18, **40.** 28.

29. *No castell . . . touris*. Cf. **62.** 29–32.

33–6. *Thocht all this warld . . . dres*. Cf. *Everyman*, ed. A. C. Cawley, 1961, ll. 906–7, 'They all at the last do Eueryman forsake, / Saue his Good Dedes there dothe he take'; Douglas, *The Palice of Honour*, ll. 1994–6:

> Nathing remanis bot fame of thair Estaitis,
> And nocht ellis bot verteous warkis richt
> Sall with thame wend, nouther thair Pompe nor micht.

42–6. *Thow sall in deathis port . . . steiris*: with these images of voyage, storm, and salvation by a 'ransonner with woundis fyve', cf. **6.** 165–8, **60.** 13–15.

62. *Timor Mortis conturbat me*. One of the great elegiac expressions of a melancholy age, in which the universal and the personal are poignantly fused. The poem is a meditation upon death; the refrain 'Timor mortis conturbat me' is drawn from the Office of the Dead (responsorium to the seventh lesson in the third nocturn): 'Peccantem me quotidie et non me poenitentem timor mortis conturbat me: Quia in inferno nulla est redemptio, miserere mei, Deus, et salva me.' Cf. J. Huizinga, *The Waning of the Middle Ages*, 1924, ch. xi; T. S. R. Boase, *Death in the Middle Ages*, 1972. On the popularity of this theme in verse see Woolf, pp. 333 ff. Dunbar had a probable model in Lydgate's 'So as I lay this othir nyght', a personal meditation on the 'lessoun' *timor mortis conturbat me*, moving through *exempla*—Adam Noah, Moses and the Jewish leaders, the Nine Worthies, ladies 'that were so fressh of face'—to the universal evidence of mutability in youth–age, summer–winter, 'tresour and greet pocessioun', and an exhortation to 'thynke on Cristes passioun' against the fear of death But Dunbar deepens his meditation in two ways: (1) he universalizes and dramatizes the catalogue of the dead as a *danse macabre* (ll. 17 ff.) (2) he intensifies and personalizes the significance of this by reducing the catalogue to poets dead—and turning his mind, in the climax, on himself. Miss Woolf (p. 335) finds in Dunbar some (implicit) suggestion that 'death's power is seen at its most intense in the fact that a poet dies, though his work continues to be read . . . surely even in the fifteenth century the effect . . . would have been different if Dunbar had been, for instance, a lawyer, and enumerated the names of other dead lawyers'. I think this is to see too much, and wrong: the 'makaris' are Dunbar's 'faculte' (l. 47), his 'brether' (l. 93), who fall in the 'stour' and leave Dunbar 'on forse . . . his nyxt pray' (l. 95). It is, however, interesting that he places himself with poets, and not with priests; it is as a priest that he would be buried. But his procession of dead poets takes its start from the implicit contrast between the pageant-playing of the poet in life and the last, real passage to the grave (ll. 45–6). The traditional number of *morts*—type-figures of prince and prelate, knight and lady, and many more—is restricted to make room for the column of dead poets; elegy for Chaucer and the older 'makaris' rises into lamentation for Henryson and Sir John the Ross, and Kennedy lying 'in poynt of dede'; and a meditative vision ends in a *cri de coeur*.

On the history of the *danse macabre* see J. M. Clark, *The Dance of Death* (1950), and (for a comprehensive bibliography) H. Rosenfeld, *Der mittel-alterliche Totentanz* (1954). Dunbar may have known the famous *danse macabre* painted in 1425 in the colonnade at the Église des Innocents in Paris, or the similar murals in the cloister round Pardon Churchyard near St. Paul's painted a few years later, and the French and English verses (by Lydgate) associated with these (*La Danse macabre*, ed. E. F. Chaney, 1945; *The Dance of Death*, EETS); cf. Brant, *Narrenschiff*, (1494), section 85. See W. F. Schirmer, *Lydgate*, 1961, pp. 127–9; for murals which may be close to the lost Parisian *danse* see Grete Ring, *A Century of French Painting 1400–1500*, 1949, figs. 20–1 (*c.* 1470), in which the figure of Death, as a corpse, entices, drags away, or strikes each representative man or woman in turn as in Dunbar, ll. 21 ff. But there were many visual representations of the theme in the churches of the time—cf. M. D. Anderson, *Drama and Imagery in English Medieval Churches*, 1963, pp. 75 ff.; E. C. Williams, 'The Dance of Death in Sculpture and Paintings in the Middle Ages', *Brit. Arch. Assn. Jour.* l. 229–57—including the carvings at Roslin near Edinburgh; and the *danse macabre* was sometimes performed as a masque. On the stanza see **18.**

6–7. *This fals warld . . . the Fend is sle.* Cf. Lydgate's *Testament*, st. 26:

> Our flesshe is freel, but short abydyng here,
> The olde serpent malicious and wood,
> The world vnstable, now ebbe, nowe is flood,
> Eche thyng concludyng on mutabilite . . .

10–11. *Now sound, now seik*, etc. For the use of rhetorical oppositions to express mutability cf. **60.** 17–24, and numerous illustrations in Whiting, N179.

14–15. *As with the wynd . . . vanite*. Cf. Dante, *La Divina Commedia*, 'Purgatorio', xi. 91 ff., 'O vanagloria dell' umane posse . . . Non è il mondan romore altro che un fiato / Di vento, che or vien quinci ed or vien quindi . . .'; Lydgate's confession, in his *Testament*, of being 'Wawed with eche wynd, as doth a reedspere' (st. 86).

17. *On to the ded gois all estatis*. Cf. the *Vado mori*, in which twelve representatives of the estates of society speak in turn; e.g. 'Vado mori, rex sum; quid honor, quid gloria regum? / est via mors hominis regia. Vado mori.'

18. *Princis . . . He takis*, etc. Cf. Langland, *Piers Plowman*, B. xx. 99–104:

> Deth cam dryuende after and al to doust passhed
> Kynges and kny3tes kayseres and popes;
> Lered ne lewed he let no man stonde,
> That he hitte euene that euere stired after.
> Many a louely lady and lemmanes of knyghtes
> Swouned and swelted for sorwe of Dethes dyntes.

potestatis. For this sense cf. Henryson, *Fabillis*, ll. 1574–5, 'ane prince or empriour / Ane potestate, or 3it ane king with croun'.

37. *Art magicianis*: practitioners of the art of magic. Cf. Gower, *Confessio Amantis*, vi. 1957, 'the craft of Artemage'.

38. *Rethoris . . . theologgis*. Cf. Irlande, *Meroure of Wysdome*, STS, ii. 91, 'to þat concordis all clerkis, logicianis, philosophouris and theologis'.

46. *Playis heir ther pageant*. Cf. **61.** 13. Whiting cites (?) Skelton, *Kynge Edwarde* (1483), 'I have played my pageyond, now am I past' (P5).

51. *The monk of Bery*: John Lydgate (1370–1449), monk of Bury St. Edmunds.

53–5. *The gud Syr Hew*, etc. The beginning of a roll of Scotch poets: Sir Hugh Eglinton of that Ilk (d. 1377), brother-in-law of Robert II, and not otherwise known as a poet; Heryot unknown —the attributive use of 'Ettrik' in the MSS is almost certainly an error for 'Et eik', and anyhow does not help; and Andro of Wyntoun, prior of Lochleven till 1422 and author of the long verse *Oryginale Chronykil of Scotland*.

58. *Johne Clerk*. A number of poems in the Bannatyne MS are attributed to 'Clerk' (a common name); Affleck is unknown.

61. *Holland*: Sir Richard Holland, secretary to the Earl of Moray, rector of Halkirk in Caithness and Abbreochy in Moray, canon of Kirkwall, and author of the allegorical *Buke of the Howlat* (1447–55). *Barbour*: John Barbour (d. 1395), archdeacon of Aberdeen, author of *The Actes and Life of Robert Brus* (1376) and probable translator of *The Buik of Alexander*.

63. *Schir Mungo Lokert of the Le*: (d. ? 1489), of Lanarkshire; not otherwise known as a poet.

65. *Clerk of Tranent*. This Clerk and his work are unknown. The Maitland Folio MS has, less specifically, 'The clerk of Tranent'; but this is unrhythmical.

66. *Gawane*. See *Arthurian Literature in the Middle Ages*, ed. R. S. Loomis, 1959, pp. 360 ff., 493 ff., 528 ff.

67. *Schir Gilbert Hay*: (*fl.* 1450), priest, translator of *The Buke of the Law of Armys* and other prose works, and of *The Buik of Alexander*; 'chaumerlayn umquhile' to Charles VII of France (see J. H. Stevenson's introduction to *Gilbert of the Haye's Prose Manuscript*, STS, i).

69. *Blind Hary*: author of *The Actis and Deidis of Schir William Wallace* (1478); as much as possible has been done for his shadowy life and character by his editor, M. P. McDiarmid (STS, i). Sandy Traill is unknown.

70. *Slane . . . haill*. Cf. Lydgate, *Timor Mortis conturbat me*, st. 10, 'Deth . . . with his dedly mortal schours / Abatyd hath ther fresshe flours'.

71. *Patrik Johnestoun*: official receiver of revenues from West Lothian crown lands, paid for producing 'certis joccis et ludis factis coram rege' in 1476–7 (*Exchequer Rolls*, viii. 333, 404, 512) and for plays before the king at Linlithgow (*LHTA*, i. 91, 118). *The Thre Deid Pollis* is attributed to him by Bannatyne (*Bannatyne MS*, STS, ii. 142–4; Henryson, *Poems*, ed. H. Harvey Wood, 1933, pp. 205–7).

73–5. *He has reft Merseir . . . hie*. A number of poems are ascribed to Mersar in the Bannatyne MS (STS, iii. 245, iv. 48 and 73), but he is not otherwise known.

75. An adaptation of Chaucer, *CT*, I. 306, 'short and quyk and ful of hy sentence'.

77–9. *Roull of Aberdene*: unknown. *Roull of Corstorphin*: (near Edinburgh); perhaps the author of *The cursing of Sr Iohine Rowlis* 'upoun the steilaris of his fowlis' (*Bannatyne MS*, STS, ii. 277–84; *c.* 1500), and if so a notable 'flytar'.

82. *Maister Robert Henrisoun*: 'scholmaister of Dunfermling', author of *The Morall Fabillis of Esope* and *The Testament of Cresseid*. Interpretations of Bannatyne's 'taie broun' as 'tane Broun' or 'laid Broun' introduce another (unidentifiable) poet and do violence to the clear sense of the print.

83. *Schir Johne the Ros*. See **23**, intro. note.

86. *Stobo*: John Reid, 'alias Stobo', rector of Kirkcrist in Kirkcudbright, secretary to James II, James III, and James IV (cf. **23**. 331); noted as sick in May 1505 (*LHTA*, iii. 138, 142) and as dead in July (*Exchequer Rolls*, xii. 372). *Quintyne Schaw*: author of a poem in the *Maitland Folio MS* (STS, i. 385) and recipient of a pension of £10 in 1504 (*LHTA*, ii. 445).

89. *Walter Kennedy*. see **23**, intro. note.

63. *Into this Warld may none assure*. The sentiment in the refrain is proverbial; for many variants see Whiting, W671. On the stanza see **19**.

2. *kyth . . . or mo*: '(at least) declare, give vent to, my troubles to—or more'.

7. *For lang service . . . none*. Cf. Tilley, S254, 'Service unrewarded is a punishment' (1616).

11. *ane rowt*: here, a fine company. Cf. **48**. 53–4; Chaucer, *CT*, I. 2494–5, 'And to the paleys rood ther many a route / Of lordes upon steedes and palfreys'.

13. *spending*: money to spend.

17–18. *And bot . . . And nane bot . . . injure*: 'And only . . . And none except just men have to endure injustice'.

19. *wit . . . and ressoun*. Cf. **26**. 20. Dunbar intends a distinction; *wit* = sense, wisdom; cf. **14**. 257, 463, and **78**. 44.

23. *cairlis*: peasants. Cf. Lindesay MS (*c*. 1586), f. 44b, 'ane evill carle that is vngentill, that is to say, ane churle' (*DOST*).

28. *On fredome is laid foirfaltour*: freedom (with its noble associations) is taken away by forfeiture. The phrasing is legal: cf. *Criminal Trials in Scotland*, i. 13 (1489), 'the process of forfaltour led upon oure cousingis Johne, Earl of Leuenax . . .' (*DOST*).

29. *pety*: another attribute of nobility. Cf. **14**. 315–16 and *n*.

38. *trewth . . . dure*. Cf. Lindsay, *Ane Satyre of the Thrie Estaits*, ed. Kinsley, 1954, p. 165, 'Quhy that my lustie Ladie Veritie / Hes nocht bene weill treatit in this cuntrie'.

41–2. *Fra everilk mowth . . . hairt*: the opposition is proverbial. For many examples see Whiting, M755.

46. *quhyte quhaill bone*: ivory from the walrus or other marine beast, confused with the whale. Cf. *The Squire of Low Degre* (*c.* 1400), l. 537, 'lady as whyte as whales bone'; *The Destruction of Troy* (*c.* 1400), l. 3055, 'alse qwyte . . . as any qwalle bon'.

48. *asure*: lapis lazuli, exemplifying not only blueness but hardness; *blew asure* is not tautological. Bannatyne (or his source) seems to have tried desperately to emend the metaphor he misunderstood.

49. *adamant*: 'extremely hard, so that it scratches all metals except the hardest steel' (Albertus Magnus, *Book of Minerals*, I. ii; transl. Dorothy Wyckoff, 1967, p. 40. Cf. *Lapidaries*, pp. 66–7.

51–3. *ȝit . . . future*. Cf. 2 Cor. v. 10, 'omnes enim nos manifestari oportet ante tribunal Christi, ut referat unusquisque propria corporis, prout gessit, sive bonum, sive malum'.

54. *or than de sall*: i.e. at the Day of Judgement.

56. *cravis*. *DOST* glosses 'ask, beg' (1. c); but the sense is surely 'demand, claim' (2), referring to ll. 52–3 *supra*.

59. *as wind hyne wavis*. Cf. *The Castell of Perseverance* (*c.* 1450; *Macro Plays*, EETS), l. 380, 'As wynde in watyr I wave'.

63. *Quhen the angell . . . sture*: at the 'last trump'; 1 Cor. xv. 52, Rev. xi. 15, and 1 Thess. iv. 16, 'Quoniam ipse Dominus in jussu, et in voce Archangeli, et in tuba Dei descendet de coelo . . .'.

71–5. For a comment on Dunbar's effective contrasts between Latin and the vernacular, here and elsewhere, see Denton Fox in D. S. Brewer, *Chaucer and the Chaucerians*, 1970, pp. 182–4. Lines 71–2 may be from a hymn, or are Dunbar's own Latin. Line 73 is reminiscent of Job iii; l. 74 is from Matt. vi. 23, 'Si ergo lumen, quod in te est, tenebrae sunt: ipsae tenebrae quantae erunt?'

77. *frak*: roll swiftly. Cf. **10.** 237. The emphatic simplicity of diction and alliteration in ll. 76–80 lift Dunbar's argument to a climax. *flude and fyre*. Cf. Wyntoun, *Orygynale Cronykil*, i. 231, 'In prophecy . . . That fyre and flwde sulde all oure-ga'.

64. *For to be Blyth me think it best.* One of a notably small group of poems on being cheerful and contented (**65**, **66**); the cheerfulness is measured—a defensive consolation in a world of 'frawdfull fary'. Maitland's text is manifestly inferior to Bannatyne's, with the omission of ll. 16–20, weaker readings in ll. 6, 8, 24, 27, clumsy inversions in ll. 11–12, and an 'improvement' in l. 37 which destroys the emphatic repetition in 'evir . . . nevir . . . Bot evir'. On the stanza see **19.**

6. *This warld . . . vary*. Cf. **62**. 5–16.

7–8. *Fortoun . . . rest*. See **53**. 14–15 *n*.

17. *dois his dayis in dolour dryfe*. Cf. **67**. 17–18.

28–9. *Sen to the lyfe . . . twynklyng of ane e*. Cf. 1 Cor. xv. 52 (part of the service for the burial of the dead), 'In momento, in ictu oculi, in nouissima tuba: canet enim tuba, et mortui resurgent incorrupti, et nos immutabimur'. For *twynklyng of ane e*, used early to translate 'ictu oculi', see Whiting, T547. Cf. **57**.

65. *Without Glaidnes avalis no Tresure*. The Aberdeen MS of this poem was discovered by J. W. Baxter in the Aberdeen Minute Book of Seisins in the Town Clerk's office, vol. iii (1507–13); see *TLS*, 8 April 1939, p. 208. The poem is a little more than half-way through the volume, after entries for October and November 1511 and before two pages dated August 1510 and January 1510 respectively. Despite this slight muddle, it seems safe (with Baxter) to associate the Aberdeen text with Queen Margaret's visit to the city in May 1511, the poet in attendance (see **48**). This text is not only the earliest of the three surviving versions; it is arguably superior to one or both of the others at a number of points (cf. ll. 6, 10, 12, 14, 17, 20, 27, 30, 33, 34). Bannatyne's version is not merely a careless copy of the Aberdeen MS (cf. ll. 6, 11, 31), though some variants may be 'improvements' by Bannatyne (cf. l. 14); it is far closer to the Aberdeen text than is the markedly inferior Maitland version. On the stanza see **4**.

5. *His chance . . . to morow*: 'hodie mihi, cras tibi', Ecclus. xxxviii. 22; 'an old hempen proverb' (Marlowe, *The Jew of Malta*, IV. ii. 18).

18. *famous*: reputable. Cf. **14**. 307 *n*.; Edinburgh Burgh Records, 1484, 'That nane of the commoun rentis be set bot till famous men, inhabitantis of this toun and of substance' (*DOST*).

20. *ane cry*: the space of a shout, a short time.

29. *to spend . . . grace*: who (by grace) have the fortune to spend it.

37. *Ane raknyng . . . small*: prob. proverbial. Cf. Tilley, S965, 'A small sum will serve to pay a short reckoning'.

39. *strang as ony wall*: a favourite simile of Lydgate's; Whiting, W14–18.

66. *He hes anewch that is Content*. On the stanza see **19**. Reidpeth's text is markedly different from the Maitland Folio text, which I follow, and was presumably copied from the lost quire of the Maitland Folio MS. Apart from the confusion of l. 34, there are a number of metrically inferior lines (6, 7, 33), what look like attempts to correct

›y simplifying (ll. 2, 12, 17, 19, 27), and a number of weaker readings ll. 4, 11–12, 15, 24, 28, 31).

;. *He . . . content*: proverbial. Cf. Caxton, *Book of Curtesye* (*c.* 1477), EETS, p. 25; Whiting, E120; Tilley, E162.

:1–14. *Thairfoir . . . gud cheir*. Reidpeth's text apparently attempts o simplify, and attracts Baxter (p. 197). The Folio text may be construed: 'I therefore beg you . . . not to look for delight in a great ariety of pleasures, but to thank God for whatever (little) is sent to ›ou . . .'.

:7. *Withe gall in hart and hunyt hals*. For numerous illustrations of his proverbial opposition see Whiting, G12 and H433; cf. Lydgate, *Troy Book*, Prologue, ll. 277–8, 'With sugred wordes vnder hony oote / His galle is hidde lowe by the rote'. *hals*: neck; prob. here throat'.

9. *subchettis*: (?) subcharges, second dishes. Cf. Henryson, *Fabillis*, l. 281–2, 'Till eik thair cheir ane subcharge furth scho brocht, / Ane ›lait off grottis and ane disch full of meill'; Douglas, *Eneados*, XIII. x. 118.

:9. *Gif we . . . fall*: proverbial; Whiting, C295, C296; Tilley, C412.

;3. *of his intent*: in his mind, disposition.

›7. *Thyne awin Gude spend*. Mackenzie doubts Dunbar's authorship ›f this poem: it is anonymous in the Maitland Folio MS, and 'the heme is scarcely congruous with Dunbar's usual utterances'; the xposition, moreover, is 'awkward'. Scott attacks it as the 'worst' poem ttributed to Dunbar, 'mean and vile' in sentiment and weak in style pp. 258–60). Congruity is not, however, an infallible test in Dunbar: e expresses a wide range of moods and sentiments; and the style of this oem is nowhere quite uncharacteristic. Lines 5–8 and 33–4, for ıstance, are clumsy; but on the other hand ll. 21–4 seem to me unıistakably Dunbar. A number of correspondences with other poems y Dunbar are noted below, and there is nothing untypical in the iction or phrasing. There is a strain of cynicism and bitterness in the oem, notably in ll. 33–40, but nothing which is unthinkable in)unbar; the mood is sadly and painfully human. On the stanza see **18.**

. *thy lyfe . . . in weir*. Cf. **61.** 22.

–16. The sequence in the Maitland Folio MS is perhaps an attempt › keep the link in sentiment between ll. 1–4 and 9–10; but ll. 5–8 emain a break in the circuit between 9–12 and 13–16.

o. *And . . . wend*: metrically clumsy; not materially improved in the Maitland Folio MS.

9–12, 31. *Thow may . . . space: Bot his . . . grace*. Cf. **65**. 27–9.

17–18. *Sum all . . . pane*. Cf. **64**. 16–17, **65**. 25–6.

23. *mirrynais/mirrey face* [Maitland]. Cf. **65**. 31 and textual note.

27. *settis on ane es*: risks in play (*es*: ace, the one in dice).

68. *Cuvetyce*. This poem is anonymous in the Bannatyne MS, but is attributed to Dunbar in the Maitland Folio MS and set there in the midst of a large group of his poems. The stanza is peculiarly Dunbar's (see **18**). In the diction of the poem, there are a few words not otherwise used by Dunbar ('hors rynning', 'houshaldis', 'to landwart', 'vennesoun', 'wyld fowill', 'spyce', 'husbandis' (farmers), 'grangis', 'ȝemen'; but these are not significant in either number or character. There is nothing in the style to argue against Dunbar's authorship, and the sentiments are not uncharacteristic. It is probable, however, that the poem was written after Flodden (1513), when 'the Realme now in sik distres, al drew to factiounis and pairties, sum to defend the quene, sum the nobilitie, al studiet to thair particular proffet, outher occupieng his nychtbours landis, with force, or his nychtbouris gudes wrangouslie, how euer he could' (Leslie, *The Historie of Scotland* (1570), STS, ii. 155). Cf. Lindsay, *Testament . . . of our Soverane Lordis Papyngo* (1530), ll. 523–7, 535–41, 'Of Flodoun feilde the rewyne to reuolfe':

> So may ȝe knaw the courtis inconstance
> Quhen prencis bene thus pullit frome thair seis;
> Efter quhose deith quhat strainge aduersiteis,
> Quhat gret mysreule, in to this regioun rang,
> Quhen our ȝong prince could noder spek nor gang . . .
>
> Sum tyme the realme was reulit be regentis,
> Sum tyme, Lufetenentis, ledaris of the law;
> Than rang so mony Inobedientis
> That few or none stude of ane vther aw:
> Oppressioun did so lowde his bugyll blaw
> That none durst ryde bot in to feir of weir:
> Ioke Vponeland, that tyme, did mys his meir.

5. *weilfair, welth and wantones*. With the phrasing cf. **14**. 479, **22**. 36, 70.

29. *in silk harlis to the heill*: go in trailing silk cloaks. Cf. **52**. 19–21; Lindsay, *Syde Taillis*, l. 88, 'Harland thare claggit taillis so syde'.

33–6. *Quha that dois . . . cuvetyce*. Cf. **65**. 17–20.

41–2. *Man . . . chirry*. Cf. **65**. 1–2, **70**. 21–2.

69. *In Winter*. In its present state, the text of the Maitland Folio MS begins with l. 23 of this poem. The text was apparently complete wher

Reidpeth copied parts of the MS in the 1620s; he begins his own manuscript with a transcript of ll. 1–22 and goes on erroneously, without a break, to **43**. I follow the second (complete) version in Maitland. On the stanza see **21**.

The sentiment here is of course characteristic of the age; but cf. the twelfth century 'Mirie it is while sumer ilast . . . this nicht is long / And ich with wel michel wrong / Soregh and murne and fast' (MS Rawlinson G. 22), and, from the thirteenth century (MS Harl. 2253),

Wynter wakeneth al my care;
Nou this leves waxeth bare;
Ofte I sike and mourne sare
  When hit cometh in my thoght
Of this worldes ioie, hou hit geth al to noht.

Nou hit is, and nou hit nys,
Also hit ner nere ywys.
That moni man seith, soth hit is,
  Al goth bote Godes wille.
Alle we shule deye, thah us like ylle . . . .

2. *sabill*: (1) black (cf. the application to clouds in **14**. 433, **16**. 2); (2) mourning (cf. **14**. 418, 447; **36**. 7). I take l. 3 not with ll. 1–2 but with ll. 4–5.

3. *mystie vapouris . . . skyis*. For the effects of cloudy or misty air see Burton, *The Anatomy of Melancholy*, I. 2. ii. 5.

4–5. *curage . . . off*: disposition to, heart for.

9. *langour*: misery, low spirits. Cf. **9**. 33–4 *n*., **19**. 7, **51**. 21–5.

11–15. *I walk*, etc. Cf. Chaucer, *The Book of the Duchess*, ll. 1–8, 'I have gret wonder . . . How that I lyve, for day ne nyght / I may nat slepe wel nygh noght . . .'.

17. *Despair*: hopelessness; without prospect of pension or benefice.

23–5. *Fortoun . . . hir glas*: hour-glass, sand-glass; symbols of time and death.

27. *Quhy . . . away*. Cf. Chaucer, *Troilus and Criseyde*, iv. 1628, 'For who may holde a thing that wol awey'; Whiting, H413.

29–35. *Thow tending . . . spendit heir*. Cf. *The Dance of Death*, EETS, ll. 381–2: 'ȝe mote accounte towchyng ȝowre laboure / How ȝe haue spente hit in dede worde and thowght'; *Everyman*, ed. A. C. Cawley, 1961, ll. 103–12:

Dethe. On the thou must take a longe iourney;
Therfore thy boke of counte with the thou brynge,
For tourne agayne thou can not by no waye.
And loke thou be sure of thy rekenynge,

For before God thou shalte answere, and shewe
Thy many badde dedes, and good but a fewe;
How thou hast spente thy lyfe, and in what wyse. . . .

31–45. *And than sayis Age . . . sowp.* Contrast Henryson, *The Prais o Aige*, ll. 15–16, 'I am content that youthede is ago: / The more of age the nerar hevynnis blisse'. 'Nothing could better stress the differenc between the two poets, and of the two eras they express. Dunbar' *Angst* is as sincere as Henrysoun's serenity, his melancholy as profoun as Henrysoun's humour' (Scott, pp. 246–7).

36–40. *Syne Deid . . . his ȝettis wyd*, etc. The menace half-hidden i Age's brotherly gesture is open now. Cf. **4.** 3 *n.*; Matt. xvi. 18. Fo the gates of death, see Job xxxviii. 17, Ps. cvii. 18, Isa. xxxviii. 10 With l. 39 cf. **3.** 118–19.

41. *For feir . . . I drowp.* Cf. **62.** Scott (pp. 314–15) notes how the ol four-stress measure underlying Dunbar's verse stands out in thi stanza.

42. *No gold in kist.* Contrast **70.**

70. *Ane wirkis Sorrow to him sell.* Attributed to Dunbar by Banna-tyne; anonymous in Maitland. Dunbar uses this stanza form wit notable frequency (see **19,** intro. note). The metrical pattern inter-laced with alliteration, the blend of simplicity and strength in style, ar characteristic; there is little in the diction that is not otherwise to b found in Dunbar ('expell', 'prop', 'mank or menȝie'); and there ar parallels in sentiment and phrasing. I accept Bannatyne's attribution

6. *sturt or stryfe.* Cf. **52.** 31.

8. *with mariege . . . mell.* Cf. the alliterative pattern in **14.** 56.

11–15. *He that hes . . . sell*: 'He, on the other hand, who has a pleasin and virtuous wife ('but mank or menȝie')—a target for his own arrow-shaft ('genȝie')—and goes shooting at an unknown target, and is wor out with the pox, is the author of his own sorrow'. Cf. Carmichaell *Proverbs in Scots*, ed. M. L. Anderson, 1957, no. 786, 'He that hes wif of his awin and gois to this town, that is a lown'. With the rhym in ll. 11–12, cf. **21.** 3–4. For *prop* (shooting-butt) in Scots see *OED* s.v. sb.[1], 2.b. The sexual quibble on *schell* follows the Latin 'concha (= 'cunnus'; cf. Plautus, *Rudens*, III. iii. 42); the correspondenc between the cowrie shell and the female *pudendum* is a familiar them in folklore. With Dunbar's metaphor cf. Lindsay, *Answer to the Kingi Flyting* (1536), ll. 36–7, 45–9:

Thocht ȝe rin rudelie, lyke ane restles Ram,
Schutand ȝour bolt at mony sindrie schellis . . .

> Tholand ȝow rin schutand frome schell to schell,
> Waistand ȝour corps, lettand the tyme ouerslyde:
> For, lyk ane boisteous Bull, ȝe rin and ryde
> Royatouslie lyke ane rude Rubeatour,
> Ay fukkand lyke ane furious Fornicatour.

the fleis of Spenȝie: possibly the dried beetle *Cantharis vesicatoria*, used as a genital stimulant and 'ministered . . . to drink *ad venerem excitandam*' (Burton, *Anatomy of Melancholy*, I. 2. v. 4); but Dunbar is more probably referring to the 'Spanȝie pockis' (cf. Montgomerie, *Flyting*, l. 314, 'The feavers, the fearcie, with the Speinȝie flees' and innumerable other ills).

18–19. *ane maister . . . rewth*: James IV. Cf. **25**. 9.

21–2. *Now . . . chirry*. Cf. **68**. 41–2.

71. *Thir Ladyis fair that in the Court ar kend*. An equivocal satire on ladies who 'solist' in the courts—or rather, on 'the middle-class landed gentry . . . the men of property [who] care more about their property than the honour of their womenfolk' (Scott, pp. 71–2). The stanza is twelve-line tail-rhyme, based on Latin and French models; see J. Schipper, *History of English Versification*, 1910, pp. 299–300.

3. *kend*: well-known, familiar; with a probable double entendre, 'known carnally'. Cf. Lindsay, *The Monarche* (1552), ll. 3417–19: 'Thay purposit thame for to ken / And abuse thame vnnaturally / With thare foule stynkand Sodomye'.

16. *myld and moy*. Cf. Douglas, *Eneados*, XIII. xi. 1–2, 'Venus . . . rycht myld and moy'.

21. *collatioun*: (bedtime) repast, here with amorous implications. Cf. Lindsay, *In Contemptioun of Syde Taillis*, ll. 146–9, 'Quhen thay wald mak collatioun / With only lustie companȝeoun / ...Ȝe may considder quhat I mene'; Lindsay, *Ane Satyre of the Thrie Estaits*, ed. Kinsley, 1954, p. 54 (Solace to Sensualitie):

> Ȝes lustie ladie thocht he war never sa seik
> I wait ȝe beare his health into ȝour breik:
> Ane kis of ȝour sweit mow in ane morning
> Till his seiknes micht be greit comforting,
> And als he maks ȝow supplicatioun
> This nicht to mak with him collatioun.

28. *Trest as the steill*: proverbial: Whiting, S702–712.

46. *spend*: give something away; an obvious double entendre. Earlier ME usage supports the sense, 'dissipate, wear out'; the early Scots sense, 'spring, leap', which would be equally appropriate in Dunbar's word-play, is not recorded before 1533 (*OED*).

48. *geir*: (1) property; (2) (sexual) apparatus. Cf. Wyntoun, *Orygynale Cronykil* (*c.* 1420), iii. 866, 'Thay wyvis . . . poyntyt to thaire preva gere / That betwene thaire lymys stud'; Lindsay, *Satyre*, ed. Kinsley, 1954, p. 55, '. . . preif ȝon gallant geir'.

54. *compositouris*: (a legal term) those who settle disputes and arrange agreements; conventionally described as 'amiable', 'freyndsome', etc. (*DOST*).

58–60. *With expeditioun . . . pendit*: 'With despatch, and with all stipulations met, their seals are appended'. If innuendo is intended, it is clumsily done. *conditioun*: a common legal term.

61. *Alhaill almoist*: (1) 'almost completely'; (2) 'undamaged—almost'.

65–6. *get indoist . . . evidens*: (1) 'get inscribed all the documents establishing their legal rights'; (2) 'get marked all that they display'.

71. *suppryis*: harm, destroy. Mackenzie cites the heading to Douglas, *Eneados*, XI. x, 'Turnus . . . gan devys / Practikis of weir, the Troianys to supprys'.

72. *In Prays of Wemen*. Scott (p. 56) reads this poem as a piece of court flattery. In view of the emphatic (and possibly connective) ll. 1–2—'this now is *my* opinion of women'—I take it rather as a supplement or a rejoinder to another poet's praise or blame of women: an exercise in a familiar mode, perhaps part of a court contest or entertainment. In the Middle Ages 'femininitee' is suspended between the two poles of Eve and Mary: 'þe ȝates of parais / Þoruth Eue weren iloken, / And þoruth oure swete Ladi / Aȝein hui beoþ nouþe open' (John Peter, *Satire and Complaint in Early English Literature*, 1956, pp. 86 ff., where the tradition is ably summarized). Dunbar himself was capable of energetic anti-feminist satire; cf. **14.** This is his only exercise in the Chaucerian decasyllabic couplet.

23. *That fowll his nest he fylis*: proverbial; Whiting, B306. Cf. *Of Women cometh this Worldes Weal* (Vernon MS; Carleton Brown, *Religious Lyrics of the Fourteenth Century*, 1924, no. 110), ll. 73–6:

I holde þat brid muche to blame
Þat defouleþ his oune nest;
Þou wost wel a wommon was þi dame,
I-boren and fed of hire brest.

73. *Tway Cummeris*. 'This is a curious picture from the life, in the style of Flemish paintings' (Pinkerton, *Ancient Scotish Poems*, 1786, ii. 414). Cf. R. L. Greene, *The Early English Carols*, 1935, no. 419). On the stanza see **19.**

The earliest version of this poem is in the Aberdeen Minute Book of Seisins in the Town Clerk's office, vol. ii (1503–7), where it appears on the same page as **31**. I have followed Bannatyne's text, as a little superior (metrically and in one or two substantive readings) to the Aberdeen MS. Maitland's version is markedly different, especially in the variable refrain which adjusts to the context of each stanza with superficial cleverness. But the modification is obviously wrong in l. 5 (Lent is just beginning on Ash Wednesday); and the variations lose the force of the simple reiteration in Bannatyne, there sustaining the irony of a poem in which 'all talk is double talk' (Scott, p. 67). The hypermetrical variation in l. 30 in the Aberdeen MS looks like a clumsy attempt at what the Maitland Folio MS does more systematically; and it muddles the sense of l. 29, which is self-sufficient—the object of the cummers' 'howp' is 'to mend'.

14. *mavasy*: malmsey, wine originally produced in Malvasia (Greek Monemvasia), and at this time imported from the Netherlands; first recorded in the burgh records of Aberdeen in 1412, and in those of Edinburgh in 1468. With the preference of the cummer's mother cf. Pitscottie, i. 186: 'And then the Duik of Albanie send his familiear servand to the said Frincheman for the wyne and prayit him to send of the best and starkest quho grantit the samin werie heartfullie and send him the tuo bossis of mavasie.'

23. *nocht wirth a bene*: proverbial; Whiting, B92. Cf. **14.** 128.

26–7. *Off wyne . . . sowp.* They drank two quarts of wine, turn about, using a half-pint glass.

74. *Tydingis hard at the Sessioun.* In the Bannatyne MS this is the first of 'certane ballattis aganis the vyce in sessioun court and all estaitis'. The Session originated in the special court set up by James I in 1426, ordaining 'þat his chancellar and with hym certane discret personis of the thre estatis to be chosyn ande depute be oure souerane lorde þe king sall syt fra hyne furthe thre tymis in þe ȝere . . . quhilk sal knaw, examyn, conclude and finally determyn all and sindry complayntis, causis and querellis þat may be determynit befor þe kingis counsal' (*Acts of the Parliaments*, 1814–75, ii. 11, c. 19). The modern Court of Session, the supreme civil tribunal, derives from the College of Justice set up by James V in 1532. On the stanza see **13.**

5. *undir confessioun*: as under the seal of confession. Probably at this time, as later, the public was not allowed to hear the proceedings of this court, and those present were sworn not to reveal them.

18–19. *Sum patteris . . . oppressioun.* Cf. Burns, *The Holy Fair*, ll. 82 ff., 'Here, some are thinkan on their sins', etc.

23. *super expendit.* Cf. **14.** 397.

29–31. *Sum castis*, etc. 'One interprets writs (issued by the court under the royal signet) and one makes objections ('exceptionis and causis defensall') to the court's ruling; one stands aside and picks up the incidental pronouncements of the lawyers; some cases are adjourned, some win, some lose'.

37. *Sum in ane lambskin is ane tod.* See **14.** 423 *n.*; cf. **37.** 59.

41. *sait*: court. Cf. Scott, *The Heart of Midlothian*, ch. iv, 'A lord of seat—a lord of Session'.

45. *Carmeleitis and Cordilleris*: White-friars, of the order of Our Lady of Mount Carmel, founded in Palestine *c.* 1154 but claiming continuity with earlier hermit settlements on Mount Carmel; and the Franciscan Grey-friars or Observantines, who wore girdles of knotted cord (founded *c.* 1368); see J. H. Moorman, *A History of the Franciscan Order*, 1968, esp. ch. 43. The first Grey-friars house was established at Berwick in 1231, and the first Carmelite house at Tullilum, near Perth, in 1262. On the religious orders in Scotland at and after Dunbar's time see Anthony Ross's essay in McRoberts, pp. 185–233 and appendices.

50. *he complexioun*: vigorous constitution. Cf. Henryson, *Fabillis*, ll. 2826–9:

> For clerkis sayis the inclinatioun
> Of mannis thocht proceidis commounly
> Efter the corporall complexioun
> To gude or euill, as nature will apply.

55. *All mercyfull wemen thair eirandis grantis.* See. **9.** 49 and **14.** 315, 497–502, *nn.*

75. *To the Merchantis of Edinburgh.* The medieval city of Edinburgh extended east down the long high ridge from the Castle, through the Lawnmarket and the High Street, to the burgh of Canongate and Holyrood Palace. The houses, generally wood-framed with a plaster infilling, often stood at right angles to the street; and temporary booths, erected against the gables, lined the thoroughfare. The old Tolbooth, where the Parliament and Court of Session met, stood to the west of St. Giles' Kirk (l. 16), leaving a narrow street between the Lawnmarket and the High Street. To the east the luckenbooths, or permanent shops, ran down to the head of the High Street. The commercial quarter of the city was crammed and odoriferous. For a good account of burgh life at this period see W. Croft Dickinson, *Scotland from the Earliest Times to 1603*, ch. xxv. Dunbar's address to the merchants is related to the homiletic tradition of 'sermones ad status'; and it moves typically from rebuke (*increpatio*) through warning (*comminatio*; ll. 57–63) to *exhortatio* (ll. 64 ff.); cf. J. H. Fisher, *John Gower*, 1965, pp. 141 ff. The poem is a fine illustration of Dunbar's facility (not equalled in Scots till Burns) in interweaving natural diction and rhythm with metrical form. This stanza ($aaab_4b_2ab_4$) is not used elsewhere by Dunbar.

9. *stink of haddockis and of scaittis*. The fishmongers and butchers threw their trimmings into the streets, which were piled high with middens on both sides. On 4 July 1505, for instance, the burgh council ordered 'purgeing and clengeing of the hie streitt . . . of all maner of muk, filth of fische and flesche, and fulyie weit and dry'; and in October ordered 'that the furrouris and skynneris dicht nor schaik thair skynis on the hie gaitt, nor hing thame on forestairis [*infra*, l. 17], for til eschew the evil sauour thairof . . .' (*Extracts from the Records . . . of Edinburgh*, ed. J. D. Marwick, 1869, pp. 105, 107). Cf. C. H. Talbot, *Medicine in Medieval England*, 1967, pp. 154–5.

11. *fensum*: origin uncertain. *DOST* takes this as an error (? by Reidpeth) for *fowsum*, foul, loathsome. Cf. Boece, *History*, II xii. 82b, 'twa bredir . . . be fowsum flytingis lichtlying vtheris'.

15. *stinkand scull*. Reidpeth's transcript has *scull* altered from *stull*, which is probably a scribal error caused by *styll* (l. 38). The school has not been identified. The 'summa scola grammatica', now the Royal High School, was at this time in the Vennel of the Church of St. Mary in the Fields, or Kirk o' Field Wynd (W. C. A. Ross, *The Royal High School*, 1934, p. 19), well to the south of the 'parroche kirk' of St. Giles. The *stinkand scull* may have been part of the ecclesiastical establishment, a 'little' or elementary school (see John Durkan in McRoberts, pp. 145 ff.).

17. *foirstair*: an external stair on the front of a house; first recorded about 1500.

20. *polesie*: improvement. Cf. *St. Giles' Charters*, 1475 (1859), p. lxviii, 'For reparacioun, beilding and polesy to be maid in honour of . . . sanct Johan' (*OED*, s.v. *policy* sb.[1] II. 6a).

22. *hie croce*: the Mercat Cross, to the north-east of St. Giles'. It was rebuilt in 1555 and 1617; demolished in 1756, and the shaft removed to the grounds of Drum till 1869, when it was returned to St. Giles'; and set up on its present platform in 1885. See *The Stones of Scotland*, ed. G. Scott-Moncrieff, 1938, pp. 82–4 and illustrations. The mercat-cross was the central point in the main market-place, where proclamations were made and punishments meted out; 'the symbol of the burgh's jurisdiction and . . . its legal centre' (Dickinson, op. cit., p. 246); degraded in Dunbar's Edinburgh by vulgar and trivial chaffering.

24. *trone*: the site of the king's 'tron', or public weighing-beam; sometimes also associated with the 'jougs', an iron collar and chain serving as a pillory. Cf. **23.** 400.

30. *Now the Day dawis*: a popular song, transformed into a pious one in *The Gude and Godlie Ballatis* at the Reformation. Cf. Douglas, *Eneados*, xiii, Prologue, l. 182, 'menstralis playing "The ioly day now dawys" '. *Into Joun*: not identified.

31–2. *Cunningar men . . . clame*: more skilled men have to spend their time serving S. Cluanus, and never claim the right to practise other and higher crafts. S. Cluanus, a sixth-century Irish abbot, was apparently associated with eating and drinking (see Lindsay, *Ane Satyre*, ed. Kinsley, 1954, pp. 88 and 189).

34. *mowaris on the moyne*: those who deride, mock at, the moon. Cf. the proverbs, 'to bark against the moon', 'the moon does not heed the barking dog'; Whiting, M654, and Tilley, M1119 and M1123.

36. *Tailȝouris, soutteris and craftis vyll.* Cf. **52.** 124–5, 138, 164–8, *nn.*

38. *the stinkand styll*: probably the Old Kirk Style, an alley through the luckenbooths. Professor Kenneth Cameron has drawn my attention to a substantial number of place-names with 'stinking' as a first element; 'stigel', a stile, occurs in names which suggest it also means a 'steep ascent'.

39. *hamperit in ane hony came*: cramped like bees in a honeycomb.

57–9. *Sen . . . burgh*: 'Since the countryside resorts to this town because the king's court and the court of session are here . . .'. On the *sessioun*, see **74**, intro. note.

67. *proclame*: declare outlawed, denounce. Cf. **23.** 24.

77. For Reidpeth's lacuna Laing proposed 'reconqueis', which is too strong and requires the emendation of *ȝow* to 'ȝour'. Small (STS) proposed *win bak to*, which is persuasive (cf. *supra*, ll. 42, 56).

76. *Dunbar at Oxinfurde.* The colophon in the Maitland Folio MS (*b*) is the only evidence that Dunbar visited (or studied at) Oxford. For the stanza see **4.**

9. *curius probacion logicall*: subtle logical proof.

11. *The naturall science filosophicall*: the study of natural phenomena. Cf. Gilbert of the Haye, *Prose Manuscript*, STS, i. 67, 'alsua the gretest clerkis philosophouris naturale that ever was, sayis in thair naturale science of phisik . . .'.

22. *ȝour sawis ȝour dedis contrar*: proverbial; Whiting, W642.

77. *He Rewlis weill that weill him self can Gyd.* Advice to a young friend at court. For the stanza see **4.** With the refrain cf. *The Life and Martyrdom of Beket* (*c.* 1300), ed. W. H. Black, 1845, 261–2, 'For he thoghte he mighte wel of othere habbe maistrie / If he hadde of his owne flesch thurfout seignurye'.

12. *Ane freind may be thy fo*: proverbial; Whiting, F635.

15. *The psalme . . . eiris*: Ps. xviii. 25.

19. *Be thow content . . . no neid*: proverbial; Tilley, C623, C624.

21. *Chakmait*: proverbial metaphor. See Whiting, C196; cf. Chaucer on Fortune's 'chek . . . mat', *The Book of the Duchess*, ll. 618 ff.; Lydgate, *The Dance of Death*, l. 459, 'O cruel dethe . . . To my beaute thou haste i-seide checke-mate'.

28. *Sic art thow . . . thy cumpany*: proverbial. Cf. Barclay, *The Ship of Fools* (1509), 1874 edn., ii. 35, 'For eche man is reputyd of the same sort / As is the company wherto he doth resort'; Whiting, C395, C396; and later examples in Tilley, M248, M382.

36. *stryk . . . in the neck*: rebound on, overtake. Proverbial; Whiting, N43.

78–80. *Of Discretioun.* The three poems on discretion are linked in the Bannatyne MS by tags at the end of the first and second; the attribution to Dunbar at the end of the third must apply to all three. In the Maitland Folio MS they are set out as a single poem; but Dunbar's authorship is not in question. The allusion in **79.** 36–7 has been taken to refer to Damian and to indicate a date 1502–7 (see **53**), but it may well be quite general. On the stanza see **19.**

Bannatyne's drafts of the first two poems are occasionally close to Maitland's texts; variations between the drafts and Bannatyne's own final versions are not significant. In many places Maitland's versions are inferior to Bannatyne's metrically (see **78.** 1, 6, 9, 26, **79.** 16, 17, 27, 58, **80.** 22, 29, 39); rhetorically (see **78.** 12, 21, 22, **79.** 21, 41, 49, 58, **80.** 1, 21, 32, 38); or in sense (see **78.** 14, 23, 28, 34, 36–9, **79.** 6, 28, 36, 38, 39, 54, **80.** 2, 28, 31). Maitland's versions of the first two poems each lacks a stanza; in **80** Maitland's additional stanzas after ll. 15 and 35 are of poor quality and are probably not Dunbar's.

78. *Discretioun in Asking.* 9. *dull as stane*: proverbial. Cf. Whiting, S759–62 (as deaf, dumb, as a stone); Douglas, *Eneados*, xi, Prologue, l. 40, 'dolf [dull] as ony stane'.

17. *To ask . . . blame*: 'to ask for payment for service is not culpable, is justified'.

24. *Few wordis may serve the wyis.* Cf. *The Paston Letters*, ed. J. Gairdner, 1904, vi. 60, 'I can nomore but *sapienti pauca* etc.'.

27. *Na thing is gottin but wordis sum*: proverbial; Whiting, M276. Cf. Gower, *Confessio Amantis*, i. 1293, and vi. 446–9:

> He was no fol that ferst so radde,
> For selden get a domb man lond:
> Tak that proverbe, and understond
> That wordes ben of vertu grete.

79. *Discretioun in Geving.* 8. *in practik for supple*: with practical cunning, artfully, to procure their own advantage.

27. *all ourlaidin is his berge.* Cf. *Die Burgsche Cato-Paraphrase*, 'Men seen al day: the litell boot and barge / Wol drench a-non, whan it is over-freiht' (Whiting, B422); Chaucer, *Legend of Good Women*, ll. 619–21.

28–9. *Than vyce . . . dischairge*: 'Then, from this, vice and prodigality destroy his honour'. *Dischairge* also carries forward, from l. 27, the metaphor of a cargo.

51. *[gud] kewis*: prudent conduct. I reject Bannatyne's 'gud', which is apparently accidental repetition; but I retain *kewis* (which Mackenzie thought unintelligible). To keep one's *kewis* is to play one's part well, like a good actor. Cf. Wantonnes in Lindsay, *Ane Satyre of the Thrie Estaits*, ed. Kinsley, 1954, p. 56: 'To kis hir and clap hir sir be not affeard . . . Will ȝe leif me Sir first for to go to, / And I sall leirne ȝow all kewis how to do'.

80. *Discretioun in Taking.* 2. *Bot littill . . . forsaiking*: construable as 'leaving little of value behind'; but that suits ill with the line following.

13. *mailis*: usually rents paid in money rather than in kind; but the context suggests the latter here. See *DOST*, s.v. *male* n.[1] 2b, 'victale male mele' (1498). *gersomes*: additional rents paid in advance for a lease of one or more years. 'Male' and 'gersum' are often conjoined in legal documents.

36–9. *Grit men . . . successioun.* Cf. Higden, *Polychronicon*, transl. Trevisa, Rolls Society, 1865–86, iii. 357, 'Zenocrates seygh oon i-lad to the honging, and lowh and sede, "the gretter theeves punscheth the lasse" '. *sessioun*. See **74**.

81. *May na Man now undemit be.* In the Bannatyne MS this poem follows Dunbar's three poems *Of Discretioun* (**78–80**) and is ascribed to him. There are two versions in the Maitland Folio MS. The first follows **16**, and is left anonymous. The second comes between a poem attributed to Stewart and a sequence of nine poems by Dunbar; and it is ascribed to Stewart. This may be an error due to placing, but the problem of anonymity in the first version remains. The stanza is a popular one with Dunbar (see **19**). The theme is close to that of **82**, and may be modelled like **82** on Lydgate's *A wicked Tunge wille sey Amys* (see *infra*, ll. 16–17, 21–3, 26–30, *nn.*). The opening is typical of Dunbar; it is unlike him, however, to abandon his 'voce that said on hicht' at the outset. But the sentiment and the style are not uncharacteristic of him, though the ending is stylistically weak. The poem contains only a few words and uses which are not to be found elsewhere in Dunbar (the construction 'lord lyk', l. 11; ll. 17, 'gentillmen'; 19, 'jaipit'; 22, 'cumis' (becomes); 28, 'quantetie'; 32, 'streiche'). There are on the other hand some indications of Dunbar's hand (see ll. 1–2, 8–9, 12–14, 24, 41 *nn.*)—not perhaps decisive, but enough to strengthen Bannatyne's attribution.

Manifest errors (e.g. l. 2) and trivial variants aside, the first Maitland version is closer to Bannatyne's than is MFb, differing from Bannatyne at only a few points; and MFb has a number of inferior readings peculiar to itself (ll. 4, 6, 9, 17, 22, 26, 27, 28, 32, 33, 41, 43, 46, 48). The cancellation of l. 26 and the omission of ll. 26–30 in MFa suggests that the copyist had these lines before him and dropped them because they interrupt the moral theme, and break the natural link between 'prydfull' dress (ll. 21–5) and 'ornat . . . speiche' (ll. 31–5). The omission of ll. 41–5 from Bannatyne's MS may be due to inattention—or incomprehension.

1–2. *Musing . . . mirry day.* Cf. the opening of **13**, **37**, **51**; **14.** 211, **50.** 24.

8–9. *Sum . . . Sum*: a favourite rhetorical device of Dunbar's; cf., e.g., **14.** 480 ff., **20** *passim*, **78.** 11–13, **79.** 2–3, 6–9 *et passim*, **80** *passim*.

12–14. *Than every pelour . . . leid a tyk*: with the phrasing and association cf. **23.** 113–14 and 237–8.

16–19. *Be I ane lady . . . air.* Cf. Lydgate, quoted *infra*, **82.** 21–30 *n.* *jaipit.* Cf. Lindsay, *The Historie of Squyer Meldrum*, ed. Kinsley, 1959, ll. 61–2, 'it is no happie lyfe, / Ane Man to jaip his Maisteris wyfe'.

21–3. *Be I ane courtman . . . me.* Cf. Lydgate, quoted *infra*, **82.** 21–30 *n.* *cumis me richt.* Cf. *Bannatyne MS*, STS, iii. 295, ll. 65–6, 'Na weid will cum hir better / Nor this garmond'.

24. *a widdy wicht.* Cf. **56.** 72.

26–30. *Be I bot littill*, etc. Cf. Lydgate, *A wicked Tunge*, st. 7:

> ȝif thow be fatte owther corpolent,
> Than wille folke seyn thow art a grete glotoun,

A deuowrer or ellis vinolent; [drunken
Ʒif thow be lene or megre of fassioun,
Calle the a negard yn ther oppynyoun . . .

32. *Towsy*: some unkempt, dishevelled woman.

41. *War nocht*: were it not that. For the construction cf. **14.** 332, **19.** 8.

46–7. *Gude James . . . ȝing*: James IV (born 1473). Lines 49–50 are an application, hardly 'subtill', of Matt. vii. 1–2.

82. *How sould I Governe me.* Baxter (p. 192) reads this poem on slander as autobiographical. But although the tone is characteristically personal, the poem belongs to a minor didactic tradition. It is perhaps modelled on Lydgate's *A wicked Tunge wille sey Amys*, which concludes with an allusion to Cato's *Distichs*, 'virtutem primam esse puta conpescere linguam; / proximus ille Deo est, qui scit ratione tacere' (cf. Whiting, T366 *et seq*). On the stanza see **19.** I have preferred the text in the Maitland Folio MS, which (despite flaws) has superior readings at ll. 4, 8, 14, 26, 28, 34, 39, 41, 44, 46. But I have followed Bannatyne's sequence: ll. 36–40 are an obvious complement to ll. 31–5 (cf. the stanza pairs 6–15, 21–30). I do not regard Maitland's ll. 16–20 as integral: they disturb the rhetorical pattern of the poem, l. 19 repeats l. 8, and the sentiment in ll. 16–20 is more succinctly expressed in ll. 43–4.

9. *confort*: probably here, 'strong drink'. Cf. **14.** 509, **22.** 11–12; Henryson, *The Testament of Cresseid*, l. 37, '[I] tuik ane drink, my spreitis to comfort'; Douglas, *Eneados*, vii, Prologue, l. 91, 'mychty drink and metis confortyve'.

13. *drowpe as I wald de.* Cf. **14.** 420, **64.** 26.

21–30. *Giff I be lustie*, etc. Cf. Lydgate, *A wicked Tunge*, sts. 2 and 4:

For yn thi port or yn thyn apparaile,
Ʒif thow be glad or honestli be-seyne,
A-noon the peple of malis wille not faile,
With-owte aduyse or resoun, for to seyne
That thyn arrai is made, or wrowght yn veyne
. . . . .
Ʒif thow be feire, excellyng of beaute,
Than wille they seyne that thow art amerous.
Ʒif thow be fowle and owgle vn-to see,
They wille afferme that thow art vycious,
The peple of langage is so despitous.
Suffre al ther speche and truste right wel this,
A wicked tonge wille alwey sey a-mys.

28. *Evill gydit*: ill-conducted, disordered. Cf. *The Spektakle of Luf*, vii (Asloan MS; STS, i. 294), 'a man of weir . . . quhilk in his ȝouth-heid had bene folich and evill gydit þat he had lyin with a nun . . .'.

33. *not worthe ane fle*. Cf. Henryson, *Fabillis*, ll. 2045, 2286.

83. *Foure Maner of Men ar evill to Pleis*. In the Bannatyne MS this poem follows **82**, but it is left anonymous and ends at l. 24. The version in Bannatyne's draft (p. 47) is defective, beginning at l. 9 at the top of the page (preceding leaves are missing), and is also anonymous and ends at l. 24. Reidpeth's copy from the Maitland Folio MS (from which the poem is now missing) supplies an additional stanza and is ascribed to Dunbar (presumably following Maitland). If we assume that Reidpeth followed Maitland's sequence in copying the poems now lost, **83** was preceded by fifteen of Dunbar's poems in Maitland, and was followed by a further eight. Its attribution to Dunbar by Maitland/Reidpeth is therefore unequivocal. The STS editors omitted it from the canon: but—apart from the additional stanza (see *infra*)—it contains only one word ('welthfull', l. 19) which does not appear elsewhere in Dunbar, and the style and sentiment are characteristic.

Mackenzie says curiously that Bannatyne's versions are 'defective and inferior' to Reidpeth's. It is difficult to see superiority in Reidpeth's sequence in ll. 3, 9–16, or in his readings at ll. 13, 14, 20. I have confined his additional stanza to the *apparatus criticus*, for I am dubious about it. The word 'regres' occurs nowhere else in Dunbar, and its sense here is a bit strained; the personification of 'Schir Gold' is uncharacteristic; and the change of tense in the third line is obviously wrong. Lines 21–4, with Dunbar's recurrent self-pitying complaint, are the natural ending of the poem. On the stanza see **18.**

3. *Gold . . . corne, cattell and ky*. Cf. **38.** 77–8.

7. *rewill nor gy*. Cf. **36.** 6.

14. *lusty lady fair*. Cf. **10.** 58, **48.** 54.

15. *wyis and womanly*. Cf. **14.** 496.

A NOTE ON *DUBIA*

A LARGE number of poems have been attributed to Dunbar, on grounds of style, theme, or association, without adequate evidence. More than twenty of these are discussed and rejected by Baxter (pp. 225–8), and I accept his general verdict. Two poems call for additional comment.

(1) 'Devorit with Dreme', entitled *A Generall Satyre* by Allan Ramsay (Mackenzie, no. 77). This poem is ascribed to Dunbar by Bannatyne, and to Sir James Inglis in the Maitland Folio MS. Of the two men of this name in the court records, one must prefer the James Inglis who became abbot of Culross and was murdered on 1 March 1530/1, to whom Lindsay (*Testament of . . . the Papyngo*, ll. 40–2) ascribes 'ballattis, farses, and . . . plesand playis'. What is to be said in favour of Bannatyne's attribution to Dunbar? (i) With its allusions (ll. 6–15) to priests and prelates, it is obviously pre-Reformation. (ii) At least some of the instances of corruption have parallels in the Dunbar canon. (iii) There are a few parallels in phrase and sentiment between this and other poems indisputably Dunbar's. What is to be said, in view of Maitland's attribution to Inglis, against Dunbar's authorship? (i) Mackenzie argues that 'Dunbar adopts a brisker metre in all his undoubted satirical poems and nowhere else uses this . . . stanza', and that he nowhere writes throughout 'with inner or sectional rhymes': but he does use internal rhyme, the canon is doubtless incomplete, and it is dangerous to argue in this way about so inventive and experimental a poet. (ii) Mackenzie argues that the hits at the nobility (ll. 2–5, and doubtless also 21–5, 36–8) are contrary to Dunbar's general criticism, 'which is rather that of the usurpation of nobility by upstarts'; but there are occasional criticisms of the aristocracy elsewhere (cf. **80.** 11–15). (iii) Mackenzie is on firmer ground in arguing that the phrases 'commoun caws', 'commoun weill' (ll. 27, 48) suggest a date later than Dunbar. (iv) An argument for a later date may also be based on the lines on the lack of patriotic courage (ll. 36–8); it would be difficult at any rate to apply these to the years before Flodden.

There are two additional arguments, almost conclusive, for a date in the 1530s or later and against Dunbar's authorship. (i) I have listed a large number of less usual words, constructions, and alliterative and other phrases in the poem, and collated them with the accepted Dunbar canon. Only three of these were to be found in the canon; fifty were not. This is not indeed decisive evidence; some of the contexts are themselves uncommon, and there are other poems, indisputably by

Dunbar, from which one could extract large numbers of 'unique' words over a run of eighty lines. But this poem is not, in theme or diction, a special case like the religious poems or the *Flyting*, which have vocabularies of their own. It hits at targets not uncommon in Dunbar, but it does so in a manner which seems not to be his. (ii) The poem ridicules (ll. 71–5) 'fartingaillis' (hooped petticoats) and 'fuck sailis' (foresails, skirts). Maxwell and Hutchison (*Scottish Costume 1550–1850*, 1958, p. 9) place the heyday of the farthingale in the second half of the sixteenth century; James Laver (*Costume of the Western World: Early Tudor*, 1951, p. 11) attributes its popularity to Spanish influence in England in the 1550s. The earliest English reference in *OED* is to Latimer, 1552; the earliest in Scots is *LHTA*, 1560. For 'fuck sailis', the earliest quotation in *OED* is from Skelton (1529); in *DOST*—apart from the *Generall Satyre* itself—the earliest quotation is from Sir Richard Maitland (a boy of seventeen at the time of Flodden), Maitland Quarto MS, f. 1[r], l. 14, where 'fuck sailis' exemplify 'newfangilnes of geir'. I have reluctantly rejected Bannatyne's ascription to Dunbar.

(2) *Quhen the Gouvernour past in Fraunce*. Mackenzie, no. 65. This poem was probably written after the disaster at Flodden (1513). If we accept the title (Maitland's), it refers to the regent John Stewart, Duke of Albany and Admiral of France, a nephew of James III and cousin of James IV, who arrived in Scotland in May 1515 and, having established some degree of order, returned to France in June 1517; he made later visits in 1521 and 1523. I do not believe this poem to be Dunbar's. (i) None of his undisputed work can be dated after 1513. (ii) He does not appear in *LHTA* after Flodden; and although the records are not continuous for the periods 1513–15, 1518–22, it is improbable that he would drop into total obscurity, as either priest or civil servant, after Flodden. (iii) Denton Fox argues (in my view rightly) against Dunbar's authorship on grounds of technical incompetence, bad metre, awkwardness of style, banality, and an uncharacteristic mixture of 'whining servility and currish snapping' (*Philological Quarterly*, xxxix (1960), 420–4). Some of the metrical infelicity may be due to faulty transmission, and Dunbar's verse is not invariably smooth. But little else that is attributed to him is as clumsy and undistinguished as this, though the theme is one to which he could be expected to rise with far greater power and feeling. (iv) The theme is well within Dunbar's range of interest and sensibility; but there are more than twenty words and phrases of a religious/moral kind which do not occur elsewhere in his work (and 'pennance and contritioun', l. 36, is an odd sequence from a priest-poet; see **5**. 48 *n*.). I have excluded this poem.

GLOSSARY
AND INDEX OF NAMES

THE Glossary is not an *index verborum omnium* but an aid to the reading of the text. It does not include forms which are still standard, or words in near-standard spellings with meanings which are still current. For recurrent words, it provides a selection of references sufficient to illustrate the range of Dunbar's forms and usage. It includes most of the names of persons and places which occur in the text. No attempt has been made to gloss variants which occur only in the *apparatus criticus*. Kennedy's part of the *Flyting* (**23**) has been lightly glossed: I have omitted words which occur also in Dunbar's verse in like form and sense, and words which are readily intelligible; those words which appear only in Kennedy are marked by an asterisk. In etymologies, the asterisk signifies a hypothetical form. References are to poem and line.

ABBREVIATIONS

adj.	adjective	orig.	originally
adv.	adverb, -ial	pa. t.	past tense
app.	apparently	perh.	perhaps
art.	article	phr.	phrase
attrib.	attributive	pl.	plural
auxil.	auxiliary	pp.	past participle
coll.	collective	ppl. adj.	participial adjective
comp.	comparative	prec.	preceding (word)
conj.	conjunction	pref.	prefix
contr.	contracted	prep.	preposition
corresp.	corresponding	pres.	present
def.	definite	pres. p.	present participle
gen.	genitive	prob.	probably
imper.	imperative	pron.	pronoun
indef.	indefinite	sg.	singular
infin.	infinitive	subj.	subjunctive
interj.	interjection	suff.	suffix
med.	medieval	sup.	superlative
mod.	modern	v.	verb
n.	noun	var.	variant
nth.	northern	vbl. n.	verbal noun
num.	numeral		

AN	Anglo-Norman	ME	Middle English
Da(n)	Danish	MHG	Middle High German
Du	Dutch	MLG	Middle Low German
F	French	Norw	Norwegian
Flem	Flemish	OE	Old English
Gael	Gaelic	OF	Old French
Ger	German	OHG	Old High German
Gk	Greek	ON	Old Norse
Heb	Hebrew	ONhb	Old Northumbrian
It	Italian	OScand	Old Scandinavian
L	Latin	Sc	Scots
LG	Low German	Sw	Swedish
MDu	Middle Dutch	WS	West Saxon

GLOSSARY

a *adj.* all **28.** 9 [ONhb *all*]

a *prep.* of **41.** 9, **51.** 62 [reduced form of *of*; OE]

abaising *n.* dismay **10.** 155 [see **abasit**]

abak *adv.* back, backwards **10.** 180, **14.** 223 [OE *on bæc*]

abasit *pa. t.* **14.** 112; *pp.* **5.** 47, **11.** 17, **78.** 34 dismayed, cast down [ME *abaisse;* OF *esbaïss-*]

abayd *n.* stay, delay **39.** 7 [ONhb *ābidan*]

abbais *n. pl.* abbeys' **39.** 85 [ME; OF; late L *abbadia*]

abbeit, abeit, abyte, habeit *n.* dress of a religious order **54.** 11, **55.** 3, **55.** 6, **55.** 18, **55.** 35 [ME, OF *abit*]

Aberdeane, Aberdein, Aberdene Aberdeen **48.** 1, **48.** 8, **62.** 77

abell, abill *adj.* able, having power **5.** 20, **5.** 66, **43.** 29; liable, likely **5.** 61; qualified, fit **35.** 42, **50.** 131 [ME, OF *able;* L *habilis*]

***Abiron 23.** 250 (Num. xvi)

aboif, abufe *prep.* above **22.** 66, **23.** 3, **35.** 29, **53.** 50 [ME *above,* reduced from *aboven;* OE *abufan*]

aboin, abone *prep.* above, beyond, over **1.** 55, **6.** 127, **14.** 23, **14.** 142, **14.** 326, **28.** 12. Cf. **aboif** [ME *abovin* contracted; OE *abufan*]

abouchtpp. *pp.* of *aby;* paid for, suffered for **14.** 143 [OE *ābycgan*]

aboundance *n.* abundance, plenty **18.** 6, **83.** 18 [ME; OF; L *abundantia*]

abowt *adv.* on all sides, everywhere **23.** 134; **45.** 40, **63.** 12 [OE *onbūtan*]

Absolone Absalom, son of David **61.** 12

abufe. See **aboif**

abusioun *n.* wrong-doing **44.** 71 [ME; OF; L *abusio*]

abusit *pp.* misused, neglected **6.** 25 [F *abuser*]

abyd *v.* wait, stay, dwell **20.** 5, **49.** 15, **69.** 20; **abydis** *3 sg.* **59.** 37, **60.** 17; submit to **32.** 4 [OE *ābidan*]

accusar *n.* one who accuses **76.** 23 [ME; OF; L *accusare*]

accusit *pa. t.* charged, prosecuted **3.** 123 [prec.]

Achill Achilles **35.** 57, **61.** 10

acquentance, acquyntance *n.* acquaintance, friendship **15.** 13, *pers.* **10.** 220 [ME; OF *accointance*]

Adam(e) Adam **14.** 521, **23.** 294; **Adame and Ev(e) 42.** 38, **48.** 31

adamant *n.* diamond **63.** 49 (see Commentary) [ME; OF; L *adamas*]

addres *v.* prepare, make ready **49.** 30; **addrest** *pp.* **64.** 38 [ME; OF *adresser*]

adew *interj.* farewell, goodbye **14.** 208, **14.** 413 [ME; F *a dieu*]

adir *adj.* each, either **52.** 187 [OE *æȝðer*]

adjutorie *n.* helper, aid **35.** 25, **42.** 84 [ME; L *adjutorius*]

ado *adv.* to do **5.** 51, **71.** 36 [nth. ME *at do*]

adore *v.* pray earnestly **2.** 55 [L *adorare*]

adultre *n.* adultery **6.** 54, **14.** 179 [L *adulterium*]

adversite *n.* adversity **50.** 182 [ME; OF; L *adversitas*]

advocat *n.* advocate, intercessor **25.** 25; **advocattis** *pl.* **20.** 19 [ME; L *advocatus*]

advysit *ppl. adj.* counselled, guided by reflection **11.** 2 [later form of *avisit*; OF *aviser*]

aep *n.* ape, monkey **33.** 6; ***aip** fool **23.** 36; **aipis** *pl.* **50.** 109 [OE *apa*]

aferit *ppl. adj.* afraid **10.** 279 [OE *āfǣran, āfǣred*]

affeir. See **effeir**

Afflek unknown Scotch poet **62.** 58

afforow *adv.* before, previously **65.** 7 [nth. ME *forwith*]

affrayit *pa. t.* alarmed, scared **10.** 207; *pp.* **10.** 134, **10.** 142; **affrayde** *ppl. adj.* terrified **10.** 242 [ME; AF; OF *effreer*]

affrey *n.* state of alarm, fear **50.** 187 [ME; OF *effrei*]

affy *v.* trust, put confidence in **36.** 30 [ME; OF *afier*; late L *affidare*]

afor . . . or *conj.* before **5.** 55 [ME; OE *on foran*]

Agamenon Agamemnon, king of Mycenae **35.** 60

agane, agayn, aganis *prep.* against, in resistance to, in readiness for, over against **2.** 66, **6.** 14, **6.** 76, **6.** 90, **10.** 29, **10.** 44, **10.** 50, **14.** 58, **14.** 83, **16.** 5, **16.** 11, **26.** 25 [nth. ME]

agane, agayn *adv.* again, anew **3.** 33, **3.** 43, **4.** 19, **4.** 25, **6.** 68, **10.** 192, **14.** 208 [nth. ME]

agast *pa. t.* frightened **37.** 34; *pp.* **47.** 17, **52.** 153, **56.** 1, **69.** 21 [ME *agasten;* OE *gǣstan*]

ago *ppl. adj.* gone, past **39.** 22 [ME *ago* depart]

aige *n.* (old) age **16.** 38, **17.** 1 *et seq.* [ME; OF *aage*]

ail(l) *n.* ale **22.** 13, **56.** 53, **83.** 10; *attrib.* **38.** 110 [OE *ealu*]

aipis. See **aep**

Air Ayr **38.** 36; ***Aire 23.** 371

air, are *n.* the element, air; the atmosphere **1.** 13, **1.** 33, **1.** 50 [OF; L *aer*]

air *n.* male heir **9.** 105, **23.** 209, **23.** 241, **52.** 227, **59.** 22; **airis** *pl.* **67.** 26 [ME; OF *(h)eir*]

air *n.* circuit court held by itinerant judges **47.** 19 [ME, OF *eire*; L *iter*]

air *adv.* early **3.** 132, **38.** 30, **81.** 19 [nth. OE, ON *ār*]

aird. See **erde**

airis. See **air**

airlie, airly *adv.* early in the day **14.** 528, **59.** 2, **73.** 1 [ME; ON *ārliga*]

airmour *n.* arms **36.** 23 [ME; OF *armure*]

aisur, azure, *adj.* clear, deep blue **10.** 41 (see Commentary), **16.** 11 [ME; OF; med. L *azura*; Persian]

aithis *n. pl.* oaths, profanity, **6.** 106, **56.** 3 [OE *āþ*]

aitis *n. pl.* oats **23.** 133 [OE pl. *ātan*]

aix *n.* (battle) axe **23.** 72 [OE *æx*]

akword *adj.* backhanded, perverse **14.** 286 [ME; ON *afugr*]

aland. See **upaland**

***Alathya 23.** 322 (see Commentary)

albeid *conj.* even if **69.** 38 [ME]

ald, auld, awld *adj.* old, aged **5.** 70, **10.** 114, **14.** 89, **14.** 102, **14.** 105, **14.** 277, **15.** 14, **17.** 9, **67.** 27; old fellow **14.** 286 [ONhb]

Alexander the Great **61.** 11

alhaill *adv.* completely **71.** 61, **71.** 66 [ME; see **haill**]

all ther *adj.* of all **14.** 138 [ME *alther*; OE *eallra*, gen. pl. of *eall*, all]

allace, allece, allais, *interj.* alas **3.** 102, **6.** 22, **10.** 214, **12.** 6, **51.** 97, **52.** 140 [ME; OF *a las*]

allane, allone *adj., adv.* alone, only **13.** 26, **14.** 2, **16.** 16 *et seq., with poss. pron.* **22.** 17, by itself **78.** 29 [nth. ME; OE *eall+ān*]

allegance *n.* fealty, loyalty **15.** 21 [ME; from *lege*, loyal subject; OF]

allevin *num. adj.* eleven **55.** 26 [ONhb *ællefne*]

allkin *adj.* of every kind **52.** 66 [**all+kyn**; OE *ealra cynna*]

allowit *pa. t.* praised, commended **14.** 240 [ME; OF *alouer:* L *allaudāre*]

***allya** *n. coll.* allies, associates **23.** 324 [ME *alye;* OF *alié*]

almaser *n.* almoner, official who distributes alms **28.** 15 [ON *almusa* alms]

almous *n.* money given in charity or piety; *attrib.* **79.** 1 [as prec.]

Alphais *n. gen.* God's **2.** 14 [L *alpha;* Gk (Rev. i. 8)]

als, alse *adv.* as **10.** 54, **14.** 388; **al(l)s . . . as** as . . . as **3.** 58, **10.** 51, **10.** 59, **10.** 261, **14.** 180–3, **33.** 12; **als** also **39.** 19, **77.** 6, **77.** 27 [ME; reduced form of *alsa;* OE *eall swā*]

alter *n.* altar **56.** 8 [ME; OF; L *altare*]

alway *adv.* always, at all times **11.** 6 [ME; ONhb *all*+OE *weȝ*]
alyt *pa. t.* ailed, suffered (some sickness) **14.** 222 [OE *eȝlan*]
alyve *adv.* alive, in the world **24.** 3 [OE *on life*]
amang, amangis, *prep.* **3.** 1, **10.** 56, **10.** 206, **10.** 243, **14.** 241, **14.** 368, **20.** 21, **52.** 5 [OE]
amendis *n.* compensation, satisfaction **52C.** *title* [ME; OF pl. *amendes*]
amene *adj.* pleasant, delightful **2.** 37, **10.** 249, **50.** 70 [ME; L *amoenus*]
amiable. See **amyable**
amis *adv.* out of order, wrong **11.** 6 [ME *a mis* (misdeed)]
amourouse *adj.* amorous, expressing love **10.** 104 [OF; L *amorosus*]
amyable, amiable, *adj.* friendly, loving, lovely, attractive **14.** 265; **16.** 5; *as. n.* friendly person (ironic) **14.** 239 [ME, OF]
An, Sanct the mother of the Virgin **25.** 31 (see Commentary)
anamalit, annamalit *pa. t.* enamelled **14.** 31; *ppl. adj.* enamelled, glossy, brilliant, **10.** 13, **10.** 257, **50.** 42; **anamalyng** *vbl. n.* enamelling **10.** 251 [OF *anamaler*]
anarmyng *pres. p.* arming, equipping **6.** 76; **anarmyt** *pp.* **62.** 22 [var. of *enarm;* OF *enarmer*]
and *conj.* and, if **5.** 21, **5.** 22, **5.** 24, **14.** 237, **23.** 13, **25.** 28, **46.** 20 [OE]
ane *num. adj., pron.* one, a **3.** 1, **3.** 3, **5.** 5, **5.** 21, **11.** 1, **13.** 7; of one **14.** 48; **ane . . . ane** one . . . an **5.** 35; **at ane, in ane,** together, as one **13.** 47, **13.** 61 [OE *ān*]
aneuch, anewch, annuche *adj., n.* enough **23.** 137, **66.** 5, **66.** 20 [ME; OE *ȝenōȝ*]
angeilik. See **angellik**
angelicall *adj.* like an angel **2.** 6 [L *angelicus*+*-al*]
angellik(e), angeilik *adj., adv.* like an angel **10.** 10, **31.** 12, **50.** 146 [ME *aungel-lyke;* L *angelus*]
anger *v.* make angry; **angrit** *pa. t.* became angry **14.** 301 [ME; ON *angra*]
Angers French town **22.** 56
anis, anys *adv.* once **6.** 86, **14.** 54, **14.** 177, **14.** 313, **17.** 26, **41.** 14; at some time, one day **59.** 19 [OE *ānes* adv. gen.]
anker *n.* anchor *fig.* **61.** 46; *pl.* **10.** 187 [OE *ancer*]
annamalit. See **anamalit**
annuche. See **aneuch**
anone, annone *adv.* forthwith **44.** 86, **50.** 22, **50.** 72, **55.** 19, **60.** 11 [ME]
anser *v.* answer, reply to a charge **63.** 52; **answerit** *pa. t.* **74.** 9 [OE *andswarian*]
Antane, Sanct, S. Antony's preceptory in Leith **38.** 60
***antecessouris** *n. pl.* ancestors' **23.** 311 [OF; L *antecessor*]
Antechrist Christ's chief enemy **53.** 29 (see Commentary)
***Antenor** betrayer of Troy **23.** 539
anteris *n. pl.* adventures **62.** 66 [ME; OF *aventure*]
anter(o)us, aunterus *adj.* adventurous, bold **27.** 31, **35.** 42, **35.** 91, **36.** 4 [prec.]
Aphrycane Africa **39.** 71
apirance *n.* appearance, aspect **76.** 12 [see **appeir**]
apon(e), aupone *prep.* upon, on, in **10.** 218, **10.** 242, **14.** 1, **14.** 35, **14.** 211, **50.** 177, **54.** 75 [ME]
***apostata** *n.* apostate **23.** 523 [ME; L]
apparalit *ppl. adj.* arrayed, dressed **10.** 12 [ME; OF *aparailler*]
apparrall *vbl. n.* attire **33.** 11 [prec.]
appeir, appere *v.* present oneself, seem **9.** 54, **10.** 215, **50.** 51, **51.** 52, **55.** 2; *3 sg.* **77.** 10; **apperand** *pres. p.* **14.** 265, **14.** 305 [ME; OF *apereir;* L *apparere*]
***appelle** *v.* challenge **23.** 405 [OF; L *appellare*]
appelling *pres. p.* appealing (at law) **6.** 163 [prec.]
appere. See **appeir**
appetyt(e) *n.* natural desire, pleasure **23.** 108, **34.** 35 [ME; OF; L *appetitus*]
appill ruby *n.* a variety of apple **13.** 57 (see Commentary) [OE *æppel*+ OF *rubi*]

applyid *ppl. adj.* attached, inclined **13.** 55 [OF *aplier;* L *applicare*]
Appollo 4. 22, **10.** 75 (see Commentary); **Appollois** *gen.* **16.** 78
appostillis *n. pl.* apostles, twelve chief disciples of Christ **22.** 45 [OE *apostol;* L *apostolus*]
approch(e) *v.* come near **10.** 50, **14.** 16 [OF *aprochier*]
Aprile, Appryll *n.* the month of April **10.** 83, **50.** 2 [ME; L *aprilis*]
ar *v. pres.* are **4.** 3, **4.** 6, **4.** 30, **8.** 5, **16.** 92 [ONhb *aron*]
aray. See **array**
arayed, ar(r)ayit, arreyit *pp., ppl. adj.* adorned, dressed, drawn up in order **10.** 42, **10.** 127, **14.** 30, **14.** 68, **14.** 268, **48.** 10, **68.** 27 [ME; OF *arreyer*]
arbe(i)r, *n.* garden **14.** 17, **14.** 525 [ME; L *herbarium*]
archangellis *n. pl.* the highest hierarchy of heaven **1.** 9 (see Commentary) [L *archangelus*]
arche(a)ris *n. pl.* bowmen **10.** 137, **10.** 185 [ME; OF *archier*]
***arestis** *v. 3 pl.* cause to stop **23.** 435 [ME; OF *arester*]
***argh** *adj.* reluctant, unwilling **23.** 477 [nth. ME; OE *earȝ*]
argone, argown *v.* argue (against) **16.** 100, **77.** 30 [ME, OF; L *arguere*+*-n*]
armes, armys *n. pl.* arms of the body **14.** 101, **14.** 209, **14.** 220 [OE *earm*]
armes, armis, armys *n. pl.* arms of war, chivalry **35.** 10, **35.** 42, **44.** 7, **52.** 210 [ME, OF; L pl. *arma*]
armipotent. See **armypotent**
armit *pp., ppl. adj.*, armed, protected **23.** 87, **63.** 31 [ME, OF; L *armare*]
armony *n.* harmony **1.** 50, **10.** 46, **16.** 17, **50.** 7 [ME; OF *harmonie*]
armypotent, armipotent *adj.* mighty in arms **10.** 112, **10.** 152, **35.** 73 [ME (Chaucer); L *armipotens*]
arowis *n. pl.* arrows **10.** 111, **10.** 178, **10.** 195 [OE *arwe*]
ar(r)ay *n.* readiness, order, dress **10.** 174, **16.** 23, **51.** 2, **59.** 13; **arrayis** *pl.* attire **14.** 365, **79.** 46 [OF *arei*]
arrayit, arreyit. See **arayed**
arrest *n.* apprehension, durance **1.** 22 [OF; late L *arresta*]
arrest *v.* lay hands on **10.** 138 [OF *arester*]
arrivit *pa. t.* came to land **10.** 57 [ME; OF *ariver*]
art magicianis *n. pl.* practitioners of the art of magic **62.** 37 (see Commentary) [ME *art magic*]
artelȝie. See **artilye**
Arthur British king **35.** 59
***Arthuris Sete** in Edinburgh **23.** 336
artickillis *n. pl.* clauses in a document or creed **6.** 57 [L *articulus*]
artilye, artelȝie *n.* variant of *artailȝerie,* artillery, ordnance **10.** 161, **10.** 179, **48.** 15 [OF *artillerie*]
artistis *n. pl. prob.* alchemists **44.** 6 [F *artiste;* L *artista*]
as *n.* ash, ashes **59.** 6, **59.** 7, **60.** 22, **61.** 2; **Ask** *attrib.* Ash (Wednesday) **73.** 1 [OE *asce*]
ascendit *pp.* ascended, gone up **48.** 3 [ME; L *ascendere*]
askar *n.* suppliant **51.** 81; **askaris** *pl.* **44.** 43 [ME; OE v. *āscian*]
askis *3 sg.* asks **51.** 83; **askit** *pa. t.* asked for, requested **10.** 185 [OE *āscian*]
aspyit *pp.* observed, caught sight of **10.** 137 [OF *espier*]
assaile *v.* attack **54.** 3; **assalis** *3 sg.* **65.** 13 [ME; OF *assaillir*]
assailȝeit *pa. t.* attempted, made trial of **54.** 57 [OF *assaillir, lȝ* for *ll*]
assay *n.* attack, assault **16.** 83; **assayes** *pl.* **10.** 170 [OF *assai*]
assay *v.* try, test, assail **47.** 9, **54.** 26, **54.** 43; **assayit** *pa. t., pp., ppl. adj.* **10.** 130, **10.** 144, **10.** 201, **69.** 16 [OF *assayer* put to trial]
assege, maid, *pp.* beleaguered **9.** 79 [ME; OF *asegier*]
assemblit *pa. t.* brought together, marshalled **9.** 91 [OF *assembler*]
ass(e)ure *v.* trust, have confidence **15.** 4, **63.** 5; assure **77.** 47;

assured *ppl. adj.* certain **12.** 1 [ME; OF *asurer*]

asswage, assuage *v.* alleviate, relieve **12.** 26, **14.** 167 [OF *assouager*]

astrolog(g)is *n. pl.* astrologers **44.** 6, **62.** 37 [F *astrologue;* L *astrologus*]

asur(e) *n., adj.* deep blue **50.** 42, **63.** 48 (see Commentary) [ME; OF; med. L *azzurum* (Persian origin)]

at *prep.* from (after vbs. of asking etc.) **5.** 33, **11.** 21, **14.** 257, **50.** 3, **71.** 54; in accordance with, with **1.** 36, **10.** 183 [OE *æt*]

at *conj.* that **6.** 159 [nth. ME; ON]

atonis, attonis *adv.* at the same time, together **35.** 23, **50.** 159 [ME *at ones;* substituted for *at* **anis**]

atour. See **at(t)our**

atteir *n.* dress, costume **50.** 18 [ME *atire;* OF v. *atirer*]

attemperit *ppl. adj.* mild **10.** 249 [L *attemperare*]

***attircop** *n.* spider; venomous person **23.** 523 [OE *āttorcoppe*]

attonis. See **atonis**

at(t)our *prep.* above, beyond, over **1.** 31, **3.** 15, **14.** 22, **52.** 188 [app. prep. *at*+*our* (over)]

atyrit *ppl. adj.* attired, adorned **31.** 26 [ME; OF *atirer*]

aucht *n.* possession **38.** 49 [OE *ǣht*]

aucht *pa. t.* owned **9.** 110; *pa. t. as pres.* deserve to be **10.** 279 [OE *āh*]

aucht *adj.* eight **39.** 43 [nth. ME; OE *eahta*]

auditoris *n. pl.* listeners, audience **14.** 527 [ME; L *auditor*]

aufull, awfull *adj.* terrible, dreadful **3.** 19, **10.** 113, **10.** 148, **10.** 171, **10.** 202, **36.** 23, **48.** 35, **50.** 92 [ME; ON *age*]

Augustyne, S., of Canterbury (d. 604) **23.** 125

auld. See **ald**

aunterus. See **anter(o)us**

aupone. See **apon(e)**

aureate *adj.* golden, fine as gold **10.** 71, **10.** 263 [L *aureatus*]

Aurora, Aurore, Awrora, *n.* goddess of the dawn, dawn **1.** 38, **2.** 53, **10.** 16, **10.** 74, **16.** 1, **50.** 9, **50.** 62, **54.** 1; *fig.* Christ **4.** 21 [L]

***austerne** *adj.* stern **23.** 540 [ME; L *austerus*]

availȝeit *pa. t.* helped, profited **54.** 59 [var. of **availl**]

availl *n.* ready service **39.** 14 [ME; see next]

availl *v.* help **16.** 117; **avalis** *pres. 3 sg.* helps, profits **5.** 23, **5.** 25, **65.** 8, **65.** 10 [ME; OF *valoir, vaill-*]

avance *v.* promote, make more distinguished **15.** 19 [ME; OF *avancer*]

avaryce *n.* covetousness, greed **59.** 34 [ME; OF; L *avaritia*]

aventur(e) *n.* event, unusual occurrence **14.** 528, **65.** 6; **into aventeure** in danger, at risk **77.** 11 [ME; OF]

aver, avoir *n.* cart-horse, old horse **14.** 114, **14.** 387, **28.** 11, **43.** 3; **aviris** *pl.* **23.** 229 [OF; L *averum*]

averill *n.* cart-horse **23.** 185 [as prec.]

avys *v. refl.* bethink (thyself) **5.** 43 [OF *aviser*]

aw *adj.* all **23.** 95, **23.** 178, **62.** 85; **with aw** along with the rest **20.** 12 [OE *eall*]

awalk *v.* awake, wake up **16.** 20, **50.** 13, **50.** 22; *pa. t.* **awoi(l)k** **50.** 184, **53.** 41, **55.** 50 [OE *āwacian, āwōc*]

awfull. See **aufull**

awin, awne *adj.* own **1.** 23, **5.** 50, **14.** 93, **14.** 456, **16.** 44, **16.** 55, **38.** 62 [ME; OE *āȝen*]

awld. See **ald**

awoi(l)k. See **awalk**

awppis *n. pl.* bullfinches **50.** 122 [ME *alpe;* origin unknown]

Awrora. See **Aurora**

awtoritie *n.* authority, power **79.** 53, **80.** 3 [ME; OF *autorité;* L *auctoritas*]

ay(e) *adv.* always, continually **2.** 41, **2.** 60, **3.** 101, **6.** 20, **9.** 18, **11.** 7, **40.** 4 [ON *ei;* OE *ā*]

ayr *n.* air **39.** 35 [ME, OF; L *aer*]

ayrtis *n. pl.* quarters, points of the compass **39.** 69 [nth. ME; origin obscure]

***Baal** pagan god **23**. 541
bab *n.* baby **13**. 44, **62**. 27 [ME]
babill, babile *n.* fool's bauble **9**. 36, **26**. 23 [OF *babel*]
bace *n.* bass; *fig.* **37**. 19 (see Commentary) [ME; F *bas;* L *bassus*]
bachilleris *n. pl.* young knights **14**. 477 [ME; OF *bacheler*]
Bacus Bacchus, god of wine (son of Jupiter and Semele) **10**. 124
bad. See **bid**
bae *n.* baa, cry of a sheep **23**. 204 [imit.]
baggis *n. pl.* money-bags **65**. 27, **67**. 11 [ME; ON *bagge*]
bagit *adj.* having testicles (of a stallion) **52**. 80 [ME *bagged*]
baid *pa. t.* remained, stayed **3**. 39, **9**. 111 [OE *bīdan*]
baid *n.* bed **51**. 20 [OE *bed*]
baid. See **bid**
baid *n.* waiting, delay **14**. 143 [nth. ME *bād;* see **byde**]
bailful(l) *adj.* miserable, wretched **14**. 51, **14**. 416 [OE *bealoful;* next]
baill *n.* misery **49**. 15; **balis** *pl.* **65**. 12 [OE *bealu*]
bair *n.* boar **14**. 95; **baris** *pl.* **3**. 58 [OE *bār*]
bair, bar, bare *adj.* naked, destitute **3**. 23, **10**. 269, **23**. 155, **23**. 210, **49**. 7, **52**. 28, **65**. 27, **74**. 20; without flesh **23**. 165 [OE *bær*]
baird *n.* bard, minstrel (pejorative in Dunbar) **23**. 17, **23**. 49, **23**. 63, **23**. 96, **23**. 120, **23**. 183, **23**. 208, **23**. 244 [Gael *bard*]
baire *pa. t.* brought forth, gave birth to **2**. 46, **2**. 72 [OE *beran*, *bær*]
bairne. See **barne**
baith(e), bayth *adv., conj.* both **2**. 12, **5**. 36, **5**. 66, **6**. 68, **8**. 8, **13**. 61, **40**. 12, **44**. 24 [nth. ME; ON *bāðer*]
bak *n., adj., adv.* back **14**. 236, **14**. 275, **23**. 199, **32**. 24, **45**. 57; **bak and syd, syd and bak** all over **3**. 57, **23**. 191, **30**. 18 [OE *bæc*]
***bak** *v.* support, help **23**. 448 [prec.]
bakbyttaris *n. pl.* slanderers **52**. 50; **bakbytting** *n.* slander, calumny **23**. 22 [OE *bæc*+*bītan*]
bakwart *adv.* backwards **39**. 75 [ME]
balat. See **ballat**
bald. See **ba(u)ld**
baldlie *adv.* boldly, with assurance **9**. 42 [OE *baldlīce*]
Balioll, John (d. 1313) **23**. 265
balis. See **baill**
ball *n.* globe **2**. 79 [ME; ON *bǫllr*]
ballade. See **ballat**
ballat, ballet *n.* poem, song, hymn, song to accompany dancing **2**. *title*, **30**. 5, **35**. *title, attrib.* **51**. 69, *pl.* **10**. 103, **10**. 129, **14**. 480, **19**. 6, **42**. 48, **42**. 69 [OF *ballade*]
ballingaris *n. pl.* small ships **44**. 12 [ME; OF *baleinier*, whaler]
balme *n.* balm, balsum, fragrance **10**. 15, **12**. 26 [OF *baume;* L *balsamum*]
balmit *ppl. adj.* embalmed, anointed **50**. 20 [prec.]
balmy *adj.* fragrant **1**. 2, **10**. 97, **16**. 10 [see **balme**]
ban *v.* curse **14**. 154, **38**. 26 [ME; ON *banna*]
bancat *n.* banquet *fig.* **14**. 430 [ME; F *banquet*]
band *n.* compact, bond **9**. 103, **14**. 47, **14**. 50, **14**. 154, **14**. 235, **14**. 346; dog chain **28**. 45 [ME; ON]
band *pa. t.* bound, made fast **3**. 34 [OE *bindan*]
bandis *n. pl.* headbands **10**. 60 [F *bande*]
bandoun *n.* authority, domination **9**. 4 [OF *bandun*]
bane *n.* bone **13**. 33, **23**. 165, **72**. 18; **banis** *pl.* **23**. 186, **56**. 77 [OE *bān*]
baneis *v.* banish, put away **49**. 15; **banist** *pp.* banished, exiled **9**. 82, **39**. 29; **banyst** *pa. t.* **10**. 206, **14**. 404 [ME; OF *banir*, *baniss-*, proclaim]
baner, benner *n.* battle-flag **9**. 59, **10**. 177, **52**. 133, **52**. 163, *pl.* **baneris 38**. 111 [ME; OF *banere*]
banesoun *n.* blessing **41**. 15 [ME; OF *beneisson;* L *benedictio*]
banist. *See* **baneis**
baptasing *vbl. n.* baptism **6**. 44, **54**. 9 [ME; OF *baptiser;* L *baptizare*]
bar. See **bair**

Barbary *n.* **54.** 6
Barbour, John, archdeacon and poet (d. 1395) **62.** 61
bard *pp.* barred, secured **37.** 46; **barrit** *pp.* debarred, shut out **63.** 38 [ME; OF *barrer*]
bar(e), baris. See **bair**
baret, barat. See **barrat**
***barefut.** See **berfute**
barell *n.* barrel **38.** 100; *attrib.* **38.** 33 [ME; OF *baril;* med. L *barellum*]
barganeris *n. pl.* quarrellers, wranglers **52.** 34 [ME; OF *bargaigner*]
barge, berge *n.* small vessel **10.** 187, **79.** 27 [OF; L *bargia*]
barkis *n. pl.* barks of trees **10.** 27 [ME; ON *bǫrkr*]
barkis *n. pl.* barques, small vessels **44.** 12 [ME; F *barque*]
barkis *3 sg.* barks **29.** 6, **29.** 14 [OE *beorcan*]
barkit *ppl. adj.* tanned **52.** 163; hardened as if tanned **23.** 202, **23.** 239 [ME]
Barnard, Sanct ? of Clairvaux (1090–1153) **79.** 57
barne, bairne *n.* child **1.** 26, **14.** 338, **67.** 37; *pl.* **barnis 14.** 402 [OE *bearn*, ON *barn*]
barnheid *n.* childishness **42.** 49 [ME; prec.]
baronis, barronis, barrounes *n. pl.* barons, nobles (of lowest rank) **14.** 402, **14.** 476, **48.** 54, **80.** 11 [ME; OF]
barrat, bar(r)et *n.* distress, trouble, anger **14.** 51, **14.** 346, **23.** 189 [ME; OF *barat*]
barres, barrowis *n.* enclosure, lists **52.** 126, **52.** 139, **52.** 148 [ME; OF *barras*]
barrit *pp.* See **bard**
barronis, barrounes. See **baronis**
barrou *n.* hand-barrow *attrib.* **30.** 19 [? OE **bearwe*]
Bartane, Britane, Bretane *n.* Britain **10.** 255, **23.** 69, **25.** 11; **Bertan** Brittany **35.** 85 [OF *Bretaigne*]
Bartilmo, S. Bartholomew **23.** 126
***Bas** rock in the Firth of Forth **23.** 461
batalrus *adj.* bellicose, warlike **35.** 89 [cf. ME *batailous*, OF *bataillos;* see **battale**]
bathit *pp.* drenched *fig.* **10.** 32; *adj.* bathed, wet **3.** 99 [OE *baðian*]
battale, bataill, batall, battell *n.* conflict, encounter **2.** 30, **4.** 1, **4.** 33, **9.** 57, **10.** 197, **35.** 61, **54.** 92 [OF *bataille*]
batteret *pp.* struck with heavy blows **30.** 19 [ME; OF *batre*]
battering *vbl. n.* hammering **54.** 52 [ME *bater;* OF *batre*]
bauchlis *n. pl.* documents **14.** 347 (see Commentary [? v. *bauchill;* origin obscure]
ba(u)ld, bawld *adj.* bold, fierce **14.** 253, **23.** 22, **27.** 27, **43.** 18, **50.** 65; *adv.* strongly, fiercely **17.** 8 [OE *bald*]
bausy *adj.* ? big and clumsy **45.** 56 [origin obscure]
bawch *adj.* poor, weak **14.** 143 [? ON *bagr* clumsy]
bawd. See **bid**
bawis *n. pl.* testicles **23.** 104, **54.** 87 [ON *ball-*]
bawsy *n.* ? clumsy fellow **13.** 38 (see Commentary) [origin obscure; cf. **bausy**]
Bawsy Broun name of a fiend ? **52.** 30
baxstar *n.* baker **56.** 36 [OE *bæcere*, fem. *bæcestre;* cf. MDu *bacster*]
bayth. See **baith**
be *v.* be, are **5.** 45, **9.** 16, **11.** 1–3, **11.** 9–11; **beis** *2 sg.* **53.** 22; **bein, byne** *3 sg.* **58.** 16, **24.** 3; **bene** *3 sg.* is **2.** 36, **10.** 89, **16.** 8, *3 pl.* are **8.** 15, **10.** 71, **10.** 264, **bein(e), bene, beyn** *pp.* been **9.** 18, **13.** 4, **14.** 341, **17.** 1, **27.** 22, **32.** 9, **35.** 71, **39.** 65, **43.** 28, **43.** 53, **47.** 21, **55.** 28 [OE *bēon*]
be *prep. and conj.* by means of, through **2.** 4, **2.** 18, **2.** 24, **5.** 13, **5.** 35, **10.** 224; according to **9.** 39, **51.** 46; concerning **39.** 17; not later than, by **3.** 71; by the time **14.** 303, **52.** 112; by (in oaths) **14.** 380; by the number of, to the extent of **2.** 50, **10.** 90; **be meikill** by much, far **14.** 60; **be ful mekill** very much **14.** 376; **be this (that)** by this (that) time **9.** 105, **10.** 229 [OE]
beautee. See **bewt(i)e**

beckis *3 pl.* bow **74.** 20; **bek** *n.* gesture of respect, curtsy **14.** 277 [ME *becknen*]

beclip *v.* embrace **14.** 104 [OE *beclyppan*]

becum *v.* come, come to be; **become** *pa. t.* **3.** 129, befitted **48.** 10 [OE *becuman*]

bed *n.* bed; childbed **72.** 14; **beddis** *pl.* **58.** 15 [OE]

bedene *adv.* completely **2.** 41, **10.** 85 [ME; origin uncertain]

bedirtin *ppl. adj.* fouled with excrement **28.** 20 [ME *dirt;* ON *drit*]

bedrate, bedret. See **dryte**

bedroppit *ppl. adj.* spattered **13.** 9 [ME; OE *dropian*]

befoir, befor *prep.* before, in front of, previous to **2.** 16, **6.** 3, **12.** 20, **14.** 34, **14.** 493; **beforne 45.** 46, **53.** 12 [OE *beforan*]

beft *pa. t.* struck, buffeted **52.** 40, **54.** 78; *pp.* buffeted, beaten **3.** 103 [nth. ME]

befyld *pa. t.* fouled **27.** 48 [OE *befȳlan*]

beggar *n.* beggar **23.** 242; *pl.* **23.** 135, **75.** 43 [ME]

beggartie *n.* beggary **78.** 18 [prec.]

beggis *2 sg.* beg **23.** 133, *pl.* **23.** 147; **beggand** *pres. p.* **23.** 142 [ME; origin uncertain]

begonne, begouth, begowth. See **begyn**

begyle *v.* deceive **55.** 45; **begylis** *3 pl.* **34.** 16; **begyld(e), begylit** *pp.* **5.** 36, **14.** 199, **23.** 98, **60.** 2 [ME; OF *guiler*]

begyn *v.* begin, start **17.** 3, **22.** 22, **50.** 5; **begyn(n)is** *3 sg.* **14.** 413, **52.** 13; **begouth, begowth(e)** *pa. t.* (on analogy of **can, couth**) **21.** 7, **28.** 1, **28.** 44, **52.** 15; **begonne** *pp.* begun **10.** 158 [OE *beginnan, begunnen*]

behald *v.* behold, regard, look **3.** 102, **3.** 111, **10.** 88, **12.** 22, **15.** 1; **behaldis** *1 sg.* **14.** 230; *3 pl.* **14.** 436; **beheld** *pa. t.* **50.** 129; **behaldin** *pp.* indebted **71.** 33 [nth. OE *behalda*]

behechtis *n. pl.* promises **63.** 59 [ME *behiȝt;* see **hecht**]

behud. See **behuf**

behuf *v.* be necessary for; **behuffit** *pa. t.* needed **14.** 386, **behud** *pa. t.* was forced **14.** 334 [OE *behōfian*]

behufe *n.* regard, purpose **16.** 57 [OE **behōf;* cf. Du *behoef*]

beid *n.* bed **14.** 237 [OE *bed*]

beidis *n. pl.* a rosary **74.** 18 [OE *ȝebed*]

beild *n.* protection, relief **35.** 61 [ME *belde;* ONhb *bældo;* OE adj. *beald* bold]

beild *pp.* suppurated **14.** 164, swollen with rage **14.** 345 [origin obscure]

beildaris *n. pl.* builders **44.** 12 [ME *bilder;* OE *byldan*]

bein. See **be**

beir *n.* bear **52.** 33, ***23.** 259 [OE *bera*]

beir *n.* barley **23.** 133 [OE *bere*]

beir *n.* clamour, din **54.** 126 [OE *ȝebǣre* behaviour]

beir. See **bere**

beis *n. pl.* bees **23.** 217, **56.** 82 [OE *bēo*]

be(i)st *n.* animal **1.** 54, **5.** 47, **50.** 71, **50.** 86, **50.** 92, **52.** 196; beast of burden **14.** 330; *reduced pl.* **68.** 23; **beistis** *pl.* **50.** 79, **50.** 108, **50.** 114 [OF *beste;* L *bestia*]

beist *n.* ? basting thread, tacking **52.** 130 [? ME *baste;* OF *bastir;* cf. OHG *bestan*]

beit *v.* mitigate, relieve, assist **14.** 128, **75.** 69 [OE *bētan*, ON *bœ̄ta*]

beittir. See **bettir**

bejaip *v.* befool, deceive **14.** 452 [ME]

bek. See **beckis**

bekis *n. pl.* ? corner teeth **43.** 18 (STS edn.) [? OF *bec*]

belang *v.* pertain to **40.** 18 [nth. ME; OE *ȝelang*, belonging]

belief *n.* faith, trust **39.** 25 [OE *ȝelēafa*]

beleif, beleiff, belief *v.* believe, credit **14.** 406, **42.** 83, **60.** 3 [OE *belēfan*]

Belȝebub *n.* Satan **14.** 112 (see Commentary)

Beliall *n.* a devil **52.** 74 (see Commentary), ***23.** 250; *gen.* **52.** 219

Bell, Allan 27. 28

bellis *n. pl.* fool's bells **27.** 54, funeral bells **38.** 107 [OE *belle*]
bellokis *n. pl.* testicles **23.** 119 [OE *bealluc*]
belly *n.* paunch; *attrib.* **13.** 38, **52.** 70 [OE *bæliȝ* bag]
belyf(f), belyve *adv.* at once **14.** 49, **22.** 72, **51.** 95 [ME]
beme *n.* beam **24.** 15, **49.** 14; **bemes, bemis, bemys** *pl.* **10.** 5, **10.** 24, **10.** 32, **16.** 5, **50.** 20 [OE *bēam*]
ben *adv.* through to the inner room **14.** 485, **14.** 487 [OE *binnan* within]
bend *v.* draw a bow, sail etc. **60.** 13; *pa. t.* **9.** 67; **bendit** *pp.* drawn tight, stretched **3.** 73; stretched with exultation **23.** 6 [OE *bendan*]
bene. See **be**
bene *n.* bean (something of no value) **14.** 128, **17.** 57 [OE *bēan*]
benefice, benifice *n.* ecclesiastical office, living **40.** 1, **41.** 1, **42.** 58, **47.** 25, **53.** 22; **beneficis** *pl.* **39.** 46, **80.** 6 [ME; L *beneficium*]
beneth *prep.* below **54.** 104 [OE *beneoðan*]
benigne, bening, benyng *adj.* gracious **1.** 26, **2.** 13, **10.** 167, **48.** 26, **49.** 26, **50.** 32; **benignite** *n.* **62.** 27 [OF; L *benignus*]
benner. See **baner**
benyng. See **benigne**
berand. See **beris**
berd *n.* beard **13.** 8, **14.** 95, **54.** 91 [OE *beard*]
berd. See **bird**
berdin *n.* burden **14.** 165 [OE *byrden*]
berdles *adj.* beardless **23.** 208 [see **berd**]
bere, beir, beire *v.* bear, carry, endure, put up with **3.** 50, **9.** 43, **14.** 165, **14.** 348, **45.** 56; **be(i)ris** *2 sg., 3 sg.* **10.** 256, **35.** 43, **39.** 34; **bur(e)** *pa. t.* **9.** 59, **10.** 168, **10.** 169, **63.** 73; **born** *pp.* **52.** 133 [OE *beran*]
berevit *pp.* taken away by force **62.** 61 [*bereāfian*]
berfute *adj.* with bare feet **23.** 210 [OE *bærfōt*]
berge. See **barge**
beriall *n.* beryl, crystal **31.** 34 (see Commentary), *fig.* **48.** 1; *attrib.* sparkling, clear **10.** 23, **10.** 39 [OF; L *beryllus;* Gk]
beris *3 sg.* cries, carries on **20.** 15; **berand** *pres. p.* **52.** 80 [OE *ȝebǣran*]
bern(e) *n.* fellow, lover **13.** 2, **14.** 237, **14.** 429, **23.** 210, **27.** 27; *pl.* men **14.** 60, **14.** 74 (see Commentary), **14.** 494 [OE *beorn*]
Bertan. See **Bartane**
Berwick, *Berwik on the English–Scotch border **55.** 34, ***23.** 267
Bery Bury St. Edmunds **62.** 51
bery *v.* bury **6.** 30 [OE *byriȝan*]
besalie *adv.* diligently, actively **12.** 15 [ME; OE *bisiȝ*]
***beschate.** See **beschittin**
beschittin *pp., ppl. adj.* defiled with excrement **23.** 195, **23.** 239, **52.** 191, **52.** 218; ***beschate** *pa. t.* **23.** 460 [OE **scitan, besciten*]
beseik *v.* ask earnestly **22.** 24, **26.** 14; **beseikand, beseiking** *pres. p.* **12.** 20, **81.** 53 [ME]
besene, besein *pp., ppl. adj.* arrayed, ranked **10.** 250, **16.** 86, **48.** 46, **50.** 45, **82.** 26 [ME *be-se*, see to, provide]
bespewit *pp.* spewed upon **52.** 200 [ME]
best. See **be(i)st**
***bestiall** *adj.* brutish **23.** 256 [ME; L *bestialis*]
beswakkit *ppl. adj.* drenched **23.** 188 [echoic]
beswik *v.* deceive, beguile **14.** 226 [OE *beswīcan*]
besy *adj.* busy, diligent **10.** 217, **51.** 81, *adv.* **20.** 18 [variant of **bissy**]
besyd(e) *prep.* close to **14.** 3, **32.** 26, **37.** 62, **50.** 112, **56.** 14, **69.** 40; *adv.* at hand, near by **54.** 116 [OE *be sīdan*]
besynes. See **bissines**
bet- *v.* beat, overcome **51.** 91 [OE *bēatan*]
betaknis *3 sg.* signifies **35.** 89 [ME; OE **betācnian*]
***betrasd, *betrasit** *pa. t.* betrayed **23.** 267, **23.** 299 [ME *betrais;* OF *trahir*]

betteis *n. pl.* remedies **32.** 4 (see Commentary) [OE v. *bētan;* ON *bǿta*]
bet(t)ir, beittir *adj. and adv.* better **14.** 46, **14.** 52, **14.** 60, **14.** 360, **14.** 460, **23.** 56, **32.** 28, **56.** 33, **72.** 2 [OE *betera*]
betue(e)ne, betwene *prep.* between **14.** 133, **39.** 58; *adv.* among other things **17.** 34, to and fro **22.** 75 [ONhb *bitwīen*]
betuix *prep.* between **3.** 81, **9.** 104, **10.** 83, **14.** 312 [OE *betwyx*]
betyd *v.* befall **23.** 234 [OE *ȝetīdan*]
beuche. See **bewch**
Bevis, Sir, 27. 35
bewar *imper. phr.* be ware, vigilant **11.** 4, **77.** 9 [**be**+**war**]
bewch, beuche *n.* bough, branch **14.** 6, **14.** 205, **27.** 25; **bewis** *pl.* **10.** 32, **10.** 39, **14.** 242, **14.** 518, **16.** 113, **50.** 35; *fig.* limbs **13.** 61 [OE *bōh, bōȝ*]
bewrie *v.* reveal **14.** 41 [ME *bewreye*]
bewt(i)e, bewty, beautee *n.* beauty **8.** 3, **9.** 9, **9.** 15, **9.** 104, **14.** 482, **16.** 58, **62.** 31; *pers.* **10.** 146, **10.** 192, **10.** 210 [ME; OF *beauté*]
beyn. See **be**
bichis *n. pl.* bitches **23.** 220, *gen.* **23.** 237 [OE *bicce*]
bicker *n.* beaker, drinking vessel **38.** 47 [ME; ON *bikarr*]
bickerit. See **bikkerit**
bid *v.* command, desire, seek **23.** 137; **biddis** *3 sg.* **7.** 4, **23.** 131; **ba(i)d, bawd** *pa. t.* **9.** 42, **10.** 137, **10.** 182, **10.** 186, **16.** 70, **32.** 4, **38.** 34, **50.** 122, **73.** 14 [OE *biddan*]
biggingis *n. pl.* buildings **14.** 338 [ME next]
***biggis** *3 sg.* builds, makes a nest **23.** 290 [ME; ON *byggja*]
bikkerit, bikkrit, bickerit *pa. t.* skirmished with arrows **10.** 194; attacked (with missiles) **23.** 204, **54.** 91 [ME; origin obscure]
bikkir *n.* attack with missiles **10.** 144 [ME; prec.]
bill *n.* letter **9.** 42, **45.** 2, **billis** *pl.* **14.** 347 [ME; Anglo-L *billa*, L *bulla*]
billie *n.* friend, companion **13.** 31 [origin obscure]
bind *v.* constrain **75.** 76, **bindis** *3 sg.* constricts painfully **5.** 54, ties together **14.** 47; ***boundin** *ppl. adj.* **23.** 303 [OE *bindan*]
***binkis** *n. pl.* benches **23.** 289 [OE *benc*]
bird, berd *n.* bird; (every) bird **1.** 54; *pl.* **10.** 10, **10.** 20, **10.** 234, **14.** 205, **14.** 516, **16.** 113, **50.** 30 [OE *brid*]
bird *n.* lady, maiden **14.** 238 [? OE *byrde* well-born]
birn *v.* be on fire **23.** 14, **birnis** *3 sg.* **17.** 8, **birnand** *pres. p.* **52.** 87, **birnyng** *ppl. adj.* glowing **10.** 24 [OE *byrnan*]
birs *n.* bristles (of a boar etc.) **14.** 95 [OE *byrst*]
birst *v.* burst **41.** 8; **birstis** *3 sg.* **39.** 83; *pa. t.* **3.** 35, **14.** 346, flowed out, poured **14.** 5 [OE *berstan*]
birth *n.* child **2.** 82; child-bearing **72.** 16 [ME; ON]
bischop *n.* bishop **42.** 62, *gen.* **55.** 29, *pl.* **55.** 27 [OE *bisceop;* L *episcopus*]
bischoprik *n.* episcopal see **39.** 51; **bischopperikis** *gen.* **51.** 109 [OE *bisceoprice*]
bissart *n.* buzzard (*buteo buteo*) **54.** 85 [ME, OF *busart*]
bisselye. See **bissy**
bissines, besynes *n.* industry, diligence; *pers.* **9.** 60, **9.** 67, **10.** 166; **16.** 85, **39.** 2 [ONhb *bisiȝnis*]
bissy *adj.* busy, active **54.** 85; **bisselye** *adv.* **28.** 40 [OE *bisiȝ*]
bittirnes *n.* bitterness **22.** 82 [OE *biternys*]
bla *adj.* blue from cold **23.** 210 [nth. ME; ON *blār*]
blabbar *v.* babble, mutter **23.** 112 [ME; Dan *blabbre*]
bladȝeanes *n. pl.* ? clowns **45.** 23 [origin and meaning obscure]
blaiknit *ppl. adj.* made pale, pallid **23.** 165 [ON *bleikna; bleikr* pale]
***blait** *adj.* spiritless **23.** 256 [origin obscure]
blait-mouit *adj.* weak-, loose-mouthed, stupid-looking **45.** 23 [origin of **blait** obscure; OE *mūþ*]
blak *adj.* black in colour, evil **4.** 1,

56. 81, 60. 19, negro 33. 2 [OE *blæc*]

Blak Belly ? a fiend 52. 30

blaksmyth *n.* iron-smith 54. 51, 54. 67 [late ME; OE *blæc+smið*]

blandit *pp.* mixed, associated 42. 77 [OE *blandan*, ON *blanda*]

blasflemyng *n.* blasphemy, calumny 6. 106 [OF; L *blasphemare*]

blasphemar *n.* evil-speaker 23. 63 [prec.]

blast *n.* blowing of a trumpet 10. 231, violent wind 50. 3; *pl.* 8. 11, 50. 34, 50. 67 [OE *blǣst*]

blaw *v.* blow 23. 93, spread, make widely known 14. 74; **blawis** *3 sg.* 63. 63; *pres. p.* 48. 23; **blawin owt** *pp.* 23. 69 [OE *blāwan*]

***blawe** *n.* blow, stroke 23. 436; **blawis** *pl.* 54. 91 [nth. ME; origin obscure]

ble *n.* complexion 23. 165 [OE *blēo*]

bledder *n.* bladder; *attrib.* bladder-like 45. 23 [OE *blǣdre*]

bleid *v.* bleed 35. 31 [OE *blēdan*]

***bleir eit** *adj.* blear-eyed, stupified 23. 256 [ME]

bleit *n.* bleat 23. 204 [OE *blǣtan*]

blek *n.* black mark 9. 82; leather blacking 52. 179, 56. 34 [ON *blek* ink]

blenk *v.* glance 14. 428; **blenkis** *3 pl.* 14. 487; **blenkand** *ppl. adj.* 14. 181; **blenkit** *pa. t.* 52. 148 [OE *blencan* deceive]

blenk *n.* glance, look 14. 228, **blenkis** *pl.* 14. 111, 14. 494 [prec.]

blent *v.* glance, look (poet.) 35. 75; *pa. t.* 14. 112, 52. 139 [OE pa. t. *blencte;* see **blenk**]

bler *v.* blear, beguile 14. 277 (see Commentary), 38. 79; **blerde** *ppl. adj.* bleared 14. 111 [ME *blerien;* origin obscure]

blew out on *pa. t.* denounced (lit. by blowing a horn) 9. 96 [see **blaw**]

blew *adj.* blue 50. 19, 63. 48 [ME; OF *bleu*]

blinde, blynd(e) *adj.* sightless 5. 35, 10. 205; *fig.* lacking discernment 5. 33, 40. 16 [OE *blind*]

blindis *3 sg.* makes blind 16. 90; **blindit, blyndit** *pp.* 10. 214, 63. 19 [ME; OE adj. *blind*]

blinkis *3 sg.* gleams 33. 12 [late form of **blenk**]

blis(e) *v.* bless 14. 154 [OE *blētsian*, infl. by OE n. *blis*]

blis(e), blys *n.* happiness, blessed state 6. 100, 7. 8, 14. 51, 14. 205, 14. 238, 22. 20, 49. 7, 69. 43 [prec.]

blisfull *adj.* happy 4. 23, 16. 6, 48. 8, 49. 26; *sup.* **blissfullest** 10. 94 [ME; **blis(e)**]

blissit, blissed, blist *ppl. adj.* blessed 3. 10, 3. 50, 3. 104, 6. 59, 6. 165, 14. 47, 14. 235, 18. 5 [ME; **blis(e)**]

blith, blyth(e) *adj.* glad, cheerful 10. 81, 14. 416, 14. 477, 48. 1, 62. 10, 64. 5, 82. 6 [OE *blīðe*, ON *blīðr*]

blode. See **blude**

blome, blowme *n.* flower 10. 96, *fig.* 49. 2, 50. 153, *pl.* 10. 12; **blumys** *pl.* 14. 524 [nth. ME; ON *blōm*]

blomyt *ppl. adj.* blossomed 10. 55; **blumyng** *ppl. adj.* flourishing 14. 477 [ME; ON *blōma*]

blos(s)um, blosome *n.* blossom, flower 10. 51, *fig.* 49. 4, 49. 33, 50. 167 [OE *blōs(t)ma*]

blowme. See **blome**

blud(e), bluid, blode, *n.* blood 1. 21, 2. 82, 3. 35, 3. 53; birth, family 14. 298, 14. 312, 14. 407, 14. 464, 45. 64; kinsman 35. 15 [OE *blōd*]

bludy *adj.* bloody, bloodstained 3. 108, 6. 3, 35. 76, 56. 12 [*blōdiȝ*]

bluid. See **blud(e)**

blumyng. See **blomyt**

blumys. See **blome**

Blunt, Johne 14. 142 (see Commentary)

blynd(e). See **blinde**

blyndit. See **blindis**

blynis(of) *1 sg.* cease (from) 14. 428 [OE *blinnan*]

blys. See **blis(e)**

blyth(e). See **blith**

blythfull *adj.* joyful, glad 3. 27, 49. 2; *comp.* **blythfullar** 14. 6; **blythlie** *adv.* 19. 6 [OE *beīðe*]

blythnes *n.* happiness, gladness 13. 25, 19. 4, 48. 2 [OE *blīðnes*]

bo *v.* make a face **14.** 276 [cf. ME interj. *bo*]
bocht. See **by**
bodin *ppl. adj.* furnished with arms **52.** 36 [OE *bēodan*, pp. *boden*]
***bogane** *n.* ? fellow **23.** 334 [? Gael *boghainn* person]
bogill *n.* hobgoblin, nightly spectre **14.** 111 (see Commentary) [origin uncertain; cf. Welsh *bwg* ghost, *bwgwl* terror]
***bois.** See **boy**
boist. See **bost**
boith *adv.* both **16.** 31 [midl. ME; cf. **baith**]
boll *n.* a grain measure **56.** 54 (see Commentary) [OE *bolla;* ON *bolli* bowl]
bonet *n.* bonnet, cap **14.** 180, **52.** 17; **bonettis** *pl.* **52.** 37 [OF]
bonk *n.* bank (poet., after English models) **10.** 96 [ME var. of *bank;* ON **banke*]
bontie *n.* goodness **8.** 3, **16.** 61 [ME; OF *bonté*]
bony *adj.* pretty, beautiful **13.** 7, **13.** 14, **37.** 8 [origin obscure]
bordell *n.* brothel **32.** 29 [ME; OF *bordel* hut, brothel]
bordour *n.* edge of a field **10.** 197, frontier **39.** 29 [ME; OF *bordure*]
borne *pp. of* **bere** *and ppl. adj.* born **6.** 60, **23.** 210, **24.** 11, **45.** 45, **72.** 31
bor(r)ow *v.* lay in pledge, forgo **19.** 4, borrow **65.** 4; **borrowit** *pp.* pledged, redeemed **4.** 6, *ppl. adj.* borrowed **23.** 201 [OE *borȝian*]
bost, boist *n.* bragging, vaunting **23.** 6, **23.** 96 [ME; origin obscure]
bostaris *n. pl.* boasters, brawlers **52.** 34 [ME; origin obscure]
bosum *n.* bosom **38.** 33 [OE]
bot, bott, *prep., conj.* except, unless, other than **5.** 19, **5.** 51, **10.** 234, **13.** 17; without **6.** 101, **12.** 27, **14.** 48; = but **9.** 34, **9.** 94, **10.** 64, **13.** 9, **23.** 208, **32.** 3, **32.** 8; *adv.* only **9.** 77, **10.** 233, **14.** 57, **14.** 202, **14.** 285, **16.** 98 [nth. ME; see **but**]
botingis *n. pl.* boots **23.** 212, **23.** 220 [F *bottine*, dim. of *botte*]
bott. See **bot**
***botwand** *n.* (obscure) **23.** 474 (see Commentary)
boucht. See **by**
boun *ppl. adj.* ready, prepared **23.** 233, **52.** 126, **72.** 14, **75.** 59; ready to go **22.** 44 [ME; ON *būa*, *būenn*]
***boundin.** See **bind**
boundis *n. pl.* boundaries, lands **14.** 404, **54.** 6 [ME; OF *bunde*]
***boune** *v.* prepare, get ready **23.** 474 [prec.]
bountie *n.* goodness, moral excellence **48.** 2 [ME; OF *bunté*]
bour(e) *n.* bower, inner chamber **14.** 184, **29.** 1, **39.** 23, **62.** 31; **bouris** *pl.* (of foliage) **10.** 11, **58.** 15 [OE, ON *būr*]
bourd(e), bowrd *n.* jest, cause for laughter **14.** 238, **14.** 385, **14.** 476, **51.** 84, **52.** 220; *v.* **30.** 5 [ME; OF *bourde* deception]
bourdour *n.* jester **9.** 35 [ME; OF *bordeor*]
bow *v.* incline, kneel **1.** 26, stoop **3.** 118 [OE *būȝan*]
bowdyn *pp.* swollen, affected by anger **14.** 345 [ME *bollin*]
bowgle. See **bugill**
bowis *n. pl.* archers' bows **10.** 140 [OE *boȝa;* ON *bogi*]
bowk *n.* body **13.** 25 [ON *būkr;* OE *būc* belly]
bownes *v. 2 sg.* set out, take your way **18.** 17 [ME; from **boun**]
boy *n.* lad, groom; **bo(y)is** *gen.* **14.** 330, *pl.* **23.** 217, **23.** 225 [ME; LG *boi*]
***brace.** See **brais**
braek. See **brek**
braggaris *n. pl.* braggarts **52.** 34 [ME; origin obscure]
braid, bred *n.* sudden movement, start **28.** 45, **50.** 185 [OE *ȝebreȝd*]
braid *pa. t.* tossed up **14.** 348;
braidis (of) *3 sg.* has the qualities (of); **as braidis of me** as my own nature is **78.** 13 [OE *breȝdan*]
braid *adv.* plainly, amply **14.** 347 [OE *brād*]
brais, *brace *v.* embrace **67.** 11, *fig.* ***23.** 376; **braisit** *pa. t.* **37.** 8 [ME; OF *bracier*]

brak. See **brek**

branch(e), bran(s)ch(e), brench(e) *n.* bough **10.** 15, **10.** 96, **14.** 5, **16.** 6, **35.** 68; *pl.* **10.** 27 [OF]

brand *n.* piece of burning wood, torch **17.** 3 (see Commentary) [OE; ON *brandr*]

brand *n.* sword **27.** 9, *pl.* **52.** 40 [ON *brandr*; perh. as prec.]

brand *adj.* brawned, muscled **14.** 429 [ME n. *brawne;* OF *braon*]

brandeist *pa. t.* bore himself with gestures **52.** 33 [ME; OF *brandir, brandiss-*]

brane *n.* brain **39.** 83 [OE *bræȝen*]

brane *n.* bran **43.** 23 [ME; OF *bran*, origin obscure]

brankand *ppl. adj.* prancing, proud **14.** 180 [ME; origin obscure]

bransche. See **branch(e)**

bras *n.* brass **61.** 7 [OE *bræs*]

brattis *n. pl.* ragged garments **23.** 49 [ONhb *bratt* cloak]

bravelie *adv.* splendidly **48.** 44 [F *brave;* It *bravo*]

brattill *n.* clatter **52.** 193 [imit.]

brawlis *n. pl.* brawls, uproar **80.** 6 [nth. ME *bralle;* origin obscure]

brayd *adj.* broad, patent, plain **44.** 78 [OE *brād*]

bred. See **braid**

bredest *sup. adj.* broadest **14.** 429 [see **brayd**]

bredir. See **brethir**

breid *n.* bread **70.** 24, **80.** 31 [OE *brēad*]

breid *n.* breadth **14.** 234; **of breid and lenth** over the whole extent **3.** 65; **on breid** in breadth, openly **3.** 73, abroad **14.** 74; **one breid** open **14.** 424 [OE *brǣdu*]

breid. See **gallow breid**

breid *v.* propagate, transmit **32.** 10; **breidis** *3 sg.* **63.** 42 [OE *brēdan*]

breif *n.* summons, indictment **23.** 79; **breif of richt** writ fixing a legal right to property **52.** 108 [ME, OF *bref;* L *breve*]

breif, breve *v.* write **9.** 42, **19.** 6, **42.** 48; tell **14.** 385 [ME; med. L *breviare*]

breik. See **polk breik**

breik *n.* breeches **23.** 104, **23.** 119; **breikis** *pl.* **45.** 24 [OE pl. *brēc* (sg. *brōc*)]

breik, breikis. See **brek**

breist *n.* breast (esp. as the seat of thought and feeling) **5.** 45, **12.** 25, **14.** 104, **14.** 165, **14.** 345, **17.** 40; pap **62.** 26; **breistis** *pl.* **23.** 6, = bodies **72.** 14 [OE *brēost*]

breith *n.* anger **38.** 26 [ME *brethe;* ON *bræði*]

brek, braek, breik *v.* break, rupture, crack **12.** 47, **13.** 7, **23.** 183, **30.** 14, **44.** 81; **breikis** *3 sg.* **39.** 83; **brekand** *ppl. adj.* **49.** 4, **breking** *pres. p.* **50.** 167; **brak** *pa. t.* **3.** 74, **9.** 84, **10.** 241, **32.** 13, **51.** 114; **brokin** *pp.* **4.** 3, **4.** 34, deformed **52C.** 29 [OE *brecan*]

brekar *n.* breaker, destroyer **12.** 3 [prec.]

***brekeles** *adj.* without breeches **23.** 384 [nth. ME; see **breik**]

bremys *n. pl.* bream, variety of carp (*abramis brama*) **10.** 35 [ME, F *breme*]

brench(e). See **branch(e)**

Bretane. See **Bartane**

brethir, brether, bredir *n. pl.* of *brother* **14.** 404, **62.** 93, **66.** 11, **66.** 26, brethren in religion **55.** 16 [OE *brōðor*]

breve. See **breif**

brewis *3 sg.* brews, *fig.* **23.** 189 [OE *brēowan*]

bricht, brycht, bryght *adj., adv.* bright, shining, glorious(ly) **1.** 3, **2.** 23, **2.** 25, **4.** 27, **10.** 33, **10.** 66; *n.* fair lady **13.** 2, **14.** 236; **brichtest** *sup.* fairest **14.** 181 [OE *briht*]

bridill, brydill *n.* bridle, restraint **14.** 348, **14.** 354; *attrib.* **42.** 49, **52.** 74 [OE *brīdel*]

***brigantis** *n. pl.* robbers **23.** 436 [ME; OF *brigand*]

brilȝeane *n.* ? *pudendum muliebre* **13.** 44 [obscure]

brim, brym *adj.* furious, fierce **3.** 58, **14.** 95 [ME]

brint *pp.* burnt, consumed by fire **9.** 76 [ON *brinna*]

brist *v.* burst, rupture **14.** 164, *pa. t.* **3.** 74, **52.** 222; **bristis** *3 sg.* **44.** 69 [var. of **birst**; ON *bresta*]

Britane. See **Bartane**

brocht, broght, broucht *pa. t.* brought, conveyed **9.** 60, **10.** 192, **10.** 197, **14.** 237, **52.** 189, **71.** 24 [OE *bringan*]

broddit *pa. t.* goaded **14.** 330 [nth. ME; ON n. *broddr*]

brodir *n.* brother, friend **69.** 33; **bruder 30.** 3 [OE *brōðor*]

brokin See **brek**

broud *pp.* embroidered **10.** 90; **browderit 48.** 44 [ME; OF *brouder*]

broun *adj.* dark-coloured, dusky **50.** 19, **68.** 26 [OE *brūn*]

***brow** *n.* broth, liquid **23.** 458 [nth. ME; OF *bro*]

browderit. See **broud**

browk *v.* have possession of **39.** 49 [OE *brūcan*]

browstar *n.* brewer **56.** 51 [ME; OE v. *brēowan*]

***Bruce,** Robert de, husband of Marjory Countess of Carrick and father of Robert I **23.** 265

Bruce, Robert I, king of Scots (1274–1329) **48.** 33

bruder. See **brodir**

bruikit *ppl. adj.* blackened, streaked with black **54.** 51 (see Commentary) [origin obscure]

bruke, bruik *v.* enjoy possession, have the use of **54.** 72, **54.** 87; **brukis** *2 sg.* **65.** 12, *3 pl.* **63.** 24; **bruikit** *pp.* possessed, enjoyed **46.** 17 [var. of *broke;* ME]

bruke *n.* brook, stream **10.** 35, **10.** 234 [OE *brōc*]

brukill, brukle *adj.* fragile, readily yielding **14.** 262, **62.** 7 [OE *brucol*]

brukis. See **bruke**

***bruntstane** *n.* brimstone **23.** 291 [ME; OE *byrnan,* to burn; cf. ON *brennisteinn*]

brybour *n.* vagabond, rascal **23.** 79; attrib. **23.** 49 [AF]

brybrie *n.* begging **23.** 63 [ME; OF *briberie*]

brycht. See **bricht**

brychtnes *n.* brightness, radiance **49.** 14 [ONhb *brihtnise,* OE *beorhtnes*]

Bryd, Sanct S. Bride, abbess of Kildare (d. *c.* 523), 'the Mary of the Gael' **79.** 57

bryd *n.* bride **23.** 189 [OE *brȳd*]

brydallis *n. pl.* weddings **27.** 19 [OE *brȳd-ealo*]

brydill. See **bridill**

brym. See **brim**

***brynt.** See **brint**

buddis *n. pl.* rewards, bribes **14.** 142 [origin obscure; ? from *bud-*, variant stem of OE *bēodan*]

buffat *n.* blow **3.** 21; **buffettis** *n. pl.* **54.** 78 [OF *buffet*]

bugill, bowgle *n.* hunting horn, trumpet **10.** 230, **63.** 63; wild ox **50.** 110 [ME; OF *bugle*]

***bugrist** *n.* one who buggers **23.** 526 [ME, OF *bougre;* L *Bulgarus*]

buikis. See **buke**

buill *n.* bull **26.** 27 [ME *bule*]

buke *n.* book **14.** 424; **buikis** *pl.* **40.** 23; **be this buke** an oath sworn on the Gospels **9.** 39 [OE *bōc*]

bukky *n.* shell of a whelk; **a bukky in my cheik** tongue in cheek **14.** 276 [origin obscure]

buklar *n.* small round shield **27.** 9 [ME; OF *bucler;* ON *buklare*]

bumbart *n.* lazy fellow **14.** 91; *attrib.* **bumbard 52.** 70; **bumbardis** *pl.* **63.** 24 [? f. *bum* to hum like a bee]

bund, bundin *pp.* bound, in bonds **9.** 17, **14.** 236 [OE *bindan*]

***bune** *n.* buttocks, fundament **23.** 467 [cf. Gael *bun* bottom; E *bum*]

bung *n.* stopper of a barrel **38.** 33 [ME; MDu *bonghe*]

bur, bure. See **bere, beir**

burch(t), burgh *n.* borough, town **23.** 201, **39.** 23, **46.** 17, **48.** 8, **48.** 32; *pl.* **burghis 68.** 17 [OE *burh*]

***burd** *n.* board, table **23.** 364 [OE *bord*]

burd, hard on *adv. phr.* close at hand **10.** 55 [prec.]

burdclaith *n.* tablecloth **23.** 206 [OE *bord*+*clāþ*]

***burdoun** *n.* staff **23.** 431 [ME; OF *bourdoun*]

bure. See **bere**

burgeoun *v.* make to bud, increase **14.** 88; *intr.* flourish **31.** 3 [ME; F *bourgeonner*]

urges *n.* citizen; *as pl.* company of citizens, freemen **48.** 9 [ME; OF *burgeis*]
urgh(is). See **burch(t)**
buriawe *n.* hangman **23.** 437 [F *bourreau*]
urrow *attrib. n.* of, pertaining to a borough **14.** 338 [OE *burh*]
usche *n.* clump, bush **50.** 130; **bussis** *pl.* **14.** 186 [var. of *busk;* ME; ON *buskr*]
usk v. dress, array *intr.* **14.** 416; **buskit** *pa. t. trans.* **14.** 402 [nth. ME; ON *būask* (*būa*)]
ussis. See **busche**
ussome *n.* besom, broom **53.** 34 [OE *besema*]
usteous, bustious *adj.* rough, harsh **13.** 31, **50.** 34, **50.** 110 [ME; origin obscure]
ut *prep.* without **2.** 22, **6.** 124, **9.** 10, **9.** 26, **14.** 215, **17.** 85; **but sicht** unseen **2.** 31 [OE *būtan*]
ute, John court fool **28.** 19
ute *n.* remedy, use **14.** 309 [OE *bōt*]
uthman *n.* shop-keeper **14.** 309 [ME; OScand *bōþ*]
utis *n. pl.* boots **23.** 230, **56.** 33 [ME; OF *bote*]
y *v.* buy, redeem **1.** 21; **bocht** *pa. t.* bought, ransomed, redeemed **6.** 98, **16.** 111, **36.** 27, **38.** 49, **43.** 53; **boucht** *pp.* paid for **10.** 135 [OE *bycgan*]
y *prep.* beside, near **10.** 197, **14.** 428, **50.** 10; *adv.* near at hand **43.** 53, besides **83.** 4 *et seq.* [OE *bī*]
yd, byde *v.* wait **5.** 68, stay, remain **19.** 22, **54.** 34, stay away (from) **32.** 29; **bydand** *pres. p.* awaiting the result of, enduring **74.** 22 [OE *bīdan*]
ydding *vbl. n.* command, order **14.** 327 [OE v. *biddan*]
yle *n.* boil *fig.* **14.** 164 [OE *bȳl*]
ynd *v.* fasten, tie **38.** 45 [OE *bindan*]
yne. See **be**
yrkis *n. pl.* birch trees **42.** 69 [OE *byrc*]
yt *v.* bite **74.** 16, munch **43.** 23 [OE *bītan*]
byt buttoun *n.* button-biter **23.** 241 [prec.+OF *boton*]
bytin *vbl. n.* biting **29.** 10 [see **byt**]
byttaris *n. pl.* biters **52.** 130 [see **byt**]

***caa** *n.* jackdaw (*corvus monedula*) **23.** 521; **kayis** *pl.* **54.** 89 [nth. ME *ka;* ? ON **kā*]
cabeld *pa. t.* secured, fastened **14.** 354 [ME; F n. *câble*]
cabroch *adj.* scraggy **23.** 190 [? Gael *cabrach; cabar* pole, slender tree-trunk]
cace *n.* affair, situation **12.** 33, **19.** 32, **37.** 7, **67.** 39, **81.** 52; **cacis** *pl.* events, states of affairs **14.** 123 [OF *cas;* L *casus*]
caerfull. See **carefull**
caf *n.* chaff *attrib.* **14.** 355 [OE *ceaf*]
***cahute** *n.* cabin **23.** 449 [F]
caiger *n.* travelling dealer, carrier *attrib.* **23.** 229 [? ME *cagge* to bind]
caiges *n. pl.* cages **42.** 23 [ME, F]
caild. See **cald**
cair *n.* distress, misery, anxiety **14.** 470, **19.** 9, **23.** 16, **23.** 190, **80.** 8; *attrib.* mourning **14.** 422; *pl.* **cairis** **58.** 17, **kairis** **63.** 2 [OE *caru*]
cairfull. See **carefull**
cairlis. See **carle**
cairt *n.* cart **23.** 228; **cart** **14.** 356 [OE *cræt*]
cairt *n.* playing card **42.** 68; **cartis** *pl.* **68.** 11 [ME, OF *carte*]
cald. See **call**
cald, caild, cauld, cawld *adj.* cold **8.** 11, **14.** 522, **17.** 7, **50.** 67, **58.** 15; *n.* sickness **43.** 60, cold weather **43.** 66 [OE *cald;* ON *kaldr*]
Calȝecot Calicut (Malabar) **39.** 62
Calis Calais **26.** 6
call *v.* call, name, summon; **callis** *2 sg.* **23.** 97, *3 pl.* **32.** 20, **32.** 35; **cal(l)it, cald, calit** *pp.* **14.** 210, **42.** 62, **50.** 88, **50.** 127, **51.** 61 [ME; ON *kalla*]
Callyng, Fair *n.* Courteous Welcome *pers.* **10.** 188, **10.** 218; **14.** 489 (corresp. OF *Bialacoil*) [prec.]
calsay *n.* paved part of a street **23.** 216 [ME; ONF *caucié*]

cam. Se **cum**
came *n.* (honey)comb **75.** 39 [OE *camb*]
campio(u)n *n.* champion **4.** 2, **35.** 44, **48.** 36, **62.** 29 [ME; ONF *campium;* L *campio*]
can(e) *v.* is, are able to **4.** 6, **13.** 5, **19.** 34; *forming a pa. t.* did (poet.) **9.** 20, **56.** 9; **cold, coud, cowld, cowd** *pa. t.* could, is, was able **10.** 64, **10.** 67, **10.** 224, *forming a pa. t.* did (poet.) **10.** 226, **23.** 93, **52.** 42, **52.** 212, **56.** 39; **couth(e), cowth, cuth, co(u)ght** *pa. t.* **14.** 256, **14.** 275, **14.** 281, **17.** 27, **31.** 21 [OE *can, cūðe*]
candill *n.* candle; *fig.* the sun **10.** 4 [OE *candel;* L *candela*]
canker *n.* ulcerous sore; **cankerit** *ppl. adj.* poisoned, corrupt **3.** 124; evil, malignant **54.** 127 [OF; L *cancer*]
Canterberry Canterbury **55.** 38
cape *n.* cope, outer vestment **10.** 7 [ON *kāpa;* med. L *capa*]
capircalȝeane *n.* wood-grouse; term of endearment **13.** 43 [Gael *capull coille*]
capitane *n.* military captain **9.** 27, **62.** 30 [OF *capitain*]
cappill *n.* horse **14.** 355 [Gael *capull*]
caprowsy *n.* ? undergarment **23.** 202 [origin obscure]
cardinall *adj.* principal **6.** 75 [L *cardinalis; cardo* hinge on which something turns]
cardinall *n.* cardinal-bishop **39.** 50 [prec.]
carefull, caerfull, cairfull *adj.* dismal, distressing **10.** 243, **14.** 418, **22.** 22 [OE *carful*]
carioun *n.* vile body **23.** 139 [ME; ONF *caroine*]
carle, carll, carill *n.* rustic, fellow of little worth **14.** 89, **14.** 118, **14.** 131, **14.** 274; **cairlis** *pl.* peasants **63.** 23 [ME; ON *karl*]
carleche *adj.* churlish, rude **42.** 19 [ME; **carle**]
carlingis *n. pl.* old women **23.** 221, **75.** 10; *gen.* **23.** 247 [ON *kerling*]
Carmeleitis *n. pl.* White-friars **74.** 45 (see Commentary)

carnale *adj.* corporeal **2.** 39 [L *carnc lis*]
***carnicle** *n.* chronicle **23.** 272 [meta thetic var. of ME *cronicle;* L p *chronica*]
carpand *pres. p.* talking **37.** 52 **carpit** *pa. t.* conversed, talked **14** 510 [ME; ON *karp* boasting]
carpentaris *n. pl.* carpenters **4ϵ** 11 [ME; OF *carpentier*]
Carrik, Karrik *n.* southern Ayı shire **23.** 112 (see Commentary **23.** 134, **23.** 158, *attrib.* **23.** 211
cartis. See **cairt**
carvit *pa. t.* sliced through **54.** 2 [ME; cf. **kerffis**]
carvouris *n. pl.* carvers in wood **4ϵ** 11 [ME *carve;* cf. **kerffis**]
cary *v.* carry, bear **64.** 7 [ME med.L *cariare*]
carybald, caribald, carrybald *n* (pejorative) **14.** 94 (see Commen tary), **14.** 137, **23.** 184; *attrib.* **14** 131 [origin obscure]
cassin *ppl. adj.* cast, thrown **14.** 23 **cassyne** *pp.* **38.** 40 [next]
cast, kast *v.* apply, set (oneself) **14** 81; throw **14.** 227, **14.** 494, **4** 52; consider, search **69.** 13; **cas tand** *pres. p.* devising, plannin **14.** 123; **castis** 1 *sg.* cast **14.** 434 3 *pl.* throw off **23.** 229; **keist kest** *pa. t.* **35.** 77, **56.** 68 [ME ON *kasta*]
***cast** *n.* throw, discharge **23.** 46 [prec.]
castell *n.* castle, stronghold **9.** 12 **61.** 29 [ME; L *castellum*]
castingis *n. pl.* cast-off clothes **45** 43 [ME; **cast**]
catall. See **cattell**
catherein. See **katherene**
catif *n.* villain **81.** 44; **catyvis** *p* **52.** 58; **catyve** *adj.* miserable wretched **81.** 27 [ME; OF; L *captivus*]
catt *n.* cat; *attrib.* catlike, snub **33** 8; **cattis** *pl.* **68.** 23 [OE]
cattell, catall *n.* cattle, livestoc **29.** 15, **38.** 77, **68.** 22, **83.** 3 [ME OF *chatel*]
catyve, catyvis. See **catif**
cauld. See **cald**

aus *n.* cause, origin **16.** 81; sake, reason **68.** 4; good reason **23.** 206, **78.** 2 *et seq.;* accusation, fault **6.** 139 [L *causa*]
aus *v.* make; **caussis** *3 sg.* **5.** 16 [L *causare*]
ausles *adv.* without cause **45.** 28 [prec.]
awandaris *n. pl.* entertainers of some sort **44.** 10 [meaning and origin obscure]
awf *n.* calf **13.** 23 [OE *cælf*, ON *kalfr*]
awkit *pa. t.* excreted, shat **54.** 101 [ME *cakke;* MDu *cacken;* L *cacare*]
awld. See **cald**
Caym Cain **23.** 513
Cayphas Jewish high priest **23.** 534
cedull *n.* document **23.** 48 [ME; OF; L *scedula*]
eis, seis *v.* come to an end, stop **4.** 33, **16.** 33, **77.** 31 [ME; F *cesser;* L *cessare*]
elestiall *adj.* of the sky **1.** 33 [L *coelestis*]
elicall *adj.* heavenly **10.** 257 [late L *coelicus*]
elsitud, selcitud *n.* majesty **2.** 76, **31.** 7 [L; title of honour]
ertane *adj.* sure, safe **14.** 285 [ME; OF *certain*]
certify *v.* confirm **23.** 320 [ME; OF; late L *certificare*]
ertis *adv.* assuredly **14.** 448 [ME; OF]
essioun. See **sessioun**
ete. See **cite**
hace, chece *v.* pursue, put to flight **23.** 235, **49.** 9, **50.** 56, **67.** 15; *pres. p.* **chassand 29.** 15; *ppl. adj.* **chest** chased **23.** 219; **chest** *pa. t.* **9.** 100; **chasit, chaist** *pp.* **4.** 33, **27.** 13 [ME; OF *chascier*]
hace, chaise *n.* pursuit **37.** 54, **60.** 12 [OF]
haftis *n. pl.* jaws **14.** 108, **14.** 290 [nth. ME; OE *ceaft]
haingit *pa. t.* changed, altered **52.** 141 [ME; OF *changer*]
haip *v.* escape, get away **14.** 55, **56.** 71 [aphetic f. *eschape;* OF *eschaper*]
chaise. See **chace**
chaist, chaste, chest *adj.* pure, continent **10.** 76, **14.** 293, **22.** 30, **23.** 166 [ME; L *castus*]
chaist. See **chace**
chakmait *n.* checkmate **77.** 21 [ME *chekmate;* OF *eschec mat*]
chalker *n.* annual audit, court of exchequer **46.** 1 (see Commentary) [reduced form of ME, AF *escheker*]
chalmer, chalmir *n.* bed-chamber **14.** 183, **14.** 194, **14.** 370, **20.** 19, **28.** *title, fig.* **14.** 431 (see Commentary); **chalmeris** *pl.* **29.** 23 [ME *chawmer*]
chalmirleir *n.* chambermaid **9.** 86 (see Commentary) [prec.]
chamerlane *n.* chamberlain, high steward **35.** *title* [ME; OF *chamberlain*]
chance *n.* accident, luck, fortune, fate **15.** 1, **18.** 5, **65.** 5 [ME; OF]
changeis *n. pl.* changes **14.** 53 [OF]
chengit *pp.* changed, turned **68.** 6, **68.** 10 [ME var. of *change;* OF *changer*]
channoun *n.* canon of a cathedral, church dignitary **54.** 53 [ME; OF; L *canonicus*]
channoun *adj.* canonical, prescriptive **54.** 54 [prec.]
chapell *n.* chapel; *attrib.* **10.** 21 [ME; OF *chapele*]
char, on *adv.* ajar, slightly open **4.** 11 [ME; OE *c(i)err* a turn]
charbuckell *n.* ruby *fig.* **36.** 24 (see Commentary); **charbunkle 31.** 5 [ME; L *carbunculus*]
charge *n.* task, commission **10.** 189; imposition, duty **5.** 57 [ME, OF]
chasis. See **chace**
chastite *n.* chastity **14.** 208 [OF; L *castitas*]
Chaucer(e) *n.* the English poet (d. 1400) **10.** 253, **62.** 50
***chaumir.** See **chalmer**
cheif *n.* head, chief; **at cheif** in the principal place **42.** 23 [ME; OF]
cheif *adj.* most important, principal **14.** 292, **23.** 77. See **chymys** [prec.]
cheipit *pa. t.* chirped, squealed **37.** 55 [imit.]

cheir. See **chere**

cheis(e) *v.* choose, select **14.** 46, **14.** 52, **14.** 75, **14.** 208; **cheset** *pa. t.* **48.** 11; **chosin** *pp.* **14.** 75, **50.** 178, *ppl. adj.* **31.** 5 [OE *cēosan*]

cheke, cheik *n.* cheek **14.** 276, **14.** 291, *attrib.* **23.** 165; *pl.* **3.** 133, **14.** 107, **14.** 278, **14.** 438 [OE *cēc*]

chenȝie *n.* chain **52.** 73; **che(i)nȝeis** *pl.* chains, shackles **14.** 53, **14.** 55, ornamental chains **14.** 366 [var. of ME **cheyne**]

chenȝeit *pp.* furnished with chains **52.** 38 [prec.]

cherarchy *n.* hierarchy **50.** 57 (see Commentary) [late L *ierarchia*]

chere, cheir *n.* expression, mood, demeanour **10.** 94, **10.** 211, **14.** 282, **14.** 423, **20.** 23, **50.** 92; *pers.* **10.** 150, **10.** 167; entertainment **18.** 3, **22.** 69; **guid cheir** cheerfulness **48.** 7, **55.** 35, **65.** 9 [ME; OF; late L *cara*]

cheris, chirreis *v.* cherish, handle kindly **14.** 291, **42.** 29 [ME; OF *cherir*, *cheriss-*]

cheris(s)ing *n.* affection, loving care **44.** 24; *pers.* **10.** 189, **10.** 219 [prec.]

cheritable *adj.* charitable, generous **65.** 19 [ME]

cherite, cheritie, cheretie *n.* charity, love; one of the three theological virtues **6.** 74, **16.** 66, **19.** 3, **22.** 38, **68.** 34 [ME; L *caritas*]

chesit. See **cheis**

***chessone** *v.* find fault with, accuse **23.** 273 [ME *cheson*, reduced form of OF *enchesoun* cause]

chest. See **chaist**

chest. See **chace**

chevalouris *n. pl.* 'blackleg' minstrels **44.** 10 (see Commentary) [? satiric use of ME, OF *chevalere* knight]

chevalry, chevelrie, chevelry *n.* company of knights, fighting force **10.** 193; knightly virtue **27.** 3, **35.** 18, **35.** 82, **36.** 8 [ME; OF *chevalerie*]

chevilrous *adj.* knightly, bold **36.** 19 [ME; OF *chevalerous*]

chevist (to) *pp.* obtained, acquired (for) **14.** 292 [ME; OF *chevir cheviss-*]

cheyne *n.* chain **9.** 26 [ME]

chid *v.* reproach, scold **14.** 290 [OE *cīdan*]

chiftane *n.* chieftain **35.** 21, **35.** 63 *pl.* **36.** 23; ***lordis chiftanis** noble commanders **23.** 273 [(lord +) AF *chevetaine*]

chirreis. See **cheris**

chirry *n.* cherry **13.** 52, **68.** 42, **70.** 22 [ME; OE *ciris*]

chittirlilling *n.* (? pejorative) **23.** 243 (see Commentary) [origin uncertain]

choip *n.* jaw **23.** 166 [origin obscure]

chois(e) *n.* choice, the most excellent **10.** 185, **10.** 193, **31.** 19, **35.** 82 **36.** 23; chance to choose **14.** 46 **14.** 52 [ME; OF]

choll *n.* jowl **23.** 166 [ME; origin uncertain]

choppyne (stowp) *n.* vessel holding a Scotch half pint **73.** 26 [ME; OF *chopine*]

chosin. See **cheis**

Chryst, Crist **3.** 112, **4.** 2, **4.** 7, **6.** 79, **14.** 380, **48.** 26, **50.** 182, **72.** 27; **Christys** *gen.* **3.** 137

chuf(f) *n.* churlish fellow **14.** 290 *attrib.* **45.** 25 [ME; origin obscure]

chuk *v.* chuck under the chin, fondle **14.** 291; **chukkit** *pa. t.* **13.** 1 [origin obscure]

churle, churll *n.* rude or miserl[y] fellow (mainly poet.) **14.** 55, **14.** 293, *pl.* **45.** 25 [OE *cēorl*]

churlichenes *n.* rudeness, rusticit[y] **50.** 139 [OE *cierlisc* (prec.)+*-nis*]

chymys *n.* (chief) mansion, manor house **14.** 292 [OF *chymois*, *che[…] més*]

chyn *n.* chin **14.** 291 [OE *cin*]

circumstance, sircumstance *n.* elaborate detail **46.** 3, **55.** 20 [ME; OF; L *circumstantia*]

cite, cete *n.* city **3.** 86, **35.** 55 [OF; L *civitas*]

clacht. See **claith**

claem. See **clame**

claid. See **cleith**

claif *pa. t.* stuck fast **3.** 59. Se[e] ***clevis** [OE *cleofian*]

claif. See **cleif**
claight. See **claith**
clairettis. See **clarat**
clais. See **claith**
claith, clayth, clacht, claight *n.* woven fabric, cloth **3.** 59, **14.** 139, **14.** 366, **65.** 35; **clais, clayis, cla(y)this** *pl.* garments, clothes **3.** 23, **14.** 371, **45.** 53, **52C.** 21, 'washing' **23.** 224 [OE *clāþ*]
clame, claem *v.* lay claim (to), assert a right **33.** 24, **44.** 50, **47.** 2, **52C.** 33 [OF *clamer*]
***clamschellis** *n. pl.* scallop shells (of pilgrims) **23.** 431, **23.** 509 [origin obscure]
clap *v.* draw **14.** 104; **clappis** 3 *pl.* fondle **14.** 483; **clappit** *pa. t.* patted fondly **13.** 11, **43.** 63; **clapping** *vbl. n.* **14.** 274 [ME; ON *klappa*]
clarat *n.* claret, red Bordeaux wine; *attrib.* **44.** 42; **clairettis** *pl.* **22.** 55 [OF]
clarefeid *ppl. adj.* made clear, clarified **50.** 155 [ME; L *clarificare*]
clarioun *n.* clarion trumpet **35.** 22 [ME; OF *claron*]
clarkis. See **clerk**
claschis 3 *pl.* strike, slap **23.** 232 [imit.]
clatter *v.* chatter, rattle out **14.** 90, **52.** 116, 3 *pl.* **20.** 10; **clatteraris** *n. pl.* chatterers **44.** 40 [OE **clatrian;* MDu *klateren*]
claver, clever *n.* clover **13.** 29 (see Commentary) **43.** 4 [OE *clāfre*]
clayis. See **claith**
clayth(is). See **claith**
cled. See **cleith**
cleif(f) *v.* cleave, split **19.** 9, **23.** 88, **42.** 18; **claif** *pa. t.* **3.** 83 [OE *clēofan*]
cleik *v.* snatch, grab **23.** 62; **clekis** 3 *sg.* **45.** 28 [ME; ? OE **clǣcan*]
cleik *n.* haul at cards; *fig.* **42.** 67 [ME; cf. prec.]
cleir, cler(e) *adj.* clear, bright, fair **1.** 5, **1.** 13, **3.** 59, **10.** 5, **10.** 36, **10.** 129, **14.** 21, **14.** 227, **14.** 433; *adv.* **2.** 35, **10.** 266, **58.** 13 [OF *cler;* L *clarus*]
cleirkis. See **clerk**
cleith *v.* clothe, dress **53.** 23, **55.** 4; **cled** *pa. t.* **3.** 26, **3.** 41, **6.** 29, **54.** 11; **cled, claid** *pp. and ppl. adj.* **14.** 422, **33.** 11, **45.** 43, **48.** 42, **60.** 22, **81.** 22 [OE *clǣðan*, ON *klæða*]
clek *v.* hatch **42.** 24 [ME; ON *klekja*]
***cleke** *v.* put on **23.** 510 [see **cleik**]
clemence *n.* clemency, mildness, mercy **35.** 94 [OF]
clene, clein(e), cleyne *adj.* free from stains, pure **2.** 41, **5.** 10, **5.** 67; *adv.* completely, utterly **14.** 103, **14.** 325, **17.** 16, **48.** 30; *adv.* **clenely 54.** 21 [OE *clǣne*]
clenge *v.* clean **23.** 190, **56.** 35; **clengit** *pp.* **5.** 18 [ME var. of *clense;* OE *clǣnsian*]
Cleo *n.* the muse of history **10.** 77
cler(e). See **cleir**
clergie, clergy *n.* clerkly learning **23.** 62; clerks in holy orders **1.** 25 [ME; OF]
clerit *pp.* cleared away **4.** 28 [**cleir**]
Clerk, Master Johne 38. 81 (see Commentary)
Clerk, Johne Scotch poet **62.** 58
Clerk of Tranent Scotch poet **62.** 65
clerk *n.* cleric **56.** 9; scribe, secretary, scholar **23.** 417, **35.** 7, **62.** 34; **cle(i)rkis, clarkis** *pl.* minor clergy **10.** 21, **80.** 6, scholars **14.** 435, **76.** 17 [OF *clerc;* L *clericus*]
clething *n.* clothing, dress **14.** 182, **14.** 268, **82.** 29 [ME; OE v. *clǣðan*]
clever. See **claver**
cleverus *adj.* nimble **54.** 86 [ME *clever*]
***clevis** 3 *sg.* sticks **23.** 452 [see **claif**]
clewch *n.* ravine; side of a ravine **43.** 4, **clewis** *pl.* cliffs **10.** 243 [nth. ME *cloghe, clowes;* OE **clōh*]
cleyne. See **clene**
clip *n.* big awkward fellow, 'big softie' **13.** 36 [origin obscure]
clippis *n.* eclipse **33.** 13 [ME; L *eclipsis*]
clips 3 *sg.* calls out for, demands **7.** 5 [OE *clipian*]
***clocis** *n. pl.* closes; courtyards,

vennels **23.** 499 [ME; OF *clos;* L *clausum*]

cloddis *3 pl.* pelt with clods etc. **23.** 232 [ME n. *clod(de)*]

clog *n.* block of wood, wooden shoe **29.** 11 [origin obscure]

clok(e) *n.* cloak **10.** 126, **14.** 426, **14.** 470; **clokis** *pl.* **14.** 418, **14.** 434, **14.** 437 [ME; OF; med. L *cloca*]

closet *n.* small room, secret place; *transf.* the Virgin's womb **2.** 78 [OF; L *clausum*]

closit *pp.* enclosed (for defence) **62.** 30 [ME; OF; L *claudere*]

clothit *pp.* dressed, adorned **16.** 23 [ME; replacing Sc *clethit;* see **cleith**]

Cloun, Sanct S. Cluanus **75.** 31 (see Commentary)

***cloutit** *ppl. adj.* patched **23.** 509 [OE *ȝeclūtod*]

clowis *n. pl.* cloves **23.** 192 (see Commentary) [ME; OF *clou* (*de gilofre*)]

clowis *n. pl.* claws **4.** 13 [ME (Chaucer) pl.; OE *clāwu*]

clowt, *clout *n.* piece of cloth, rag **23.** 380; **clowttis** *pl.* **52.** 134 [OE *clūt*]

clowttar *n.* patcher, cobbler **52.** 125 [ME; OE v. *clūtian*]

clubfacet *ppl. adj.* heavy-faced **45.** 24 [ME *clubb* (ON *klubba* a staff)+ ME, OF *face*]

clucanes *n. pl.* ? yokels **45.** 24 [origin and meaning obscure]

clud *n.* cloud in the sky **1.** 5, **2.** 27, *fig.* **49.** 11, **54.** 89; **clud(d)is** *pl.* **1.** 38, **14.** 433, **16.** 2, **53.** 29, **69.** 3 [ME; corresp. to OE *clūd* hill]

cluik *n.* claw **54.** 86; **cluikis** *pl.* **54.** 118 [ME *cloke;* origin obscure]

clutit *ppl. adj.* patched **45.** 24 [OE *clūtian, ȝeclūtod*]

cluvis *n. pl.* (cloven hoofs) paws **50.** 99 [OE *clēofan;* cf. Da *klov*]

clym(e) v. climb, mount **14.** 131, **14.** 137, **23.** 240, **39.** 50, **66.** 29; *3 sg.* **14.** 142 [OE *climban*]

clynk *v.* make a clinking sound **23.** 16 [ME; cf. Du *klinken*]

cockis. See **cok**

coclinkis *n. pl.* whores **32.** 26 [origin obscure]

coft *pa. t.* bought **52.** 173 [MDu *copen, cofte*]

coillis *n. pl.* coals **23.** 229 [OE *col*]

coist *n.* expenditure; **mak the coist** meet the expense, pay out **71.** 62 [ME; OF]

co(i)st *n.* coast, shore **9.** 100, **23.** 94 [ME; OF; L *costa*]

coistly. See **costlie**

cok *n.* (barnyard) cock **14.** 326, **23.** 248 (see Commentary); **co(c)kis** *pl.* **23.** 156, *fig.* victors **32.** 8 [OE *coc*]

***Cokburnis peth** Cockburnspath in Berwickshire **23.** 258

Cokelbeis gryce title of a farcical tale of a feast **44.** 66 (see Commentary) [see **gryce**]

cokill *n.* cockle (shellfish) **75.** 24 [ME, OF *cokille*]

***cokkatryce** *n.* cockatrice **23.** 295 [ME; OF *cocatris*]

cold. See **can**

***collapis** *n. pl.* slices of meat **23.** 427 [ME *collop;* origin obscure]

collatioun *n.* repast at bed-time **71.** 21 (see Commentary) [ME; OF; L *collatio*]

collep *n.* ? drinking vessel **52.** 95 [origin obscure]

colleveris *n. pl.* horses for carrying coal **43.** 59 [OE *col*+**aver**]

collouris. See **colour**

***collum** *n.* ship **23.** 468 [? = *collvin,* origin obscure]

colour, cullour *n.* colour, complexion **16.** 76, **49.** 34; *pl.* hues, colours of flowers and vegetation **10.** 13, **50.** 172; painted devices, disguises *fig.* **14.** 456; **collouris** *pl.* style **26.** 11 [ME, OF; L *color*]

com(e). See **cum**

comfortable. See **confortable**

commandit *pa. t.* ordered **50.** 80, *pp.* have commanded **9.** 11 [OF; late L *commandare*]

commendis *1 pl.* recommend (ourselves) to kindly remembrance **22.** 3 [ME; L *commendare*]

commirwald *adj.* ? henpecked **23.** 129 [see **cummer**]

commissar *n.* delegate, representative **23.** 131 [ME *commissarie;* med. L *commissarius*]
commones *n. pl.* the common people **48.** 55 [next; and L *commune*]
commoun, commone *adj.* communal, public **23.** 16, **75.** 4, **75.** 29; general **50.** 176; notorious **23.** 76, **74.** 12 [ME; L *communis*]
commoun *adj.* common **40.** 12 (see Commentary) [L *commune*]
compair *v.* compare **50.** 140 [ME; OF; L *comparare*]
comparesone, comparisoun *n.* distinction *pers.* **9.** 27 (see Commentary) **9.** 63, **9.** 83, **10.** 174 [OF; L *comparatio*]
compasand *pres. p.* considering, contriving **14.** 123 [ME; OF *compasser*]
compassioun *n.* pity *pers.* **3.** 97 [OF; L *compassio*]
compeir *v.* make a formal appearance (e.g. before a king or court of justice) **50.** 72, **50.** 82 [ME; OF *comparoir;* L *comparere*]
compile *v.* give an account of, describe **10.** 72; **compild** *pp.* composed **23.** 1; **compilit** *ppl. adj.* **35.** *title* [OF *compiler;* L *compilare*]
compleit *adj.* entire, full **5.** 31, **6.** 67; *adv.* completely **6.** 5 [ME; L *completus*]
complene, compla(i)ne *v.* make complaint **17.** 55, **26.** 1, **45.** 1, **51.** 69, **73.** 3; **complenis** *3 sg.* **74.** 25; **complenit** *pa. t.* **53.** 6 [ME; OF *complaindre*]
complexioun *n.* bodily constitution **74.** 50 [ME; OF; L *complexio*]
compositioun *n.* agreement for the settlement of a dispute **71.** 55 [ME; OF; L *compositio*]
compositouris *n. pl.* those who settle disputes **71.** 54 (see Commentary) [AF; L *compositor*]
comprehendit *pa. t.* included **6.** 58 [OF; L *comprehendere*]
compt, coumpt *n.* account, reckoning **5.** 57, **40.** 30, **46.** 2, **46.** 15, **63.** 53, **65.** 36, **69.** 34 [ME; OF respelling of *conte* after L *computum*]
comptis *3 sg.* reckons, regards **23.** 129 [ME; OF; L *computare*]
concedring, conciddering. See **considdir**
concluding *pres. p.* bringing to an end, resolving **6.** 102 [ME; L *concludere*]
conclusioun *n.* satisfactory end **71.** 24; **conclusionis** *pl.* inferences, arguments **62.** 39 [ME; OF; L *conclusio*]
condamnit *pp.* condemned **3.** 17 [OF; L *dampnare*]
conditio(u)n *n.* state **14.** 43, **49.** 18; kind, category **50.** 79; agreement, a bargain **14.** 138, **25.** 18, **71.** 59; *pl.* dispositions **14.** 409, **16.** 39 [OF *condicion;* L *conditio*]
confermit *pp.* established **4.** 35 [OF *confermer;* L *confirmare*]
confes(e) *v.* acknowledge (sin, truth) **6.** 129, **14.** 153, **16.** 97, **61.** 37; **confessioun** *n.* formal acknowledgement of sin **5.** 10, **5.** 42, **5.** 49, **63.** 64, *pers.* **3.** 122 [OF; L *confessio*]
confessour *n.* a priest who hears confession **5.** 14, **5.** 29; one who has suffered for confessing his faith **55.** 25 (see Commentary), *pl.* **22.** 46 [OF, L *confessor*]
confirmacioun *n.* one of the seven Sacraments, in which the grace of the Spirit is given more fully to those who have already received it in Baptism **6.** 44; **confirmatioun** testament, document confirming a grant **9.** 109 [L *confirmatio*]
confort, confurt *n.* encouragement, consolation, strength **13.** 5, **17.** 32, **18.** 2, **33.** 24, **39.** 6, **50.** 25, *pers.* **51.** 32, **65.** 15; ? strong drink **82.** 9 (see Commentary) [ME; OF; L *confortare*]
confort *v.* console, encourage **14.** 521, **69.** 47; **confortis** *3 sg.* **50.** 61; **confortand** *ppl. adj.* **8.** 15; **conforting** *vbl. n.* comfort, strength **6.** 36 [ME; OF; L *confortare*]
confortable, comfortable *adj.* comforting, fortifying, delightful **14.** 509, **16.** 4, **36.** 5 [ME; prec.]
confortative *adj.* comforting **22.** 12 [ME; OF]
confoundit *pp.* overthrown, cast

down **4.** 2, **4.** 31 [OF *confondre;* L *confundere*]
confurt. See **confort**
conȝie. See **cunȝie**
conjuratioun *n.* use of spells, magic power **19.** 27 [ME; OF; L *conjuratio*]
conjure *v.* exhort, command **23.** 168; *pa. t.* **50.** 83 [ME; OF; L *conjurare*]
connyng *adj.* learned, skilful **10.** 273 [var. of **cunning**]
conqueir, conqueis, conquys *v.* obtain by conquest, acquire **6.** 126, **42.** 34, **45.** 13 [OF *conquerre;* L *conquirere*]
conquis *n.* conquest **35.** 69 [OF *conquise*]
consaif *v.* conceive **72.** 13; ***consavit** *pp.* **23.** 489 [ME; OF *conceveir;* L *concipere*]
consall. See **counsall**
consaloure *n.* counsellor, adviser **35.** *title* [ME; OF *conseilleor*]
***consavit.** See **consaif**
consciens *n.* conscience, scruple **59.** 35 [ME; OF; L *conscientia*]
conselit *pp.* hidden **5.** 24 [ME; OF *conceler;* L *concelare*]
consentit *pp.* agreed **43.** 54 [ME; OF *consentir;* L *consentire*]
consequent *adj.* following **10.** 109 [OF; L *consequent-*]
conserf *v.* preserve **50.** 182 [ME; OF *conserver;* L *conservare*]
considdir, considder, consydder *v.* reflect upon, take into account **5.** 34, **17.** 86, **22.** 83; *pres. p.* **concedring 50.** 131, **concidder-ing** seeing (that) **50.** 144 [ME; OF; L *considerare*]
considerance *n.* consideration *pers.* **10.** 165, **15.** 9, **51.** 56 [OF; L *considerantia*]
consolatioun *n.* consolation, comfort **22.** 39, **22.** 78 [ME; OF; L *consolatio*]
constance *n.* steadfastness **10.** 169, **76.** 17 [ME; OF]
consuetude *n.* custom, habit **14.** 64 [OF; L *consuetudo*]
consydder. See **considdir**
contene *v.* hold within **17.** 40, **48.** 62 [ME]
contempcioun *n.* impudent disregard of authority **6.** 117 [L *contemptio*]
contenence *n.* chastity *pers.* **10.** 164 [OF; L *continentia*]
conteyne *v.* continue, endure **2.** 41 [ME; L *continuare*]
continance, countenance, contynance *n.* countenance, bearing, manner, **6.** 130, **14.** 278, **15.** 2, **28.** 32 [ME; OF]
continuall *adj.* perpetual, constant **20.** 4 [ME; OF; L *continuus*]
continuatioun *n.* succession to an inheritance **9.** 106 [OF; L *continuatio*]
continuit *pp.* adjourned, postponed **74.** 31 [ME; OF *continuer;* L *continuare*]
contrair *n.* contrary, opposite **58.** 10, **79.** 48 [ME, OF adj.; L *contrarius*]
contra(i)r *prep.* against, at variance with **6.** 123, **16.** 67, **16.** 69, **17.** 16, **76.** 22 [elliptic use of *in contrare;* OF *contraire*, L *contrarius*]
contrariously *adv.* in opposition **53.** 7 [ME, OF *contrarious*]
contrit *adj.* penitent **6.** 47 [OF; L *contritus* crushed]
contritioun, contrycioun *n.* interior repentance **5.** 48, *pers.* **3.** 99, **3.** 121 [ME, OF; L *contritio*]
contynance. See **continance**
convenabille *adj.* appropriate **58.** 2 [ME, OF]
convenient *adj.* suitable (to), in accord (with), fitting **44.** 21, **78.** 31 [ME, OF; L *conveniens*]
convoy *v.* lead, conduct **22.** 59, **71.** 14; **convoyis** *3 pl.* conduct, administer **14.** 453; **convoyed, convoyid, convoyit** *pp.* **48.** 53, **52.** 128, **52.** 158 [OF *convoyer*]
convoy *n.* deportment, carriage **28.** 32 [OF *convoi;* v. *convoyer*]
cop. See **co(w)p**
corce, cors *n.* coin with a cross on one side **19.** 22, **46.** 4 [OE *cros*]
corchet *n.* crotchet in music **42.** 18 [ME; OF *crochet* hook]
corde *n.* rope, string **3.** 52 [OF; L *chorda*]

Cordilleris *n. pl.* Franciscan Greyfriars **74.** 45 (see Commentary)
coreck *v.* correct, admonish **77.** 37 [ME *correcte;* L *corrigere*]
corne *n.* corn, grain **38.** 77, **83.** 3 [OE *corn*]
corpolent *adj.* stout **10.** 113 [OF; L *corpulentus*]
corporall *adj.* concerned with the human body (Matt. xxv. 35) **6.** 26 [ME; OF; L *corporalis*]
corps, corpis *n.* living, human body **3.** 77, **19.** 9, **50.** 94 [OF; L *corpus*]
correctioun *n.* correction by reproof **6.** 35 [OF; L *correctio*]
correnoch *n.* outcry in Gaelic **52.** 112 (see Commentary) [Gael]
corruptit *ppl. adj.* rotten **23.** 139 [ME; L *corrumpere*]
cors. See **corce, croce**
cors(e) *n.* body **14.** 104, **14.** 137, **14.** 419, **52.** 79 [ME; OF *cors*]
***Corspatrik** Gospatrick, earl of Northumberland (depr. 1072) **23.** 257 (see Commentary)
Corstorphin Corstorphine near Edinburgh **62.** 78
cost. See **coist**
costlie, coistly *adj.* valuable **48.** 62, **50.** 155; **costly** *adv.* expensively **14.** 268 [ME; OF *cost*]
cote *n.* coat; *fig.* plumage **42.** 16 [ME, OF]
coud. See **can**
cought. See **can**
couhirttis *n. pl.* ? cowards **45.** 22 [meaning uncertain; but cf. OF *cowairt*, e. mod. E *cowherd* coward]
coumpt. See **compt**
counȝie *n.* (obscure) **52.** 78
counsall *v.* advise **16.** 101, **51.** 71, **77.** 37 [ME; OF *conseiller;* L *consiliari*]
counsall, counsale, consall *n.* advice, body of advisers, council **6.** 35, **6.** 134, **6.** 142, **14.** 353, **44.** 53, **73.** 21 [OF *conseil;* L *consilium*]
countaris *n. pl.* counters for reckoning with **46.** 8 [ME, AF *countour*]
countbittin. See **cuntbittin**
coup. See **co(w)p**
cour *v.* cower **23.** 330 [ME]
cours(e) *n.* passage by water **10.** 237; course of a meal **22.** 57, *pl.* **22.** 14 [ME; OF]
courtas *adj.* courteous, courtly **82.** 43 [ME; OF *curteis*]
courtȝour *n.* courtier **56.** 11 [ME; prob. AF]
courtly, cortly *adj.* elegant, refined **14.** 268, **14.** 369, **14.** 419, **14.** 435 [OF n. *court*]
court man *n.* courtier **81.** 21, *gen.* **22.** 34, *pl.* **44.** 3 [ME]
courtyns *n. pl.* curtains **10.** 11 [ME; OF *courtine;* L *cortina*]
***cousing.** See **cusing**
cout *n.* colt **14.** 354 [OE *colt*]
couth(e). See **can**
covanis *n. gen.* assembly's **41.** 15 [ME, OF *covin*]
covat *v.* covet, desire to have **6.** 54 [nth. ME; OF *coveiter*]
covatice, covatyce, covetyce, cuvatyce *n.* covetousness (*avaritia*) **6.** 19, **20.** 14, **52.** 55, **66.** 9; **covatus** *adj.* **66.** 31 [OF *coveitise*]
coverit *pp. and ppl. adj.* covered **14.** 34, **39.** 86, **48.** 63 [ME; OF *covrir*]
cowart *n.* coward **23.** 76; **cowardis** *pl.* **16.** 82 [ME; OF]
cowch *n.* bed **73.** 6 [ME; OF *couche*]
cowd. See **can**
cowffyne *n.* (obscure) **13.** 23 (see Commentary)
cowhuby *n.* ? booby, fool **13.** 58 (see Commentary)
cowkin *ppl. adj.* ? shitten **45.** 16 [cf. **cuk**]
cowld. See **can**
cowle, cowll *n.* friar's cowl **34.** 12, **45.** 28 [OE *cuȝele*]
co(w)p, coup *n.* wine-cup **14.** 125, **14.** 484, **14.** 510, **48.** 62, **52.** 95, **69.** 42; *pl.* **14.** 35; **playand cop out** drinking the cup empty **38.** 101, **41.** 13 [ME; OF *coupe*]
cowrt *n.* royal court **45.** 13, **68.** 3 [ME, OF *court*]
cowth. See **can**
coy *adj.* quiet **71.** 17 [ME; OF *coi*]
crab(b)it *adj.* ill-natured, cross, angry **10.** 114, **14.** 227, **14.** 445 [ME; ? OE *crabba* a crab]
cradoun. See **craudone**

craft *n.* skill **71.** 9, **76.** 1; *pl.* **31.** 20 [OE *cræft*]

craftely *adv.* cunningly, artfully **14.** 369, **50.** 83 [OE *cræftlīce*]

craftismen *n. pl.* members of crafts, skilled workers **44.** 3 [**craft**]

***crag.** See **craig**

craif(e) *v.* ask humbly, beg, demand **6.** 146, **39.** 54, **69.** 28; **cravis** *3 sg.* **63.** 56, **81.** 9 [OE *crafian*]

craig, *crag *n.* neck **23.** 169 [MLG, MHG *krage*]

craikaris *n. pl.* clamorous fellows **44.** 40 [ME *crake* croak; imit.]

crak *v.* break (with a sharp noise) **3.** 77 [OE *cracian*]

crak *n.* sudden loud noise, explosion **4.** 3, **10.** 243, **51.** 115, **63.** 79; **crakkis** *pl.* shouting **78.** 22 [prec.]

cramase *adj.* crimson **48.** 13 [OF *crameisi*]

cran *n.* crane (*grus grus*) **22.** 51; **crennis** *pl.* **50.** 123, **53.** 24 [OE]

crap *pa. t.* of *crepe* crept, crawled **10.** 133, **37.** 60 [OE *crēopan, crēap*]

crauch *interj.* 'beaten!' **23.** 245 [origin obscure]

craudo(u)n(e), cra(w)doun *n.* coward **14.** 215, **23.** 50, **23.** 129, *pl.* **45.** 22 [ME *crathon;* origin obscure]

cravis. See **craif(e)**

crawis *n. pl.* crows (*corvus*) **23.** 219, **54.** 71 (see **hudit**) **54.** 89, **54.** 115 [OE *crāwe*]

creatur(e) *n.* created being, person **14.** 454, **14.** 521, **15.** 20, **16.** 55 [ME; L *creatura*]

creddens *n.* trust, credit **74.** 34 [ME, OF *credence;* L *credentia*]

***credis** *n. pl.* recitations of the Creed **23.** 318 [OE *creda;* L *credo*]

cre(i)lis *n. pl.* creels, wicker baskets carried on horseback **14.** 355, **23.** 229 [origin obscure]

***creip** *v.* come in unobtrusively **23.** 301 [OE *crēopan*]

creische *n.* grease, fat **52.** 99 [OF *creisse*]

crennis. See **cran**

creuell, crewall, cruell *adj.* cruel **4.** 10, **14.** 260, **26.** 12, **60.** 20 [ME; OF *cruel;* L *crudelis*]

creuelte, crewaltie. See **cruelte**

crevar *n.* one who asks **79.** 17 [**craif(e)**]

***criant** *pres. p.* crying **23.** 383 [**cry**]

cripill *n.* cripple **23.** 134 [OE *crypel*]

cristall *n.* crystal **14.** 515; *attrib. as adj.* clear, bright as crystal **10.** 17, **10.** 37, **16.** 2, **35.** 67, **50.** 9, **54.** 1 [OF; L *crystallum*]

cristallyne *adj.* clear as crystal **10.** 5, **16.** 10 [ME; OF; L *crystallinus*]

Crist. See **Chryst**

Cristin, Crystyn *adj.* **35.** *title*, **36.** 1; *as n. pl.* Christians **4.** 30 [OE *cristen*]

***croapand** *ppl. adj.* croaking **23.** 393 [imit.?]

croce, crose, cors *n.* cross (of Christ) **3.** 49, **3.** 65, **3.** 77, **3.** 107, **4.** 4; market cross **23.** 211, **48.** 58, **75.** 22; **crocis** *pl.* signs of the Cross **14.** 117 [OE *cros*]

croce *v.* cross (oneself) **14.** 103 [nth. ME var. of n. *crois;* OF]

crok *n.* old ewe **23.** 248; **crockis** *pl.* **32.** 18 [origin obscure]

crop *n.* top of a plant; *fig.* highest manifestation **36.** 21; **croppis** *n. pl.* highest parts of plants **10.** 20 [OE]

***crop** *v.* cut the end from **23.** 393 [prec.]

croppit *ppl. adj.* cut short **13.** 8 [ME; prec.]

croun(e), crown(n)e *n.* crown **3.** 46, **3.** 108, **9.** 108, **31.** 6, **45.** 8, *pl.* **10.** 80; crown of the head **14.** 103, **23.** 88; **crownes** *n. pl.* gold coins **18.** 18 (see Commentary) [ME, OF *corune;* L *corona*]

crownit *pa. t.* crowned **50.** 101, **50.** 120; **cround** *pp.* **50.** 153, **crownit, crownyt 1.** 55, **35.** 67, *ppl. adj.* **81.** 6 [ME; OF *coroner;* L *coronare*]

crows *adv.* in high spirits, jauntily **37.** 52 [nth. ME; origin obscure]

croynd *pa. t.* bellowed, roared **27.** 42 [nth. ME; MDu *krônen*]

crud(d)is *n. pl.* curds **75.** 23, ***23.** 427 [ME; origin obscure]

cruelte, creuelte, crewaltie *n.* cruelty, violence **6.** 141, **12.** 13, **56.** 3 (see Commentary] [OF]

cruik, cruke *n.* a hook; curvature, lameness **43.** 60, **52C.** 34 [ME *crōc;* ON *krōkr*]

cruke *adj.* crooked **14.** 275; **cru(i)-kit** *ppl. adj.* **16.** 38, **75.** 53 [ME; ON *krōkr*, a crook]

cry *n.* loud lamentation **75.** 53, **79.** 34; **cryis** *n. pl.* shouting **75.** 10, **78.** 22 [ME, OF *cri*]

cry *v.* shout, sing **1.** 53, call (to . . . for) **12.** 7, **12.** 43, **23.** 184; **cryis** *3 pl.* **23.** 136, **23.** 218; *pa. t.* **cryd, cryit** **9.** 70, **37.** 13, **52.** 100, **52.** 109; **cryid** *pp.* proclaimed **52.** 122 [OF *crier*]

***cry . . . doun** *v.* suppress by proclamation **23.** 31 [prec.]

***crya** *n.* proclamation **23.** 325 [OF *criée;* cf. **allya**]

cryaris *n. pl.* those who shout in their own interest **44.** 40 [**cry**]

cryminall *adj.* criminal, guilty **6.** 139 [ME; L *criminalis*]

crynd, crynit *ppl. adj.* shrivelled **14.** 278, **23.** 187 [? Gael *crīon* withered]

Cryst. See **Chryst**

Crysthinmes *n.* Christmas **43.** 66 [ME *Crystenmas(se)*]

Crystyn. See **Cristin**

Cuddy Rug a fool **26.** 24

cuill *v.* cool, weaken **43.** 39; **culit** *pa. t.* cooled **14.** 509, *ppl. adj.* **17** 3 [OE *cōlian*]

cuir. See **cure**

***cuk** *v.* shit **23.** 469; **cukkis** *2 sg.* foul with excrement **23.** 499 [ME *cuckyn*]

cukkald, kuckald *n.* cuckold **14.** 380, **30.** 17; **cukcald** *attrib.* **23.** 76 [ME; OF **cucuald*]

culd. See **can**

culit. See **cuill**

cullour. See **colour**

culpabill, culpabile *adj.* guilty, deserving punishment **6.** 55, **6.** 105, **6.** 140, **26.** 22 [ME; L *culpabilis*]

culroun *n.* rascal; *attrib.* **45.** 16 [origin obscure]

***cultur** *n.* coulter of a plough **23.** 366 [OE *culter*]

cum *v.* come **5.** 43, **5.** 46, **5.** 49, **10.** 160, **16.** 62; **cum to** approach **1.** 19; **come** *3 sg.* **1.** 15; **cum(m)is** *3 sg.* **17.** 1, **23.** 218, **39.** 57, **60.** 11; **cumis** *3 sg.* befits, suits **81.** 22; **cam, come** *pa. t.* **10.** 146, **10.** 151, **10.** 194, **32.** 3, **48.** 41; **cumin(g), cummyn, cumyne** *pp.* **1.** 7, **1.** 20, **9.** 106, **14.** 227, **39.** 61, **39.** 69; **cuming of** sired by **45.** 25; **cuming** *vbl. n.* **48.** 57 [OE *cuman*]

***cumbir** *n.* trouble, nuisance **23.** 479 [ME]

cumeris. See **cummer**

cumlie, cumly *adj.* fair, pleasing **14.** 34, **50.** 156 [nth. ME; cf. OE *cȳmlic*]

cummer *n.* woman friend, gossip **23.** 224, **73.** 9 *et seq.;* **cummaris, cumeris** *pl.* **14.** 353, **73.** 2 [OF *commere*]

cummerans *n.* distress, annoyance **14.** 118 [ME *cumberaunce*]

cummerid *pp.* harassed **27.** 14 [ME; reduced form of *encumber;* OF]

cummerlik *adv.* like gossips **14.** 510 [**cummer**]

cumpany *n.* companions, company **6.** 137, **22.** 15, **77.** 13, **77.** 28 [OF *cumpaignie*]

cumyng *n.* coming, visit **35.** *title* [**cum**]

cunȝeitt *ppl. adj.* coined **48.** 63 [v. **cunȝe**; OF *cungner*]

cunȝie, conȝie *n.* coin **46.** 4, **83.** 22 [OF *cuigne*]

cunȝouris *n. pl.* coiners at the mint **44.** 11 [OF v. *cungner, coignier*]

cunnaris *n. pl.* expert tasters of liquor **44.** 42 [OE *cunnere*]

cun(n)ing, cunnyng *n.* skill **44.** 50, **45.** 11, **45.** 47, **54.** 26, **76,** 2; *adj.* skilled **44.** 17, **44.** 61; **cunningar** *comp.* **75.** 31 [OE v. *cunnan*]

cuntbittin, countbittin *ppl. adj.* poxed **23.** 50, **23.** 239 [ME *cunte*, ON *kunta;*+OE *bītan*]

cuntre, cuntray *n.* region, district, country **14.** 82, **14.** 459, **39.** 17, **52C.** 39; **cuntreis** *pl.* **23.** 24, **35.** 51 [ME; OF *cuntrée*]

Cupide *n.* god of love, son of Venus **10.** 110

cur. See **cure**

curage *n.* aggressive spirit, strength, ability, sexual desire **10.** 158, **14.** 67 (see Commentary), **14.** 188, **14.** 215, **14.** 485, **14.** 522, **17.** 13, **21.** 12, **32.** 11, **35.** 12, **35.** 57, **43.** 39 [OF]

curat *n.* priest with the charge (cure) of a parish **6.** 85, **14.** 306 [med. L *curatus*]

curche *n.* kerchief, head covering **14.** 138; *pl.* **14.** 23 (see Commentary), **23.** 221 [reduced f. *courchef;* OF *couvrechef*]

cur(e), cuir *n.* guardianship, office, task, pastoral charge **10.** 228, **14.** 325, **15.** 16, **40.** 21, **63.** 23; *pl.* **39.** 89, **42.** 71, **44.** 2, **44.** 51; concern, labour **65.** 30 [ME, OF; L *cura*]

curi(o)us(e) *adj.* elaborately modulated, subtle **10.** 21; **76.** 9; **curiys, curyus** artful, beautiful **14.** 419, **31.** 18; **curiouslie** *adv.* artfully **14.** 21 [OF *curius;* L *curiosus*]

curledoddy *n.* ribwort plantain **13.** 29 (see Commentary) [origin uncertain; prob. *curly*+*doddy* (round-headed)]

Curry court fool **27.** 43–8

cursis *3 sg.* curses **74.** 41; **cursit** *ppl. adj.* accursed, execrable **6.** 137, **14.** 54, **54.** 14 [OE *cursian*]

cursouris *n. pl.* war-horses **43.** 64 [ME; OF *coursier*]

curtasli, curtasly *adv.* courteously, with good behaviour **14.** 318, **14.** 356, **14.** 484 [ME; OF *curteis*]

curtly *adj.* refined, elegant **14.** 182 [ME; OF *c(o)urt*]

cury *n.* cooked dish **14.** 455 [ME; OF *queurie*]

cuschettis *n. pl.* wood-pigeons **54.** 69 [OE *cūsceote*]

cusing *n.* cousin, kinsman **9.** 93, **38.** 62 [OF *cousin*]

cuth. See **can**

cutis *n. pl.* ankles **23.** 232 [MDu *cote*, Flem *keute*]

cuvatyce. See **covatice**

cuver *v.* cover, conceal **52C.** 31 [ME; OF *covrir*]

dagone *n.* villain **23.** 66 (see Commentary)

daill *n.* dale, valley **14.** 10 [OE *dæl*, ON *dalr*]

daill *n.* dealing; sexual intercourse **14.** 421 [OE *dāl*]

daine, dane *adj.* haughty, reserved **14.** 132, **14.** 253 [ME; var. of *digne;* L *dignus*]

dainte. See **daynte**

dais. See **day**

dait *n.* time **55.** 32 [ME, OF *date;* L *data*]

dam *n.* mill-dam **30.** 15 [ME; OFris]

dame *n.* lady (used as title) **10.** 42, **10.** 100, **10.** 102; **damis** *n. pl.* mothers **23.** 152 [OF; L *domina*]

damiesall *n.* damsel **51.** 18; **dameselis, damysellis** *n. pl.* young female attendants, young women **10.** 147, **14.** 457 [ME; OF *damisele*]

dampnage *n.* damage, injury **12.** 23 [med. L *dampnagium*, var. of *damnagium*]

***dampnit** *ppl. adj.* damned **23.** 283 [ME; OF; L *dampnare*]

damys *3 sg.* makes water **14.** 186 [ME *dam* mill-dam]

danceand, danceing, dansand *pres. p.* dancing **28.** 40, **51.** 26, **62.** 11; **dance(i)t, dansit** *pa. t.* **27.** 21, **28.** 24, **51.** 9 [ME; OF *dancer*]

danceis. See **dans**

dandillie *n.* a pet **42.** 62 ME v. [*dandle*]

dane. See **daine**

dang. See **ding**

danger *v.* be endangered **14.** 500 [next]

danger(e), denger *n.* reluctance, disdain **10.** 223, **13.** 6, **17.** 39, **17.** 56, **17.** 62, **45.** 74 [OF *dangier*]

dangerus *adj.* disdainful **14.** 132 [ME; OF *dangereus*]

dans, dance *n.* dance **52.** 55; **danceis** *pl.* **14.** 511 [ME, OF]

dansand. See **danceand**

***Danskyn** Danzig **23.** 446

dantis *3 pl.* subdue **74.** 52 [ME; OF *danter;* L *domitare*]

dar *v.* dare, venture **9.** 23, **14.** 109, **14.** 125, **16.** 95, **71.** 34; *pa. t.* **durst** **9.** 29, **14.** 319, **17.** 49 [ME; OE *dearr*]

darett *v.* ? for *direct*, send **45.** 2 [ME; L *dirigere, directum*]

dartis *n. pl.* light spears, javelins **10.** 199 [OF]
daseyne *n.* daisy (*bellis perennis*) **2.** 43 (var. for rhyme) [OE *dæȝes ēaȝe*]
dastard, dastart *n.* coward, sot **23.** 65, **45.** 34 [ME; origin obscure]
***Dathane** a devil **23.** 249
dautit *pp.* petted, treated with affection **43.** 27 [origin obscure]
David, king of Israel **61.** 12
daw *n.* lazy person, slattern **52.** 71 [origin obscure]
daw, (up) *v.* dawn **14.** 512; *3 sg.* **75.** 30 [OE *daȝian*]
dawing *vbl. n.* dawn **55.** 1 [OE *daȝung*]
day *n.* time of daylight; **dayis, dais** *pl.* days, time, lifetime **5.** 1, **6.** 110, **14.** 421, **27.** 47, **54.** 119, **56.** 58; *gen.* **52.** 2, **60.** 9; *adv.* **daylie 75.** 50 [OE *dæȝ*]
daynte, dainte, denty, dyntie *n.* regard, favour, esteem, delight **14.** 376, **14.** 413, **14.** 458, **22.** 57, **50.** 141; **daynteis** *pl.* pleasures, luxuries **66.** 12 [ME; OF; L *dignitat-*]
de, dee *v.* die **3.** 94, **12.** 27, **16.** 103, **17.** 80, **62.** 11; **deit** *pa. t.* **6.** 119, **6.** 143, **14.** 411, **16.** 45 [OE **dēȝan*]
***dearch** *n.* dwarf **23.** 33 [OE *dweorh*]
debait *n.* argument, conflict **65.** 17, **77.** 20, *pl.* **75.** 10; **at debaittis** in strife, dissension **23.** 135 [ME; OF *debat*]
debait *v.* fight in defence of, protect **3.** 135, **52.** 202, **63.** 32 [ME; OF *debatre*]
decay *v.* fall away, decline **75.** 63; **decayid** *pp.* fallen away, deteriorated **68.** 20 [ME; OF *decair*]
declair *v.* announce, state openly **58.** 6 [ME; OF *declarer;* L *declarare*]
decore *adj.* beautiful **2.** 49 [L *decorus*]
ded(e), deid *n.* death **1.** 46, **3.** 137, **6.** 98, **14.** 370, **16.** 111, **26.** 12, **54.** 46, **62.** 90; murder **6.** 140; *pers.* **69.** 36; **deidis** *pl.* **51.** 94 [nth. ME var. of **deth**]
ded(e), deid *adj.* dead **3.** 86, **14.** 410, **17.** 7; funereal **51.** 22; *as n. pl.* **6.** 30, **6.** 62, **62.** 97 [OE *dēad*]
Dedalus 54. 65 (see Commentary)
dedis. See **deid**
defame *n.* defamation **75.** 11 [ME; OF; late L *diffamia*]
defamit *pp.* disgraced, made infamous **77.** 25 [ME; OF *defamer;* med. L *defamare*]
defamows *adj.* defamatory **26.** 10 [ME; AN; L *defamare*]
defend *v.* offer resistance (to) **9.** 65, *pa. t.* **10.** 201; *pa. t.* defended, protected **10.** 153 [OF *defendre;* L *defendere*]
defender *n.* champion **52.** 159 [ME; OF]
def(f)ence *n.* protection **34.** 25, **35.** 14, **35.** 38 [ME; OF *defens*]
deflorde *pp.* disfigured **3.** 53 [OF; L *deflorare*]
defowll *v.* trample down; *fig.* **23.** 236 (see Commentary) [ME; OF *defouler*]
degest *pp.* grave, settled at rest **1.** 30, **53.** 21, **64.** 3 [L *digestus*]
degre(e), degrie *n.* rank *pers.* **10.** 172; **14.** 497, **42.** 29, **50.** 87, **62.** 19, **63.** 27, **77.** 2; kind **52C.** 19, way **82.** 3 [ME; OF *degré*]
deid *n.* deed, act **6.** 139, **6.** 142, **12.** 11, **14.** 192, **14.** 450, *as pl.* **61.** 35; **de(i)dis** *pl.* **6.** 26, **6.** 33, **6.** 118, **14.** 97, **51.** 65, **63.** 44 [OE *dǣd, dēd*]
deid. See **ded**
deidlie, deidly *adj.* fatal, causing death, mortal **4.** 9, **6.** 18, **12.** 17, **12.** 29, **52.** 14 [OE *dēadlic*]
deiff *v.* deafen with noise **51.** 79; *pp.* **devit 52.** 118 [OE *dēafian*]
deill *v.* have to do, busy oneself (with) **13.** 6 [OE *dǣlan*]
deill *n.* devil ***23.** 259; **deill a bitt** not a bit, nothing at all **52.** 174 [OE *dēofol*]
deill *n.* part, bit **5.** 18, **14.** 48, **71.** 29 [OE *dǣl*]
deip *adj.* deep **9.** 25; **depest** *sup.* **52.** 119 [OE *dēop*]
deir, dere *adj.* dear, beloved, costly, precious **3.** 87, **6.** 143, **8.** 4, **12.** 49, **14.** 145, **14.** 270, **14.** 511, **24.**

10, **50.** 101; *adv.* dearly **10.** 135, **14.** 143, **52.** 173; **derer** *comp.* more dearly **14.** 376 [OE *dēore*]

deis, dies *n.* dais, platform at the end of a hall **27.** 21, **51.** 74 [ME; OF *deis*]

deit. See **de**

deithe. See **deth**

delayit *pa. t.* put off **10.** 138 [ME; OF *delaier*]

delice, delyce. See **flour delice**

deligent *adj.* assiduous, constant **5.** 7, **5.** 11 [OF; L *diligens*]

delis *3 pl.* have to do (with) **14.** 458 [OE *dǣlan*]

delit. See **delyt(e)**

deliver, delyver *v.* liberate, rescue **22.** 25, **deliverit** *pp.* **4.** 30; **deliverit** *pa. t.* delivered, handed over **9.** 19, **10.** 227 [L *deliberare*]

deliverance *n.* liberation **5.** 27; decision, judgement **6.** 133; action, agility **50.** 95 [OF; L *deliberare*]

deliverly, delyverly *adv.* smartly, swiftly **9.** 73, **55.** 9 [ME; OF adj. *delivre*]

delyt(e), delit *n.* delight, joy **3.** 28, **10.** 264, **16.** 74, **17.** 15, **22.** 7, **24.** 14, **31.** 35, **37.** 23, **50.** 7 [ME, OF]

delyt *v.* delight, take pleasure **66.** 12 [ME; OF *delitier*]

delytable *adj.* delightful, delectable **10.** 120 [ME; OF]

delytsum *adj.* delightful **8.** 2, **49.** 5 [ME]

demair *n.* judge, censurer **81.** 42 [OF]

demane *v.* deal with, maltreat **39.** 39 [ME; OF *demener*]

deme *n.* dame (title) **53.** 11 [var. of **dame**]

deme, deyme *v.* judge, form an opinion **45.** 40, **82.** 14; **demyng** *pres. p.* judging, considering **6.** 109; **demit** *pp.* **81.** 55 [OE *dēman*]

deming *n.* judging, judgement **81.** 7, **81.** 15 [prec.]

denger. See **danger(e)**

dengerous *adj.* disdainful, perilous **9.** 37 [OF *dangereus*]

dennar *n.* dinner **52.** 173 [ME, OF *diner*]

Denseman *n.* Dane **23.** 51 [OE *denisc mon*]

denty *n.* See **daynte**

denyis *3 sg.* refuses **69.** 4 [ME; OF *denier*; L *denegare*]

depairtit *pa. t.* went away **50.** 43; *pp.* separated, divided **4.** 23 [ME; OF *departir*]

depant *v.* paint, depict **31.** 21; **depaynt, depent** *pp.* coloured, painted **10.** 40, **10.** 66, **10.** 248, **50.** 16, **51.** 3 [ME; OF *depeindre*]

departing *pres. p.* leaving, going away **10.** 226; **depairting** *vbl. n.* **49.** 29 [ME; OF *departir*]

depaynt, depent. See **depant**

depest. See **deip**

depictour *n.* painting **31.** 14 [L *depictura*]

depurit *ppl. adj.* purified **10.** 5 [ME; OF *depurer;* L *depurare*]

deray *n.* disorderly merriment, revelry **21.** 14 [ME; OF *desrei*]

dere, derer. See **deir**

derect *pp.* destined (for) **51.** 93 [ME; L *dirigere*]

derene *v.* engage in conflict **17.** 56 [ME; OF *dereiner*]

dergy. See **dirige**

deris *3 sg.* harms, hurts **45.** 74 [OE *derian*]

derisioun *n.* ridicule, disdain **6.** 116 [OF; L *derisio*]

derne *n.* darkness, secrecy, secret **2.** 3, **14.** 9, **14.** 192; *adj.* dark, secret **14.** 242, **14.** 450, **14.** 457 [OE *dyrne*]

Derntoun Darlington **55.** 38 (see Commentary)

dertis *n. pl.* darts, spears *fig.* **50.** 121 [ME; OF *dart*]

desarvit. See **deservis**

descendyd *ppl. adj.* derived by lineage **24.** 6 [ME; OF; L *descendere*]

descepcioun, disceptioun *n.* deception, deceit **6.** 125, **63.** 42 [OF; L *deceptio*]

descryve. See **discrive**

desert *ppl. adj.* empty, waste **23.** 95 [ME; OF; L *desertus*]

deservis *3 sg.* **78.** 11; **desarvit, deservit** *pa. t.* deserved, merited **12.** 4, **54.** 23 [OF *deservir*; L *deservire*]

desir *v.* wish strongly for **14.** 336;

desyrd *pp.* **55.** *title* [ME; OF *desirer*]
dessaveabille *adj.* deceitful **58.** 5 [ME; OF *deceveir*]
desyr(e) *n.* desire, passionate longing **20.** 16, **53.** 40, **77.** 20 [ME; OF *desir*]
desyrouse (of) *adj.* ardent, eager (for) **10.** 54 [ME; OF *desireus*]
deth(e), deith(e), deathe *n.* death **4.** 26, **8.** 13, **12.** 4, **14.** 48, **35.** 39, **59.** 10, **60.** 14; **de(a)this** *gen.* **2.** 20, **61.** 42 [OE *dēaþ*]
detressit *ppl. adj.* untressed, loose **48.** 43 [OF *detrecié*]
dett *n.* debt, duty **40.** 16 [ME; OF; L *debita*]
devill, dyvill *n.* Satan, devil **19.** 29, **45.** 32, **56.** 2, **70.** 25; **devellis** *gen.* **45.** 20; **devillis** *pl.* devils **56.** 81, **divillis** **4.** 5, **23.** 11 [OE *dēofol*]
***devis** *2 sg.* deafen **23.** 360 [**deiff**]
devise, devy(i)s *v.* design, contrive **10.** 104, **71.** 70, **82.** 2; **devysit** *pp.* **82.** 41 [ME; OF *deviser*]
devit. See **deiff**
devocio(u)n. See **devotioun**
devoid, devoyd *v.* discharge, eject **14.** 166, **49.** 8 [ME; OF *devoyder*]
devoit *adj.* devout, pious **22.** 23, **74.** 51; **devotely** *adv.* **22.** 48 [ME; OF; L *devotus*]
devore, devoir, devour *v.* devour, destroy **2.** 59, **36.** 18, **49.** 35, **50.** 126, **62.** 49; **devouris** *3 sg.* **1.** 5, **61.** 28; **devouring** *pres. p.* **59.** 11 [OF; L *devorare*]
devotioun, devocio(u)n *n.* prayer, meditation, piety **14.** 428, **20.** 17, **25.** 3, **45.** 31 [ME; L *devotio*]
devyce, at *adv. phr.* in accordance with (his) design, **53.** 45; **eftir his devyce** **68.** 15 [ME; OF *devis(e)*]
devydit *pp.* distributed **39.** 46 [ME; L *dividere*]
devyne *adj.* holy, sacred, of God **1.** 27, **2.** 4, **22.** 32 [ME; OF *devin*; L *divinus*]
devys. See **devise**
dew *adj.* due, proper **50.** 77 [ME; OF *deu*]
***Dewlbeir, Deulbere** 'Devil-bear' **23.** 260 *et seq.*
dey sterne. See **sterne**
deyme. See **deme**
deyne *n.* disdain, scorn **9.** 28 [ME]
diamaunt *n.* diamond **31.** 35 [ME; OF; late L *diamas*]
dicht *v.* make ready; *pp.* **4.** 18; *ppl. adj.* prepared, treated, dealt with **2.** 35, **3.** 87 [OE *dihtan*]
did away *pa. t.* put, drove away **14.** 242 [OE *dōn*]
diedie *adj.* doing (evil) **44.** 58 [**deid** deed]
dies. See **deis**
digne, ding, dyng *adj.* worthy, deserving **2.** 15, **35.** 45, **36.** 3, **44.** 23 [OF; L *dignus*]
dignite(e), dignitie *n.* high rank, standing **50.** 147, *pers.* **10.** 173; ecclesiastical office **45.** 48 [OF; L *dignitas*]
din *n.* noise, loud talk **21.** 14 [OE *dyn*]
ding *v.* strike, beat, overcome **52.** 146; **dang** *pa. t.* **23.** 125, **54.** 109; **dungin** *pp.* **4.** 9 [nth. ME; ON *dengja*]
ding. See **digne**
dink *adj., adv.* dainty, finely **14.** 377 [origin obscure]
dirige, dergy, dregy *n.* office of the dead, dirge **22.** *title*, **22.** 23, **22.** 28 [Ps. v. 8, *dirige;* see Commentary]
dirk *adj.* dark **2.** 20, **3.** 85, **49.** 11, **58.** 18, **69.** 1 [OE *deorc*]
dirkin *v.* lurk, lie hid **14.** 9 [ME; prec.]
dirkit *pp.* darkened **54.** 121 [ME *dirke;* ? OE **dyrcan*]
dirknes *n.* darkness **2.** 28, **4.** 28, **76.** 20 [OE *deorcnes*]
dirrydan *n.* name of a dance, copulation **13.** 60 (see Commentary) [origin obscure]
dirrye dantoun *n.* a lively dance **28.** 24 [cf. prec.]
***dirtfast** *adj.* covered in dirt **23.** 33 [ME *dirt*, ON *drit*]
dirtin *adj.* dirtied, filthy ***23.** 25, **23.** 248 [prec.]
discend *v.* come down **53.** 36;

discendit *pa. t.* **6.** 60, **23.** 7 [L *descendere*]
disceptioun. See **descepcioun**
discerne *v.* perceive, see **2.** 3 [OF; L *discernere*]
discha(i)rge *v.* free, relieve **5.** 30, **79.** 29 (see Commentary); *pres. p.* **dischairgeing** dismissing **52.** 213 [OF *descharger*]
discimilit *adj.* feigned, disguised **6.** 113 [OF *dissimuler*; L *dissimulare*]
disciplyne *n.* branch of learning **76.** 4 [ME; OF; L *disciplina*]
discirnyng *pres. p.* distinguishing **50.** 128 [ME *discerne*; OF; L *discernere*]
discordis *3 sg.* disagrees, is at variance with **26.** 11 [ME; OF *descorder*; L *discordare*]
discrecioun, discretioun *n.* discernment, judgement **6.** 123, **15.** 9, **78–80** *passim*, *pers.* **10.** 165, **51.** 43 [OF; L *discretio*]
discreit, discret *adj.* discreet, judicious **5.** 29, **17.** 74, **49.** 3, **50.** 134, **75.** 66 [OF; L *discretus*]
discrive, descryve *v.* describe, delineate **10.** 64, **22.** 71, **33.** 4, **50.** 39 [ME; OF *descrivre*]
discry *v.* describe **35.** 87 [ME; F *descrire*]
discure *v.* discover, reveal **17.** 50, **77.** 9 [ME; OF *descovrir*]
disdenȝie *n.* disdain, contempt **79.** 44 [ME; OF *desdain*]
dise(i)s *n.* hardship, distress **14.** 281, **17.** 39 [ME; OF *desaise*]
***diserth** *n.* (obscure) **23.** 283
disheris *v.* disinherit **39.** 38 [back formation f. *disherisoun*; OF *disheriteison*]
disjone *n.* breakfast **19.** 17 [OF *desjeun*]
dismemberit *pp.* broken up, dislocated **26.** 8 [ME; OF *desmembrer*]
dispair *v.* despair of obtaining **47.** 15 [ME; OF *despeirer*; L *desperare*]
dispensationis *n. pl.* ecclesiastical licences **42.** 72 [ME; L *dispensatio*]
dispensit *pp.* dealt (with) by granting exemption **54.** 54 [ME; OF *dispenser*; L *dispensare*]
dispern *v.* disperse **2.** 7 [L *dispernere*]
dispise, dispy(i)s *v.* despise, scorn **14.** 396, **45.** 64, **63.** 21, **82.** 4; **dispysit** *pp.* **82.** 42 [ME; OF *despire, despis-*]
dispitois *adj.* cruel, pitiless **14.** 253; **dispituouslie** *adv.* cruelly **3.** 29 [OF *despitos*]
displeis *v.* displease, make unhappy **17.** 37 [ME; OF *desplaire, desplais-*]
dispone *v.* order, arrange, deal with, make ready **38.** 90, **62.** 98, **63.** 6, **67.** 13, hand over **63.** 49 [ME; OF *disponer*; L *disponere*]
disport *n.* pastime, diversion **48.** 19; *pl.* **51.** 10 [ME; OF *desport*]
dispulit *pp.* stripped, deprived **4.** 39 [ME; OF *despuillier*]
dispy(i)s. See **dispise**
dispyt(e) *n.* animosity, hatred **34.** 34, **44.** 88, **52.** 45, **77.** 23 [ME; OF *despit*]
dispyt *v.* hate **23.** 172; **dispytit** *pa. t.* **14.** 271 [ME; OF *despiter*]
dispytfull *adj.* malicious, scornful **77.** 45 [ME; n. **dispyt(e)**]
dissaif *v.* deceive, beguile **14.** 256; **dissavis** *3 sg.* **63.** 57; **dissavand, dissavyng** *ppl. adj.* **15.** 2, **17.** 87 [ME; OF *deceveir*]
dissait *n.* deceit **60.** 7 [ME; OF *deceite*]
dissaitfull *adj.* deceitful **23.** 75 [ME; prec.]
dissever *v.* become separate **12.** 5 [OF *dissevérer*]
dissever *n.* separation **38.** 22 [prec.]
dissimilit, dissym(b)lit *pp., ppl. adj.* disguised, hidden under pretence **6.** 129, **14.** 254, **52.** 47; **dissymyland** *pres. p.* concealing, holding back **14.** 157 [OF *dissimuler*; L *dissimulare*]
dissimulance, dissymilance, dissymulance *n.* dissimulation, feigning, deceit **15.** 3, **54.** 13; *pers.* **10.** 182, **10.** 217 [L *dissimulantia*]
dissimulatour *n.* dissembler **34.** 31 [L]
dissolvit *pp.* resolved into elements **60.** 22 [ME; L *dissolvere*]

distelling. See **distill**
distemperance *n.* disordered, ill-regulated way **15.** 18 [ME; OF; med. L *distemperantia*]
disteynit *ppl. adj.* stained, discoloured **10.** 278 [ME; OF *desteindre*]
distill *v.* let fall in drops **1.** 2; **distelling** *pres. p.* falling in drops **6.** 15 [OF; L *distillare*]
distitud *adj.* deprived, destitute; as *n. pl.* **6.** 35 [ME; L *destitutus*]
distres *n.* affliction **21.** 10, **22.** 6; *pers.* **51.** 18, **51.** 41 [ME; OF *destresse*]
distributioun *n.* distribution (of wages, goods etc.) **51.** 63 [ME, OF; L *distributio*]
divers(e), dyvers *adj.* different, various **10.** 148, **16.** 39, **20.** 1, **44.** 2, **52.** 135 [ME; OF; L *diversus*]
divillis. See **devill**
divinouris *n. pl.* diviners, those who practise divination **44.** 5 [ME; OF; L *divinator*]
do *v.* make, perform, give **1.** 27, **9.** 52, **9.** 71, *auxiliary with infin.* (*pl.*) **1.** 25; **dois** *1 sg.* **6.** 10, **6.** 18, **22.** 71, *2 sg.* **16.** 73, *3 sg.* **4.** 7, **8.** 13, **17.** 10, *3 pl.* **14.** 457, **51.** 41; **doing** *pres. p.* **22.** 24; **doin** *pp.* **30.** 21; **doar** *n.* one who does **74.** 12 [OE *dōn*]
docht. See **dow**
dochter, dochtir *n.* daughter **24.** 10, **31.** 12, **50.** 149, **50.** 166 [OE *dohtor*]
doctouris *n. pl.* men holding academic doctorates, eminent scholars **44.** 4 [ME; OF; L *doctor*]
doctring, doctryne *n.* dogma, instruction **11.** 7, **76.** 2 [OF *doctrine*; L *doctrina*]
Dog, James, the Queen's wardrober **28.** 44, **29, 30**
dogonis *n. pl.* worthless fellows **14.** 458 [origin obscure]
doig *n.* dog **23.** 113; *attrib.* **23.** 71 [OE *docga*]
doin. See **do**
doingis *n. pl.* deeds, goings-on **14.** 454 [ME; OE *dōn*]
dois. See **do**
dok *n.* arse, fundament **23.** 248 [ME]
dollin *pp.* delved, interred **14.** 410 [OE *delfan, dolfen*]
dolly. See **dully**
dolor(o)us *adj.* sorrowful, sad, bringing sorrow **6.** 3, **12.** 29, **36.** 17 [OF; L *dolorosus*]
dolour *n.* sorrow, mourning **14.** 413, **30.** 23, **49.** 23, **64.** 17, **65.** 14 [ME; OF]
dome *n.* (last) judgement **6.** 67 [OE *dōm*]
dominatioun *n.* authority, power **19.** 29 [ME; L *dominatio*]
domisday *n.* day of judgement **38.** 22 [OE *dōmes dæȝ*]
dompnationis *n. pl.* dominations, one of the orders of angels **1.** 9 (see Commentary) [OF; L *dominatio*]
done *infin.* do **10.** 159; *pp.* finished, over **4.** 1, **14.** 412; *auxiliary with infin.* = has, have **4.** 33, **55.** 13, **62.** 49; **(sa) done** *ppl. adj.* (so) very, utterly **39.** 82, **42.** 2 [OE *dōn*]
***dong** *v.* drop dung **23.** 395 [ME *dunge*; OE n. *dung*]
donk *adj.* damp, moist **10.** 97; **donkit** *pa. t.* dampened **14.** 10, **14.** 512 [ME; origin obscure]
dotit *ppl. adj.* stupid, silly **14.** 186, **14.** 377, **14.** 457 [ME *dote* think stupidly]
doubilnes, dowbilnes *n.* deceitfulness, duplicity **10.** 184, **59.** 30 [ME; OF *double*]
doublett *n.* close-fitting garment for men **29.** 2 [ME; OF *doublet*]
douchtie. See **dughti**
doun(e) *adv.* down **2.** 17, **3.** 3, **3.** 76, **5.** 47, **6.** 47, **9.** 68, **10.** 28, **10.** 84, **14.** 22, **41.** 12 [OE *dune*]
Dounteboir, Dame 28. 36 (see Commentary)
dour(e) *adj.* sullen, unwilling **14.** 132, **14.** 253, **25.** 29, **29.** 2; **dourly** *adv.* sullenly, heavily **83.** 9 [origin doubtful]
dout *v.* fear, suspect **8.** 11 [ME; OF *douter*]
dout(e), dowt *n.* uncertainty, apprehension **5.** 30, **23.** 66, **51.** 47, **54.** 96, **69.** 14; **but, bot dowt**

assuredly **52.** 103, **77.** 36; **dowtles doutles** *adv.* undoubtedly **42.** 79, **64.** 34 [OF] [ME; OF *doute*]

Dover in Kent **55.** 39

dow *n.* dove; term of endearment **12.** 36; *pl.* **14.** 263 [ME; ON *dūfa*]

dow *v.* is of value, use *3 sg.* **81.** 14; **docht** *pa. t.* **14.** 370 [OE *duȝan*, *dohte*]

dowbart *n.* fool, stupid fellow **23.** 66 [origin obscure]

dowbilnes. See **doubilnes**

***dowcare** *n.* diver **23.** 379 [ME v. *douke*; MLG *duken*]

dowsy *adj.* stupid; *as n.* **23.** 158 [cf. later *dozy;* Du *dösig*]

dowt. See **dout(e)**

draf(f) *n.* refuse of malt after brewing **38.** 39; *attrib.* **38.** 37 [ME; MDu]

drago(u)n, dragone *n.* dragon **53.** 27; the Devil **4.** 1, **4.** 9; death **36.** 17, **40.** 28, **61.** 28; *pl.* **14.** 263 [OF]

draif. See **dryf**

draik *n.* male duck **44.** 46 [ME]

dram *adj.* sad, dejected **30.** 23 [origin obscure]

draucht *n.* draught, drawing (a cart etc.) **14.** 85 [ME; rel. to OE *draȝan*]

drave. See **dryf**

draw *v.* pull (in a cart) **43.** 10; *pp.* drawn, hoisted **23.** 90; **drawis** *1 sg.* pull, **14.** 426, *3 sg.* **14.** 356; **drawand** *pres. p.* coming **67.** 2 [OE *draȝan*]

drawkit *pp.* drenched **54.** 102 [origin obscure]

dre *v.* endure, suffer **5.** 2, **14.** 443, **73.** 19 [OE *drēoȝan*]

drede, dreid, dreyd *n.* apprehension, fear **11.** 4, **17.** 31, **80.** 28; *pers.* **10.** 156; **dreid** = for fear that **54.** 23; doubt, uncertainty **51.** 82; **but dreid** certainly, without doubt **27.** 10, **55.** 15 [OE *andrǣdan*]

dredefull, dreidfull *adj.* causing dread, fearsome **10.** 111 [ME; prec.]

dregar *n.* dredger **23.** 242 [Du v. *dreggen*]

dregy. See **dirige**

dreid. See **drede**

dreid *v.* fear, be afraid **36.** 13, **39.** 74; **dred** *pa. t.* **10.** 159 [OE *ondrǣdan*]

dreidfull. See **dredefull**

dreme *n.* dream **53.** 41; *gen.* **dremes** **10.** 49; **dremyng** *vbl. n.* **53.** 10 [OE *drēam*]

drene *n.* drone, monotonous voice **78.** 7 [imit.]

***drepis** *3. sg.* drips **23.** 519 [OE *drēopan*]

drerie, drery *adj.* dismal, sad **14.** 411, **51.** 18, **53.** 47, **58.** 14 [OE *drēoriȝ*]

dres, dresse *v.* prepare, turn, proceed, betake yourself **10.** 226, **21.** 7, **30.** 11, **52.** 93, **60.** 10, **61.** 36; **dressit** *pa. t.* dressed up **14.** 377, **drest** proceeded **52.** 157; *pp.* **37.** 67, **75.** 48; *pp.* cruelly treated **3.** 111 [ME; OF *dresser*]

drevellis *n. pl.* worthless fellows **45.** 19 [ME]

dreyd. See **drede**

dron *n.* drone (bee) **14.** 91 [imit.]

dronis *3 sg.* talks monotonously **78.** 8 [imit.]

droppis *n. pl.* drops (of dew) **10.** 14, **10.** 23 [OE *dropa*]

drownd, drownet, drownit *pa. t.* drenched **3.** 100; *pp.* drowned **9.** 87, **30.** 15, drenched **54.** 102 [ME; origin obscure]

drowp. See **drup**

drowth *n.* prolonged dry weather **59.** 19, thirst **73.** 28 [OE *drūȝoþ*]

drublie *adj.* clouded **69.** 1 [ME]

drug *v.* drag with force **43.** 10; **druggit** *pa. t.* **54.** 70 [ME *drugge*]

Drumfres, *Drumfrese Dumfries **23.** 425, **26.** 24

drunckart *n.* drunkard **52.** 94; **druncartis** *pl.* **45.** 19 [OE *drincan*, *druncen*]

drunkyn *adj.* overcome by drink **10.** 204, *fig.* soaked **16.** 92 [OE *druncen;* cf. prec.]

drup, drowp(e) *v.* droop, be dispirited, feeble **14.** 420, **64.** 26, **69.** 41, **82.** 13 [ME; ON *drūpa*]

drup *adj.* drooping, impotent **14.**

192; **drupe** *as n.* feeble fellow **14.** 370 [ME; as prec.]
drye *v.* wither **76.** 15; **dryit** *ppl. adj.* dried out by exposure **23.** 51 [OE *drȳȝan*]
dryf(e), dryve *v.* drive, spend **64.** 17, *3 sg.* **67.** 17; break by force **61.** 44; **drave** *pa. t.* **27.** 17, **draif . . . our** spent **14.** 511 [OE *drīfan*, ON *drīfa*]
drynk *n.* drink, drinking **19.** 17 [OE *drinc*]
drynk *v.* drink **22.** 53, **52.** 100, **56.** 62; *pres. p.* **38.** 101, **73.** 2 [OE *drincan*]
***dryte** *v.* shit, void excrement **23.** 395; **bedret** *pa. t.* **52.** 203, ***bedrate** **23.** 450 [OE *drītan*, ON *drīta*]
dryve. See **dryf**
dryver *n.* driver, drover **23.** 246 [ME; OE *drīfan*]
dub *n.* small stagnant pool **54.** 119 [MLG *dobbe*]
***duddis** *n. pl.* ragged clothes **23.** 384 [ME sg. *dudde*]
duddroun *n.* sloven **52.** 71 [origin obscure]
duell *v.* dwell, stay **57.** 2; *3 sg.* **14.** 181, **27.** 51; **dwellis** *3 sg.* **51.** 100, **77.** 10, *3 pl.* **34.** 6; **duelling** *ppl. adj.* **60.** 10 [OE *dwellan*]
***duerch(e)** *n.* dwarf **23.** 395, **23.** 408 [OE *dweorh*]
dughti, douchtie *adj.* valiant **35.** 21, **35.** 45 [late OE *dohtiȝ*]
dughtines *n.* valour **35.** 92 [prec.]
duik, duke *n.* duck (*anas*) **40.** 6, **44.** 46; **dukis** *pl.* **54.** 119 [OE *dūce*]
duilfull *adj.* causing sorrow **36.** 17, **51.** 23; **dulfullie** *adv.* dolefully **36.** 18 [ME; **dule**]
duill. See **dule**
duir. See **dure**
duk *n.* duke, ranking next to a prince **28.** 34 [ME; OF *duc*]
duke, dukis. See **duik**
dulce *adj.* sweet **50.** 47; ***dulcely** *adv.* **23.** 339 [L *dulcis*]
dule, duill *n.* sorrow, grief, mourning **14.** 242, **14.** 281, **14.** 411, **43.** 10, **47.** 21; *attrib.* mourning **14.** 420 [ME]
dule *v.* lament, be sorrowful **14.** 450 [cf. prec.]
dule *adj.* var. of **dully**
dullit *ppl. adj.* made dull **21.** 10 [ME]
dully, dolly, dule *adj.* doleful, dismal **1.** 37, **14.** 412, **27.** 15, **50.** 60, **69.** 8 [origin obscure]
dulnes *n.* heaviness **21.** 10 [ME]
dum *adj.* dumb, silent **52.** 152, **78.** 26 [OE *dumb*]
***Dumbar, Archbald** **23.** 299
***Dumbar, Dunbar** the poet **23.** 25, **28.** 22, **35.** *title*
***Dumbar, *Dunbar** Dunbar castle **23.** 275, **23.** 285, **23.** 288, **23.** 300, **23.** 411
Dumferm(e)ling, Dunfermelyne Dunfermline, Fife **37.** 1, **37.** 70, **62.** 81
***Dunbar,** Sir Alexander, of Westfield **23.** 388
dungeoun *n.* deep, dark prison **4.** 36, **9.** 25, **52.** 211 [OF *donjon*]
dungin. See **ding**
dure, duir *n.* door **51.** 111, **63.** 38, **80.** 14; **dur(r)is** *pl.* **32.** 13, **37.** 46, **44.** 52 [OE *duru*]
dures *n.* harm **10.** 170 [ME, OF *duresse*]
durst. See **dar**
dwamyng *vbl. n.* fainting **52.** 170 [see next]
dwawmes *n. pl.* swoons **12.** 17 [cf. OSax *dwalm* confusion; OHG *twalm* giddiness]
dwellis. See **duell**
dyademe *n.* crown **50.** 101 [ME, OF; L *diadema*]
Dyane *n.* Diana, daughter of Jupiter and Latona, patron of virginity and the chase (cf. **Lucina**) **10.** 76
dyce *n.* dice used in gambling **68.** 11 [ME pl.; OF *de*, pl. *dez*]
dyk *n.* wall of turf or stone **14.** 9 [OE *dic*]
dyng. See **digne**
dynis *3 sg.* dines out **74.** 34; **dynd** *pp.* dined, feasted **23.** 52 [ME; OF *disner*]
dynnit *pa. t.* sang loudly **14.** 10 [OE *dynnan*]
dynt *n.* heavy blow **54.** 76 [OE]
dyntie. See **daynte**

dysour *n.* dice-player **56.** 66; *pl.* **45.** 19 [ME *dysar*; see **dyce**]
dyt *n.* composition, writing **47.** 21 [ME; OF *dit*; L *dictum*]
dyt *v.* compose, write **21.** 7 [ME; OF *diter*; L *dictare*]
dyvers. See **divers(e)**
dyvour *n.* bankrupt **14.** 410, **39.** 39; *pl.* **45.** 19 [origin obscure]

e, e(y)e *n.* eye **6.** 79, **10.** 235, **14.** 227, **14.** 277; **ene, eyn(e)** *pl.* eyes **2.** 39, **6.** 15, **10.** 212, **10.** 203, **35.** 75 [nth. ME reduced form of *eye*; OE *ēaȝe*]
eb *n.* ebb of the tide **60.** 20 [OE *ebba*]
ebbis *3 sg.* ebbs in a tide **52.** 137 [OE *ebbian*]
ecclippis *n.* eclipse **23.** 14 [ME, OF; L *eclipsis*]
edder *n.* adder **23.** 240, **58.** 9; *pl.* **14.** 266 [ME; aphetic form of OE *nædre*]
***eddirstangit** *ppl. adj.* adder-stung, poisoned **23.** 546 [prec.+**stang**]
Edinburch(t), Edinburgh(e) Edinburgh **22.** 5, **22.** 64, **23.** 217, **35.** *title*, **47.** 11, **74.** 7, **75.** 2; *attrib.* **23.** 211
***Edwart Langschankis** Edward I of England (d. 1307) **23.** 270, **23.** 410
effect *n.* greater part **40.** 8, worth ***23.** 289; **in (gud) effek** in fact, in reality **56.** 31 [ME; L *effectus*]
effectioun *n.* affection, loyalty **35.** 37; *pers.* partiality **51.** 58 [var. of *affectioun*; OF; L *affectio*]
effeir, affeir *n.* equipment **14.** 401, bearing **52.** 39; **effeiris** *pl.* manners, behaviour **14.** 49, **50.** 128, **52.** 185 [ME; OF *afere*]
effeiritly *adv.* in alarm **52.** 182 [OE pp. *āfæred*]
effek. See **effect**
eff(e)ray *n.* alarm, terror **3.** 140, **50.** 125 [OF *effrei*]
effray *v.* alarm, terrify **50.** 68 [OF *effrayer;* cf. **affrayit**]
efter, eftir *prep.* after the time (that) **10.** 212, **14.** 341, **14.** 370, **58.** 19; according to **14.** 508, **42.** 29, **51.** 44; in search of **14.** 9, **23.** 127 [OE *æfter*]
***Egeas** Roman pro-consul **23.** 537
egill, egle *n.* eagle (*aquila chrysaetos*) **42.** 26, **50.** 120, **54.** 99 [ME; OF *egle*]
***Egipya** wife of Potiphar **23.** 530
Eglintoun, Sir Hugh (d. 1377) **62.** 53
eik. See **eke**
eild, eld *n.* age, maturity, legal age **9.** 105, **14.** 297, **14.** 465; old age **16.** 42, **35.** 63, **43.** 17, **59.** 9 [OE (Angl) *eldo*]
eir *n.* ear **3.** 101, **9.** 41, **69.** 26; **eris** *pl.* **10.** 264, **14.** 115, **14.** 527 [OE *ēare*]
eirand(is). See **erand**
eird. See **erd**
eis *n.* comfort, pleasure **17.** 38, **83.** 2; **at ese** in comfort **14.** 414 [ME; OF *eise*]
eist. See **est**
eit, ete *v.* eat **22.** 51, **23.** 207, **68.** 22; **eitis** *3 pl.* **22.** 11 [OE *etan*]
eith *adj.* easy (to)+*infin.* **46.** 18 [OE *ēaðe*]
eivry. See **every**
eke, eik *adv.* also (poet.) **10.** 96, **14.** 323, **16.** 52, **16.** 70, **31.** 37, **44.** 36 [ONhb *ēc*; OE *ēac*]
eldar *comp. adj.* elder **74.** 48; **eldaris** *n. pl.* ancestors, forefathers **45.** 46 [OE (Angl) *eldran*]
eldnyng *n.* jealousy **14.** 119, **14.** 126, **14.** 204 [var. of *endling*; ? OE *ęlnung*]
electioun *n.* choice, election to office **51.** 59 [ME, OF *election*; L *electio*]
***elf** *n.* elf, fairy **23.** 36, **23.** 345 [OE *ælf*]
ellevin, ellevyn *adj.* eleven **2.** 58, **51.** 89, **52C.** 1 [OE *ellefne*]
ellis *adv.* besides, otherwise **14.** 309, **14.** 391, **44.** 80, **51.** 12, **51.** 79 [OE *elles*]
ellummynit. See **illumynate**
elrich *adj.* elvish, supernatural **10.** 125 [? OE **elfrice* fairy kingdom (used attrib.)]
elyk *adv.* alike, equally **50.** 109 [nth. ME]

embassat *n.* embassy **35.** *title* [ME; med. L *ambassata*]
***eme** *n.* uncle **23.** 360 [OE *ēam*]
emerant *n.* emerald **31.** 37 (see Commentary), *attrib.* **10.** 39 [ME; OF *esmeralde*]
empryce, emprys *n.* empress (title of the Blessed Virgin) **2.** 38, **2.** 61, **50.** 160 [OF *emperesse*]
enbracit *pa. t.* embraced **10.** 220; **enbrast** *pp.* **62.** 83 [ME; OF *embracer*]
enchessoun *n.* cause, objection **44.** 64 [ME, OF]
enclynyng *pres. p.* bowing **10.** 98 [OF *encliner*; L *inclinare*]
endar *n.* one who brings to an end **12.** 2 [ME; OE *endian*]
endis *3 sg.* ends; **endit** *pp.* **14.** 239, **14.** 304, **14.** 505 [as prec.]
endite, endyte, indyte *n.* writing **10.** 270, **23.** 109, **62.** 73; **endyt(e)** *v.* compose, write **10.** 64, **44.** 80 [ME; OF *enditer*]
endlang *prep.* along, by the side of **10.** 131 [OE *andlang*; ON *endelangr*]
endyt. See **endite**
***Eneas** Aeneas of Troy **23.** 539
ene. See **e**
enemys, ennemeis *n. pl.* **2.** 65, **9.** 90 [OF]
enermit *ppl. adj.* equipped with arms **9.** 99 [ME; OF *enarmer*]
enforsit *pa. t.* added power to **14.** 383 [ME; OF *enforcier*]
engranyt *ppl. adj.* dyed scarlet or crimson **14.** 139 (see Commentary) **14.** 366 [ME *engreyned*; F *en graine* cochineal dye]
engyne *n.* ingenuity, contrivance **14.** 121, **14.** 452, **54.** 31 [ME; OF *engin*; L *ingenium*]
enlumynit *pa. t.* illuminated, lit up **10.** 45 [ME; OF *enluminer*]
enprent *v.* imprint **14.** 442 [ME; OF *empreinter*]
enschesoun *v.* accuse, blame **51.** 65 [see **enchessoun**]
ensence *v.* perfume with incense **1.** 29 [OF *ensenser*; med. L *incensare*]
entencioun *n.* intent, resolve **6.** 114 [ME; OF *entenciun*]
entent, intent *n.* intention, design, disposition **6.** 6, **6.** 78, **12.** 40, **56.** 44, **66.** 33 [ME; OF]
enterand *pres. p.* entering, joining a religious order **45.** 31; **enteris** *3 sg.* enters **79.** 34; **enter(r)it, entrit, entirt** *pa. t.* **3.** 2, **50.** 44, **51.** 7, **52.** 85, **52.** 108 [ME; OF *entrer*]
entre(e), entr(i)e *n.* entrance, right of entry, entering **9.** 62, **10.** 120, **48.** 19 [ME; OF *entrée*]
Eolus *n.* god of the winds, son of Jupiter and Menalippa **10.** 122, **23.** 91, **50.** 33, **50.** 65
epistell *n.* epistle, letter **22.** 8; **epistillis** *pl.* **55.** 17 [ME; OF *epistle*]
erand, eirand *n.* business, concerns **25.** 27; the business he came on **78.** 39; **e(i)randis** *pl.* **45.** 44, **74.** 55 [OE *ǣrende*]
erd(e), e(i)rd, aird *n.* (the) earth **1.** 13, **1.** 54, **3.** 83, **3.** 138, **14.** 168, **14.** 234, **14.** 352, **52.** 206; **erdit** *pp.* buried **9.** 83 [OE *eard*]
erdly, erthly *adj.* earthly, worldly **59.** 4, **64.** 13, **72.** 2, **72.** 4 [ME var.; OE *eorðlic*]
eris. See **eir**
erle, erll *n.* earl, nobleman corresponding to *count* **28.** 34, **35.** *title*, **45.** 41 [OE *eorl*]
ernis *n. gen.* eagle's **53.** 23 [OE *earn*]
errour *n.* erroneous (religious) beliefs **4.** 31, **16.** 97 [OF; L *error*]
ers *n.* arse, fundament **23.** 56, **23.** 131, **52.** 203, **52.** 219; *pl.* **52.** 89 [OE *ears*]
ersch(e), iersche *adj.* 'Irish', Gaelic, highland **23.** 49, **23.** 145; the Gaelic language **52.** 116; **erschemen** *n. pl.* highlanders **52.** 113; **erschry** *n.* the highlands **23.** 107 [reduced form of *erisch;* ME *irisc*]
erth(e) *n.* earth, the world **31.** 15, **53.** 37 [OE *eorþe*]
erthly. See **erdly**
es *n.* ace, the 'one' in dice **67.** 27 [ME; OF *as*; L]
eschame *1 sg.* am ashamed **23.** 18, **schame** be ashamed **75.** 75; **(es)-chamit** *pp.* **77.** 27, **80.** 39 [var. of *aschame*; OE *āscamian*]

eschew *v.* avoid, abstain from **6.** 82, **10.** 224, **14.** 53, **51.** 42; **eschewit** *pa. t.* **52.** 199 [ME; OF *eschever*]

ese. See **eis**

est, eist *n.* east **1.** 6, **64.** 23 [OE *ēast-*]

estait, estate *n.* rank, order **10.** 173, **60.** 2, **65.** 19; *pl.* **esta(i)t(t)is 62.** 17, **75.** 13 [ME; OF *estat*]

ete. See **eit**

eterne *adj.* eternal; *as n.* eternity **2.** 1 [OF; L *aeternus*]

***Etrike Forest** in Selkirkshire **23.** 425

eucarist *n.* mass, the sacrament of the altar **6.** 43 [L *eucharistia*; Gk (thanksgiving)]

***Eustase** Pseustis **23.** 321 (see Commentary)

everie, every, evere, eviry, eivry *adj.* every, all **8.** 2, **40.** 1, **10.** 89, **10.** 260, **27.** 50, **31.** 10; **every deill** altogether **5.** 18 [OE *ǣfre*]

evermoir. See **evirmair**

everrilk, everilk, everylk *adj.* every, each **6.** 135, **63.** 41, **63.** 43 [nth. ME; OE *ǣfre*+*ylc*]

evidens *n.* (*in pl. form*), **evidentis** *n. pl.* documents establishing legal right **14.** 344, **71.** 66 [ME; L *evidentia*]

evill *adj.* wicked, depraved **6.** 109, **11.** 10, **14.** 119, **14.** 450, **23.** 21; ill, difficult **21.** 8, **83.** 1; *n.* **14.** 122, **14.** 126; *adv.* seriously, ill **52.** 196 [OE *yfel*]

evin *n.* evening **14.** 1, **14.** 197, **19.** 2, **20.** 8, **23.** 116; **evyns 71.** 18 [OE *ǣfen*]

evin *adv.* quite, fully **38.** 101 [OE *efne*]

evin and od *adj. phr.* one and all **56.** 37 [OE *efn*+ME *od* (ON *oddi*)]

evinlie *adv.* on the level **51.** 102 [ME; OE adj. *efen*]

evir *adv.* always, at all times **3.** 110, **9.** 34, **56.** 71; **evir quho** whoever **10.** 255 [OE *ǣfre*]

evirmair, evirmare, evermoir *adv.* always, for all time **12.** 21, **12.** 23, **38.** 18, **54.** 18, **59.** 21 [ME *auere mære*]

evyne *adj.* even (of numbers) **2.** 56 [OE *efen*]

exaltit *ppl. adj.* elevated, haughty **6.** 115 [OF; L *exaltare*]

exampill *n.* example, exemplar, pattern **5.** 4, **14.** 507, **45.** 30 [OF; L *exemplum*]

exceid *v.* increase to excess **3.** 75; *pres. p.* **6.** 127 [OF; L *excedere*]

excellis *3 sg.* is pre-eminent **34.** 1 [ME; OF *exceller*; L *excellere*]

exceptioun *n.* plea, defence **61.** 15 [ME; L *exceptio*]

exceptis *3 sg.* makes objections **74.** 29 [OF *excepter*; L *excipere, exceptum*]

excersing. See **exerce**

exces *n.* a great amount, immoderation **73.** 28 [ME; OF; L *excessus*]

excus *v.* seek to clear oneself from fault **5.** 39 [OF *excuser*; L *excusare*]

excusationis *n. pl.* excuses **55.** 20 [ME; L *excusatio*]

exellence *n.* high quality or worth **6.** 43 [OF; L *excellentia*]

exelling *ppl. adj.* surpassing **6.** 10 [OF; L *excellere*]

exeme *v.* examine **14.** 156 [reduced form of ME *examyn*; OF; L *examinare*]

exerce, exers *v.* practise, administer **50.** 106, **56.** 64; *pres. p.* **6.** 21, **76.** 7 [OF *exercer*; L *exercere*]

***exilde** *pp.* exiled, expelled from **23** 412 [ME; OF *exilier*; L *exiliare*]

expeditioun *n.* execution, speed, dispatch **71.** 58 [ME; L *expeditio*]

expell *v.* drive out **49.** 6, **70.** 3 [ME; OF *expeller*; L *expellere*]

expence *n.* expenditure, administration **35.** 62 [ME; late L *expensa*]

expendit. See **super**

expreme *v.* express, name **6.** 161 [OF *exprimer*; L *exprimere*]

expremyng *vbl. n.* expression, speech, **6.** 108 [prec.]

expres *adv.* expressly, directly **16.** 37, **71.** 45 [ME; OF adj.; L *expressus*]

expyrd *pp.* come to an end **79.** 19 [ME; OF *expirer*; L *exspirare*]

extold, extollit *pp.* elevated, uplifted **6.** 114, **77.** 38 [L *extollere*]

extortiounes *n. pl.* extortions, taking by force **75.** 67 [ME; OF; L *extortio*]

extreme *adj.* last **6.** 45, most rigorous **6.** 163 [OF; L *extremus* (see **uncioun**)]
exul *adj.* exiled **63.** 39 [L *exul*]
exultive *adj.* given to rejoicing **6.** 164 (see Commentary) [L *exsultare*]
exyll *v.* cast away **49.** 39; **exylit** *pp.* **72.** 24 [ME; OF *exilier*; L *exiliare*]
eyn(e). See **e**
***Eyobulus** Eubulus Aurelius **23.** 541

fa *n.* enemy **14.** 383, **74.** 17; **fais** *pl.* **14.** 405 [OE *gefā*]
fablis *n. pl.* fictitious tales **76.** 13 [ME; OF; L *fabula*]
faceis, facis *n. pl.* faces **14.** 26, **14.** 70, **52.** 49, **74.** 44, *fig.* **39.** 10 [OF *face*]
faculte *n.* profession **62.** 47 [ME; OF; L *facultas*]
fader, fathir *n.* father, God **3.** 82, **6.** 51, **6.** 58, **22.** 29; sire **23.** 74; old fellow **14.** 279 [OE *fæder*]
faderlyk *adv.* in a fatherly manner **74.** 53 [prec.]
fadit. See **faid**
faggottis *n. pl.* faggots, bundles of sticks for fuel **9.** 74 [ME; OF *fagot*]
faid *v.* make to fade **49.** 36; **fadit** *ppl. adj.* faded, enfeebled **14.** 171 [ME *fade;* OF *fader*]
fa(i)lȝe *v.* fail, weaken, decline **14.** 203; **falȝeis** *3 sg.* **14.** 401; **failȝeit** *pa. t.* failed, lost strength **14.** 84, **54.** 58; **falȝeid** *ppl. adj.* enfeebled **14.** 173; **failȝeand** *ppl. adj.* declining **39.** 2, **39.** 94 [OF *faillir*]
faill, but *adv. phr.* without fail, assuredly **16.** 35 [ME; OF *faile*]
faill *v.* cease to help **12.** 44 [ME; OF *faillir*]
***failye.** See **fa(i)lȝe**
faine. See **fenȝe**
fain, (be) *adv.* (with) willingness, gladly **33.** 14; **faine 47.** 2 [cf. **fane**]
fair *v.* make (his) way **53.** 25; **faris** *3 sg.* gets on **14.** 460; **fur(e)** *pa. t.* **9.** 46, **40.** 22; **fair weill** goodbye **12.** 49; **farne** *pp.* **14.** 153 [OE *faran*]
fair(e), fayr(e), fare *adj.* beautiful, handsome, pleasant, fine **1.** 35, **2.** 42, **3.** 18, **10.** 117, **17.** 73; **fa(i)rar** *comp.* **23.** 111, **17.** 61, **56.** 38; **fairast, farest** *sup.* **9.** 2, **42.** 21 [OE *fæȝer*]
fair *adv.* civilly, courteously, finely, elegantly **9.** 71, **10.** 67, **10.** 267, **14.** 280; **fair mot hir fall** may she prosper, good luck to her **37.** 20 [OE *fæȝere*]
Fair Callyng. See **Callyng**
Fair Service *n. pers.* **9.** 44, **9.** 46 (**fair** = eloquent, persuasive) [see **fair(e)**]
fairheid, fayrehede *n.* loveliness, beauty **14.** 27, **24.** 7 [ME]
fairis *n. pl.* periodic fairs for buying and selling **14.** 70 [ME; OF *feire*]
fairnes *n.* beauty **14.** 299, **14.** 400 [OE *fæȝernys*]
faith. See **fayth**
falco(u)ne *n.* falcon **10.** 54, **53.** 25; **falcounis** *gen.* **42.** 11 [ME; OF *falcun*; L *falco*]
fald *n.* enclosure, small field **43.** 12; *pl.* folds, pens **23.** 151 [OE *falod*]
falȝe, falȝeid. See **fa(i)lȝe.**
falis. See **fals**
fall *v.* meet with, fall into **5.** 61; **fell** *pa. t.* turned out **37.** 70; **fallis ȝow** it comes to you as a task **14.** 151; **fair . . . fall** (see **fair** *adv.*) [OE *feallan*]
fallow *n.* fellow, neighbour **41.** 9, **74.** 15; *pl.* equals **14.** 298, friends **62.** 79 [ME; ON *fēlage*]
fallow *v.* associate (with), take as a mate **50.** 138 [ME; *felowe*; ON n. *fēlage*]
fallowschip *n.* company, companionship **77.** 25 [ME; prec.]
fals, falis *adj.* false, deceitful **6.** 53, **6.** 118, **9.** 95, **14.** 121, **14.** 307, **17.** 87, **34.** 31; **falslie, fasly** *adv.* **3.** 17, **74.** 27 [OE; L *falsus*]
falset(t) *n.* falsehood **34.** 20, **55.** 43; *pers.* **63.** 11, **63.** 37 [OF; med. L *falsatum*]
falsheid *n.* falsehood, fraud **14.** 460 [ME; OF *fals*; L *falsus*]
falt *n.* offence **34.** 8, **44.** 77; lack, want **79.** 33; **fa(u)ltis** *pl.* defects **52C.** 14, **52C.** 35, **75.** 60 [ME; OF *faulte*]

fame *n.* reputation, good repute *pers.* **9.** 87 (*gen.* **9.** 105); **10.** 164, **14.** 461 [ME, OF; L *fama*]

famist *pp.* starved **23.** 95 [ME]

famous *adj.* reputable **14.** 307, **65.** 18 [ME; L *famosus*]

fand. See **fynd**

fane *adj.* glad, pleased **14.** 363, **23.** 116, **39.** 87, **59.** 31; *adv.* gladly, willingly **14.** 341, **17.** 82, **23.** 103, **42.** 39 [OE *fæȝen*]

fang *n.* capture, prey **4.** 15 [OE, ON]

fang *v.* take, get at **14.** 363, **32.** 7, **40.** 8, **43.** 12; embrace **14.** 66, **14.** 88, **14.** 209; **fangis** *3 sg.* **67.** 23, *3 pl.* **14.** 62 [OE *fōn, fangen*]

fannoun *n.* a piece of embroidered material worn with ecclesiastical vestments, esp. a maniple worn over the left arm **54.** 55 [ME, F *fanon*; med. L *fano*]

fant *adj.* faint, weak **14.** 86 [ME; OF]

fantasie, fantasy *n.* imagination, fancy **10.** 49 [ME; OF *fantasie*; L *phantasia*]

fantastik *adj.* mad **44.** 57; fanciful ***23.** 35 [ME; med. L *fantasticus*]

fantesy *n.* product of imagination, a fancy **53.** 10 (see Commentary) [ME; OF; L *phantasia*]

farar. See **fair(e)**

farcy *n. attrib.* having the farcy (a disease of horses) **14.** 114 [F *farcin*]

fare *n.* expression, demeanour **10.** 225 [ME; OE *fær*]

fare. See **fair(e)**

farest. See **fair(e)**

farie *n.* fairy; *attrib.* **27.** 5 [ME; OF *fae(rie)*]

faris, farne. See **fair**

farit, (evill) *ppl. adj.* (ill) favoured **23.** 51 [**fair**]

farrest *adj. sup.* furthest, most distant **42.** 21 [OE *feorr*]

fartis *n. pl.* breaking of wind **52.** 155 [ME; OE v. **feortan*]

fartit *pa. t.* broke wind **52.** 207 [see prec.]

fary, phary *n.* fairy; a vision as of fairies, illusion, unreality **51.** 11, **51.** 111, **64.** 39 [ME; OF *faerie*]

***fasert** *n.* hermaphrodite fowl, coward **23.** 517 [origin obscure]

fasly. See **fals**

fas(s)o(u)n *n.* fashion, way **14.** 491, **48.** 69, sorts **50.** 82, **50.** 94; *pl.* **fass(i)onis** **50.** 128, **54.** 57 [ME; OF *façon*]

fassoun *v.* fashion, make **52C.** 27 [F *façonner*]

fast *v.* abstain from food **5.** 6; *pa. t.* **5.** 4; *pres. p.* hungry **40.** 7 [OE *fæstan*]

fast *adv.* firmly, persistently, vigorously **13.** 11, **14.** 47, **14.** 493, **37.** 32 [OE *fæste*, ON *fast*]

Fasternis, Fasterennis evin *n.* Shrove Tuesday **32.** 2, **52.** 8 [ON-hb *fæstern* a fast + OE *ǣfen*]

fathfull *adj.* sincere, loyal **35.** 33 [ME *faithful*; OF *feit*]

faucht. See **fecht**

fault(is). See **falt**

favo(u)r *n.* act of good will **9.** 71; aspect, look **14.** 26; good will displayed (to) **14.** 324; prejudice in favour **74.** 26; *pl.* sexual favours **14.** 364 [ME; OF; L *favor*]

favouryt *pa. t.* treated well, was well disposed to **10.** 221 [ME; OF *favorer*; med. L *favorare*]

fawd *suffix* -fold, times **34.** 37 [OE *-feald*]

faynt *v.* become weak **14.** 210 [ME; OF adj. *faint*]

fayr(e). See **fair(e)**

fayrehede. See **fairheid**

fayth, faith *n.* religious faith **4.** 28; fidelity, troth **14.** 45, **14.** 323, **14.** 459; **faythfull** *adj.* **30.** 3, **49.** 20 [ME; OF *feit, feid*]

fe n. property, wealth **38.** 77 [ON; OE *fēoh*]

febill, feble *adj.* feeble, weak **14.** 86, **73.** 8; **feblit** *ppl. adj.* enfeebled **14.** 171, **62.** 3 [ME; OF *feble*]

febilnes *n.* weakness, inadequacy **14.** 300 [prec.]

Februar *n.* the month of February **52.** 1 [ME; L *februarius*]

feche *v.* go for, bring **50.** 81, **52.** 110 [OE *fecc(e)an*]

fecht *v.* fight **23.** 65, **78.** 44; **faucht** *pa. t.* **33.** 14 [OE *feohtan*]

fedder *n.* feather, plume **58.** 8; **fedderis, feddiris** *pl.* **14.** 379, **16.** 14, **42.** 21 [OE *feðer*]
fedrem. See **fethreme**
feest. See **feist**
feght, ficht *n.* fight **2.** 29, **35.** 44 [OE *feohte*]
fegour. See **figour**
feid *n.* hostility, enmity **6.** 100, **6.** 130, **14.** 324, **14.** 405, **52.** 44, **74.** 26 [OF *fe(i)de*]
feid *v.* feed, nourish **72.** 17, flourish **61.** 26 [OE *fēdan*]
feild. See **felde**
feill *n.* understanding **23.** 109, **71.** 26; shrewd suspicion **52.** 185, ***23.** 257 [ME; OE v. *fēlan*]
feill, fiell *v.* feel, suffer **5.** 16, **64.** 14; *3 sg.* **51.** 39, **51.** 49; **feiling** *pres. p.* suffering **6.** 156 [OE *fēlan*]
feill *adj.* many (poet). **14.** 364 [OE *fela*]
fe(i)nd, feynd, fieind *n.* devil, Satan **1.** 22, **2.** 66, **16.** 102, **19.** 23, **23.** 23, **55.** 47; *pl.* **2.** 30, **16.** 35, **38.** 115, **52.** 5; **feindlie, feyndly** *adj.* devilish **23.** 84, **23.** 173 [OE *fēond*]
feir *n.* fear, dread **9.** 46, **52.** 141, **54.** 15, **54.** 101, **69.** 41 [OE *fǣr*]
feir, feyr *n.* comrade, mate **14.** 62, **14.** 209; adversary **9.** 30; *pl.* **14.** 63, **14.** 66, **61.** 30, **77.** 13; **but feir** without equal **50.** 94 [OE *ȝefēra*]
feir *n.* bearing **51.** 107, show of violence **52.** 207; **feiris, feris** *pl.* manners, behaviour **3.** 97, **13.** 13, **39.** 33, **45.** 61; **feir of weir** warlike array **52.** 36 (see **weir**) [reduced form of **effeir**]
feir *adj.* well, vigorous **51.** 51 [OE **fēre*; ON *fœrr*]
feist, feest *n.* festival **40.** 1, **41.** 1, **52.** 8; *fig.* **32.** 7; *pl.* **40.** 11 [ME, OF *feste*; L pl. *festa*]
feistit *pa. t.* feasted **44.** 66 [ME; OF *fester*]
feit. See **fut(e)**
fek *n.* main part **9.** 85 [reduced form of **effect**]
eld(e), feild(e) *n.* open country **10.** 13, **10.** 250, *pl.* **10.** 65; battle **4.** 38, **10.** 141, **10.** 192, **62.** 21, *fig.* **32.** 8; surface of a shield (in heraldry) *fig.* **50.** 97 [OE *feld*]
felȝe (of) *v.* miss, fall short **4.** 15 [OF *faillir*]
felicit(i)e *n.* happiness **18.** 10, **50.** 181 [ME; OF; L *felicitas*]
fell *v.* strike down; *fig.* **23.** 246 [OE *fellan*]
fell *adj.* cruel, savage **14.** 342, **22.** 49, **23.** 78, **34.** 19, **52.** 5, **62.** 57 [OF *fel*]
***fellis** *n. pl.* hills **23.** 512 [nth. ME; ON *fjall*]
fellony *n.* ferocity, cruelty **52.** 44 [ME; OF *felonie*]
felloun *adj.* great **51.** 11 [ME, OF *felon*]
femynyne *adj.* womanly **2.** 10 [OF; L *femininus*]
fen *n.* mire, midden **23.** 84 [OE, ON]
fend. See **fe(i)nd**
fend *v.* defend **50.** 133 [ME abbrev. form of **defend**]
fenȝe, fene, fenȝie, feynȝe, faine, fayne *v.* feign, dissimulate **12.** *title*, **14.** 423, **23.** 137, **51.** 68, **42.** 47; **fenis** *3 sg.* **74.** 27, **feynȝeis** *3 sg.* **42.** 17; **fenȝeing** *pres. p.* **45.** 61; **fenyt** *pa. t.* **54.** 17; **fenȝeit** *pp.* pretended **14.** 343; **feynȝeit, fenȝeit, fenȝeid, feynit** *ppl. adj.* false, counterfeit **17,** 4, **17.** 15, **39.** 6, **54.** *title*; **fenȝing, fenȝening** *vbl. n.* **14.** 151, **38.** 65 [ME; OF *feign-*; L *fingere*]
fenȝeouris *n. pl.* dissimulators, pretenders **44.** 39 [ME; see prec.]
fensum *adj.* offensive, vile **75.** 11 (see Commentary)
fepillis *3 sg.* puts out the lower lip **14.** 114 [origin uncertain]
fer *adv.* far **14.** 487, **44.** 79, **50.** 54, **65.** 1; **alls fer as, sa fer as,** to such an extent as **6.** 46, **10.** 261; **one far** afar **14.** 436 [OE *feorr*]
ferd(e) *adj.* fourth 35. *title*, **81.** 46 [OE *fēorða*]
fere, in, *adv.* in company, together **10.** 91 [ME; OE *ȝefēr*]
***ferily** *adv.* actively, smartly **23.** 477 [*fery* adj.; rel. to *fere*, OE **fēre* vigorous]
feris. See **feir**

ferleit *pa. t.* marvelled, wondered **54.** 63 [ME; ON adj. *ferligr*]
ferlifull *adj.* wonderful **14.** 26, **31.** 15 [as prec.]
ferly *n.* marvel, wonder **23.** 106, **52.** 143; *adj.* marvellous, strange **14.** 323, **37.** 7 [ME; ON *ferligr*]
ferme *adj.* fixed, constant **64.** 3 [ME, OF]
fers(e), feyrse *adj.* fierce, violent, forceful **14.** 203, **14.** 342, **35.** 57, **50.** 65, **54.** 80; **fersly(e)** *adv.* **3.** 61, **61.** 44 [OF; L *ferus*]
ferst *adv.* first **14.** 152 [OE *fyrst*]
fervent *adj.* glowing with heat **52.** 63 [ME, OF; L *fervens*]
fessoun *n.* form, appearance, show **14.** 189 [ME; OF *façon*]
festinit *pp.* fastened, bound **14.** 45 [OE *fæstnian*]
festuall *adj.* festival **6.** 83 [OF *festival*; L *festivalis*]
fethreme, fedrem, feddreme *n.* coat of feathers, plumage **53.** 45, **54.** 60, **54.** 105, **54.** 109 [OE *feðer-hama*]
fetter *v.* secure with fetters; **fetterit** *pa. t.* **9.** 26, *pp.* **9.** 30; **fetrit** *pp.* secured *fig.* **14.** 25 [ME; next]
fetteris *n. pl.* fetters, bonds **4.** 36 [OE *feter*]
feulis. See **foull**
feure *n.* furrow **80.** 12 [OE *furh*, gen. sg. *fure*]
fewte *n.* fealty, faithful allegiance **50.** 117 [ME; OF *feauté*]
feynd(is), feyndly. See **fe(i)nd**
feyne, feynȝe(id), feynit. See **fenȝe**
feyr. See **feir**
feyrse. See **fers**
ficht. See **feght**
fiellis. See **feill**
figour, fegour *n.* image **6.** 3, **16.** 44 [OF *figure*; L *figura*]
figurit *ppl. adj.* rhetorical, 'fine' **39.** 10 [ME; L *figurare*]
fild. See **fillis**
fill *n.* enough to satisfy **32.** 7 [OE *fyllu*]
fillaris *n. pl.* fillers, loaders **45.** 25 [late ME; OE *fyllan*]
fillis *v.* fills up **14.** 125; **fild** *pa. t.*, *pp.* filled **52.** 44, **52.** 65 [OE *fyllan*]
filosophicall *adj.* pertaining to a philosopher (cf. **philosophouris**) **76.** 11 [perh. F *philosophique*]
finale *adj.* absolute, complete **12.** 2 [OF; L *finalis*]
fingaris *n. pl.* fingers **14.** 25 [OE *finger*]
finyng *vbl. n.* settlement, contract, composition **6.** 132 [OF *finer*; L *finis*]
firit *pp.* set on fire *fig.* **31.** 28 [OE *fȳrian*]
firmament *n.* vault of heaven **1.** 12, **10.** 37, **10.** 108, **10.** 239, **23.** 9 [L *firmamentum*]
***firmance** *n.* custody, imprisonment **23.** 274 [OF *fermance*; L *firmus*]
first *n.* delay **14.** 341 [OE; ON *frest*]
firth(e) *n.* wood **43.** 12; *pl.* **1.** 35 [OE *fyrþ*]
fische *v.* fish **40.** 18 [OE *fiscian*]
fishe, fische *n.* fish **22.** 52, **22.** 95; *coll.* **1.** 51; *attrib.* **23.** 231, **56.** 76 [OE *fisc*]
flaid *pa. t.* flayed **23.** 126 [OE *flēan*]
Flanderis Flanders **79.** 37
flane. See **flayn**
***flaskynnis** *n. pl.* flea-skins **23.** 445 [OE *flēa*+ON *skinn*]
flatteraris, flattereris *n. pl.* flatterers, sycophants **44.** 39 [ME; OF *flater*]
flatteris *3 sg.* flatters **20.** 9 [ME; as prec.]
flattry *n.* flattery *pers.* **63.** 36, **77.** 26 [ME; as prec.]
flayn, flane *n.* arrow **10.** 188, **39.** 59 [ME; OE *flān*]
fle *v.* fly **42.** 27, **53.** 24, **53.** 44, **54.** 61; **fleand** *pres. p.* **54.** *title*; **flew** *pa. t. fig.* **79.** 37 [OE *flēoȝan*]
fle, flie *v.* flee, avoid, refrain from **6.** 53, **12.** 16, **19.** 23, **62.** 35, **65.** 17; **fleis** *2 sg.* **23.** 219 [OE *flēon*]
fle(y) *v.* frighten off, scare **23.** 152, **23.** 235, **38.** 115; **fleit** *pp.* **4.** 34 [var. of *fley*; ME]
fleggar *n.* flatterer ? **23.** 242 [origin obscure; cf. Da dial. *floegre* to flatter]
fleichit *pp.* flattered, cajoled **55.** 36 [origin obscure]

fleichouris *n. pl.* coaxers, cajolers **44.** 39 [origin obscure]
fleis *n. pl.* (Spanish) flies **70.** 14 (see Commentary) [OE *flēoȝe*]
fleise *n.* fleece **14.** 423 [OE *flēos*, *flīes*]
fleit. See **flete**
flemis *3 pl.* banish, drive away **74.** 26; **flemit** *pp.* **4.** 34, **55.** 44 [OE *flīeman*]
***flend** *adj.* (obscure) **23.** 518
flesch(e) *n.* flesh **3.** 61, **6.** 68, **6.** 158, **14.** 134, **16.** 110, **56.** 77; meat **56.** 43; mortal flesh, humanity **62.** 7 [OE *flǣsc*]
fleschely *adj.* bodily, carnal **6.** 127 [OE *flǣsclīc*]
fleschour *n.* butcher **56.** 41 [ME; see **flesch(e)**]
flet *n.* inner part of a house **23.** 242 [OE; ON]
flete, fleit *v.* flow with moisture **10.** 15, *fig.* **10.** 70, **50.** 49; float *fig.* **37.** 50 [OE *flēotan*]
flett. See **flyt(e)**
flewme *n.* phlegm **14.** 91, **14.** 272 [ME; OF *fleume*]
***fleyit.** See **fle**
fleys. See **fle**
flicht. *n.* flight in the air; **of flicht** flying **1.** 51 [OE *fliht*]
flicht *n.* flight, fleeing **2.** 29 [OE *flyht*]
flicht *v.* flutter **64.** 6 [imit.]
flicir *v.* flicker, quiver **38.** 43 [OE *flicerian*]
flie. See **fle**
flingaris *n. pl.* dancers **44.** 10 [ME *fling*; origin obscure]
flirdis *3 pl.* ? talk idly **20.** 9 [origin obscure]
flit *v.* shift, change; **flittis, flytis** *3 sg.* **39.** 95, **60.** 18; **dois flit** is unstable **39.** 26 [ME; ON *flytja*]
flocht, (on) *n.* (in) a flutter, perturbation **52.** 186, **64.** 2 [prob. early ON **flohte*, later *flōtti*]
flockis *n. pl.* flocks, crowds **32.** 3 [OE *floc*]
Flora *n.* goddess of flowers **10.** 42, **10.** 74, **10.** 100, **16.** 21, **50.** 62; **Florais** *gen.* **10.** 48
flour(e) *n.* flower **1.** 4, **2.** 10, **8.** 10, *fig.* **62.** 50; **flouris, flowris** *pl.* **1.** 4, **1.** 41, **8.** 7, **10.** 17, **10.** 59, **10.** 248, **14.** 170 (bloom, flourish); embellishments, ornaments of rhetoric **10.** 117; flourishing age **17.** 88 [OF; L *flos, flor-*]
flour(e) delice, delyce *n.* lily (*lilium*), more specifically iris (*iridaceae*), the Virgin's flower **2.** 42, **2.** 71, **50.** 138; **flour delycis** *pl.* **50.** 98 [OF *flour de lys*]
flouris *v.* flourish **49.** 33 [ME *flourishe*; OF *florir*]
flowis *3 sg.* flows in a tide **52.** 137 [OE *flōwan*]
***floyte** *n.* flute **23.** 507 [ME; OF *flaüte*]
flud(e) *n.* flood, river, stream **1.** 51, **3.** 47, **10.** 237; rising tide **60.** 20; *pl.* **10.** 121 [OE *flōd*]
flure *n.* floor **28.** 23, **55.** 9 [OE *flōr*]
flureis *v.* grow, blossom **50.** 165; **flur(e)ist, flurising** *ppl. adjs.* blooming, flowery **14.** 27, **14.** 172, **16.** 28; **flurising** *vbl. n.* blossoming **2.** 13 [ME *flurische, floris*; OF *florir*]
flur(e)ist, flurising. See **flureis**
flurest *pp.* caused to flourish, adorned **16.** 21 [ME *floris*]
flynt *n.* flintstone **54.** 80; **flynt stone 63.** 47 [OE *flint*]
***flyrdom** *n.* object of scorn **23.** 494 [ME *flyre* jest at, mock]
flyrit *pa. t.* leered **14.** 114 [ME; Da *flire*]
flyrok *n.* ? deformed fellow **52C.** 17 [meaning and origin obscure]
flyt(e) *v.* scold, abuse **14.** 342, **23.** 13, **44.** 79; **flett** *pa. t.* wrangled, spoke abusively **56.** 76; **flyt(t)ing** *vbl. n.* **23.** 18, **23.** 23, *pl.* **75.** 11 [OE *flītan*]
flytis. See **flit**
fo *n.* foe, enemy **4.** 33, **4.** 38, **12.** 1, **22.** 34, **36.** 11, **50.** 60 [from Eng. poetry replacing Sc *fa*]
fog *n.* grass left in the fields in winter **43.** 12 [ME; cf. med. L *fogagium*]
foir *adj.* front **9.** 68 [OE *fore-*]
foirfaltour *n.* loss of lands by forfeiture **63.** 28 [ME, OF *forfeture*]

foirstair *n.* (*as pl.*) external stair **75.** 17 [OE *fore*+*stǣʒer*]
fold *n.* earth, ground **50.** 68 [ON; OE *folde*]
folie *adj.* foolish **51.** 85 [ME; OF *fol* fool] See **foly**
folkis *n. pl.* people, persons **9.** 94, **77.** 14 [OE *folc*]
fol(l)owis *3 sg.* comes after **44.** 36, **78.** 1; *pa. t.* **10.** 147, **10.** 173, **52.** 94 [OE *folʒian*]
foly, folie *n.* foolishness **14.** 210, **17.** 4, **23.** 197, **38.** 73, **44.** 56 [ME; OF *folie*]
***fond** *n.* ? fool **23.** 518 [ME adj.; origin obscure]
fone *v.* play the fool **14.** 274 [ME; origin obscure]
***fontayne** *n.* fountain, spring **23.** 339 [ME; OF; L *fontana*]
for *prep.* because of, for the sake of **6.** 23, **10.** 19, **10.** 25, **11.** 17, **12.** 13; despite **10.** 171, **71.** 9; in order to seize **4.** 12; *conj.* in order that, so that **14.** 318 [OE]
for thy *adv.* therefore **72.** 23 [OE *forþi*]
for to *prep. with infin.* to **2.** 3, **2.** 7, **2.** 28, **3.** 22, **4.** 15, **5.** 16, **9.** 4 [OE]
***forbearis** *n. pl.* ancestors **23.** 257 [OE *fore*+*bēon*]
forbeir *v.* do without, abstain, refrain **79.** 32, **80.** 29; **forborne** *pp.* refrained, avoided **50.** 35 [OE *forberan, forboren*]
force *n.* strength, power, violence **4.** 2, **14.** 189; **forcely** *adv.* strongly **14.** 430 [OF]
forcye, forsy *adj.* forceful, strong **14.** 85, **61.** 10 [**force**]
ford, I stand I guarantee **45.** 62 [contraction of *for it*]
fordir *adj.* fore, front **37.** 9; **forder** *adv.* further on **52.** 175 [var. of *forthir*; OE *furður*]
forfairn *pp.* brought to ruin, destroyed **70.** 14 [OE *forfaran*]
forflittin *ppl. adj.* thoroughly scolded **23.** 239 [**flyte**]
forg(e)it *ppl. adj.* formed **14.** 430, **50.** 18 [ME; OF *forgier*]
forgevinnes *n.* forgiveness **6.** 38 [OE *forʒifnes*]
forgif(e) *v.* forgive **6.** 39, **6.** 150; **forgaife** *pa. t.* **6.** 149 [OE *forʒiefan*]
forʒet(t) *v.* forget **5.** 21, **14.** 300, **16.** 75, **36.** 31; *3 sg.* **5.** 63; **forʒet** *pp.* forgotten **6.** 162, **42.** 11 [OE *forʒietan*]
forky *adj.* (obscure; perh. for *forthy*; see Commentary) **14.** 85
forlane *pp.* set aside, worthless, despicable **14.** 137, **23.** 132 [pp. of *forly*; OE *forlicgan*]
forleit *pp.* abandoned, discarded, rejected **14.** 258, **14.** 381 [OE *forlǣtan*]
forloppin *ppl. adj.* runaway, renegade (especially of monks, friars) **54.** 7 [pp. of *lepe*; OE *hlēapan, hlēop*]
forlore, forloir *ppl. adj.* lost, destroyed **2.** 51, **42.** 2; *v.* become forlorn **69.** 9 [OE pp. *forloren*]
forme *n.* shape, body **14.** 87, **14.** 189, **14.** 263 [OF; L *forma*]
formest *adj.* foremost, first **39.** 97 [OE]
forrest *n.* forest **58.** 13, **59.** 27; *pl.* **1.** 35 [OF; med. L *foresta*]
forriddin *ppl. adj.* over-ridden, tired out **43.** 40 [OE *for-*+*rīdan*]
forrow, (to) *adv.* previously **50.** 188 [reduced form of *forouth*; nth. ME *forwith*]
fors *v.* take into account, care **40.** 22 [ME; OF *forcer*]
forsaik *v.* renounce **56.** 36, **56.** 46; *3 sg.* **74.** 36; *pres. p.* **80.** 2; **forsaekin** *pp.* forsaken, given up **32.** 19 [OE *forsacan*]
forse, on, *adv. phr.* necessarily, inevitably **62.** 95 [ME, OF *force*]
forsy. See **forcye**
fort *n.* fort, fortress **9.** 53 [F]
forthwart *adv.* forward **14.** 426 [OE *forðweard*]
fortifyit *pa. t.* supported **14.** 383 [ME; L *fortificare*]
fortoun(e) *n.* fortune, chance **18.** 10, **20.** 6, **54.** 95, *pers.* **53.** 6, **69.** 23 [ME; OF; L *fortuna*]
Fortuna maior a figure of the stars **35.** 79 (see Commentary)
fortunable *adj.* fortunate, successful **35.** 41, **35.** 63 [ME; L *fortuna*]

forvayit *pa. t.* went astray **10.** 204 [ME; OF *forvoier*]
forworthin *adj.* deformed, shapeless **23.** 105, **23.** 193 [OE *forweorðan, forworden*]
***fostirit** *ppl. adj.* nurtured **23.** 517 [ME]
foule, fowll, fowle *adj.* filthy, vile **6.** 125, **23.** 126, **23.** 138, **23.** 184, **34.** 8; **fowlar** *compar.* **23.** 84, **27.** 40 [OE *fūl*]
foull, fow(i)ll *n.* bird; *coll.* birds **1.** 51, **54.** 63; *gen.* **10.** 46; *pl.* **1.** 33, **10.** 6, **10.** 85, **feulis 14.** 10, **42.** 21, **50.** 68 [OE *fuȝel*]
foundit (of) *pp.* based (on) ***23.** 314, **77.** 29 [ME; F *fonder*; L *fundare*]
foure, fowyr *num. adj.* four **6.** 75, **34.** 20, **51.** 92 [OE *fēower*]
fourty *num. adj.* forty **5.** 1, **52.** 181 [OE *fēowertiȝ*]
fow *adj.* full **13.** 18, **41.** 8, **73.** 24; *adv.* very **13.** 28, **13.** 42, **13.** 56, **13.** 62 [OE *full*]
fowill. See **foull**
fowle, fowll, fowlar. See **foule**
***fowmart** *n.* polecat; *fig.* **23.** 517 [OE **fūl mearð* 'foul marten']
fowyr. See **foure**
fox(e) *n.* fox **14.** 423, **34.** 31 [OE]
fra *prep.* from **1.** 41, **2.** 83, **4.** 29, **5.** 63; from the time when, when **9.** 89, **14.** 80, **14.** 203, **14.** 310 [ON]
frackar *comp. adj.* readier, smarter **28.** 23 [OE *fræc*]
frak *v.* move swiftly **51.** 111, **63.** 77; *pa. t.* **10.** 237 [OE *fræc*]
Francis, Sanct of Assisi (c. 1182–1226), founder of the Order of Friars Minor **55.** 2 *et seq.*
frane *v.* ask, enquire **39.** 79 [OE *freȝnan*]
***frank** *n.* French franc **23.** 439 [F]
fratour *n.* refectory in a monastery **34.** 11 [ME; OF *fraitur*]
Fraunce *adj.* French **18.** 18 [OE *frencisc*]
frawart *adj.* froward, perverse **23.** 81, **52.** 39 [ME]
frawd *n.* deceit **34.** 38; **frawdfull** *adj.* **34.** 15, **64.** 39 [ME; L *fraus*]
frayit *pp.* alarmed, frightened **52.** 196 [ME; aphetic; see **effray**]
fre *adj.* noble **3.** 54; generous **66.** 21, **82.** 43; free, unrestricted **14.** 52, **14.** 65, **57.** 4; *adv.* **38.** 73, **56.** 28 [OE *frēo*]
fredom(e) *n.* gentility, generosity of disposition **10.** 176, **14.** 299, **35.** 81, **63.** 28, **68.** 1; liberty **59.** 29 [OE *frēodōm*]
freik. See **freke**
freind. See **frend**
freindlie, freyndly *adj.* friendly **6.** 130 [OE *frēondlic*]
freindlyk *adv.* in a friendly way **29.** 13 [OE *frēondlice*]
freir *n.* friar **11.** 23, **38.** 4, **54.** *title*, **55.** 5; *pl.* **3.** 1, **55.** 27, **74.** 46 [OF *frere*]
freke, freik *n.* man (poet.) **14.** 210, **14.** 324; fellow **52.** 47 [OE *freca*]
frely *adv.* unrestrainedly **63.** 78 [OE *frēolice*]
fremyt, fremmit *adj.* strange, distant **10.** 225, **53.** 11 [OE *fremede*]
frend, freind, freynd *n.* friend **30.** 3, **60.** 3, **63.** 4; *pl.* **7.** 8, **14.** 405, **14.** 436, **23.** 85 [OE *frēond*]
frendschip *n.* kinship, kindred **14.** 298 [OE *frēondscipe*]
fresch(e) *adj.* fresh, lovely **2.** 10, **2.** 13, **2.** 42, **8.** 7, **9.** 9; *adv.* **14.** 172; **freschest** *sup.* **50.** 160 [OF]
fro *prep.* from **1.** 44, **1.** 46, **2.** 20, **4.** 23, **10.** 106, **16.** 45 [ME]
frog *n.* cloak **29.** 3 [ME; origin uncertain]
frome *prep.* from **12.** 32, **22.** 94, **34.** 41, **49.** 12 [adopted from English in place of **fra**; OE *from*]
front *n.* forehead, brow **23.** 84, **23.** 126, **23.** 173 [ME; OF; L *frons*]
fruct *n.* fruit **72.** 9; *fig.* **59.** 11, **64.** 22, **80.** 12 [ME; var. of **frute**, after L *fructus*]
frustar *n.* vanity, worthlessness **76.** 21; **fruster** *v.* bring to nothing **63.** 78; **fruster, frustir** *adj.* vain, useless **14.** 190, **14.** 400, **16.** 54 [F *frustrer*; L *frustrari*]
frustrat *adj.* frustrated, purposeless, vain **6.** 107, **53.** 40, **79.** 19 [ME; L *frustratus*]
frute *n.* fruit *fig.* **1.** 43, **12.** 38 [OF *fruit*; L *fructus*]

frutles(e) *adj.* fruitless, without profit **14.** 401, **39.** 2, **39.** 34 [ME; prec.]
fry *n.* spawn, progeny **14.** 403 [ME; OF *fraie*]
fudder *n.* cart-load **52.** 62 [OE *fōður*]
fude *n.* food **2.** 80, *fig.* **3.** 54 [OE *fōda*]
fukkit *pp.* copulated **13.** 13 [origin uncertain]
fule, fulle, fuill *n.* fool **10.** 205, **14.** 294, **14.** 300, **20.** 10, **26.** 8, **26.** 18; *pl.* **14.** 403, **44.** 57, **44.** 65 [ME; OF *fol*]
fulfild, fulfillit *ppl. adj.* completely filled (with) **2.** 80, **77.** 26 [OE *fulfyllan*]
fulȝeid, fulȝeit *ppl. adj.* worn out, exhausted **14.** 63, **14.** 86, **14.** 173 [ME *foyle;* OF *fuler* trample]
ful(l) *adj.* filled **10.** 162; *adv.* very, completely **1.** 20, **6.** 41, **9.** 91, **10.** 10, **10.** 53, **14.** 219, **14.** 376 [OE]
fulle. See **fule**
fullelie *adv.* vilely **3.** 51 [OE *fūl*]
fummyll *v.* handle, feel sexually **14.** 134 [cf. LG *fummeln*, Du *fommelen*]
fund, fundin. See **fynd**
***funling** *n.* foundling **23.** 38 [ME; **fynd**]
fur(e). See **fair**
fure *n.* furrow **63.** 78 [OE *furh*, gen. *fure*]
fure *n.* (conject. = *man*; but see Commentary) **14.** 85
furght *adv.* forth **14.** 424, **14.** 481 [OE *forþ*]
furius *adj.* furious, raging **35.** 57, **35.** 73 [ME; OF *furieus*; L *furiosus*]
furnyse *v.* provide, supply **14.** 430 [ME; OF *furnir, furniss-*]
furrit *ppl. adj.* trimmed with fur **14.** 139, **63.** 36 [ME; OF *forrer*]
furth *adv.* forward, onward **3.** 11, **3.** 52, **5.** 35, **14.** 2; out **3.** 37, **9.** 8, **9.** 70, **14.** 157, **33.** 3, **43.** 4; further **14.** 84; into view, notice **5.** 32, **5.** 56 [OE *forþ*]
furth bering *vbl. n.* conduct **14.** 299 [cf. OE v. *forð beran* maintain]
furtheyet *pa. t.* poured forth **35.** 78 [OE *forþ*+*ȝēotan*]
furthwart *adj.* forward, to the fore **14.** 85 [OE *forðweard*]
fut(e), futt *n.* foot **3.** 36, **14.** 493, **28.** 4, **28.** 10, **34.** 48, **63.** 12; **feit** *pl.* **3.** 55, **6.** 7, **6.** 68, **34.** 25, **45.** 54, **52C.** 14 [OE *fōt, fēt*]
futher *n.* cartload; number, company (of people) **74.** 13 [OE *fōður*]
futt syd *adj.* reaching to the feet **29.** 3 (see Commentary) [cf. ON *fōtsīðr*, Dan *fodsid*]
fy (one) *interj.* fie (on) **14.** 461, **16.** 36, **23.** 83, **23.** 173, **54.** 95 [ON]
fycket *pa. t.* fidgeted, wriggled **52.** 89 [? ON *fīkjast* be restless]
***fyftenesum** *n.* fifteen in all, a company of fifteen **23.** 471 [OE *fiftēne*]
fyiftene *adj.* fifteenth **52.** 1 [as prec.]
fyle, fyll *v.* make foul, pollute **14.** 134, **23.** 240, **75.** 37; *3 sg.* **72.** 23; **fyld(e)** *pa. t., pp.* **5.** 38, **23.** 100, **27.** 47 [OE (*ȝe*)*fȳlan*]
fyllis *3 pl.* pour out **14.** 479 [OE *fyllan*]
fynaly *adv.* in the end, completely **71.** 15, **71.** 57 [ME; L *finalis*]
fynd *v.* find, discover **8.** 10, **23.** 197, gain **14.** 364; **fand** *pa. t.* **10.** 216, **14.** 42, devised **10.** 117; **fund, fundin** *pp.* **12.** 41, **14.** 192, **14.** 202, **14.** 503, **39.** 62 [OE *findan*]
fyne *n.* end, purpose, result **76.** 7 [ME; OF *fin*; L *finis*]
fyne *adj.* excellent, splendid **10.** 8, **10.** 150, **14.** 26, **44.** 3; **fynest** *sup.* **14.** 33, **14.** 138 [ME; OF *fin*]
fyre *n.* the element, fire **1.** 13, **52.** 23, **52.** 67; *fig.* fire of love **17.** 2, **17.** 8, **32.** 12; fire on a hearth **73.** 6 [OE *fȳr*]
fyreflawcht *n.* lightning **52.** 63 [OE *fȳr*+? *fleaht*]
fyrie, fyry *adj.* fiery, burning **35.** 75, **53.** 31, **55.** 48 [ME; OE *fȳr*]
fyrit *pa. t.* set on fire **9.** 73, fired **10.** 238 [OE *fȳrian*]
fyve *num. adj.* five **28.** 43, **51.** 92, **61.** 45 [OE *fīf*]

ga, gane *v.* go **27.** 8; move, enter **14.** 133; become **20.** 15; **ga bet-**

weyne intercede **2.** 47; **gais** *2 sg.* **23.** 216, *3 sg.* **15.** 14; **ȝeid, gaid** *pa. t.* **28.** 4, **28.** 47, **54.** 20, **55.** 30; **gane** *pp.* **14.** 293, **23.** 101, **39.** 74; **gane** *ppl. adj.* impotent **14.** 129 [OE *gān*]

Gabriell, Sanct 22. 74

gadderaris *n. pl.* gatherers, pickers-up **52.** 59 [ME; OE v. *gaderian*]

gaddir *v.* collect, hoard **65.** 26; **gadderis** *3 sg.* **67.** 25, **68.** 38; *pres. p.* **67.** 18; **gadderit** *pa. t.* collected, assembled **9.** 98, **52.** 113 [OE *gaderian*]

gaff. See **gif(e)**

gaid. See **ga**

gaif. See **gif(e)**

gaip *n.* gape, greedy opening of the mouth **52.** 100 [ME v., ON *gapa*]

gaip *v.* open the mouth wide (in death) **56.** 57, **56.** 72; *3 pl.* are hungry **23.** 127, **23.** 222; **gaipand** *ppl. adj.* **23.** 98, **59.** 10 [ON *gapa*]

gairding. See **garding**

gais. See **ga**

gaist *n.* ghost **13.** 19, *fig.* **14.** 100, **23.** 168, **27.** 14, **55.** 7, spirit **53.** 21; Holy Ghost, third person of the Trinity **6.** 94, **22.** 29 [OE *gāst*]

gait *n.* road, street, way **23.** 225, **60.** 4; **gaittis** *pl.* **75.** 8 [ME; ON *gata*]

gaittis. See **get(t)**

galland *n.* smart young fellow **14.** 83, **14.** 287; *pl.* **14.** 375, **52.** 10; **galland** *adj.* **82.** 6 [ME; F *galant*]

gallous. See **gallowis**

gallow breid *n.* one destined for the gallows **23.** 141 [OE *galȝa*+*brēdan* nurture]

gallow treis *n. pl.* gallows **34.** 23 [OE *galȝa*+*trēow*]

Galloway 23. 141

gallowis, gallous *n.* gallows **23.** 127, **23.** 222, **56.** 57, **74.** 40, **80.** 19 [OE pl. *galȝan*]

gam *n.* game, sport, pleasure **30.** 7; **gammis** *pl.* **32.** 19 [ME, with short vowel; OE *gamen*]

gamaldis *n. pl.* leaps, capers **43.** 52 [F *gambade*; cf. **gamountis**]

game *n.* sport, fun **14.** 241, **14.** 360, **37.** 4 [ME; reduced form of OE *gamen*]

gamis, *gammys *n. pl.* large teeth; jaws **23.** 363, **37.** 34 [origin obscure]

gamountis *n. pl.* gambols, capers **52.** 11 [var. of *gambat*; see **gamaldis**]

gane *n.* ugly face **13.** 28, **13.** 42, **23.** 167, **23.** 199, **45.** 59 [origin obscure]

gane *v.* be suitable, fitting (for) **23.** 113, **39.** 51; **ganyt** *pa. t.* **14.** 360 [ME *gayne*; ON *gegna*]

gane. See **ga**

ganest *adj.* fittest, most suitable **14.** 78 (only in sup.) [ME; ON *gegn*]

ganestanding *vbl. n.* opposition, resistance **6.** 13; **ganestude** *pa. t.* resisted **3.** 63 [late OE *aȝēnstandan*]

gang *n.* going, walk **29.** 23 [OE]

gang *v.* go **14.** 277, **23.** 146, **82.** 34 [OE *gangan*, ON *ganga*]

gangarall *n.* toad **33.** 7 [**gang**+ ending of obscure origin]

ganȝie, genȝie *n.* arrow, bolt **21.** 4, *fig.* **70.** 11; **ganyeis** *pl.* **10.** 168 [Gael *gainne*]

ganis, ganyt. See **gane**

gar, ger *v.* cause, make, give instructions to **3.** 66, **3.** 75, **9.** 53, **19.** 28, **23.** 23, **23.** 215, **38.** 87; *3 sg.* **13.** 34; *3 pl.* **23.** 166; **gart, gert** *pa. t.* **3.** 68, **10.** 215, **14.** 274, **48.** 25, **52.** 6 [ON *gera*]

gardevyance *n.* trunk, chest **54.** 40 [ME; F **gardeviandes* food-chest]

garding, gairding, gardyng *n.* garden **10.** 84, **14.** 16, **50.** 44; *pl.* **10.** 118 [ONF *gardin*; med. L *gardinum*]

garisoun, garesoun *n.* company, troop **52.** 132, **53.** 35 [ME; OF]

garlandis. See **gerland**

gart. See **gar**

garth(e) *n.* enclosed garden **8.** 6, **10.** 40, **14.** 3, **50.** 47, **81.** 3 [ON *garðr*]

gast *adj.* frightened **12.** 19 [ME v. *gaste*]

gat. See **get(t)**

gatherit *pp.* collected **63.** 62 [see **gaddir**]

gaude flore. 3. 7. (see Commentary]
gaw *n.* gall (bladder) **23.** 183 [OE *galla*, ON *gall*]
Gawane Arthurian knight **62.** 66 (see Commentary)
gawf *n.* guffaw **13.** 22 [imit.]
gawsy *n.* (obscure; see Commentary) **13.** 39, **13.** 41
geangleiris. See **janglar**
geir *n.* apparatus, tackle; (sexual) implements **14.** 232; wealth **45.** 31, **48.** 68, **56.** 73, **79.** 31; merchandise **56.** 16; (double entendre) **71.** 48 [ME; ON *gerve*]
geis. See **guse**
geist *n.* tale, story **40.** 4 [ME, OF; L *gesta*]
geit *n.* jet bead **14.** 201 [ME; OF *jaiet*]
gekkis *n. pl.* derisive gestures, gibes **52.** 29 [LG, Du *gek*]
geldit *pp.* castrated *fig.* **14.** 392 [ME; ON *gelda*]
geme *n.* jem, jewel **14.** 201 [ME, OF; L *gemma*]
generale, in *phr.* generally, without specific reference **23.** 2 [ME; L *generalis*]
generit. See **gennar**
genȝie. See **ganȝie**
genitrice *n.* mother **2.** 44, **2.** 63 [OF; L *genetrix*]
genner *v.* generate **74.** 46; **generit** *pp.* **14.** 316, **54.** 32 [OF *genrer*; L *generare*]
gent *adj.* elegant, fine (poet.) **10.** 41, **14.** 69, **50.** 44 [OF]
gentill *adj.* gentle, excellent, fine **2.** 34, **8.** 12, **12.** 34, **14.** 316, **16.** 26, **42.** 14; of high rank **42.** 32 [ME; OF]
gentilnes *n.* high birth; excellence **8.** 1, **35.** 81, **50.** 175 [ME]
gentrice, gentrise *n.* gentility, aristocratic behaviour **63.** 26, *pers.* **10.** 165 [ME; OF *genterise, gentelise*]
ger, gert. See **gar**
***gere.** See **geir**
gerland *n.* wreath, garland **10.** 276; **garlandis** *pl.* **14.** 18 [OF *gerlande*]
germyng *pres. p.* budding **31.** 3 [ME; OF *germer*]
gers *n.* grass **23.** 196 [OE]
gersomes *n. pl.* additional rents **80.** 13 (see Commentary) [OE *gærsuma*]
***gersone** *n.* fellow **23.** 407 [ME; F *garçon*]
gert. See **gar**
gesse *v.* guess, conjecture **10.** 230 [ME; MDu *gessen*]
gest *n.* guest, lover **14.** 233, **14.** 359 [ME; ON *gestr*]
***geste** *v.* play or sing as a minstrel **23.** 507 [ME; OF *geste* tale, exploit; L *gesta*]
get(t) *v.* obtain, engender **5.** 20, **13.** 5, **51.** 30, **53.** 29, **69.** 18, **74.** 46; **gaittis** *3 sg.* **45.** 35; **gat(t)** *pa. t.* received, obtained **9.** 82, **9.** 109, **23.** 70, **32.** 30; **gottin** *pp.* got **14.** 78, **14.** 201, **14.** 338; begotten **14.** 293, **27.** 6, **38.** 3 [ON *geta, gat, getenn*]
geve, gevin, geving. See **gif(e)**
giand. See **gyane**
Gibbonis *n. gen.* **23.** 209 (see Commentary)
gif(e), giff *v.* give **1.** 14, **29.** 2, **40.** 5; **givis** *3 sg.* **19.** 7; **giffis** *3 pl.* **14.** 484; **gaif, gaff** *pa. t.* **3.** 21, **3.** 50, **3.** 81, **6.** 27, **6.** 34, **13.** 22, **13.** 57, **16.** 52, **28.** 18; **gevin** *pp.* **14.** 527, **34.** 38; **geving** *vbl. n.* **79.** 5 *et seq.*; **gife our** abandon **15.** 15; **God gif, Cryst gif** *vbl. phr. expressing a wish* **14.** 56, **14.** 64, **23.** 158, **25.** 4 [ME; ODan *givæ*]
gif(e), giff *conj.* if, whether **3.** 30, **5.** 15, **5.** 27, **5.** 32, **14.** 16, **14.** 43, **42.** 42, **50.** 143, **55.** 30; **(bot) gife** unless **16.** 51 [OE *ȝif*]
giftis *n. pl.* presents **14.** 364 [nth. ME; ON]
gild *n.* clamour, din **23.** 225 [origin obscure]
gillot *n.* mare **14.** 114 [origin obscure; ? f. the name *Gill*]
gilt *n.* guilty action **6.** 135 [OE *gylt*]
giltin *ppl. adj.* gilded, yellowed **23.** 99 [ME]
girdill *n.* ? waist-belt **13.** 45 [OE *gyrdel*]
girn *v.* show the teeth, snarl; *3 sg.* **29.** 10; **gyrnd** *pa. t.* **52.** 24;

girnand *ppl. adj.* **14.** 290, **37.** 34 [nth. ME]

girnall *n.* granary; meal-chest **23.** 246 [ME *gerner* (OF), perh. infl. by F *grenaille* refuse corn]

Girnega a devil **52.** 164 (see Commentary]

glad *v.* make glad; *pres. p.* **2.** 23, **10.** 6; **gladit** *pa. t.* **14.** 287, **14.** 517; **glaidid** *pa. t.* rejoiced **48.** 39 [nth. ME; OE *ȝegladian*]

gladder *n.* one who makes glad, cheers **10.** 124 [ME (Chaucer); prec.]

gladderit *ppl. adj.* besmeared **14.** 98 [origin obscure]

gladethe *v. imper.* rejoice **31.** 1; **gladdith** *3 pl.* **10.** 85 [ME form; **glad**]

glaid *adj.* glad, happy **1.** 17, **3.** 113, **14.** 7, **14.** 20, **16.** 17, **41.** 11, **45.** 32; *adv.* **69.** 45; **glader** *comp.* **51.** 36; **glaidlie** *adv.* **65.** 4 [OE *glæd*]

glaidid. See **glad**

gla(i)dnes *n.* happiness **18.** 2, **39.** 5, **57.** 6, **62.** 1, **64.** 24, **65.** 8 [OE *glædnes*]

glaidsum *adj.* happy **1.** 39, **14.** 359 [ME; OE *glæd*]

glaiking *vbl. n.* folly **80.** 4 [origin obscure]

glaikkis *n. pl.* sexual desire, lasciviousness **13.** 12; ***glaykis** trickery, folly **23.** 497 [origin obscure]

glance *n.* flash of light **50.** 96 [ME v. *glaunche*; origin obscure]

glar *n.* slime, mud **14.** 99, **54.** 108 [origin obscure]

glaschane *adj.* (obscure) **45.** 59 [origin obscure]

glaschewe hedit *ppl. adj.* (obscure) **45.** 26 [origin obscure]

glas(e) *n.* glass **14.** 202, **61.** 5; hour-glass, sand-glass ***23.** 460, **69.** 25; wine-glass **73.** 24 [OE *glæs*]

glasing wrichtis *n. pl.* glaziers **44.** 15 [OE *glæsen*]

glawmir *n.* outcry, scandal **20.** 20 [? = *clamour*; but cf. ME *glam* noise, ON *glamm*]

***glaykis.** See **glaikkis**

gle *n.* rejoicing; melody (poet.) **14.** 518 [OE *glēo*]

gled *n.* kite (*milvus milvus*) **23.** 128, **23.** 237, **42.** 13 (see Commentary), **54.** 77; *pl.* **23.** 52, **23.** 146 [OE *glida*]

gledaris *n. pl.* (obscure) **44.** 41 (see Commentary)

gleme *n.* gleam **14.** 517, *pl.* **10.** 31 [OE *glǣm*]

gleme *v.* gleam (poet.) **14.** 20; **glemand** *ppl. adj.* **14.** 108; **glemyng** *vbl. n.* **14.** 202 [ME]

glemen *n. pl.* minstrels, entertainers **52.** 104 [OE *glēoman* (*glēo* mirth)]

glemys *3 sg.* looks askance **14.** 228 [nth. ME]

glen *n.* valley **23.** 153; **glen(n)is** *pl.* **23.** 159, **27.** 15 [OGael *glenn*]

glengoir *n.* venereal disease; *attrib.* poxed **23.** 83 [OF *grand gorre*]

glete *v.* gleam, glitter (poet.) **10.** 66 [ON *glita*]

gletering *ppl. adj.* glittering **10.** 61 [ME; ON *glitra*]

gleyd *n.* a live coal, ember **14.** 108 [OE *glēd*]

glitterand *ppl. adj.* glittering **14.** 517; **glitterit** *pp.* (*trans.*) made to glitter **14.** 19 [ON *glitra*]

***glod** *adj.* (meaning and origin obscure) **23.** 343

gloir, glor(i)e, glory *n.* glory, honour, celestial bliss **2.** 4, **2.** 51, **3.** 4, **40.** 11, **42.** 82, **59.** 13 [OF; L *gloria*]

***glorificate** *adj.* glorified **23.** 528 [ME; late L *glorificare*]

glori(o)us, gloryus *adj.* in glory **2.** 32; full of glory, **3.** 27; splendid **2.** 72, **4.** 22, **14.** 19, **14.** 518, **16.** 17 [OF *glorieus*; L *gloriosus*]

glour, glowir *v.* stare **13.** 19, **34.** 24; **glowrand** *pres. p., ppl. adj.* **14.** 100, **23.** 98, **23.** 176 [origin obscure]

glowis *3 pl.* glow redly **14.** 108 [OE *glōwan*]

gluntoch *adj.* ? bare-kneed **23.** 99 (see Commentary)

glutteny *n.* one of the seven deadly sins (*gula*) **52.** 91 [ME; OF *glutanie*]

gluttoun *n.* glutton **23.** 241 [ME; OF *gluton*; L *gluto*]

glyd(e) *v.* go, ride, smoothly **3.** 92, **52.** 164, **52.** 188, **54.** 108; *3 sg.* **61.** 6 [OE *glīdan*]

gnawin *pp.* gnawed, chewed **43.** 36 [OE *gnazan*]

go, gone *v.* go **16.** 62; **gois** *2 sg.* **16.** 37, *3 pl.* **62.** 17, **62.** 46; **gon** *pp.* over, past **4.** 35, **36.** 8 [ME; adopted in Sc poetry in place of **ga**]

God *n.* God **16.** 16, **16.** 32 *et seq.*; **God(d)is** *gen.* **2.** 2, **2.** 76, **3.** 87, **38.** 83 [OE]

goddes *n.* goddess **50.** 69 [ME *god(d)-esse*]

Gog ma Gog *n.* chief of the giants **29.** 19 (see Commentary); ***Gog and Magog** **23.** 528

goif. See **gove**

goishalk *n.* goshawk (*astur palumbarius*) **42.** 14 (see Commentary) [OE *gōs-hafoc*]

goist *n.* spirit **12.** 16 [ME *gost*; OE *gāst*]

goldin, goldyn *adj.* golden **10.** 4, **10.** 62, **14.** 366, **14.** 517, *fig.* eloquent **23.** 97 [ME; OE *gold*]

goldit *ppl. adj.* wealthy **14.** 361 [as prec.]

goldsmythis *n. pl.* workers in gold **44.** 15 [OE]

golk *n.* cuckoo (*cuculus canorus*) **13.** 51 (see Commentary), **54.** 77 [ME; ON *gaukr*]

***Golyas** *n.* Goliath **23.** 529

gone. See **go**

gone *n.* gun, cannon **51.** 112 [ME; origin obscure]

gor *n.* slime, filth **14.** 98 [ME; OE]

gorge-millaris *n. pl.* (obscure) **45.** 26 [origin obscure]

gorgeit *pp.* choked, stopped up **14.** 99 [ME; OF *gorger*]

gormaw *n.* cormorant (*phalacrocorax carbo*) **54.** 77 [*gor-* (obscure)+ **maw**]

gossep *n.* god-father, -mother; a form of address **74.** 3 [OE *godsib*]

gottin. See **get(t)**

goulis *n.* heraldic red **10.** 41 [ME; OF]

goun(e) *n.* gown, dress **10.** 87, **14.** 139, **23.** 201, **56.** 27; *pl.* **14.** 366, **48.** 12 [OF; med. L *gouna*]

gove, goif *v.* gaze (at), stare **14.** 287, **14.** 393; **govit** *pa. t.* **9.** 5 [origin obscure]

governance, govirnance *n.* management, conduct **5.** 58, **6.** 135, **9.** 13, **15.** 10, **14.** 259, **35.** 60, **51.** 60, **54.** 14 [OF *gouvernance*]

governing *vbl. n.* conduct **11.** 2 [ME; OF *governer*]

gowdy *n.* ? gold piece **13.** 45 [see **goldin**]

Gower, John, English poet (d. 1408) **10.** 262, **62.** 51

grace *n.* favour, God's supernatural help **2.** 4, **6.** 69, **10.** 216, **12.** 20; *pers.* **3.** 113, **3.** 129; sexual satisfaction **37.** 47 [OF; L *gratia*]

graceles(e) *adj.* ill-favoured **13.** 28, **13.** 42, **14.** 393, **23.** 127, **52.** 132, (*as n.*) **23.** 222 [prec.]

graciows *adj.* gracious, benevolent **20.** 25 [ME; OF]

graep *v.* feel, handle **33.** 7 [OE *grāpian*]

graif(e) *n.* grave **6.** 148, **38.** 113, **62.** 46 [OE *græf*]

graith *v.* make ready, prepare **52.** 10; **grathing** *pres. p.* **60.** 4; **grathit** *pa. t.* arrayed, adorned **14.** 365, *ppl. adj.* **14.** 18, **71.** 42 [ME; ON *greiða*]

gramercy *interj.* thanks **13.** 58, **56.** 29 [OF *grant merci*]

grane, grayne *n.* seed(s) **39.** 99, *fig.* **2.** 72, **59.** 11 [ME; OF *grein*]

grane *v.* groan **13.** 19; **graneand** *pres. p.* **73.** 4 [OE *grānian*]

grangis *n. pl.* granaries; farms **68.** 21 [ME; OF *grange*]

granis *n. pl.* groans **52.** 24, **56.** 76 [see **grane**]

grantis *3 pl.* consent to **74.** 55; **grantit** *pa. t.* **14.** 159, *pp.* **14.** 314 [ME; OF *granter*]

grathing, grathit. See **graith**

gratious *adj.* gracious **82.** 50 [see **grace**]

gratitud *n.* benefit, favour conferred **6.** 97 [late L *gratitudo*]

gravetie *n.* grave, serious bearing **19.** 18 [F]

grayne. See **grane**

grayth *n.* materials, goods; wealth **39.** 85 [nth. ME; ON *greiðe*]

gre *n.* first place, victory **27.** 20, **27.** 33 [ME; OF *gré*]
gredines *n.* greed **51.** 99 [ME; next]
gredy, gredie *adj.* greedy **23.** 146, **44.** 57, **45.** 59, **52.** 92, **80.** 33 [OE *grǣdiȝ*]
gree *v.* agree, accord **28.** 5 [ME; OF *gréer*]
greiff *n.* grief, sorrow **42.** 3 [ME, OF *gref*]
greif(f) *v.* trouble, vex **42.** 53, **42.** 63 [ME *greif*; F *grever*]
Greik sie the Mediterranean **52.** 137
grein. See **grene**
greis *n. pl.* academic degrees **23.** 397 [ME; OF *gré*]
greit, grit, gret, gryt(t) *adj.* great **2.** 68, **3.** 69, **3.** 137, **9.** 28, **9.** 60, **27.** 34, **29.** 19; **gretly** *adv.* **10.** 142, **gritly 23.** 18 [OE *grēat*]
greitand. See **grete**
greiting *n.* greeting, salutation **3.** 113 [OE *grēting*]
grene, grein, greyn(e) *adj.* green, flourishing, fresh, young **2.** 43, **5.** 65, **8.** 9, **10.** 155, **14.** 3, **31.** 37 [OE]
grephoun *n.* griffin; fabulous creature with a lion's body and an eagle's head and wings **53.** 26 [OF *griffon*]
gress *n.* grass **14.** 24; *pl.* herbs, plants **14.** 20 [OE *græs*]
gret. See **greit**
gretast, grittest *adj. sup.* greatest, highest **50.** 87, **52C.** 7 [see **greit**]
grete *v.* weep, shed tears *fig.* **10.** 16; **gre(i)tand** *pres. p.* **23.** 141, **38.** 103 [OE (Angl) *grētan*]
grevance *n.* hurt, injury **10.** 168, **42.** 42 [ME; OF]
greve *v.* harass, distress, vex **51.** 41; *3 sg.* **19.** 2; *pres. p.* **6.** 13; **grevit** *pp.* **9.** 98 [ME; F *grever*]
greyne. See **grene**
grip *n.* firm grasp; **in grippis** into a close embrace **33.** 18; **hald no grippis** *fig.* lose all cohesion, firmness **23.** 15 [ON]
grip, gryp(e) *v.* grasp, clutch, lay hands on **39.** 37, **43.** 24; *3 sg.* **14.** 100; **grippit** *pa. t.* **37.** 29 [ONhb; cf. OE *gripan*, ON *gripa*]
gris *n.* grass **43.** 24 [nth. ME; var. of **gress**]
***grisis.** See **gryce**
grit, gritly. See **greit**
gritheidit *ppl. adj.* big-headed **13.** 41 [**greit**+**heid**]
grittest. See **gretast**
grome *n.* fellow **14.** 78, **14.** 392 [ME; origin uncertain]
***grotis** *n. pl.* husked grain **23.** 427 [ME; OE pl. **grotan*]
groukaris *n. pl.* (obscure) **44.** 41 [origin obscure]
growf(e), on flat on the ground **37.** 12, **37.** 58 [ME; ON *ā grūfu*]
growis *3 sg.* grows **38.** 64 [OE *grōwan*]
grugeing *vbl. n.* reluctance **79.** 7 [ME]
grund *n.* earth, ground **23.** 196, **52.** 188, **52.** 192; *fig.* **52.** 56, **72.** 32 [OE]
grundyn *ppl. adj.* ground, sharpened **10.** 111, **10.** 199 [OE *grindan*, *ȝe-grunden*]
grunȝ(i)e *n.* snout **23.** 123, **52.** 69 [ME *groney*; OF *groign*]
gruntill *n.* 'grunter', snout **23.** 127 [ME]
gryce *n.* sucking pig **44.** 66; ***grisis** *pl.* **23.** 427 [ME; ON *griss*]
grym *adj.* fierce **14.** 98 [OE *grim*; ON *grimmr*]
gryp(e). See **grip**
gryslie *adj.* horrible (poet.) **23.** 163 [OE *grislic*]
gryt(t). See **greit**
grytast *adj. sup.* greatest **28.** 34, **76.** 17 [var. of **greit**]
guberne *v. imper.* govern, guide **2.** 11 [L *gubernare*]
gud man *n.* husband **14.** 233, *pl.* **71.** 7 [OE *gōda mon*]
gud(e), guid *adj.* good, worthy, fitting **5.** 53, **9.** 41, **10.** 90, **13.** 41, **14.** 259, **17.** 73, **18.** 1, **81.** 8; *absol.* goods, wealth **6.** 122, **14.** 296, **14.** 361, **14.** 392, **38.** 34, **64.** 21, **83.** 18, **83.** 21; **guddis** *pl.* **16.** 95; **men of gude** men of importance, substance **44.** 48, **79.** 51 [OE *gōd*]
gudlie, guidlie, gudly *adj.* distinguished, fine, handsome **14.** 3, **14.** 365, **22.** 16, **44.** 8, **50.** 138,

51. 13; **guidlie** *adv.* fitly, well **48.** 22; **gudliest** *sup.* loveliest, finest **9.** 5 [OE *gōdlic*]

gudnes *n.* excellence, whatever is good **16.** 62, **72.** 32 [OE *gōdnes*]

guerdoun, gwerdon *n.* reward **17.** 63, **82.** 34 [ME; OF]

guid. See **gud(e)**

***gukkis** *3 sg.* behaves foolishly **23.** 497 [next]

gukkit *adj.* foolish **13.** 10 (cf. **hony-gukkis**) [f. n. *guk*, imit. or mocking word]

gulesnowt *n.* yellow nose **23.** 52 [ON *gul-r*+ME *snute*]

gulsoch *n.* jaundice; *attrib.* **23.** 199 [ME *gule* yellow (cf. prec.)+ *sought* sickness]

gumes *n. pl.* gums **43.** 36 [OE *gōma*]

gunnaris *n. pl.* gunners **44.** 41 [ME]

gunnis *n. pl.* guns, cannon **10.** 238 [ME; origin obscure]

guse *n.* goose **23.** 159; ***geis** *pl.* **23.** 427 [OE *gōs*]

gusting *vbl. n.* tasting **6.** 12 [ME; L *gustare*]

gutaris *n. pl.* (street) gutters **14.** 99 [ME; OF *gutiere*]

gwerdon. See **guerdoun**

Gy Guido de Corvo **23.** 172

Gy off Gysburne 27. 28

gy *v.* guide, govern **36.** 6, **83.** 7 [ME; OF *guier*]

gyane, giand, jyane *n.* giant **4.** 20, **13.** 36 (term of endearment), **27.** 4; **gyans, gyandis** *pl.* **32.** 21, **54.** 32 [ME; OF *geant*]

gyd *n.* guide **3.** 129, **49.** 10 [OF *guide*]

gyd(e) *v.* guide, steer **32.** 27, **77.** 8, **79.** 59; **gydis** *3 sg.* directs, manages **17.** 88; **gydit** *pp.* **39.** 45, **82.** 28; **gyd(d)ing** *vbl. n.* **45.** 12, **82.** 41; **gydingis** *n. pl.* ways of acting **14.** 451 [ME; OF *guider*]

gyis. See **gyse**

gymp *adj.* slender, graceful **14.** 69 [origin obscure]

gyn *n.* military engine, contrivance **9.** 60, **9.** 67 [ME; reduced f. OF *engin*, L *ingenium*]

gyng *n.* company, gang **38.** 98 [OE *genge*]

gyngill *v.* jingle **23.** 119 [ME; imit.

gyrnd. See **girn**

gyse, gy(i)s *n.* fashion, custom masquerade **10.** 103, **38.** 95, **52** 10, **52.** 26 [OF *guise*]

ȝa, ȝe *interj.* yes **9.** 15, **78.** 36 [ON *jā*]

ȝadswyvar *n.* mare-buggerer **23** 246 [ON *jalda*+ME *swyve* copulate with]

ȝaid. See **ȝald**

ȝaip *adj.* astute, nimble **14.** 79, **14** 170 [OE *ȝēap*]

ȝak *v.* ache **21.** 1 [OE *acan*]

ȝald *n.* old horse *fig.* **43.** 2 *et passim* **ȝaid** *attrib.* worn out **43.** 3 [ON *jalda* mare]

ȝallow *adj.* yellow **26.** 26 [OE *ȝeolu*]

ȝarrow *n.* milfoil (*achillea millefolium* **50.** 83 [OE *ȝearwe*]

ȝawmeris *n. pl.* yells, outcry **54.** 12 [ME *ȝomer*, OE *ȝeōmrian*; cf. MLG *jammeren*]

ȝe. See **ȝa**

ȝe, ȝie *pron. 2 pers. sg. and pl.* you **1.** 11, **1.** 19, **5.** 36, **8.** 5, **9.** 24, **14** 41–7, **52C.** 40 [OE]

ȝeid. See **ga**

ȝeild *v.* repay, recompense **14.** 12 [OE *ȝieldan*]

ȝeir, ȝe(a)r, ȝer *n.* year **5.** 62, **6.** 86 **9.** 3, **14.** 56, **14.** 386; *pl.* **5.** 65 **10.** 86, **81.** 47, as to years **16.** 3 [OE *ȝēar*]

ȝell *n.* outcry, yowling **52.** 118 [OE *ȝiellan*]

ȝelp *n.* yelp, shrill bark **37.** 10 [OE *ȝielp*]

ȝemen *n. pl.* freeholders, commoners of good standing **68.** 25 [ME; prob reduced form of *ȝongman*]

ȝemit *pa. t.* kept, guarded **4.** 39 [OE *ȝieman*]

ȝerd *n.* straight branch; penis **14** 130, **14.** 220 [OE *ȝyrd;* cf. L *virga*]

ȝerne *adv.* diligently, swiftly **2.** 11 eagerly, gladly **14.** 129 [OE *ȝeorne*

ȝester *adj.* yester, belonging to yesterday **21.** 1 [OE *ȝeostran*]

ȝesterday, ȝisterday *n.* yesterday **58.** 6, **79.** 37 [OE; see prec.]

ȝet, ȝete. See **ȝit**
ȝet *n.* gate **9.** 17; **ȝettis** *pl.* doors **3.** 126; gates **4.** 3, **9.** 73, **69.** 36 [OE]
ȝetland *n.* Jutland **23.** 94
ȝewth. See **ȝouth**
ȝing, ȝoing, ȝ(o)ung, ȝhyng, ying, yo(u)ng(e) *adj.* young **2.** 13, **5.** 64, **10.** 22, **10.** 154, **14.** 79, **14.** 306, **16.** 35, **24,** 5; **ȝungar** comp. **74.** 48 [nth. OE *ȝing*]
ȝit, ȝitt, ȝet(e), yit *adv.* yet, still **3.** 89, **5.** 26, **6.** 30, **10.** 69, **31.** 27, **34.** 24, **45.** 74 [OE *ȝiet*]
ȝockis. See **ȝolk**
ȝok *n.* yoke **14.** 79, **50.** 112 [OE *ȝeoc*]
ȝoldin *ppl. adj.* submissive, exhausted **14.** 220 [OE *ȝieldan, ȝolden*]
ȝolk *v.* link, embrace **14.** 220; **ȝockis** *3 pl.* copulate **32.** 33 [OE *ȝeocian*]
ȝone *adj., adv.* yonder **9.** 38, **9.** 51, **9.** 53, **14.** 354, **14.** 442 [OE *ȝeon*]
ȝou. See **ȝow**
ȝoulis. See **ȝowle**
ȝoull. See **ȝule**
ȝoung. See **ȝing**
ȝour, ȝowr *adj.* your **1.** 2, **1.** 18, **8.** 6, **14.** 269, **26.** 4 [OE *ēower*]
ȝouth(e), ȝewth, ȝowth, yhouth *n.* youth **2.** 59, **14.** 170, **16.** 34, **17.** 1, **31.** 3, **35.** 63, **59.** 9 [OE *ȝeoȝuþ*]
ȝow, ȝou *pron.* you **1. 20, 9.** 70, **11.** 3, **32.** 31; *pl.* yourselves **1.** 42, **9.** 72 [OE *ēow*]
ȝowis *n. pl.* ewes; *fig.* women **37.** 24, **37.** 62 [OE *eowu*]
ȝowle *v.* yell, howl in distress **23.** 236; *n.* **54.** 75, *pl.* **42.** 22, **54.** 122, **ȝoulis 63.** 69; **ȝowling** *vbl. n.* **37.** 57 [ME **ȝoȝele**]
ȝowllis. See **ȝule**
ȝuke *v.* itch (with desire) **14.** 130 [app. alteration of nth. ME *ȝeke*, infl. by MDu *jeuken*]
ȝule, ȝoull, ȝu(i)ll *n.* Christmastide **22.** 89, **26.** 25, **27.** 49, **43.** 6, **47.** 22, *gen.* **43.** 2 *et seq.* [OE *ȝeōl*; ON *jōl*]
ȝung, ȝungar. See **ȝing**

habitakle *n.* habitation **2.** 14 [OF *habitacle*]
hace *adj.* hoarse **51.** 79 [OE *hās*]
hache *n.* pain, pang **14.** 224 [ME]
had. See **hald**
hadder *n.* heather **39.** 86 (see Commentary) [origin uncertain]
haem. See **hame**
haff. See **haif**
haggarbaldis *n. pl.* (obscure) **45.** 18 [origin obscure]
haggeis *n.* haggis **23.** 128 (see Commentary) [ME *hagas*; origin unknown]
haif, heff *v.* have, possess **9.** 48, **9.** 62, **11.** 18, **28.** 30, **29.** 4; **hais, hes** *1 sg.* **64.** 1; *2 sg.* **48.** 66; *3 sg.* **8.** 12, **34.** 48; **hes** *pl.* **3.** 111, **9.** 10, **12.** 18, **14.** 60; **haifand** *pres. p.* **51.** 98; **ha(i)d, hed** *pa. t.* **14.** 207, **14.** 390, **32.** 9, **43.** 5; **haff e** have an eye, take heed **45.** 69 [OE *habban*]
haiknay *n.* riding or ambling horse **54.** 35 [ME; OF *haquenée*]
haile, haill, hayle *n.* hail **54.** 1, **69.** 7; *attrib.* **10.** 178; *fig.* **62.** 70 [OE *hæȝl*]
***Hailis** Hailes near Haddington **23.** 299
haill, hal(e) *adj.* healthy **5.** 17, **51.** 51; whole, entire **14.** 386, **14.** 472, **25.** 26, **44.** 29; *adv.* wholly, entirely **14.** 325 [nth. ME; OE *hāl*]
haill, haile, hale *interj.* hail! **2.** 1, **2.** 10, **23.** 104, **50.** 62–3 [ON *heill*; OE *hāl*]
hairbis *n. gen. pl.* plants' **50.** 160 [ME, OF *herbe*; L *herba*]
haird *ppl. adj.* -haired **37.** 16 [nth. ME; ON n. *hār*]
hair(e) *adj.* hoary, grey-haired **10.** 114, **14.** 272 [OE *hār*]
hairis *n. pl.* hairs of the head **10.** 61, **10.** 140, **16.** 77 [nth. ME; ON *hār*]
hairt. See **hert**
hairtly *adj.* heartfelt, sincere **22.** 3 [OE *heorte*]
hais. See **haif**
haist *n.* haste **5.** 46, **14.** 13, **78.** 33 [ME; OF]
haistalie, hastely *adv.* quickly **14.** 224, **42.** 59 [ME; OF n. *haste*]
hait *v.* hate, abhor **14.** 169; **hatit** *pa. t.* **14.** 232, **14.** 273 [OE *hatian*]

hait *adj.* hot, passionate **20.** 16, **52.** 101, **74.** 52 [OE *hat*]

hald(e), had, hawd *v.* hold, conduct **6.** 62; consider, believe **5.** 36, **11.** 10, **50.** 135; keep **14.** 210, **14.** 349, **23.** 15; keep quiet **28.** 39, **82.** 47; stay **44.** 28; hold off **34.** 42; *3 sg.* **15.** 7, *3 pl.* **14.** 458; ***hald of,** am a vassal, tenant, of **23.** 322; **held** *pa. t.* stayed in **23.** 201; **haldin** *pp.* held, practised **14.** 64, regarded **14.** 256, **14.** 399, kept **14.** 450; **haldin owt** barred **52.** 104 [ONhb *halda*]

hale. See **haill**

hal(e)sum *adj.* health-giving, beneficial **8.** 9, **10.** 248 [nth. ME]

halflingis *adv.* half **3.** 140, **50.** 187 [ME]

halie. See **haly**

halines *n.* holiness **72.** 31 [OE *hāliȝnes*]

halk *n.* hawk; the little red merlin (*falco columbarius*) **42.** 7; **halking** *n.* hawking **68.** 9 [OE *hafoc*]

halok *adj.* guileless **14.** 465 [origin unknown]

hals *n.* neck **13.** 33, **14.** 339, **37.** 36, throat **66.** 17 [OE; ON]

halsing *pres. p.* greeting **3.** 7; **halsit** *pa. t.* hailed **50.** 11 [ON *heilsa*]

halsit *pa. t.* embraced **37.** 9 [ON *halsa*]

halsum. See **hal(e)sum**

haltane *adj.* haughty, arrogant **23.** 59 [ME; OF *hautain*]

haly, halie *adj.* holy, devout **1.** 30, **14.** 472, **39.** 41; **haly day** sabbath **6.** 52; **haly writ** scripture **5.** 3; **Haly Gaist, Haly Spreit** the third person of the Trinity **22.** 29, **6.** 65 [OE *hāliȝ*]

***Halyrudhous** in Edinburgh **23.** 278

hame, haem *n.* home **32.** 5; *adv.* back to home **14.** 524, **23.** 96, **23.** 116, **47.** 1 [OE *hām*]

hamely *adv.* kindly, graciously **14.** 230 [nth. ME; prec.]

hamelynes *n.* intimacy, familiarity *pers.* **10.** 190 (see Commentary) [nth. ME]

hamperit *pp.* cramped, confined **75.** 39 [ME; origin uncertain]

hanchis, henchis *n. pl.* haunches **23.** 181, **45.** 55 [ME; OF]

hand *n.* the human hand; *pl.* **14.** 295, **45.** 56, **63.** 44; **at my hand** *adv. phr.* close by **14.** 12, **out of hand** excessively **14.** 378 [OE]

handill *v.* handle (roughly) **14.** 223; **handlit** *pa. t.* **37.** 30, *pp.* **37.** 32 [OE *handlian*]

hang. See **hing**

hangit *pp.* hanged **56.** 32, **80.** 38; **hangitman** hanged man **23.** 187 [ME; OE *hangian*]

hankersaidilis *n. pl.* anchorets, hermits **22.** 9 [OE *āncersetl* hermit's cell]

hansell, hansill *n.* present, reward at New Year **18.** 4 *et seq.* [OE *handselen*, ON *handsal*]

hanyt *pp.* held back **14.** 386 (see Commentary) [ON *hegna*]

happinnit *pa. t.* befell **14.** 528; **happinit** *pp.* befallen, come about **14.** 224 [ME; ON n. *happ*]

happis *n. pl.* little jumps **10.** 19 [var. of *hop*; OE *hoppian*]

happit *pp.* wrapped up against the cold **43.** 65 [nth. ME; origin obscure]

happy *adj.* fortunate **14.** 464 [ME, ON *happ*]

***happyn.** See **happinnit**

hard. See **heir**

hard(e) *adj.* harsh **25.** 7, severe, ungenerous **25.** 29 [OE *heard*]

hard *adv.* close, near **10.** 55 (see **burd**), **10.** 197, **14.** 13, **56.** 14; fiercely, vigorously **32.** 12; securely, fast **37.** 48 [OE *hearde*]

hardely *adv.* stoutly, boldly **38.** 115 [ME; F *hardi*]

hardines *n.* boldness **16.** 99 [ME; F *hardi*]

hardly *adv.* confidently; **hardly mot it be** certainly, so be it **56.** 63 [OE *heardlīce*]

hardy *adj.* bold, valiant **10.** 191, **16.** 83, **50.** 89 [ME; F *hardi*]

hardyment *n.* courage, valour **52.** 140 [ME, OF]

harlis *3 pl.* go in trailing garments **68.** 29; **harlit** *pa. t.* dragged violently **3.** 52 [nth. ME, to drag origin unknown]

harlotrie *n.* ribaldry, loose living **23.** 59 [ME; OF *harlot*]
harlott *n.* rascal **52.** 161; *pl.* whores **32.** 32, knaves, profligates **52.** 25, **52.** 214 [ME; OF *harlot*]
harme *n.* pain, distress **14.** 222; **harmis, harmes** *pl.* **23.** 8, **56.** 13 [OE *hearm*]
harmyt *pa. t.* harmed, damaged **10.** 157 [OE *hearmian*]
harnas, harnes *n.* armour **52.** 193, *attrib.* **52.** 167 [ME, OF *harneis*]
harnis *n. pl.* brains **23.** 8 [ME; ON *hjarne*]
harpis *n. pl.* harps **51.** 33 [OE *hearpe*]
hart. See **hert**
harth *adj.* ? rough **23.** 181 [meaning and origin obscure]
hartit *ppl. adj.* -hearted, having a heart of this or that disposition **13.** 32 [ME; OE *heorte*]
hartlie. See **heartlie**
Hary, Blind Scotch poet **62.** 69
has. See **haif**
haschbaldis *n. pl.* (obscure) **45.** 18 [meaning and origin obscure]
hasknes *n.* harshness **42.** 19 [ME *harsk*; MLG *harch*]
hastely. See **haistalie**
hatrent *n.* hatred **14.** 333, **52.** 46 [OE *hēte*+*rǣden* condition]
hattis *n. pl.* hats **48.** 44 [OE *hæt*]
hautand, hawtane *adj.* haughty **14.** 12, **52.** 25 [ME, OF *hautain*]
havines. See **hevynesse**
having *n.* bearing, behaviour, manner **9.** 9, **16.** 50; *pers.* **10.** 149 [ME]
havy(e). See **hevy**
haw *adj.* livid, bluish **23.** 164, **23.** 181 [OE *hāwi*]
hawd. See **hald**
hawkit *adj.* spotted, streaked (of cattle) **54.** 103 [origin obscure]
hawtane. See **hautand**
hawthorne *n.* hawthorn **14.** 14; *attrib.* **14.** 4 [OE *haȝaþorn*]
Hay, Schir Gilbert (*fl.* 1450) **62.** 67
hayle. See **haile**
he, heast. See **hie**
he *pers. pron.* he, the one **11.** 22 [OE *hē*]
heartlie *adv.* heartily **47.** 29; **hartlie** earnestly **25.** 2 [ME; OE *heorte*]
heavines. See **hevynes(se)**
heavinlie. See **hevinlie**
hechar *comp. adv.* higher **14.** 160 [OE *hēh*]
hecht *v.* be called, have as one's name **9.** 27; *pa. t.* **51.** 38 [OE *heht*, pa. t. of *hātan*]
hecht *v.* (I) avow, dare say **9.** 55; pledge **23.** 67; promise **38.** 47; *pa. t.* **47.** 10, **52.** 145; *pp.* **39.** 77 [as prec.]
Hector, Trojan prince **35.** 58, **61.** 9
hed. See **haif**
***hede point** *n.* crest of a coat of arms **23.** 414 [OE *hēafod*+F *point* (L *punctum*)]
hedit *ppl. adj.* -headed **45.** 15, **45.** 26, **45.** 60 [ME; OE *hēafod*]
hee. See **hie**
heff. See **haif**
heft *n.* haft **52.** 41 [OE *hæft(e)*]
hege *n.* hedge **14.** 13; **hegies** *pl.* **10.** 34; **hegeit** *ppl. adj.* hedged round **14.** 4 [OE *hegg*]
heggirbald *n.* (obscure; abusive) **23.** 149 [meaning and origin unknown]
heich *adv.* high **74.** 21 [OE *hēah*]
heid, hede, heyd *n.* head **3.** 44, **14.** 331, **14.** 348, **14.** 377, **21.** 9 (see Commentary), chief **38.** 51, **38.** 53; *pl.* **74.** 20 [OE *hēafod*]
heildit *ppl. adj.* covered, concealed **14.** 14 [var. of *hele*; OE *helian*]
heill *n.* heel **52.** 20, **52.** 38, **52.** 204, **68.** 29; **heilis** *pl.* **23.** 226 [OE *hēla*, ON *hæll*]
heill *n.* (source of) health **13.** 3, **62.** 1 [OE *hǣlu*]
heilie *adj.* proud, arrogant **52.** 25 [OE *hēalic*]
heir, here *v.* hear **5.** 51, **10.** 132, **23.** 12, **51.** 40; **heiris** *2 sg.* **23.** 159, *3 sg.* **45.** 4; **hard, herd** *pa. t.* **9.** 89, **13.** 2, **14.** 11, **50.** 30; *pp.* favourably considered **42.** 12; **hard** *pp.* **14.** 6, **45.** 72, **63.** 69 [OE (Angl) *hēran*]
heir *adv.* here, in this place, at this

point **3.** 20, **3.** 123, **6.** 161, **7.** 8, **9.** 14, **11.** 18 [OE *hēr*]
heirar *n.* listener **78.** 9 [**heir**]
heirof *adv.* of this, concerning this **6.** 46 [OE *hērof*]
heit. See **hete**
heklis *v.* scratches as with a flax-comb **14.** 107 [ME n.; cf. MLG and MDu *hekele*]
heland, heleand, helland *adj.* highland (Gaelic) **23.** 55, **23,** 168, **27.** 14, **52.** 109 [OE *hēa*+**land**]
held. See **hald**
helme *n.* helmet (poet.) **35.** 43, **35.** 67, **62.** 22 [OE *helm*]
help(e) *v.* help, succour **2.** 8, **12.** 33, give relief **14.** 130; **helpis** *3 sg.* **45.** 65, *3 pl.* **52C.** 34; **helpit** *pa. t.* **35.** 26 [OE *helpan*]
helth *n.* health **59.** 25 [OE *hǣlþ*]
hely *adv.* highly, greatly **14.** 368, **52.** 145 [ME *heȝliche*; OE *hēaȝ-*]
hen *n.* domestic fowl, chicken **14.** 269; **hen(n)is** *pl.* **23.** 149, **23.** 156, **34.** 41 [OE]
henches. See **hanchis**
hende, heynd(e) *adj.* skilful, expert **10.** 191; pleasant **14.** 14; *as n.* gentle one **14.** 32 [ME; aphetic; OE *ȝehende*]
henes, hienes *n.* highness, majesty (as a title) **26.** 7, **30.** 9, **44.** 20, **44.** 36, **50.** 72 [OE *hēa*]
Henniball Hannibal, Carthaginian general **35.** 61
Henrisoun, Robert Scotch poet **62.** 82
hepit *pa. t.* piled up, accumulated **14.** 334 [OE *hēapian*]
herbe *n.* herb **8.** 12; *pl.* **8.** 9 [OF]
herbr(e)it *pp.* harboured, sheltered **3.** 119, **6.** 29 [? ON *herbergja*]
Hercules Greek hero **61.** 9
***herefore** *conj.* therefore, for this reason **23.** 359 [ME]
heremeitis *n. pl.* hermits **22.** 9 [ME; OF; med. L *heremita*]
heretage *n.* inheritance in the world to come **52.** 107; **heritagis** *pl.* inheritance **14.** 344 [ME; OF *(h)eritage*]
hering. See **heir**
herle *n.* heron (*ardea cinerea*) **14.** 382 [origin obscure]
***Herode** king of the Jews **23.** 537
herreit. See **heryit**
herretyk *n.* heretic **23.** 247 [ME; eccl. L *haereticus*]
hert, ha(i)rt *n.* heart, esp. as seat of the emotions **5.** 9, **6.** 47, **6.** 149, **8.** 13, **12.** 41, **14,** 301, **19.** 8; = dear **12.** 18, **13.** 3, **13.** 15; *gen.* **6.** 157, **12.** 1, **12.** 49; *pl.* **39.** 11, **51.** 10; *attrib.* **14.** 224 [OE *heorte*]
hertit *ppl. adj.* -hearted **14.** 498 [prec.]
hertly *adj.* heartfelt **14.** 230 [ME; OE *heorte*]
heryit, herreit *pp.* plundered, reduced to poverty **14.** 378, **74.** 34 [OE *herȝian*]
Heryot unknown Scotch poet **62.** 54
hes. See **haif**
hest *n.* haste, urgency **37.** 30; **hestely** *adv.* **50.** 45, **67.** 10 [ME; OF *haste*]
hete *n.* heat **10.** 18, **14.** 222; **heit** heating, roasting **52.** 77 [OE *hǣtu*]
hett *adj.* heated, hot **52.** 62 [OE *hǣtan, hǣtte*]
***heve** *v.* lift, hold up **23.** 333 [ME; OE *hebban, hōf*]
hevely *adv.* greatly, sadly **53.** 6 [OE *hefiȝlīce*]
hevin, hev(e)yn(e), heavin *n.* the sky **14.** 32, *pl.* **1.** 2; the habitation of God **1.** 49, **1.** 54, **2.** 25; **10.** 26, **10.** 66, **16.** 76, **45.** 6, **51.** 100; *gen.* **6.** 100, **7.** 8, **10.** 8; **hevynnis** *pl.* **50.** 56 [OE *heofon*]
hevinlie, hevinly, hevynly *adj.* celestial, divine, splendid **1.** 7, **1.** 11, **2.** 38, **3.** 14, **10.** 132, **14.** 11, **16.** 11, **18.** 13 [OE *heofonlic*]
hevy, havie, havy(e) *adj.* weighty, burdensome, severe **5.** 57, **14.** 165, **29.** 11, **53.** 4, **69.** 7 [OE *hefiȝ*]
hevynes(se), he(a)vines, havines, hivines *n.* misery, dejection, depression **10.** 227, **51.** 19, **51.** 35, **57.** 7, **59.** 26 [OE *hefiȝnes*]
hevynnis. See **hevin**
hew *n.* hue, colour **8.** 7, **10.** 89, **12.** 30; *pl.* **14.** 20, **14.** 32, **14.** 243; **hewit, hewd** *ppl. adj.* **14.** 11, **23.** 171 [OE *hīew*]
hewand *pres. p.* cutting wood **44.** 14 [OE *hēawan*]

heyd. See **heid**

heynd(e). See **hend(e)**

hicht *n.* height **1.** 49, **14.** 4; **on hicht, upoun hicht,** *adv. phr.* **1.** 34, **2.** 25, **4.** 20, **4.** 25, **10.** 34, **10.** 276; **unto the hicht** on high **53.** 16 [var. of *hechte*; OE *hēahþu*]

hiddill *n.* concealment **38.** 53 [ME; OE *hȳdels*]

hiddir *adv.* hither, to this place **22.** 84 [OE *hider*]

hiddous, hiddow(u)s, hiddowis, hoddous *adj.* hideous **4.** 5, **6.** 100, **12.** 30, **14.** 101, **22.** 94, **23.** 164, **28.** 18, **37.** 57, **54.** 126 [OF *hidos*]

hiddy giddy *adv.* topsy-turvy **54.** 44 (see Commentary) ['a riming jingle' (*DOST*)]

hie *v.* raise, exalt **14.** 378 [eME *heie*]

hie, he, hy(e) *adj.* high **2.** 38, **2.** 63, **2.** 75, **43.** 18, **63.** 27; great, noble **14.** 310, **14.** 464, **18.** 19; exalted **6.** 43; loud **14.** 12, **23.** 139; vigorous **74.** 50; *adv. phr.* **on h(i)e 3.** 78, **56.** 78; **he** *adv.* **48.** 5; *sup.* **heast** highest **42.** 27 [OE *hēa*]

hienes. See **henes**

Hilhous Sir John Sandilands of Hillhouse **23.** 241, ***23.** 515

him *refl. pron.* himself **4.** 20 [OE]

hindir, hinder *adj.* recent, the other (night, day) **13.** 1, **37.** 1, **51.** 1, **81.** 1 [ME; ON *endr*]

hing, hyng *v.* hang (down) **10.** 17, **48.** 43; **hingis** *3 pl.* **23.** 104, **23.** 213; **hingand** *pres. p.* **23.** 226; **hang** *pa. t.* **52.** 20, **54.** 82; **hingit** *ppl. adj.* hanged **23.** 175 [ME; ON *hengja*]

hint *n.* grip, clutch **54.** 88 [OE v. *hentan*]

hippis *n. pl.* hips, buttocks **23.** 99, **23.** 110, **23.** 200, **28.** 18, **28.** 38, **33.** 23, **45.** 55, **54.** 44 [OE *hype*]

hippit *ppl. adj.* furnished with hips **23.** 179 [prec.]

hir *pron.* her **3.** 7, **6.** 149, **9.** 2, **13.** 57; *poss. adj.* **10.** 17, **14.** 7; *reflex.* herself **10.** 226 [OE *hire*]

hirklis. See **hurkland**

hirpland *ppl. adj.* limping **23.** 179 [origin obscure]

hivines. See **hevynes(se)**

hobbell *n.* part of a shoe **52.** 125 [origin uncertain; cf. next]

hobland *pres. p.* jogging clumsily along **23.** 212 [ME; MDu *hobbelen*]

hoddous. See **hiddous**

hodiern *adj.* hodiernal, of the present day **2.** 5 [L *hodiernus; hodie*]

hog *n.* yearling sheep, not yet shorn **29.** 7 [nth. ME]

hogeart *n.* ? tired-out old man **14.** 272 [? MF *hachart;* cf. mod. Sc *haggart* old horse; *hag* to fatigue]

hoip. See **houp**

holkand *ppl. adj.* piercing, digging **23.** 186; **holkit** *ppl. adj.* hollowed out **23.** 164 [nth. ME; MLG *holken*]

***holl** *n.* ship's hold **23.** 458; **hollis** *pl.* apertures **37.** 48 [OE *holl*]

Holland 23. 94

Holland, Sir Richard, Scotch poet **62.** 61

holsum *adj.* wholesome, salubrious **50.** 32 [midl. ME; cf. **hal(e)sum**]

holyn(e) *n.* holly tree **14.** 11, **38.** 64 [OE *holeȝn*]

homecyd *n.* manslayer **54.** 33 [ME; OF; L *homicida*]

homege *n.* formal declaration of allegiance **50.** 117 [ME; OF *hommage*]

hommiltye jommeltye *adj.* awkward **28.** 16 [imit.]

honest *adj.* worthy, honourable **10.** 166 [OF; L *honestus*]

honestie, honesty *n.* virtue, goodness **22.** 37, **71.** 72, **79.** 43 [ME; OF; L *honestas*]

honorabilly *adv.* in an honourable way **48.** 21 [ME; OF *honorable;* L]

honoris *n. pl.* position of eminence **14.** 378 [ME; OF; L *honor*]

hony. See **huny**

honygukkis *n.* sweet idiot **13.** 39 [see **huny, gukkis**]

***hoo** *n.* halt, pause **23.** 491 [ME; OF *ho* stop!]

hoppet *pa. t.* bounded, capered **28.** 25 [OE *hoppian*]

hoppir *n.* hopper in a mill; *attrib.* shaped like a hopper **45.** 55 [ME; OE v. *hoppian*]

hopschackellt *ppl. adj.* hobbled **28.** 12 [origin obscure]

hore *n.* hoariness **2.** 59 [var. of **hair(e)** adj.; ME; OE *hār*]

horne *n.* animal horn **23.** 212, wind instrument **50.** 34; *pl.* **50.** 110 [OE *horn*]

hornit howle *n.* long-eared owl (*asio otus*) **54.** 74 [prec.+ME *howle*]

horreble *adj.* dreadful, frightful **53.** 26, **63.** 69 [ME; L *horribilis*]

hors *n.* horse **23.** 209, **52.** 80, **68.** 9; *fig.* **43.** 9; **hors** *pl.* **43.** 11 [OE]

hos *n. coll.* pair of hose, worn by men and boys on loins and legs **23.** 200 [ME; ON *hosa*]

hospitall *n.* hospice, lodging **2.** 77 [OF; med. L *hospitale*]

hostit *pa. t.* coughed **14.** 272; **hostand** *ppl. adj.* **23.** 200 [nth. ME; ON *hōsta*]

houp, hoip, howp *n.* hope, expectation **9.** 41, **19.** 8, **39.** 97, **42.** 82, **69.** 22, **73.** 29; *pers.* source of desire **13.** 3 [OE (*tō-*)*hopa*]

houp *v.* expect, intend, mean **9.** 56 [OE *hopian*]

houre *n.* hour; *as pl.* **6.** 51, **61.** 22; **houris, howris** *pl.* times **50.** 161, services said or sung at the canonical hours **10.** 10, **50.** 5 [ME, OF; L *hora*]

hous *n.* cloth covering a horse's back and flanks **43.** 65 [ME *howse;* OF *huche*]

hous *n.* dwelling **3.** 119, **3.** 127, **37.** 53, **50.** 21, **55.** 49, **63.** 67; *attrib.* household **81.** 33; **howses** *pl.* **32.** 27 [OE, ON *hūs*]

houshaldis *n. pl.* families **68.** 13 [nth. ME; cf. MDu *huysholt*]

housit *pp.* provided with shelter **43.** 6; ***hows** *infin.* **43.** 73 [ME; OE *hūsian*]

howbeit *conj.* although **23.** 6 [ME]

howis *n. pl.* houghs (pl. of *hoch*) **23.** 190 [ME *hough*]

howlat *n.* owl **23.** 219 [ME; F]. See **hornit howle**

howp. See **houp**

howphyn *n.* clumsy, stupid fellow (mod. Sc *howffin*) **13.** 24 [origin obscure]

howses. See **hous**

hud pykis. See **huidpyk**

huddroun *n.* heifer; **belly huddroun** big-bellied glutton **13.** 38, **52.** 70 [origin unknown]

hudit crawis *n. pl.* hooded or grey crows (*corvus cornix*) **54.** 71 [ME *hodid* (OE *hōd*); **crawis**]

huge *adj.* great; *adv.* greatly **14.** 334, **14.** 345; **hugeast** *sup.* **14.** 168 [ME; OF *ahuge*]

huidpyk *n.* miser **79.** 23; **hud pykis** *pl.* **52.** 59 [app. OE *hōd* (hood)+ ME *pyken*; cf. **purspyk;** allusion obscure]

hukebanis *n. pl.* hucklebones **23.** 181 [ME *hoke bone*]

humile, humill, hummle, humyll *adj.* humble, lowly **2.** 48, **6.** 4, **5.** 48, **65.** 3; **humelie** *adj.* **51.** 107; **humly, humblie** *adv.* **1.** 20, **51.** 69 [L *humilis*]

humilite *n.* humility **50.** 116 [ME, F; L *humilitas*]

hummellis *n. pl.* (obscure; but see Commentary) **45.** 18 [origin obscure]

hummle. See **humile**

hund *n.* hound, dog **14.** 273 [OE]

hundreth, hundrithe, hunder, hundir *num. adj.* hundred **10.** 58, **12.** 18, **14.** 465, **23.** 93, **27.** 22, **52.** 134, **54.** 103 [ON *hundrað*]

hungert *ppl. adj.* starved **23.** 168 [ON *hungraðr*, v. *hungra*]

huntaris *n. pl.* scroungers in the dining hall **44.** 46 [ME; OE *huntian*]

huny, hunny, hony *n.* honey **13.** 15; sweetheart **13.** 3, **14.** 223; *attrib.* **10.** 106, **13.** 30, **75.** 39 [OE *huniȝ*]

hunyt *ppl. adj.* honeyed *fig.* **66.** 17 [ME; OE *huniȝ*]

hur, hure *n.* whore **63.** 58; **hur maister** a frequenter of whores **14.** 168 (see Commentary) [OE *hōre*, ON *hōra*]

hurcheoun *n.* hedgehog **23.** 179; **hurcheone** *attrib.* **14.** 107 [ME; ONF *herichon*]

hurdaris *n. pl.* hoarders of money **52.** 59 [OE *hordian*]

hure. See **hur**
hurkland *ppl. adj.* drawn close together **23.** 186; **hirklis** *3 pl.* crouch together **23.** 181 [ME *hurkel*]
hurle *n.* violent rush; **13.** 38 (see Commentary); **hurle behind** diarrhoea **23.** 194 [origin uncertain]
hurlit *pa. t.* pushed violently **3.** 20 [nth. ME; origin uncertain]
***hursone** *n.* son of a whore **23.** 359 [ME *hores sone;* see **hur**]
hurtis *3 sg.* harms, injures **14.** 269, **78.** 16; **hurt** *pp.* **50.** 143 [ME; OF *hurter* knock together]
hurtmanis *n. gen.* sick man's **54.** 35 [ME, OF *hurte* stroke]
husband *n. correlative of* **wif, 14.** 441; **husbandis** *gen.* **14.** 436, *pl.* **14.** 452; *pl.* farmers **68.** 21 [ON *hūsbōndi*]
hutit *ppl. adj.* hooted at, mocked **14.** 465 [ME]
hy. See **hie**
***hyar**. See **hie**
hyd *n.* skin **3.** 59, **23.** 186, **23.** 239, **43.** 29, **52.** 163, **54.** 35 [OE]
hyd(e) *v.* hide, protect **23.** 8, **49.** 12, **54.** 120; **hid** *pa. t.* **3.** 27 [OE *hȳdan*]
hym *pron.* him **10.** 205, **10.** 206 [OE]
hyn(e) *adv.* from here **23.** 93, **26.** 6, **61.** 6; from there **10.** 233, **54.** 20 [ON *heðan;* vowel assim. to **syne**]
hynting *vbl. n.* getting **23.** 8 [OE *hentan*]

idilnes *n.* idleness, indolence **6.** 110 [OE]
iersche. See **ersch(e)**
ile, yle *n.* island (Britain) **10.** 269, **39.** 62 (see Commentary); **ilis, ylis** *pl.* (Western Isles) **34.** 17, **39.** 71 [OF]
ilk *adj.* same **14.** 235, **75.** 27 [OE *ilca*]
ilk(a) *adj.* each, every **14.** 61, **14.** 206, **23.** 53, **38.** 39, **54.** 82 [OE (Mercian) *ylc*]
ilk. See **everrilk**
illumynit *pa. t.* shone **50.** 21, **50.** 157; *pp. and ppl. adj.* **10.** 258, **50.** 41; **illumynate** *pp.* made bright **10.** 266; **ellummynit** *ppl. adj.* **14.** 425 [F *illuminer;* L *illumenare, illuminatus*]
***illusion** *n.* deceit **23.** 262 [ME, F; L *illusio*]
illustare, illuster *adj.* illustrious, renowned **36.** 1, **50.** 150 [F; L *illustris*]
illwillie *adj.* bearing ill-will, malevolent **13.** 32 [cf. ON *illvili*]
imbrace *v.* embrace, clasp **37.** 5 [ME; OF *embracer*]
imperatrice *n.* empress **2.** 61 [16th-cent. F; L *imperatrix*]
imperfyte *adj.* incomplete, defective **10.** 267 [ME; cf. L *imperfectus*]
imperiall, imperiale, imperyalle *adj.* highest, empyrean **1.** 49; excellent **2.** 73, **10.** 254, **24.** 6, **31.** 5, **50.** 168 [ME; med. L *empyreus*]
implore *v.* entreat **2.** 55 [L *implorare*]
imprent *v.* keep in mind **17.** 19, remain fixed **66.** 28 [ME]
impyre *n.* empire, dominion **53.** 37 [ME, OF *empire*]
in *prep.* into **14.** 229, on **14.** 331, **23.** 156, **23.** 226; **in till** during, in **10.** 9, **52.** 3; at **6.** 107; **in to, into** in **1.** 15, **3.** 26, **9.** 76, **10.** 11, **10.** 49; during **5.** 65; unto **45.** 70 [OE]
inclinacioune *n.* disposition **35.** 34 [L *inclinatio*]
inclois *v.* surround, confine **50.** 156 [ME, OF *enclose*]
include *v.* enclose, contain **2.** 78 [L *includere*]
incluse *v.* close up **12.** 46 [L *includere, inclusum*]
inclyne *v.* bend, bow **1.** 25, **3.** 6, **50.** 90; **inclynnand** *pres. p.* **50.** 77; **inclynning** *vbl. n.* inclination **16.** 52 [OF; L *inclinare*]
inconstance *n.* inconstancy **15.** 5 [ME, OF; L *inconstantia*]
incontricioun *n.* lack of contrition **6.** 91 [eccles. L]
incres *n.* increase **23.** 21 [ME; L *increscere*]
incres *v.* increase **17.** 10, **49.** 38, **52.** 99, **75.** 50; **incress** *3 sg.* **50.** 26; **incressing** *pres. p.* raising,

enlarging **11.** 8, **11.** 16, **11.** 24 [as prec.]

incubus, incuby *n.* **10.** 125 (see Commentary), **38.** 3 [L]

indeficient *adj.* unfailing **35.** 25 [L *indeficiens*]

indeflore *adj.* undeflowered, virgin **2.** 55 [OF; L *deflorare*]

indigence *n.* lack, poverty **66.** 2 [ME, OF; L *indigentia*]

indoce *v.* endorse **4.** 7; **indorsit, indo(i)st** *pp.* **9.** 103, **26.** 15, ***43.** 75, **71.** 65 [ME; OF *endosser*; med. L *indorsare* write on the back]

***induellar** *n.* resident **23.** 551 [ME; OE *dwellan*]

indure *v.* last, survive **15.** 12, **61.** 43, **63.** 8, **63.** 33; suffer, bear **12.** 34, **51.** 70; **induris** *pl.* **45.** 10 [ME; L *indurare*]

indyt(t) *v.* write **33.** 2, **50.** 26; **indyting** *vbl. n.* writing, composition **26.** 15 [ME; OF *enditer*]

infek *v.* corrupt, poison **62.** 57; **infeck** *pp.* (is) infected **53.** 30 [ME; L *inficere*, *infectum*]

infermite *n.* sickness, weakness, **62.** 3 [ME; L *infirmitas*]

inferne *adj.* infernal **2.** 7 [L *infernus*]

infineit *adj.* infinite, unending **57.** 6 [ME; L *infinitus*]

Ingland *n.* England **39.** 18

ingle *n.* fire burning on the hearth **23.** 117 [Gael *aingeal*]

Inglis, Inglisch *adj. and n.* English; the vernacular language of lowland Scotland and of England **10.** 259, **23.** 111 [nth. ME; OE *englisc*]

ingyne *n.* talent, ingenuity **48.** 60 [ME; L *ingenium*]

ingynouris *n. pl.* inventors, contrivers; alchemists **44.** 55 [ME; prec.]

inhibitioun *n.* formal prohibition **50.** 64 [ME, OF; L *inhibitio*]

injur(e) *n.* injustice, offence **63.** 18, **65.** 38; *pl.* **26.** 1, **45.** 9 [OF *injure*]

inlaik *n.* deficiency, shortcoming **56.** 49 [ME *lake;* see **laik**]

innis *n. pl.* house, residence **30.** 13 [OE *inn*]

innocent *adj.* free from guilt, harmless **6.** 158, **14.** 252; **innocentis** *n. pl.* **14.** 267 [ME; OF; L *innocens*]

inobedience *n.* disobedience **6.** 117 [OF; L *inobedientia*]

inoportunitie *n.* unseasonable solicitation *pers.* **51.** 76; **78.** 23 [late L *inop(p)ortunitas*]

inopportoun *adj.* unseasonable **44.** 43 [prec.]

inpres *v.* impress, imprint **61.** 39 [ME]

inquyrit *pp.* enquired **19.** 31 [ME; OF *enquerre*]

***insensuate** *adj.* senseless **23.** 321 [late L *insensatus*]

inspir, inspyr *v.* inspire, vitalize, influence **14.** 247, **39.** 93; **inspirit** *pp.* **31.** 31 [ME; L *inspirare*]

instrument *n.* weapon of war **10.** 148; musical instrument **51.** 22, *pl.* **51.** 9 [OF; L *instrumentum*]

intencioun *n.* disposition, spirit **35.** 36 [ME; OF *entenciun*]

intent. See **entent**

intercessioun *n.* prayer, entreaty **36.** 26, **74.** 54 [L *intercessio*]

inthrang *pa. t.* pushed in **14.** 13 [*in*+OE *þringan*, *þrang*]

into. See **in to**

intollerabill *adj.* unbearable **12.** 22 [L *intolerabilis*]

invencionis *n. pl.* fabrications, fictions **6.** 125 [OF; L *inventio*]

invy *n.* envy, one of the seven deadly sins **6.** 19, **9.** 95, **16.** 69, **52.** 43, **74.** 16, **77.** 29, **82.** 37 [L *invidia*]

invy *v.* envy **77.** 2 [ME *envye*; med. L *invidiare*]

inwart *adj.* heartfelt, fervent **35.** 37 [OE *innanweard*]

ire, yre *n.* wrath, one of the seven deadly sins **3.** 20, **6.** 19, **50.** 119; *pers.* **52.** 31 [OF; L *ira*]

irische. See **ersch(e)**

irke *v.* grow weary, tire **5.** 69 [eME; origin uncertain]

irke *adj.* weary **2.** 36 [cf. prec.]

irne *adj.* iron **3.** 69 [OE *iren*]

***irregular** *adj.* lawless **23.** 36 [ME; OF; L *irregularis*]

is *v.* are **14.** 97. See **be**

ische *v.* issue, pour **44.** 85 [ME *issh*]

ja *n.* jay (*garrulus glandarius*) **54.** 97 (see Commentary) [ME, OF *jay*]
jaipit *pp.* seduced **81.** 19 [ME; origin obscure]
jakkis *n. pl.* padded leather jerkins **52.** 37 [ME; OF *jaque*]
jalous *adj.* envious, resentful **9.** 94 [ME; OF]
James IV king of Scots **35.** *title*
janglar, jangler *n.* gossip, detractor **17.** 70; **ȝeangleiris** *pl.* **9.** 94; *pl.* **37.** 44, **79.** 44 [ME; OF *jangleor*]
Janus *n.* Roman deity of gates and doors **10.** 120
Jeill S. Giles (Aegidius) **22.** 59 (see Commentary)
jelosy, jelusy *n.* **14.** 121, **17.** 43 [ME; OF *jelousie*]
jemis *n. pl.* gems **50.** 153 [ME; cf. **geme**]
Jerusalem *n.* place of the Crucifixion **75.** 74
Jesu(s) *n.* **3.** 93, **5.** 3, **6.** 1, **6.** 23, **6.** 59, **6.** 143; **Jhesu 2.** 44, **2.** 64, **51.** 15
jevellis *n. pl.* ruffians **45.** 15 [ME; origin obscure]
jevellouris *n. pl.* jailers **4.** 34 [cf. OF *jaioleur*]
Jhesu. See **Jesu(s)**
jocound *adj.* cheerful, gay **51.** 71 [ME; OF; L *jucundus*]
Johnestoun, Patrik Scotch poet **62.** 71
Johnis ene, Sanct 23. 124 (see Commentary)
Johnne the reif hero of a popular tale **42.** 33
jolie, joly *adj.* gay, merry **14.** 69; presumptuous, conceited **6.** 113, **44.** 55 [eME; OF *jolif*]
jolyus *adj.* jealous, suspicious **14.** 452 [ME, OF *jelous*]
Jonet the weido 53. 34
josit *pa. t.* possessed, had **14.** 201 [var. of *jois;* OF *joir, joiss-*]
Joun *n.* the month of June **75.** 30 [ME; L *Junius*]
journay *n.* day's travel **69.** 30 [ME; OF *journee*]
Jow *n.* Jew **3.** 9, *pl.* **3.** 111, **4.** 31; **jow** *n. and adj.* infidel **45.** 15, **54.** 31 [ME]
jowell *n.* precious ornament **14.** 140 [ME; OF *jouel*]
jowrdane. See **jurdane**
joyfull *adj.* rejoicing **10.** 245 [ME; OF *joie*]
joyis *3 pl.* enjoy, possess with enjoyment **14.** 61 [ME; OF *joir*]
joyus *adj.* gay, joyful, giving joy **14.** 69 [ME; OF *joieus*]
Judas Iscariot **3.** 9, ***23.** 506, ***23.** 524
juffler *n.* clumsy fellow **28.** 16 [? imit.]
juge *n.* judge **3.** 17, **6.** 71, **9.** 77, **63.** 53, **65.** 36 [OF]
jugement *n.* the last judgement **6.** 62; **juging** *vbl. n.* **6.** 131 [OF]
jugit *pp.* judged **82.** 46 [ME; OF *jugier*]
***juglour** *n.* conjurer; wizard **23.** 524 [ME; OF *jouglere*]
Julius Gaius Julius Caesar (d. 44 B.C.) **35.** 17, **35.** 62
Juno *n.* Roman deity; daughter of Saturn and wife of Jupiter **10.** 75 (see Commentary), **50.** 69
jupert *n.* feat of arms, valour **35.** 62 [ME *jeupardy*; OF *ju parti* 'even game' (chess)]
jurdane *n.* chamber-pot; (abusive) **27.** 38; **jowrdane** *attrib.* **45.** 15 [ME; med. L *jurdanus*]
jure *n.* law, jurisprudence **44.** 4, **76.** 3 [L *jus, juris*]
justice court *n.* court of justice **6.** 163 [OF; L *justitia*]
justing *n.* jousting, tilting **27.** 32, **52.** 226 [ME; OF *jouster*]
jyane. See **ȝyane**

kaill *n.* cabbage (soup); broth **13.** 9 [ON *kāl*]
kairis. See **cair**
Kalice Calais **55.** 34
karlingis. See **carlingis**
Karrik. See **Carrik**
kast. See **cast**
katherene, catherein *n.* cateran, highland reiver **23.** 145, **27.** 13 [med. L *katheranus*; Gael *ceatharn*]
***Katryne** a ship **23.** 449 (see Commentary)
kayis. See **caa**
keik (to) *v.* glance (at), look about **14.** 81, **14.** 125, **14.** 434 [ME]

***keild** *pp.* killed, slain **23.** 271 [ME; var. of *kill*]

kein. See **kene**

keip(e), kepe *v.* keep, guard **3.** 130, **14.** 118, **14.** 369, **23.** 221; observe **6.** 83, **11.** 7; preserve **5.** 67, **19.** 18; **ke(i)pit** *pa. t.* held, kept to **9.** 58, **47.** 13 [OE *cēpan*]

keist. See **cast**

***kelde** *ppl. adj.* ? **23.** 431 (see Commentary)

kell *n.* caul, close-fitting netted cap **10.** 60 [ME]

kemm *v.* comb **14.** 275; **kemd, kemmit** *ppl. adj.* combed **13.** 8, **14.** 21; **kemmyng** *vbl. n.* combing **14.** 182 [OE *cemban*]

ken *v.* make known, know **71.** 10; come to know (himself) **14.** 318; *3 sg.* **5.** 52, **14.** 454, **27.** 18, is given to **14.** 356; *3 pl.* acknowledge, respect **44.** 48; **kend** *pp.* imparted, made known **5.** 14, **54.** 13; **kend with** known by **14.** 409; **kend** *ppl. adj.* familiar **71.** 3 (double entendre; see Commentary) [OE *cęnnan*]

kene, kein, keyn(e) *adj.* fierce, savage, piercing **3.** 42, **4.** 11, **8.** 11, **10.** 199, **10.** 137, **14.** 260, **14.** 354, **27.** 4, **35.** 3 [OE *cēne*]

Kennedy, Andro 38

Kennedy, Kennedie, Walter, Scotch poet **23** *passim*, **62.** 89

kennis. See **ken**

kenrik *n.* kingdom **14.** 216; **kinrikis** *pl.* **23.** 24 [OE *cynerīce*]

kenseis *n.pl.* ? rascals **45.** 16 [origin obscure]

kepair *n.* keeper **29.** *colophon* [ME; see **keip**]

keping *n.* guard, watching, holding **35.** *title*, **65.** 28 [as prec.]

kepit. See **keip**

keppis *3 sg.* catches (something falling) *fig.* **74.** 30 [nth. ME var. of **keip**]

kerffis *3 pl.* carve, serve as carvers at table **14.** 484; **kervit** *pa. t.* carved, shaped **31.** 18 [OE *ceorfan*]

kers *n.* the cress plant, 'type of something of negligible significance' (DOST) **23.** 129 [OE *cerse*]

kersp. See **kirsp**

kervit. See **kerffis**

***kest.** See **cast**

kest *pa. t.* cast, threw **3.** 108, **3.** 124, **9.** 25, **10.** 39, **10.** 203, **14.** 355 [ME; ON *kasta*]

kethat *n.* ? overgarment, cloak **52.** 21 [origin obscure]

kevellis *n. pl.* rogues **45.** 16 [ME; origin obscure]

kewis *n. pl.* cues **79.** 51 (see Commentary) [origin uncertain]

keyne. See **kene**

kewt *ppl. adj.* trimmed, polled **14.** 275 [nth. ME *coll* cut hair]

kiddis *n. pl.* young goats **23.** 151 [ME; ON *kið*]

kill *n.* kiln, fire for drying grain in making malt **56.** 49, **56.** 52 [ME *cylene*]

kindill *v.* arouse, stir up **14.** 522; **kyndillis** *3 sg.* is aroused **14.** 94; **kindilland** *ppl. adj.* kindling **17.** 2 [ME; ON *kynda*]

kindly *adj.* innate, natural **14.** 456 [OE *gecyndelīc*]

kinrick(is). See **kenrik**

kirk *n.* the Catholic church **6.** 66, **6.** 81, **39.** 45; parish church **1.** 30, **6.** 84, **14.** 81, **14.** 152, **14.** 306, **14.** 422; *pl.* **42.** 67, **51.** 88 [ME; ON *kirkja*]

kirkmen *n. pl.* churchmen, clergy **39.** 41, **44.** 3; **kirkmenes** *poss.* **51.** 94 [prec.]

kirsp, kersp *n.* fine fabric, gauze **14.** 23, **14.** 138 [metathetic var. of *crisp;* ME; med. L *crispum*]

Kirtillis *n. pl.* close gowns, dresses **10.** 60 [ON *kyrtill*]

kis, kys *v.* kiss **14.** 278, **23.** 131, **33.** 18, **37.** 33; *3 sg.* **14.** 94; *3 pl.* **14.** 483; **kist** *pa. t.* **13.** 11 [OE *cyssan*, ON *kyssa*]

kist *n.* chest **69.** 42 [ME; ON *kista* corr. to OE *cyst*, L *cista*]

kith *n.* country, nation **14.** 64 [OE *cyðð*]

***knaif, kneff** *n.* rogue, rascal **23.** 254, **27.** 43; **knaiffis, knavis** *pl.* **52C.** 39, **79.** 53 [OE *cnafa*]

knaip *n.* manservant, groom **14.** 125 [OE *cnapa*]

knaleging *vbl. n.* erudition **76.** 18 [nth. ME v. *knawlege*]

knapparis *n. pl.* biters, snappers **52.** 130 [echoic; cf. LG *knappen* snap]

knavis. See **knaif**

knaw *v.* know, confess, acknowledge, recognize **6.** 55, **6.** 105, **6.** 140, **10.** 274; **knawih** *pp.* **14.** 409, confessed **5.** 14, ill-reputed **26.** 6 [OE *ȝecnāwan*]

knawlege *n.* intelligence, understanding **14.** 300, **14.** 455 [ME; origin uncertain]

kne *n.* knee **14.** 424, **28.** 12, **42.** 61, **50.** 100; **kneis** *pl.* **12.** 20, **23.** 184 [OE *cnēo;* ON *knē*]

kneff. See **knaif**

kneling *pres. p.* kneeling **3.** 3 [OE *cnēowlian*]

knightheyd, knightheid, knychtheid *n.* knighthood, knightly prowess **35.** 18, **35.** 82, **36.** 19, **52.** 176, **52.** 212 [ME; OE *cnihthād* boyhood]

knitchell *n.* small bundle **42.** 72 [OE *ȝecnycce*]

knop *n.* bud **31.** 26; *pl.* **10.** 22 [ME; cf. OFris *knop*]

knowll *n.* swollen toe *attrib.* **52C.** 19 [cf. OSw *knula*, Da dial. *knūl*]

knycht *n.* knight, gentleman, warrior **27.** 1, **52.** 142; *pl.* **14.** 216, **14.** 435, **14.** 476, **16.** 83, **22.** 15, **44.** 7, **62.** 21 [OE *cniht*]

knycht(heid). See **knycht, knightheyd**

knychtlie. See **knyghtli(e)**

knyfe *n.* knife **23.** 72, **52.** 32, **56.** 67; **knyvis** *pl.* **52.** 42 [OE *cnīf*, ON *knīfr*]

knyghtli(e) *adj.* knightly, valiant **33.** 22, **35.** 59, **35.** 94; **knychtly** *adv.* **52.** 180 [OE *cnihtlīc*]

knyp *v.* crop grass, graze **43.** 57 [cf. LG and Du *knippen* clip]

knyt *pa. t.* joined, coupled **14.** 215 [OE *cnyttan*]

kokenis *n. pl.* rogues **44.** 48 [OF *coquin*]

koy *n.* quey, young cow **23.** 142 [ME; ON *kviga*]

krych *v.* scratch **14.** 275 (see Commentary)

kuckald. See **cukkald**

kuke *n.* cook **54.** 68 [ME *kok*; OE *cōc*]

ky *n.* cows (pl. of *kow*) **83.** 3 [OE *cū*, pl. *cȳ*]

kyind, kynd *adj.* affectionate, fond **14.** 278, **14.** 434, **65.** 3, **82.** 16; native, natural **42.** 24 [OE *ȝecynde*]

***Kyle** in Ayrshire **23.** 284

kyn(e) *n.* relatives, kinsfolk **14.** 214, **14.** 521, **38.** 51, **42.** 33 [OE *cynn*]

kynd *n.* nature, human character **14.** 58, **16.** 37, **17.** 75, **23.** 50, **34.** 32, **45.** 22, **66.** 9; sort **3.** 63, **42.** 11, **44.** 43, **50.** 114 [OE *ȝecynde*]

kynd. See **kyind**

kyndillis. See **kindill**

kyndnes *n.* affection, love **14.** 459, **14.** 483; nature **17.** 16; generosity **47.** 2, **52C.** 33 [OE *ȝecynde*]

kyng *n.* king **35.** *title*; *gen.* **14.** 82; *pl.* **35.** 3 [OE *cyning*]

kys. See **kis**

kyth(e) *v.* show, declare **63.** 2, **82.** 9; *3 sg.* displays **14.** 433; *2 pl.* **52C.** 37; **kythit** *pp.* revealed, expressed **16.** 46 [OE *cȳðan*]

lachtter, lawchtir *n.* laughter **28.** 39, **52.** 222, **54.** 38 [OE *hleahtor*]

lad, lawd *n.* serving-man, menial **14.** 381, **43.** 48; **ladis** *pl.* **26.** 27; **laidis** *pl.* boys **23.** 203, **23.** 227 [ME; origin obscure]

ladie, lady(e) *n.* consort of a gentleman, mistress **12.** 8, **12.** 49, **33.** 5, **62.** 31; **ladeis** *gen.* lady's **9.** 16, **9.** 40, **9.** 86, **16.** 58; *pl.* **ladeis, ladyes, ladyis** **10.** 58, **10.** 91, **14.** 17, **14.** 191, **16.** 50, **51.** 26, **71.** 1 [ME; OE *hlǣfdīȝe*]

laeffe. See **laif**

laid *pa. t.* set aside, abandoned **14.** 352; **laid doun** *pp.* set aside **68.** 13 [OE *lecgean*, *leȝde*]

laidis. See **lad**

laif(f), laeffe *n.* remainder, rest **5.** 23, **14.** 395, **20.** 21, **28.** 30, **38.** 92, **44.** 25, **50.** 133; others **14.** 506 [OE *lāf*]

laik *n.* lack, want **12.** 27, **69.** 10, **75.** 3 [ME; cf. MLG, MDu *laken* to be wanting]

laip *v.* lap, drink greedily **52.** 101 [OE *lapian*]

lair *n.* branch of learning, 'subject' **76.** 4 [OE *lār*]
laird *n.* lord, baron **68.** 14; *pl.* **40.** 13, **68.** 29, **71.** 31 [OE *hlāford*]
lait *adv.* late in the day **3.** 132, **20.** 8, **60.** 5, **81.** 19, lately **37.** 3 [OE *late*]
laith *n.* ill-will, hatred **38.** 28 [OE *lāð*]
laith, layth *adj.* reluctant, unwilling **11.** 6, **14.** 308, **14.** 387, **23.** 17, **63.** 49 [OE *lāð*]
la(i)thly *adj.* loathsome, horrible **23.** 102, **23.** 154, **23.** 161, **23.** 182, **52.** 79 [OE *lāðlic*]
laitlie, laitly *adv.* recently, not long ago **21.** 6, **74.** 6 [OE adj. *latu*]
lait(t)is, latis *n. pl.* manners, behaviour **14.** 37, **14.** 147, **23.** 132, **50.** 118, **52.** 166 [ON *lāt*; in pl. manners]
lak *n.* lack, want (of) **63.** 13, disparagement **72.** 11, **72.** 22 [ME; cf. MLG *lak*]
lak *v.* lack, want **14.** 67; **lakkis** *3 sg.* disparages **72.** 6; **lakit** *pa. t.* lacked, were without **9.** 77 [ME; see **laik**]
lam(e) *n.* lamb **30.** 4, **37.** 3; **lammis** *pl.* **32.** 17; **lambis** *gen.* lamb's **14.** 423 [OE *lamb*]
lampis *n. pl.* lamps **76.** 20; *gen. pl.* **51.** 6 [ME, OF *lampe*]
land *n.* holding of burgage land; *pl.* tenements **14.** 338 (see Commentary) [OE]
landis *3 pl.* land, disembark **10.** 57; **landet** *pa. t.* **33.** 3; **landit** *pp.* endowed with lands **42.** 76 [ME; OE n. *land*]
landwart, to *adv. phr.* in the country **68.** 17 [cf. late ME *landward*; MDu *te landewært*]
lang *adj.* long **14.** 77, **14.** 341, **23.** 169, **37.** 17, **39.** 14 (see **large**) [OE]
lang(e) *adv.* long (in time) **4.** 12, **9.** 6, **13.** 4, **14.** 149, **14.** 343, **51.** 45 [OE *lange*]
langage *n.* language, vernacular **10.** 266; speech, talk **11.** 15, **14.** 445 [F]
langar *comp. adj., adv.* longer **3.** 66, **14.** 348, **38.** 93, **54.** 87 [see **lang**]
langit *pa. t.* belonged **14.** 407 [nth. ME; aphetic f. OE adj. *ʒelang* (*on*) belonging to]
langit (eftir) *pa. t.* longed, yearned (for) **53.** 5 [OE *langian*]
langour, langar *n.* dispirited indifference, misery, wretchedness **9.** 33, **9.** 84, **19.** 7, **49.** 8, **51.** 45, **66.** 28 [OF; med. L *langor*]
languissing *vbl. n.* pining, sorrow **2.** 23 [ME; OF *languir, languiss-*]
lanis *3 sg.* conceals, keeps secret **9.** 95 [ME; ON *leyna*]
lap. See **leip**
lapidaris *n. pl.* jewellers, artificers in precious stones **44.** 15 [OF; L *lapidarius*]
larbar *n.* exhausted, impotent man **14.** 133; *pl.* **14.** 67; *adj.* impotent **14.** 175, **23.** 121, **23.** 169 [origin obscure]
***lard.** See **laird**
large, lerge *adj.* ample, wide **14.** 166; generous, lavish **11.** 19 (see Commentary), **79.** 26; **large and lang** massive **3.** 49; *adv.* abundantly, much **5.** 59; **at large** freely, unhindered **10.** 186 [OF]
larges *n.* ceremonial giving of presents **43.** 45 (see Commentary) [ME, F *largesse*]
lark, lork *n.* skylark (*alauda arvensis*) **10.** 8, **50.** 24; *pl.* **10.** 25 [reduced f. *laverok*; OE *lāferce*]
lasar. See **laser**
lascht *pa. t.* lashed, thrashed **52.** 75 [ME]
lase *n.* girl **14.** 465; **lassis** *pl.* little girls **14.** 503 [nth. ME; etymology uncertain; cf. Sw *lōsker* unmarried]
lase(i)r, lasar *n.* opportunity, respite **6.** 8, **9.** 6, **78.** 32 [nth. ME; OF *leisir*; repr. L *licere* to be permitted]
lassis. See **lase**
last, lest *adj. and adv.* last; **at the lest** **1.** 46 [OE *latost* sup. of *læt*]
lat(t) *v.* let go, liberate, allow, leave **9.** 21, **9.** 51, **14.** 308, **16.** 54, **32.** 2, **32.** 10, **42.** 60, **43.** 1, **50.** 139; **lattis** *3 pl.* **14.** 63, **23.** 200; **lettis** *1 sg.* behave as if, pretend **14.** 228; **leit, lete, lute** *pa. t.* **3.** 76, **10.**

139, **14.** 133, **14.** 289, **37.** 33, pretended, behaved as if **14.** 445; **lat be** abandon, give up **81.** 40, **81.** 45; **lat se** let's see **52.** 13, **73.** 9 [OE *lǣtan*, *lēt*; ON *lāta*, *lēt*]

lathand *adj.* disgusting **23.** 102 [cf. **laithly**]

lathit *pa. t.* detested **14.** 328 [OE *lāðian*]

lathly. See **la(i)thly**

lathlyit *pa. t.* loathed **14.** 381 [OE adj. *lāðlic*]

latis. See **lait(t)is**

lat(t) *v.* hinder, prevent **23.** 119, **69.** 44 [OE *lętten*; adj. *læt*]

latt. See **lat**

Latyne *n.* the Latin language **14.** 504 [L *Latinus*]

laubour *n.* work, toil **14.** 330 [ME, OF; L *labor*]

lauch *v.* laugh; **lauchis** *3 sg.* **14.** 417; **lauchand** *pres. p.* **14.** 240; **leuch, lewch(e), luche** *pa. t.* **14.** 147, **52.** 27, **52.** 29, **56.** 39 [OE *hlæhhan*, *hlōȝ*]

laureat(e) *adj.* worthy of the laurel crown for distinction in poetry **10.** 262, or in arms **35.** 4 [ME; L *laureatus*]

***lave** *v.* remove (liquid) with a bucket **23.** 471 [OE *lafian* pour]

law *adj. and adv.* low **3.** 118, **6.** 7, **14.** 497, **50.** 77, **53.** 17, **77.** 18 [nth. ME; ON *lāgr*]

Lawarance, S. (d. 128) **23.** 123

lawboring *pres. p.* labouring **44.** 18 [ME; F; L *laborare*]

lawchtir. See **lachtter**

lawd. See **lad**

lawd(e) *n.* praise **35.** 8 *et seq.*, **50.** 115 [ME, OF *laude*; L *laus, laudis*]

lawis *n. pl.* laws, precepts **55.** 13 [OE *laȝu*]

lawland *adj.* lowland **23.** 56 [**law**]

lawlines, lawlynes *n.* humility *pers.* **9.** 43, **10.** 163 [ME; ON adj. *lāgr*]

lawrŷ *n.* laurel **16.** 6, **35.** 67 [ME; OF *lorier*; L *laurea*]

lawte *n.* loyalty, fidelity **45.** 14 [ME; OF *leaute*]

laxatyve *n.* looseness of the bowels, flux **54.** 41 [ME, F; L *laxativus*]

lay *v.* lay down in pledge, wager, vow **9.** 23; set aside, put a stop to **23.** 96; **layis** *3 sg.* places **74.** 22; **lay ane sege unto** besiege **9.** 53; **lay out** spread, unfold **1.** 45; **layid** *pa. t.* **55.** 8 [OE *lecgan*]

layth. See **laith**

lazarus *n.* resurrected corpse **23.** 161 (see Commentary)

le, ley *v.* lie, tell untruth **14.** 308, **27.** 36, **52.** 51, **56.** 23, **leis** *2 sg.* **23.** 86; **leid** *pa. t.* **23.** 138 [OE *lēoȝan*]

lear *n.* liar **11.** 9 [OE *lēoȝere*]

lecheing. See **leiching**

lechis. See **leiche**

ledder *n.* (gallows) ladder **23.** 174, **23.** 240 [OE *hlǣdder*]

ledder *n.* leather **56.** 33 [OE *leðer*]

leding *vbl. n.* putting about, promulgating **6.** 125 [OE *lǣdan*]

lef(e), leif *n.* leaf **8.** 10, **23.** 196, *as pl.* **10.** 27; **leves lev(e)is, leiffis** *pl.* **1.** 45, **8.** 15, **10.** 15, **10.** 93, **14.** 14, **14.** 241, **16.** 114 [OE *lēaf*]

legeand *n.* biography of a saint **14.** 504; **legendis** *pl.* **55.** 26 [ME; med. L *legenda*; L *legere*]

legeis, leigis, leggis *n. pl.* loyal subjects **42.** 28, **48.** 52, **50.** 105, **75.** 64 [ME *lege*; OF *liege*]

leggis *n. pl.* legs **14.** 133, **52.** 38 [ME; ON *leggr*]

leich, leisch *n.* (dog) leash **23.** 71, lash **23.** 100; ***leichis** *pl.* lashes with a leash **23.** 45 [ME *lesh*; OF *lesse*]

leiche *n.* physician, doctor **5.** 17, **54.** 17, **81.** 34; **lechis** *pl.* **62.** 42 [OE *lǣce*]

leichecraft *n.* art of medicine, surgery **54.** 33 [OE *lǣcecræft*]

leiching *vbl. n.* medical treatment **5.** 23, **51.** 50 [OE *lǣcung*]

leid *n.* language **54.** 16 (see Commentary); ***lede** national language **23.** 346 [OE *lēoden*]

leid, le(y)d *n.* person; man **13.** 27, **14.** 283, **14.** 407, **14.** 497, **35.** 29; **led** woman **14.** 441 [OE *lēod*]

leid *n.* the metal, lead **51.** 20, **51.** 25, **52.** 101 [OE *lēad*]

leid *v.* lead, conduct **14.** 155, **23.** 113, **52.** 81; **leidis** *3 sg.* **42.** 49,

68. 15, **74.** 17; **leid** *pa. t.* **3.** 14 [OE *lǣdan*]

leid. See **le**

leif *n.* permission, licence, leave **19.** 7, **42.** 8, **42.** 73, **50.** 3 [var. of leve]

leif *v.* live **23.** 166, **42.** 39, **42.** 76, **49.** 8, **70.** 7; **leivis** *2 sg.* subsist **23.** 205, *3 pl.* **68.** 31; **levis** *3 sg.* **64.** 19, **65.** 23, **70.** 4; **leifand** *pres. p.* **42.** 82 [OE *lifian*]

leif(f), lefe, leve *v.* leave, abandon **6.** 54, **35.** 83, **38.** 18; avoid **12.** 13; bequeath **38.** 36, **38.** 41; **leves** *3 sg.* neglects **20.** 17; **levit** *pa. t.* **62.** 62 [OE *lǣfan*]

leigis. See **legeis**

leik *n.* the vegetable, leek **23.** 102 [OE *lēac*]

leill. See **lele**

leip, liep *v.* leap, caper **39.** 25, **52.** 15; **lap** *pa. t.* leapt, jumped **9.** 84, **55.** 10; **loppin** *pp.* mounted (in copulation) **14.** 387 [OE *hlēapan*]

leir, lere, leyr *v.* learn, teach **11.** 21, **14.** 257, **14.** 503, **44.** 54; **leiris** *3 sg.* **74.** 48; **lerit** *pa. t.* **14.** 318 [OE *lǣran*]

leis *n. pl.* lies, untruths **26.** 13, **27.** 24 [OE *lyȝe*]

leis. See **le**

leis me *phr.* dear is to me **13.** 28, **13.** 42, **13.** 56, **13.** 63 [contraction of *leif is*; OE *lēof*]

leisch. See **leich**

leist. See **lest**

leit. See **lat**

Leith near Edinburgh **51.** 114

lele, lell, liell *adj.* faithful **14.** 478, **39.** 13; lawful **14.** 155; **leill** *adv.* **39.** 46; **lelely** *adv.* **14.** 441 [ME; OF *leal*; L *legalis*]

leme *n.* brightness, radiance; **lemys** *n. pl.* rays of light **10.** 29, **50.** 21 [OE *lēoma*; ON *ljōme*]

leme *v.* shine, glow **10.** 30; **lemand** *ppl. adj.* **10.** 79 [prec.]

len *v.* lend **65.** 4; **lent** *pp.* bestowed (on), granted **47.** 26, **57.** 3 [OE *lǣnan*]

***lendis** *n. pl.* flanks, buttocks **23.** 45 [OE **lęnden*]

lene *adj.* lean, meagre, skinny **14.** 120, **23.** 121, **23.** 161, **23.** 182, **37.** 15, **73.** 5 [OE *hlǣne*]

lene *v.* lean, press **14.** 492, **50.** 100; **lenyt** *pa. t.* got (up) **50.** 187 [OE *hleonian*]

lent *pp.* set, fixed **14.** 499 [OE *lęndan*]

lent. See **len**

Lentern. See **Lentren**

lenthin *v.* lengthen, prolong **69.** 6 [OE n. *lęngðu*]

Lentren, Lentern *n.* Lent, the penitential season before Easter **59.** 1, **73.** 5 *et seq.* [nth. form of OE *len(c)ten*]

leonyne *adj.* lion-like **50.** 91 [ME; F *léonin*; L *leoninus*]

lerge. See **large**

lergenes *n.* liberality, generosity **16.** 84 [ME; OF *large*]

lerit *ppl. adj.* educated **45.** 41 [ME *lered*; f. **leir**]

lerit. See **leir**

lern *v.* teach **28.** 9; **lernit** *pp.* **28.** 30 [OE *leornian*]

les *adj.* (*n.*) less, lower in estimation **14.** 322, **52.** 102, **71.** 48, *adv.* **75.** 51 [OE *lǣs*]

les of *v.* alleviate, relieve **44.** 76 [ME; prec.]

lesing *n.* a lie, lying **9.** 99, **11.** 14; **les(s)ingis** *pl.* **6.** 106, **37.** 43, **38.** 58, **52.** 52 [OE *lēasung*; v. *lēasian*]

lessing *n.* alleviation **39.** 100 [ME]

lesson *n.* instructive example, counsel **14.** 257; *pl.* **14.** 503 [ME; OF *lecon*; L *lectio*]

lest *v.* endure **64.** 13, **64.** 28; **lestis** *3 sg.* **59.** 38, **65.** 20; **lestand** *ppl. adj.* **57.** 7 [OE *lǣstan*]

lest, leist *adj.* of lowest station, humblest **1.** 14, **50.** 73 [OE *lǣst*]

lete. See **lat(t)**

lettis. See **lat(t)**

leuch. See **lauch**

leuket. See **luk(e)**

levand. See **liffand**

leve *n.* leave, departure **10.** 222, **51.** 45; **leveis** *pl.* **14.** 67 [OE *lēafe*]

levefull *adj.* right, proper, lawful **10.** 166 [ME *lefull*; OE *lēaf*]

lev(e)is. See **lefe, leif(f), leve**

lever, levir, (had) *comp. adj.* (would)

rather **38.** 30, **52.** 215 [OE comp. *lēofra*]
Leves. See **leif(f)**
Levir. See **lever**
Levis, levit. See **leif(f)**
Lewch. See **lauch**
Ley. See **le**
Leyd. See **leid**
Leyr. See **leir**
Lib *v.* cure by a potion or charm **32.** 5 (see Commentary), **32.** 15; **libbin** *vbl. n.* **32.** 20 [OE *lybb* potion]
libertee *n.* liberty of action, freedom from restraint, *pers.* **10.** 175 [ME, F; L *libertas*]
licherus *adj.* lecherous **27.** 41 [ME; OF *lecheros*]
lichery, lichory *n.* lust (*luxuria*), one of the seven deadly sins **6.** 20, **14.** 445, **52.** 79 [ME; OF *licherie*]
licht, lycht *n.* light, illumination **1.** 39, **2.** 27, **3.** 84, **7.** 3, **10.** 30, **10.** 259 [ON *lēoht*]
licht *v.* descend, be brought low **53.** 17; **lichtit** *pp.* dismounted **74.** 6 [OE *līhtan*]
licht, lycht *adj.* slight, trivial **42.** 51; agile **50.** 95; happy **51.** 10, **52.** 143 [OE *lēoht*]
lichtlyit *pa. t.* disdained, despised **14.** 328; **lychtleit** *pp.* **27.** 45 [OE *lēohtlic* contemptuous]
liep. See **leip**
lif, liffis. See **lyfe**
lif *v.* live, be alive **62.** 94, **62.** 99 [see **leif**]
liffand, levand, livand *ppl. adj.* living, alive **14.** 497; **16.** 25, **35.** 29, **65.** 33 [OE *lifian*]
lifly *adv.* briskly, vividly **62.** 74 [OE *liflīce*]
lift *n.* sky **51.** 6, **53.** 49 [OE *lyft*]
liftis *3 sg.* lifts **14.** 187; **liftit** *pa. t.* **50.** 99 [ME; ON *lypta*]
lig *v.* lie; (for sexual intercourse) **14.** 500 [OE *licgan*]
***lik** *v.* lick **23.** 396 [OE *liccian*]
lik. See **lyk**
likit *v. pa. t.* liked **14.** 373, **14.** 407; **likit, lykit**+*pers. pron.* it pleases me, us etc. **14.** 66, **14.** 75, **14.** 207, pleased me **14.** 237 [OE *lician*]
liknes *n.* semblance, appearance **14.** 254, **55.** 47 [OE *ȝelīcnes*]
lilly, lyllie *n.* white lily, symbol of purity **8.** 2, **50.** 150; **lilleis** *gen.* lily's **50.** 140; **lil(l)ies** *pl.* **10.** 65, **14.** 28 [OE *lilie*]
lind *n.* linden, lime tree; in tags, a tree **23.** 196 [OE]
linege, linnage, lynnage *n.* family, tribe, race **9.** 101, **35.** 13, **50.** 150 [OF *linage*, *lignage*]
lipinit *pp.* trusted, relied on **45.** 70 [ME *lipnien*; ? ON *hlīta*]
lippir *n.* leper *attrib.* **23.** 154 [ME, OF *lepre*; L *lepra* leprosy]
lippis *n. pl.* lips **10.** 69, **10.** 263, **23.** 97, **23.** 112, **33.** 5 [OE *lippa*]
liquour *n.* liquid; = water **16.** 10 [ME, OF *licur*; L *liquor*]
lisk *n.* groin **23.** 121 [nth. ME; cf. OE *lesca*, ON *ljōski*]
list *v.* choose, wish **14.** 258, **52.** 228, **77.** 1, **79.** 38; *pa. t.* **12.** *title* (*colophon*), **14.** 187 [OE *lystan*]
listly *adv.* elegantly **50.** 100 [ME; OE *listelīce* (*list* skill); ON *listulega*]
litill, littill, litle, lytill *adj. and adv.* little, scant **6.** 41, **10.** 271, **14.** 185, **14.** 288, **14.** 373, **52.** 149, **54.** 16, **82.** 42 [OE *lȳtel*; ON *lītill*]
livand. See **liffand**
lob *adj.* loutish, clumsy **14.** 387 [attrib. use of n., bumpkin; MLG *lobbe*]
lockis. See **lok**
lod steir *n.* lodestar; *fig.* shining example, paragon **31.** 10 [ME; cf. ON *leiðarstjarna*]
Lodovick Louis XII (1462–1515) **36.** 1
loffit. See **luf**
loft, (ap)on(e) *adv. phr.* into the air **3.** 71, **4.** 22, **13.** 34, **14.** 147, **14.** 187; **one loft** above (in copulation) **14.** 388 [OE; ON]
logicianis *n. pl.* logicians, philosophers **62.** 38 [ME; F *logicien*]
loik hertit *adj.* ? warm-hearted **14.** 498 [? ME *luke* warm; origin uncertain]
loikman *n.* executioner, hangman **23.** 174 [origin uncertain; see *DOST*]

loist. See **losit**

lok *n.* lock, padlock **9.** 26; **lockis** *pl.* **32.** 13 [OE *loc*]

Lokert, Sir Mungo, of the Lee (d. ? 1489) **62.** 63

***lollard** *n.* heretic **23.** 524 [ME; MDu *lollaerd*]

lomp *n.* lump, gobbet **23.** 462 [ME; origin uncertain]

lonȝe, lunȝie *n.* loin **23.** 121, **52.** 75 [OF *loingne*]

loppin. See **leip**

lord *n.* nobleman, gentleman; **lordis** *gen.* **38.** 20; *pl.* **14.** 36, **22.** 15, **23.** 77, **46.** 1 [OE *hlāford*]

lordschip *n.* landed property **64.** 18, **66.** 27, **77.** 17; **lordschippis** *n. pl.* estates **63.** 66 [OE *hlāfordscipe*]

lork. Irreg. var. of **lark**

losingeris *n. pl.* flatterers, deceivers **14.** 258 [ME; OF *losengeour*]

losit *ppl. adj.* forfeited, perished, ruined **12.** 14; **lossit, loist** *pp.* **63.** 9, **71.** 64 [OE *losian*]

louket. See **luk(e)**

loun, lown *n.* rascal, wretch, ruffian **23.** 83, **23.** 132, **23.** 178, **23.** 203, **52.** 129, **68.** 14; *pl.* **23.** 178, **23.** 227 [nth. ME; cf. e. mod. Du *loen*]

loungand *pres. p.* slouching **23.** 174 [origin obscure]

loungeour *n.* lay-about **23.** 121 [prec.]

lounry *n.* rascality, knavery **23.** 100 [f. **loun**]

lour *v.* cower, crouch, grovel **9.** 69; **lowrit** *pa. t.* **37.** 12 [ME; cf. MDu *loeren* lurk]

lous, low(i)s *v.* loose, free **1.** 22, **9.** 56, **14,** 362; **lousit, lowsit** *pa. t.* let loose, fired off **10.** 178, **52.** 205; *pp.* unbound **4.** 36 [ON adj. *lǫuss, lauss*]

***louse** *adj.* incontinent, lax-bowelled **23.** 467 [ME; ON *lauss*]

loutt, lowt *v.* bow **48.** 52, **69.** 39; **loutit** *pa. t.* humbled (himself) **14.** 322 [OE *lūtan*]

love *v.* praise, extol; **lov(e)it** *pa. t.* **36.** 25, loved **37.** 24; *ppl. adj.* **2.** 54; **loving** *vbl. n.* praise, glory **1.** 14, **55.** 21; *pl.* praises **2.** 58 [OE *lofian*; ON *lofa*]

lovery *n.* bounty dispensed to a retainer **52.** 102 [var. of *livery;* OF *livree*]

low *n.* flame, blaze **10.** 45 [ME; ON *loge*]

lowd(e) *adj. and adv.* loud **2.** 58, **14.** 506, **16.** 105, **43.** 45, **52.** 116 [OE *hlūd*]

lowrit. Sel **lour**

lowry *n.* fox **37.** 16 [= *Lawrence* name given to a fox; cf. ME and F *Renard*]

lowsy *adj.* infested with lice **23.** 102, **23.** 121, **23.** 178, **52.** 161 [ME; OE n. *lūs*]

lowt. See **loutt**

Lowthiane *n.* the area of Lothian; *attrib.* **23.** 110

Loys Louis XII of France (1462–1515) **35.** *title*

lucerne *n.* lantern **2.** 3 [OF; L *lucerna*]

luche. See **lauch**

Lucifer the morning star; the Devil (Isa. xiv. 12) **4.** 9, **23.** 7 [L]

Lucifera *n.* the morning star **10.** 81 (converted to a classical goddess by fem. ending)

Lucina *n.* the moon **10.** 79, **53.** 1 (see Commentary); **Lucyne** (vernacular form) **10.** 2 (see Commentary) [L]

Ludgate the English poet John Lydgate (d. 1449) **10.** 262

ludgeing. See **lugeing**

ludly *adv.* loudly **14.** 240 [ME; OE adj. *hlūd*]

luf(e), luff, luif(f), luve *n.* love **3.** 16, **10.** 18, **12.** 8, **15.** 1, **28.** 26, **39.** 6, **45.** 14; *attrib.* **14.** 111, **14.** 228; **lufis, luiffis, luvis** *gen.* **9.** 96, **10.** 102, **15.** 16, **69.** 43; **luf** lover **14.** 120 [OE *lufu*]

luf *v.* love **6.** 53; **luffit, luvit, loffit** *pa. t.* **13.** 27, **14.** 406, **14.** 441, **14.** 506; *pp.* **14.** 185, **16.** 51, **17.** 69 [OE *lufian*]

lufar, luvar *n.* lover, paramour **11.** 1, **13.** 4; *gen.* **luvaris** **50.** 60; **luffaris, lufferis, luvaris** *pl.* **14.** 375, **14.** 478, **16.** 20, **43.** 45 [prec.]

luff. See **luf(e)**

lufliare *comp. adj.* fairer, more beautiful **10.** 213 [OE *luflic*]
lufsum *adj.* lovable **49.** 3, **49.** 21; **lufsummar** *comp.* **14.** 283 [OE]
lug *n.* ear **54.** 82 [Scand origin]
luge *n.* dwelling, hut **9.** 76, **23.** 154 [ME; OF *loige*; med. L *logia*]
lugeing, ludgeing *n.* town house, residence **14.** 478, **48.** 59 [as prec.]
lugget *pp.* lodged, been set **32.** 28 [var. of *loge*; F *logier*]
luif(f). See **luf(e)**
luik(is). See **luke**
luk(e), luik *v.* look, gaze, glance **9.** 6, **9.** 28, **14.** 120, **21.** 5, **40.** 9; **luikis** *3 sg.* **20.** 12; **lukand** *pres. p.* **9.** 37; **leuket, louket, lukit** *pa. t.* **10.** 225, **28.** 9, 37, **50.** 10, **luikit** looked to see **14.** 15; **luikit** *pp.* examined **46.** 20; **luking** *vbl. n.* **9.** 14; **luke furth** look out, i.e. live **14.** 308 [OE *lōcian*]
luke *n.* look, glance, stare **9.** 37, **10.** 115, **10.** 123, **14.** 188; *pers.* **10.** 167; **lukis** *pl.* **14.** 434, **63.** 43; **luke, luik** appearance, aspect **23.** 152, **23.** 175, *pl.* 'looks' **23.** 169 [ME; prec.]
Lumbard *adj.* Lombard **54.** 16 (see Commentary); **lumbart** *n.* financier **14.** 362 (see Commentary); **Lumbardy** Lombardy **35.** 49, **35.** 85, **36.** 22, **54.** 7 [ME]
lume *n.* tool; penis **14.** 96, **14.** 175 [OE *ȝelōma*]
lunatyk *n.* lunatic, madman **23.** 247 [ME; late L *lunaticus, luna*]
lunȝie. See **lonȝe**
lurdane *n.* rogue, villain **27.** 37, **38.** 87 [ME; ? OF *lourdin* dullard]
lurk *v.* shrink, cower **69.** 8 [ME; app. f. **lour**]
***luschbald** *n.* ? (abusive) **23.** 501 [meaning and origin obscure]
lust *n.* pleasure, desire, appetite *pers.* **9.** 59 *et seq.*, **14.** 188, **14.** 283, **14.** 499 [OE]
lusti(e). See **lusty(e)**
lustilie, lustely *adv.* gaily **48.** 20, **50.** 98 [ME; f. **lust**]
lustines *n.* gaiety, charm **8.** 2, **31.** 10, joy **49.** 8 [ME; f. **lust**]
lustlese *adj.* joyless **14.** 441 [f. **lust**]
lusty(e), lusti(e) *adj.* gay, lovely **8.** 8, **10.** 58, **10.** 104, **14.** 425, **48.** 6; vigorous **10.** 144, **35.** 13; *as n.* fair one **14.** 49; **lustely, lustily** *adv.* beautifully **1.** 45, **10.** 29, **10.** 91; cheerfully **9.** 77; vigorously **10.** 53 [f. **lust**]
lusum *adj.* lovesome, beautiful **24.** 9 [OE *lufsum*]
lut *adj.* bowed, stooping **45.** 57 [ON *lūtr*]
lute. See **lat(t)**
luttard *adj.* bent, crooked **45.** 57 [nth. ME; ? OE *lūtan*]
luvar. See **lufar**
luvit. See **luf**
ly *v.* lie **14.** 213; lie hid, lurk **9.** 75; **lyis** *2 sg.* **23.** 191, *3 sg.* **14.** 175, rests, is centred **51.** 50; **lyand** *pres. p.* quartered, employed **44.** 13; **lyne** *pp.* lain **4.** 12 [OE *licgan*]
***lyart** *adj.* streaked with grey; *as n.* **43.** 72 [ME; OF *liart*]
lyce, lys *n. pl.* lice **68.** 27 [OE *lūs*, pl. *lȳs*]
lychour *n.* lecher, libertine **14.** 174 [OF]
lycht. See **licht**
lychtleit. See **lichtlyit**
lychtsum *adj.* bright, shining **49.** 10 [ME *liȝtsum*; OE *lēoht*]
lyf(e), lyff, lif, lyve *n.* life **1.** 46, **12.** 2, **14.** 421, **36.** 30, **54.** 42; *gen.* **liffis 65.** 26; **on lyf (lyve), upone lyf** alive **3.** 89, **14.** 44, **61.** 47; **with lyf** keeping his life, staying alive **3.** 45 [OE *lif*]
lyflett *n.* means of living, subsistence **47.** 26 [OE *līflād*]
lyk(e), lik *adj.* like, resembling **3.** 13, **4.** 18, **10.** 123, **23.** 243, **42.** 7; likely **10.** 115; as if **44.** 44 [OE *ȝelīc*]
lykand *ppl. adj.* pleasant, delightful **10.** 29 [ME *lyking*; OE *līcian*, ON *līca*]
lyllie. See **lilly**
lymis *n. pl.* limbs **23.** 182 [OE *lim*]
lymmar *n.* scoundrel, rascal; *attrib.* **52.** 129 (***lymmer 23.** 313, ***lymare 23.** 501) [origin obscure]
lymmerfull *adj.* villainous **23.** 152 [f. **lymmar**]

lyis, lyne. See **ly**
lynnage. See **linege**
lynning *adj.* linen **23.** 224 [OE *linnen* made of flax (*līn*)]
***lynt** *n.* flax (used as a combustible) **23.** 335 [ME]
lyntall, lyntell *n.* lintel over a door **3.** 118, **69.** 39 [OF *lintel*]
lyone, lyoun *n.* lion **4.** 19, **50.** 87; *pl.* **3.** 19 [AF *liun*]
lyre *n.* face, skin **14.** 499 [OE *hlēor*]
lyte *adj.* slight, inadequate **10.** 71 [OE *lȳt*]
lyth *v.* listen, give ear **14.** 257; **lythis** *imper.* **27.** 1 [ME; ON *hlȳða*]
lythenes *n.* laziness, evil (?) *pers.* **52.** 81 [ME *lythernes*]
lytill. See **litill**
lyve. See **lyf(e)**

ma, mai *v.* may **5.** 13, **14.** 488; **micht, mycht** *pa. t.* **1.** 19, **3.** 45, **20.** 12, **23.** 22, **25.** 13, **28.** 3 [OE *maȝan, meahte*]
ma *n., adj., adv.* more **23.** 195, **23.** 198, **55.** 27; **may** *adj.* **3.** 79 [OE *mā*]
***Machomete,** Muhammad = Satan **23.** 526, **23.** 538 (see **Mahoun**)
macull, makle *n.* blemish, flaw **2.** 22, **50.** 152 [F *macule*; L *macula*]
madinis *n. pl.* virgins, maids **48.** 41 [OE *mæȝden*]
maed. See **mak**
maest. See **maist**
maesteres, mastres *n.* mistress **28.** 29, **31.** 13 [ME, OF *maistresse*]
Magdalyn, (the) Mary of Magdala **6.** 146
magellit *pp.* mangled, botched **26.** 3 [origin obscure]
magryme *n.* migraine, headache **21.** 3 [F *migraine*; L *hemicrania*]
Mahoun, Mahowne *n.* Satan, the Devil **14.** 101 (see Commentary), **23.** 233, **52.** 6, **52.** 27, **52.** 109, **52.** 142, **52.** 208 [ME, OF; shortened f. *Mahomet*]
maid. See **mak**
maik *n.* mate, consort **14.** 61; **maikles** *adj.* matchless, incomparable **13.** 52 [OE *ȝemaca*, ON *make*]
maik. See **mak**
mailis *n. pl.* rents **80.** 13 (see Commentary) [OE *māl*]
maille *n.* chain-mail, armour made up of metal rings **10.** 152 [ME, F]
maine *n.* mane **43.** 21 [OE *manu*]
mair, mar(e), mor(e) *adj. and adv.* more **6.** 101, **14.** 44, **14.** 183, **14.** 295, **18.** 11; **nevir mare (mair)** never again **10.** 222, **11.** 12 [OE *māra*]
mais *3 sg.* makes, does **34.** 43 [nth. ME; reduced form of **mak**]
maist, maest, mo(i)st *adj. and adv.* most, of the highest station **2.** 37, **3.** 82, **5.** 44, **6.** 10, **6.** 43, **33.** 17; **most and lest** every one **1.** 14; **most of hicht** highest **1.** 49 [nth. OE *māst*]
maister, maistir *n.* master, controller **11.** 13, **14.** 168, **28.** 15; superior **23.** 114, **38.** 60, **45.** 45; Master of Arts **28.** 8, **35.** *title*, **38.** 1, **62.** 58, **62.** 82 [OE *mæȝester*; L *magister*]
mak, maik *v.* make, do **1.** 50, **2.** 56, **5.** 10, **10.** 182, **35.** 30; compose, write poetry **21.** 2, **50.** 28; cause, arrange **8.** 14; **makis** *3 sg.* **16.** 38; **makand** *pres. p.* **14.** 279; **maid** *pa. t.* **2.** 15, **4.** 15, **14.** 241, **med** *pa. t. reflex.* set himself (to) **28.** 46; **maid** *pp.* **7.** 2, **9.** 107; rendered, paid **4.** 37, **14.** 371; **maed** *pp.* written **33.** 1; **makin** *pp.* was drawn up, concluded **14.** 346; **maid** *ppl. adj.* instituted, inducted **54.** 53 [OE *macian*]
mak *n.* build, appearance **74.** 1 [ME; prec.]
makar, mackar *n.* creator **1.** 18, **68.** 41; poet **28.** 22; *pl.* poets **10.** 77, **10.** 256, **62.** 45, **62.** 50 [ME; f. **mak**]
makdome *n.* form, comeliness **14.** 73 [OE *macian*+*-dōm* (suffix of state)]
makin. See **mak**
making *vbl. n.* composing, verses **26.** 3 (***23.** 40) [**mak**]
makle. See **macull**
malancolie, malancoly *n.* sickness caused by excess of black bile; depression, dejection, rage **44.** 76,

44. 84, **65.** 21 [ME; OF; L *melancholia*]
maledie *n.* malady, sickness *fig.* **42.** 56 [ME; F]
maling *adj.* malign, baleful **2.** 17 [OF *maligne*; L *malignus*]
malis, malyce *n.* wickedness **26.** 3, **52.** 45, **77.** 5 [ME; OF *malice*]
malisone *n.* curse **38.** 83 [ME; OF *maleison*; L *maledictio*]
malitius *adj.* malicious, spiteful **23.** 89 [ME, OF *malicius*]
maltman *n.* maltster, who prepared grain for the brewer **56.** 46 [ME; OE *m(e)alt*]
malyce. See **malis**
man *n.* mankind **1.** 54; servant, vassal, lover **12.** 6, **12.** 13; **man(n)is** *gen.* man's **6.** 54, **14.** 421, **22.** 34, **31.** 23; **men(n)is** *gen. pl.* **14.** 42, **23.** 154, **38.** 69, **68.** 37, **80.** 16 [OE]
man, mane. See **mon(e)**
manasing *pres. p.* menacing **35.** 76; **manassing** *vbl. n.* threats, menaces **3.** 15 [OE *manacer*]
mandrag *n.* mandrake, poisonous plant with a human shape ***23.** 29; *pl.* **45.** 21 [OE, L *mandragora*]
mane *n.* man, people **51.** 65, **51.** 66 [OE *man*]
maneir, maner(e) *n.* manner, way **1.** 15, **10.** 95, **37.** 45, **53.** 12; sorts **83.** 1; **man(n)eris** *pl.* behaviour **14.** 250, **14.** 259, **14.** 328, **14.** 447 [ME; OF *maniere*]
***manesuorne** *ppl. adj.* perjured **23.** 526 [OE *mān-swęrian, -sworen*]
mangit *ppl. adj.* crazed, imbecile **14.** 118 [f. *mang* v. bewilder, go frantic; etym. uncertain]
manheid *n.* manhood, manliness, courage **16.** 82, **36.** 12, **68.** 2 [ME]
mank *n.* flaw, defect **70.** 12 [OF adj. *manc*]
manly *adj.* fitting for men **14.** 352; *adv.* valorously **10.** 202 [OE *mannlīce*]
mannace *n.* threat, menace **23.** 4 [ME; OF *menace*]
mannis. See **man**
manslaar, man slayar *n.* murderer **6.** 50, **12.** 5 [OE *man*+Nhb *slān* (OE *slēan*)+*-er*]
mansuetude *n.* gentleness, meekness **50.** 17 [ME; F; L *mansuetudo*]
mantene *v.* continue, carry on with **51.** 57 [ME; F *maintenir*; L *manu tenere*]
mantill *n.* mantle, loose sleeveless cloak, plaid **50.** 46; *fig.* **10.** 48; *pl.* **10.** 139, **14.** 24 [OF *mantel*; L *mantellum*]
mar. See **mair**
***Mar** ancient district of south-west Aberdeenshire **23.** 261
***Marciane** ? Marcion the heretic **23.** 538
marcifull *adj.* mercifull **6.** 1 [**marcy**]
Marcurius. See **Mercurius**
marcy *n.* mercy **6.** 8 *et seq.* [OF *merci*]
mard *pp.* confounded, thwarted **37.** 45 [OE *męrran*]
mare. See **mair**
Maria, Mary the Blessed Virgin **1.** 4, **1.** 44, **2.** 9 *et passim*, **6.** 60, **22.** 30
mariege, maryage *n.* marriage **14.** 42, **70.** 8 [ME, F *mariage*]
mariit, mary(i)t *pa. t.* married **14.** 296, *pp.* **14.** 303, *ppl. adj.* **14.** *title* [F *marier*]
markat. See **mercat**
markis *n. pl.* signs, seal **29.** 5 [OE *mearc*]
marleȝonis *n. pl.* merlins (the stone falcon, *falco columbarius*) **54.** 90 [ME *merlion*, aphetic f. OF *esmerillon*]
***marmaidyn** *n.* mermaid; ? grotesque **23.** 514 [ME; cf. OE *męrewīf* sea-woman]
marrit *pp.* astonished, affrighted **55.** 7 [OE *męrran* hinder]
Mars the god of war **10.** 112, **10.** 152, **35.** 12, **35.** 73; **Martis** *gen.* **54.** 67 [L]
***marschall** *n.* farrier; **horse marschall** horse doctor **23.** 475 [ME, OF; med. L *marescallus*]
martir *n.* martyr (ranking first among the saints) **3.** 94; **marte(i)ris** *pl.* **1.** 10, **22.** 46 [OE, eccl. L *martyr*]
martir *v.* inflict pain upon, torment **14.** 329 [OF *ȝemartyrian*]

marvelus *adj.* wonderful **54.** 66 [ME; OF *merveillos*]

Mary. See **Maria**

maryage. See **mariege**

mary(i)t. See **mariit**

Maryland *n.* fairyland **13.** 51 (see Commentary) [origin obscure; perh. f. folklore]

***marynaris** *n. pl.* mariners, seamen **23.** 463 [ME; med. L *marinarius*]

masounis *n. pl.* stonemasons **44.** 13 [ME; OF *maçon*]

mastevlyk *adj.* like a great lolloping dog **28.** 47 [see **mastive**]

mastis *n.* mastiff, large dog; *attrib.* **45.** 21 [late ME; cf. Prov. *mastis*]

mastive *n.* mastiff, large dog **29.** 17 [ME; cf. OF *mastin*]

mastres. See **maesteres**

mater, meter *n.* matter, theme, subject **10.** 258, **44.** 30; **45.** 68; evidence **23.** 137; legal issue **71.** 6; *pl.* **14.** 40, **14.** 122, **14.** 196, **14.** 211, **14.** 352, **14.** 453 [OF *matere*; L *materia*]

matern *adj.* maternal, being a mother **2.** 11 [L *maternus*]

matremony *n.* marriage, one of the seven sacraments **6.** 45, *pers.* **9.** 97, **9.** 102, **9.** 108 [OF; L *matrimonium*]

matutyne *adj.* morning **10.** 4 [L *matutinus* (*Matuta* Aurora)]

matynnis *n.* the early morning office, one of the canonical hours **54.** 54 [ME, F; med. L *matinae*]

mauch *n.* maggot; *attrib.* 'mauchie', maggoty **23.** 241 [ON *maðkr*]

maugre *n.* odium, ill-will **17.** 33 [ME; OF]

mavasy *n.* malmsey, the wine **73.** 14 (see Commentary) [ME, OF *malvesie*]

mavis, mavys *n.* song-thrush (*turdus ericetorum*) **14.** 513, **50.** 164 [ME; OF *mauvis*; med. L *malvitino*]

maw *n.* gull, mew (*larus*); **mawis** *pl.* **54.** 90 [ON *mār*, *mav-*; cf. **gor-maw**]

***Maxencius** executioner of S. Catherine **23.** 538

May *n.* the month of May **50.** 4, **50.** 15, **50.** 62; **Mayis** *gen.* **50.** 38, **76.** 15 [F *Mai*; L *Maius*]

mayit *pa. t.* sported, danced in celebration of May **10.** 131 [prec.]

mayne *n.* complaint, lament **12.** 31 [nth. ME *man*; OE **mān*]

me *pron.* (*as reflex.*) myself **6.** 4, **6.** 9, **6.** 18, **56.** 28 [OE]

med. See **mak**

medecyne, medicyne *n.* art of healing **44.** 4, **62.** 41; medicine, remedy **42.** 54, **54.** 30 [ME, OF; L *medicina*]

mediatrice *n.* (female) intercessor **2.** 67 [F; L *mediatrix*]

mednycht. See **midnicht**

meid *n.* reward, recompense **17.** 33, *pl.* **79.** 2; deserving reward, merit **68.** 2 [OE *mēd*]

meid *n.* meadow **14.** 514; **medis** *pl.* **10.** 55 [OE *mǣd*]

meik *adj.* meek, humble, modest **1.** 15, **6.** 4, **12.** 40, **14.** 26, **22.** 23; *adv.* **14.** 513; **mekar** *comp.* **14.** 250 [ME; ON *mjūkr*]

meikle. See **mekle**

meill *n.* (oat)meal **23.** 147, **68.** 30 [OE *melo*, ON *mjǫl*]

mein *n.* means, expedient **48.** 70 [ME; OF adj. *meien*]

meir *n.* mare **74.** 6, ***23.** 261 [OE *mēre*]

meit, met *n.* food **6.** 27, **22.** 11, **65.** 35, **75.** 65; meat *attrib.* **44.** 44 [OE *mete*]

meit *adj.* fitting, good **17.** 75, **52C.** 13 [OE (Anglian) **ȝe-mēte*]

meit *v.* meet, come together **13.** 61, **23.** 67, **48.** 47, **53.** 27, **53.** 32; **mett** *pa. t.* **48.** 9, **48.** 17 [OE *mētan*]

mekar. See **meik**

mekle, mekill, meikle *adj.* much, great **2.** 31, **14.** 240, **23.** 189, **33.** 5, **54.** 36, **75.** 65; *adv.* **14.** 291, **14.** 376, **14.** 506 [OE *micel*; ON *mikell*]

***mele.** See **meill**

mell *v.* mix, mingle; copulate **14.** 56; *3 sg.* involve himself **34.** 2, **70.** 8 [ME; OF *meller*]

mell-hedit *ppl. adj.* blockheaded **45.** 60 [nth. ME *mell* heavy hammer; F *mail*]

melle *n.* close combat **62.** 23 [nth. ME; OF *mellée*]

mellifluate *adj.* flowing with honey, honeyed (poet.) **10.** 265 [L *mellifluus*]
memberis *n. pl.* 'limbs', agents **45.** 20 [ME; OF *membre*; L *membrum*]
memor(i)e *n.* memory **3.** 5, reminder **2.** 53 [OF *memoire*; L *memoria*]
men of weir *n. pl.* soldiers **36.** 6; ***men of were** warships **23.** 466 [late ME; F *homme de guerre*]
menatair *n.* the minotaur **54.** 66 [ME; L *minotaurus*]
mene, meyne *v.* mean, refer to, signify **22.** 4, **31.** 39 [OE *mǣnan*]
mene *v.* lament (for) **17.** 64; **of mene 8.** 12 **menys** *1 sg.* take pity on **14.** 501 [OE *mǣnan*]
mene *adj.* middling, low **14.** 297 [ME; cf. OF *meien*]
menes *n. pl.* solicitations, exertions **71.** 12; **menis** (*as sg.*) influence **74.** 24 [ME; OF adj. *meien*]
menȝie *n.* company, retinue **78.** 33, **81.** 33 [ME; OF *mesnie*]
menȝie *n.* flaw, lack **70.** 12 [ME *mayne*; OF *meshaigne*]
menȝie *v.* wound, disable **21.** 3 [ME *maynhe*; OF *mahaignier*]
mening *n.* intention **49.** 28 [ME; OE v. *mǣnan*]
men(n)is. See **man**
mensk *n.* honour, dignity **14.** 352 [ME; ON *mennska* humanity]
menskit *pa. t.* favoured, graced **14.** 152 [as prec.]
menstrale, menstrall *n.* professional entertainer, musician, singer **10.** 8, **56.** 61; *pl.* **44.** 9, **48.** 23, **52.** 103, **75.** 29 [OF *menestral*]
menstrallie *n.* minstrelsy, music **21.** 13 [prec.]
mensweir *v.* repudiate, renounce **52.** 210 [OE *mānswęrian* (*mān* wicked, false)]
menys. See **mene** lament
mercat, markat *n.* market **14.** 81, **56.** 4 [ME; cf. L *marcatus*]
merchand *n.* merchant, trader **14.** 296, **56.** 16, **56.** 19; **merchantis** *pl.* **75.** 1 [ME; OF *marchand*]
Merche *n.* the month of March **8.** 11, **50.** 1 [ME, OF *Marche*]
merciabill *adj.* compassionate **45.** 68 [ME, OF *merciable*]
Mercurius, Marcurius son of Jupiter and Maia, messenger of the gods and god of eloquence **10.** 116, **35.** 78
mercye, mersy *n.* mercy, pity **42.** 52, merciful disposition **25.** 21 [ME; OF *merci*]
mercyles *adj.* without pity, ruthless **8.** 5, **12.** 42 [prec.]
mereit *n.* merit, virtue **41.** 6, **79.** 2 [ME, OF *merite*; L *meritum*]
Mergreit Queen Margaret (= the margarite) **31.** 33 (see Commentary), **31.** 39 [ME; OF *margarite*]
meridiane *adj.* midday, noontide **2.** 70 [ME, F; L *meridianus*]
merily *adv.* merrily, cheerfully **10.** 245 [OE adj. *mer(i)ȝe*]
merk. See **mirk**
merle *n.* blackbird (*turdus merula*) **16.** 3, **16.** 29 *et seq.*, **50.** 169 [L *merula*]
Merlyne Arthurian prophet and magician **53.** 33 (see Commentary)
***merreit** *pa. t.* contracted marriage **23.** 296 [ME; F *marier*]
merrens *n.* nuisance, vexation **14.** 57 [OF *marrence*]
merse *n.* top-castle of a ship **10.** 52 [MDu; MLG]
Merseir Scotch poet **62.** 73
mersy. See **mercye**
mervalous, mervellus, mervel(o)us *adj.* extraordinary, amazing **12.** 31, **48.** 42, **50.** 163, **72.** 15 [ME; OF *merveillos*]
mery *adj.* merry, cheerful **10.** 6, **10.** 46, **14.** 147, **14.** 282, **14.** 391, **62.** 11 [OE *mer(i)ȝe*]
mes(s) *n.* mass, eucharist **6.** 84, **20.** 17, **21.** 6, **54.** 49 [OE *mæsse*]
messan *n.* lap-dog **29.** 21, *attrib.* ***23.** 495 [Gael *measan*]
messour *n.* measure; bounds, limits **3.** 15, **6.** 127 [ME; F *mesure*]
met. See **meit**
meter *n.* metre, poetry **26.** 8 [ME, OF; L *metrum*]
meter. See **mater**
meter *comp. adj.* more suitable **30.** 9 [**meit** adj.]
methis *3 sg.* adjoins, is a neighbour **9.** 38 [ON *miða*]

methocht *pa. t.* it seemed to me **3.** 9, **3.** 97 [OE *mē þyncþ*]
mett. See **meit**
meyne *v.* negotiate; ? relieve by intercession, mediation **2.** 47 [ME; OF *meenner*]
meyne. See **mene**
mi *poss. pron.* my **14.** 344, **14.** 486 [reduced form of **myn**]
michane *n.* ? stomach **13.** 37 [meaning and origin uncertain]
micht, mycht *n.* power, strength **1.** 36, **2.** 24, **2.** 31, **3.** 82, **29.** 17, **66.** 4 [OE *miht*]
micht. See **ma**
michti(e), mychty, mychti, myghti *adj.* powerful, mighty **5.** 5, **10.** 80, **10.** 102, **36.** 5, **48.** 36; having divine power **3.** 4; strong, loud **10.** 129; opulent **14.** 296; **michtely** *adv.* **65.** 23 [OE *mihtiȝ*]
midding. See **myddyng**
midnicht, mednycht, mydnycht n. midnight **10.** 261, **14.** 2, **14.** 211, **58.** 18 [OE *midniht*]
milhous *n.* building housing a mill **23.** 243 [ME *milnehous*; OE *myln*+*hūs*]
Minerva. See **Pallas**
mir *n.* myrrh, aromatic gum-resin **48.** 27 [ME, OF *mirre*; L *myrrha*]
mirakle *n.* miracle **2.** 24; **mirakillis** *pl.* **52C.** 37 [OF; L *miraculum*]
mirk *adj.* dark **23.** 92, **75.** 17; **merk** *n.* darkness **23.** 221 [OE *mirce*]
mir(r)ines, mirrynais, mirrynes *n.* mirth, cheerfulness **22.** 5, **48.** 7, **64.** 22, **67.** 23, **70.** 2 [ME]
mirrouris *n. pl.* mirrors; *fig.* models, patterns **76.** 19 [ME, OF *mirour*]
mirry, mirrie, myrrie *adj.* merry, gay, happy **16.** 3, **16.** 26, **18.** 3, **22.** 21, **44.** 9, *as n.* **41.** 12; **mirrear** *comp.* **28.** 7; **mirriest** *sup.* **14.** 1 [var. of **mery**]
mirrynais, mirrynes. See **mir(r)ines**
mirth, myrth *n.* joy, gladness **10.** 19, **10.** 246, **18.** 3; **mirthis** *pl.* entertainment **14.** 9; **mirth(e)full, myrthfull** *adj.* **1.** 36, **1.** 52, **22.** 30, **58.** 18; **myrthles** joyless **14.** 391; *sup.* **myrthfullest** **10.** 9 [OE *myr(i)ȝð*]
mis, mys *n.* harm, wrong, sin **6.** 147, **7.** 6, **71.** 19 [? prefix *mis-*; cf. MLG *misse* mistake]
misaventeur *n.* misfortune, adversity **77.** 44 [ME, OF]
mischance *n.* wretchedness, misery **51.** 35 [ME; OF *meschaunce*]
mischeif(f) *n.* harm, wickedness, evil **23.** 74, **23.** 234, **34.** 14, **42.** 5; **mischeifaislie** *adv.* harmfully **12.** 17 [ME; OF *meschief*]
miscuke *v.* spoil in cooking **14.** 455 [ME *mis-*+*coke*]
misdemyng *n.* wrong judgement **11.** 4 [ME; cf. ON *misdǣma*]
miserabell, miserabill *adj.* wretched **43.** 28, **44.** 37 [F; L *miserabilis*]
misfassonit *ppl. adj.* ill-designed, mis-shapen **52C.** 25 [ME; OF *façon*]
misgydit *ppl. adj.* ill-behaved **45.** 20 [ME]
miskennyt *pa. t.* disowned, neglected **14.** 380 [*mis-*+**ken**; cf. ON *miskenna* not to recognize]
mismakkis *3 sg.* makes wrongly **52C.** 10; **misma(i)d** *ppl. adj.* mis-shapen **23.** 53, **45.** 21 [ME; see **mak**]
mispendit, mispent *ppl. adj.* misspent, wasted **15.** 19, **39.** 3; **myspent** *pp.* wastefully used **6.** 110 [ME; OE *spendan*; L *expendere*]
mist *pp.* missed **71.** 30 [*mis* feel the want of; OE *missan*]
misteris, mystirs *n. pl.* business, affairs **14.** 362; sexual desires, needs **14.** 128 [ME; OF *mestier*]
misteris *3 sg.* has need of **81.** 34 [ME; prec.]
mittanis. See **myttell**
mo *adj.* more **69.** 28 [sth. ME; adopted in place of **ma**]
moder, modir, muder, muddir *n.* mother **2.** 22, **6.** 51, **9.** 110, **45.** 6, **50.** 4, **67.** 37, **73.** 12; *gen.* **13.** 37, **62.** 26 [OE *mōdor*]
modern *adj.* alive today **2.** 5 [F *moderne*; late L *modernus*]
modir. See **moder**
moir *adj., adv., n.* more **17.** 10, **17.** 76, **22.** 93, **31.** 35, **34.** 35, **50.** 31 [midl. and sth. ME; cf. **mair**]

moist. See **maist**
mok(k)is *n. pl.* derisive speech, gestures **14.** 279, **34.** 45 [ME; OF v. *mocquer*]
molet *n.* ? lip, muzzle **14.** 113 (see Commentary) [origin uncertain; cf. ON *mūle* muzzle]
molet *n.* bit, curb, **14.** 349 [origin obscure]
moltin *adj.* melted **52.** 62 [ME; OE *meltan*, *ȝemolten*]
mone, moyne *n.* moon **14.** 432, **23.** 14, **53.** 50, **75.** 34; (as making men lunatic) **23.** 53; *pl.* **53.** 49 [OE *mōna*]
mon(e), man(e) *auxil. v.* must **14.** 447, **16.** 68, **19.** 18, **23.** 167, **43.** 59, **44.** 81, **51.** 54, **60.** 6 [ME; ON *munu*, *mon* shall]
moneles *adj.* moonless **23.** 92 [**mone**]
moneth *n.* month **10.** 252, **14.** 80; *pl.* **10.** 82 [OE *mōnað*]
monkis *n. pl.* monks **74.** 50 [OE *munuc*]
monsouris *n. pl.* messieurs, French gentlemen **44.** 42 [F]
monster, monstir, monstour *n.* repulsively deformed creature **23.** 53, **52.** 91, **54.** 110; *pl.* **45.** 27, **53.** 28 [ME, OF; L *monstrum*]
monstrowis *adj.* monstrous, grotesque **81.** 29 [ME; F *monstrueux*; L *monstruosus*]
mont *v.* soar, rise **54.** 62 [ME; OF *monter*]
***montayn** *n.* mountain **23.** 337 [ME; OF *montaigne*]
mony *adj.* many **3.** 9, **3.** 11, **3.** 21, **5.** 63, **5.** 68, **9.** 30; many a **14.** 425 [OE *maniȝ*, *mǫniȝ*]
monyast *adj.* most **40.** 2 [sup. of **mony**]
morall *adj.* concerned with morality **10.** 262 [ME; L *moralis*]
morgeownis *n. pl.* grotesque capers **28.** 38 [? var. with intruded *r* of *mudgeoune* motion; L *motio*]
morne, to *n.* tomorrow (used adverbially) **67.** 10 [OE *morȝen*]
morow, morrow *n.* morning **10.** 9, **10.** 261, **14.** 513, **58.** 18, **65.** 5, [ME; reduced var. of *morwen*; OE *morȝen*]
morowing *n.* morning (poet.) **10.** 247 [prec.]
morsall *n.* tasty mouthful; *fig.* **37.** 23 [ME; OF *morsel* bite]
mortall *adj.* deadly, fatal **4.** 10, **62.** 70 [OF; L *mortalis*]
mortar stane *n.* hollowed-out stone used for pulverising **45.** 60 [nth. ME; cf. MDu *mortiersteen*]
morthour *n.* murder **23.** 74 [OE *morðor*]
moryis *n.* 'moorish' dance **20.** 8 (see Commentary) [ME]
most *v.* must **51.** 52 [pa. t. of **mot,** as pres.; OE *mōste*]
most. See **maist**
mot *v.* may **22.** 64, **37.** 20, **51.** 91, **56.** 18, **56.** 63, **82.** 50 [OE pret. pres. *mōt*]
mouit. See **blait-mouit**
***Mount Barnard** etc. in the Alps **23.** 433–5
***Mount Falconn** the gallows-hill in Paris **23.** 368, **23.** 369
mouthis. See **mowth**
mowaris *n. pl.* **75.** 34 mockers [late ME]
mowitt. See **tute mowitt**
mowlis *n. pl.* chilblains (esp. on the heels) **52C.** 19 [ME; F pl. *mules*; med. L *mula*]
***mows,** in *phr.* in fun, as a joke **23.** 29 [ME; MDu *mouwe* pout]
mows *n.* mouse **37.** 55; **myce** *pl.* **68.** 23 [OE *mūs*, *mȳs*]
mowt *v.* moult **42.** 9 [ME; OE **mūtian*]
mowth *n.* mouth **59.** 10, **63.** 41; **mowthis, mouthis** *pl.* **13.** 47, **14.** 509, **39.** 9 (*meton.*) words, language **10.** 265 [OE *mūþ*]
moy *adj.* meek, submissive **14.** 349, **71.** 16 [? MDu *mooy*]
moyne. See **mone**
muder(is), muddir. See **moder**
muill *n.* mule **43.** 40 [OE *mūl*; L *mulus*]
***muk** *n.* dung **23.** 472 [ME; Scand origin]
muk *v.* to clear of dung **45.** 52 [ME; cf. ON *moka*]
***muldis** *n. pl.* burial mounds **23.** 378 [OE *molde*]

murdir *v.* murder, slay **12.** 10 [OE *myrðrian*]
murdris *v.* murder, slay; *1 sg.* torment **14.** 212; **murdreist** *pa. t.* **54.** 30 [OF *murdrir, murdriss-*]
murlandis *adj.* from the moor, rustic **74.** 1 [OE *mōrland*]
murnys *1 sg.* grieve **14.** 212; **murning, murnyng** *vbl. n.* sorrow **12.** 31, **14.** 417, **72.** 15 [ME; OE *murnan*]
***Murray,** earls of **23.** 386
murtherer *n.* murderer **34.** 43; **murthour** *n.* murder **34.** 43 [OE *morðor*]
mus *v.* ponder, reflect **14.** 211, **64.** 1; **musand** *pres. p.* **20.** 11 [OF *muser*]
Musgraeffe, maesteres 28. 26, **28.** 29
musicians *n. pl.* musicians **44.** 9 [ME; OF *musicien*]
musing *n.* ? complaint **13.** 40 [ME; OF *muser* meditate]
***mute** *n.* assembly, law-court **23.** 475 [OE *ʒemōt*]
***mutis** *2 sg.* speak, utter **23.** 375 [OE *mōtian*]
muttoun *n.* dead sheep **23.** 241, ? sheep for slaughter **23.** 246 [ME; OF *moton*]
muvit *pa. t.* passed, went **14.** 2 [OF *movoir*; L *movere*]
myance *n.* means, resource **54.** 36 [var. of *moyen*; ME, MF]
myce. See **mows**
mycht. See **micht; ma**
mychtely, mychttelye *adv.* doughtily **33.** 17, **50.** 97 [OE *mihtiʒlīce*]
mychti, mychty. See **michti(e)**
myd *adj.* middle **14.** 297 [OE *midd*]
mydding, midding *n.* midden, heap of refuse **14.** 355, **38.** 37, **52.** 68; *attrib.* **29.** 14, **45.** 25 [ME; ON **myki-dlyngja*]
mydlis *n. pl.* waists **10.** 63 [OE *middel*]
mydnycht. See **midnicht**
myght *v.* might, could **14.** 349, **14.** 375 [pa. t. of *may;* OE *maʒan, meahte*]
myghti. See **michti(e)**
myld(e) *adj.* gentle, kind, soft **10.** 167, **14.** 513 [OE *milde*]
myle *n.* mile **10.** 221; **myll** *pl.* **23.** 93 [OE *mīl*]
mylne *n.* corn-mill **23.** 147 [OE *myln*]
***mymmerkin, mymmerken** *n* ? dwarf **23.** 29 (see Commentary), **23.** 514 [origin obscure]
myn(n), myne *poss. adj.* my **6.** 1, **6.** 15, **14.** 209, **14.** 327, **14.** 439, **16.** 97, **51.** 59; **myne alone** by myself **51.** 64 [OE *mīn*]
mynd(e) *n.* mind, attitude **1.** 30, **5.** 12, **6.** 129, **12.** 43; wits **23.** 53, **44.** 44; memory **44.** 28; *pl.* **14.** 57, **39.** 9; **haif mynd** remember **59.** 5, **59.** 9 [OE *ʒemynd*]
myne *poss. pron.* mine **56.** 24. See **myn(n)** [OE *mīn*]
mynʒeoun *n.* woman's darling, lover **13.** 52 [F *mignon*]
mynny *n.* mother **13.** 16 [prob. f. baby talk]
mynting *vbl. n.* attempt, move **23.** 4 [ME *myntan*]
myre *n.* swampy ground, bog **54.** 107 [ME; ON *mȳrr*]
***myrit** *pa. t.* bespattered, fouled **23.** 472 [ME; ON *mȳrr* bog]
myrrie. See **mirry**
myrth, myrthfull(est), myrthles. See **mirth**
myspent. See **mispendit**
myst *n.* mist **14.** 514; **mystie** *adj.* **69.** 3 [OE *mist*]
mystirs. See **misteris**
myswent *pa. t.* went wrong, erred **6.** 70 [pres. *misga* (*mis-*+OE *gān*); pa. t. f. OE *wēndan*]
***myten** *n.* dwarf, runt **23.** 494 (see Commentary) [? OE *mīte* the insect]
myttane, myttell *n.* a bird of prey **42.** 12 (see Commentary), **54.** 73; **mittanis** *pl.* **54.** 90 [origin obscure]

na *adj., adv.* no, not any **5.** 70, **6.** 50, **6.** 54, **13.** 27, **14.** 90, **32.** 8; **na thing** not at all **14.** 271 [reduced form of **nane**; OE *nān*]
na, ne *conj.* than **5.** 52, **14.** 60, **14.** 176, **14.** 377, **16.** 26, **31.** 36, **51.** 82 [origin uncertain; perh. spec. use of *na* other than; OE *nā*]

naceoun. See **natioun**
naem. See **name**
nagus *n.* stingy fellow **23.** 177 [origin obscure; cf. 19th cent. Lancs. dial. *nagus*]
nailis, nalis *n. pl.* human nails **23.** 148, iron nails **3.** 107 [OE *næȝel*]
nain. See **nane**
nakit, naikit *adj.* naked **3.** 70, **23.** 120; *as n. pl.* **6.** 29 [OE *nacod*]
name, naem *n.* fame, reputation **11.** 8, **11.** 16, **11.** 24, **12.** 14, **33.** 22 [OE *nama*]
namelie *adv.* especially **5.** 44, **36.** 29 [ME; cf. ON *nafnliga*]
nane, nain, non *pron.* not one, none **8.** 10, **13.** 5, **14.** 504, **17.** 85, **28.** 39, **63.** 16 [OE *nān*]
nanis, for the *adv.* fittingly, assuredly, indeed **52.** 21 [ME; eME *to þan anes*]
Naplis Naples **35.** *title*, **35.** 85
nar *prep.* close to **55.** 10 [ME; ON comp. adv. *nærre*]
narrest, nerrest *sup. adj.* shortest, most direct **47.** 18, **54.** 25, **59.** 22 [ME; OE *nēarra* (comp. of *nēah* near)]
nathing *n.* nothing **78.** 29 [OE *nā þing*]
natioun, naceoun *n.* nation **19.** 26, **35.** 26, **36.** 29 [ME, OF *nacion*; L *natio*]
nativite *n.* occasion of a birth **35.** 74 [ME; L *nativitas*]
natur(e), natour, nator *n.* nature, the natural order **6.** 90, **34.** 9; character, disposition **14.** 321, **23.** 244; sexual power **14.** 174, **14.** 392, *gen.* **14.** 198; the goddess Natura **10.** 73, **10.** 87, **10.** 95, **16.** 22, **16.** 39, **31.** 17, **50.** 63, *gen.* **10.** 251, **50.** 173 [L *natura*]
naturaly *adv.* in accordance with nature **1.** 42 [OF; L *naturalis*]
naught. See **nocht**
necligent *adj.* neglectful, careless **6.** 46, **6.** 118 [F; L *negligens*]
ned, neid *v.* need, be obliged to, require *3 sg.* **23.** 206, *3 pl.* **79.** 4; **it nedis ȝow** it is necessary for you **14.** 264; **most nedis** must necessarily **44.** 83; **neidis to be** is required **56.** 38; **neding** *vbl. n.* want, indigence **6.** 124 [OE *nēodian*]
nedis, neidis. See **neid**
nedy *adj.* needy, poor **66.** 33 [ME; OE *nīed*]
neid *n.* lack, want **23.** 140, **77.** 19; **neyd** time of need **35.** 26; **nedis** *pl.* (sexual needs) **14.** 467 [OE *nīed*]
neid *adv.* of necessity, unavoidably **55.** 12 [OE *nīede*]
neidfull *adj.* necessary **78.** 26 [ME]
neiff *n.* fist **14.** 486 [nth. ME; ON *hnefe*]
neir, nere *adv.* near, close by **9.** 38, **10.** 133, **14.** 116, **50.** 54; almost **10.** 208, **14.** 2, **14.** 346, **20.** 14, **52.** 222; **neir hand** *prep.* close to **42.** 79 [ME; ON *nǣr*]
neir. See **nevir**
neis *n.* nose **74.** 16 [ME *nese*; cf. MLG *nese*]
nek, neck *n.* neck **9.** 84, **52.** 178, **52.** 204, **56.** 32, **77.** 36; *pl.* **52.** 28 [OE *hnecca*]
nemmyt *pp.* named, uttered **14.** 117 [OE *nemnan, nemde*]
Neptunus *n.* god of the sea, brother of Jupiter **10.** 121, **23.** 91, **50.** 65
nere. See **neir**
***Nero** Roman emperor **23.** 529
nerrest. See **narrest**
nether *conj.* neither **46.** 4, **75.** 41 [ME]
nettill *n.* nettle **50.** 137 [OE *netele*]
nevir, neir *adv.* at no time **10.** 222, **11.** 12, **13.** 17, **14.** 388, **17.** 8, **53.** 21 [OE *nǣfre*]
***nevow** *n.* nephew, descendant **23.** 529 [ME, OF; L *nepos*]
nevyne *v.* name, declare **2.** 60 [ME; ON *nefna*]
new *adj.* inclined to novelty, change **15.** 13 [OE *nīwe*]
new *adv.* newly, freshly **10.** 22, **13.** 24, **14.** 29, **52.** 65 [prec.]
neyd. See **neid**
nicht, nycht, nyght *n.* night **1.** 37, **2.** 27, **4.** 23, **10.** 36, **13.** 1, **14.** 412, **25.** 1, **37.** 1, *pl.* **14.** 1 [OE *niht*]
nichtbour, nighbouris. See **nychtbour**
nigirtnes *n.* niggardliness, meanness **73.** 12 [ME *negard*]

nill *v.* to be unwilling; *1 sg.* **39.** 85 [OE *nylle* (*ne wille*)]

nipcaik *n.* cake-pincher, miser **23.** 177 [ME *nyp*+OE *kaka*]

nixt, nyxt *adj.* nearest, following **3.** 41, **14.** 83, **14.** 246, **35.** 47, **58.** 16–19, **62.** 95 [OE *nēahsta*]

no thing *adv.* not at all **10.** 157 [ME; OE *nan þing*]

nobillis *n. pl.* noblemen **45.** 10, **63.** 23 [ME; f. next]

nobil(l), noble *adj.* of noble rank, splendid **9.** 97, **12.** 42, **10.** 88, **10.** 99, **10.** 153, **10.** 251; **nobillie, nobily** *adv.* splendidly **10.** 43, **14.** 31 [F *noble*; L *nobilis*]

nobilitee, nobilitie *n.* noble rank, excellence in virtue; *pers.* **10.** 176; **63.** 26 [OF]

nobilnes *n.* nobility of rank, and character **12.** 38, **16.** 87, **31.** 13, **35.** 91, *pers.* **51.** 27, **51.** 50 [ME; as **nobil(l)**]

nocht, not *n.* nothing **5.** 51, **16.** 44, **60.** 17; **no(u)cht, nought** *adv.* not at all, not **1.** 19, **4.** 14, **6.** 34, **10.** 67, **10.** 142, **14.** 109, **14.** 128; **for nocht** of no avail **9.** 63 [OE *nōht*]

noddill *n.* head, pate **14.** 275 [origin obscure]

nois, nos *n.* nose **9.** 81, **33.** 8 [OE *nosu*]

nolt *n. coll.* cattle **42.** 73, **54.** 103 [ME *nowte*; ON *naut*]

non. See **nane**

none *n.* noon, time of mid-day meal **19.** 19 [OE *nōn*]

none *pron. adj.* no one **7.** 7, **63.** 5 *et seq.* [ME; in place of **nane**]

nor *conj.* than **14.** 45, **23.** 134, **23.** 196, **32.** 10, **34.** 20; **nor I** may I **56.** 32 [origin obscure]

nor . . . not *conj.* and not (even) **5.** 37 [ME; perh. contracted f. OE *nōðer*]

norising *vbl. n.* nourishment **10.** 99 [OF *norir*]

Norny, Schir Thomas **27.** 2 (see Commentary)

***Northumbir** Northumberland **23.** 478

northwart *adv.* to the north **52.** 111 [OE *norðweard*]

Northway Norway **23.** 94

nos. See **nois**

not. See **nocht**

note, not(t) *n.* musical note; **not(t)is** *pl.*, **1.** 34, **10.** 104, **10.** 129, **14.** 5, **14.** 516, **16.** 3 [F; L *nota*]

note *v.* use, employ **14.** 264 [ME; OE *notian*]

nothir, nothair *pron.* neither **27.** 8, **14.** 358; **nother . . . nor** *adv.* neither . . . nor **14.** 86 [OE *nōðer*, *nowðer*]

nottit *ppl. adj.* celebrated **48.** 5 [ME v. *note(n)*; OF *not(t)er*; L *notare*]

nou *adv.* now **32.** 17, in consequence **32.** 6, next after this **33.** 2 [OE *nū*]

noucht, nought. See **nocht**

nowder, nowdir, nowthir *conj.* neither **22.** 7, **23.** 19, **23.** 72, **23.** 207, **37.** 15, **54.** 19, **66.** 3 [OE *nōhwæðer*, *nowðer*]

noy *n.* vexation, distress **14.** 116, **22.** 25, **59.** 22, bother **71.** 13 [ME; aphetic form of *anoye*; OF *anoi*]

noyis *n.* noise, din **16.** 25, **23.** 56, **23.** 227, **50.** 113, **54.** 93 [ME; OF *noise*]

***noyis** *3 sg.* injure, distress **23.** 344 [ME; OF *noire*]

nuk(e) *n.* obscure corner **20.** 13, **40.** 7, **44.** 45, **52.** 111, **77.** 33 [ME *noke*; origin obscure]

nummer *n.* number, company **44.** 27 [nth. ME *noumer*; OF *nombre*]

nureice *n.* nurse; *attrib.* wet-nurse's **42.** 61 [ME, OF *nurise*]

nurissing *vbl. n.* rearing **72.** 21 [ME *norisse*; OF *norir, noriss-*]

nurtur(e), nurtir, nurtour *n.* courtesy, good breeding **31.** 13, **44.** 54, **50.** 174; *pers.* **10.** 163 [OF *nourture*]

nybbillit *pa. t.* bit, nipped repeatedly **54.** 93 [nth. ME; MLG *nibbelen*]

nyce, nys(e) *adj.* silly, preposterous **15.** 22, **16.** 65, **23.** 177, **44.** 65, **53.** 41, **68.** 35 [ME; OF *nice*]

nychell *n.* nothing **42.** 74 (see Commentary) [L *nihil*]

nycht, nyght. See **nicht**

nychtbour, nichtbour *n.* neighbour **16.** 70, **65.** 4, **74.** 2; **nighbouris,**

nychtburis *pl.* **6.** 39, **6.** 53, **6.** 109, **75.** 69 [OE *nēahezebūr*]

nychtingall, nycht(t)ingale, nychtingaill *n.* nightingale (*megarhyncha luscinia*) **2.** 34, **16.** 13, **16.** 26, **16.** 33, **16.** 57, **50.** 173, *attrib.* **42.** 17 [OE *nihtegale*]

nyne *num. adj.* nine **14.** 117, **22.** 31; **nynte** *adj.* ninth **50.** 189 [OE *nizon*]

nys(e). See **nyce**

nyxt. See **nixt**

o *prep.* on **16.** 20 [reduced var. of *on*; OE]

obediens *n.* submission, allegiance **50.** 76 [ME; F *obédience*; L *obedientia*]

obscure *adj.* dark **63.** 68 [ME, OF; L *obscurus*]

obscurit (of) *pp.* dimmed, darkened **3.** 84 [L *obscurare*]

observance, observans *n.* worship, due ritual **1.** 27, **10.** 132, **15.** 15, **50.** 37, **52.** 9 [OF; L *observantia*]

obtene, opteyn *v.* gain, win **17.** 82, **35.** 66 [ME; F *obtenir*; L *obtinere*]

oceane *n.* ocean; *as adj.* **39.** 67 (see Commentary) [L *oceanus*]

ocht, oucht *n.* anything **5.** 24, **9.** 61, **14.** 336, **56.** 62, **71.** 36, **72.** 10 [OE *ōwiht*]

ockeraris *n. pl.* usurers (pejorative) **52.** 58 [ME; ON *okr* usury]

od. See **evin and od**

oddis *n. pl.* odds; **mak our oddis evyne** level our inequalities, remit our sins **2.** 56 [pl. of adj. **od**; ON *oddi*]

odouris *n. pl.* scents (= fragrant flowers) **50.** 6 [ME, OF *odur*; L *odor*]

of, off *prep.* from **1.** 7, **1.** 22, **6.** 11, **6.** 18, **13.** 5, **54.** 80; because of **6.** 97, **23.** 16; for **10.** 99, **55.** 22; on **9.** 48; as regards **14.** 182; **of before** *adv.* formerly **2.** 49, **10.** 213 [OE]

office *n.* official status, authority **39.** 26 [ME; L *officium*]

officiaris *n. pl.* servants, agents, of the king **44.** 2 [med. L *officiarius*]

***Olibrius** Roman prefect **23.** 540

olyve *n.* olive **35.** 68 [ME; L *oliva*]

ombesett *pa. t.* surrounded, beset **37.** 53 [OE *ymbe*+*besettan*; cf. MDu *ombeset*]

Omer the Greek poet Homer **10.** 67

on *pron.* one **16.** 38, **25.** 14 (for **ane**)

on(e) *prep.* on **14.** 106, **14.** 112, **14.** 205; of, about **14.** 301; **on(e) syd** aside **14.** 357, **77.** 14 [OE]

on to, on(e)to, ontill *prep.* unto **3.** 82, **9.** 12, **9.** 23, **11.** 12, **14.** 528, **50.** 105 [ME]

onie. See **ony**

onis *adv.* once **50.** 115 [midl. ME; for **anis**]

onlie *adj., adv.* only **3.** 136, **8.** 5, **65.** 34 [ME]

onone *adv.* forthwith **14.** 239, **14.** 264 [ME; OE *on ān*]

onrycht *adv.* wrong **28.** 4 [OE *on-*, *un-*+*riht*]

onsair *adj.* free from pain **47.** 23 [**sair**; cf. OE *unsār*, ON *ūsārr*]

onto, ontill. See **on to**

ony, onie *adj.* any **3.** 58, **3.** 85, **6.** 142, **12.** 34, **13.** 53, **14.** 475, **51.** 47 [OE *ǣniz*]

onywayis *n. phr.* by any means **17.** 20 [OE *on ǣnize wīsan*]

operationis, operatiounes *n. pl.* forces, agencies **1.** 11, **20.** 1 [L *operatio*]

opinȝoun *n.* opinion, view **13.** 55 [F; L *opinio*]

opnyt *pa. t.* opened **10.** 97; *pp.* **10.** 106; **oppin** *adj.* **50.** 59, **69.** 37 [OE *opnian*]

opprecioun, oppressioun *n.* molestation **6.** 121, **80.** 17; tyranny, extortion **63.** 62; malice **74.** 19 [OF; L *oppressio*]

oppres *v.* crush, afflict **49.** 22; **opprest** *pa. t.* **51.** 35; **oppressit** *ppl. adj.* afflicted **14.** 432, **51.** 29, **69.** 48 [ME; OF; L *opprimere* crush]

opteyn. See **obtene**

or *conj.* before **5.** 43, **10.** 7, **10.** 268, **12.** 14, **12.** 21, **14.** 116; (**afor . . .**) **or 5.** 55; lest **23.** 235, **47.** 18 [ON *ār*]

oratouris *n. pl.* orators; ambassadors, envoys **44.** 6 [ME; L *orator*]

oratrice *n.* (female) intercessor **2.** 48, **2.** 67 [AF; L *oratrix*]
ordane *v.* prepare, make ready **3.** 115; **ordand** *pa. t.* decreed **50.** 71, *pp.* **52C.** 5 [OF; L *ordinare*]
ordinance, ordynance *n.* principle, rule **15.** 22; army in battle order **10.** 171 [OF *ordenance*; med. L *ordinantia*]
ordinare *adj.* official, permanent **35.** *title* [OF; L *ordinarius*]
ordour *n.* orders, ordination (one of the seven sacraments) **6.** 45; order, discipline **39.** 30, **75.** 69; array **48.** 46; *pl.* hierarchy **22.** 31 [ME; F *ordre*]
organe *n.* organ (musical instrument) **35.** 22; **vane organis** *pl.* jugular veins **54.** 21 [ME, OF; L *organum*]
orientale *adj.* eastern, in the east **2.** 26 [L *orientalis*]
orisoun *n.* prayer **36.** 31 [ME; OF *orison*]
oritorie *n.* chapel for prayer **3.** 2 [L *oratorium*]
Orliance Orleans **22.** 56
ornat *adj.* ornate, highly ornamented, splendid **14.** 505, **76.** 10, **81.** 31 [L *ornare*]
ost *n.* host, army **9.** 98 [ME; OF]
ostir *n.* oyster *attrib.* **23.** 242 [ME; OF *oistre*; L *ostrea*]
othir. See **uder**
oucht. See **ocht**
ouirhie. See **ourhie**
ouirpast *pp.* crossed **12.** 18 [OE *ofer*+F *passer*]
ouirsie. See **ourse**
ouir word *n.* burden, refrain **40.** 4 [OE *ofer*+*wōrd*]
oule, owle *n.* owl **34.** 7, *fig.* **23.** 236; *pl.* **42.** 24, **50.** 122 [OE *ūle*]
oulkis. See **owk**
our, ower *prep., adv., prefix* over, too **11.** 20, **13.** 31, **14.** 165, **29.** 21, **32.** 25; throughout **14.** 76 [OE *ofer*]
ourcast *v.* turn over, become upset **52.** 150 [ME]
ourcoverd *pp.* covered over **59.** 15 [ME *overcover*; **our**+OF *covrir*]
ourcumin, ourcummyn *pp.* overcome, vanquished **4.** 38, **14.** 325 [OE *ofercuman*]
ourdrife *v.* waste time **6.** 20 [OE *oferdrīfan*]
oure *poss. pron.* our **5.** 3, **5.** 4, **10.** 259 [OE *ūre*]
ourgane *ppl. adj.* overcome **13.** 12, **51.** 99 [OE *ofergān*]
ourgilt *pa. t.* gilded over **10.** 27, *pp.* **10.** 267 [OE *ofer*+ME *gild*]
ourhelit *pp.* covered over, hidden **10.** 93 [OE *ofer*+*helian*]
ourhie, ouirhie *adj., adv.* too high **23.** 188, **80.** 13 [OE *oferhēah*]
ourlaidin *ppl. adj.* overloaded **79.** 27 [OE *hladan, ȝehladen*]
ourscailit *pp.* scattered, sprinkled, dappled **10.** 26 [OE *ofer*+ME *scail* (prob. Scand)]
ourse, ouirsie *v.* overlook, tolerate **44.** 77; oversee, administer **79.** 58 [OE *oferseōn*]
oursettis *v. 3 sg.* puts off, passes over **5.** 62; **oursett** *pp.* defeated **23.** 245 [ME]
ourstred *pa. t.* bestrode **23.** 209 [cf. nth. ME *ouire-stride*; OE *strīdan*]
ourtak *v.* overtake, catch up with **60.** 14 [ME; **our**+**tak**]
ourthort *adv.* across, over **9.** 55 [nth. ME; OE *ofer*+ON *þvert*]
outthrow *prep.* throughout **16.** 28 [OE adv. *ūt*+prep. *ðurh*]
ower. See **our**; **slyd**
owk *n.* week **13.** 27; **oulkis** *attrib.* weeks **14.** 177 [OE *wice*]
owl(e). See **oule**
owsprang *pa. t.* sprang forth **54.** 111 [ME; see **spring**]
owt *adv.* out, aloud **20.** 10, **23.** 53, **37.** 46; *prep.* **28.** 2 [OE *ūt*]
owther *adv.* either **44.** 81 [ME; OE *ōhwæðer*]
Owyr Donald Owre **34.** 19
ox *n.* an ox **23.** 142; **oxin** *pl.* **27.** 17, **39.** 43 [OE *oxa*]
Oxinfurde (University of) Oxford **76.** *colophon*
oxstar *n.* armpit; (upper) arm **74.** 17 [OE *ōhsta*]
***oyis** *n. pl.* grandchildren **23.** 308 [var. of *o*; Gael *ogha*]

pacience, patience, patiens *n.* constancy, calm endurance **65.** 22; *pers.* **10.** 164, **69.** 21 [OF; L *patientia*]
pacient *adj.* forbearing, longsuffering **6.** 38 [OF; L *patient-em*]
pacok, pako *n.* peacock **14.** 379, **16.** 14, *attrib.* **58.** 8; *pl.* **50.** 123 [ME *pa-cock*; OE *pāwa* (L *pavo*)+ *cok*]
padȝane, pageant *n.* pageant **52.** 109, *fig.* **62.** 46; **padgeanes** *pl.* tableaux, stage scenes **48.** 51 [ME *pagyn*; Anglo-L *pagina*. Origin obscure; see *OED*, s.v. *pageant*]
***padok** *n.* toad *attrib.* **23.** 342 [ME; OE *pade*+dim. suffix]
page *n.* low fellow, knave **14.** 313, **45.** 36 [OF]
pageant. See **padȝane**
paikis *n. pl.* due thrashing **23.** 70 [origin unknown; cf. *paik* to beat]
paile, paill *adj.* wan, pallid **4.** 27, **50.** 11, **54.** 2 [OF *pale*; L *pallidum*]
paill *n.* canopy of fine cloth **48.** 13 [OF; L *pallium*]
pairis *n. pl.* pairs, couples **52.** 35 [ME, F; L *par*]
pairt, part, pert *n.* part, share **42.** 46, **56.** 17, **65.** 34, **69.** 47, **77.** 4; *pl.* **61.** 13; **in a pairt** partly, for a time **47.** 17 [ME; F *part*; L *partem*]
pairt *v.* divide, share **40.** 5 *et seq.* [ME; F *partir*; L *partire*]
pairtie *adj.* particoloured **42.** 16 [ME; F *parti*; L *partire*]
Pais, pasche, pesche *n.* Pasch, Easter **5.** 63, **27.** 49, **67.** 19 [ME; med. L *pascha*]
Paislay Paisley **23.** 78 (see Commentary)
pak *n.* bundle, pedlar's pack ***23.** 445, **45.** 58 [ME; MLG]
pako. See **pacok**
palestrall *adj.* magnificent **2.** 73 (app. misuse for *palatial*; see Commentary) [L *palaestra*]
palfrayis *n. pl.* saddle-horses for ladies **43.** 46 [ME; OF *palefrai*]
palice, palis *n.* palace **26.** 4, **63.** 68 [ME; OF *palais*; L *palatium*]
Pallas Minerva, goddess of war and wisdom **10.** 78, **31.** 12
pallatt *n.* pate, head **54.** 51 [ME; OF *palet* headpiece]
pamphelet *n.* wench, strumpet **32.** 14 [OF; title of med. L comedy; Gk *πάμφιλος* beloved of all; cf. obs. Du *pampoelie*]
pane *n.* pain, suffering **3.** 75, **3.** 134, **8.** 13, **12.** 22, **12.** 46, **42.** 3; *pers.* **3.** 109; *pl.* **5.** 16, **19.** 35, **22.** 63; **panefull** *adj.* **19.** 5 *et seq.*, **22.** 19 [OF *peine*; L *poena*]
panence. See **pennance**
pans *v.* think, consider **40.** 24; **pansing** *vbl. n.* meditating, thinking **19.** 13 [OF *panser*]
pansches *n. pl.* entrails; tripe **75.** 25 [ME, ONF *panche*; L *pantex*]
pansing. See **pans**
panting *pres. p.* (painting) displaying **45.** 50 [ME; OF *peindre*; L *pingere*]
panton *n.* slipper **28.** 27 [origin uncertain; cf. F *pantoufle*]
papingay *n.* parrot **14.** 382; **papingais** *pl.* **50.** 123 [OF; see *OED*, s.v. *popinjay*]
pappis *n. pl.* breasts **10.** 63 [ME]
par de *interj.* by God, indeed **82.** 28 [ME; OF]
paradice, parradyis, paradyce, peradis, *n.* the celestial paradise, Heaven **2.** 40, **2.** 71, **57.** 4, **68.** 43, *fig.* **22.** 4, **31.** 9; the earthly paradise, Eden **48.** 30 [L *paradisus* a park]
parage *n.* noble lineage **35.** 15 [ME, F; med. L *paraticum*]
paramour *n.* lover **16.** 47; **paramoris** *pl.* **82.** 22 [ME; OF *par amour*]
parcialitie *n.* prejudice, bias **74.** 25 [ME, OF; L *partialitas*]
***pardoun.** See **perdoun**
***Parise** Paris **23.** 437
parlament, perliament *n.* parliament **6.** 134, **35.** 65 [ME; OF; med. L *parlamentum*]
parrell, perrell *n.* risk, danger **5.** 68, **77.** 39 [ME; F *péril*; L *periculum*]
parroche *n. attrib.* parish **6.** 84, **75.** 16 [OF; late L *parochia*]
parrochynnis *n. pl.* parishes, livings **79.** 56 [prec.; suffix obscure]

parsiall *adj.* biased, unfair **6.** 131 [OF *parcial*; late L *partialis*]

***part** *n.* particular, matter **23.** 406; **partis** *pl.* portions **41.** 2 [OE; L *pars*]

party *n.* company (in combat) **10.** 143 [F; L *pars*]

pas *v.* go **57.** 2, **59.** 5, **60.** 6; **pasis** *3 pl.* **19.** 17; **passit** *pa. t.* went in procession **52.** 35; *pp.* past, gone **1.** 37, **63.** 27; **passing (of)** *vbl. n.* going on **14.** 474 [F *passer*]

pasche. See **Pais**

passioun *n.* suffering (of Christ) **3.** 5, **3.** 109, **12.** 29 [ME; L *passio* (*patior*)]

passit. See **pas**

pastance *n.* pastime, recreation **14.** 526, **19.** 12 [prob. phonetic repr. of F *passe-temps*]

pastouris *n. pl.* pastures **43.** 16 [ME, OF *pasture*; L *pastura*]

pater noster *n.* (a recital of) the Lord's Prayer in Latin **3.** 3, **6.** 95 [Matt. vi. 9]

patiens. See **pacience**

patriarchis *n. pl.* Abraham, Isaac, and Jacob **22.** 45 (see Commentary) [ME; OF; L *patriarcha*; Gk]

patroun *n.* protector, patron, advocate **31.** 14; **patronis** *pl.* **40.** 13 [ME; L *patronus*]

patteris *3 sg.* mumbles (his) prayers **74.** 18 [ME; L **pater noster**]

pavys *n.* large shield; *fig.* protection, defence **2.** 65 [OF *pavais*; app. f. *Pavia* where the *pavais* originated]

Pawlis, Sanct S. Paul **80.** 7

payntit *pa. t.* adorned, beautified **14.** 379 [ME; OF *peindre, peint*; L *pingere*]

payntouris *n. pl.* artists **44.** 16 [ME; OF *peintour*; L *pictor*]

peax, pece, peis *n.* peace, concord **4.** 35, **7.** 8, **50.** 181, **68.** 34, **74.** 3 [OF *pais*; L *pax*]

***pece, the** *phr.* apiece, each **23.** 439 [ME, OF; F *la pièce*]

pechis *n. pl.* laboured breaths **74.** 53 [onomat.]

peciable *adj.* (*as adv.*) peaceably, quietly **50.** 112 [ME; OF *paisible*; L *pax*]

peddir *n.* pedlar, packman **14.** 302 [? *ped* pannier]

peilit *ppl. adj.* mean, meagre **23.** 170; disfeathered, bald **23.** 237; plundered, destitute **23.** 241; **peld** *ppl. adj.* stripped bare **43.** 16 [ME *pelen* pillage]

peip *n.* cheep, squeak **37.** 64 [ME; cf. L *pipare*]

peir *n.* equal, rival **11.** 20, **14.** 314; **peirles** *adj.* matchless **2.** 74 [OF *peer*]

peirt. See **pert**

peirtrikis. See **pertrik**

peis *n. coll.* pease, pea plants **23.** 115 [OE *pise*; L *pisa*]

peis. See **peax**

peld. See **peilit**

pelf(f)e *n.* spoil, booty **40.** 5, **40.** 10 [ME; OF *pelfre*]

pelour *n.* plunderer, robber **23.** 70, **23.** 80, **23.** 114, **81.** 12 [ME]

pendit *pp.* attached, appended **71.** 60 [F *pendre*; L *pendere*]

pene *n.* quill pen **14.** 526, **pennis** *pl.* **10.** 268; **pen(n)is** *pl.* feathers **23.** 157, **50.** 121, **53.** 23, **54.** 83, **54.** 102 [OF; L *penna*]

pene *n.* peg; *fig.* penis **14.** 135 [late OE *pinn*; LG]

penis. See **pene**

pennance, pennence, panence *n.* penance, act of self-mortification or discipline **3.** 134, **5.** 2, **6.** 44, **6.** 93, **9.** 12, **22.** 10, **22.** 67, **44.** 73 [OF; L *paenitentia*]

pennis. See **pene**

pennyis *n. pl.* (silver) pence **56.** 58 [OE *pęning*]

pensioun *n.* regular payment to a servant **47.** 27 [ME; F; L *pensionem*]

penuritie *n.* poverty, destitution **19.** 13 [L *pęnuria*]

pepill, peple, peopill *n.* people **14.** 73, **14.** 332, **14.** 368, **14.** 475, **39.** 33, **48.** 50, **52C.** 34 [OF *poeple*; L *populus*]

peradis. See **paradice**

peralous. See **perilouse**

***perambalit** *pa. t.* walked about **23.** 337 [L *perambulare*]

percaice *adv.* perhaps, by chance **71.** 52 [ME; OF *par cas*]

perchance *adv.* maybe, perhaps **9.** 15 [ME; OF *par chance*]

perdoun *n.* pardon, indulgence **14.** 475 [ME; OF; med. L *perdonum*]

perfurneis *v.* perform, carry out **14.** 84 [OF *parfournir*]

perfyt(e), perfytt, perfit *adj.* perfect, mature, full **10.** 68, **14.** 305, **16.** 79, **17.** 14, **23.** 111; *adv.* fully **33.** 4 [OF *parfite*; L *perfectus*]

perilouse, peralous, perrell(o)us *adj.* dangerous, dreadful **10.** 196, **23.** 150, **32.** 34, **76.** 8, **77.** 29 [ME; OF *perillos*; L *periculosus*]

perle *n.* pearl; *fig.* **14.** 443, **31.** 4, **50.** 180 [F; med. L *perla*]

perliament. See **parlament**

perly *adj.* round and lustrous like a pearl **10.** 14 [F *perle*; med. L *perla*]

***Pernaso** Mt. Parnassus in Phocis, sacred to the Muses **23.** 337

peronall *n.* wanton young woman **14.** 231 [OF; L name *Petronilla*]

perqueir *adv.* by heart, perfectly **5.** 32 [F *par cueur*]

perrell. See **parrell**

perrellus. See **perilouse**

persaif *v.* perceive **83.** 17; **persavit** *pp.* become aware of **10.** 181; **persaveing** *vbl. n.* perception, observation *pers.* **51.** 38 [ME *perceive*; OF *perçoivre*; L *percipere*]

pers(e) *v.* pierce, penetrate **10.** 107, **10.** 183, **13.** 40, **14.** 249; **persit** *pa. t.* **14.** 389; *pres. p.* **3.** 44, **21.** 4; **perst** *pp.* **1.** 38; **persing** *ppl. adj.* **50.** 93 [OF *percer*]

perseveir *v.* continue in constancy **18.** 7 [ME, F; L *perseverare*]

persew *v.* attend, enter **6.** 84, **8.** 6, come in **16.** 12; *3 pl.* **14.** 478; *pa. t.* went **10.** 172 [ME; OF *porsievre*; L *prosequere*]

personage *n.* parson's benefice **45.** 35 [ME; OF]

perso(u)n(e) *n.* person, body, self **14.** 16, **14.** 219, **14.** 299, **14.** 314, **35.** 39, **49.** 21; = selves **48.** 68; *pl.* **14.** 435, **14.** 473 [OF; L *persona*]

persute *n.* attack, assault **10.** 182 [OF *poursieute*]

pert. See **pairt**

pert, peirt *adj.* forward, saucy **13.** 10, **14.** 305; *comp.* **pertlyar** more impudently **14.** 244 [aphetic f. *apert*; OF]

***Perth** Perth **23.** 281

pertlyar. See **pert**

pertrik *n.* partridge (*perdix cinerea*) **22.** 51; **peirtrikis** *pl.* **42.** 13 [ME; OF *perdriz*; L *perdix*]

perverst *ppl. adj.* perverted, wicked **6.** 131, **14.** 249 [L *perversus*]

Pesche. See **Pais**

pet *n.* spoiled child **23.** 247 [origin unknown]

pete. See **petie**

pete(w)ous, pet(e)ous(e) *adj.* lamentable, deplorable **8.** 13, **9.** 31, **23.** 163, compassionate **14.** 473; **petewouslie, petuously, piteuslie** **40.** 9, **62.** 49, **75.** 46 [ME; OF *piteus*]

peticionis *n. pl.* clauses in the Lord's Prayer **6.** 95 [OF; L *petition-em*]

pet(i)e, pety, pietie *n.* compassion **12.** 28; *pers.* **3.** 110, **9.** 49, **9.** 54; cause for pity **3.** 62, **14.** 442 [ME; OF *pité*; L *pietas*]

Petir, Sanct S. Peter **80.** 7

petous. See **pete(w)ous**

petuously. See **pete(w)ous**

peur(e). See **pure**

phane *n.* weather-vane **39.** 95 [OE *fana*]

Phanus Faunus, god of fields and fertility; identified with Pan **10.** 119

***Pharao** Pharaoh of Egypt **23.** 530

phary. See **fary**

Phebus Apollo; the sun **1.** 6, **10.** 7, **10.** 16; *gen.* **10.** 33, **10.** 246, **50.** 20, **50.** 165

philosophouris *n. pl.* philosophers, scientists **44.** 5 [ME; OF *philosophe*]

phisicianis *n. pl.* physicians, healers **62.** 42 [ME, OF *fisicien*; L *physica*]

phisnomy *n.* countenance (as an index to character) **23.** 81 [ME; OF]

Piccardy, Pikkardy Picardy **35.** 84, **55.** 40

pik *n.* pitch (from tar) **56.** 81, ***23.** 335 [OE *pic*; L *pix*]

***Pilate,** Pontius, Roman procurator of Judaea 26–36 A.D. **23.** 523
pilgrame *n.* pilgrim **60.** 9 [ME; OF **pelegrin*; L *peregrinum*]
pilgrymage *n.* devotional journey to a sacred place **14.** 474 [ME; OF *pelerinage*]
pillie *n.* ? colt **28.** 25 [? OF *poulain*]
pingill *v.* strive, vie **23.** 114 [origin obscure]
piscence *n.* puissance, strength **50.** 108, **62.** 33 [F *puissance*]
pische *v.* piss **14.** 187 [ME; OF *pisser*]
piteuslie. See **pete(w)ous**
pitht *n.* vigour, mettle **14.** 80 [OE *piþa*]
place *n.* residence, mansion, home **2.** 73, **60.** 6, rendezvous **71.** 49; *pl.* rendezvous **14.** 285 [ME; med. L *placia*]
plait, plate *n.* iron, armour **10.** 152, **63.** 31; **plaitis** *pl.* plates of iron in armour **52.** 167 [ME, OF *plate*; late L *plattus*]
plane *n.* open country **34.** 39, **39.** 23; treeless waste **59.** 27; *pl.* battlefields **9.** 92 [ME; L *planum*]
plane *v.* express, lament **50.** 31; **ple(i)nȝie** complain **42.** 46, **79.** 41; **pleyne** complain of injury **9.** 29; **plenis** *3 pl.* make lovers' plaints **14.** 482 [ME *plenȝe*; OF *pleindre*; L *plangere*]
plane *adj.* clear, unobstructed, open **6.** 70, **39.** 55, **43.** 16; sheer **50.** 181; *adv.* entirely, fully **6.** 70; **in plane** plainly, clearly **14.** 244 [OF *plain*; L *planus*]
planeit *n.* planet, carried round the earth by the rotation of its sphere **1.** 12 [OF; late L *planeta*]
planis. See **plane**
plant(is). See **plaunt**
plat *pa. t.* fell down flat **37.** 58 [ME; cf. Ger *platten*]
plate. See **plait**
plaunt *n.* plant, scion *fig.* **31.** 2, **31.** 30; **plantis** *pl.* **50.** 48 [OE *plante*; L *planta*]
play, pley *n.* brisk action, entertainment, delight **13.** 59, **18,** 3, **21.** 13, **22.** 37, **32.** 34, **50.** 181, **54.** 27; *pl.* stage plays **14.** 71, **69.** 5 [OE *pleȝa*]
playis *v. 3 pl.* plead, contend for **39.** 55 [ME; AN n. *plai*]
playis *v. 3 sg.* plays **41.** 13, **42.** 74; *3 pl.* **20.** 10, **62.** 46; **playand** *pres. p.* **38.** 101, **48.** 45; **playit** *pa. t.* **10.** 128, **10.** 205, **37.** 4, **48.** 51, **51.** 9; *pp.* **61.** 13 [OE *pleȝan*, *plaȝian*]
pleasance. See **plesance**
plece *n.* place **45.** 76 [ME, F *place*]
pled, pleid *n.* plea, excuse **32.** 14; discussion **16.** 115; legal dispute **71.** 38 [ME *plaiden*; OF *plaidier*]
pleid *v.* wrangle, argue **26.** 5 [as prec.]
pleinȝe. See **plane**
pleis, ples *v.* please, choose, like **14.** 63, **26.** 5, **46.** 1, **48.** 70, **68.** 41; *3 sg.* **51.** 40; *pa. t.* **14.** 57 [ME; OF *plaisir*]
pleisand. See **plesand**
plenȝie. See **plane**
plenis. See **plane**
ples. See **pleis**
plesance, pleasance, plesans *n.* delight, joy **14.** 443, **15.** 11, **17.** 14, **18.** 3, **22.** 7, **22.** 37, **50.** 145, **50.** 180, **64.** 33; *pers.* **10.** 150, **51.** 32 [OF *plaisance*; L *placentia*]
plesand, pleisand, plesant *adj.* pleasing, delightful **10.** 143, **14.** 16, **14.** 80, **14.** 207, **24.** 2, **44.** 19, (*as n.*) **14.** 158; **plesandest** *sup.* **61.** 18; **plesandly** *adv.* **14.** 374 [OF *pleisant*; pres. p. of *plaisir*]
plesere, plesour *n.* delight, enjoyment **10.** 92, **68.** 18 [OF *plesir*; L *placere*]
plesit *pp.* pleased, satisfied **41.** 5 [ME; as prec.]
plet *ppl. adj.* intertwined **14.** 15 [ME v. *playt*; OF n. *plait*]
***pleuch.** See **pluch**
plever *n.* (? golden) plover (*pluvialis apricaria*) **22.** 51 [ME; OF *plovier*; late L *plovarius*]
pley *n.* action at law **71.** 39 [ME, AN *plai*; L *placitum*]
pley. See **play**
pleyne. See **plane**
plicht, plicht anker, plycht anker

n. main anchor of a ship *fig.* **2.** 31, **61.** 46, *pl.* **10.** 187 [OE *pliht*+*ancer*; LG *plicht-anker*]

pluch, *pleuch *n.* plough ***23.** 366; *attrib.* **50.** 111 [OE *plōȝ*]

plukkis *v. 2 sg.* steal, snatch **23.** 157;

pluckit *pp.* snatched, pulled **63.** 17; **plukit** *ppl. adj.* plucked **14.** 382 [*pluccian*]

plum *adj.* plump, fat **27.** 38 [? ME v. to swell]

plumis *n. pl.* feathers **42.** 9 [ME; OF; L *pluma*]

plunge *n.* deep pool, depth **54.** 113; **plungeing** *vbl. n.* throwing violently forward **14.** 356 [OF v. *plunjer*]

Pluto king of the lower world, husband of Proserpina **10.** 125, ***23.** 535

ply *n.* condition **23.** 170, **43.** 51 [OF *ploi*]

plycht. See **plicht**

pockis *n.* (*pl.*) pox, syphilis **32.** 5 *et seq.* [OE *poc* pustule]

point(i)s *n. pl.* articles, items **6.** 63, **6.** 87 [F; L *punctum*]

polesie *n.* improvement in buildings, amenity **75.** 20 [ME; L *politia* government; in Sc infl. by L *policies* elegance]

polist *ppl. adj.* polished **2.** 62 [ME *polis-*; L *polire*]

polk breik *n.* ? tartan, chequered bag **23.** 145 [Gael *poca*+*breacan*]

polkis *n. pl.* bags, sacks **23.** 147 [ME; Gael *poca*]

Pollexen Polyxena, daughter of Priam king of Troy **31.** 11

port *n.* city gate **48.** 17 [ME; F; L *porta*]

port *n.* harbour; *fig.* **61.** 42 [OE; L *portus*]

port *n.* bearing, mien **23.** 163, **31.** 11, **61.** 18 [ME; F; L *portare*]

portar, porteir *n.* porter, doorkeeper **9.** 18, **9.** 22; **porter** *attrib.* porter's **9.** 76 [OF *portier*; L *portarius*]

portratour, portrature *n.* appearance, figure, form **10.** 150, **48.** 35 (see Commentary) [ME; OF]

posceding *vbl. n.* possessing, seizing **6.** 122 [cf. F *posséder*; L *possidere*]

posseid *v.* hold, occupy **36.** 15, **45.** 48, **61.** 33, **77.** 17 [as prec.]

possessioun *n.* property, wealth **63.** 61, **74.** 33 [ME; OF; L *possessio*]

possessoris *n. pl.* owners, holders **14.** 198 [ME; F *possesseur*; L]

possest (in) *pp.* put in legal possession (of) **51.** 88, **53.** 22, **64.** 18 [ME; OF *possessier*; L *possidere*]

possoddy *n.* broth **13.** 30 [origin obscure; perh. related to *posset*]

postponit *pp.* deferred, put off **6.** 90 [L *postponere*]

pot *n.* deep hole, abyss **52.** 119 [perh. f. OE *pott* vessel]

potestatis *n. pl.* the sixth order of angels **1.** 10; rulers, lords **62.** 18 [L *potestas*]

potingaris *n. pl.* apothecaries **44.** 16 [ME; med. L *apothecarius*]

pottingry *n.* pharmacy, the apothecary's art **54.** 29 [prec.]

pount *n.* point; mark, sign, characteristic **15.** 17 [ME; F *point*; L *punctum*]

povertie *n.* poverty, want **66.** 8, **66.** 22 [ME; OF; L *paupertas*]

pow *v.* pull, drag, tear **3.** 110 [OE *pullian*]

powder *n.* gunpowder **10.** 238; **powderit, powdirit** *pp.* powdered, sprinkled, spangled **10.** 23, **23.** 192 [F; L *pulvis, pulveris*]

power(e) *n.* authority, jurisdiction **5.** 31; vigour, force **10.** 183 [AF *pouair*; late L *potere*]

poynt *n.*; **in poynt of dede** about to die **62.** 90 [see **pount**]

poysone *n.* poison; *fig.* treason **23.** 78 (see Commentary) [ME; OF; L *potio*]

poysonid *pp.* poisoned **26.** 9; **poysonit** *ppl. adj.* full of poison, malignant **23.** 70 [ME; OF *poisonner*]

practicianis *n. pl.* practical men **62.** 41 [F *practicien*; L *practica*]

practik *n.* policy, stratagem **34.** 26, **79.** 8; *pl.* **54.** 45 [ME; OF; Gk]

prasis *3 pl.* praise, extol **14.** 482 [ME; OF *preisier*; late L *preciare*]

prattelie *adv.* ingeniously, skilfully **48.** 51 [ME; OE *prættiȝ*]

pray *n.* prey, spoil, victim **10.** 180,

50. 126, **57.** 5, **62.** 95 [OF *preie*; L *praeda*]

prayis *3 pl.* pray, supplicate **14.** 482 [ME; OF *preier*; L *precari*]

prays *n.* praise **72.** *colophon* [ME; see **prasis**]

preching *vbl. n.* religious discourse, exhortation **6.** 37, (ironic) **14.** 249, **16.** 33; **preichingis** *pl.* sermons, public services **14.** 71 [OF *prechier*; L *praedicare*]

prechour *n.* preacher, one who proclaims **11.** 23 [ME; OF; L *praedicator*]

precius, pretius *adj.* of great value, dear **6.** 145, **6.** 151, **14.** 374, **31.** 33, **50.** 168 [OE *precios*; L *pretiosus*]

preclare, preclair *adj.* illustrious **24.** 2, **47.** 27, **48.** 65 [L *praeclarus*]

preiche *v.* preach, proclaim **53.** 37, **55.** 14; **preichit** *pp.* **55.** 37 [ME; OF *preichier;* L *praedicare*]

preichingis. See **preching**

preif(f) *n.* test, trial **54.** 45; evidence, example **34.** 18, **46.** 19 [ME; OF *prueve*]

preif(f) *v.* make a trial, test **42.** 58; try, taste **42.** 13; demonstrate, establish **23.** 80, **23.** 86, **73.** 9; turn out to be **32.** 8, **42.** 43; proves, turns out *3 sg.* **33.** 17 [ME *prover*; L *probare*]

preis *n.* crowd, throng **14.** 72, **78.** 33 [ME; cf. F *presse*, L *pressare*]

preis *v.* urge, drive **53.** 14, **77.** 5 [ME; OF *presser*; L *pressare*]

preist *n.* priest **56.** 7; confessor with authority to absolve **5.** 43, **5.** 51; *pl.* **38.** 105, **52.** 28 [OE *prēost*; L *presbyter*]

prelat, prelot *n.* ecclesiastical dignitary **54.** 49, **14.** 307; **prelottis** *gen.* **45.** 50, **45.** 53; **prelotis** *pl.* **62.** 18 [ME; OF *prélat*; L *praelatus*]

premocione *n.* promotion, advancement **20.** 18 [ME; L *promotio*]

prenecod *n.* pin-cushion; *fig. mons pubis* **37.** 39 (see Commentary) [OE *prēon*+ON *kodde*]

prent *n.* stamp, imprint **52.** 66 [ME; OF *priente*]

prentit *pp.* stamped, imprinted **5.** 45 [ME; OF pp. *preint*; L *premere*]

pres, prese *n.* affray, melée, the thick of battle **10.** 149, **10.** 172; dense crowd, throng **14.** 475, **48.** 50 [ME; L *pressare*]

pres *v.* struggle, strive **61.** 3; **pressit** *pa. t.* hastened forward **54.** 49 [ME; OF *presser*; L *premere*]

presandlie *adv.* at once, quickly **14.** 15 [OF *present*; L *praesens*]

prese. See **pres**

presence, presens *n.* presence, physical closeness **52.** 123; *pers.* **10.** 187, **10.** 196, **10.** 203 [ME; OF; L *praesentia*]

present *pp.* presented **26.** 4 [ME; OF *presenter*; L *praesentare*]

presente *adj.* directly recalled, immediate **5.** 12 [OF; L *praesens*]

presome *v.* venture, dare, take the liberty **14.** 313 [F *presumer*; L *praesumere*]

presone *n.* prison **4.** 34 [ME; OF *prisun*; L *prehensio*, v. *prendere*]

presoneir, prisonnere *n.* prisoner **9.** 1 *et passim*, **10.** 209; *pl.* **4.** 37 [F; med. L *prisionarius*; prec.]

pressit. See **pres**

***prestyt** *pp.* ordained to priest's orders **23.** 309 [OE n. *prēost*]

presumpcioun *n.* arrogance, effrontery **6.** 117 [OF; L *praesumptionem*]

***pretendis** *2 sg.* profess, claim a right to **23.** 42; **pretendand** *pres. p.* **23.** 26 [ME; L *praetendere*]

pretius. See **precius**

preve *adv.* secretly **14.** 273 [OF *privé*]

preveit *pp.* tried, tested **14.** 80; **preving** *vbl. n.* trying out **54.** 28 [OF *prover*; L *probare*]

prevelege *n.* dispensation, special right **14.** 207 [ME; L *privilegium*]

prevely, privaly *adv.* secretly, stealthily **14.** 525, **82.** 39 [ME; F *privé*; L *privatus*]

prevene *v.* forestall, supplant **17.** 70; **prevenis** *3 sg.* **74.** 13 [L *praevenire*]

Priapus god of fertility **10.** 118 (see Commentary)

price. See **prys**

prickill *v.* prick, sting, affiict **19.** 30

priclis, pric(k)illis *3 sg.* **19.** 5, **19.** 10, **19.** 35 [OE n. *pricel*]
***prickit** *ppl. adj.* skewered, impaled **23.** 548 [OE *prician*]
pricklous *n.* tailor, 'louse-killer' (derisive) **52.** 125 [OE *prician*+*lūs*]
prid, pryd *n.* pride (*superbia*), the primary sin **6.** 19, **23.** 236, **50.** 111, **56.** 11; *pers.* **52.** 16 [late OE *prȳto* sb. from adj. *prūd*; OF *prut*]
prik *n.* skewer **9.** 81 [OE *prica*]
princes *n.* princess **24.** 2, **24.** 11, **30.** 1, **31.** 4, **48.** 65, **50.** 63 [ME; F]. See **princis**
principall *n.* chief, ruler **50.** 178 [ME; F; L *principalis*]
princis *n. pl.* princes, kings **62.** 18, **63.** 29; **princes** *gen.* prince's **50.** 166 [ME, F; L *princeps*]
prising *pres. p.* valuing, esteeming **6.** 109; **prysit** *pp.* **82.** 44 [cf. **prys**; OF *prisier*; L *pretiare*]
prisonnere. See **presoneir**
privaly. See **prevely**
probacion *n.* demonstration, proof **76.** 9 [ME, OF; L *probatio*]
proceidis *3 pl.* come forth **63.** 41 [ME; F *procéder*; L *procedere*]
proces *n.* discussion, argument **55.** 19 [ME, F; L *processus*]
processioun *n.* moving company on a festive occasion **48.** 17 [ME, F; L *processio*]
prochin *n.* parishioner **40.** 24 [ME; OF *parochien*]
proclame *v.* declare, publish **11.** 14, **50.** 24; denounce **23.** 24, **75.** 67; **proclamit** *pp.* celebrated **35.** 54 [ME; L *proclamare*]
prodissioun *n.* treason, treachery **34.** 4 [ME; OF; L *proditio*]
profeitis *n. pl.* prophets (who spoke for God) **22.** 45 [ME; L *propheta*; Gk]
proferis *3 pl.* offer **14.** 483 [ME; OF *purofrir*]
professioun *n.* religious vow **74.** 47 [ME; L *professio*]
proffeit(t) *n.* benefit, gain **67.** 7, **75.** 4, **75.** 50, **75.** 71 [ME, OF; L *profectus*]
prolixitnes *n.* prolixity, tediousness **35.** 83 [F *prolixité*; L *prolixitas*]
promocioun *n.* advancement, preferment **45.** 32 [ME; L *promotio*]
promyt *v.* promise **50.** 38 [ME; L *promittere*]
***pronunciate** *ppl. adj.* pronounced, declared **23.** 525 [ME *pronounce*; OF; *pronuntiare*]
prop *n.* shooting butt, target *fig.* **70.** 12 (see Commentary) [ME; cf. MDu *proppe*]
proper, propir *adj.* one's own **6.** 85, **40.** 12 (see Commentary) [F *propre*; L *proprius*]
prophane *adj.* unholy; unclean, polluted **39.** 35 [F; L *profanus*]
propois *v.* state, intend, purpose **32.** 6 [F *proposer*; L *proponere*]
proporcioun *n.* balance, symmetry **10.** 90 [ME; L *proportio*]
propyne *v.* present **48.** 61 [perh. orig. offer a present of wine; ME; L *propinare* drink one's health]
Proserpyna daughter of Jupiter and Ceres, wife of Pluto **10.** 75
prosperit(i)e *n.* good fortune, success **7.** 8, **18.** 9, **76.** 8 [ME; OF; L *prosperitas*]
protest *v.* request, demand, stipulate **14.** 158; *pres. p.* **37.** 68 [F; L *protestari*]
***prouvait** *pp.* furnished, provided **23.** 465 [ME *porvaien*, *provei*; OF *porveioir*; L *providere*]
provyd *v.* provide, supply **20.** 6, **60.** 6, **69.** 17 [ME; L *providere*]
prowd *adj.* proud, arrogant **11.** 20, **43.** 46 [OE, OF *prūd*]
prunȝa *v.* preen, prink, deck out **14.** 374 [ME *proyne*; see *OED*, s.v. *prune* v.[1]]
pryce *n.* value, worth **50.** 135 [ME; OF *pris*; L *pretium*]
pryce *v.* account for, reckon up **5.** 42 [see **prising**]
pryd. See **prid**
prydfull *adj.* proud, arrogant **81.** 23 [see **prid**]
prydles *adj.* devoid of pride **23.** 115 [see **prid**]
pryis *v.* value, esteem, extol **71.** 68 [ME; OF *prisier*, form of *preisier*; see **prasis**]
prymros *n.* primrose (*primula*

vulgaris) or cowslip (*primula veris*) used medicinally **23.** 192 [on problem of identification see *OED*, note; ME; OF; L *prima rosa*]

prynce *n.* chief, primary representative **35.** 81 [ME; L *princeps*]

pryntouris *n. pl.* printers **44.** 16 (see **44,** introductory note) [ME; OF n. *priente*; L *premere* to press]

prys, price *n.* price, value, merit **14.** 313, **36.** 15; **of prys,** price worthy, excellent **2.** 46, **2.** 61, **31.** 4 [OF; L *pretium, precium*]

prysit. See **prising**

pryvie *adj.* hidden, secret **52.** 46 [ME; F *privé*; L *privatus*]

***psaltris** *n. pl.* selection of psalms (in the Office of the Dead) **23.** 318 [OE *psaltere*; L *psalterium*]

pudingis *n. pl.* entrails stuffed with meat, oatmeal etc. **75.** 25 [ME; origin uncertain; see note in *OED*, s.v. *pudding* sb.]

pulcritud(e) *n.* beauty **2.** 74, **24.** 5, **31.** 2 [L *pulcritudo*]

pulder *n.* powder **10.** 203 [OF *puldre*; L *pulvis, pulveris*]

***pule** *n.* pool of standing water **23.** 342 [OE *pōl*]

pullis *3 sg.* pulls, plucks **23.** 157 [OE *pullian*]

pulpet *n.* pulpit for preaching **55.** 37 [ME; L *pulpitum*]

pultre *n.* poultry, fowls **23.** 157 [ME; OF *pouletrie*]

punes *v.* punish **26.** 22 [ME; F *puniss-*; L *punire*]

pur. See **pure**

purast. See **pure**

purchas, purches *v.* obtain, acquire **16.** 82, **71.** 53, **82.** 36 [ME; OF *pourchacier*]

pure *adj.* true, perfect, clear **6.** 95 [OF; L *purus*]

pure, p(e)ur(e) *adj.* poor **6.** 124, **9.** 24, **23.** 135, **23.** 170, **40.** 17, **62.** 19, **65.** 22, **68.** 38; *as n.* **the p(e)ur(e) 14.** 473, **77.** 45, **79.** 33; *sup.* **purast 66.** 32; **purly** *adv.* **14.** 135 [ME, OF *povere*; AF *poure*]

purgatioun *n.* aperient medicine **54.** 47 [ME; OF; L *purgatio*]

purgatorie, purgatory *n.* intermediate state *post mortem* where souls are purified from sin **22.** 2, **42.** 81 [ME; med. L *purgatorium*]

purpest *pa. t.* intended, planned **23.** 77 [ME *purpose*; OF]

purpos *n.* intention, resolve **39.** 27 [ME; OF; L *propositum*]

purp(o)ur, purpyr *n.* purple **10.** 41; purple cloth, robe **3.** 41; *adj.* purple, crimson **10.** 7 (see Commentary), **10.** 26, **50.** 50 [L *purpura* shellfish from which Tyrian dye was taken]

purs *n.* purse **19.** 5 *et seq.*, **46.** 19; *pl.* **19.** 16, **74.** 39 [OE; ? late L *bursa*]

purspyk *n.* pickpocket **23.** 238, **23.** 247, **81.** 12 [OE *purs* (? L *bursa*)+ ME *pyken*]

purteth *n.* poverty **23.** 118 [OF *poverteit*; L *paupertas*]

puscence *n.* strength, force **34.** 26 [ME; F *puissance*; L *posse*]

pusoun *n.* poison **53.** 30 [ME; OF *puison*; L *potio*]

put *n.* thrust, push (in copulation) **14.** 231; **puttis** *3 pl.* **43.** 11; **put . . . to nocht** reduce, degrade **72.** 9; **put out (owt) of** expelled from **12.** 40, **74.** 33 [OE v. *putian*]

puttar *n.* one who puts (to flight) **2.** 29 [prec.]

***Puttidew** the Wandering Jew **23.** 541

pyat, pyot *n.* magpie (*pica pica*) **42.** 16, **54.** 83 [ME *piot*; ME, OF *pie*; L *pica*]

pykis *n. pl.* sharp points, spikes **3.** 44, **14.** 15, **25.** 23 [OE *pic*]

pykis *3 sg.* picks, steals **74.** 39 [ME *pyken*]

pykpuris *n.* pickpocket; *attrib.* **23.** 114 [ME; see **purspyk**]

pykthank *n.* one who 'picks a thank', curries favour; flatterer **42.** 43, **45.** 53 [ME *pyken*+**thank**; *OED*]

pyne *n.* punishment, torture (of hell) **19.** 30; anguish **22.** 33, **54.** 29 [OE **pin*; L *poena*]

pynhippit *ppl. adj.* sharp-, narrow-buttocked **23.** 185 (cf. later *pin-buttocked*) [OE *pinn* peg+**hippit**]

pynit *ppl. adj.* wasted **23.** 114, **23.** 170 [OE *pīnian*]
pyot. See **pyat**

quaik *v.* quake, tremble violently **23.** 11 [OE *cwacian*]
quair *n.* small book consisting of a single quire; poem of such a size **10.** 271 [OF *quaer*; L *quattuor*]
quantetie *n.* size, bulk **81.** 28 [ME; OF; L *quantitas*]
quein. See **quene**
queir *adj.* odd, dubious **23.** 218 [origin obscure]
quell *v.* slay, destroy **23.** 248 [OE *cwęllan*]
quene, quein, queyne, qwene *n.* queen **2.** 37, **10.** 42, **10.** 73, **10.** 98, **16.** 22, **27.** 5, **31.** 1, **45.** 6, **48.** 6; *gen.* **28.** 6; *pl.* **10.** 80 [OE *cwēn*]
quene *n.* woman; jade, hussy **23.** 146 [OE *cwene*]
querrell, quarrell *n.* cause **4.** 26, **17.** 22, **33.** 14 [OF; L *querella*]
queyne. See **quene**
quha, quhai, quho *pron.* who **3.** 31, **5.** 52, **10.** 64, **32.** 33, **33.** 16; **quho so evir** whoever **10.** 201; **quham, quhome** whom **1.** 5, **3.** 28, **10.** 85; **quhais, quhois(e)** whose **6.** 103, **8.** 13, **15.** 3, **27.** 4, **30.** 3, **35.** 94, **49.** 30 [OE *hwā*, *hwām*, *hwæs*]
quhaill *n.* whale (ie. walrus) *attrib.* **63.** 46; **quhalis** *gen.* **13.** 33 [OE *hwæl*]
quhair, quhar(e) *adv.* where **3.** 138, **5.** 54, **6.** 70, **9.** 75, **10.** 216; **quhair evir, quharevir** wherever **18.** 17, **23.** 67; **quhar fro** from where **10.** 57 [OE *hwǣr*]
quha(i)rfo(i)r *adv.* because of which **15.** 11, **16.** 95, **16.** 101, **53.** 20, **65.** 15 [ME; cf. ON *hvar fyrir*]
quhairin *adv.* where **52.** 134, **52.** 164 [**quhair**]
quhairon *adv.* on which **14.** 5 [**quhair**]
quhairthrow *adv.* on account of which **3.** 139, **52.** 223 [OE *hwǣr*+*þurh*]
quhairto *adv.* for what reason, to what end? **50.** 29 [**quhair**; cf. Du *waartoe*]
quhais. See **quha**
quhalis. See **quhaill**
quham. See **quha**
quhare. See **quhair**
quharfor. See **qua(i)rfo(i)r**
quhat *pron., adj.* what **3.** 143, **5.** 23, **5.** 41, **9.** 38, **12.** 9, **14.** 336 [OE *hwæt*]
quhat throu, quhat throw *adv. phr.* what with, as a result of **10.** 46, **14.** 7 [OE *hwæt*+*þurh*]
quhattrak, quhat rek *interrog.* (*adv.*) what does it matter, for all that **52C.** 30, **71.** 22 [**quhat**; OE **rec(c)an** heed]
quheill *n.* wheel **52.** 19, **53.** 14, **64.** 7, **64.** 12; **quheilis** *pl.* **23.** 228 [OE *hweoȝol*]
quheit *n.* wheat **23.** 205 [OE *hwǣte*]
quhelp *n.* young dog, pup **37.** 11 [OE *hwelp*]
quhen, quhone *adv., conj.* when **3.** 73, **5.** 38, **10.** 2, **10.** 181, **10.** 205, **12.** *colophon*, **12.** 44, **40.** 10, **42.** 13 [OE *hwanne*]
Quhettane Clan Chattan **27.** 16
quhi. See **quhy**
quhiddir *conj.* whether **41.** 6 [OE *hwæþer*]
quhile *n.* (for) some time **10.** 220 [OE *hwīl*]
quhilis *adv.* at times **14.** 334, **14.** 433 [ME]
quhilk *rel. pron.* which **2.** 19, **3.** 38, **4.** 12, **6.** 22, **10.** 18, **12.** 23, **14.** 528 [OE *hwilc*]
quhill, *adv., conj.* while, till **2.** 59, **3.** 47, **3.** 61, **10.** 15, **10.** 108, **52.** 28 [OE *hwīle*]
quhillylillie *n.* (familiar word for) penis **13.** 34 [origin obscure]
quhilum *adv.* at times **14.** 302 [OE *hwīlum*]
quhinge *n.* whine, cry **37.** 10 [OE v. *hwinsian*]
quhip *n.* whip, lash **43.** 58 [ME; origin uncertain; see *OED*, s.v. *whip* v.]
quhispir *v.* whisper **82.** 32 [OE *hwisprian*]
quhit(e), quhyt(e), quhytt *adj.* white

3. 26, **8.** 8, **10.** 12, **10.** 51, **10.** 63, **10.** 250, **12.** 36, **14.** 426, **33.** 1, **63.** 46 [OE *hwīt*]

quhithir *conj.* whether **16.** 46 [OE *hwæþer*]

quho. quhois(e), quhom(e). See **quha**

quhone. See **quhen**

quhou, quhow *adv.* how **28.** 47, **31.** 21, **33.** 4, **45.** 39, **48.** 29 [OE *hū*]

quhryne *v.* whine, squeal **38.** 87 [OScand **hwrīna*, ON *hrīna*]

quhy, quhi *adv.* **10.** 214, **12.** 24; **for quhy** *conj.* because **60.** 11 [OE *hwī*]

quhyle, quhyll *n.* while, time, season **39.** 61, **50.** 38 [OE *hwīl*]

Quhynfell, Simon of **27.** 29

quhyt(e), quhytt. See **quhit(e)**

quik, quyk *adj.* living **9.** 83; lively, vital **62.** 75; *as n. pl.* **6.** 62 [OE *cwic*]

Quintene, Quenetyne, Quinting Scotch poet **23.** 2, **23.** 34, **23.** 131

quintessance, quintiscence *n.* the 'fifth essence', of which the celestial bodies were composed, believed capable of extraction by alchemy **44.** 55, **54.** 58 [F; L *quinta essentia*]

quitt. See **quyt**

quo, quod, quoth *pa. t.* said **9.** 22, **13.** 15, **13.** 29, **14.** 223, **16.** 29, **28.** 6 [OE *cweðan, cwæð*]

quyet *adj.* private, secluded **71.** 49; **quyetly** *adv.* subtly, without tumult **14.** 453 [ME; OF *quiete*]

quykkin *v.* animate, invigorate **14.** 247 [OE adj. *cwicu*]

quyt *v.* repay, recompense **51.** 54; **quitt** *pa. t.* **52.** 180, **52.** 208 [ME; OF *quiter*; med. L *quietare*]

quyt, quyte *adv.* quite, entirely **12.** 14, **39.** 74 [ME; OF *quite*]

quytclame *v.* renounce, give up **23.** 62 [ME; OF *quite* free+*clamer* declare]

quyte *adj.* free, clear **52.** 54, ***23.** 479 [ME, OF; L *quietus*]

qwene. See **quene**

racis *n. pl.* types, kinds **52.** 50 [F; origin obscure]

rad (for) *adj.* afraid (of) **14.** 320 [ON *hrǣddr*]

radis. See **raid**

radius, radyous *adj.* radiant, bright **4.** 21, **50.** 102, **50.** 132 [F *radieux*; L *radiosus*]

raeff. See **rif**

rage *v.* take sexual pleasure **14.** 386; **rageing** *vbl. n.* wanton play **14.** 194 [ME; F; L *rabia, rabies*]

raggis *n. pl.* rags, tatters **68.** 27 [ME; cf. next]

raggit *adj.* broken-feathered **23.** 57 [ME; cf. ON *rǫgg* tuft of fur]

ragment *n.* long discourse **14.** 162; list, catalogue **65.** 37 [ME; origin obscure]

raid *n.* inroad, foray (*fig.* sexual) **14.** 141, **14.** 391; **radis** *pl.* **14.** 194 [OE *rād*]

raid. See **ryd**

raif. See **rif**

raif *v.* talk boisterously, rant, declaim **16.** 73, **38.** 93; **raiffis** *3 pl.* **14.** 481 [ME; OF *raver*]

raip *n.* rope, halter **3.** 52 **14.** 331, **56.** 56, **56.** 74 [OE *rāp*]

raird *v.* resound **51.** 113 [OE *reordian*]

rais *v.* cause to rise, call up **23.** 23; **rais(s)it, rasit** *pa. t.* set on end **3.** 71, **3.** 78; *pp.* **4.** 4, increased **80.** 13 [ON *reisa*]

rais(e). See **ris**

rak *n.* shock, crash **10.** 240, **52.** 155 [ME; prob. Scand]

rak *v.* go off, fire **51.** 112 [cf. prec.]

rak *v.* stretch, strain **14.** 350; **rak sauch** *n.* gallows-bird **23.** 245 [? MDu *recken*; see **sauch**]

rakit (of) *pa. t.* heeded, thought of **14.** 322 [OE *reccan*]

rakit *pa. t.* went, proceeded, wandered **14.** 524 [OE *racian*]

rakles. See **rekles**

raknyng *n.* computation, account **65.** 37 [ME; OE v. *ȝerecenian*; cf. Du *rekening*]

rakyng *ppl. adj.* vagabond **26.** 2 [ME; ON *reika* wander about]

ralis *3 sg.* jests **14.** 193; **ralȝeis** *3 pl.* jest, rally **14.** 480; **ralȝeit** *pa. t.* **14.** 149 [F *railler*; origin uncertain]

rame *n.* ram **37.** 6; **rammis** *pl.* **32.** 16 [OE]

rame *v.* shout persistently **75.** 46; **ramyis** *3 sg.* gets by persistent demand **45.** 33; *pres. p.* shouting repeatedly **23.** 142 [ON *hreimr* a scream]

***ramowd, raw mowit** *adj.* raw-mouthed, abusive **23.** 27, **23.** 401 [OE *hrēaw*+*mūþ*]

ramyis. See **rame**

rane, rayn *n.* rain **10.** 195, **39.** 27, **59.** 19 [OE *reȝn*]

rane. See **rin**

ranebow, raynbow *n.* rainbow **10.** 241, **51.** 113 [OE *rēnboȝa*]

rangat *n.* disorder, disturbance **39.** 30 [origin obscure]

rankild *ppl. adj.* festered **14.** 163 [ME; OF *rancler*]

ransonit, raunsound *pp.* redeemed, restored **2.** 84, **3.** 38, *pa. t.* **9.** 88 [OF *ransonner*]

ransonner *n.* redeemer, Christ **61.** 45 [ME; OF v.]

ransoun *n.* ransom, the paying of money to release a prisoner **4.** 37; **ransonis** *pl.* **4.** 7 [OF; L *redemption-em*]

rap *v.* drive (in) **14.** 177; **rappit** *pa. t.* struck, drove **10.** 195 [ME; ? echoic]

rare *v.* cry, yell **23.** 236 [OE *rārian*]

rasit. See **rais**

rasoun. See **resoune**

rasour *n.* razor **14.** 105 [OF]

rattill *n.* noise, racket **52.** 194 [ME; LG v. *ratelen*]

rattillis *3 pl.* rattle, knock **23.** 180 [ME; cf. LG, Du *ratelen*; prob. echoic]

rattis *n. pl.* wheels used for execution **23.** 51 (see Commentary) [MLG, Da *rat*]

raucht, rawcht *pa. t.* (of *reach*) held out and passed **14.** 148; handed, gave **54.** 100 [OE *rǣcan, rǣhte*]

Rauf Colȝard hero of a popular tale **42.** 33

raunsound. See **ransonit**

ravin, ravyn(i)s. See **revin**

ravyne *n.* robbery; **fowll of ravyne** bird of prey **50.** 125 [ME; F; L *rapina*]

raw, on *adv. phr.* in order, in succession **23.** 180; **apon rawis** in lines **14.** 35 [? OE *rāw*]

raw mowit. See **ramowd**

rawcht. See **raucht**

rawchtir *n.* rafter, roof-beam **54.** 37 [OE *ræfter*; MLG *rachter*]

rax *v.* stretch **28.** 44, **80.** 19; **raxit** *pp.* **4.** 20 [OE *raxan*]

rayn. See **rane**

realme *n.* kingdom **18.** 14, **35.** 14, **51.** 75; *pl.* **43.** 53 [ME; OF; L *regalis*]

rebald *n.* varlet, scurrilous rascal **23.** 54, **63.** 22; *attrib.* knavish **23.** 68, **52.** 165; *pl.* rascally menials **39.** 31 [ME; OF *ribaut*]

rebaldrie *n.* coarse language, obscenity **23.** 57 [prec.]

reboytit *pp.* foiled, deprived, by repulse **10.** 180 [OF *rebouter*]

rebuik *n.* check, stop **54.** 85 [ME; ONF *rebuker*]

rebute *n.* repulse **10.** 181 [prec.]

receaves *3 sg.* receives, meets with **33.** 21 [ME; OF *reçoivre*; L *recipere*]

reche. See **riche**

recidence *n.* stay, abode **35.** 30 [ME; L *residentia*]

recompens(e) *n.* compensation, return **14.** 136, **71.** 63; ***recompansing** *vbl. n.* reward **23.** 46 [ME, OF; L *recompensare*]

reconfort *v.* strengthen, put heart into **16.** 117; **reconforting** *vbl. n.* **49.** 31 [F *reconforter*; L *confortare*]

recryat *v.* ? surrender **23.** 88 [origin uncertain; perh. f. OF *recreant*, pres. p. of *recroire* give up]

red *v.* clear, sweep away **23.** 68, arrange, see to **45.** 44 [cf. MLG, Du *redden*]

red. See **reid**

red (for) *adj.* afraid (of) **29.** 10 [ME; ON *hrǣddr*]

reddie, red(d)y *adj.* ready, prepared **3.** 79, **3.** 131, **5.** 45, **14.** 320, **55.** 45, **64.** 38 [ME *rædiȝ*; OE *ȝerǣde*+*-iȝ*]

rede *n.* fear **10.** 241 [ON *hrǣddr*]

rede *v.* read, consider, discern; **redis** *3 sg.* **10.** 255, *3 pl.* **14.** 480 [OE *rǣdan*]

rede, reid, rid *adj.* red **6.** 103, **8.** 8, **10.** 12, **10.** 24, **10.** 250, **26.** 26, **37.** 16, **42.** 7, **50.** 50, **56.** 52; **rede wod** *adj.* stark staring mad **14.** 141 [OE *rēad*]

redeme *v.* redeem, buy back, deliver; *pa. t.* **6.** 28, *pp.* **4.** 37; **redeming** *vbl. n.* redemption **6.** 111; **redemer** *n.* redeemer **6.** 2 [F *rédimer*; L *redimere*]

redempcioun *n.* deliverance from sin and death by Christ **6.** 119 [F; L *redemptio*]

redis *n. pl.* reeds **10.** 56 [OE *hrēod*]

redly *adv.* clearly, certainly **38.** 5 [OE *rǣdlice*]

redolent *adj.* fragrant **10.** 40, **10.** 275, **50.** 47 [OF; L *redolere*]

redomyt *adj.* wreathed; beautiful **16.** 77 [L *redimere*]

redoun *v.* pass, penetrate **51.** 17; **redoundis** *3 sg.* accrues, attaches (to) **16.** 63 [ME; F; L *redundare*]

redour *n.* terror **23.** 11 [ME adj. *rad*; ON *hrǣddr*]

redy. See **reddie**

refferis *3 sg.* commits, submits **20.** 24 [ME; OF; L *referre*]

reffus *v.* deny, renounce **55.** 5; **reffuse (of)** *adj.* rejected (by) **23.** 105 [ME; OF *refuser*]

refing *ppl. adj.* thieving **26.** 2 [OE *rēafian*]

reflex *n.* reflection **10.** 33 [late L *reflexus*; *reflectere*]

refoundit *pp.* established again **4.** 28 [OF *refonder*; L *fundare*]

refrene *v. reflex.* restrain (yourself), abstain **73.** 18 [ME; OF *refrener*; L *refrenare*]

reft. See **revis**

refuse *n.* refusal, rejection **42.** 36 [ME; OF *refuser*]

refusis *2 sg.* abandons, deserts **67.** 6 [ME; F *refuser*]

refute *n.* protection, defence **10.** 185 [OF *refuite*]

regall *adj.* royal **2.** 75 [OF; L *regalis*]

regio(u)n, regeone *n.* part of the world or universe, country **27.** 51, **31.** 1, **47.** 5, **53.** 31; *pl.* **1.** 50, **45.** 72 [AF; L *regio*]

regyne *n.* queen **2.** 6 [L *regina*]

rehator *n.* ? knave **23.** 244 (se Commentary) [origin and meanin obscure]

rehers *v.* repeat, relate **37.** 44 [ME OF *rehercer*]

reid, red *v.* counsel, advise **5.** 8, **5** 39, **5.** 53, **5.** 64, **23.** 224, **29.** 22 **71.** 37; read **1.** 29, **54.** 12 [O *rǣdan*]

reid. See **rede**

reif *n.* plunder, robbery **6.** 121 [O *rēaf*]

reik. See **reke**

reikit *ppl. adj.* smoked, fumigate **56.** 52 [OE *rēcan*]

reill *v.* whirl round **52.** 195 [origi uncertain; perh. related to O *hrēol* reel for yarn]

reird, rerd *n.* uproar, din **23.** 23 **39.** 31, **52.** 205, **54.** 94 [OE *reord*]

reistit *ppl. adj.* dried, cured in smok *fig.* **23.** 187 [origin obscure; cf. D *riste* to grill]

reiv *v.* tear at **43.** 30 [*OED*, *rea* v.[2]; app. a confusion of *rei* plunder and *rive*]

reive *v.* plunder, despoil **68.** 37 [O *rēafian*]

reiwll. See **rewle**

rejo(i)s *v.* be glad **31.** 17, **50.** 15 **rejoysyng** *pres. p.* gladdening 2 15; **rejos(e)ing** *vbl. n.* **25.** 26, 5 34 [ME; OF *rejoir*, *rejoiss-*]

rek. See **quhattrak**

reke, reik *n.* smoke **10.** 239, **5** 36 [OE *rēc*]

rekkyning *vbl. n.* reckoning, coun ing up **46.** 6 [ME; OE *ȝerecenia* cf. Du *rekening*]

rekles, rakles *adj.* careless, heedle **5.** 58; imprudent, rash **14.** 43, **7** 34 [OE *recceleās*]

relationis *n. pl.* narrative accour **55.** 17 [ME; L *relatio*]

releif *v.* relieve, succour **42.** 28 [M OF *relever*; L *relevare*]

remanent *n.* rest, remainder **65.** [ME; L *remanere*]

remanes *n. pl.* remainder **46.** 18 [(*remain*; L *remanere*]

rema(y)ne *v.* remain, stay **10.** 2 **59.** 23; *3 sg.* **9.** 93 [OF *remanoir*; *remanere*]

remeid *n.* remedy, compensation **26.** 14, **26.** 28, **52.** 90, **62.** 97; cure, salvation **57.** 3; redress **75.** 73 [ME; OF; L *remedium*]

remeid *v.* redress, amend **6.** 101, **19.** 34, **26.** 7, **42.** 56, **60.** 5 [OF *remedier*; L *remediare*]

remember, remembir *v.* recall (sins) **6.** 153, remember **59.** 6; **remembir the** remind yourself **16.** 41 [ME; OF *remembrer*; L *rememorari*]

rememb(e)rance *n.* recollection **5.** 60, **15.** 14, *pers.* **3.** 105 [F]

remissioun *n.* forgiveness, pardon **5.** 20, **5.** 26, **34.** 3, **36.** 28, **44.** 60, **71.** 56 [OF; L *remissio*]

remord *v.* contemplate with remorse **45.** 42 [ME; F *remordre*; L *remordere*]

remuffit *pa. t.* passed away **14.** 514 [ME; OF *remouvoir*; L *removere*]

renewis *3 sg.* resumes, begins again **14.** 116 [ME; after L *renovare*]

renȝie, reynȝe *n.* rein *fig.* **42.** 49, **52.** 74; **renȝeis** *pl.* **14.** 350 [ME; OF *regne*; L *retinere*]

renoun(e), reno(w)ne *n.* distinction, celebrity, reputation **6.** 42, **10.** 88, **14.** 72, **14.** 332, **27.** 34, **45.** 66; *pers.* **10.** 175 [OF *renon*; L *renominare*]

renownit, renownd *ppl. adj.* celebrated, famous **35.** 1, **35.** 65, **50.** 154 [ME; OF *renoumer*]

rent *n.* income, revenue, wealth **6.** 54, **6.** 126, **12.** 39, **40.** 26, **47.** 25, **51.** 109, **66.** 3; *pl.* **46.** 6, **80.** 8 [OF *rente*; med. L *rendere*]

rent *pp.* torn asunder, tattered **6.** 111, **10.** 278, **56.** 13 [OE *rendan*]

renunce *v.* renounce, give up **23.** 54, **56.** 5 *et seq.*; **renuncit** *pa. t.* **56.** 17 [ME; OF; L *renuntiare*]

repair *n.* resort, haunt, sojourn **9.** 107, **71.** 2, **75.** 58, **81.** 17 [OF *repaire*; L *repatriare*]

repell *v.* drive back **57.** 5 [ME; L *repellere*]

repet *n.* uproar, noisy disturbance **14.** 193 [? imit.]

repreiff *v.* reprove, reproach **42.** 78; **reprovit** *pa. t.* accused **23.** 85 [ME; OF *reprover*; *reprobare*]

reput *pp.* reckoned, considered **68.** 3 [OF *reputé*; L *reputatus*]

requeir *v.* ask, request **9.** 70, **69.** 32; **requyrd** *pp.* **79.** 16 [OF; L *requirere*]

requeist *n.* petition; **mak requeist** beg **40.** 2 [ME; OF *requeste*]

rerd. See **reird**

resave. See **ressaif**

***reskewit** *pa. t.* recovered by force **23.** 303 [ME; OF *reskeure*]

resoune, ressoun, rasoun *n.* reason, rational faculty **6.** 123, **7.** 4, **69.** 24; *pers.* **10.** 151 *et seq.*, **51.** 61; = reasonable (cf. OF *il est raison*) **9.** 111, **44.** 63 [OF *reisun*; L *ratio*]

resownyt *pa. t.* resounded, echoed **10.** 108, **10.** 240 [ME; L *resonare*]

respyt *n.* delay, reprieve **34.** 33 [ME; OF *respit*; L *respectus*]

ressaif, res(s)ave *v.* receive (in the eucharist) **6.** 151; accept (in place of) **16.** 76; greet **26.** 25, **48.** 69, **50.** 118; *pa. t.* **48.** 20, **56.** 8; **ressaveing** *vbl. n.* **46.** 10 [OF *reçoivre*; L *recipere*]

ressait *n.* receipt (of the sacrament) **6.** 92 [ME; OF *recete*; L *recipere*]

res(s)ave, ressavit. See **ressaif**

ressoun. See **resoune**

rest *v.* remain, stay **9.** 4, **10.** 3; cease (from) **14.** 141 [OE *ræstan*]

restles *adj.* perpetually active **50.** 80 [ME; OE *ræst(e)*; cf. Fris *restleas*]

rethorike *n.* art of eloquence, elegance in language **10.** 70, **10.** 117, **10.** 270, **10.** 274 [ME; OF; L *rhetorica*]

rethory(e) rhetorician, master of eloquence **23.** 97; *pl.* **10.** 253, **44.** 5, **62.** 38; oratory **76.** 10 [F *rethore*; L *rhetor*]

returne *v.* come back **66.** 24; **returnis (in)** *3 sg.* turns (into) **59.** 4 *et passim* [OF *returner*; L *tornare*]

reull, *reule. See **rewle**

reuth, rewth(e), ruth *n.* pity, compassion **2.** 12, **6.** 124, **12.** 33, **12.** 38, **14.** 316, **25.** 9, **62.** 91, **70.** 19; *pers.* **3.** 101; **rewthfull** *adj.* **17.** 74; **reuthles** *adj.* **25.** 23 [OE *hrēowan*]

revaris *n. pl.* robbers, plunderers **44.** 44 [OE *rēafere*]
***reve.** See **reive**
reveil(l) *v.* disclose, reveal **14.** 43, **14.** 162; **reveild** *pp.* **54.** 117 [OF *reveler*; L *revelare*]
rever. See **rivir**
reverence, reverens *n.* respect, veneration **10.** 162, **14.** 310, **50.** 77 [ME, OF; L *reverentia*]
reverend *adj.* worthy of respect **10.** 253 [OF; L gerundive of *revereri*]
reverentlie *adv.* with great respect **48.** 47 [OF *reverent*; see **reverend**]
revert *v. imper.* spring up afresh **1.** 42 [L *revertere*]
revest *pp.* arrayed, apparelled **10.** 7 (see Commentary) [OF *revestir*; L *revestire*]
revin, ravin *n.* raven (*corvus corax*) **52.** 117, **54.** 114, *fig.* **23.** 57; **ravynis** *pl.* **54.** 70 [OE *hræfn*]
revin. See **rif**
revir. See **rivir**
revis *3 sg.* takes away, removes **19.** 14; **reft** *pp.* **62.** 73 [OE *rēafian*]
revoik *v.* recant, withdraw **6.** 70 [ME; OF *revoquer*; L *revocare*]
rew *n.* rue (*ruta graveolens*) shrub used medicinally **8.** 10 [F *rue*; L *ruta.* Dunbar puns on *rue* (pity) f. OE *hrēow*]
rew (on) *v.* take pity (on) **6.** 23, **49.** 39; feel remorse, repent **6.** 87, **60.** 5; deplore **14.** 43, **54.** 18 [OE *hrēowan*]
rewaird, rewarde *n.* recompense, profit **17.** 34, **23.** 19, **44.** 24, **44.** 34, **51.** 54, **63.** 7, **78.** 2 [ME; OF *reguard*]
rewardit *pa. t.* rewarded **52.** 198; *pp.* **44.** 63 [ME; OF *reguarder*]
rewle *n.* rule **39.** 29; ***reule** conduct, behaviour **23.** 381 [ME; OF; L *regula*]
rewle, reiwll, reull, rewill *v.* govern, manage, administer **18.** 14, **30.** 11, **51.** 105, **79.** 58; *3 sg.* **77.** 8; *pp.* **77.** 7; **be rewlit** submit to counsel, listen to reason **11.** 7 [ME; OF *riuler*; L *regulare*]
rewth, rewthfull. See **reuth**
reynȝe. See **renȝie**
riall, riale, ryall, ryell *adj.* royal, noble, **2.** 77, **10.** 256, **14.** 140, **14.** 523, **31.** 6, **35.** 1, **35.** 92, **50.** 151; **rialest** *sup.* **2.** 8; **royaly, ryallie** *adv.* splendidly, **14.** 30, **14.** 72, **14.** 367 [ME; OF *rial, roial*; L *regalis*]
riatus. See **ryat(o)us**
***ribald.** See **rebald**
riche, reche, ryche *adj.* wealthy, splendid, abundant, fine, choice **14.** 30, **14.** 361, **14.** 367, **33.** 11, **40.** 17; **richelie, richely** *adv.* **14.** 136, **48.** 10; **riches, ryches** *n. pl.* **20.** 26, **64.** 21 [OE *rīce*]
richesse *n.* opulence; *pers.* **10.** 176 [ME, OF; OE *rīce*]
richt, rycht *adj.* right, true **2.** 27, **6.** 61, **50.** 164; *as n.* **34.** 29 [OE *riht*]
richt, rycht *adv.* right, precisely **3.** 142, **5.** 19, **5.** 24, **10.** 1, **10.** 47; very **10.** 123, **14.** 69, **26.** 10, **48.** 35; **rycht so** in the same way **72.** 10 [OE *rihte*]
rid. See **rede**
riddill *n.* riddle, coarse sieve **38.** 55 [OE *hriddel*]
riddin. See **ryd**
rif, ryff, ryfe *v.* tear apart, open up, split **3.** 91, **14.** 350, **23.** 15, **56.** 61; **revis** *3 sg.* tears **19.** 14; **raeff, raif** *pa. t.* **3.** 60, **32.** 13; **revin** *pp.* **3.** 55, **54.** 118 [ON *rīfa*]
rigbane *n.* backbone **23.** 180 [OE *hrycg*+**ban**]
rilling *n.* shoe(s) made of undressed hide **23.** 145, **23.** 243 [OE *rifeling*]
rin, ryn(e) *v.* run, run away **3.** 122, **14.** 320, **45.** 44; *2 sg.* **23.** 225, *3 sg.* **34.** 47, *3 pl.* **23.** 228; **rynnand** *pres. p.* **52.** 162; **rane** *pa. t.* ran, thrust **3.** 90, flowed **48.** 58; **rynning** *vbl. n.* racing **68.** 9 [OE *rinnan, ran*]
ring, ryng *n.* reign, kingdom **2.** 19, **81.** 9 [OF *regne*; L *regnum*]
ring *v.* rule **50.** 33; *3 sg.* **39.** 30, **68.** 44, **72.** 30 [OF *regner*; L *regnare*]
ringis *n. pl.* finger rings **14.** 367 [OE *hring*]
rink *n.* (fighting) man; *as pl.* men of valour **47.** 5 (see Commentary) [OE *rinc*]

ris, ryis, rys(e) *v.* arise, get up **6.** 67, **7.** 4, **13.** 34, **14.** 471, **63.** 22; *3 sg.* **17.** 6, **23.** 227, turns in disgust **14.** 163; **rysing** *pres. p.* **50.** 151; **rais(e)** *pa. t.* **1.** 44, **9.** 92, **10.** 3, **10.** 34, **10.** 239, **10.** 255, **14.** 523, **54.** 94, increased **14.** 368; **rissin** *pp.* **1.** 3, **1.** 39, **4.** 19, **4.** 25 [OE *rīsan*; ME pa. t. *ras*]

rise. See **ryce**

rispis *n. pl.* sedge **10.** 56 [origin obscure]

rivir, rever, revir, ryvir *n.* river **10.** 28, **10.** 44, **10.** 131, **16.** 9, **16.** 27, **22.** 52; *gen.* **10.** 47 [ME; OF *rivere*; L *ripa*]

ro *n.* small deer (*capreolus capræa*) **50.** 78 [OE *rā*]

robbis *n. pl.* robes **30.** 11 [ME; OF *rob(b)e*]

Robein under bewch ? Robin Hood **27.** 25

roch *n.* rock, cliff **10.** 44; *pl.* **10.** 240, **23.** 15 [OF]

rocht. See **wrocht**

rockis, rokkis *n. pl.* distaffs **32.** 23, **34.** 46 [ME; cf. Du *rokken*]

***rod** *n.* spawn **23.** 342 [origin obscure]

Roger off Clekniskleuch 27. 26

rois. See **ros(e)**

Rois Ross **27.** 12

***roist** *n.* roast; *fig. app.* a contest **23.** 27 (see Commentary) [ME; OF]

rokkat *n.* bishop's rochet, linen vestment **45.** 33 [ME, OF *rochet*]

rokkis. See **rockis**

rolpand *pres. p.* shouting, roaring **23.** 142 [origin Scand; cf. Icel *raupa*]

Rome 14. 331

rong *pa. t.* rang, resounded **16.** 19 [OE *hringan*]

rong *pa. t.* reigned **35.** 74 [ME *regn*; OF *regner*; L *regnare*]

ronk *adj.* dense, abundant **10.** 93 *ranc*]

ros(e), rois, roys *n.* rose **1.** 4, **1.** 44, **2.** 40, **2.** 79, *fig.* **10.** 253, **31.** 6, **31.** 25; *fig.* the queen **50.** 39 *et passim*; *pl.* **10.** 22, **10.** 275, *fig.* **14.** 523 [ME; L *rosa*]

Ros, Johine John (the Ross) **23.** 1, **23.** 39, **62.** 83 (see Commentary, **23** headnote)

rosere *n.* rose-bush **10.** 3 [OF *rosier*; L *rosarium*]

rostit *pa. t.* tortured by fire, grilled **23.** 123 [ME; OF *rostir*]

rosyne *n.* rose **2.** 8 [L *rosa*; after *regina* etc.]

rottin *adj.* affected with sheep-rot (a disease of the liver) **23.** 248 [ME; ON *rotinn*]

Roull of Aberdene Scotch poet **62.** 77

Roull of Corstorphin Scotch poet **62.** 78

roumes. See **rowme**

roundar *n.* whisperer **77.** 33; **rownaris** *pl.* **52.** 52 [See **roun(e)**]

roundit, rowndit *ppl. adj.* cropped, shorn **26.** 19, **26.** 26 [ME; OF *rond*; L *rotundus*]

roun(e), rown *v.* whisper, discourse **62.** 81; *3 sg.* **20.** 13, **63.** 37; *3 pl.* **14.** 480, **rownand** *pres. p.* **56.** 84; **rounde, rownit** *pa. t.* **3.** 101, **9.** 41, **74.** 4 [OE *rūnian*]

roust *n.* canker; rust, decay **44.** 32; rancour **14.** 163 [OE *rūst*]

rousty *adj.* rusted, feeble **14.** 141 (see Commentary) [OE *rūstiȝ*]

***rowis** *n. pl.* rolls, papers **23.** 32 [ME; OF *roulle*]

rowme *n.* space **39.** 42, **52.** 114, **83.** 11; **rowmis, roumes** *pl.* farms, property ***23.** 301, **46.** 6, **68.** 37 [OE *rūm*]

rownaris. See **roundar**

rownd *prep.* all about **34.** 21 [ME; OF; L *rotundus*]

rownis, rownit. See **roun(e)**

rowp *v.* croak **52.** 117 [Scand origin; cf. Icel *raupa*]

rowt(t), rowte, routt *n.* company, retinue **48.** 53, **52.** 165, **54.** 127, **63.** 11 [ME; OF *route*; L *rupta*]

rowt *n.* violent stroke **23.** 68, **54.** 100 [cf. OE *hrūtan* hurl, cast]

rowttit *pa. t.* scoured, rode over in troops **9.** 92 [OF *(ar)router*; L *ruptus* detachment]

roy *n.* king **45.** 33, **47.** 6, **48.** 34 [OF]

royis *2 sg.* talk nonsense **23.** 54 [origin obscure]

rubbit *pp.* rubbed out **23.** 117; *ppl. adj.* **23.** 205 [ME; LG *rubben*]
rubeis *n. pl.* rubies **50.** 132 [ME; OF *rubi*]
ruch *adj.* rough, hairy, shaggy **13.** 44, **23.** 243 [OE *rūh*]
rude *n.* rood, Christ's cross **2.** 84, **3.** 68, **6.** 103, **6.** 111, **56.** 56 [OE *rōd*]
rude *n.* extent **39.** 42 [OE *rōd*]
rude *adj.* rough, harsh, violent **3.** 60, **3.** 90, **10.** 266, **10.** 278, **14.** 368; **rudlie, rudly, ruidlie** *adv.* **3.** 105, **14.** 481, **51.** 112 [OF; L *rudis*]
ruffie *n.* ruffiian **45.** 42 [OF *rufyen*]
ruffill *n.* impairment, destruction **14.** 332 [origin uncertain]
rug *v.* pull violently, tug **54.** 83; *pres. p.* **3.** 106; *pa. t.* **54.** 71 [? Scand origin]
ruge *n.* roar **3.** 19 [L *rugire*]
ruggis *n. pl.* tugs, violent pulls **3.** 60 [? Scand origin]
ruidlie. See **rude**
ruke *n.* rook (*corvus frugilegus*) **23.** 57, **52.** 117; **ru(i)kis** *pl.* **54.** 70, **54.** 117 [OE *hrōc*]
rumour *n.* widespread talk, gossip **14.** 332 [OF; L *rumor* noise]
rumple *n.* tail **23.** 125 (see Commentary); **rumpillis** *pl. fig.* **52.** 20 [ME *rump*; Scand origin]
runsyis *n. pl.* horses **23.** 228 [ME; OF *ronci*]
rusche *v.* rush, dash **44.** 53 [ME; OF *rehusser*]
ruse *n.* boasting, bragging **14.** 431 [ME; ON *hrōs*]
ruse *v.* boast **42.** 37; **rusing** *pres. p.* (*reflex.*) boasting (himself), vaunting **14.** 194 [ON *hrōsa*]
rut(e) *n.* root **1.** 41, **2.** 12, **8.** 14; core **14.** 162, **14.** 224; source **10.** 184, **23.** 73, **52.** 56; **rutis** *pl.* **68.** 31 [late OE *rōt*]
ruth. See **reuth**
ry *n.* rye, the cereal **28.** 17 [OE *ryȝe*]
ryall(i)e, ryally. See **riall**
ryat(o)us, riatus *adj.* noisy, turbulent, wanton, extravagant **14.** 149, **14.** 193, **14.** 481, **32.** 16 [ME; OF *rioteus*]
ryce, rise *n. coll.* small branches, brushwood **10.** 28, **68.** 31, *attrib.* **14.** 524 [OE *-hrīs*]
ryche. See **riche**
rycht *n.* legal title, due, standing **14.** 310, **42.** 52 [OE *riht*]
rycht. See **richt**
ryd *v.* ride on horseback **27.** 8, **32.** 1, **49.** 13; *3 sg.* **63.** 11; *pres. p.* **48.** 34, **53.** 34; **raid** *pa. t.* **52.** 175; **riddin** *pp.* (in copulation) **37.** 6, (with double entendre) **43.** 48 [OE *rīdan*]
ryell. See **riall**
ryfe, ryff. See **rif**
ryis. See **ris**
ryme *v.* make verses **23.** 23; **rymyng** *vbl. n.* versifying **23.** 54, **23.** 68 [ME; OF]
ryne *n.* rind, bark *fig.* **2.** 12 [OE *rind*]
ryn(e), ryn(n)is. See **rin**
Ryne the river Rhine **22.** 54
ryng. See **ring**
rynning. See **rin**
rype *v.* search, ransack **5.** 40 [OE *rȳpan*]
rys. See **ris**
ryve. See **rif**
ryver *n.* plunderer **23.** 246 [ON *rifa*]

sa, sua *adv., conj.* so, thus **5.** 19, **5.** 24, **5.** 36, **5.** 42, **6.** 46, **11.** 3, **11.** 18, **13.** 20, **27.** 45; as long as **14.** 450 [OE *swa*]
sabill, sable *n.* black (colour of mourning), blackness, darkness **10.** 126, **14.** 418, **14.** 433, **36.** 7, **49.** 12, **50.** 56, **69.** 2; *adj.* **14.** 447, **16.** 2 [F (heraldic term)]
Sabot *n.* God **14.** 502 (see Commentary) [L (Vulgate) *sabaoth*]
sacrament, the *n.* holy communion **6.** 86, **56.** 41; *pl.* the seven sacraments **6.** 42 [F; L *sacramentum*]
sacrand, sacring (bell) *adj.* (bell) used at the elevation of the host **23.** 160, **54.** 50 [ME *sacre* to consecrate; L *sacrare*]
sad, said *adj.* sorrowful, lamentable **5.** 48, **14.** 447, **51.** 20, **60.** 21; **sadlye** *adv.* **61.** 39 [OE *sæd*]
sadall, sadell *n.* saddle **27.** 47, **52.** 191 [OE *sadol*]

sadnes, saidnes *n.* melancholy, sorrow **49.** 22, **65.** 13 [ME; f. **sad**]
saed. See **say(n)**
saek. See **saik**
saep *n.* soap **33.** 9 [OE *sāpe*]
saffrone, saphron *n.* saffron **23.** 191 (as a sudorific); *attrib.* **23.** 171 [ME, F; Arabic]
said. See **sad**
saif(e), saiff *v.* save, rescue, deliver **5.** 25, **6.** 167, **12.** 13, **20.** 22; protect **14.** 284, **14.** 461 [ME; OF *salver;* late L *salvare*]
saif *adj.* saved, delivered, in a state of salvation **6.** 69, **14.** 502 [ME; F *sauf*; L *salvus*]
saif, sauf *quasi-prep.* except, but **13.** 26, **65.** 11 [ME; F *sauf*; L *salvo*]
saik, saek *n.* sake, account **4.** 17, **25.** 10, **28.** 33, **33.** 16, **35.** 31, **49.** 30 [OE *sacu*]
saikles, sakles *adj.* innocent, harmless **3.** 43, **12.** 10, **14.** 97 [OE *saclēas*]
sailȝeit *pa. t.* assailed, attacked **9.** 66, **9.** 85; ***sailit** *pa. t.* tried **23.** 379 [aphetic form of *assail*; OF *assaillir*]
saill *n.* ship's sail **10.** 51, **23.** 90, **60.** 13; **salis** *pl. fig.* **65.** 15 [OE *seȝel*]
saillis *3 sg.* sails **6.** 166 [OE *siȝlan*]
sair, soir *adj.* painful, grievous **3.** 21, **34.** 30, **46.** 15; sorrowful **3.** 99, **22.** 86; grieved **14.** 446; (as *n.*) sufferers **54.** 19; *comp.* **sarar** **10.** 198; *adv.* **6.** 87, **14.** 223, **21.** 3, **41.** 7, **52.** 153, **53.** 5 [OE *sār*]
sairis *2 sg.* savour, smell (of) **56.** 34; **savrand** *pres. p.* flavouring, giving a spice to **23.** 192 [ME; OF *savourer*; L *sapor*]
sais. See **say(n)**
sait(t) *n.* assembly, court **22.** 47, **74.** 41 [ME; ON *sǣti*]
sakles. See **saikles**
salbe *v.* shall be **12.** 23, **14.** 192, **14.** 308, **14.** 502, **17.** 76, **23.** 69 [OE *sceal*+**be**]
sald *pa. t.* sold **68.** 30, ***23.** 443 OE *sęllan, sealde*]
sald. See **suld(e)**
salis. See **saill**
sall *v.* shall **2.** 60, **3.** 118, **3.** 119, **6.** 147, **9.** 54, **11.** 14, **12.** 43 [OE *sceal*]
salpeter *n.* potassium nitrate **26.** 9 [ME; OF]
sals *n.* sauce, adding piquancy *fig.* **66.** 19 [ME; F *sauce*; L *salsa*]
salt *n.* aphetic form of *assault* **10.** 198 [ME]
saluse *v.* salute, hail **10.** 101; *pres. p.* **48.** 47; **salust** *pa. t.* **10.** 95, **16.** 18 [OF; L *salutare*]
salvatour, salviour, salvitour *n.* saviour **3.** 10, **3.** 104, **3.** 128, **6.** 1, **6.** 9, (as present in the mass) **6.** 92; **sanct salvatour** Christ **19.** 1 [late L *salvator*; *salvare*]
salvatrice *n.* (female) saviour **2.** 67 [med. L *salvatrix*]
salviour. See **salvatour**
sam, samin, samyn *adj.* same **10.** 100, **14.** 156, **14.** 491, **30.** 11 [ME, ON *same*]
Sampsone Samson **61.** 10 (Judges xiii–xvi)
sanative *adj.* healing, curative **14.** 8 [OF *sanatif*; L *sanare*]
sanct *n.* saint **14.** 206, **14.** 444, **19.** 1, **22.** 59; **sanctis** *gen.* **14.** 254; *pl.* **16.** 35, **22.** 65, **40.** 11 [OF; L *sanctus*]
sane *v.* make the sign of the cross (on) **14.** 444; **sanis** *3 sg.* blesses **74.** 41 [OE *seȝnian*]
sang *n.* song **14.** 7, **16.** 4, **42.** 22, **51.** 16; *pl.* **49.** 31, **50.** 28, **69.** 5 [OE]
sanyne *vbl. n.* making the sign of the cross, blesssing **14.** 102 [see **sane**]
sapheir *n.* sapphire **31.** 36 (see Commentary); **sapher** *adj.* transparent blue, like a sapphire **10.** 37 [OF *safir*; L *sapphirus*]
saphron. See **saffrone**
sapience *n.* wisdom **76.** 1 [ME, OF; L *sapientia*]
***saraȝene** *n.* Muslim; infidel **23.** 525 [ME; late L *saracenus*]
sark. See **serk**
sary(e), sory, sorie *adj.* worthless, wretched, lamentable **10.** 207, **14.** 96, **32.** 18, **35.** 27, **51.** 19, **62.** 10, **64.** 9, **64.** 37 [OE *sāriȝ*]

satefeit, satisfeit *pp.* satisfied, contented **66.** 7, **80.** 32 [ME; OF *satisfier*; L *satis+facere*]

Sathan(e) Satan, the Devil ***23.** 309; devil **14.** 102; *gen.* **Sathanis 54.** 4 [L (Vulgate)]

satisfactioun *n.* act of reparation; together with contrition and confession, a necessary part of the sacrament of penance **6.** 93 [ME; F; L *satisfactio*]

Saturn(us) the most ancient king of Latium, honoured as god of agriculture **10.** 114 (see Commentary), **35.** 75, **53.** 31 (see Commentary), **54.** 68

sauch *n.* sallow; rope of twisted sallow-withes **23.** 245 (see **rak**) [OE *s(e)alh*]

sauf. See **saif**

saul(e), saull, sawle *n.* soul **5.** 25, **7.** 2, **14.** 502, **36.** 26, **38.** 18, **55.** 30; *pl.* **1.** 21, **4.** 6, **6.** 37, **12.** 5, **38.** 69 [OE *sāwol*]

sauld *pp.* sold **43.** 54 [OE *sęllan, seald*]

savrand. See **sairis**

saw *n.* speech, talk **14.** 115; *pl.* **11.** 19; moral discourse **76.** 22, utterances **81.** 37 [OE *saȝu*]

sawle. See **saul(e)**

sawsy *adj.* sauced, flavoured, coated **23.** 191 [ME, OF *sause*; L *salsa*]

sax *adj.* six **3.** 71, **28.** 43 [OE *sex*]

say *v.* assay, attempt **14.** 197; **saying** *pres. p.* **45.** 49 [ME; OF *assayer*]

say(n), sane *v.* declare, tell, say **10.** 198, **14.** 157, **17.** 67; *3 sg.* **5.** 3, **9.** 55, **14.** 221; *3 pl.* **19.** 33; **sayand** *pres. p.* **9.** 47, **56.** 4; *pa. t.* **saed, sayd 28.** 48, **56.** 36; **said** *pp.* **11.** 18 [OE *sęcgan*]

***saynit.** See **sane**

scabbit *adj.* covered in scabs **14.** 92, **43.** 60 [ON **skabbr*]

scaffaris *n. pl.* beggars, spongers **44.** 45 [origin obscure; perh. f. Du and G *schaffen* to procure food]

scaith *n.* hurt, harm **14.** 358 [ME; ON *skaðe*]

scaittis *n. pl.* skates, the fish (*raia*) **75.** 9 [ME; ON *skata*]

***scald** *n.* noisy brawler, lampooner **23.** 322 [ME; ON *skāld* poet]

scaldit *ppl. adj.* scalded, inflamed **23.** 58 [ME; ONF *escalder*; late L *excaldare*]

scale, *scaile, skail *v.* disperse, scatter **2.** 28, **23.** 215,* **23.** 398; **skaild** *ppl. adj.* scattered, spilt *fig.* **74.** 30 [origin uncertain; perh. Scand]

scamleris *n. pl.* parasites, spongers **44.** 45 [perh. f. *scamble* kitchen bench; but cf. Gael *sgiomlair* stealer out of pots]

scant *adv.* scarcely, hardly **21.** 5, **39.** 86 [ON *skammr* neut. *skamt*]

scapit *pa. t.* escaped, avoided **14.** 358 [aphetic form of *escape*; ME; OF *eschaper*]

scart *v.* scratch **14.** 93 [metathesis of *scrat*; ME]

scarth. See **skarth**

scawpe *n.* scalp, head **38.** 52 [nth. ME; ? Scand origin]

schaddow *n.* reflection, image **61.** 5; **schadow** companion **14.** 191 [OE *sceaduwe*]

schadowit *pa. t.* reflected **10.** 31 [OE *sceadwian*]

schaem. See **schame**

schaiffyne *pp.* shaven, shaved **14.** 105; **schevin** *ppl. adj.* **52.** 28 [OE *sceafan*]

schaik *n.* man, fellow **14.** 105 (see Commentary) [OE *scealc*]

schaik *v.* shake, quake **23.** 9; *pa. t.* **schuk-(e)** brandished **9.** 36, wagged **37.** 10; **schake, schuke** shook off, down **10.** 14, **14.** 515 [OE *scacan, scōc*]

schaip *n.* physical form, figure **50.** 95 [ME; OE *ȝesceap*]

schaip *v.* form, make **52C.** 26 [OE *scieppan*]

schame, schaem *n.* shame **3.** 102, **14.** 110, **17.** 49, **23.** 13, **34.** 5, **44.** 49; disgrace **33.** 21; a shameful thing **11.** 6 [OE *sceamu*]

schame. See **eschame**

schamefull *adj.* modest, shamefaced **10.** 155; disgraceful **3.** 12 [see **schame**]

scharp *adj.* sharp, keen **3.** 42, **3.** 107,

10. 111, 14. 105, 14. 109, fierce 10. 170 [OE *scearp*]

Schau, Robert 28. 8

schau. See **se**

Schaw, Quintyne Scotch poet **62.** 86

schaw *n.* thicket, copse **14.** 516, **54.** 116; *pl.* **50.** 104 [OE *sceaȝa*]

schaw(e) *v.* show, display, reveal **5.** 32, **5.** 56, **14.** 72, **14.** 158, **29.** 5; *3 sg.* **34.** 29, *3 pl.* **74.** 20; *pres. p.* **schawand 48.** 28; *pa. t.* **schew 14.** 252, **54.** 2; *pp.* **schawin 5.** 13, **5.** 19 [OE *scēawian*]

sche, scho(u) *pron.* she **6.** 146, **10.** 57, **10.** 86, **10.** 161, **13.** 22, **28.** 37, **30.** 15; *adj.* she- **53.** 27 [prob. OE fem. pron. *sīo*]

sched *v.* cause, make to flow; *pa. t.* **3.** 43; *ppl. adj.* **14.** 21; **schedis** *3 sg.* parts, sets apart **14.** 106 [OE *scēadan*]

scheild. See **scheld(e)**

***scheild** *ppl. adj.* shelled, husked, *fig.* exposed **23.** 30 [ME; origin obscure]

scheir *v.* cut **52.** 42; **schewre** *pa. t.* rent, tore **54.** 105 [OE *sceran*]

scheld(e), scheild *n.* shield **10.** 151, **10.** 200, **33.** 16, **35.** 14, **35.** 43, **52.** 127, **62.** 22 [OE *sceld*]

schell *n.* target; *fig.* **70.** 13 (see Commentary) [OE *sciell*]

schene, shene *adj.* lovely, (*quasi-n.*) beauty, fair one **2.** 39, **10.** 45, **10.** 74, **10.** 246, **14.** 252, **14.** 515, **24.** 7, **31.** 34 [OE *sciene*]

schent *pp.* shamed, reviled, punished **6.** 22, **9.** 51, **10.** 146, **66.** 8 [OE *ȝescendan*]

schepe *v.* prepare, make ready **23.** 71 [OE *scieppan*]

scherp *adv.* sharply, keenly **52.** 42 [OE *scearp*]

scherpit *pa. t.* sharpened **50.** 121 [OE *scerpan*]

schevill *adj.* distorted, twisted **14.** 106 [rel. to *shevel* distort; origin unknown]

schevin. See **schaiffyne**

schew. See **schaw(e)**

schill *adj.* resonant, shrill **14.** 516 [ME; OE **scielle*]

schilling *n.* husked grain; husks of oats etc. **23.** 147, **23.** 243 (cf. ***scheild**) [cf. OE *sciell* shell]

schining. See **schyne**

schinnis *n. pl.* shins **30.** 14, **32.** 23 [OE *scinu*]

schip, scip *n.* vessel, ship **10.** 235; *fig.* soul **6.** 165; **schippis** *pl.* **33.** 3 [OE *scip*]

***schiphird** *n.* shepherd *attrib.* **23.** 254 [OE *scēaphirde*]

schipwrichtis *n. pl.* shipwrights **44.** 14 [OE *scipwyrhta*]

schir, ser *n.* sir **9.** 15, (the king) **21.** 6, **23.** 1, **25.** 1, **26.** 1, **41.** 1, **42.** 1, **43.** 1, **44.** 1 [reduced form of OF *sire*; L *senior*]

***schit** *n.* shit; term of contempt **23.** 496 [OE v. **scītan*; ON *skīta*]

scho. See **sche**

schog *v.* shake to and fro **29.** 23 [ME *shogge*; cf. OHG *scoc* swinging]

schoir. See **schore**

schoirt. See **schort**

schomd *pp.* ? groomed **43.** 47 [meaning and origin obscure]

schone *n. pl.* shoes **52C.** 13 [ME pl. of OE *scōh*]

schone. See **schyne**

schore, schoir *n.* threatening, menace **14.** 110, **69.** 8 [origin obscure]

schort *v.* shorten, grow short **69.** 46 [OE *sceortian*]

schort, schoirt *adj.* short, brief **6.** 99, **9.** 50, **15.** 11, **33.** 8, **39.** 5, **57.** 6, succinct **62.** 75; *comp.* **schortar 39.** 61; *adv.* quickly, soon **3.** 117; briefly **10.** 136, **63.** 8; at once **63.** 56 [OE *sceort*]

schot. See **schute**

schot(e) *n.* discharge **10.** 199, **52.** 64 [OE *sceot*]

schot *n.* shooting (with arrows etc.) **27.** 30 [OE *ȝesceot*]

schou. See **sche**

schoud, evill *adj.* ill-(?) **43.** 30 [meaning and origin obscure]

schour *n.* shower **10.** 178, **10.** 195, **62.** 70; **schouris, schowris** *pl.* showers **1.** 2, **10.** 14, **14.** 515, **50.** 2, **50.** 67, **69.** 7, **69.** 48 [OE *scūr*]

schout, schowt(e) *n.* shout, vehement cry **48.** 55, **50.** 183, **54.** 125, **56.** 78 [next]

schout, schowt *v.* cry out **14.** 109, **23.** 71, **42.** 7, **52.** 112; **schoutit** *pa. t.* sang out **14.** 516; **schoutyng** *vbl. n.* clamour, loud calling **10.** 25 [ME; cf. ON *skūta* a taunt]

schovaris *n. pl.* pushers, thrusters **44.** 49 [OE *scūfan*]

schow *n., v.* push, thrust **3.** 11, **3.** 126; **schowis** *3 sg.* **14.** 106 [as prec.]

schowris. See **schour**

schowte. See **schout**

schrenk *v.* cower, curl up **14.** 109; *pa. t.* **52.** 149 [OE *scrincan*]

schrevin. See **schrif(e)**

schrew *n.* malignant rascal **14.** 110, **14.** 126; scolding wife **14.** 251; *pl.* **52.** 7, **77.** 27, **79.** 52 [OE *scrǣwa* the *sorex vulgaris* (shrew); cf. MHG *schröwel* devil]

schrew *v.* curse **27.** 36, **38.** 52 [f. prec.]

schrif(e), schrive, schryfe *v.* make (one's) confession, renounce **5.** 10, **5.** 46, **6.** 4, **6.** 9, **6.** 18, **6.** 25, **6.** 137; **schrevin** *pp.* confessed, absolved **52.** 7 [OE *scrīfan*]

schrift *n.* confession to a priest **5.** 19, **5.** 24, **6.** 90, **14.** 251 (ironic) [OE *scrift*]

schrive. See **schrif(e)**

schroud *pp.* dressed, decked out **43.** 47 [OE *scrȳdan*; ME pp. *shrud*]

schrowd *n.* clothing, gown **14.** 252 [OE *scrūd*]

schryfe. See **schrif(e)**

schuk(e). See **schaik**

schulderaris *n. pl.* fellows who make their way by pushing with their shoulders **44.** 49 [OE *sculdor*; cf. Du *schouderen*]

schulderis *n. pl.* shoulders **14.** 22, **14.** 429, **23.** 177, **45.** 57 [OE *sculdor*]

schup(e) *pa. t.* prepared, took measures **9.** 65, **10.** 268, **37.** 27, **54.** 61 [OE *scieppan, scōp*]

schut(e) *v.* shoot **10.** 188, **39.** 59, discharge excreta ***23.** 451; **schuttis** *3 sg.* **70.** 13 (*fig.*); **schot (furth)** *pa. t.* drove out **3.** 11, kept shooting **10.** 179, fired **51.** 112, vomited **52.** 61; **schott** *ppl. adj.* driven out **43.** 4 [OE *scēotan*]

schyne *v.* shine **2.** 2, **10.** 1; *3 sg.* **4.** 27, **33.** 9; **schynnyng** *pres. p.* **53.** 1; *ppl. adj.* **14.** 22, **35.** 94; **schone** *pa. t.* **16.** 14, **16.** 78, **50.** 53; **schining** *vbl. n.* illumination **76.** 20 [OE *scinan*]

schyre *n.* shire, region, district **14.** 472 [OE *scīr*]

schyre *adj.* bright, shining **14.** 22; meagre ***23.** 496 [OE *scīr*]

science, sciens *n.* knowledge, learning **23.** 60, **76.** 1, **76.** 11, **54.** 28 [ME; L *scientia*]

scippis *3 sg.* skips, springs **14.** 357 [? Scand]

sclander. See **sklander**

scoir *n.* score, groups of twenty **27.** 16 (see Commentary), **52.** 134 [OE *scoru*]

***Scone** near Perth **23.** 277

scorde *pp.* cut **3.** 55 [ON *skora*]

scorne, skorne *n.* derision, contempt *pers.* **9.** 35, **9.** 61; **14.** 358; *gen.* **9.** 81 [ME; OF *escarn*]

scorpio(u)n(e) *n.* scorpion, stinging arachnid *fig.* **14.** 92, **23.** 58; *fig.* death **62.** 57 [OF; L *scorpio*]

***Scota** *n.* Scotland **23.** 348 [med. L *Scotia*]

Scottis *adj.* Scots, Scotch **31.** 1 *et seq.*, **35.** 21, **36.** 29 [late OE *Scottisc*; as prec.]

scowlis *n. pl.* malevolent looks **54.** 123 [ME v.; prob. Scand origin]

scull *n.* school **75.** 15; **sculis** *pl.* **23.** 215 [OE *scōl*; L *schola*]

scunner *n.* loathing, disgust **14.** 93, **52.** 154 [origin obscure]

scurge *n.* scourge, whip **3.** 107 [OF *escurge*; L *excoriare*]

scurgit *pa. t.* scourged **3.** 36 [prec.]

scurrilitie *n.* coarse invective **23.** 58 [F; L *scurrilitas*]

scutarde *n.* skitterer **14.** 92 [origin uncertain]

scyne. See **skyn**

se, sey, sie *n.* sea **1.** 54, **6.** 71, **9.** 100, **23.** 14, **23.** 95, **36.** 13, **68.** 17; **seyis** *pl.* **34.** 21 [OE *sǣ*]

se, se(i)ne, seyne, sie *v.* see, behold **3.** 22, **3.** 28, **3.** 62, **8.** 8, **10.** 43, **10.** 143, **23.** 61, **31.** 36, **51.** 99; look to it, make sure **5.** 11, **5.**

29; **seis, seyis** *2, 3 sg.* **6.** 149, **77.** 41; **schau** *pa. t.* **28.** 31; **se(i)ne** *pp.* looked at, seen **5.** 18, **5.** 68, **10.** 80, **16.** 54, **17.** 52, **48.** 22; **seing** *vbl. n.* **6.** 12 [OE *sēon*]

seasoun. See **sessone**

secreit, secrete *adj.* secret, private, close **11.** 8, **13.** 1, **14.** 284, **14.** 466; **secreitlie** *adv.* **82.** 38 [ME; OF; L *secretus*]

secund, secound *adj.* second, other, additional **10.** 32, **14.** 319, **35.** 17, **37.** 68, **52.** 67 [F; L *secundus*]

sege *n.* man **14.** 469, **23.** 13 [OE *sęcg*]

sege *n.* siege, beleaguering **9.** 53 [OF]

sege *v.* talk, speak **14.** 196 [OE *sęcgan*]

seid *n.* semen, progeny **54.** 4 [OE *sǣd*]

seik *v.* try to find, look for **6.** 148, **28.** 13, **57.** 3, **58.** 1; **socht** *pa. t.* **48.** 70, **52.** 183, **52.** 192, **54.** 115; **socht** *pp.* **16.** 109, **69.** 15, searched **64.** 4 [OE *sēcan, sōhte*]

seik *adj.* sick **62.** 10; *as n. pl.* **6.** 28, **54.** 19 [OE *sēoc*]

seiknes *n.* malady, illness **14.** 446, **59.** 25, **62.** 2, **76.** 8 [OE *sēocnesse*]

seilis *n. pl.* seals attached to documents **71.** 60 [ME; OF *seel*; L *sigillum*]

seill *n.* happiness, good fortune **22.** 61 [OE *sǣl*]

seimes. See **seme**

seimlie. See **semely**

seir *adj.* divers, each in particular **1.** 10; many **54.** 57, **66.** 12 [ME; ON *sēr*]

seis. See **ceis, se**

sek *n.* sack, bag **9.** 87 [OE *sacc*; L *saccus*]

sekir. See **sicker**

Seland Zealand **23.** 94, ***23.** 380

selcitud. See **celsitud**

seldin *adv.* rarely, infrequently **5.** 57 [OE *seldan*]

self(fe) *pron.* self **42.** 83; *as pl.* **62.** 43, **79.** 59; **selffis** *pl.* **32.** 21 [OE *self*]

selfin *pron.* self **14.** 212 [OE *self(a)*]

seling *vbl. n.* sealing, attestation **6.** 133; **selit** *pp.* sealed **14.** 344, **14.** 347 [ME; OF *seeler*]

sell *pron.* self **5.** 39, **5.** 52, **17.** 25, **23.** 80, **45.** 71, **70.** 5 [OE *self*]

sely *adj.* innocent, pitiable (and in danger of divine judgement) **5.** 25, **14.** 502 [OE *ȝesǣliȝ*]

seme *n.* seam, sewing **52.** 130 [OE *sēam*]

seme *v.* appear (to be) **10.** 216, **14.** 225; **semys** *1 sg.* **14.** 444; **seimes, semys** *3 sg.* **14.** 184, **14.** 200, **51.** 13; **seimeit, semyt** *pa. t.* **10.** 211, **10.** 241, **14.** 255, **51.** 24 [ME; ON *søma*]

semely, se(i)mlie, semly *adj.* fine, excellent **9.** 91, **14.** 28, **14.** 68, **31.** 36, **48.** 46; *quasi-subst.* **14.** 146 (see Commentary); **semelyar** *comp.* **14.** 217, **14.** 469; **semeliest** *sup.* **9.** 79 [ME; ON *sømiligr*]

sempill, sympill, symple *adj.* guileless, innocent **14.** 255, **14.** 468; of low degree **42.** 32, humble **10.** 272, **42.** 64; **sempillnes** *n.* simplicity, innocence **20.** 21 [OF; L *simplex*]

sempitern *adj.* everlasting **2.** 5 [L *sempiternus*]

sen *prep.* since, considering that **2.** 52, **5.** 5, **9.** 1, **12.** 42, **13.** 16, **14.** 42, **15.** 19 [contracted form of *sithen*; OE *siþþan*]

sence *n.* incense **35.** 22, **48.** 27 [ME; eccl. L *incensum*]

sendis *3 sg.* sends, gives **65.** 9; **send** *pa. t.* sent **50.** 78, *ppl. adj.* **35.** *title* [OE *sęndan*]

sene *v.* say **9.** 31 [OE *sęcgan*]

sene. See **se**

senȝeour *n.* lord **23.** 104 [ME; OF *seignor*; L *senior*]

senȝie *n.* war-cry **23.** 139 (see Commentary) [OE *seȝn* standard, mixed with ME *enseigne*]

sensualite *n.* indulgence in the pleasures of the senses **7.** 1 [F; late L *sensualitas*]

sensyne *adv.* since then **54.** 127 [ME **sen**+**syne**]

sentence, sentens *n.* theme, substance **16.** 7, **16.** 15, **16.** 30, **21.** 8, **62.** 75, **81.** 48; opinion, judgement **58.** 2, **58.** 4; discourse **14.** 146, **14.** 248 [ME, F; L *sententia*]

sepulture *n.* grave, tomb **15.** 24 [ME, OF; L *sepultura* burial]
ser. See **schir**
serene *adj.* clear, cloudless **10.** 108; (as honorific title) **2.** 37, **35.** 1 [L *serenus*]
serf(f) *v.* minister to, gratify **14.** 491, **51.** 97 [ME; OF *servir*; L *servire*]
serk, sark *n.* shirt, chemise **14.** 471, **23.** 223, **50.** 46 [OE *sęrc*; ON *serkr*]
sermon *n.* discourse, exhortation **76.** 13; *pl.* **55.** 17 [ME, OF; L *sermo*]
serpent *n.* reptile; the Devil (Gen. iii. 1–5, Rev. xii. 9) **4.** 10; *gen.* **23.** 75 [ME; OF; L *serpens*]
servand *n.* vassal, servant **47.** 31, **49.** 27, **51.** 67, **55.** 4; vassal in love, paramour **14.** 466; *pl.* servants **45.** 69 [ME; OF; L *servire*]
servatour *n.* servitor; squire **35.** 7 (see Commentary); **servitouris** *pl.* **44.** 1 [ME; OF and late L *servitor*]
service. See **Fair Service**
servis *3 sg.* serves **66.** 18; deserves **22.** 81, **26.** 12; **servit** *pa. t.* deserved **6.** 22; *pp.* provided for **42.** 6, **42.** 31, **51.** 80 [ME; OF *de)servir*]
servitouris. See **servatour**
serviture *n.* servitude **15.** 8 [med. L *servitura*]
servy(i)s, service *n.* service rendered to a master **45.** 14, **78.** 16, **78.** 21 [ME, OF *servise*; L *servitium*]
sessioun, cessioun *n.* court of justice (see **74.** *note*) **6.** 134, **51.** 62, **51.** 74, **75.** 57 [F; L *sessio*]
sessoun, ses(s)one, seasoun *n.* season, time **14.** 24, **50.** 33, **58.** 7; time of maturity **14.** 289 [ME; OF *seson*; L *satio*]
set(t) *v.* set; direct **14.** 449, **19.** 11, sit **51.** 74; **sett . . . by** count . . . worth **17.** 57, **23.** 238, **70.** 22; **settis** *3 sg.* becomes, suits **14.** 196; *3 pl.* gamble **67.** 27; **set(t), settin** *pp.* placed, worked, fitted **10.** 276, **23.** 108, **32.** 18; *ppl. adj.* settled **14.** 327, **40.** 20, **45.** 51; assessed, regarded **11.** 18, **68.** 7; imposed **14.** 176 [OE *sęttan*]
seve *n.* sieve, strainer **38.** 55 [OE *sife*]
severit *pp.* separated, parted **14.** 337 [ME; OF *sevrer*; L *separare*]
severance *n.* distinction, difference **14.** 311 [OF *sevrance*]
sevin, sev(e)yne *num. adj.* **6.** 18, **6.** 26, **6.** 33, **14.** 177, **22.** 66, **39.** 47, **45.** 5, **51.** 88; **be sic s.** seven times more **2.** 50, **14.** 218, **55.** 27 [OE *seofon*]
sew *v.* accompany, attend upon (one) **14.** 285 [ME; AF *suer*; L *sequi*]
sex *num. adj.* six **56.** 54 [OE]
sexty *num. adj., pron.* **14.** 256 [OE *sextiȝ*]
sey, seyis, seyne. See **se**
shene. See **schene**
***shere** *v.* cut off, remove *fig.* **23.** 398 [OE *sceran*]
sib *adj.* akin, closely related **38.** 55 [OE]
sic, sik *adj.* such **2.** 50, **5.** 5, **8.** 13, **9.** 78, **10.** 169, **12.** 17, **14.** 196 [reduced form of OE *swilk*]
sich, sych *v.* sigh **14.** 218, **14.** 446; **sichand** *vbl. n.* sighing **49.** 39 [OE *sican*]
sicht, sycht *n.* sight, display **2.** 2, **2.** 18, **2.** 25, **10.** 207, **10.** 277, eyesight **12.** 45, glimpse **65.** 35; **but sicht** unseen **2.** 31 [OE *sihð*]
sic(k)er, sic(k)ir *adj.* secure, safe **3.** 130, **14.** 285, **14.** 468, **62.** 13, firm **38.** 41; *adv.* **77.** 47 [OE *sicor*; L *securus*]
siclyk *n.* such kind of person **77.** 36 [**sic**+**lyk**]
sie. See **se**
signakle *n.* sign (the Cross) **2.** 18 [late L *signaculum*]
signe *n.* standard, emblem **4.** 4 [F; L *signum*]
sik. See **sic**
sile, syle *v.* cover the eyes; beguile **10.** 217, **14.** 449 [OF *ciller*]
silk *n.* garment made of silk **14.** 365; *pl.* **14.** 68 [OE *sioloc*]
sillie, silly *adj.* simple, helpless **37.** 18, **37.** 40, **39.** 91 [ME; see **sely**]
silvir *adj.* silvery **10.** 14, **10.** 26 [OE *siolfor*]
Sinclair, Sir Jhon 28. 1

sindrie, sindry *adj.* various **14.** 38, **39.** 89, **51.** 8, **52.** 26, **52.** 50, **52.** 136 [OE *syndriȝ*]

sing *v.* sing **1.** 29; **singand** *pres. p.* **38.** 103, **48.** 45; **song** *pa. t.* **50.** 58, **50.** 162 [OE *singan*]

singaris *n. pl.* singers **44.** 9 [ME; prec.; cf. MDu *singer*]

single *n.* small bundle of gleanings **23.** 116 [ME adj.; OF; L *singulum*]

singula(i)r *adj.* special **47.** 31, private **75.** 71 [ME, OF; L *singularis*]

sinkis *3 sg.* sinks, penetrates **14.** 115 [OE *sincan*]

sirculit *ppl. adj.* encircled, enclosed **50.** 98 [ME; F *circuler*; L *circulare*]

sircumstance. See **circumstance**

sistir (*as n. pl.*) sisters **10.** 83; **sisteris** *pl.* **14.** 145, **14.** 251 [OE *sweostor*]

sit *v.* sit; disregard, neglect **14.** 319 (see Commentary); **sittis** *3 sg.* is seated **14.** 490, **14.** 492; *3 pl.* **14.** 440, **14.** 487; **sittin** *pp.* seated **52.** 190 [OE *sittan*]

skaffis *2 sg.* sponge, beg contemptibly **23.** 133 [? Du *schaffen*; see *OED*, *scaff* v.[1]]

skaild. See **scale**

***skaitbird** *n.* perh. the skua (*stercorarius parasiticus*), in later Scots *skatie-goo* **23.** 37 (see Commentary)

skaith *n.* harm, damage **50.** 107 [ON *skaðe*]

skaldand *ppl. adj.* scalding, scorching **52.** 23 [ONF *escalder*; L *calidus*]

***skaldit** *ppl. adj.* scabby, affected with scall, a skin disease **23.** 26, **23.** 37 [ME *scall*; ON *skalle* bald head]

***skamelar** (**23.** 37). See **scamleris**

skar *v.* frighten, terrify **23.** 214; **skarris** *2 sg.* are terrified **55.** 11; **skarrit** *pa. t.* took fright **55.** 6 [ME *skerre*; ON *skirra*]

skarth, scarth *n.* hermaphrodite, monster **14.** 92, **23.** 58, **23.** 194 [OE **scratta*; cf. ON *skratte*]

skeich *adj.* spirited, inclined to shy **14.** 357 [cf. OE *scēoh*]

skeilis *n. pl.* wooden tubs **23.** 231 [ME; ON *skjōla* pail]

skellat *n.* small hand-bell **54.** 50 [ME; OF *esqualette*; OHG *scella*]

sker *adj.* restive **14.** 357 [cf. ON *skiarr*]

skerche *adj.* scarce, niggardly **11.** 5 [ONF *escars*; L *excerpere*]

skillis *n. pl.* sculls, round wicker baskets **23.** 231 [origin obscure; ? OF *escuelle* dish]

skippis *n. pl.* skips, slight jumps **10.** 19 [ME; cf. MSw v. *skuppa*]

skippis, up *3 sg.* turns up **33.** 8; **skippit** *pa. t.* leapt, danced **52.** 23 [prec.]

***skirle** *v.* scream, shriek **23.** 39 [? Scand origin; cf. Norw dial. *skrylla*]

sklander, sklandir *v.* slander, decry **11.** 22, **82.** 39; **sklander, sklandir, sclander** *n.* slander, calumny, scandal **23.** 21, **26.** 12, **75.** 21; *pers.* **9.** 89, **9.** 100 [OF *esclandre*; L *scandalum*]

sklender *adj.* thin, scraggy **37.** 24 [ME; origin obscure]

skolderit *ppl. adj.* scorched **23.** 122, **23.** 171 [origin obscure; but cf. **skaldand**]

skomer *v.* defecate (of a dog or fox) **23.** 113 [ME; aphetic form of OF *descombrer*]

skornar *n.* scorner, mocker **77.** 35 [ME; see **skornit**]

skorne *n.* derision; **skornes** *gen.* **9.** 81; *pl.* insults **50.** 107 [ME *skarn*; OF *escarn*]

skornit *pa. t.* mocked, derided **54.** 98 [ME; OF *escarnir*; cf OHG *skernôn*]

skowry *adj.* 'scourie', scruffy, broken-down **37.** 15 [origin obscure]

skrippit *pa. t.* mocked, jeered at **54.** 97 [origin obscure]

***skrowis** *n. pl.* scrolls, writings **23.** 26 [ME; aphetic form of AF *escrowe*]

skrumple *n.* wrinkle, crease **23.** 122 [var. of *crumple*; ME v. *crump*]

skryke *n.* screech **54.** 97; **skryking** *vbl. n.* **54.** 123 [ME; prob. Scand origin; cf. Norw v. *skrika*]

skrymming *vbl. n.* darting **54.** 123 [OF (*e*)*scrimir*]

***skryp** *n.* pilgrim's wallet **23.** 509 [ME; OF *escreppe*]

skyn, scyne *n.* skin **14.** 93, **19.** 21, **23.** 122 [ME; ON *skinn*]

skyre *n.* score; line, crease in the skin **23.** 122 [ON *skor*]
skyttand *ppl. adj.* shitting, excreting **23.** 194 [ON *skīta*]
slais *3 sg.* slays, kills **34.** 44; **slane, slayn** *pp.* **8.** 12, **10.** 196, **12.** 24, **34.** 44, **58.** 12, **62.** 70 [OE *slēan*, pp. *slæȝen*]
slasy *adj.* (obscure) **13.** 39 [origin and meaning obscure]
slauchter, slauchtir, slawchtir *n.* murder **6.** 140, **12.** 6, **54.** 39 [ME; ON **slahtr*]
slaw *adj.* slow **52.** 76 [OE *slāw*]
slayar *n.* killer, murderer **12.** 5 [see **slais**]
sle. See **slie**
sleif *n.* sleeve **42.** 68 [OE *slīefe*]
sleip *n.* sleep **56.** 1; **on sleip** asleep **37.** 65 [OE *slǣp*]
sleip *v.* sleep **14.** 221; **sleipand, sle(i)ping** *pres. p.* **16.** 116, **50.** 8, **51.** 1, **53.** 40; **sleipeing** *ppl. adj.* **21.** 12; **sle(i)pit** *pa. t.* fell asleep, slept **3.** 8, **9.** 34, **10.** 48 [OE *slǣpan*]
slepy *adj.* sleepy, drowsy **52.** 69, **52.** 71 [OE n. *slǣp*; cf. MDu, MLG *slapich*]
sleuth, slewth *n.* sloth, laziness (*accidia*), one of the seven deadly sins **6.** 20, **70.** 17 [OE *slǣwð*]
slicht *n.* art, skill **31.** 18; cunning, trickery **34.** 28; **slichtfull** *adj.* crafty **39.** 7 [ME *slēȝþ*; ON *slœgð*]
slie, sle *adj.* skilled, expert **23.** 60, **27.** 30, **52C.** 31; cunning **56.** 83, **62.** 7, **62.** 39, **79.** 13 [ME *slēȝ*; ON *slœgr*]
slippis *3 sg.* escapes, breaks away **28.** 41; *pa. t.* **54.** 106 [ME; MLG *slippen*]
sloknyt *pp.* stamped out, quenched **14.** 522 [ME; ON *slokna*]
slokyn *v.* allay, satisfy **14.** 283 [OE *slacian*]
slomering *vbl. n.* slumbers, sleep **50.** 13 [ME v. *slumeren*; cf. Du *sluimering*]
***slong, staf** *n.* staff-sling, powerful sling with cords attached to a staff **23.** 358 [OE *stæf*+Ger *slinge*; cf. OHG *stapaslinga*]
sloppis *n. pl.* ? small clouds **10.** 26 (see Commentary) [MDu, MLG]
slugird *n.* lazy fellow, sloth **50.** 22; **sluggirdis** *pl.* **16.** 86 [ME; cf. Norw *sluggjie* slow person]
slummer *n.* slumber, sleep **53.** 9 [ME; cf. MDu v. *sluymeren*, MLG *slômeren*]
slute *adj.* sluttish, dirty **52.** 71 [ME n.; cf. Ger dial. *schlutt*]
slyd, (ower) *v.* slip (by) **32.** 2; **slydand, slyding** *ppl. adj.* **39.** 5, **57.** 3 [OE *slīdan*]
smakes *n. gen.* rogue's **14.** 113 (see Commentary) [? MDu, MLG *smeiker* flatterer]
small *adj.* narrow, slender **10.** 63, **32.** 23; weak (of beer) **22.** 13 [OE *smæl*]
smellit *pa. t.* gave off a scent **14.** 514 [ME; prob. OE]
***smoch** *adj.* (obscure) **23.** 364; perh. var. of *moch* fusty
smorit *pa. t.* smothered **52.** 120; **smord** *pp.* concealed **34.** 28 [perh. MLG *smōren*; cf. OE *smorian*]
smowk *n.* smoke **55.** 48; **smowking** *vbl. n.* smoking **54.** 56 [prob. Flem *smuiken*]
smuke *n.* reek, smoke **52.** 120 [prob. Flem *smuik*]
smy *n.* knave, scoundrel **14.** 113 [origin obscure]
smydy *n.* smithy, forge **54.** 56 [ON *smiðja*]
smyle, smyll *v.* smile, look on with favour **10.** 218, **50.** 36; **smyling** *vbl. n.* **14.** 230, *pl.* **63.** 58 [ME; OHG *smîlan*]
smyrkis *3 sg.* simpers **14.** 113 [OE *smearcian*]
smyt *v.* smite, strike **3.** 29 [OE *smītan*]
smyth *n.* blacksmith **56.** 56 [OE *smið*]
snaill *n.* snail, sluggard **14.** 176 [OE *snæȝel*]
***snawe** *n.* snow **23.** 434 [OE *snāw*]
***snevillis** *3 sg.* runs with mucus **23.** 550 [OE **snyflan*]
sobir *adj.* quiet, calm **10.** 249, **12.** 36, **14.** 466, **50.** 17; **sobirly** *adv.* gravely, solemnly **50.** 36 [OF *sobre*; L *sobrius*]

sobirnes *n.* gravity, temperate disposition; *pers.* **10.** 167 [prec.]
socht. See **seik**
***sodomyt(e)** *n.* bugger **23.** 253, **23.** 527 [ME, OF; Gen. xviii–xix]
soft *v.* mollify, make lenient **25.** 22 [OE adj.]
soft *adj.* mild, calm, balmy **10.** 247; *adv.* gently **9.** 71 [see prec.]
soin. See **sone**
soir. See **sair**
solace *n.* consolation, delight **18.** 2, **52C.** 6; *v.* take enjoyment **65.** 13 [ME; OF *solas*; L *solatium*]
solist *v.* plead, petition **71.** 27; **solistand** *pres. p.* entreating, inciting **56.** 82 [ME *solicite*; OF *solliciter*]
solistationes *n. pl.* petitions **20.** 2 [OF *sollicitation*; L]
solitar *adj.* solitary, lonely **22.** 17 [ME; OF *solitaire*; L *solitarius*]
somer, symmer *n.* season of summer **23.** 115; *attrib.* **61.** 26, **68.** 30; *pers.* **69.** 10, **69.** 49 [OE *sumor*]
son. See **sone**
sonce *n.* abundance, prosperity **22.** 61 [Gael *sonas* good fortune]
sondir, in to *adv. phr.* apart, in pieces **14.** 350; **in sounder, sowndir** **12.** 47, **51.** 114 [OE *on sundran*]
son(e), soune *n.* sun **1.** 5, **1.** 39, **3.** 84, **4.** 27, **14.** 471, **33.** 13, **35.** 43, *attrib.* **24.** 15 [OE *sunne*]
sone, sonne, soun *n.* son **3.** 30, **3.** 87, **6.** 59, **14.** 292, **22.** 29, **26.** 2, **35.** 12; *pl.* **14.** 402, **54.** 4 [OE *sunu*]
sone, so(i)n *adv.* soon, shortly **9.** 91, **10.** 49, **22.** 26, **22.** 33, **28.** 41, **32.** 4, **55.** 9 [OE *sōna*]
song. See **singand**
sonȝie *n.* excuse, plea **46.** 3 [var. of *soign*; F *soigne*]
sonis. See **sone**
***sonkyn** *pp.* sunk **23.** 455 [OE *sincan, suncen*]
soppis *n. pl.* (pieces of) soaked bread **13.** 30 [OE v. *sūpan*]
sore *n.* pain, affliction **2.** 53; *adv.* severely, greatly **10.** 159 [OE *sār*]
sorie. See **sary**
sorow *n.* misery, trouble **14.** 94 [OE *sorȝ*]
sort *n.* band, company **9.** 91, **48.** 46, **52.** 82 [OE *sorte*; L *sors*]
sory. See **sary**
sossery *n.* sorcery, witchcraft **27.** 6 [ME; OF *sorcerie*]
soukaris *n. pl.* suckers, parasites **44.** 41 [OE *sūcan*]
sould. See **suld**
soume *n.* sum, amount **46.** 12; **soumes, sowmis** *pl.* amount, accounts **46.** 10, **68.** 38 [ME; OF *summe*; L *summa*]
sounde *adj.* healthy **5.** 17 [OE *ȝesund*]
sounder. See **sondir**
soundit *pp.* rung out, proclaimed **4.** 29 [OF *suner*; L *sonare*]
soune, soun, sowne *n.* sound, music **10.** 47, **14.** 519, **22.** 22, **35.** 22, **50.** 57, **50.** 113, **50.** 163 [ME; AF; L *sonus*]
soun(e). See **sone**
sounȝie *n.* excuse; hesitation **52.** 72 [var. of *soign*; OF *soigne*]
soupill *adj.* soft, pliant **14.** 96 [ME; OF; L *supplex*]
sour *adj.* bitter, unpleasant **14.** 144 [OE *sūr*]
south. See **suth**
soutteris. See **sowt(t)ar**
so(u)verane, sovera(y)ne *n.* ruler **35.** *title*, **50.** 170; *adj.* supreme **2.** 64, peerless **14.** 221, **14.** 507, **23.** 104 [ME; OF *soverain*]
sowch *n.* murmuring sound of wind **14.** 519 [ME]
sowdane *n.* sultan, pagan ruler **29.** 19 [ME; OF *soldan*; Arabic]
sowk *v.* suck **72.** 18; *pres. p.* **62.** 26; **sowk** *n.* sucking, milk **13.** 24 [OE *sūcan*; L *sugere*]
sowld. See **suld**
sowmis. See **soume**
sowndir. See **sondir**
sowp *n.* sup, sip of liquor **73.** 27 [ON *saup*]
sowp *v.* take supper **69.** 45 [ME, OF; origin obscure]
sowr *adj.* cross, sullen **28.** 37 [OE *sūr*]
sowt(t)ar *n.* shoemaker, cobbler **52.**

124, **52.** 146, **56.** 31; *gen.* **23.** 155; **soutteris** *pl.* **43.** 35, **75.** 36; **sowttarlyk** *adj.* like a cobbler **52.** 166 [OE *sūtere*; L *sutor*]

sox *n. pl.* short stockings **23.** 144 [OE *socc*; L *soccus* slipper]

space, spaice, spais *n.* extent, interval of time, opportunity **6.** 99, **7.** 6, **10.** 210, **10.** 232, **37.** 61, **65.** 26, **67.** 4, **67.** 8, **69.** 28; **ane space** at an interval **51.** 27 [ME; OF *espace*; L *spatium*]

spair *v.* leave unused, keep back **48.** 67; **sparis** *3 sg.* **67.** 25 [OE *sparian*]

spak, spack. See **speik**

spald *n.* shoulder; limb of a beast **43.** 42 [ME; OF *espalde*; L *spatula*]

span *n.* the measure across the extended hand; 9 inches **14.** 160 [OE]

spane *v.* wean **13.** 54; **spaind** *ppl. adj.* weaned **13.** 24 [ME; MDu, MLG *spanen*]

Spane *n.* Spain **39.** 19; **Spanȝie, Spenȝie** *attrib.* Spanish **32.** 30, **70.** 14 [AF *Espaigne*; L *Hispania*]

spar *v.* spare, hold back **14.** 161; *3 sg.* **62.** 33; *pa. t.* avoided, abstained from, forbore **14.** 40; *pp.* **62.** 47 [OE *sparian*]

sparhalk *n.* sparrow-hawk (*accipiter nisus*) **54.** 79 [OE *spearhafoc* (*spearwa* sparrow)]

speciall, in *adv. phr.* separately, individually, specifically **14.** 495, **23.** 5 [ME; OF *especial*]

sped. See **speid**

spedelie *adv.* quickly, hurriedly **14.** 40 [OE *spǣd*]

speid *v.* attain one's desire, prosper **17.** 32, **25.** 27, **51.** 77, **51.** 81, **80.** 34; hasten **60.** 11; *3 sg.* **74.** 24; **sped** *pp.* brought to a desired end **78.** 28 [OE *spēdan*]

speid, (gud) *adv. phr.* successfully, luckily **54.** 24 [prec.]

speik, speke *v.* speak, say, tell **10.** 136, **12.** 44, **14.** 205, **14.** 495, **29.** 13; **spa(c)k** *pa. t.* **14.** 40, **14.** 49, **30.** 6, **51.** 58, **56.** 14; **spokin** *pp.* **51.** 73; **speiking** *vbl. n.* talk, speech **6.** 107 [OE *sprecan*]

speir *n. coll.* sphere(s), the concentric globes revolving round the earth and carrying the heavenly bodies **1.** 12, **50.** 165 [ME, OF; L *sphaera*]

speir *n.* spear, lance **33.** 16, **52.** 127; *pl.* **52.** 184, *fig.* **50.** 130 [OE *spere*]

speir *v.* put questions, ask **5.** 33, **5.** 37, **14.** 52; *2 sg.* **23.** 65 [OE *spyrian*]

***spelunk** *n.* cavern **23.** 275 [ME; L *spelunca*]

spend *v.* give something away, expend **71.** 46 [double entendre); *2 sg.* **65.** 11; *pa. t.* **69.** 35; **spendit, spent** *pp.* **46.** 13; expended, employed **10.** 274; **spending** *vbl. n.* money to spend, cash **63.** 13 [OE **spendan*; L *expendere*]

Spenȝie. See **Spane**

sperkis, ruby *n. pl.* small rubies **10.** 24 [OE *spærca*]

spill *v.* spoil, waste **78.** 22 [OE *spillan*]

spiritualite *n.* religious or moral feeling **7.** 3 [OF; L *spiritualitas*]

spirituall *adj.* concerned with the soul **6.** 33 [OF; L *spiritualis*]

spirling *n.* smelt (*osmerus eperlanus*) **22.** 95 [MLG]

spittit *pa. t.* spat **3.** 18, **14.** 396 [nth. OE *spittan*]

splene *n.* spleen; **fro the splene** from the heart **2.** 43, **10.** 106, **16.** 70, **17.** 6 *et seq.*, **50.** 12 [ME; OF *esplene*; L *splen*]

spokin. See **speke**

***Spottismuir** east of Haddington **23.** 269

spousage *n.* wedlock **14.** 155 [ME; OF *espousaille*]

spowt *n.* violent discharge **54.** 104 [ME; origin uncertain]

spraidis. See **spredis, sprang.** See **spring**

spray *n. coll.* small twigs on trees, stems **10.** 51, **14.** 29 [origin obscure]

spredis, spraidis *3 pl.* stretch, reach out **10.** 59, **40.** 17; **spreding** *pres. p.* **10.** 22; *pa. t.* **10.** 97; **spredding** *vbl. n.* spreading, laying **23.** 206 [OE *sprǣdan*]

spreit *n.* spirit, soul **3.** 81, **12.** 19;

mind, feelings **3.** 140, **6.** 4, **14.** 112, **14.** 247; spirits **14.** 160; third person of the Holy Trinity **6.** 65, **6.** 89; ghost **23.** 172; creature, devil **14.** 397 [ME *spirit*; OF *esprit*; L]

sprent *pa. t.* sprang, leapt **10.** 242 [e. Scand **sprenta*]

spring *n.* attack, contest **54.** 79 [OE]

spring *v.* rise up **10.** 158; **sprang** *pa. t.* arose **10.** 4, **14.** 160; **sprungin** *ppl. adj.* above the horizon **4.** 21; **spruning** *pp.* sprung, sticking out **43.** 18 [OE *springan*]

spryng *n.* dance-tune **38.** 109 [ME; prob. OE *espringuer* to dance]

spulȝeit *ppl. adj.* despoiled, deprived **14.** 397 [OF *espoillier*]

spumis *n. pl.* fragments **61.** 44 [OF; L *spuma*]

spunge *n.* sponge **14.** 437 [OE; L *spongia*]

spurrit *pa. t.* pricked with spurs **52.** 187; *pp.* **43.** 42 [ME *spure*; cf. MHG *sporen*]

spy *v.* watch covertly **14.** 427; **spyit** *pa. t.* espied, discovered **14.** 271 [ME; OF *espier*]

spyce *n.* spice, aromatic substance; *fig.* **2.** 71; = spices **68.** 19 [ME; OF *espice*]

spynist *ppl. adj.* opened **14.** 29 [OF *espanir*, *espaniss-*]

***spynk** *n.* chaffinch; term of abuse, ? 'twitterer' **23.** 552 [ME; imit.]

spynnand *pres. p.* spinning wool or flax **34.** 46 [OE *spinnan*]

square *adj.* having an equilateral rectangular section **10.** 111 [ME; OF *esquarré*]

***squeill** *v.* scream in pain **23.** 39 [ME; imit.]

squische *v.* crush **43.** 4 [origin obscure]

stabell *n.* stable **43.** 27, **45.** 52 [ME; OF *estable*; L *stabulum*]

stabill *adj.* firm, secure, fixed **60.** 17, **77.** 43 [ME; OF *estable*; L *stabilis*]

stackarand *pres. p.* staggering, reeling **28.** 17; **stackeret** *pa. t.* **28.** 11 [ME; ON *stakra*]

stafische *adj.* rigid; *fig.* unruly **45.** 17 (see Commentary) [OE *stæf* a stick]

***staggis** *n. pl.* young horses **23.** 428 [OE **stacga*]

staiffis *3 pl.* thrust **14.** 486 [etym. obscure]

staigis *n. pl.* steps on Fortune's wheel **53.** 18 [ME; OF *estage*; L *stare*]

stait *n.* condition **3.** 130, **6.** 69, **62.** 9; estate, rank **38.** 32, **39.** 37 [OF *estat*; L *status*]

***stakkis** *n. pl.* grain-stacks **23.** 362 [ME; ON *stakkr*]

stald *pp.* put into a stall **43.** 6 [ME; OF *estaler*]

stalkaris *n. pl.* prowlers **23.** 156 [OE **stealcian* walk stealthily]

stalkis *n. pl.* stems **8.** 9, **49.** 4 [ME; ? OE *stalu*]

***stall** *pa. t.* stole **23.** 361, **23.** 428 [see **steilis**]

stalwardly *adv.* boldly **14.** 485 [OE *stǣl+wierðe*]

stalwart *adj.* stout **14.** 384 [as prec.]

***stanch** *v.* stop, put an end to **23.** 378; *3 pl.* cease **23.** 543 [ME; OF *estanchier*]

stanchell *n.* kestrel (*falco tinnunculus*) **54.** 82 [var. of *staniel*; OE *stān-ȝella*]

standis *3 sg.* stands **20.** 13; is, remains **6.** 69, **62.** 13, **66.** 22; **standand** *ppl. adj.* erect **14.** 486 [OE *standan*]

stane *n.* stone, precious stone **2.** 62, **13.** 40, **14.** 140, **45.** 60, **78.** 9; **stanis, stonis** *pl.* **3.** 55, rocks **3.** 83, precious stones **14.** 367, **50.** 155 [OE *stān*]

stane *v.* pelt with stones **23.** 216 [ME; prec.]

stang *n.* sting **4.** 10; *fig.* penis **13.** 48 [OE *stǫng*; ON *stanga* prick, spear]

stang *v.* sting mortally **40.** 28; *3 sg. fig.* **58.** 9; **stangand** *ppl. adj.* stinging, piercing **14.** 266 [ON *stanga*]

stanneris *n. pl.* small stones and gravel at a river's edge **10.** 36 [prob. OE *stān;* cf. ONhb *stǣner*]

stark *adj.* strong, robust, sturdy **5.** 64, **23.** 176, **32.** 21, **56.** 72 [OE *stearc*]

***starn** *n.* ship's stern **23.** 450 [ME; ON *stjōrn*]
start. See **stert**
starvit. See **stervis**
statur *n.* height **14.** 297 [OF; L *statura*]
staw *n.* stall, standing-place in a stable **43.** 11 [OE *steall*; ON *stallr*]
stayd. See **steid**
sted, hard . . . *pa. t.* beset **32.** 12 [ME; OE n. *stęde* place]
stedfastnes *n.* constancy, fidelity *pers.* **10.** 164 [OE *stędefæst*]
steid, stayd *n.* place **3.** 139, **38.** 111, **71.** 41; *pl.* **51.** 93; ***stedis** *pl.* lands, farms **23.** 365 [OE *stęde*]
steidfast *adj.* steady, resolute **16.** 47, **49.** 28 [OE *stędefæst*]
steik *v.* shut **12.** 46 [ME; OE **ste-can*]
steilis (in) *3 pl.* come stealthily upon **23.** 156 [OE *stelan*]
steill, stele *n.* steel **47.** 14, **52.** 37, **52.** 201, **71.** 28; *attrib.* **14.** 340, **50.** 121 [OE *stǣli*]
steillaris *n. pl.* workers in steel **52.** 131 (see Commentary) [OE *stǣli*; cf. ON v. *stǣla*]
steir *n.* commotion, tumult **52.** 172; **on steir** in a state of commotion **3.** 112, **9.** 78 [ONhb *ȝestir*; ON *styrn*; OE v. *styrian*]
steir *v.* move, utter **12.** 48; move, control **53.** 15; *3 sg.* **77.** 12; ***ster-and** *pres. p.* stirring **23.** 543 [OE *styrian*]
steir *v.* guide, govern **18.** 15; *3 sg.* **45.** 3, **61.** 14 [OE *stieran*]
steiris *n. pl.* rudders *fig.* **61.** 46 [OE **stēor*]
stele. See **steill**
stent *pa. t.* stretched, set **10.** 236 [origin obscure]
steppis *3 pl.* march, proceed **14.** 485 [OE *stęppan*]
ster *n.* star **1.** 12; **day ster** morning star **1.** 3; **sterris** *pl.* **22.** 66, **35.** 5, **35.** 52 [OE *steorra*]
Sterling. See **Strivilling**
stern(e) *n.* star **2.** 1, **2.** 53, **2.** 70; **day sterne, stern of day** morning star **2.** 26, **10.** 1, **10.** 52, **49.** 9; *pl.* **10.** 36, **23.** 3 [ON *stjarna*]
stern(e) *adj.* grim, fierce **10.** 113, **52.** 201 [OE *styrne*]
***stere** *n.* rudder, helm **23.** 450, **23.** 460 [see **steiris**]
stert *v.* jump, move **14.** 234, *pa. t.* **14.** 339; **start** *pa. t.* **52.** 194 [OE *styrtan*, **stiertan*]
stervis *3 sg.* perishes **78.** 14; **starvit** *pa. t.* perished **54.** 22 [OE *steorfan*, *stearf*]
stevyne, stevin *n.* voice, sound of singing **2.** 54, **38.** 103, **52C.** 3, **63.** 69 [OE *stefn*]
stew *n.* ? stink **14.** 339 [cf. *OED*, s.v. *stew* sb.[3]]
Stewart, Barnard lord of Aubigny (d. 1508) **35, 36**
Stewartis the royal house **48.** 37
stif *adj.* stiff, rigid **14.** 95, **14.** 486 [OE]
stik *v.* stab, pierce **56.** 67 [OE *stician*]
stilis *n. pl.* writing, compositions **10.** 68 [ME; OF *style*; L *stilus*]
still *n.* style, appellation **52.** 215 [as prec.]
still *adj.* calm, quiet **9.** 47, **11.** 15, **13.** 23; *adv.* at rest **9.** 111, in the same place **32.** 6 [OE *stille*]
stinkand *ppl. adj.* stinking **75.** 15, **75.** 38; **stinckett** *pa. t.* stank **28.** 48 [OE *stincan*]
stirk *n.* young bullock **28.** 17; *pl.* ***23.** 428 [OE *stirc*]
Stobo John Reid 'alias Stobo' **62.** 86 (see Commentary), ***23.** 331
stok *n.* stock (of a plant) **50.** 151; **stok and stone** sacred images (*lit.* gods of wood and stone) **22.** 18; **stockis** *pl.* stocks, instrument of punishment **32.** 28 [OE *stōc* stump]
stole *n.* liturgical vestment, a long strip of silk worn over the shoulders **54.** 55 [ME; L *stola*]
stomok, stommok *n.* stomach **14.** 163, **52.** 172; stomacher (chest covering for a horse) *attrib.* **52.** 131 [OF *estomac*; L *stomachus*]
stonis. See **stane**
stoppell *n.* stopper, bung *fig.* **14.** 339 [ME; aphetic form of *estoppel*; OF]
stoppit *pp.* closed up, blocked **14.** 99, **37.** 48 [OE **stoppian*]

storie *n.* history, legend **40.** 12; **storyis** *pl.* tales **20.** 7 [ME; OF *estoire*; L *historia*]
storkyn *v.* grow, stiffen **13.** 48 [ON *storkna*]
stound *n.* time (of trial); sharp pain **3.** 98, **6.** 157, **14.** 109, **14.** 340 [OE *stund*]
stour(e), store *n.* conflict, combat **10.** 202, **35.** 9, **36.** 21, **48.** 33, **62.** 29; struggle with pain or death **2.** 59, **3.** 39 [ME; OF *estour*]
stout *adj.* bold, brave, fierce **50.** 93, **52.** 159, **69.** 38 [ME; OF *estout*; Teut origin]
stowin *pp.* stolen **52.** 136 [OE *stelan*, pp. *stolen*]
stowp *n.* drinking vessel, tankard **73.** 26 [ME; ON *staup*]
stra(e) *n.* straw **43.** 30, *attrib.* **23.** 213; **strais** *pl.* **23.** 214 [ON *strā*]
straik, strak, strok *n.* stroke, blow **3.** 37, **6.** 157, **54.** 22, **62.** 35; thrust **14.** 234; wound, injury **51.** 49; *pl.* **9.** 78 [ME *strāk*; OE **strac*]
straik *pa. t.* struck **9.** 68, **52.** 206, **54.** 84 [OE *strican, strāc*]
strait *adj.* stingy, mean **23.** 209 [ME *streit*; OF *estreit*; L *strictus*]
straitit *pa. t.* stretched (limbs) **3.** 67 [OE *stręccan*]
stramp *v.* tread on, trample **14.** 493 [perh. suggested by *tramp*, *stamp* . . . (*OED*)]
Stranaver, Strenever Strathnaver in Sutherland **28.** 13, **43.** 5
strand *n.* stream (of blood) **3.** 37 [?; cf. ME *strind*]
strandis *n. pl.* edges of a lake or river **10.** 61, shores **35.** 52 [OE]
strang *adj.* strong, powerful **4.** 13, **6.** 73, **26.** 9, **48.** 35, **52.** 147; secure **23.** 151 [OE]
strange, strenge *adj.* wonderful, odd **52.** 86, **67.** 35; aloof **69.** 32; **strangenes** *n.* aloofness **9.** 18 (see Commentary), **9.** 22, **9.** 75; **strangeris** *pl.* strangers **75.** 13, **79.** 36 [ME; OF *estrange*; L *extraneus*]
stranthis. See **strenth**
straught. See **stricht**
stray *n.* straw (cf. **stra(e)**); **stray breid** straw's breadth **14.** 234 [OE *strēaw*]
streiche *adj.* polite, 'proper' **81.** 32 [ME *streȝt*; pp. of OE *stręccan*]
streittis *n. pl.* streets **48.** 20, **48.** 49, **75.** 37, **75.** 52 [OE *strǣt*; L (*via*) *strata*]
strekouris *n. pl.* ? lean dogs; prob. pejorative application of *streaker* a hunting dog **45.** 17 [AF *stracur*; cf. OF *estrac* track]
stremys *n. pl.* currents of water **10.** 28, **14.** 519 [OE *strēam*]
strene *v.* distress, urge **73.** 28 [ME; OF *estreindre*; L *stringere*]
Strenever. See **Stranaver**
strenewite *n.* strenuousness, vigour **35.** 93 [ME; L *strenuitas*]
strenge. See **strange**
strenȝe *v.* bind; afflict, distress **6.** 158 [ME *streynen*; OF *estreindre*; L *stringere*]
strenth *n.* strength **5.** 65, **14.** 171, **14.** 383, **16.** 95, **36.** 21; **stranthis** *pl.* virtues **14.** 264; **strenthis** *pl.* (barren) fastnesses **43.** 5 [OE *stręngðu*]
stricht, straucht *adj.* straight, direct, true **2.** 35, **57.** 1 [adj. use of pp. of OE *stręccan* stretch]
strik, stryk(e) *v.* strike, knock **14.** 384, **77.** 36; dart (at) **54.** 99; **straik** *pa. t.* **3.** 31, **3.** 98; **strikkin** *pp.* **37.** 66 [OE *strican, strāc*]
Strivilling, Sterling Stirling **22.** 6, **22.** 34, **22.** 63, **22.** 93, **22.** 111, **28.** 13, **47.** 19
strok. See **straik**
strumbell *n.* ? beast **45.** 62; **strummellis** *pl.* **45.** 17 (see Commentary) [origin obscure]
strummill, strummall *adj.* (contemptuous epithet) **13.** 54, **28.** 11 [cf. later Eng dial. *strammel* gaunt, ill-favoured person]
stryfe *n.* conflict, discord **23.** 5, **52.** 31, **56.** 66, **70.** 6 [ME; OF *estrif*]
stryfe *v.* struggle **53.** 14, **64.** 16; **stryveis** *3 pl.* conflict, contend **14.** 59 [ME; OF *estriver*]
strynd *n.* character, quality, strain **23.** 55, **45.** 21, **82.** 17 [OE]

stryppis *n. pl.* ? pieces of armour **52.** 37 [ME; ? MLG *strippa* strap]
stude *pa. t.* remained **10.** 268, **53.** 7; stood erect **50.** 97, **53.** 12 [OE *standan, stōd*]
studie *n.* branch of learning, kind of study **76.** 4 [ME; OF *estuidie*; L *studium*]
study *n.* stithy, anvil **54.** 52 [ME; ON *steði*]
stuffettis *n. pl.* ? grooms, lackeys **45.** 17 [cf. F *estafette* mounted courier]
stunyst *pa. t.* was astounded, overcome **14.** 340 [etym. difficult; appar. OF *estoner*]
sture *adj.* violent, loud **63.** 63 [appar. confusion of OE *stōr* great and ME *stūr* wild]
sturt *n.* violent quarrelling **52.** 31, **70.** 6 [metathetic form of *strut* (OE *strūtian*)]
stychling *n.* rustling **9.** 78 [origin unknown; cf. Commentary]
styld *pp.* honoured with titles **23.** 3, **23.** 103 [ME, OF n. *style*; L *stilus*]
style *n.* title, appellation **55.** 41, ***23.** 282 [as prec.]
styll *n.* gateway for pedestrians **75.** 38 (see Commentary) [OE *stīʒel*]
styng *n.* pole **38.** 100 [OE *stęng*]
stynk *n.* stench, foul smell **55.** 48; **stynkand** *ppl. adj.* **52.** 83 [ME; OE v. *stincan*]
stynt *n.* ceasing, stop **54.** 84 [ME; OE v. *styntan*]
stynt (of) *v.* cease (from) **12.** 6, **16.** 29; **stynting** *vbl. n.* stop **23.** 5 [OE *styntan*]
sua. See **sa**
suallow *n.* swallow (*hirundo rustica*) **50.** 80 [OE *swealwe*]
subchettis *n. pl.* (for *subcharges*) subsidiary dishes, courses **66.** 19 (see Commentary)
subject, subjeit *adj.* submissive, obedient **10.** 272, **14.** 327 [ME; OF; L *subjicere, subjectus*]
substance *n.* wealth, possessions **6.** 132, **7.** 7, **14.** 337, **14.** 394, **20.** 5, **75.** 55 [ME; OF; L *substantia*]
substantious *adj.* weighty, effective **14.** 248 [OF; as prec.]
subtillie *adv.* subtly, cleverly **81.** 48 [ME; F *subtil*; L *subtilis*]
succeidis *3 sg.* comes next **59.** 22 [ME; OF *succeder*; L *succedere*]
successioun *n.* successors, progeny **80.** 39 [ME; OF; L *successio*]
sucker *n.* baby at the breast **13.** 53 [OE v. *sūcan*]
sudandlie, sudaynly, suddane *adv.* suddenly **3.** 8, **10.** 134, **10.** 141, **10.** 207, **10.** 232, **23.** 10 [ME; OF *soudain*; L *subitaneus*]
suddane *adj.* instant **54.** 46 [prec.]
sueir, sweir *adj.* lazy, slothful **16.** 85, **23.** 130, **52.** 70; indolent, ungenerous **18.** 19 [OE *swǣr* heavy]
sueird. See **swerd**
sueit, suetar. See **sweit**
suellit *pp.* swollen, distended **14.** 167 [OF *swellan*]
***suelly** *v.* devour **23.** 516; **swelleis** *3 pl.* **40.** 6 [OE *swelʒan*]
suer(e). See **sweir**
suetnes. See **sweitnes**
sueving *n.* dream **10.** 244 [OE *swefen*]
suey *v.* swing (of a balance) **51.** 104 [ME]
sufficiance, sufficience. *n.* satisfaction, sufficiency **20.** 26, **51.** 100, **66.** 1 [ME; OF]
suffir *v.* endure, undergo **50.** 107, **72.** 16; **sufferit** *pa. t.* **3.** 94, **4.** 17 [ME *suffren*; AF *suffrir*; L *suffere*]
suffragane, suffragene *n.* assistant, coadjutor (but prob. infl. by *suffrage* intercessory prayer) **2.** 68, **50.** 173 [OF; med. L *suffraganeus*]
sugarat, sug(g)urit *ppl. adj.* full of sweetness, eloquent **10.** 263, **14.** 7, **16.** 13, **39.** 9 [ME; OF *çucre*; cf. med. L *sugurata*]
sugeorne *n.* rest (abstinence) **14.** 176 [ME; OF *surjurner*; L *diurnum*]
suld(e), sould, sowld, sald *v.* should (*pa. t.* of **sall**) **5.** 2, **5.** 7, **12.** 34, **14.** 507, **16.** 43, **23.** 5, **54.** 63, **78.** 5 *et seq.* [OE *sceolde*]
sum *pron., adj., adv.* some **14.** 197, **14.** 480–5, **20.** 3 *et seq.*, **32.** 11, **50.** 23; **sum thing, sumthing** *adv. phr.* somewhat, a little **14.** 184,

44. 75, **52.** 199; **all and sum** entirely **5.** 56 [OE]

summondis *n.* command, citation **14.** 319; *pl.* writs **74.** 29 [ME; OF *summunse*]

sunye *v.* hesitate, refuse **35.** 31 [var. of *soign*; ME; OF; cf. **sounȝie**]

super (ex)pendit, spendit *ppl. adj.* having spent beyond (his) means, overspent **14.** 397, **74.** 23 [L *super* + *expendere*]

superne *adj.* supernal, dwelling in the heavens **2.** 1 [OF; L *supernus*]

suport *v.* sustain, stand by **35.** 28 [ME; OF *supporter*; L *sub-* + *portare*]

suppand *pres. p.* drinking in mouthfuls **73.** 4 [OE **suppan*]

supple *n.* support, the making up of a deficiency **52C.** 35; self-advantage **79.** 8 [OF *souppleier*; L *supplere*]

supple *v.* succour, deliver **62.** 43 [OF *soupleier*; L *supplere*]

suppleis *n.* punishment **34.** 22 [F *supplice*; L *supplicium*]

supplicationis *n. pl.* entreaties **55.** 16 [ME; OF; L *supplicatio*]

suppois, suppos *v. imper.* (=*hypothetical conj.*) even if, although **7.** 1, **14.** 293, **23.** 87, **42.** 22, **43.** 3, **43.** 33; conjecture, expect **25.** 22 [OF *supposer*; L *supponere*]

supportis *3 sg.* supplies **14.** 467; **supportand** *pres. p.* repairing **52C.** 35 [ME; OF *supporter*; L *supportare*]

suppryis *n.* injury, harm **7.** 7 [OF *surprise*; cf. med. L *subprisia*]

suppryis *v.* damage, subdue **71.** 71 [OF *surprendre*, pp. *su(r)prise*]

sure *adj.*, certain, assured, dependable **6.** 93, **14.** 284; *adv.* safely, securely **6.** 76 [OF; L *securus*]

surffet *n.* superfluity, indulgence **52.** 96 [ME; OF]

surminting, surmounting *pres. p.* passing above, transcending **1.** 6, **10.** 260, **31.** 11 [ME; OF; med. L *supermontare*]

surrigianis *n. pl.* surgeons **62.** 42 [ME; OF *serurgien*]

susspissioun *n.* suspicion **34.** 5 [ME; OF *souspeçon*]

sustene *v.* endure **3.** 45, **10.** 202, **17.** 22, **44.** 70 [OF *sustenir*; L *sustinere*]

suth, south *n.* truth **10.** 198, **14.** 157, **14.** 217, **14.** 448 [OE *sōð*]

suthfast *adj.* truthful **53.** 43 [OE *sōþfæst*]

suttelly *adv.* cleverly, craftily **14.** 254; **suttillar** *comp. adj.* **14.** 256 [ME; OF *sutil*; L *subtilis*]

swage *v.* assuage, relieve **44.** 88 [ME; AF *suagier*]

swaittis *n. pl.* small beer **23.** 130 [OE *swatan* beer]

swak *n.* violent bang **3.** 76 [echoic]

swalme *n.* swelling **14.** 167, **44.** 88 [ME; OE *swellan*]

swane *n.* man, fellow **14.** 226; *as pl.* men of low degree **39.** 31 [ON *sveinn*]

swanky *n.* brisk, smart young fellow **13.** 26, (ironic) **23.** 130 [OE *swancor* agile]

swanquhit *adj.* as white as the swan **14.** 243 [cf. ON *svanhvītr*]

swapit of *pa. t.* tossed off, drank off, knocked back **14.** 243 [ME; ? echoic]

swappit *adj.* ? whopping, great big **23.** 130 [obscure]

sweir, suer *v.* swear **14.** 233, **79.** 47; **sweiris** *3 sg.* **74.** 36; **swoir** *pa. t.* **37.** 38, **56.** 11, **56.** 41; **sweirit** *pa. t.* **56.** 7 [OE *swęrian*]

sweir. See **sueir**

sweirnes *n.* sloth; one of the seven deadly sins (*accidia*) **52.** 67 [OE *swǣrnes*; see **sueir**]

sweit *n.* sweat **3.** 53, **23.** 202 [OE *swǣtan, swāt*]

sweit, sueit, suete, swet(e) *adj.* gentle, gracious **3.** 114, **6.** 2, **6.** 9, **9.** 9, **10.** 247, **13.** 15, **14.** 494; lovely **10.** 12; melodious **10.** 69, **10.** 107, **16.** 7; **swetar, suetar** *comp.* **2.** 50, **16.** 25, **16.** 71, **23.** 160; **sweitlie** *adv.* **48.** 45 [OE *swēte*]

sweitnes, suetnes *n.* sweetness **22.** 81, **31.** 15 [OE *swōtnes*]

swelleis. See ***suelly**

swentȝouris *n. pl.* vagabonds, scoundrels **75.** 44 [origin uncertain; perh. e. Flem *swentsen* vagabond]

swenyng *vbl. n.* dreaming, dream **54.** 3 [OE *swefnian*]
swerd, sweyrd, sueird *n.* sword **9.** 10, **23.** 72, **35.** 69, **35.** 82 [OE *swēord*]
swerf *n.* swoon, faint **14.** 225 [? ON *svarfa*]
swering *vbl. n.* profanity **6.** 106 [OE *swęrian*]
swet. See **sweit**
swirk *v.* spring forth **50.** 84 [? onomatopoeic; origin uncertain]
swoir. See **sweir**
swonne, swoun *n.* fainting-fit **14.** 175, **52.** 209 [ME v. *swoȝene*]
swoune *v.* faint **14.** 225; **swownes** *3 sg.* **20.** 14 [ME *swoȝene*]
swyfe *v.* copulate **56.** 62 [ME; appar. OE *swīfan* to move in a course]
swyfte *adj.* swift **50.** 78 [OE *swift*]
swymis *3 sg.* swims **22.** 52 [OE *swimman*]
swyne *n.* pig **38.** 85 [OE *swīn*]
swynekeper *n.* swineherd **23.** 130 [OE *swīn*+ME *keper* (see **keip(e)**)]
swyr *n.* hollow between two hills **14.** 519 [OE *swēora* neck]
swyth(e) *adv.* forthwith, at once **3.** 121, **10.** 236, **54.** 3, **82.** 7 [OE *swīðe*]
sych. See **sich**
sycht. See **sicht**
syd(e) *n.* side **3.** 90, **10.** 34, **14.** 491, **16.** 12, **52.** 187, *pl.* **14.** 25; **on(e) syd(e)** aside **10.** 225, **14.** 357, tilted **14.** 180, **52.** 17; see **bak** [OE *sīde*]
syde *adv.* proudly, boastfully **14.** 196 [OE *sīde*]
syght. See **sicht**
syisis *n. pl.* 'sixes', throws of six on dice **56.** 68 [ME; OF *siis*; L *sex*]
syle. See **sile**
sylver *adj.* made of silver **42.** 23 [OE *siolfor*]
symmer. See **somer**
Symone Magus **53.** 32 (Acts viii; see Commentary)
***symonite** *n.* trafficker in emoluments **23.** 525 (see Commentary) [f. prec.]
sympill, symple. See **sempill**
syn, syne *n.* sin **3.** 124, **5.** 13, **6.** 89, **45.** 29, **52.** 84; **synnes, synnis** *pl.* **5.** 12, **5.** 32, **14.** 97, **52.** 14; **synfull** *adj.* **5.** 1, **5.** 7, **5.** 62 [OE]
syne *n.* sign, gesture **14.** 467; **syng** sign of divine power, miracle **2.** 23 [ME; L *signum*]
syn(e) *adv.* after that, immediately afterwards, thereupon **3.** 6, **3.** 8, **3.** 29, **5.** 47, **7.** 6, **9.** 97, **10.** 100, **12.** 49; since **64.** 34 [contracted form of ME *sethen*, perh. infl. by ON *siðan*]
synfull. See **syn**
syng. See **syne**
syng *v.* sing **1.** 49, **10.** 245 [OE *singan*]
synnar *n.* sinner **6.** 17; *pl.* **1.** 17 [OE *syngian*]
synnit *pa. t.* sinned **6.** 73 [as prec.]
***symphareit** *ppl. adj.* separated **23.** 253 [ME; L *separare*]
syphir, syphyr *n.* cipher **40.** 20 (see Commentary); worthless fellow **14.** 184 [ME; OF *cyfre*; Arabic]
syre *n.* man, fellow **10.** 196, **14.** 145, **14.** 218, **14.** 337 [ME, OF *sire*; L *senior*]
sys, syse *n. pl.* (*sg.* syith) times **10.** 101; **of sys** at times **7.** 2 [OE *sīð*]

tabernakle *n.* dwelling place (of God) **2.** 16 [ME; F; L *tabernaculum*]
tabil(l) *n.* table **14.** 34, **14.** 38; company at dinner **6.** 107; sequence, list **6.** *title*; **tablis** *pl.* **22.** 10 [ME F *table*; L *tabula*]
tag *n.* slashed or torn pieces of a garment **52.** 115 [ME; origin obscure]
***taidis** *n. pl.* toads **23.** 287 [OE *tādiȝe*]
taikinis *n. pl.* symbols, signs, evidences **53.** 20 [OE *tācen*]
tail(l) *n.* tail **14.** 266, **37.** 10; **talis** *pl.* sexual parts **14.** 262 (see Commentary) [OE *tæȝl*]
tailȝ(e)our, telȝour *n.* tailor **52.** 124, **52.** 127, **52.** 139, **56.** 26, **56.** 29; *gen.* **52.** 149; *pl.* **52.** 138, **75.** 36 [ME; OF *tailleur*]
taill *n.* tale, story, discourse **14.** 38 **14.** 246, **16.** 29; *pl.* **77.** 29 [OE *talu*]

***tailye** *n.* reckoning **23.** 446 [ME, OF *taille*]

taingis *n. pl.* tongs **30.** 14 [OE *tang*]

tais *n. pl.* toes **45.** 54, **52C.** 19 OE] *tā*]

taistit *pa. t.* tasted, experienced **22.** 82, *pp.* **22.** 85 [ME *tasten*; OF *taster*]

tak, taik *v.* take **1.** 46, **5.** 53, **13.** 50, **14.** 507, **16.** 74, **56.** 47, take on, assume **6.** 68; **tak(k)is** *3 sg.* **5.** 59, **62.** 21, **72.** 5; **towk, tuik, tuk(e)** *pa. t.* **3.** 10, **6.** 30, **10.** 187, **14.** 317, **16.** 110, **55.** 49; **tane, tein, tone** *pp.* taken **5.** 57, **6.** 50, **16.** 102, **43.** 17; **tak on (me)** assert **23.** 110; **tak up** lead to the dance **28.** 6 [ME; ON *taka*]

takkaris *n. pl.* tackers, stitchers **52.** 131 [ME v. *tacche*; OF *tache* fibula]

takkis *n. pl.* clasps **3.** 69 [doublet of OF *tache*; prec.]

takkis *n. pl.* leasehold farms ***23.** 365, **80.** 16 [f. **tak**]

taklit *pp.* rigged (as a ship) **61.** 41 [ME; MLG *takel*; cf. Da v. *takle*]

tald. See **tellis**

tane *pron.* one (of two) **44.** 83, **73.** 3 [ME *þat ān*]

tane. See **tak**

tapestrie *n.* decorated textile fabric used for hangings **48.** 49 [ME; F *tapisserie* (*tapis* carpet)]

targe *n.* light shield, buckler **10.** 157, **10.** 169, **10.** 183 [OE; ON *targa*]

tarie *v.* delay, linger **39.** 25 [ME; origin unknown]

tarmegantis *n. pl.* blustering bullies **52.** 115, **23.** 532 [ME, OF *Tervagant* imaginary Mohammedan deity; bully in mystery plays]

tarsall *n.* tiercel, male peregrine falcon(*falco peregrinus*) **54.** 81 [ME; OF *tercel*]

Tartary, 54. 5

tauch *n.* tallow, animal fat separated by melting **23.** 245 [ME *talȝ*]

taucht. See **teiche**

tauld, ta(w)ld. See **tellis**

teching. See **teiche**

tedder *n.* hangman's rope **23.** 176, **23.** 240 [ON *tjōðr*]

tegir *n.* tiger *fig.* **4.** 11; **tygris** *pl.* **14.** 261 [OF *tigre*; L *tigris*]

teiche *v.* teach, expound **55.** 13; **teichit** *pa. t.* **55.** 40; **taucht** *pp.* taught **16.** 22; **teching** *vbl. n.* instruction **6.** 34, **14.** 507 [OE *tæcan*, *tǣhte*]

tein. See **tak**

tein. See **tene**

teind *n.* tithe, tenth part of produce of land or work, paid to the Church **6.** 82 [e. ME *tende*, collat. form of *tende;* ON *teiða*]

teiris, teris *n. pl.* tears **3.** 99, **6.** 15, **10.** 17, **12.** 32, **14.** 439 [OE *tēar*]

teith *n. pl.* teeth, fangs **4.** 11 [OE *tōð*, *tēð*]

telȝour. See **tailȝ(e)our**

tellis *3 pl.* tell, relate **20.** 7, **28.** 26; **tald, tawld** *pp.* reported, told **37.** 2, **43.** 1; reckoned, counted **44.** 27; **tauld on** said of **11.** 3 [OE *tęllan*, *ȝeteald*]

teme *v.* empty **38.** 47; *3 pl.* **81.** 39; **temit** *pp.* emptied **4.** 36 [ME; ON *tœma*]

tempand *pres. p.* tempting, enticing **56.** 2, **56.** 83 [ME; OF; L *temptare*]

temporale *adj.* earthly, secular **39.** 37 [ME; L *temporalis*]

temporance *n.* temperance, moderation; one of the four cardinal virtues **6.** 77 [ME; AF; L *temperantia*]

***temptise** *v.* incite to evil **23.** 532 [ME *tempt*; L *temptare*]

tendir *adj.* delicate (because immature), youthful, early **10.** 86, **10.** 246; gentle **13.** 45, **14.** 229, **14.** 231, **35.** 15; **tendirly 14.** 219; **tendirnes** *n.* immaturity **16.** 36 [ME, F *tendre*; L *tener*]

tending *pres. p.* moving (towards) **69.** 29; **tendit** *pa. t.* **10.** 53 [OF *tendre*; L *tendere*]

tene, tein, teyne *n.* affliction, anger, vexation **2.** 47, **14.** 229, **44.** 69 [OE *tēona*]

tene *v.* vex, afflict **73.** 22 [OE *tēonian*]

tennents, tennentis *n. pl.* tenants holding lands on lease **68.** 30, **80.** 11 [ME, F *tenant*; L *tenere*]

tent *n.* attention, heed **5.** 53, **6.** 30 [aphetic form of *attent*; OF *atente*]

***ter** *n.* tar **23.** 335 [OE *teru*]
terandis. See **tyrand**
teris. See **teiris**
termis *n. pl.* words **9.** 20, **9.** 50; terms of rhetoric **10.** 70, **10.** 257 [ME; F; L *terminum*]
***termygantis.** See **tarmegantis**
tern *n.* gloom **2.** 7; **terne** *adj.* gloomy, fierce **14.** 261 [F *terne* dull; origin uncertain]
terrebill *adj.* dreadful **14.** 266 ME; L *terribilis*]
terrestriall *adj.* earthly **10.** 260 [L *terrestris*]
tersis *n. pl.* penises **52.** 88 [OE *teors*]
tesment *n.* testament **38.** *title* [L *testamentum*]
test *n.* examination, trial **9.** 7 [OF; L *testum*]
test *v.* taste **73.** 13 [ME *tasten*; OF *taster*]
***teuch** *adj.* tough, strong **23.** 367 [OE *tōh*]
teyne. See **tene**
tha(i), thay *dem. pron. and adj.* these, those **3.** 25, **10.** 29, **10.** 65, **10.** 157, **13.** 59, **14.** 34, **14.** 243, **14.** 369, **45.** 71 [OE *þā*]
thai, thay *pron.* they **3.** 14, **3.** 18, **3.** 26, **5.** 45, **9.** 17, **9.** 20, **14.** 242, **14.** 440 [ME; ON *þei-r*]
thaim, thame *pron.* them **10.** 158, **14.** 45, **14.** 458, **14.** 489, **16.** 52, **16.** 94, **23.** 152, (= themselves) **52.** 64 [ME; ON *þeim*]
thair, thar, ther *poss. pron.* their **3.** 25, **3.** 67, **4.** 30, **14.** 203, **14.** 264, **23.** 172, **45.** 10 [ME; ON gen. pl. *þeirra*]
thair, thar(e), ther *adv.* there **3.** 20, **5.** 17, **8.** 7, **10.** 57, **10.** 73, **14.** 216, **16.** 46; **thar of** thereof **10.** 277 [OE *þǣr*]
thairat *adv.* at that place, there **9.** 19 [OE *þǣr æt*]
thairfor(e), thairfoir, tharfor *adv.* therefore, for that reason, **5.** 39, **5.** 53, **14.** 169, **16.** 59, **22.** 83, **32.** 31, **61.** 31 [e. ME; OE *þǣr+for*]
thairfra *adv.* away from there, elsewhere **39.** 9, **55.** 10 [**thair+fra**]
thairfurth *adv.* by that place **9.** 66 [**thair+furth**]
thairin *adv.* in that place **9.** 65, in that **55.** 12 [OE *þǣr+in*]
thairof(f), tha(i)r of(f) *adv.* of, from that **20.** 20, **23.** 66, **40.** 27, **43.** 22 [OE *þǣr of*]
thairto *adv.* for that matter, purpose **5.** 11; to that **5.** 53, **12.** 12, **23.** 67 [OE *þǣr+to*]
thairwith *adv.* because of that **11.** 4 [OE *þærwið*]
tham(e). See **thaim**
than(e) *adv.* then **3.** 113, **9.** 49, **10.** 204, **14.** 208, **16.** 113, **43.** 46; at that time **9.** 108 [OE *þanne*]
thank *n.* gratitude **16.** 59, **16.** 63, **44.** 24, **79.** 11; *pl.* **17.** 34 [OE *þanc*]
thankand, thankit. See **thonk**
thar(e). See **thair**
tharfor. See **thairfor(e)**
that *pron.* what **31.** 29, **52C.** 10; *conj. added to rel.* **9.** 75, **10.** 93, **10.** 134, **13.** 47 [OE *þæt*]
thay. See **tha(i)**
the *pers. pron. 2 sg.* thee **3.** 16, **5.** 8, **5.** 16, **5.** 43, **6.** 1; (= thyself) **10.** 277, **16.** 41; **the selfe** yourself **5.** 13 [OE acc. *ðē*]
theif(f) *n.* thief **3.** 13, **3.** 51, **6.** 52, **23.** 76, **23.** 176, **34.** 32; *attrib.* **23.** 183; *pl.* **3.** 81, **45.** 22 [OE *þīof*]
theologgis *n. pl.* theologians, divines **62.** 38; *gen. sg.* **76.** 13 [L *theologus*]
ther *adv.* there **14.** 161 [OE *þǣr*]
ther. See **all ther, thair, thir**
thesaurair *n.* treasurer **46.** 11, **47.** 4; **47** (see Commentary) [L *thesaurarius* (*thesaurus* treasure)]
Thetes Thetis, sea deity, mother of Achilles **10.** 78
thewis *n. pl.* habits, traits **14.** 119 [OE *þēaw*]
thi *poss. adj.* thy **5.** 8, **5.** 9, **5.** 12 [OE *ðy*]
thi. See **for thy**
thik *adj.* dense, rapid **10.** 199; thick, crowded **14.** 488, **56.** 82 [OE *þicce*]
***thin** *poss. adj.* thine, your own **23.** 416 [OE *ðīn*]
thing *n.* sexual organ: vulva **14.** 389, phallus **14.** 486; **all thing** *n.* everything **1.** 31, **2.** 17, **45.** 3–5 [OE]

think *v.* hope **35.** 86; **thinkis** *2 sg.* recall **23.** 140; **thinkand** *pres. p.* believing **11.** 20, **thinking** *pres. p.* expecting, hoping **4.** 13; **tho(u)cht, thoght** *pa. t.* thought, considered **9.** 28, **10.** 95, **10.** 211, **14.** 301, **14.** 364; **thocht lang** *pa. t.* wearied **47.** 1 (see Commentary); **me think, thinkis me, ȝow . . . thinkis** *impers. with dat. pron.* it seems **12.** 19, **14.** 143, **14.** 154, **14.** 476, **16.** 68, **17.** 81; **me thocht** *pa. t.* **50.** 9, **51.** 2, **51.** 114, **56.** 2 [OE *þęncean þōhte*]

thir, ther *dem. pron., adj.* these **3.** 1, **3.** 117, **5.** 1, **6.** 55, **10.** 127, **10.** 168, **14.** 150, **14.** 408 [ME; origin obscure; see *OED*]

thirsill. See **thrissill**

this *dem. pron. pl.* these **14.** 172 [OE; see *OED*, s.v. *these*]

this *adv.* in this way, thus **9.** 82 [OE *þȳs*]

thocht. See **think**

thocht *n.* thought; *pers.* purpose, intention **9.** 55, **9.** 58; reflection, contemplation **42.** 5, **53.** 4, **64.** 1; mind **45.** 40; *pl.* thoughts **6.** 113, **16.** 115 [OE *þoht*]

thocht, thoght, thoucht, thought, *conj.* although **6.** 145, **9.** 29, **14.** 88, **14.** 103, **14.** 135, **14.** 203, **14.** 373, **14.** 463, **16.** 78, **47.** 7 [OE *ðēah*]

thol(e), thoill *v.* have to suffer, endure **14.** 231, **23.** 14, **23.** 79; *3 pl.* **63.** 18; **tholit** *pa. t.* **3.** 95, **33.** 13 [OE *þolian*]

thonk *v.* thank **10.** 99; **thankand** *pres. p.* **6.** 97; **thankit** *pp.* **55.** 22 [OE *þancian*]

thornis *n. pl.* thorns *fig.* **59.** 14 [OE]

thoucht, thought. See **thocht**

thow, thoue *pers. pron. 2 sg.* you **2.** 46, **5.** 10, **5.** 20, **5.** 34, **16.** 37, **31.** 1, **65.** 22 [OE *þū*]

thowmes *n. pl.* thumbs **46.** 7 [OE *þūma*]

thowsand *adj.* thousand **12.** 7, **23.** 151, **34.** 37 [OE *þūsend*]

thra *adv.* wildly, violently **14.** 195 [ME; ON *þrar*]

thraif *n.* two 12-sheaf stooks of corn; a large number *fig.* **39.** 55 [OE; Scand origin; cf. Icel *þrefi*, Da *trave*]

thraip *v.* contend, struggle **56.** 59 [OE *þrēapian*]

thrall *n.* captive **11.** 12; *as pl.* **6.** 28 [OE *þrǣl*]

thrang *n.* throng, crowd **14.** 488, **44.** 52 [OE *ȝeþrang*]

thraward *adj.* froward, perverse **23.** 108 [app. ME *fraward* altered under infl. of *thraw* distort]

thrawis *3 pl.* throng, turn (out) **23.** 217 [OE *þrāwan* throw]

thre, thrie *num. adj., n.* three **3.** 38, **3.** 117, **14.** 17, **42.** 71, **48.** 25; **be sic thre** three times as much **45.** 47, **52C.** 27 [OE *þrī*]

thredis, threidis *n. pl.* fine cords **10.** 62, **48.** 43; ***threid bair** *adj.* threadbare **23.** 30 [OE *þrǣd*]

threit *n.* distress, threat, menace **79.** 11 [OE *þrēat*]

thrid *num. adj.* third **6.** 61, **83.** 9 [OE *þridda*]

thrif, thryff *v.* prosper, get on **14.** 488, **51.** 91 [ME; ON *þrīfask*]

thrift *n.* prosperity, wealth (***23.** 443) **43.** 33, **53.** 48, **67.** 27 [ME; ON v. *þrīfask*]

thrimlaris *n. pl.* jostlers, hustlers **44.** 47 [app. from ME *thrum* press; OE *þrymm* multitude]

thring *v.* drive, press, thrust; **doune thring** overthrow **2.** 17; **thrungin** *pp.* **3.** 46 [OE *þringan*]

thrissill, thirsill *n.* thistle (*carduus*) **25.** 22; *pers.* James IV **50.** 129 [OE *þistill*; perh. infl. by v. *thrist*]

thrist *n.* thirst **41.** 9 [OE *þurst*]

thrist *v.* collide, copulate **53.** 28 [ME; ON *þrȳsta*]

thristaris *n. pl.* thrusters, pushers **44.** 47 [prec.]

thristis *3 sg.* thirsts **41.** 7, **41.** 13 [OE *þyrstan*]

thristy *adj.* thirsty (*as n. pl.*) **6.** 27 [OE *þurstiȝ*]

***Throp** Criseyde **23.** 540 (see Commentary)

throte, thrott *n.* throat **14.** 335, **23.** 170, **42.** 19, **52.** 65; **throttis** *pl.* **52.** 61, **74.** 39 [OE]

throu, throw, thr(o)ucht *prep.* through, by means of **6.** 102, **6.** 157, **10.** 28, **10.** 33, **14.** 8, **23.** 104; throughout **12.** 14 [OE *ðurh*]

thrungin. See **thring**

thryff. See **thrif**

***thrys** *adv.* three times, many times **23.** 30 [ME; OE *þrīwa*+adv. gen. *-s*]

***thryvin** *ppl. adj.* advanced in growth, grown **23.** 493 [see **thrift**]

thunner *n.* thunder **52.** 155 [OE *þunor*]

thy. See **for thy**

thyn(e) *adj.* thin, weak **22.** 13, **43.** 33 [OE *þynne*]

thyne *poss. adj.* your **5.** 14, **23.** 164, **35.** 74, **77.** 22 [OE *ðīn*]

thyne *adv.* thence **33.** 19 [red. form of *thethen*; ON *þeðan*]

***tigiris.** See **tegir**

till *prep., conj., adv.* to **3.** 34, for **3.** 131; (+*infin.*) **2.** 41, **6.** 20, **9.** 2, **13.** 2, **45.** 1; **till . . . till** to . . . until **5.** 68 [ON]

timberallis *n. pl.* tambourines **48.** 45 [dim. of ME, OF *timbre* (for L *tympanum*)]

tinsale *n.* forfeiture **23.** 20 (see Commentary) [ON *tȳna*]

tint. See **tyne**

tiranny *n.* violence, outrage **6.** 141 [F *tyrannie*; L *tyrannus*]

tirly mirly *n.* prob. = *pudendum muliebre* **13.** 46 (see Commentary) [origin unknown]

tirvit *pa. t.* stripped **3.** 23, **3.** 33, **3.** 57 [ME]

tit. See **tyit**

tithingis *n. pl.* news, reports **51.** 95 [ME; prob. ON *tiðendi*]

to *adv.* too, overmuch **5.** 59, **9.** 39, **10.** 71; *prep.* as **14.** 233, **72.** 27 [stressed form of prep. *to*; OE *tō*]

tod *n.* fox **37.** 3 *et seq.*, **74.** 37 [nth. ME; origin obscure]

todlit *pa. t.* played (with) **37.** 11 [origin obscure]

togidder *adv.* together **14.** 59, **52.** 189, **53.** 28 [OE *tōgædere*]

tohie *interj.* the sound of a derisive laugh **13.** 22

tolbuyth *n.* town hall **44.** 60 [OE *toll* tax+OScand *bōþ* stall]

***tome, tomit.** See ***tume**

tone, toun *n.* music **51.** 16, **75.** 29; good condition **19.** 16 [ME; OF *ton*; L: see *OED*]

***tone** *n.* fundament **23.** 502, **23.** 520 [origin obscure]

tone. See **tak**

tong, toung, towng, tung *n.* tongue, speech **5.** 66, **10.** 254, **10.** 260, **12.** 44, **12.** 48, **14.** 466, **23.** 55; **to(u)ngis** *pl.* **10.** 71, **10.** 263, **14.** 159, **39.** 11, **63.** 46 [OE *tunge*]

top *n.* platform at a mast-head **10.** 236 [OE]

tornament, turnament *n.* knightly contest fought on horseback **27.** 32, **52.** 121 [ME; OF *torneiement*]

to-schuke *pa. t.* quivered violently **10.** 231 [OE *tosceacan*]

tother, tothir, tuder *pron., adj.* the other **14.** 84, **14.** 150, **14.** 159, **28.** 5, **73.** 3, **73.** 11, **74.** 4 [ME *þe toþer*, earlier *þat oþer*]

totum *n.* all **42.** 74 (see Commentary) [L]

touch *v.* afflict **23.** 502 [ME; OF *tuchier*]

toun. See **tone**

toun(e), towne *n.* town **22.** 21, **22.** 43, **35.** 55, **38.** 36, **43.** 1, **43.** 31, *attrib.* **23.** 226; citizenry **48.** 59; *pl.* **48.** 1 [OE *tūn*]

toung(is). See **tong**

tour *n.* tower, stronghold **9.** 68, **62.** 30; *pl.* **1.** 7, **61.** 29 [l. OE; OF; L *turris*]

towdy (mowdy) *n.* prob. for *pudendum muliebre* **13.** 46, **13.** 48 [origin unknown; cf. later Sc *towdy* buttocks and *t-fee* fine for fornication]

***towis** *n. pl.* ropes **23.** 452 [cf. OFris *tow*, ON *tog*]

towk. See **tak**

townage, townysche *adj.* 'towny', bourgeois, uncourtly **9.** 39, **13.** 10 [**toun(e)**]

towng. See **tong**

towsy *adj.* dishevelled; (*as proper name*) **81.** 32 [ME v. *tuse*; OE **tūsian*]

traikit *ppl. adj.* wasted, worn out **23.** 118 [origin uncertain; prob. Scand cf. Sw *tråka* to drudge]

Traill, Sandy unknown Scotch poet **62.** 69
traist *n.* trust, confidence, assurance **12.** 24 (see Commentary), **39.** 25 [ON **trøsti*, *traust*]
traist, trest *adj.* trusty, secure, secret **14.** 159, true **71.** 28 [? ON *treystr*, pp. of *treysta* make firm]
***traistand** *pres. p.* trusting, expecting **23.** 421 [ME; ON *treysta*]
tram *n.* shaft of a barrow **30.** 19 [cf. LG *traam*]
tramort *n.* putrefying corpse **23.** 161, **52.** 83, **61.** 20 [L *trans-* and *mort-(em)*]
trance *n.* state between sleeping and waking **52.** 3 (see Commentary), **52.** 223 [ME; OF *transe* passage from life to death; L *transire*]
trane, trayne *n.* deceit, trick, enticement **39.** 7, **59.** 15; treachery **2.** 66 [ME; OF *traïne*]
transgressioun *n.* trespass, sin **5.** 8; crime **74.** 12 [F; L *transgressio*]
transitorie, transitory *adj.* transient, fleeting **60.** 23, **62.** 6 [ME; F *transitoire*; Chr L]
Transmeridiane *n.* **39.** 63 (see Commentary) [L *trans-+meridianus*]
trapperis, *trappouris *n. pl.* trappings, covers for a horse **43.** 41, **43.** 76; **trappit** *pp.* adorned with trappings **43.** 64 [ME; OF *drapure*]
tratlar *n.* chatterer, gossip **11.** 10; **tratling** *ppl. adj.* **81.** 39 [prob. echoic]
tratour *n.* traitor **3.** 13, **23.** 86, **23.** 244, **34.** 10, **52.** 46, *attrib.* **23.** 83; *pl.* **23.** 73 [ME; OF *traitre*; L *traditor*]
***trattillis** *2 sg.* chatter, gossip **23.** 313 [prob. echoic]
trava(i)ll, travale *n.* trouble, labour **16.** 31; travelling, journey **2.** 36, **16.** 116 [ME; OF]
trawe *n.* turn, twist, trick **14.** 124 [OE *þrāwan*]
tre *n.* tree **81.** 3; the Cross **3.** 70, **6.** 143, **56.** 13; **treis** *pl.* **10.** 27, **14.** 4, **23.** 182, **34.** 23 [OE *trēow*]
trece *n.* measure, dance in file **51.** 26 [ME *trace*; F (OF v. *tracier*)]
trechour *n.* traitor; *attrib.* treacherous **23.** 55 [ME; OF]
treit *v.* deal with, indulge, entertain, favour **14.** 280, **48.** 60, **75.** 64, **77.** 42, **79.** 14 [ME; OF *tretier*; L *tractare*]
***trentalis** *n. pl.* 'great numbers' **23.** 319 (see Commentary) [ME; eccles. L *trentale*]
tresour, tresur(e) *n.* wealth, riches **4.** 39, **6.** 126, **12.** 39, **65.** 8; dearest possession **12.** 1 [ME, OF *tresor*; L *thesaurus*]
trespas *n.* transgression, offence **6.** 101, **60.** 14 [ME; OF; med. L *transpassare*]
tressis *n. pl.* plaits, long locks **10.** 62, **14.** 19, **50.** 53 [ME; OF *tresce*]
tressit *ppl. adj.* braided **10.** 140, **16.** 77 [ME; OF *trecier*]
tressonable *adj.* treacherous, perfidious **23.** 73 [ME *treison*; OF *traïson*]
tressoun, tressone *n.* treason **26.** 17, **34.** 2 [as prec.]
trest *v.* expect with confidence **17.** 34, **53.** 19, **67.** 33; *3 sg.* trusts **74.** 11 [ME *traist*; ON *treysta*]
trest. See **traist**
tretable *adj.* tractable, **14.** 261 [ME; L *tractabilis*]
tretis *n.* book, account **14.** *title* [ME; AF *tretiz*]
treuth, trewth *n.* truth **6.** 57, **14.** 153, **14.** 158, **14.** 449, **63.** 12, **63.** 38, **65.** 39 [OE *triewþ*]
trew *adj.* true, sincere **6.** 85, **11.** 8, **14.** 280, **16.** 15, **16.** 46; **trewly** *adv.* **38.** 7 [OE *trēowe*]
tribbill *n.* treble *fig.* **37.** 19 (see Commentary) [OF *treble*; L *triplex*]
tribulatioun *n.* distress, affliction **22.** 40, **22.** 77 [ME, OF; L *tribulare*]
trigide *n.* (verse) tragedy, tragic narrative **62.** 59 [ME, OF *tregedie*; L *tragoedia*]
trimlye *adv.* neatly, finely **28.** 31 [adj. *trim*; origin obscure]
trimmill, trymmill, trymbill *v.* quake, quiver **3.** 83, **3.** 138, **13.** 20, **23.** 9; *3 pl.* **4.** 5; **trymlit** *pa. t.* **52.** 46 [F *trembler*; L *tremulus* (*tremere*)]

trippet, trippit *pa. t.* capered, skipped **28.** 27, **52.** 22 [ME; OF *tripper*]

trist, tryst *n.* appointed place, rendezvous, engagement **14.** 124, **47.** 13 [OF *triste*]

triumphall, tryumphale *adj.* betokening, celebrating victory **2.** 75, **4.** 4 [OE; L *triumphalis*]

trone *n.* throne, seat of state **2.** 75; **tronis** *pl.* the third of the nine orders of angels **1.** 10 [ME, OF; L *thronus*]

trone *n.* site of the public weighing beam **75.** 24 (see Commentary); *v.* ? pillory ***23.** 400 [ME, OF weighing machine]

trow *v.* believe (in) **6.** 57, **6.** 65; believe (it) **13.** 20; think **14.** 238; *3 sg.* **14.** 129; **trouand** *pres. p.* **14.** 280; **trowd, trowit** *pa. t.* **37.** 40, **46.** 16 [OE *trēowan*]

***trowane** *n.* vagabond, beggar **23.** 513 [ME *truant*; OF; ? Celtic (cf. Gael *trudanach*)]

trubill *v.* trouble, bother **77.** 6; **trublit** *pp., ppl. adj.* disturbed, distressed **53.** 21, **62.** 2 [ME, OF *trubler*; late L **turbulare*]

truble, trub(b)ill *n.* distress, affliction **17.** 28, **53.** 19, **60.** 7, **63.** 32, **65.** 17, **65.** 21 [ME; OF]

trumpour, *trumpir *n.* impostor, cheat ***23.** 30, **23.** 138, **52.** 22; *pl.* **79.** 52 [ME; F]

tryackill, tryacle *n.* salve, remedy **12.** 26, **44.** 87 [ME; OF *triacle*; L *theriaca*]

tryid *pp.* attempted, essayed **52.** 121; ***tryit** *ppl. adj.* convicted **23.** 513 [ME; OF *trier*]

trymbill, trymmill. See **trimmill**

tryst. See **trist**

tryumph *n.* victory, glory **10.** 256 [ME; OF; L *triumphus*]

tryumphing *ppl. adj.* prevailing **35.** 2 [OF *triumpher*; prec.]

tua. See **tuo**

tuch *adj.* tough **37.** 24 [OE *tōh*]

tuder. See **tother**

tuentie *num. adj.* twenty **48.** 41 [OE *twentiȝ*]

tuggit *pa. t.* pulled, dragged **54.** 69 [OE *tēohan, toȝen*]

tuich *v.* touch, lay a finger on **37.** 39; **tuichandly** *adv.* affectingly (ironic) **14.** 303; **tuiching** *vbl. n.* touching, feeling **6.** 12 [ME; OF *tuchier*]

tuik, tuk(e). See **tak**

Tullius Cicero **10.** 69 (see Commentary)

***tume** *v.* empty **23.** 520; **tomit** *pa. t.* **52.** 64 [OE adj. *tōm*]

tume *adj.* empty, void **14.** 219 [as prec.]

tung. See **tong**

Tungland religious house in the Stewartry of Kirkcudbright **54.** *title*

tuo, tua, twa(y) *num. adj.* two **3.** 81, **12.** 3, **13.** 59, **14.** 36, **39.** 10, **73.** 2 [OE *twā*]

turkas *n.* smith's pincers **52.** 87 [OF *turcaise*]

Turkas sey the Black Sea **36.** 13

Turkiland, Turky Turkey **54.** *title*, **54.** 61

turmentis *n. pl.* tortures, suffering **3.** 79 [ME; OF *tourment*; L *tormentum*]

turnament. See **tornament**

turne *n.* turning **64,** 8; *v.* **14.** 219, **14.** 229, **53.** 15, **69.** 11; *3 sg.* **29.** 6, **34.** 14; **turnyt** *pa. t.* **50.** 148, **50.** 185, *pp.* **53.** 8 [OE *tyrnan*; L *tornare*]

turs *v.* bundle, carry **46.** 18; ***turse** pack off **23.** 504; *3 sg.* **74.** 38 [ME *trusse*; OF *trousser*]

turtour *n.* turtle-dove (term of endearment) **12.** 37; **turtoris** *pl.* **14.** 262 [OE; OF; L *turtur* (echoic)]

tute mowitt *adj.* having protruding lips **33.** 6 [OE *tōtian*+*mūþ*; cf. Flem *tuyt-muyl*]

***Tutivillus** a demon **23.** 513 (see Commentary)

twa(y). See **tuo**

twelf, twell *num. adj.* twelve **6.** 57, **52C.** 1 [OE]

twyis, tuyse *adv.* twice **14.** 303, **79.** 9, [OE *twiȝes*]

twynkling *ppl. adj.* sparkling, scintillating **10.** 31; **twynklyng of ane e(ye)** an instant **10.** 235, **50.** 85, **64.** 29 [OE *twinclian*]

tyd(e) *n.* time, occasion **77.** 6, **77.** 30,

77. 46; tide, flow **23.** 188, **54.** 124 [OE *tīd*]

tydingis, tythingis *n. pl.* news **74.** 3, **74.** 8 [OE *tīdung*; ON pl. *tīðindi*]

tydis *3 sg.* befalls **14.** 246 [OE *tīdan*]

tygris. See **tegir**

tyit *pa. t.* bound **3.** 69; **tit** *pp.* **80.** 23 [OE *tīȝan*]

tyk *n.* cur, mongrel **23.** 238, **29.** 14, **81.** 14; **tykis** *gen.* **23.** 173, **23.** 235; *pl.* **23.** 226 [ME; ON *tīk* bitch]

tyme *n.* time **5.** 41, **6.** 99, **6.** 138; *pl.* **12.** 7, **12.** 18, **14.** 285 [OE *tīma*]

tyne, tyine *v.* lose **19.** 24, **51.** 84, **56.** 22, **75.** 4; **tynis** *3 sg.* **33.** 22, **51.** 83, **74.** 31; **tint, tynt** *pa. t.* **28.** 27, **52.** 140; **tynt** *pp.* lost, been deprived of **10.** 212, **26.** 20 [ON *tȳna*]

tynsall *n.* tinsel, gold-threaded material; something of no enduring worth **64.** 26 [ME; OF *estincelle*]

tyrand *n.* tyrant **62.** 25, villain **23.** 75; **terandis** *pl.* **3.** 25 [ME; OF; L *tyrannus*]

tyre *v.* tire, weary **39.** 94, **46.** 7; **tyrd** *pp.* **79.** 17; **tyrit** *ppl. adj.* **14.** 176 [OE *tiorian*]

tyrsum *adj.* wearisome, tedious **39.** 82 [prec.]

tys *v.* entice, draw away **45.** 29 [ME (aphetic); OF *atiser*]

tyt *adv.* quickly, at once **3.** 31, **44.** 87 [Scand]

uder, udder, udir, uthair, uther, uthir, othir *pron., adj.* other **13.** 17, **14.** 124, **20.** 14, **23.** 60, **50.** 141, **67.** 7; each other **14.** 59, **52.** 61; all others **14.** 78; elsewhere **14.** 82; **uderis, uthiris, othris** *pl.* others **11.** 21, **14.** 373, **52.** 41, **65.** 29 [OE *ōþer*]

uglie, ugelye, ugly *adj.* horrible, repulsive **23.** 185, **43.** 36, **52.** 82, **61.** 20 [ME; ON *uggligr*]

ugsum *adj.* loathsome **61.** 20 [ME; ON *ugga* to fear]

uly *n.* oil **52.** 168 [ME, OF *oille*]

umbrakle *n.* shadowy place, shade **2.** 20 [L *umbraculum*]

umquhile *adv.* formerly **35.** *title* [OE *ymb hwīle*]

unabaisitly *adv.* dauntlessly, boldly **10.** 194 [see **abasit**]

unaspyit *ppl. adj.* undiscovered, unnoticed **14.** 427 [ME; OF *espier*]

unblist *ppl. adj.* unhallowed, evil **52.** 219 [see **blissit**]

uncioun *n.* unction; anointing with oil in baptism, confirmation, and lastly in *unctio extrema* (unction of the sick) **6.** 45 [L *unctio*]

uncouth, uncow *adj.* strange, uncommon, marvellous **14.** 528; unknown **70.** 13 [OE *uncūþ*]

uncunnandly *adv.* without skill, clumsily **54.** 101 [see **cunning**]

undemit *pp.* unjudged **81.** 5 *et seq.* [see **deme**]

undertaker *n.* one who takes on an enterprise **51.** 87 [ME; OE *under-* +ON *taka*]

undir *prep.* under, below **3.** 118, **10.** 89, **12.** 24, **34.** 12, **50.** 28 [OE *under*]

undirnethe *prep.* underneath **35.** 51 [OE *underneoðan*]

undiscreit *adj.* lacking discretion **6.** 91 [ME; L *indiscretio*; cf. MDu *ondiscreet*]

***undought** *n.* worthless fellow **23.** 508 [OE *un-*+*dohtiȝ* valiant]

undynd *ppl. adj.* unfed **42.** 14 [*un-*+ ME *dyne*; OF *diner*]

unfaidit *ppl. adj.* not faded **49.** 34 [see **faid**]

unfulȝeit *ppl. adj.* untired, energetic **14.** 62 [see **fulȝeid**]

unȝeoun *n.* onion (*allium cepa*) **13.** 53 [F *oignon*; L *unio*]

unhelit *ppl. adj.* unhealed, uncured **5.** 22 [ME; OE *un-*+*hǣlan*]

unicornis *n. pl.* fabulous equine animals with one horn **50.** 109; gold coins stamped with the figure of the unicorn **39.** 78 (see Commentary) [ME; OF; L *unicornus*]

unkend *pp.* unknown **52C.** 9, **71.** 47 [see **ken**]

unkyndnes *n.* lack of love, cruelty **64.** 31 [see **kyndnes**]

unluffit *ppl. adj.* not loved in return **14.** 498 [see **luf**]

unmenȝit *pp.* unmaimed, uninjured **6.** 155 [OE *un-*+OF *mehaignier*]
unmerciable *adj.* unmerciful **14.** 329 [ME; OF *merci*]
unmyndfull *adj.* heedless **74.** 47 [ME; see **mynd(e)**]
unneis *adv.* with difficulty, scarcely **3.** 45 [OE *unēaðe*]
unourcumable *adj.* unconquerable **35.** 44 [ME; OE *ofercuman*]
unplane *adj.* dishonest **39.** 11 [see **plane**]
unquit, unquyt *pp., ppl. adj.* unrewarded **17.** 67, **78.** 41 [ME; *un-*+**quyt**]
unrestorit *ppl. adj.* not returned to its right owners **63.** 64 [*un-*+ME *restore*; OF *restorer*; L *restaurare*]
unrewairdit *pp.* unrequited **51.** 110 [ME; OF *reguarder*]
unsasiable *adj.* insatiable **52.** 92 [ME; OF; L *insatiabilis*]
unseyne *adj.* unseen **2.** 39 [see **se**]
unsicker *adj.* uncertain **67.** 3 [see **sicker**]
unslane *ppl. adj.* alive **54.** 20 [see **slais**]
unsleipit *ppl. adj.* not having slept **21.** 9 [see **sleip**]
***unsoupit** *ppl. adj.* supperless **23.** 382 [ME; OF *soper*]
unspaynd *ppl. adj.* unweaned **13.** 36 [see **spane**]
unstable, unstabille *adj.* vacillating, fickle **10.** 123, **23.** 75 [see **stabill**]
untrew *adj.* unfaithful **14.** 258 [see **trew**]
unweildable *adj.* ponderous, cumbrous **52.** 98 [OE *wieldan*]
unwiting *ppl. adj.* unknown to **6.** 138 [see **wittin(g)**]
up with *n.* sexual climax **14.** 401 [OE *up*+*wið*]
upaland, up aland *adv.* in the country **23.** 205, **27.** 19; **uplandis** *adj.* rustic **42.** 71, **74.** 1 [OE *uppe on londe*]
***updost** *ppl. adj.* dressed up **23.** 384 [Du *dossen*]
uphie *v.* exalt, honour, uplift **6.** 52, **19.** 8, **79.** 3; **upheyt** *pp.* **35.** 5 [OE *up-*+*hēan*]
uplandis. See **upaland**
upone, upoun *prep.* **8.** 9, **16.** 6, **23.** 138, **23.** 212, **45.** 42, **51.** 94 [ME]
upplane *adv.* out clearly **59.** 3 [see **plane**]
uprys(e) *v.* get up from bed **21.** 11, **50.** 29, **50.** 37; **uprais** *pa. t.* rose up **50.** 176 [ME; cf. MLG *uprisen*]
upsitt *v.* sit up **52.** 171 [OE *up*+*sittan*]
upspred *ppl. adj.* spread, stretched up **14.** 29 [see **spredis**]
upspring *v.* rise, dawn **16.** 1, **50.** 14, **59.** 2; shoot up as trees **48.** 38; **upsprungin** *pp.* **14.** 412 [ME; cf. MLG *upspringen*]
upstude *pa. t.* stood erect **50.** 15 [see **standis**]
upwart *adv.* upward **1.** 42 [OE *upweard*]
use *n.* custom, conduct **39.** 22 [ME; OF *us*; L *usus*]
use *v.* practise, make use of **23.** 18, **23.** 107, **67.** 5; **usit** *pa. t.* wore **10.** 126; *pp.* **76.** 6 [ME; OF *user*; med. L *usare*; L *uti*]
uthair, uther, uthiris. See **uder**

vacandis *n. pl.* 'vacant estates', free to admit mates **14.** 206 [OF; L *vacans*]
vailȝeand, vailyeant. See **valȝeand**
vaill, vale *n.* valley **16.** 28, **60.** 7, **65.** 2 [ME; OF *val*; L *vallis*]
vain. See **vane**
vakit *pa. t.* fell vacant **41.** *title* [L *vacare*]
Valentynis day 14 February, when sweethearts are chosen **14.** 206
valȝeand, vailȝeand, va(i)lyeant, valyand *adj.* stalwart, bold **14.** 183, **27.** 11, **35.** 4, **35.** 19, **35.** 59, **44.** 7; **valȝeandly** *adv.* **14.** 431 [OF *vailant*; L *valere*]
valȝeandnes, valyeantnes *n.* valour, strength **14.** 399, **35.** 93 [prec.]
valour(e) *n.* worth **14.** 185, **35.** 2 [ME; L *valor*]
valyand. See **valȝeand**
vane *n.* vein **3.** 35, *pl.* **3.** 74; **54.** 21 (see Commentary) [ME; OF *vaine*; L *vena*]

vane *adj.* vain, useless, empty, fruitless **14.** 431, **34.** 40, **39.** 3, **76.** 8; **in vane** *adv.* profitlessly **51.** 53; **tane in vane** treated with contempt **6.** 50 [ME; OF; L *vanus*]

vaneist *pa. t.* vanished, disappeared **55.** 48 [ME *vanyshe*; aphetic form of OF *evaniss-*]

vanglore, vane glory *n.* empty, unwarranted pride **6.** 118, **16.** 92, **62.** 5 [med. L *vana gloria*]

vanit(i)e *n.* vanity, futility **16.** 98, **62.** 15, **64.** 27 [ME; OF; L *vanitas*]

vapouris *n. pl.* exhalations, mists **10.** 247, **69.** 3 [ME; AF; L *vapor*]

vardour *n.* plant, green vegetation **14.** 30 [OF *verdour*]

variance, varians *n.* discord, enmity **15.** 6, **70.** 17 [ME; OF; L *variantia*]

varie, vary *v.* change **16.** 91, **39.** 26; wander, rave **51.** 12; **variand** *ppl. adj.* changing **77.** 41; shifting **10.** 123, **50.** 1 [ME; OF *varier*; L *variare*]

varite. See **veretie**

varlot *n.* attendant (on a knight) **52.** 160 [ME; OF *varlet*]

***Vaspasius** Vespasian (9–79 A.D.), Roman emperor **23.** 532

vassalage *n.* action befitting a vassal; military prowess **35.** 10, **35.** 59 [ME; OF]

vawart *n.* vanguard, forefront **9.** 58 [reduced form of *vantguard*; OF *avantgarde*]

velvot, velves *n.* velvet, textile fabric with a piled surface **48.** 12, **48.** 13 [ME; med. L *velvetum*; L *villus* shaggy hair]

vengabill *adj.* vindictive **6.** 141 [OF *venger*; L *vindicare*]

vengence *n.* vengeance **34.** 30 [ME; OF]

vennesoun *n.* venison, flesh of a beast killed in the chase **68.** 19 [ME, OF *veneson*; L *venari* to hunt]

venome, vennaum, vennim *n.* poison **14.** 166, **23.** 10, **44.** 85 [ME; OF; L *venenum*]

vent *n.* emission, discharge **14.** 166 [F; L *ventus*]

Venus (Roman) goddess of love **10.** 73, **10.** 181, **10.** 186, **17.** 3; *gen.* **10.** 21, **10.** 193, **14.** 127, **14.** 183, **14.** 431, **32.** 7, **32.** 12

veralie, verralie *adv.* truly, really **27.** 52, **42.** 57 [ME; OF *verai*; L *verus*]

veretie, varite *n.* truth **16.** 100, **71.** 69 [ME; OF; L *veritas*]

verey, verry *adj.* true **56.** 7, **59.** 24, **72.** 21 [ME; OF *verai*; L *verus*]

***verlot** *n.* knave **23.** 43 (see Commentary) [see **varlot**]

verralie. See **veralie**

verry. See **verey**

vers *n.* (line of) poetry **37.** 43; *pl.* **26.** 16 [OE *fers*; L *versus*]

vertew, vertu *n.* virtue, grace **8.** 1, **8.** 4, **11.** 11, **14.** 315, **16.** 67; power, efficacy **14.** 189, **14.** 397; *gen.* **16.** 87; **vertuis, vertewis** *n. pl.* moral qualities **6.** 75, **42.** 37; **of vertew** with healing properties **50.** 73 [ME; OF; L *virtus*]

vertewis *adj.* virtuous **83.** 15 [ME, OF; L *virtus*]

Vesper the evening star **10.** 2

vesyit. See **vissy**

vexit *pp.* troubled, afflicted **69.** 12 [ME; OF *vexer*; L *vexare*]

vice, vyce, vys *n.* vice, sin **2.** 63, **6.** 17, **16.** 67, **16.** 87, **34.** 1, **45.** 30; *pl.* **6.** 21, **11.** 12 [ME; OF; L *vitium*]

vicius *adj.* vicious, wicked **6.** 105, **34.** 1 [ME, OF; med. L *viciosus*]

victoryse *n. pl.* victories **35.** 66 [ME, OF *victorie*; L *victoria*]

victour *n.* conqueror **4.** 25, **14.** 326, **35.** 4, **35.** 20, **62.** 23 [ME; OF; L *victor*]

victrice *n.* victress **2.** 63 [L *victrix*]

vilipencioun *n.* act of despising, contempt **6.** 116 [OF; L *vilipendere*]

violence *n.* violent act **10.** 159 [ME, OF; L *violentia*]

violent *adj.* powerful **10.** 238 [ME, OF; L *violentus*]

virgene *n.* virgin **22.** 30; **virgyn(i)s** *pl.* maidens **10.** 154, **22.** 46 [ME, OF; L *virgo*]

visage, vissage *n.* face, countenance

3. 18, **3.** 100, **10.** 33, **49.** 36, **50.** 148 [ME, OF; L *visus*]
visar *n.* vizard, front of a helmet **35.** 76 [ME; F *vis* face]
vissy *v.* go to see, visit **22.** 72; **vesyit** *pa. t.* **6.** 28 [ONF *viseer*; L *visitare*]
voce *n.* voice, outcry **4.** 5, **9.** 31, **14.** 302, **16.** 4, **59.** 3; **vocis** *pl.* **14.** 244, **16.** 105, **50.** 59 [ME, OF *vois*; L *vox*]
vode *adj.* distracted **3.** 97 [see **woid**]
vowit *pp.* vowed **25.** 19 [ME; OF *vower*; L *vovere*]
Vulcanus god of thunderbolt and battle, oldest of the Latin deities **54.** 67
vyce. See **vice**
vyle, vyld, vyll *adj.* base, mean **23.** 49, **50.** 137, **75.** 36, **77.** 14 [ME; OF; L *vilis*]
vys. See **vice**

wa. See **wo**
waek, *waik *adj.* weak **32.** 22, ***23.** 43 [ME; ON *veikr*]
waes me *phr.* woe is me, alas **28.** 19 [see **wo**]
waett. See **wit**
wag *v.* stagger, sway **52.** 98 [OE *waȝian*]
waiknit *pa. t.* awoke **3.** 139 [OE *wæcnan*]
waill. See **wale**
wair *v.* expend, lay out **46.** 12; **wairis** *1 sg.* **17.** 68; **waris** *3 pl.* **14.** 39; **warit** *pp.* **14.** 394, **81.** 13 [OE *węrian*]
wairldis. See **warld**
waistie *adj.* devastated, in ruins **52.** 18 [ME, OF *wast*; L *vastus*]
waistit. See **wastit**
waistles *adj.* without a waist, obese **52.** 97 [ME; ? OE **weahst*]
wait *v.* keep watch, look out **9.** 21 [ME; ONF *waitier*; OHG *wahten*]
wait, (in a), at the wait *phr.* in ambush **4.** 12, **63.** 34 [ONF]
wait *adj.* wet **3.** 133 [nth. ME; ON *vātr*]
wait(t). See **wit**
waithman *n.* hunter; forest outlaw *attrib.* **54.** 8; **wathemanis** *gen.* **23.** 143 [ON *veiðimaðr*]
wald *v.* would (*pa. t.* of *will*), wished **4.** 14, **8.** 14, **9.** 61, **9.** 62, **13.** 13, **14.** 16 [OE *wolde*]
wale, waill choose, pick out **10.** 186, **14.** 76, **14.** 530 [ME; ON n. *val*]
walkand *pres. p.* walking, going about **22.** 17 [OE *wealcan*]
walkin *v.* awaken **21.** 15, **51.** 115; **walkynnis** *3 sg.* **7.** 4; **walkis** *3 pl.* **58.** 14; **walkand, walking** *pres. p.* **14.** 213, **16.** 116, **53.** 40; **walknit** *pa. t.* **52.** 223, **54.** 125 [OE *wæcnan*]
wall *n.* well-spring, fount, source **2.** 73, **48.** 7 [OE *wielle*]
wall *n.* rampart **6.** 73, **9.** 33, **9.** 59 [OE; L *vallum*]
***Wallace,** William, Scottish patriot executed by Edward I (1305) **23.** 272, **23.** 281
wallidrag, wallydrag *n.* worthless, slovenly fellow **14.** 89, **52.** 97 [origin uncertain]
wallowand *pres. p.* turning to and fro **23.** 175 [OE *wealwian*]
wallowed *pp.* withered, discoloured **51.** 25 [OE *wealwian*]
wally *adj.* handsome, fine **13.** 45 [origin obscure]
wallydrag. See **wallidrag**
walteris *1 sg.* tumble, toss to and fro **14.** 213 [ME; cf. ON **welta*]
wame, wambe *n.* belly **13.** 18, **14.** 131, **52.** 92, **83.** 11; **wamis** *pl.* **52.** 98 [OE *wamb*]
wan *adj.* sad, wretched **23.** 195, **51.** 25 [OE *wann* dark, gloomy]
wan. See **win, wyn**
***wan fukkit** *ppl. adj.* weakly, ill-conceived **23.** 38 [OE *wann*+**fukkit**]
wan visaged *ppl. adj.* livid-, leaden-faced **23.** 101 [OE *wann*+**visage**]
wandis *n. pl.* straight, slender sticks **10.** 63, **32.** 22 [ON *vǫndr*]
wane *n.* large wagon **39.** 43 [OE *wæȝen*]
wanis *n. pl.* dwellings **52.** 18 [ME; on origin see *OED*, s.v. *wane* sb.[2]]
want *v.* lack **14.** 463, **23.** 223; *3 sg.* **14.** 398; *3 pl.* **14.** 455, **42.** 44; **wantit** *pa. t.* lacked, needed **14.** 336, been lacking **47.** 22 [ME; ON *vanta*]

wanton(n)es *n.* insolence, arrogance **6.** 108; amorous delight *pers.* **10.** 175, **68.** 5 [ME; OE *wan-*+*tōȝen* trained]
wantoun *adj.* sportive, amorous **14.** 37 (see Commentary), **14.** 529; **wantonly** *adv.* merrily **14.** 479 [prec.]
wappin *n.* weapon **14.** 340 [OE *wǣpen*]
war, ware, wer, weir *v.* were **8.** 7, **9.** 57, **10.** 2, **10.** 23, **10.** 247, **14.** 56, **38.** 55, **61.** 7; was **14.** 21, **28.** 12; would be **14.** 57, **14.** 65, **17.** 51, **25.** 5; **war nocht** were it not that **19.** 8, **81.** 41 [OE *wæs, wǣron*]
war *adj.* conscious, vigilant, aware **16.** 93, **32.** 34, **37.** 51, **44.** 86, **60.** 1 [OE *wær*]
war, wer *adj.* worse **14.** 200, **14.** 469, weaker **14.** 321; *adv.* more uselessly **14.** 176 [ME; ON *verre*]
wardlie *adj.* worldly, earthly **45.** 7 [OE *woruldlic*]
wardraipair, wardraipper *n.* officer in charge of robes etc. at court **29.** 1, **30.** 2 [ME; OF *warderobier*, dial. var. of *garderobier*]
wardroippe, wardrope, wardrep *n.* wardrobe **29.** 18, **29.** *colophon*, **30.** 10 [see prec.]
waris, warit. See **wair**
warit *pa. t.* cursed **14.** 229; **wariand** *pres. p.* **14.** 214; **warryit** *pp.* **40.** 26; ***wary** *infin.* **23.** 312; ***wariet** *ppl. adj.* **23.** 293 [OE *wierȝan*]
wark, werk *n.* deed, action, labour **6.** 6, **6.** 78, **14.** 84, **14.** 462; *pl.* **6.** 31, **14.** 200, **14.** 351, **52.** 217 [OE *weorc*]
warld *n.* world **12.** 14, **16.** 108, **17.** 52; immensity, great quantity **10.** 161; **wa(i)rldis** *gen.* **17.** 87, **20.** 16, **31.** 19, **39.** 1; *pl.* **3.** 38 [OE *weorold*]
warldly *adj.* worldly, of this world **59.** 13; **warldlynes** *n.* worldly affairs **14.** 463 [OE *woruldlic* (+ *-nes*)]
warlo *n.* warlock, reprobate **52.** 60 [OE *wǣr-loȝa*]
warly *adv.* in a warlike manner **10.** 201 [OF *werre*+OE *-līc*]
warme *adj.* ardent, tender **13.** 32 [OE *wearm*]
warmys *3 pl.* become warm **14.** 496 [OE *wearmian*]
warne *v.* inform, caution, notify **23.** 193 [OE *warnian*]
warpit *pa. t.* uttered **14.** 150 [OE *weorpan*]
warryit. See **warit**
warsill *v.* wrestle, strive **64.** 16 [ME; metathetic var. of *wrestle*; OE **wrǣstlian*]
wasp *n.* malignant insect; *fig.* **23.** 195 [OE *wæfs*]
wastit, waistit *pp.* exhausted, used up **10.** 179; *ppl. adj.* **14.** 90, **14.** 127, **14.** 178 [ME; OF *waster*; L *vastare*]
wathemanis. See **waithman**
watiris. See **watter**
watter, wattir *n.* the element water **1.** 13, **50.** 66; body fluid **3.** 92; tears **3.** 100; *attrib.* **14.** 437; **watiris** *pl.* fishing waters **40.** 18 [OE *wæter*]
watteris *3 pl.* flow with tears, weep **14.** 439 [OE *wæterian*]
wattis *n. pl.* welts **23.** 213 [ME; ? Anglian **walt*]
wauchtit (at) *pa. t.* drank largely, quaffed **14.** 39 (see Commentary) [origin obscure; related to *quaff*]
waverand *ppl. adj.* changing, fluctuating **39.** 1; **wavering** *vbl. n.* **65.** 2 [ME; ON *vafra*]
wavill *adj.* wry, twisted **45.** 54 [OE *wafian*+*-el*]
wavis *3 sg.* moves to and fro **62.** 14, **62.** 15, **63.** 59 [OE *wafian*]
waw *n.* wough, wall of a house, partition **20.** 11 [OE *wāȝ*]
waw *n.* wave **23.** 92 [ME *waȝe* rel. to OE v. *waȝian*]
wax *v.* grow **3.** 66; *3 sg.* **17.** 9; **wox** *pa. t.* **3.** 85, **4.** 27, **14.** 329, **51.** 36; **waxit** *pp.* **14.** 175 [OE *weaxan, wēox*]
wayis *n. pl.* devices, methods **14.** 451, **56.** 83; **on no wayis** not at all **45.** 37 [OE *weȝ*]
webbis *n. pl.* pieces of woven cloth **52.** 136 [OE]
weche *n.* watchman, sentinel **9.** 33 [OE *wæcce*]

wecht *n.* (standard) weight **39.** 78; *fig.* burden **51.** 39 [OE *wiht*]
wed *n.* pledge, mortgage **74.** 22 [OE]
Weddinsday *n.* Wednesday **73.** 1 [OE *Wōdnes dæʒ*]
weddit *pp.* wedded, married **14.** 36; **woddit** *ppl. adj.* **14.** 41 [OE *węddian*]
wede, weid *n.* raiment, dress **10.** 278, **14.** 422, **14.** 447, **23.** 143, **50.** 16, **55.** 11; *pl.* **wedis** **10.** 58, **14.** 369, **14.** 374, **14.** 523 [OE *wǣd*]
wedo, weido, wedow *n.* widow **14.** 37, **14.** 41, **14.** 150, **14.** 245, **14.** 414, **14.** 505, **53.** 34 [OE *widewe*]
***wedsett** *pa. t.* mortgaged, pawned **23.** 443 [ME; ? OE **to wedde settan* to set to pledge]
***wedy.** See **widdy**
weid *n.* weed, wild plant **50.** 139 [OE *wēod*]
weid. See **wede**
weido. See **wedo**
weild, welde *v.* use, manage **14.** 77, hold **33.** 19, **63.** 61; *3 sg.* **14.** 372 [OE *wealdan*; see *OED*]
weilfa(i)r *n.* happiness, good cheer **14.** 479, **22.** 36, **22.** 70, **65.** 10, **68.** 5 [ME; cf. ON *velferð*]
weill *n.* well-being, prosperity **39.** 21 [OE adv. *well*, substituted for *weal* under infl. of F *bien*]
weill, weil, wele *adv.* well, rightly, fully **5.** 19, **5.** 34, **10.** 64, **10.** 208, **11.** 2, **14.** 203, **14.** 275, **82.** 26; *predic. as adj.* fortunate **14.** 65, **17.** 19, **60.** 21 [OE *wel*]
weilmaid *adj.* skilfully made up **56.** 27 [**weill**+**mak**]
weip(e) *v.* weep, shed (tears) **6.** 147, **14.** 415, **50.** 31; **weipit** *pa. t.* **14.** 288 [OE *wēpan*]
weir, were *n.* war, armed struggle **4.** 35, **9.** 102, **35.** 11, **36.** 6, **52.** 36, **52.** 213; *pl.* **36.** 12, **36.** 20, **50.** 131 [late OE *wyrre*; OF *guerre*]
weir *n.* doubt, uncertainty **3.** 89, **5.** 30, **55.** 50, **61.** 22, **67.** 1; **but weir** certainly, indeed **9.** 110, **22.** 70, **51.** 37 [origin uncertain]
weir *v.* wear **36.** 7, **43.** 41, **45.** 8, **55.** 12, **55.** 24, **68.** 26; *3 sg.* **63.** 36 [OE *węrian*]
weir. See **war**
weirines *n.* tiredness, fatigue **53.** 9 [OE adj. *wēriʒ*]
wekit. See **wickit**
welcum, wylcum *interj. and adj.* welcome **13.** 51, **24.** 4, **35.** 6, **50.** 61, **56.** 18, **56.** 74 [OE *wilcuma*]
welde. See **weild**
wele. See **weill**
welteris *3 pl.* stream down, flow **14.** 439 [ME; MLG *weltern* roll about]
welth *n.* felicity, well-being **48.** 7, **68.** 5; possessions, riches **14.** 394, **22.** 36, **22.** 70, **59.** 13 [ME *welþe*; perh. *weal*+*-th* on analogy of *health*]
welthfull *adj.* wealthy, prosperous **83.** 19 [prec.]
wemen *n. pl.* women **14.** *title*, **14.** 41, **14.** 65, **14.** 178, **14.** 448, **63.** 73, **72.** 1 [OE *wīfman, -men*]
wend *v.* go **53.** 39, **60.** 1, **67.** 10; **went** *pp.* gone **10.** 233, **12.** 37, **14.** 395, **16.** 93, **50.** 186 [OE *wendan*]
wend *pa. t.* (*ween*) thought, supposed **14.** 201, **54.** 74; **went** *pa. t.* **37.** 65 [OE *wēnan*]
wene *v.* think, believe **38.** 62; **I wene** *parenth. tag* **17.** 46; **went** *pa. t.* thought, expected **52.** 200 [OE *wēnan*]
went. See **wend**
weping *vbl. n.* weeping, tears **49.** 36 [**weip(e)**]
wer. See **war**
werblis *n. pl.* tunes, singing **10.** 107 [ME; OF]
were. See **weir; men of were**
werie *adj.* intensely tired, worn out **3.** 116; **wery**+*infin.* **12.** 16 [OE *wēriʒ*]
wering *vbl. n.* wasting away **44.** 31 [OE *węrian*]
werk, werkit. See **wark, wirk**
***wers** *adj.* worse **23.** 464 [OE *wyrsa*]
werslingis *n. pl.* wrestling contests **27.** 22 [see **warsill**]
werst *adj. sup.* worst, most objectionable **11.** 9; *adv.* **52C.** 22 [OE *wyrresta, wersta*]
***werwoif** *n.* a man turned at times into a wolf **23.** 251 [OE]
wes *pa. t.* was **3.** 22, **3.** 49, **4.** 18, **4.**

26, **6**. 38, **6**. 46; were **14**. 347, **37**. 46; *2 sg*. **10**. 259, **23**. 210 [OE *wæs*]
west *n*. waist **37**. 29 [ME; OE **weahst*]
wetis *1 sg*. wet, moisten **14**. 438 [OE *wǣtan*]
wey *v*. weigh out **51**. 103 [OE *weȝan*]
weycht. See **wicht**
weyng *n*. wing *fig*. **35**. 50 [ME; ON *vængr*]
wichis *n. pl*. witches **53**. 35 [OE *wicce*]
wicht, we(y)cht *n*. creature, man **2**. 35, **10**. 273, **12**. 10, **12**. 42, **17**. 55, **50**. 61, **51**. 61; *pl*. **14**. 501, **22**. 16 [OE *wiht*]
wicht, wight, wycht *adj*. strong, valiant **2**. 29, **27**. 2, **35**. 11, **36**. 12, **54**. 42, **81**. 24, potent **14**. 39 [ON *vigt*]
wichtnes *n*. strength, power **14**. 295 [prec.]
wicir, wickir *n*. willow twig, withe **38**. 45, **62**. 14 [Scand; cf. Sw *vika* to bend]
wickit, wicket, wekit *adj*. wicked, evil **6**. 135, **11**. 17, **14**. 214, **39**. 33, **70**. 9 [ME; prob. adj. use of OE *wicca* wizard]
widdefow *n*. gallows-bird, one who would fill a noose **23**. 101 [**widdy**+*full*]
widdis. See **wod**
widdy *n*. withy; hangman's rope **54**. 48, **81**. 24 [OE *wiþiȝ*]
wif, wyfe, wyve *n*. wife **14**. 178, **14**. 530, **23**. 155, **54**. 43; **wyfis** *gen*. **23**. 117; **wiffis, wyffis, wyvis** *pl*. **14**. 42, **14**. 398, **14**. 529, **32**. 3, **34**. 45, **56**. 76; **wif carll** womanish fellow **14**. 351 [OE *wīf*]
wight. See **wicht**
wilbe *v*. will be **78**. 4 [OE *willan*+*bēon*]
wildernes *n*. uncultivated land **10**. 119, **10**. 233 [OE **wild(d)ēornes*]
wilfull *adj*. eager, willing **5**. 2; perverse **77**. 30 [OE *willa*+*ful*]
wilk *n*. whelk **75**. 24 [OE *wioloc*]
will *n*. desire, longing, inclination **9**. 45, **11**. 13, **14**. 132, **14**. 321; *pers*. **10**. 175; submission ***23**. 330 [OE *willa*]
willing *ppl. adj*. yielding, pliable **32**. 22 [OE *willende*]
wilsome, wilsum *adj*. wandering, erring, perplexed **2**. 35; *as n. pl*. **6**. 29 [ON *villusamr*]
win, wyn *v*. gain, take possession of **9**. 64, **19**. 24, **41**. 15, manage **37**. 60; **wynnis** *3 sg*. **74**. 31; **wan** *pa. t*. **14**. 295, **25**. 15, **27**. 20, **56**. 58; **the feild is win** the battle has been won **4**. 38; **wynyng** *vbl. n*. **14**. 475 [OE *winnan*]
winder *n*. astonishment, perplexity **51**. 37 [OE *wundor*]
windir (thing), winder *adj*. marvellous (event) **37**. 2, **53**. 35; *adv*. **47**. 13 [as prec.; cf. G *wunderding*]
windis *n. pl*. winds **50**. 1 [OE]
windis. See **wounde**
wirchip. See **worschip**
wird, woord, wourd *n*. word **30**. 6; *pl*. **9**. 47, **14**. 12, **52**. 8, **52**. 152, **56**. 66, **59**. 31, **60**. 15, **63**. 41 [OE *word*]
wirk, werk, wyrke *v*. work, make, do **5**. 70, **14**. 51, **14**. 351, **14**. 508; **(w)rocht** *pa. t*. **16**. 44, **52**. 221, **54**. 29; **werkit** *pa. t*. heaved (in copulation) **14**. 236; **wrocht** *pp*. worked, made **3**. 116 [OE *wyrcan*, *ȝeworht*]
wirker *n*. creator **16**. 53, **16**. 60 [prec.]
wirling *n*. wretch **23**. 193 [origin unknown]
wirriand. See **wirry**
wirrok, wyrok *n*. corn on the foot **52C**. 18; *attrib*. calloused **45**. 54 [e. Flem *weerooghe*]
wirry *v*. chew, gnaw **70**. 24; **wirriand** *pres. p*. worrying, tearing at **29**. 7 [OE *wyrȝan*]
wirschip. See **worschip**
wirth. See **worth**
wirth *adj*. worth, of the value of **73** 23 [OE *weorþ*]
wirthy, wourthy *adj*. excellent **1**. 47, **35**. 20 [ME; OE *weorþ*]
wis, wyice, wyis, wys(e) *adj*. wise, skilled, expert **2**. 65, **5**. 29, **5**. 55, **11**. 21, **14**. 294, **35**. 4, **49**. 19, **68**. 39, **71**. 67; **wisly** *adv*. **14**. 496 [OE *wīs*]

wis(e), I *adv.* certainly, indeed (*taken as* = I know) **14.** 37, **14.** 245, **14.** 414, **17.** 85, **66.** 32 [OE *ȝewis*]

wise, wys(e), wyis *n.* way, manner, style **5.** 41, **10.** 100, **14.** 156, **22.** 3, **41.** 5, **50.** 177, **51.** 69, **82.** 1; *as pl.* **20.** 1 [OE *wīse*]

wismen *n. pl.* wise fellows **65.** 7, (ironic) **14.** 408 [OE *wīs*+*man*]

wisp. See **wosp**

wissitt *pa. t.* wished **28.** 33 [OE *wȳscan*]

wist, (I) *v.* (I) knew (erroneous use of *iwis*) **45.** 1, **53.** 48 [see **wis(e), I**]

wit, waett, wait(t) *v.* know **10.** 177, **14.** 195, **14.** 398, **14.** 408, **20.** 22, **38.** 12, **38.** 51, **46.** 14; *3 sg.* **28.** 37 [OE *witan*]

wit(t) *n.* understanding, wisdom, skill **7.** 4, **14.** 257, **14.** 288, **14.** 395, **14.** 463, **16.** 93, **26,** 20, **51.** 12, **75.** 41; *pers.* **51.** 46 [OE]

with(e), wyth *prep.* with **10.** 12, **10.** 13, **10.** 18, **12.** 32, **33.** 18; by **16.** 25, **23.** 219, **38.** 3, **43.** 48; of **32.** 34 [OE *wið*]

without(t)in, withoutyn, withowttin *prep.* without **3.** 106, **9.** 7, **9.** 46, **9.** 102, **10.** 60, **14.** 431 [OE *wiþūtan*]

witnes *n.* witness **45.** 73; *uninflected pl.* witnesses **23.** 198 [OE]

witt. See **wit**

***witt.** See **wit**

wittandlie *adv.* consciously, deliberately **5.** 21 [OE *witan*]

wittin(g) *ppl. adj.* known **23.** 193; known to **6.** 138 [as prec.]

wittis *n. pl.* the senses **6.** 11 [OE *ȝewit*]

wlonk *n.* lovely lady **14.** 150; **wlonkes** *pl.* **14.** 36 (see Commentary) [OE adj. *wlonc*]

wo, wa *n.* **4.** 30, **6.** 156, **12.** 30, **14.** 213, **14.** 437, **16.** 93; *adj.* miserable, distressed **9.** 29, **9.** 32, **13.** 62; **woful(l)** *adj.* **6.** 36, **9.** 32, **10.** 209, **14.** 415 [OE *wa*]

wobat *n.* hairy oubit, caterpillar; *attrib.* **14.** 89 [ME *wolbode* (? *wool*+ an obscure element]

wod *n.* wood, woodland; **widdis, woddis** *pl.* **10.** 76, **16.** 19, **50.** 104 [OE *wudu*]

wod. See **woid**

woddit. See **weddit**

wodenes *n.* frenzy; fierceness, violence **10.** 229 [OE *wōdnes*]

woful. See **wo**

woid, wod, wud *adj.* mad, crazed, furious **3.** 58, **12.** 22, **14.** 141, **14.** 294, **20.** 15, **23.** 91, **26.** 18, **44.** 47, **59.** 18 [OE *wōd*]

woir *pa. t.* wore **9.** 108 [OE *węrian*]

woisdome *n.* wisdom **23.** 64 [*wīsdōm*]

wolroun *n.* wild boar **14.** 90 [? ON *vilr* stray+*runi* boar]

womanhede, womanheid *n.* womanliness **12.** 9, **12.** 39, **14.** 77, **14.** 315, **72.** 11; *pers.* **10.** 160 [OE *wīfman*+**-hǣdu*]

womanlie *adj.* feminine **12.** 28, **16.** 50; **womanly** *adv.* **14.** 496, **51.** 28 [OE *wīfman*+*līc*]

wonder, woundir *adv.* exceedingly, very **10.** 144, **23.** 17, **50.** 53 [OE *wundor*]

wondit, woundit *pp.* wounded **9.** 10, **10.** 208 [OE *wundian*]

woord. See **wird**

workmanschip *n.* labour on a piece of work **56.** 22 [ME]

worme *n. fig.* contemptible reptile **14.** 89; **wormis** *pl.* parasites in the body **23.** 195 [OE *wyrm*]

worne *ppl. adj.* exhausted, worn out **14.** 127, **23.** 213 [pp. of *wear*; OE *węrian*]

worschip, wirschep, wir(s)chip *n.* distinction **14.** 372, veneration, honour **1.** 47, **16.** 94, **17.** 51, **22.** 36, **72.** 3; *v.* honour, revere **6.** 51 [OE *weorð*+*scipe*]

worth *v.* happen, come to pass; **weill worth the** may you prosper **51.** 56; **wo wirth** ill betide, confound **72.** 9, **72.** 10 [OE *weorðan*]

worthie, worthye *adj.* worthy, deserving **41.** 10, **61.** 9; **worthines** *n.* worth **48.** 4 [OE *wyrðe*]

wosp, wisp *n.* bunch of hay or straw used as a stopper *fig.* **14.** 335, as an alehouse sign **38.** 110; **23.** 64; *pl.* **23.** 213 [origin uncertain]

wounde *n.* wound, laceration **5.** 15; **windis** *pl.* **56.** 12 [OE *wund*]
woundit. See **wondit**
wouk(e) *pa. t.* stayed awake **9.** 34, **9.** 45 [OE *wæcnan, wōc*]
wourd. See **wird**
wourthines *n.* worthiness **35.** 95 [ME; see **wirthy**]
wourthy. See **wirthy**
wow *v.* woo **74.** 44; **wowit** *pa. t.* **13.** 17 [late OE *wōȝian*]
wowf *n.* wolf **37.** 57, **37.** 65, **37.** 67 [OE *wulf*]
wowing *n.* wooing, love affair **37.** *title* [see **wow**]
wox. See **wax**
wrachis. See **wreche**
wrachit. See **wrechit**
wraiglane *ppl. adj.* wriggling **23.** 195 [ME; imit.; cf. LG dial. *wraggeln*]
wraith *n.* wrath, anger **38.** 28 [OE *wrǣððu*]
wrak *n.* worldly possessions, rubbish **63.** 76, **65.** 10, **65.** 33 [LG, Du]
wrang *v.* wrong, do injustice to **40.** 3 [ON **wrangr, rangr*]
wrang *adj.* wrong, evil, unjust **6.** 11, **6.** 133, **63.** 61; *as n.* injury, harm *pl.* **5.** 70, **45.** 9 [late OE; cf. prec.]
wrangus, wrangous *adj.* wrong, unjust, illegal **6.** 122, **51.** 65, **68.** 10 [ME *wrangwis*; prec.]
wrayt, wret. See **wryte**
wreche, wrache *n.* wretch **11.** 5, **60.** 1; *pl.* **6.** 36, **16.** 84, **52.** 58, **65.** 25 [OE *wræcca*]
wrechit, wrachit *adj.* miserable **6.** 17, **64.** 19, **65.** 2; **wrechidnes, wre(t)chitnes** *n.* poverty, misery **39.** 1, **59.** 29, **68.** 6, **70.** 4; **wretchitly** *adv.* **79.** 21 [ME; see **wreche**]
wreik *v.* avenge **44.** 82 [OE *wrecan*]
wrennis *n. pl.* wrens (*troglodytes parvulus*) **50.** 124 [OE *wrenna*]
wretchidnes, wretchitly. See **wrechit**
***wrettingis** *n. pl.* writings, instructions **43.** 69 [see **wryte**]
wrink *n.* wrench; trick, device **55.** 42 [OE *wrenc*]
writ *n.* writing; scripture **5.** 3 [OE]
writtin. See **wryte**
wrocht, rocht. See **wirk**
wrokin *pp.* revenged **14.** 341 [OE *wrecan, wrǣcon*]
wry, upone *adv. phr.* awry, atwist **23.** 175 [OE *wrīȝian*]
wryte, wryt *v.* write, set down **17.** 13, **23.** 12, **50.** 23; **wrytis** *1 pl.* **22.** 8; **wrayt, wret** *pa. t.* **3.** 141, **9.** 45, **50.** 188; **writtin** *pp.* **14.** 529, **35.** 95, **52.** 217; **wrytin, wrytting** *vbl. n.* writing **29.** 9, **45.** 73 [OE *writan*]
wud. See **woid**
wy *n.* man, men **17.** 45, **53.** 43, **55.** 50, **83.** 19 [OE *wiȝa*]
***wycht.** See **wicht**
wyd(e) *adj.* wide, gaping **3.** 93, **14.** 335, **56.** 12; ample, full **14.** 437; broad **14.** 76, **77.** 22; **full wyde** *adv.* far and wide **54.** 112 [OE *wīd*]
wyffis. See **wif**
wyice, wyis, wys(e). See **wis**
wylcum. See **welcum**
wyld *adj.* wild, distracted **23.** 101, **45.** 18; loose, free **52.** 17 [OE *wilde*]
wyle *n.* cunning, stratagem **10.** 224, **55.** 42; *pl.* **14.** 295, **14.** 463, **34.** 15 [ME; origin obscure]
wylely *adv.* cunningly **14.** 438 [cf. prec.]
wylie *adj.* cunning **37.** 58 [cf. **wyle**]
wyll *n.* wish, resolution **75.** 41 [OE *willa*]
wyn, wynyng. See **win**
wynd *n.* wind **39.** 27, **62.** 14; *pl.* **10.** 122, **10.** 229 [OE]
wyn(e) *n.* wine **14.** 39, **14.** 243, **14.** 479, **22.** 12, **22.** 53; **wynis** *pl.* **14.** 35, **14.** 148, **74.** 32 [*wīn*]
wyn(n)yng *vbl. n.* gain, profit, getting **23.** 19, **38.** 65, **65.** 30 [ME; OE *winnan*]
Wyntoun, Andro of, Scotch poet **62.** 54
wyppit *ppl. adj.* whipped, bound round **10.** 62 [origin uncertain; see *OED, whip* v.]
wyrke. See **wirk**
wyrok. See **wirrok**
wysdome *n.* wisdom, sagacity **45.** 12 [OE *wisdōm*]

wys(e). See **wis**
wyte *n.* blame, fault **43.** 22 [OE *wite*]
wyth. See **withe**
wyve, wyvis. See **wif**

ybent *ppl. adj.* bent, drawn **10.** 110, **10.** 145 [OE *ʒe-*+*bendan*]
yeris. See **ȝeir**
yfere *adv.* in company **10.** 147 [ME; origin uncertain; see *OED*]
yhouth. See **ȝouth**
ying, yong, younge. See **ȝing**
yit. See **ȝit**
yle, ylis. See **ile**
ymagynit *pa. t.* imagined, fancied **14.** 390; **ymagynyng** *pres. p.* planning, devising **14.** 122 [ME; OF *imaginer*; L *imaginare*]
Ynd(e) India **39.** 66, **66.** 6
Yngland England **55.** 34
ynk *n.* ink **23.** 12 [ME; OF *enque*]
yoldyn *pp.* forced to surrender, subdued **10.** 209 [OE *ʒieldan, ʒolden*]
ypocreit *n.* hypocrite **16.** 36 [ME; OF *ipocreit*; L *hypocritus*]
yre. See **ire**
Yrland Ireland; *attrib.* Irish **44.** 43
***yrle** *n.* dwarf **23.** 38 [origin unknown; cf. **wirling**]
yrnes *n. pl.* irons, surgical instruments **54.** 37 [OE *īren*]
ythand *adj.* assiduous, busy **16.** 115, **60.** 12 [ME; ON *iðinn*]

INDEX OF SHORT TITLES

INDEX OF FIRST LINES